I know you "have a book"
but hope one more, won't be too
much of a burden—

Love and Happy Birthday—
Mom —

Sept. '81

A LIFE IN
OUR TIMES

BOOKS BY
JOHN KENNETH GALBRAITH

American Capitalism:
The Concept of Countervailing Power

A Theory of Price Control

Economics and the Art of Controversy

The Great Crash, 1929

The Affluent Society

The Liberal Hour

Economic Development

The Scotch

The New Industrial State

The Triumph

Indian Painting
(with Mohinder Singh Randhawa)

Ambassador's Journal

Economics, Peace and Laughter

A China Passage

Economics and the Public Purpose

Money: Whence It Came, Where It Went

The Age of Uncertainty

Almost Everyone's Guide to Economics

The Nature of Mass Poverty

Annals of an Abiding Liberal

A Life in Our Times

John Kenneth Galbraith

A LIFE IN
OUR TIMES

MEMOIRS

Boston

HOUGHTON MIFFLIN COMPANY

1981

Library of Congress Cataloging in Publication Data
Galbraith, John Kenneth, date
  A life in our times.
  Includes index.
  1. Galbraith, John Kenneth, (date)
2. Economists — United States — Biography.
3. United States — Politics and government — 1945–
I. Title.
HB119.G33A34   330'.092'4 [B]   80-27373
ISBN 0-395-30509-8
ISBN 0-395-31135-7 (special ed.)

Printed in the United States of America

To Katie and Jean and David and Andrew
with love

A Word of Thanks

A FRIEND once told me of seeing Noel Coward off to Jamaica where Coward was going to write his memoirs. He asked him if he had an abundance of notes and records. "No," Coward replied, "I have a memory like an elephant. In fact, elephants often consult me." In writing this account, I have relied similarly on recollection (though with some passing support from notes, records and published writing), and I have done so with similar confidence. My memory proved very good on the larger shape of events and also on the more salient conversations, actions, pronouncements, speeches, scenes and absurdities. However, it was sadly defective on dates, middle initials, minor geography and the other trivia so necessary, nonetheless, for verisimilitude. For help in getting things right, or nearly so, I had the help, as always, of my friend and partner Andrea Williams of whom I tell more in these pages. For more specific research I relied on a learned and lovely colleague, Londa Schiebinger of the Harvard Department of History, and my equally accomplished and attractive friend Rosamaria Toruño Tanghetti, who took up life in the United States as an alternative to the Nicaragua of the Somozas. Mrs. Tanghetti also typed and retyped and then corrected and typed yet again the manuscript of this book. I am grateful to her, and only with difficulty do I avoid being grateful to Anastasio Somoza Debayle. Edith Tucker of Wellesley, when not serving the excellent school board of that town, ran my office and otherwise made it possible for me to keep my attention on this book. I have elsewhere described her as the most comprehensively overqualified office manager in recent history. She took the place of Sarah Field-Johnson, who came to my assistance from London only to be lost, alas, to marital fidelity. Nothing can be so inconvenient.

To Mrs. Tucker and Mrs. Field-Johnson my warm and affectionate thanks.

Catherine Galbraith read these pages, provided much information and made many corrections. With our talented sons, John Alan, Peter Woodard and James Kenneth, she is a presence throughout this book. If she and they are not more visible, it is partly because this is, deliberately, a view outward on events, people and ideas. I have not turned to look within on family and personal life, perhaps partly because there isn't much on which to grieve. My life has been without the agony that sustains interest in such matters and which encourages the associated introspection. For this happy passage through a certain amount of self-centered concern and toil I have greatly to thank those who have been so enduring and tolerant in their love.

Contents

A LIFE IN
OUR TIMES

1

Above the Lakes

THE SOUTHERN ONTARIO countryside is devoid of topographic, ethnic or historical interest. It is a flattish acreage extending some two hundred miles from the Detroit River to the Niagara River in which rich land alternates with some that is sandy, ill-drained or otherwise rejected. There are no natural features worth noting. The population is ethnically only slightly more diverting; it consists in the main of Scots or, as we called ourselves there, the Scotch. Our forebears were expelled from the Highlands between 1780 and 1830 when their lairds discovered that sheep were both more profitable and, as they moved over the hillside, more rewarding to the eye. The larger history touched this favored region only when Colonel Richard Airey, nephew of Colonel Thomas Talbot, founder of the Talbot settlement midway between the two rivers, returned to the motherland to fight for Queen and country in the Crimean War, for his was the name on the orders that dispatched the Light Brigade. And less dramatically again, in World War I, when the inhabitants showed themselves generally adverse to the slaughter. My father manifested his opposition by serving on the draft board, as it would now be called, and exempting all those who did not wish to go.

There was a final brush with history when my home county of Elgin, and in some measure my father as a Liberal leader, sent Mitchell Frederick Hepburn to Parliament and to be Premier of Ontario. So disastrous was his administration that the Conservatives have been in office in the province almost unchallenged all of the thirty-nine years since.

The Scotch, even when in dense mass as in Elgin County, are the only race to which no politician ever thinks it worthwhile to appeal. Irish, Jewish, French Canadian, Welsh, German, Scandinavian, Ukrainian, black and Chicano voters are solicited by oratory, unconvincing efforts at identification and inspired banality. No vote-seeker ever dons kilts, praises the bagpipes or utters so much as a phrase of Gaelic. It is not entirely that such activities are considered ridiculous or barbaric; it would appear that we have so little political self-recognition as to make the effort not worthwhile.

The Ontario farms were of a hundred to two hundred acres and, in my youth, conscientiously tended. There was less often pride in the house, the orchard and the lawn, called the yard. The cattle were of much distinction and bred for buyers from across the United States and as far distant as the Argentine. In the autumn the small woodlands were rich in color, and in midwinter, after a fresh, deep snow, the land was wonderfully, starkly white and black. The people were diligent, given to much harmless pleasure in recounting the physical and mental disabilities of their neighbors and greatly law-abiding. No houses were ever locked, though perhaps partly because there was little in them to steal. In the neighboring village of Dutton there was a constable, but his job was widely regarded as honorary except as it involved the suppression of the violence to which certain of my countrymen, when drunk, were inclined to resort. I have told elsewhere and in detail of the Scotch.[1]

The founding member of our family in Canada, according to his gravestone in Black's Cemetery in Dunwich Township near the village of Wallacetown, was born in Argyllshire in 1771 and died in Ontario in 1874, although some later research by a clan historian suggests that, if these dates are accurate, he was born a year or two before his parents first met. My father, a former teacher who never fully rejected that profession, headed a cooperative insurance company that he had helped to organize (as he had once helped organize the first telephone service in the neighborhood) and was a moderately well-compensated township and county official. My mother, a beautiful, affectionate and decidedly firm woman, died when her children — my brother, my two sisters and I — were not yet all in their teens. Our farms, there being two, embraced 150 acres of mostly arable land to which in some years we added the unused acres of aged, infirm or temporarily disabled neighbors. In every respect they were working farms, a distinction then unknown, for there was no other kind. The centerpiece of our agriculture was a distin-

[1] In *The Scotch* (Boston: Houghton Mifflin, 1964), which was published in Britain as *Made to Last* and *The Non-Potable Scotch*.

guished, though not famous, herd of purebred Shorthorn cattle. The working aspect of the farm, the Shorthorns and my father's preeminent position in the community all greatly influenced my later existence. This I should now explain.

*   *   *

No one can understand farmers, not alone in the Americas but in all countries, unless it is known that, the rarest exceptions apart, they are afflicted with a serious sense of inferiority — what once was called an inferiority complex. This, then, is compensated for by vigorous assertion of the economic importance of agriculture and the spiritual and moral qualities that accrue from close association with the soil. Town and city dwellers regard themselves as of intrinsically superior sophistication. Working farmers, as distinct from landlords, are always struggling with the thought that they are hicks. These attitudes also carry over to academic, professional and political association with agriculture, a matter to which I will recur.

In our family, and in my case in particular, the sense of inferiority and the counterpart tendency to assertive compensation were made more complex, and possibly also more offensive, by the acknowledged social and public position of the clan. The Galbraiths were regarded, we believed rightly, as being more intelligent than others. We were also modestly more affluent. Many of our neighbors did not know their position on major political and other issues — the practical benefits of lower tariffs, cooperative buying of fertilizer or binder twine and the provincial highway system or the case against going to the trenches in World War I — until they heard my father providing it. My legacy was the inherent insecurity of the farm-reared boy in combination with an aggressive feeling that I owed it to all I encountered to make them better informed.

A more commonplace consequence of an early exposure to agriculture is a deeply valid appreciation of the nature of manual labor. It leaves all of minimal sensitivity with an enduring knowledge of its unpleasantness. A long day following a plodding, increasingly reluctant team behind a harrow endlessly back and forth over the uninspiring Ontario terrain persuaded one that all other work was easy. This early life could hardly have been in greater contrast with life at Harvard where more than six hours of teaching a week is often considered a grave impairment of academic freedom. Regularly since coming to the university, I have been approached at the faculty club, on social occasions and even in the Yard by colleagues who, with an unconvincingly worried look, have said, "Ken, aren't you working too hard?" There was a book last year, another in prospect, my teaching, something in politics. Back of the query lies their natural concern for the union rules. Only with difficulty have I suppressed my reply: "The trouble with you, my friend, is that you've never worked on a farm."

Work on an automobile assembly line, a construction crew or possibly even collecting garbage, all in the company of congenial companions and improved by the higher pay, can shine by comparison with that on a farm. It is this contrast that now brings Turks from the peasant villages of Anatolia to make Berlin one of the major Turkish cities in the world; Italians and Spaniards to do the hard toil of the Swiss; Algerians and Portuguese to man French production lines; and people from the rural South to Detroit. Detroit is not a paradise except to those who have known sharecropping in the Deep South or the meager returns beaten from the poor farms of the Appalachian plateau. If the industrially advanced countries survive, workers will eventually come to Western Europe from the farms of Egypt, Pakistan, India and Bangladesh to do what Italians, Yugoslavs and Spaniards will, in their turn, find too tedious. And routine industry in the United States will be saved by the Mexicans.

*   *   *

In rural Ontario in my youth the sons of the more prestigious clans continued in school, escaped on into schoolteaching or, more rarely, the ministry, medicine or the law. That was so of the Galbraiths. The others were withdrawn from school at an early age, for education was, quite rightly, thought inimical to the work ethic. After a leisured sojourn in a high school classroom a boy was lost to heavy farm toil. And a local (possibly universal) saying affirmed that the education was redundant: "A good farmer needs a strong back and a weak mind."

Those so prepared for farming would often go on to Detroit, frequently for a winter, sometimes forever. Movement back and forth across the Detroit River was commonplace and based on the secure knowledge that no immigration or customs official could tell a Canadian from an American by inspection alone. We were, of all the peoples of the world, the most nearly emancipated from the burdens of national passion. Our school books featured the Union Jack at the front, spoke warmly of Major General James Wolfe, William Lyon Mackenzie, Louis Joseph Papineau, Sir John Alexander Macdonald and King George V. But none of these stood against the better hours, more congenial work and vastly higher pay in the United States.

In those civilized days, indeed, it was felt by some that responsible citizenship did not involve an exclusive commitment to the political life of Canada. Canada might be a mother, but Michigan was a mistress. Canadian elections are on no fixed schedule; if a government is forced out or sees a chance of prolonging its tenure, they can be in spring, summer, autumn or even, as recently, in the Canadian winter. American elections, then as now, were always in November. This was after the crops were harvested in Canada and the seasonal migration to the assembly lines had begun. Accordingly, a man could vote in Canada in the summer and, by courtesy of the Detroit Democratic organization that assigned registered names, possibly from the local funeral directors, in Michigan in the autumn. No thought of corruption was involved. Men wished to have the best people in office in both countries. I have never understood why one's affections must be confined, as once with women, to a single country.

There is advantage otherwise. In May 1963, President John F. Kennedy and Prime Minister Lester B. (Mike) Pearson met at Hyannisport to discuss, among other things, the long-troubled question of Canadian air flights into the United States. For a decade or more, when the Canadian airlines asked to fly Canadians to Miami, Los Angeles or other centers of commerce, culture or rest, they were asked what routes they had to offer in return. The major Canadian cities are at most only a few miles from the border. There was no great American demand for a route to Moosonee on James Bay or the yet more northerly metropolis of Yellowknife. The stalemate caused by this absence of a *quid pro quo* had lasted for years, requiring Canadians going deeply into the United States to transship to American carriers at Detroit, Buffalo or, at most, New York.

The two heads of government agreed to appoint a two-man committee to investigate and recommend. That would get things off dead center. Recalling that I had frequently identified myself as a

Canadian, Kennedy appointed me the American representative. Recalling the same, Pearson, a friend of many years, said I would do as the Canadian representative. Both agreed that so efficient an arrangement called for a measure of reticence. I held meetings, first in Washington, then in Ottawa, with carriers and regulatory officials and found that the long-range jet had made everyone dissatisfied with the current transshipment arrangements. Also, in contrast with most international disputes, nothing was involved but money — prospective earnings — and these could be divided equally. After I negotiated with myself on the few serious points of difference, I rendered a judgment satisfactory to the carriers of both countries. While thus engaged, I was treated with marked courtesy by all the airlines. My recommendation then went back for more orthodox bargaining between national representatives, which, needless to say, took much more time. Clearly my dual allegiance had been advantageous.

*   *   *

In the early autumn of 1926, in my eighteenth year, and as another aspect of the influence of agriculture, in particular of the Shorthorns of which by then I was considered to have a highly professional knowledge, I enrolled in the Ontario Agricultural College. I had been attending high school since the age of ten, but my schooling was subject to numerous interruptions for farm work and once for what my family believed was bad health. My record, which did reflect an early addiction to extensive but undisciplined reading, was indifferent. In keeping with many of my contemporaries and many of that age since, I had considered myself superior to sustained intellectual effort. But in those days, given a high school diploma, admission to a college, any college, was entirely a matter of money. This our farm provided, and there was also an arrangement by which the members of the family were so spaced that the earlier could contribute to the college costs of the later.

The Ontario Agricultural College, with which were associated schools of home economics and veterinary medicine and, oddly, an academy for instruction in the science and art of baking, was then, as it is still, located in the city of Guelph, some fifty or sixty miles west of Toronto. The University of Toronto granted us our degrees.

The OAC is now the University of Guelph, and, on the occasion of its elevation to that status, I was asked back to receive the first honorary degree. In the citation I was described as "our most distinguished graduate." When the president read this to me the night before, I thought for a moment that I had heard it differently: "our only distinguished graduate." That would not have been accurate; Thomas H. Jukes, a major modern source of knowledge on vitamins, graduated in my generation. There have been others. On the next morning, that of the ceremony, I rose early and walked over the familiar shaded, shrub-grown and singularly beautiful campus. It all seemed fresh from heaven. Presently I met a professor from my day, an agronomist of vigorous aspect who recognized me immediately from thirty years before. He stopped, shook hands and said, "I see by the newspapers, Galbraith, that they are awarding you one of those *honorary* degrees."

I bowed in recognition.

He shook his walking stick in a menacing way and said, "Well, if I had my way, they'd be taking away the degree you already have." I was not, in my college years, well regarded.

*   *   *

There was a rough division in the OAC student body in my time between the farmers and the countrymen, although this terminology reflects the distinction rather than any contemporary usage. The farmers were mostly from Ontario farms, although there were also some from the Maritime Provinces, where the local agriculture did not justify colleges of our grandeur. The farmers were studying agriculture more or less without exception in order to escape it. Their highest ambition was for a job as a county agent — called agricultural representative in Ontario — which provided one with an automobile, an office at the county seat and a sublime deliverance from manual toil. One went around telling the practicing farmers how to do better, a thing in which, at the time, an astonishing number were not interested. In Canada, as across the United States, agricultural extension agents gathered to tell of the classic rebuff — the farmer who blithely told one of their number that he was already not farming half as well as he knew how.

Failing a job as an "ag. rep.," there was hope, perhaps with some added training, of one as a teacher in some vocational high school or in the Toronto stockyards grading swine, as Canadian law required.

The countrymen, in contrast, intended to farm. They were the sons of affluent Toronto families possessed of land somewhere adjacent to the city. The son in question had become enamored of the horses, cattle and inherited acres and had decided to make them his career. Or, not infrequently, his family had decided that that was about all he was good for. Countrymen similarly motivated or unmotivated came from elsewhere in Canada, from England and on occasion from plantations in the West Indies and ranches in Argentina.

The farmers wore sturdy suits of blue serge or gray worsted, white shirts and ties and exhibited in this unaccustomed attire the unmistakable culture of the farm. They — I could say we — were very serious about their work. The countrymen affected sweaters and trousers, flowing neck gear or none at all, and viewed our courses with contempt. Out of their superior social, sexual and athletic experience they were accorded an unchallenged preeminence in the community. They held all class offices and were given all nonacademic honors, and the rest of us yearned to display the slightest fraction of their sophistication. On Sundays they went to Church of England services in Guelph; some claimed, on festive occasions, to have gotten drunk. Throughout my years at the Ontario Agricultural College I never permitted myself even a glass of beer; alcohol, we had learned at home, was, in any form, for the wanton and the evil.

The countrymen had a durable effect on me. I have never ceased to concede to those of superior social assurance and grace.

*   *   *

The OAC campus is on a spacious hill across the river and above the city of Guelph, to which it was connected in my time by a streetcar that rocked up and down in a genial way as it made the journey. Through some engineering illogic, the wheels had been placed together in the middle rather than out at the two ends. The campus buildings, some of limestone, some of red brick, ranged from pleasant eccentricity to mild charm. A little beyond and out of sight were the barns and experimental plots. Reflecting the superior English tradition, everything was admirably landscaped and gardened.

Across the streetcar tracks from the main campus were the buildings where women students were taught the rudiments of home economics, with impressive attention also to feminine decorum and virtue. Their part of the college was called Macdonald Institute after the leading Canadian tobacco manufacturer, but this involved no concession whatever to his product. The girls, as they called themselves, united on ceremonial occasions to cry out in unison:

> Rootely toot; rootely toot.
> We are the girls of the Institute.
> We don't smoke. And we don't chew.
> And we don't go out with boys who do! [2]

From 1800 to 2400 students attended OAC in the several branches and classes in my time. Their mood, as also that of the faculty, was deeply anti-intellectual. Animal husbandry being the most anti-intellectual subject available, it attracted the largest number of students. This became my first field of specialization.

*　　*　　*

Colleges of agriculture began in the last century as model farms. There students (and also farmers) from farms of average competence or less could go to study the agricultural practices — soil preparation, selection of seed, animal breeding and nutrition — that reflected the best then known or what was so regarded. Presently experiment was added. Different varieties and breeds and modes of culture and feeding were tried out to see which produced the best results; hence the lasting reference to agricultural experiment stations. At a further stage scientific perception was brought to the guidance of this experiment. The Ontario Agricultural College, after a good early start, had stabilized somewhere between the second and third stages; there was experiment but little scientific research. We were instructed in the approved farm practices; we were not encouraged to ask why they were so regarded. Science in the abstract might be a good thing, but it was not something of any great practical relevance. Advanced degrees were thought unnecessary, perhaps because almost no one on the faculty had one.

---

[2] Ms. Virginia Gillham, now Librarian of the University of Guelph, has usefully checked my memory on various matters without responsibility for the result. I am most grateful to her. She assures me that there is no trace in the college records of either this manifestation or the one I cite later.

The president for most of my time was one G. I. Christie, a Canadian who had made his career at Purdue University and in the United States Department of Agriculture. He was a demonstration model of the kind of academic politician who built the land-grant college system in the United States and its Canadian counterpart. Their monuments are the appropriations they achieved and the buildings that ensued. Their special skill was in maintaining an equilibrium between the more regressive prejudices of farmers and legislators and the recurrent tendency to intellectual inconvenience on the part of the faculty. The latter involved not political but agricultural heresy. As late as 1943, economists at Iowa State College were assailed for a published finding that oleomargarine was, nutritionally speaking, a good wartime substitute for butter. The head of the Iowa Farm Bureau, Francis Johnson, announced that "Iowa wanted no Harvard in the corn belt."[3] Theodore Schultze, the chairman of the offending department and a later Nobel laureate in economics, removed himself to the more tolerant precincts of the University of Chicago.

The debt to the accomplished politicians who kept peace between faculty and farmers is great. Once the colleges were built, academic freedom could then develop. All things and all men must be judged in their time. However, G. I. Christie had an easier passage than most; his faculty was as opposed to independent thought as he.

I arrived at the college by train and trolley on a golden autumn evening to see the football team at practice on the lower side of the campus, for there was, of course, no stadium in those primitive days. It was my first view of the game, and it, along with the uniforms, seemed deeply evocative of all that I had expected in college life. My appreciation of football has declined steadily ever since. I was assigned to a room in the freshman residence, a place of unspeakable squalor as it even then seemed, and was given as a roommate a charming man, rather older than I, named Sydney Howe, who later became an important figure in Canadian dairying circles. He listened to my personal history and my political views through a long evening and promptly applied for a change. The dean of residence (one of whose predecessors had been John McCrae of Flanders Fields and the poppies) hastened to comply. My next roommate lasted until Christmas.

[3] "The Farm Bureau," *Fortune*, vol. XXIX, no. 6 (June 1944), p. 159.

It was a principle of agricultural instruction at OAC that while one might specialize in a particular field of learning such as animal husbandry, one must be accomplished in everything bearing on farm life. To this end, in the next five years — I spent an extra year compensating for high school deficiencies — I studied animal husbandry, field husbandry, poultry husbandry, dairy husbandry, butter- and cheese-making, butchering and meat-cutting, apiculture, botany, chemistry, zoology, embryology, bacteriology, physics, mathematics, agricultural economics, farm management, agricultural engineering, soil management, horticulture, forestry, surveying, veterinary medicine, as well as a range of, to me, more practical courses, of which the most durably useful were English composition and plumbing, the latter known to my more casually spoken classmates as "pumps and shithouses." Because my fellow students rightly believed that they would never have to write, I had more than my share of attention from two talented teachers of English who were also authors of some note — O. J. Stevenson and E. C. McLean. These great men labored, along with many other duties, to correct my grammar and punctuation and reduce my efforts at prose expression to normal.

However, not all of my instruction in the resources of the language came in those days from my teachers. I remember with gratitude and admiration the janitor who served the senior men's residence, Mills Hall. His name was Janitor Bill — he had, I believe, no other — and he was treated with respect for the quality of his housekeeping, for the discipline he enforced on its behalf, for the general strength of his personality and for his fine physical presence. Janitor Bill, in these respects, was an exceptional man. But I remember him mostly for his capacity for effective expression. One example is still in my mind — a carefully crafted sign posted in the entry hall which read: RESIDENTS WILL KINDLY CEASE PUTTING APPLE CORES IN THE URINALS AND THE ARSENALS AS THEY WILL NOT LOOP THE LOOP.

In partial consequence of this instruction I began to provide my hometown newspaper in St. Thomas, Ontario, with a weekly column of advice on agricultural practices. This kept me in spending money, and in time I also became the editor of the new college newspaper. I balanced as much criticism of our instruction as I thought permissible against a cautious avoidance of anything that would provoke damaging retribution. Perusal of old copies of the paper persuades me that I kept well to the side of safety. After I graduated, my successors became more forthright, and the paper was suppressed by President Christie.

Instruction in plumbing was by a modestly endowed but wholly practical scholar named Rodney Graham. An eminently generous man, he allowed me to remain in his class after I had asked him one day if a certain pump, of which he had a strongly favorable view, would pump both hard and soft water. He thought long and said yes and then realized that the question was ill-intended. To this day I can handle all ordinary plumbing emergencies with confidence and very often with competence, and always to the great astonishment of hostesses and friends.

*   *   *

So wide-ranging an education involved some sacrifice of depth. And there were many subjects where, by their nature, there was no depth at all. What can be told about the proper way of putting hay in a manger — there was, in fact, a course that we called principles of hay-feeding — can be covered rather comprehensively in an hour. Only by laboring the fairly obvious did our professors make such subject matter last for a term. Those who did it well were much admired, and we especially sang the praises of the head of the department of dairy husbandry, Professor Henry Hochel Dean, rechristened by students in accordance with his field of scholarship Henry Holstein Dean. He was a man of English provenance and resonant voice, and I can still hear his instruction, metaphorical, practical, incontrovertible:

"The dairy cow is the foster mother of the human race."

"The walls of the dairy stable should be built strongly to support the roof."

That practical instruction in the agricultural arts lacked content and thus the capacity to occupy time was, in a general way, recognized. A practical solution was at hand, which was to fill up our hours with livestock judging, and as we passed through the college years, we became ever more involved in its mysteries. Beef cattle, dairy cattle, horses, sheep and hogs were judged in classes of four to eight and ranked from best to worst. Within each category there were several breeds — of beef cattle, for example, Shorthorns, Herefords and Aberdeen Angus, often wrongly called Black Angus. Each breed had its traditional and often arcane standards of excellence, and these varied for males and females and for animals of different ages. All had to be judged in different classes so a near infinity of time could be devoted to livestock judging. And as a further advantage, the standards of excellence by which the animals were graded were so subjective they could not be learned. They existed only in the eyes of the judges and involved decisions on which no two judges, however accomplished, could fully agree.

Nor were the standards related to performance. In that time an Ayrshire or Holstein cow could become a grand champion because of her beauty — conformation it was called — even though her milk yield was nominal, a triumph of aesthetics over mere utility. Many years later a graduate student of mine at Harvard returned to the University of Missouri before getting his degree, and in the fullness of time, he became the dean of the college of agriculture. His thesis, however, continued to weigh on his mind, and eventually as part of his research he had cuts of beef from the most perfect of animals — grades of U.S. Prime and U.S. Choice — cooked by his home economics department along with cuts from Canners and Cutters, the most aged, infirm or otherwise defective beasts. All were then submitted to a discriminating panel of hungry diners. None could reliably tell by the flavor the cuts from the most distinguished animals from those from the worst. But when I suggested publication of his thesis, he was uneasy. The intrusion of performance was still a sensitive subject with his livestock men.

If there are no recognizable standards of achievement, no one is in danger of lessening his effort because he is approaching perfection. So we could spend several hours a day on practice judging with no feeling whatever that we were exhausting the possibilities of this branch of learning. Such was its importance at OAC that, as at other colleges of agriculture at the time, we had a special pavilion for the practice of livestock judging or for watching those so engaged.

There was a further reward. In the autumn of our senior year, four or five of us were selected to represent the college in competition at the International Live Stock Exposition at Chicago. I was one so selected, the greatest triumph of my college days. If anything but luck had been involved, it had come from my studying not the livestock but the preferences of the deciding judges, our professors.

This study served badly, however, where the judges were not our own professors, and as we trained at Michigan State, Purdue and the University of Illinois under local masters of the art, my performance was weak, and I was benched as a spare.

The International Live Stock Exposition at Chicago in 1930 was a vastly exciting thing, and having no responsibilities, I could enjoy it all. Great signs proclaimed the excellence of herds from all across the land. Rows of ribbons told of past triumphs. A pulsing mass of city-dwellers came to gape. Four-H boys and girls passed through the exhibition halls and paraded their animals in the ring with the peculiar self-consciousness that came from knowing that their robust health and their inexpressible virtue were as much on display as their prize steers. It was a high point of my college career.

*   *   *

Although the Ontario Agricultural College as a center of scholarly effort had grave defects and few merits, its insignificant cost apart, the shortcomings were skillfully disguised. I was later to learn that such techniques are universal. Thus, from the moment we arrived at Guelph, we were required to make institutional loyalty a substitute for thought. "College spirit" it was called, and, in their insistence on this virtue, the students were outdone only by the faculty. Criticism was equated with personality defect or disloyalty. The protection thus accorded inadequacy was nearly complete, and it was good to have the lesson in this comprehensible a form when so young. Those who criticize their university show by their doing so that they are incapable of the love the institution rightly expects. Here is the great protective apparatus of academic life. The obvious form at Guelph was an excellent preparation for its more subtle manifestation at Harvard. In the late sixties I became persuaded that Harvard was ill-prepared for coping with the student unrest then developing at other universities. The administration was mentally inert, out of touch with faculty and students. In December of 1968, I wrote to *Harvard Magazine* of the danger. I was indignantly rebuked; one did not say such things of Harvard. I was still in a chastened mood when, in 1969, the student explosion came to Cambridge and the university administration responded with unstudied ineptitude and unnecessary violence.

A second antidote for academic inadequacy is the cultivation of aggressively nonintellectual behavior styles. Excellence in these then becomes the accepted measure of success, and academic inadequacy goes unnoticed. At OAC this design had been raised to the level of an art, and while leadership was assumed by the students, the faculty greatly encouraged us. Sports, social life, intramural rioting and the condign punishment of those who displayed an insufficient commitment to these activities had a standing well above academic achievement. They showed real college spirit. On all occasions of academic ceremony we broke strongly into the favored college song:

> Put on your old red and blue sweater
> For there isn't any better
> And we'll open up another keg of beer.
> For 'twas not for knowledge
> That we came to college
> But to raise hell all the year.

Again the lesson was enduring. At Princeton before World War II, the least talented of my colleagues in the department of economics were always the first at the stadium on Saturday afternoon. For many years following my arrival at Harvard, there was a type of professor whose principal achievement was nowise academic but rather a superb identification with Harvard tradition. Often he became a house master and urged the highly implausible traditions of his house on the undergraduates. At faculty meetings he spoke firmly on which opportunities for undergraduate fornication were residentially permissible or impermissible, what were called the parietal rules.

*   *   *

In the year 1930, the first of the Great Depression, I was assailed by a pregnant thought, one which had no standing at OAC. It was not worthwhile improving livestock if it could not be sold at a decent price. And virtually nothing could be so sold. I decided to transfer my interest to farm economics. I could there come to understand the real problem, and that understanding might also help me get a job. As the Depression continued, there would, logically, be a demand for those with a remedy. To this day I regard this perception, which was not after the fact, as surprising.

The economists and agricultural economists at Guelph proved unhelpful. An amiable group of men, they spent their days in pleasant conversation but with no suggestion as to what might be wrong with the economic system or what would put it right. The head of the department did say that farm cooperatives might be the answer. My first doubts about the competence of economists were then formed.

In the summer of 1930, I was given a job studying tenant farming in Ontario. Equipped with a car, an unimaginable perquisite in those days, I traveled over the countryside searching out tenants to inquire into their lease arrangements, rents and other troubles. Tenants were not easy to find, for the value of land was everywhere so low it was hard to be too poor to own some. Later I was released from this task to design the college exhibits for the Canadian National Exhibition, the great festival held in Toronto each year as the summer ends. I had previously been thought to have shown talent in this line at a student exhibition. My most distinguished achievement was a plea to Ontario farmers to keep accounts. A large, handsomely painted sign said, "RUNNING A FARM WITHOUT BOOKS IS LIKE RUNNING A CLOCK WITHOUT HANDS," and over the sign was a large clock with an impressively swinging pendulum and a wholly blank face. At the Canadian National I manned the exhibit myself. People stopped to ask me, some in annoyance, a few in anger, why the clock had no hands.

In 1931, I graduated with distinction. I attended the commencement ceremonies only to discover that a cash prize on which I had been counting heavily had been given to a less assertive and thus more worthy candidate. I did not remain for the associated social events nor could I have been greatly missed. My mind was much on the University of California whither I was soon to proceed.

On this continent, as an aspect of the institutional loyalty and protection to which I have earlier adverted, one is required to love his alma mater. The beautiful lawns and gardens apart, I did not. Some years after graduating, I wrote a series of articles for the Toronto publication *Saturday Night* on agricultural education in Ontario, and I referred to my college as, in effect, an academic slum. But that was long ago. The Canadian instinct is for good management of public institutions, better than in the United States, and there is little doubt that things have now much improved.

As to my distaste for my teachers there is another possibility. My friend of many years David Niven, the actor, tells in his autobiography of his great dislike as a youth for his school, his masters and his fellow pupils. All were deeply repellent. But then he is assailed by the thought that he could have been a very nasty chap himself.

2

Berkeley and the
Higher Learning in America

MY LIFE has been spent in greater or less communion with five centers of higher learning, as that term, often loosely, is used. Two of these, Guelph and Princeton — respectively the least and the most aristocratic in tendency — did not engage my affection. Two, the University of California at Berkeley and the University of Cambridge, I greatly loved. Harvard, where I've spent most of my life, does not lend itself easily to classification. In all five universities, as they all now are, I suffered from a problem in personal relations that I never quite overcame. This was not so much from being more versatile, more diligent or perhaps more able than my colleagues. Such can be tolerated. The damage arose from my fear, which I earlier indicated and which I never quite suppressed, that my superiority would not be recognized.

Princeton was an especially serious case. There I was employed for three years immediately before and following the outbreak of World War II, two years of which I spent on leaves of absence. Much of Princeton I remember with distaste; even someone with a greater instinct for social grace and adjustment might so remember it from those years. The economics faculty of the time was firmly committed to teaching what a decade of depression had shown to be irrelevant. There were exceptions; one was Frank D. Graham, a professor of money and banking and the historian of the great German inflation of the early twenties. I also became very fond of Frank A. Fetter, by then retired, an old-fashioned liberal of exceptionally strong fiber. He once told me that he had never allowed the promotion to tenure of any economist in his department who testified on behalf of a corporation in an antitrust case, for such behavior meant the man's views could be had for money. He was, I think, right.

The low quality of the economics faculty was, however, less depressing than the scholarly and social tendencies of the Princeton undergraduates. They were even more deeply anti-intellectual, though in a more refined way, than those at Guelph. In Canada there was a certain sense of aspiration; at Princeton students, with rare exceptions, felt that they had already arrived. From time to time, as a conscientious young instructor, I sought to correct some of the more egregious archaisms which my Princeton colleagues had written into a set of small green-jacketed textbooks. These — "the little green terrors" — they had then assigned to their classes to exploit a financially insignificant conflict of interest. I was repeatedly and indignantly asked by students if it wouldn't be the textbook version, not my corrections, that would be required on the examinations. If so, why confuse them with the truth?

Those then responsible for admission to Princeton favored what was called "the Princeton type." So far as ever defined — ambiguity in these matters greatly enhances freedom of choice — a Princeton type was like a Princeton graduate. He was affluent, white, Anglo-Saxon and usually a Protestant; from a reasonably acceptable preparatory school, a substantial family or suburb, often on the Philadelphia Main Line; and with a commitment to sound personal hygiene. Scholarly aptitude was neither a requisite nor a handicap. Many of the faculty, reflecting the instincts, ambition or conditioning for academic achievement of the offspring of schoolteachers, ministers of the gospel, Jewish immigrants and the more eccentric of the American middle class, were much less distinguished in their social origins than those they taught. So at Princeton before World War II, quite a few faculty members looked with admiration on the superior social assurance and behavior of their students.

For a week or so each spring all academic work at Princeton, however frivolous, came to a complete halt while the precise social rank of each member of the freshman class was appraised and established. In an appalling procedure called "the bicker," social precedence was recognized by selecting students for the several dining clubs, buildings of sub-Georgian architecture which lined the two sides of Prospect Avenue near the campus. Each club had its exact position in the general order, beginning at the top with one called the Ivy. I was never quite sure which came last. Jews and other outcasts were firmly excluded from all clubs. At first I was rather indifferent to these awful proceedings. Then two or three students sought me out to confide their terrible fear that they would not be selected. For all of their bright college years they would be formally designated as undesirables. There was nothing one could do. I learned that Woodrow Wilson, when president of the university, had also been appalled but was equally helpless to change the system.

After World War II, women, racial tolerance and suspicion of prescriptive social position as adumbrated by John O'Hara — who, with his unerring sense of scene, came to live in Princeton — intruded on undergraduate life as civilizing forces. And two talented young economists, Richard A. Lester and Lester V. Chandler, became influential in the economics department and brought it abreast of the century. To the undoubted distress of many whom in a manner of speaking it had educated, the university moved on. My memory, alas, is of the earlier frame.

*   *   *

The two academic institutions that engaged my affection, Berkeley and the University of Cambridge, could have done so partly because of their beauty. Cambridge, England — Trinity Great Court, the Wren Library, King's Chapel, the other more intimate quadrangles, the Backs — has no equal in Europe, and certainly not in the spring when first the crocuses and then the daffodils cover great stretches of field and lawn. One learns also at Cambridge how architecture has declined geometrically in taste and excellence — by roughly half in each century since the first Elizabeth. There much is good because so little is new.

Berkeley depends for its enchantment less on architecture, though this is not universally offensive, than on location. The campus is so arranged that from a hundred places one can look out on the Bay, the Golden Gate and the Marin mountains, all in the hazy distance. The live oaks and lesser flora are a rich admixture of light and dark greens, and over all is an especially rich and lingering aroma of eucalyptus. Above is the gently Gothic Campanile mocking the white-to-cream Moorish façades with their tiles and arches that were once the compulsory California fashion. These buildings vastly improve on their aggressively sensible successors.

I arrived in Berkeley one late summer evening in 1931, having left Ontario by ship ten days earlier, the ship being one that plied from Port Stanley, twenty miles from our farm, to Cleveland. At the casino in Port Stanley during my youth the dance orchestra was thought by all to be very good, a shrewd judgment. It was from the nearby city of London and was led by the then uncelebrated Guy Lombardo.

The journey from Ohio to California was with another graduate student in an ancient and enfeebled Oakland automobile with an uncontrollable appetite for gasoline and oil. However, the depression was heavy on the land, and even the oil companies were succumbing to the relentless pressures of deflation so by watching attentively for the battle zones of the gasoline wars that had broken out across the country, we were able to fill up the tank and a spare can for just upward of ten cents a gallon. From Lincoln, Nebraska, west in 1931, the main crosscountry roads were unpaved to the California line.

My travel to Berkeley was to acquire a Ph.D. and to take up a research assistantship in the Giannini Foundation of Agricultural Economics. There my ultimate benefactor was Amadeo Peter Giannini, a California banker and entrepreneur, who, a year or two earlier (following a temporary loss of control of his enterprises), had launched a major effort to improve his ethnic and political image. The ethnic transformation involved the renaming of his Bank of Italy the Bank of America. The political improvement was principally accomplished by having the Bancitaly Corporation, the parent enterprise, give the University of California a million and a half dollars in what may not have been an arm's-length transaction to establish the A. P. Giannini Foundation of Agricultural Economics in honor of its president. From early in his career Giannini had been a major source of financial support to California farmers. He had also learned not to doubt their political power.

Years later, as an editor of *Fortune,* I returned the Giannini favor with a major story on his life and enterprises. The research was done by a tall, slender, highly intelligent woman named Janet McEnany to whom Giannini, by then well along in his seventies, was much attracted. Janet returned to New York to tell of going to lunch with him one rainy day in San Francisco. There was doubt as to whether the great banker's car had arrived so his secretary asked a distin-

guished-looking gray-haired man who was in the outer office to accompany her employer down to the street and get him a taxi should
this be necessary. One was needed, and when the man came back
with the vehicle, Giannini gave him a twenty-five-cent piece. The
recipient was visibly embarrassed and explained to Giannini that he
was an officer of the company, the head of the Los Angeles Bank of
America, and as such, one of the larger bankers of the nation. Giannini apologized, took back the quarter and gave his man a dollar.

I spent three utterly contented years at Berkeley.[1] During the
third I commuted into the Sacramento Valley to the university's agricultural branch at Davis, an institution now, like Guelph, promoted
to separate university rank and with the added distinction recently
of having sought to exclude the litigious Allan Bakke from its medical school. At Davis I was in charge of teaching in economics, agricultural economics, farm management and accounting and, apart
from assistance from an elderly dean, provided all the instruction in
these subjects. During that year I also wrote a Ph.D. thesis, which
was without distinction, on the expenditures of California counties.
The purpose was to get the degree.

The College of Agriculture of the University of California was
then divided between Davis and Berkeley, with a further branch at
Riverside. The Berkeley part consisted of three buildings in subdued
Moorish revival making three sides of a rectangle, one of which was
the gleaming new building of the Giannini Foundation. An older
one proclaimed its agricultural purpose: "To rescue for human society the native values of rural life." There was frequent speculation
as to why human as opposed to other society was specified, what the
native values of rural life were and why these already needed rescue
in a state where there was no land that had been farmed for more
than three or four generations. Some nitpicking is inevitable.

*   *   *

The University of California in those days existed in a unique political equilibrium in which my fellow agriculturalists played an important part. The instincts of the arts and sciences faculty members
were generally liberal; the professors expressed sympathy for the
migrant field-workers, including the Okies and Arkies who were

---

[1] Of which I have told in *Economics, Peace and Laughter* (Boston: Houghton Mifflin,
1971), pp. 344–360.

now swarming into the state from the drought and depression of the southern Great Plains. Paul Taylor, a phenomenally durable reformer in the department of economics, valiantly urged the enforcement of a law prohibiting the distribution to farms of more than 160 acres, of irrigation water that was provided by the federal government at public expense. However, since much of the water had for long gone to much larger landowners, suggestions that the law be enforced were held to be subversive. This was still the response as late as 1977, when the Secretary of the Interior held that so long as the law was on the books, it should be obeyed.

Other professors spoke sympathetically of trade unions, which in the circulation area of the *Los Angeles Times* were then regarded as instruments of extreme sedition. And of the public ownership of utilities and the writings of Lincoln Steffens. With faculty members venturing onto such dubious ground, it was inevitable that the graduate students in economics would go further. In consequence, the most distinguished of my classmates were Communists. We looked up especially to Gregory Silvermaster, who was rather older than the rest of us and who had a regular teaching job at nearby St. Mary's College, a Catholic academy of high religious and athletic reputation. Silvermaster later moved on to Washington and was much celebrated by Whittaker Chambers as a leader of the Communist underground in that city. Robert Merriman, another contemporary, had come down to Berkeley from the University of Nevada where, handsome and popular, he had been a big man on campus and a pillar of the local ROTC. At Berkeley he became the head teaching fellow in economics under Professor Ira B. Cross, a stalwart conservative who prided himself, rightly, on his tolerance of the aberrant political views of the young. In due course, Merriman was awarded one of the rare traveling fellowships in the gift of the university — foreign travel was not for everyone in those days. He turned both this and his ROTC training to unexpected use by going on to Spain where he commanded the Abraham Lincoln Battalion in the Spanish Civil War and was eventually chief of staff of the XV International Brigade. He was killed in Aragón in the retreat from Belchite in 1938, but he lives on as the Robert Jordan of Hemingway's *For Whom the Bell Tolls*. I think of him with admiration.

The mood of the university, ranging from liberal to revolutionary in those years, could have been expected to arouse the antagonism of conservative California citizens and taxpayers. The reaction was far less than might have been imagined. A tradition of academic freedom helped but not much; California conservatives were not then greatly deterred by such abstractions. More of the protection lay in the fact that much of the liberal and all of the revolutionary tendency was without serious operative effect. It expended itself verbally and within a closed circle; what filtered out was not understood. This is not exceptional in the American academic experience. Until relatively recent times, the most radical of the major economics departments in the United States was that of the University of Texas. Here in the mid-century years even active Marxists were tolerated. A few hundred yards distant from the campus was the Texas legislature. The economists at the university survived because the legislators, though politically adverse, were also intellectually obtuse, and a great and useful barrier of ignorance thus separated the enemies of academic freedom from their prey.[2]

At Berkeley, however, academic freedom had a yet more effective defense. My fellow agriculturalists were highly regarded practitioners of what Thorstein Veblen called exoteric learning. (Veblen made a distinction between esoteric knowledge, which enjoys the greatest academic prestige but is without economic or industrial effect, and exoteric learning, which, in contrast, has negligible academic prestige but is very useful.) My colleagues at Berkeley and Davis had gone on from the simple-minded empiricism of the early colleges of agriculture to a scientific and effective response to the numerous afflictions and opportunities of California agriculture. Animal disease, plant disease, declining water tables, soil disorders, bankrupt irrigation districts, even low prices, brought prompt remedial effort from the College of Agriculture. Often, if not invariably, it helped. To this part of the university the politically conservative and very influential California Farm Bureau Federation and the unabashedly reactionary and even more influential Associated Farmers of Califor-

[2] Not entirely, of course. There were recurrent outbursts in the legislature and one or two efforts to persuade the university to sack Robert H. Montgomery and Clarence E. Ayres, the most distinguished and inimical of the economics professors. Once, when under investigation by the legislature, Montgomery was asked if he favored private property. "I do," he said, "and so strongly that I want everyone in Texas to have some." The department was also not without its distinguished defenders. When he was Vice President, I commented to Lyndon Johnson that I thought the department of economics at the University of Texas was the most interesting in the country. He replied, "How long did it take you to find that out?"

nia were deeply indebted. The revolutionaries and the liberals and their rhetoric were the price the farmers had to pay for the exoteric help. Thus the balance between liberty and utility.

No one should think this a theoretical construct. In the early thirties the finances of the State of California were in very poor condition. Payrolls were being covered with tax anticipation certificates which the recipient sold at a discount. State expenditures were reduced, and this included the university budget. The university promptly announced that its savings would be achieved in the College of Agriculture — the Agricultural Extension (Farm Adviser) Service was held to be expendable. At once the legislative mood became more generous, and the budget cuts were restored. As Veblen had indicated, the agriculturalists at the University of California were, indeed, second-class citizens. But we protected the first-class citizens and never ceased to wish that we were better appreciated.

*   *   *

Within the Giannini Foundation there was also a certain balance between the esoteric and exoteric worlds. The Foundation was headed by Howard R. Tolley, recently arrived from the United States Department of Agriculture where he had headed the work on farm management. A lovable, well-loved and extremely homely man, he had the appearance and something of the posture of an elongated frog. He was soon recalled to Washington to serve in the Agricultural Adjustment Administration, of which, yet later, he became the head. When the war restored farm prices and made that activity irrelevant, he came contentedly to work for me controlling food prices.

Quite a few of the Foundation professors were new arrivals, brought in by the Giannini largesse. One recalls with wonder how much could then be done with the income from a million and a half dollars. Full professors were paid three or four thousand dollars a year, worked in narrow offices without secretaries and, when called on the telephone, dashed down the hall to the main office in response to a buzzer. Although all were judged by their usefulness, not all were useful. Peach, prune, grape, avocado, artichoke and citrus growers were told what they might expect as to prices, how in principle they might limit shipments to get higher prices, how they might better manage their cooperatives or their orchards, groves or farms. This service failed of complete success, for economics, then as now, was less than a predictive science. Our price forecasts were based almost entirely on market influences that had yet to reveal themselves. Efforts to limit shipments in order to raise prices broke down when each farmer suspected his neighbor of selling more than his quota and then proceeded to sell more himself. What a farmer could usefully be told about how to manage his farm was somewhat unclear. Still, the effort was made and appreciated.

To earn my $60 a month, I was first assigned to work with Edwin C. Voorhies, a charming bachelor wholly free from economic knowledge but with a certain distinction as the only native-born Californian on the agricultural economics faculty. Our task was to ascertain ways of improving the economic position of the California bee industry. I thought it would be useful to visit retail establishments in various parts of Los Angeles, San Francisco and their environs to see what the owners knew of their customers' tastes and preferences. To these the apiarists could then respond. Eventually we published two substantial monographs, but by neither, I judge, was the well-being of the apiarists much improved.

I did learn that for a young economist, publication, even on so exoteric a subject as the preferences of consumers for orange blossom honey over sage, is a prime measure of academic worth. Those passing judgment on a scholar avow their interest in the quality of his published work, but, in the end, most settle for counting the number of printed pages. In the depression years, the principal, indeed the nearly total, preoccupation of graduate students, outranking sex, alcohol or even revolution, was the question of an eventual job. Few expected ever to achieve one; at Berkeley many kept postponing their final examinations, for then one descended from the modestly honorific stature of a student to the wholly derogatory status of the unemployed. In addition to my more monumental work on bees, I set about writing articles for the *Journal of Farm Economics* and eventually, also, getting my thesis published. I became known as a prolific scholar, and in the spring of 1934, this reputation, unsullied by any consideration as to the quality of the contributions, brought me an offer of an instructorship at Harvard for that autumn. I could have remained happily at Berkeley, which I loved, and Davis, which I endured. But Harvard offered me a great deal more money — $2400 a year instead of the $1800 that I was now being paid for my numerous courses at Davis.

*   *   *

Agricultural economics left me with the strong feeling that social science should be tested by its usefulness.[3] This, as Veblen urged, is a considerable professional handicap. The economists who are most highly regarded in their own time have almost always been those who confined themselves to abstract speculation unmarred by social purpose. Joseph Schumpeter, in later years one of the most admired of my senior Harvard colleagues, once accused John Maynard Keynes of being, like David Ricardo, subject to the curse (his word) of usefulness. Again the prestige of the esoteric as opposed to the exoteric.

However, usefulness causes problems for the teacher. At Berkeley the instruction in agricultural economics — farm management, land economics, marketing, agricultural cooperation, prices — was intensely practical. And much of it encountered the same difficulty that had emerged at Guelph — there was nothing much to teach. All the information useful to students that was possessed by R. L. Adams, the tall and confident professor of farm management, could have been conveyed in an hour or two. So with marketing, agricultural cooperation and other practical subjects. What remained was often tedious description, which one could more easily have read. Or classroom time was spent in discussion. Discussion, in all higher education, is the vacuum which is used to fill a vacuum.

Some instruction I do remember with gratitude. Howard Tolley lectured on statistical methods and left his students with the one indispensable attribute of an economist, which is a sense of magnitudes. This allows one to respect the income tax for the money it raises and forget customs duties since they are insignificant. In personal affairs it causes one to concentrate on important items of revenue and ignore unimportant items of outgo. From Tolley I also learned to add a column of figures by inspection and know for

---

[3] Some forty years later, in a notable presidential address to the American Economic Association, the Nobel laureate and my friend Wassily Leontief surveyed the research achievements of the various branches of economics and concluded that agricultural economics had earned a special distinction in consequence of this test.

nearly all purposes that the resulting 10 percent error could be ignored. George M. Peterson, an exceptionally roughhewn product of the Minnesota farm country, drilled us in the nature of the production function — roughly the behavior of costs with different mixes of labor, capital and land. And even some of the practical information served an eventual purpose. When lecturing or making political speeches in California in later years, I could always astonish my audiences by showing that a Harvard professor could be richly knowledgeable on the details of rice cultivation in the Sacramento Valley or lemon marketing in Ventura County.

Agricultural economics forty-five years ago was an unformed subject. Provision of money to finance its teaching and research had run far ahead of the available subject matter and talent. The Berkeley agricultural economists did have one advantage over my professors at Guelph: they sensed that they were beginners with a good deal to learn.

*   *   *

The teaching of economics proper in those years was in South Hall, a tall, ungainly red-brick building at the base of the Campanile. Two lines of instruction had for me a permanent effect. The first was in the economics of Alfred Marshall, which was taught with great diligence and precision by E. T. Grether, who became a lifelong friend. Marshall, who lived from 1842 to 1924, nearly all that time at the University of Cambridge, was the preeminent figure in what has come to be called the neoclassical school. This is the economics of numerous, competitive firms, each intelligently committed to maximizing its profits and meeting in the market the even more numerous consumers, all rationally distributing their income between products so as to maximize enjoyment. This process is facilitated by an equally rational state, which recognizes the primary role of the market and confines itself to rendering those services, from education to the enforcement of laws to providing for the common defense, that are beyond the scope of the market. In this system prices settle out at cost plus a minimum necessary profit. Workers can find employment by slightly lowering their wage demands, thus making it worth the while of some employer to hire them. There are occasional flawing monopolies, but these are the exception. The Marshallian world is a tidy thing without unemployment, inflation or depression or anyhow not much. Not surprisingly, many who studied Marshall found it pleasant to live in his world forever.

By the time of my exposure, Marshall's *Principles of Economics* had reached its eighth edition and totaled 871 learned pages. We were required, more or less, to know it all. The feeling that I was meant to be an economist emerged when I discovered that I had grasped the essentials of Marshall and had escaped the despair that afflicted many of my contemporaries.

In 1937, when I was at the University of Cambridge as a postdoctoral student, Alfred Marshall had been dead for thirteen years, but Mary Marshall, his widow, survived and maintained the prophet's house on Madingley Road as a shrine. In the garden was the study where Marshall worked, one side of it open to the air, the whole structure mounted on a pivot like a Dutch windmill so that it could be turned to catch the light or the sun. Mary still rode her bicycle with perilous abandon through the Cambridge traffic until one day John Maynard Keynes, himself a protégé of Marshall, took it away from her.

Marshall's world of competitive entrepreneurs, maximizing consumers and a suitably reticent state continues to serve the ends of comfortable orthodoxy today. It does not describe the world as it is. The great modern corporation — of which a thousand do around half the American business — the unions, the farm organizations and the welfare and garrison state have captured the reality, as one day they will capture the economic mind.[4] But to have mastered Marshall was a good thing. To know what is right, one must have a firm grasp on what is wrong.

In the Berkeley years I was also introduced to Adam Smith, David Ricardo, Karl Marx, the early John Maynard Keynes and the great German economists who sought truth in history and of whom only Werner Sombart seriously entered my consciousness. This instruction was led by Leo Rogin, a teacher who established himself firmly in the affections of all of my generation. However, after Marshall, the major influence on me from those years was Thorstein Veblen.

Veblen is the most interesting social scientist the United States has produced. With Henry George, he is also one of the few with roots in the last century who still have a substantial and appreciative audience. In 1931, Veblen was two years dead, his last years having

[4] I return to this point in Chapter 32.

been spent near the Stanford campus from which he had been ejected for conspicuous philandering, as then judged, two decades before.

Veblen was perhaps dangerously attractive to someone of my background. The Scotch in Ontario owned and farmed the land, dominated the political life and, in the case of the more prestigious clans, sought educational advancement with some enthusiasm. As I have told, we felt ourselves superior to the merchants and tradesmen of the towns. But the townspeople, more often of English origin and prideful supporters of the Church of England, took their superior social position for granted. Town folk, not hicks. We disputed that eminence without being clear as to what our recourse, if any, should be. The Veblens were a highly intelligent and cultivated family, relatively affluent, at a time when Norwegian farmers in Minnesota were considered awkward, uncouth, unmannered and even slightly stupid. Veblen's scholarship was an eruption against all who, in consequence of wealth, occupation, ethnic origin or elegance of manner, made invidious claim (a Veblen phrase) to superior worldly position. I knew the mood.

Veblen's treatment of the manners and social observances of the American rich dealt with their dwellings, entertainments and dress on the same level as an anthropologist would examine the orgiastic observances and ceremonials of a primitive New Guinea tribe. In consequence, he made the rich the object not of envy, which concedes superiority, but of ridicule, which does not. The Veblenian ridicule persists in the language, most notably in the still-current reference to eye-catching social extravagance as "conspicuous consumption." In the United States, in contrast with France or Italy, a too overt display of wealth has come to be thought a trifle gauche. This — a raised eyebrow at conspicuous consumption — was the achievement of Veblen.

He was not a constructive figure; no alternative economic system and no penetrating reforms are associated with his name. There was danger here. Veblen was a skeptic and an enemy of pretense. Those who drank too deeply could be in doubt about everything and everybody; they could believe that all effort at reform was humbug. I've thought to resist this tendency, but in other respects Veblen's influence on me has lasted long. One of my greatest pleasures in writing has come from the thought that perhaps my work might annoy

someone of comfortably pretentious position. Then comes the sad-
dening realization that such people rarely read. There is a theorem
to this effect. At Harvard in 1934, I took over the course previously
given in agricultural economics by Thomas Nixon Carver, a notable
conservative of his time. Were he to be remembered for anything, it
would be for Carver's Law: "The trouble with radicals is that they
only read radical literature, and the trouble with conservatives is that
they don't read anything."

In the war years one of the recruits to the staff of the Office of
Price Administration was a leading Berkeley Veblenian, Robert
Brady. Brady came up with the sensible thought that lubricating oil
could be conserved by not having it changed every 1000 miles as the
oil companies then demanded. I did not approve the idea; such was
the pressure on my office that I never got around to his paper. As
would any good follower of Veblen, Bob accused me not of negligence but of shielding the oil companies.

And there has been yet more. In 1970, the nominating committee
of the American Economic Association entertained a proposal that I
be the next president. Nomination within the AEA is equivalent to
election; democratic centralism is not confined to the Soviet Union.
My selection was opposed by Professor Milton Friedman, and he offered as his clinching argument that Veblen had never been president. I learned after the election that this got me by. Later I wrote
the introduction for a new edition of *The Theory of the Leisure Class*
for Houghton Mifflin and Penguin Classics and led a drive to rescue
from the ravages of time and casual tenants the fine house built by
Thorstein Veblen's father with his own hands on the family homestead south of Northfield, Minnesota.

*   *   *

Over the Christmas holidays in 1933, I used some of my new wealth
from my teaching at Davis to make the first trip home to Canada in
two and a half years. (In accordance with the thrifty family compact
earlier mentioned by which the older educated the younger, I was
already using some of it to send my younger sister Catherine to college.) I went on to Philadelphia to attend the meetings of the American Economic Association. There, except among the agricultural
economists, the reputable opinion was powerfully against the New
Deal. The budget was unbalanced. The value of the dollar on the

international exchanges was being depreciated deliberately by the gold-buying program. The National Recovery Administration was allowing businessmen to get together to stabilize prices and wages in an especially egregious conflict with Marshallian market principles. The Agricultural Adjustment Administration was cutting back on agricultural production. Every one of these actions violated the accepted canons of economic wisdom. All were sternly denounced. Yet there was also a strong undercurrent of excitement at the meetings over what was going on in Washington. I decided to go down to see for myself, my first visit. Everything was entirely up to my expectations.

Early the following summer, now with a Ph.D., I left Berkeley to go back east and, eventually, take up my job at Harvard. With a fellow graduate student who, like nearly all of my contemporaries, now had a job with the federal government, I again journeyed across the country by car, this time through Yellowstone National Park, over the northern Great Plains and stopping, as was obligatory that year, to see Sally Rand at the Century of Progress in Chicago, her performance being the major current breakthrough in soft-core pornography. This was one of the years of the great drought, and in South Dakota the soil was in drifts in the manner of snowbanks behind the fence rows. Cars were being driven with last year's license plates. A stone thrown up from one of the dry gravel roads took out our windshield. One was surprised on reaching Illinois to see green fields again. Since I wasn't expected in Cambridge until the autumn, I decided to accompany my friend to Washington before going north.

3

First Glimpse of Grandeur

THE ATTRACTIONS of politics are manifold, one being its theater. Politicians play roles that are larger than life and not their own. At any moment they are giving a studied imitation of someone better or more interesting than they are themselves. Or they are enhancing their own public image. They read or hear that they are forthright, sincere, uncompromising, and so they feel obliged to seem. All this is an interesting thing to watch.

A second source of interest is that politics has come to resemble football, soccer, baseball or any other spectator sport. One develops, as to any contest, a commitment to the play and to the outcome. And in politics the rankest amateur managing a campaign or working therein is allowed to believe himself an accomplished professional. Reporters will listen with awe as he outlines strategies that only remotely support belief and as he speaks unblushingly of "what the American voter really wants." The reduction of politics to a spectator sport, I might note, has been one of the more malign accomplishments of television. Television requires reporters to seem impartial, and this, reinforced by normal mental lethargy, means that they don't get into issues of war, peace, taxes or welfare. Questions of political tactics and strategy, who is winning and who is losing, are safe and comprehensible. So television newsmen are breathless on how the game is being played, largely silent on what the game is all about. On the morning following the 1978 congressional elections, I was asked in urgent tones by an NBC commentator who I thought would win a yet unresolved electoral contest in Ohio. I said that it was a silly question; he had only to wait for a few hours and he would know for sure. The great man trembled with indignation.

For a participant, politics is also psychologically therapeutic. Being combative, it is a solvent for aggression. One can say things about others to an appreciative audience that normally would be reserved for private comment. This improves personal behavior. Arthur Schlesinger's family noted that he was always unnaturally agreeable when writing speeches for Adlai Stevenson.

Finally, with all else in politics, there is the thought that one is helping change the world. And there is a helpful element of illusion here. You are always aware of your own efforts, much less so of the efforts of the many who similarly engage themselves. From this comes a pleasantly exaggerated sense of accomplishment. It is why political memoirs must always be read with caution.

My own introduction to the enchantments of politics began well before I was ten. I was taken by my father to political meetings where I saw him, as I've often told, mount a manure pile at a farm auction and apologize for speaking from the Tory platform. By the time I left Canada, I had seen William Lyon Mackenzie King and various of the other great men in action. But my true fascination with politics began with Franklin D. Roosevelt.

On March 4, 1933, a class in land economics under Professor David Weeks had a field exercise near Walnut Creek, then an impeccably rural landscape a few miles over the hills from Berkeley and Oakland. The purpose was to instill an elementary awareness of land-surveying techniques. I was not a member of the class, but I thought this knowledge might be useful one day. A miscalculation. From the radio of a nearby farmhouse I was able to hear Roosevelt's inaugural address and, in ringing tones, his deathless affirmation that "the only thing we have to fear is fear itself." This was a gross misstatement of current fact, but at such moments people do not demand literal truth.

The fashion on the liberal left in the election of 1932, it is now forgotten, was to dismiss Roosevelt and Hoover as equally hopeless. People of perception supported Norman Thomas, and the intellectually uncompromising were for the Communists or else they disdained involvement. But as a youngster in Canada, I had a different instruction. There were two parties and you chose, or more likely were born to, one or the other. Every family was known for its party as it was known for its church. "They are Presbyterians and Liberals." On coming to the United States, I took for granted that I should so classify myself and be a Democrat.

Also in the autumn of 1932, I had gone to hear Hoover speak on the outskirts of Oakland outside one of the largest Hoovervilles in California. Housing was in some spacious sewer pipe that had been left randomly over the landscape when the city ran out of money. Hoover there told his audience of mendicants that the Depression was over. I shared their doubt. At least Roosevelt did not believe that.

By the spring of 1934, after a year of F.D.R., the views of the young professors and especially of the graduate students at Berkeley had changed. Against all learned prediction, much was being attempted in Washington; Roosevelt now seemed a wonderfully compelling leader. Word had also reached the university that a nearly unlimited number of jobs were open for economists at unbelievably high pay in the federal government. All the new agencies needed this talent. Students who had been resisting for years the completion of theses and the resulting unemployment now finished them up in weeks. Some did not even stop to do that. So a new gold rush began, back across the American River, up by Calaveras County, over the crest of the Sierras and on across the Rockies and the Plains to the Potomac. When I got to Washington in the early summer of 1934, many of my friends were already at work.

On my first day there, I went to the South Building of the Department of Agriculture. This large yellow-brick structure is on the right, across from the Bureau of Printing and Engraving as one comes in from National Airport over the bridge onto Fourteenth Street. It consists of long bays and cross-bays. The important people had their offices on the outside on Fourteenth Street or looking north to the much smaller marble-faced building that housed, as it still does, the Secretary of Agriculture. In 1934, the South Building was unfinished. Passing along a corridor, you would come suddenly to open air and a barrier protecting you from the precipice below. I went to Howard Tolley's office in the Agricultural Adjustment Administration, and he immediately suggested that I go on the payroll for the summer. I as promptly agreed. I was not a citizen, but it is not certain that one was even asked about such details in those civilized days. After filling in forms, I was, however, required to go to a small room on the upper floor and meet the resident representative of James A. Farley, the Postmaster General and custodian of Democratic patronage. There I affirmed that I was a Democrat; one could be a Democrat without being a citizen or a voter. My salary was at the rate of $3200 a year. In the next months I paid off all my college debts, and not since have I been short of money.

I shared an office with two other civil servants, one a fellow University of California economist from Maine, a man with an amused and relaxed view of life and the Latinate name of Rutilus Allen. Our other stablemate, slightly older and somewhat portly, we addressed as Doctor. He left early each day for work at American University where he was getting his Ph.D. He had previously been president of a small college in Los Angeles, and his present doctorate, he explained one afternoon, he had awarded to himself. He was getting another because a self-given degree "was not quite the same thing."

A few months earlier, President Roosevelt, reflecting a lifelong concern, had asked that serious attention be given to the state of the American land. In the Southeast it was being washed away by water, on the Plains it was being blown away by wind. Elsewhere it was suffering idleness and neglect.

The public lands of the United States, then as now, exceeded the combined areas of Germany, France, Italy, Belgium, Holland, Switzerland, Denmark, Austria, Hungary *and* Albania. Where socialized ownership of land is concerned, only the U.S.S.R., China and Brazil can claim company with the United States. This great territory was being administered by the General Land Office, an agency with a reputation for having a sharp ear for political influence and a tolerant view of outright larceny. It was still possible under the Homestead Act for a settler, if really given to suffering, to go upon these lands and prove up a farm of his own. (The public domain was finally withdrawn from entry that autumn.) Charles W. Eliot II, a grandson of President Eliot of Harvard and a friend and favorite of F.D.R., had been asked to come up with a report on what should be done to check wind and water erosion and protect the public lands. Eliot had then turned to the Secretary of Agriculture for help, who had turned the matter over to the Agricultural Adjustment Administration. It was for this work that I was hired. My particular assignment was to propose a policy for land on which no one could afford, or would think it worthwhile, to pay taxes.

This tax-delinquent land was also a vast estate. Half of Florida was theoretically subject to seizure for unpaid taxes. Elsewhere in much of the old South, in northern Michigan, Wisconsin, Minnesota and in the Dust Bowl states, delinquency was not the exception but the rule.

I got into the tax laws of the worst beset states, a dreary task, to see how valid public title to this reverted land would be. And I went out to Michigan and back to New York to look into imaginative efforts being made in those states to bring poor and tax-delinquent land into permanent public ownership.

Such public ownership seemed to me the right solution. Accordingly, I proposed that where the agricultural prospect was hopeless — a frequent situation — the federal government, acting either by itself or through a state, should purchase the land for the amount of the unpaid taxes and add it to the public domain. It was my thought that one day this acreage, now scorned, would be a public asset.

Meanwhile much-needed revenue would go back from Washington to the local governments and school districts. It was not an easy case to make. A wilderness is now thought a valuable thing; then it was only a wilderness. Additionally I was surrounded by sensible men, who thought the whole idea irresponsible. To clear tax titles would require special legislation. Good money would then go out and worthless land would come in. I did not fight very hard, for I was concerned to show that, though young, I was a very responsible chap. In review my plan was compromised into banality. Perhaps it didn't matter greatly. In Washington nothing or not much ever happens in response to a report. Something only happens when someone obsessed by belief fights the proposal through. This I did not yet know.

*   *   *

The most prestigious of my California contemporaries, as I've told, were Communists. Now they had come to Washington to save the free enterprise system. Some found their view of capitalism substantially improved by the $3200 a year. Others, more stalwart, continued to gather to discuss the forthcoming revolution.

The revolutionaries from California at the Department of Agriculture found kindred if more moderate spirits from other universities and colleges, and most notably from the Harvard Law School. These included Lee Pressman, John J. Abt, Nathan Witt and, most famous of all, Alger Hiss. There were others at the U.S.D.A., including Abe Fortas, later a Supreme Court Justice; Jerome N. Frank, later a highly regarded federal judge; Thurman W. Arnold, a law professor, judge, public official and eminently successful Washington lawyer;[1] Paul A. Porter, Arnold's future law partner, of whom there will be much mention later; George W. Ball, later an Undersecretary of State, Ambassador to the United Nations and my colleague in numerous enterprises; and Adlai Stevenson.

It was a remarkable convocation because the Agriculture Department in those days was a remarkable place; there may never have been a bureaucracy quite like it. Partly this was owing to Henry Agard Wallace, who was Secretary of Agriculture as his father had been a decade earlier. But even in the Harding-Coolidge-Hoover years the Department had been a haven for liberal economists and scientists and other progenitors of social change. It sustained its own graduate school, and any idea, however radical, could at least have a hearing. As at the University of California, the exoteric contribution to agriculture was widely observed and appreciated by farmers and legislators. This accorded it protection.[2]

During my first months at the USDA I met none of the famous subversives. I was not important enough. Doubtless had I been invited to their meetings, I would have gone, for in Washington there is always a powerful yearning to be in — to be with those who are turning the wheels. The Washington radicals of those days had a deep sense of their role or potential role. They did not proselytize. Rather, they regarded themselves as members of a very special club for which only a few were qualified by revelation and commitment.

---

[1] A friend who did not cultivate modesty either in himself or in others. I treasure a small book, a fragment of autobiography, from Thurman. It is inscribed: "To Kenneth Galbraith, the world's greatest economist from the only man qualified to say."

[2] The protection was not complete; there was one notable witch hunt in the Republican years. Econometric methods were then, for the first time, being applied systematically to prospective domestic and world supplies of crops and livestock products, likewise to demand and to forecasting prices. One such forecast concluded that the price of cotton would fall. On the release of the forecast, it did. Two of the most formidable demagogues in the history of the Republic, Senator J. Thomas (Tom Tom) Heflin of Alabama and Senator Ellison D. (Cotton Ed) Smith of South Carolina, were aroused. They launched an investigation and discovered that the guilty men were Mordecai Ezekiel, one of the founders of modern statistical method, and Louis Bean, one of the inventors of modern polling techniques. Both were Jewish. Neither, under examination, knew the color of the cottom blossom when in bloom. Worse, it was established beyond doubt that Bean had been born in Russia. Firm remedial action was taken: a law was passed making the release of forecasts of cotton prices by a public agency a criminal offense.

When, after World War II, they came under mortal attack, I first reflected gratefully on the accident of fortune that had kept me out. But then it occurred to me that even if I had asked, perhaps they would not have allowed me in.

I did not see Roosevelt that summer nor did anyone for whom I worked. My image of the man was no less complete — he was there, a massive figure back of his desk, his cigarette and cigarette holder rising at a jaunty angle, telling you how important was the work you were doing and how much he approved the result. The impression was one of great physical strength. That was because not then or during the twelve years he was President do I remember seeing a news photo of Roosevelt in a wheelchair, his normal recourse for movement.

* * *

Writers on Roosevelt speak compulsively of a father figure. My view was of a man who saw the United States as would a kindly and attentive landlord, concerned in all aspects for the lives of his tenants and the estate on which they dwelt. He was not the source of all wisdom; indeed, one considered him greatly open to petition and persuasion, and no man could ever have had more of both. But when he had decided, that was truth. Once a few years later at the University of Cambridge when I was there as a Social Science Research Fellow, I dined one evening with some lawyers at the High Table at Gonville and Caius College. Afterward in the Senior Combination Room we joined in talk about the President's court-packing proposal, a matter of major contention and debate at the time. I defended it as a matter of course; all of F.D.R.'s own arguments I had accepted and had fully in hand. My hosts were impressed and astonished — no American had ever said anything good about court-packing before. I was invited to lecture on the subject at the law school. Back at our house, it occurred to me that perhaps it had been supposed that I was a lawyer. When I asked next morning, this turned out to be the case, and the invitation was gratefully withdrawn.

Only after Roosevelt's death did I realize that a President could be wrong. In the summer of 1945, at a meeting in London with William L. Clayton, a brilliant, civilized and charming Texas businessman turned public official, I heard that Harry Truman had canceled Lend-Lease. It was a premature, ill-considered and unwise action urged on the President by those who thought we were being too kind to our allies and in particular to the Russians. Clayton was aghast. So was I. Suddenly the thought assailed me: no longer does one come automatically to the President's defense. One must decide whether he is right or wrong.

*   *   *

When F.D.R. came to office in March 1933, so desperate was the economic position that for the business and financial community he was an angel of rescue. Even the House of Morgan publicly rejoiced. By 1934, things were enough better so that his efforts on behalf of farmers and the unemployed, his tendency to make light of economic orthodoxy, could be disliked and even feared. Roosevelt had become "that man in the White House" and "the traitor to his class."

There was a characteristically American quality to the attack. Italians, Frenchmen, Germans and even many Englishmen seek more income and property because of the pleasure it imparts. Affluent Americans always seek more because of the social good it will accomplish, the support it will give to incentives and investment. Roosevelt was unmoved by the criticism of those who shared his own privileged past and equally by the moral or functional case for personal pecuniary gain. The Roosevelt response to criticism and to special pleading in whatever disguise had a deep effect on me and, I believe, on others who were part of his time.

The business attacks on Roosevelt and the Roosevelt response had larger consequences, ones as far-reaching as anything in American history. For when Roosevelt countered, a whole generation joined on his side. If the privileged were against Roosevelt, we obviously must be against privilege. If Roosevelt found the moral posture of big business unconvincing or fraudulent, it must be so. Roosevelt is assumed to have made hostility toward business an American intellectual norm. But it was the business attacks on him that made it inevitable.

*   *   *

During the summer of 1934, with two other economists of similarly subordinate rank, I lived outside Alexandria in the house of a mid-level official in the Department of Agriculture named Ernst H. Wiecking. Every night we settled into a discussion of our work of the day. Or we had a more general seminar on how American agriculture was to be rescued and the nation saved. Each morning we left early for work. There was much to do and Wiecking wanted an hour for thought before he was caught up in the daily routine. I thought myself especially important because of the President's interest in land. Perhaps it was from this that I developed the image of F.D.R. as a landlord. The United States was an extension of his Hyde Park estate. He would wish to take charge of those tax-delinquent acres. It was only that my colleagues and superiors, no less devoted to his interest, did not want to load him up with worthless real estate.

The summer passed despite my best efforts to adhere to every moment. Outwardly Washington was much as now, although streetcars passed along the streets and, though it did not then seem possible, there were fewer automobiles. The Senate and the House of Representatives had but one office building each; going by their doors, one saw secretaries and assistants idling in the outer offices. The Commerce Building was new and the Federal Triangle just approaching completion. The pseudo-classical façades were thought very bad, partly because they were attributed to Hoover. All now agree that they improve greatly on the new functional monstrosities to the south of the Mall. Down toward the Capitol was open space; Andrew Mellon's generosity, improved by his difficulties with his income tax, had not yet brought the National Gallery.

Beneath the surface, however, Washington was a far less pleasant place than it is now. Once, walking through the distant recesses of the South Building in search of one of Rexford Tugwell's acolytes who had some relation to my failed land, I saw a black woman working at a typewriter. In the Washington of 1934, one never imagined that black men or women were allowed up to such levels. Sometimes, after working late, I took the bus home to our Alexandria seminar sessions; blacks moved dutifully to the back, as a firm notice required.

Franklin D. Roosevelt won the affection and support of northern blacks because he gave them jobs. He did nothing in the South that would disturb the great southern baronage in the Senate — Joseph T. Robinson of Arkansas, Pat Harrison of Mississippi, Tom Connally of Texas, Walter George of Georgia — for out of party loyalty, agricultural interest and a shared perception of the obligations of fellow members of the ruling class, these men gave the President his prime congressional base. Any movement toward civil equality and this base would have gone. Mrs. Roosevelt was greatly criticized for being seen, on occasion, with "colored" people in the South. The New Deal remembered the forgotten man but not the truly forgotten. Looking back, I am astonished at how little we were concerned.

*   *   *

When eventually I went on to Cambridge and Harvard, it became evident, to my joy, that our report on saving the land would require a great deal more work. And every word would have to be scrutinized by higher and wiser authority and revised accordingly. It was thought that I would be useful in this effort, the unique advantage of the individual who can write. I was provided with a resource of infinite wonder, a book of travel requests. One had only to fill out a form and present it at the window at South Station in Boston. The agent regarded you with respect and gave you a railroad ticket and a lower berth in the Pullman to Washington. The government was billed direct. Sometime around midnight you awakened to a jolting about, voices outside, and you knew you were in New York. A little after dawn you joined the assembly in the Pullman washroom, chins held elevated and being scraped before the mirrors, and then a twenty-cent taxi ride took you to breakfast in the South Building cafeteria. There a colleague told of the great events of the preceding week. Almost every Friday evening that fall and winter I managed to be on the train to Washington.

4

Harvard Before Democracy

In mid-September 1934, perhaps because I had not at the time seen the Atlantic Ocean, I journeyed to Baltimore and took passage to Boston on the Merchant and Miners Transportation Company Line. This allowed for a day's stopover in Norfolk, and I went out to Virginia Beach for its unsurpassed view of the water. Then or later I was inoculated against any desire ever in the future to find rest and recreation on such landscape. Three or four times in my adult life I have ventured for a weekend to Martha's Vineyard, Wellfleet or some other nesting place of the weary literate. The need to engage in seemingly intelligent conversation while sitting under the hot sun, on hot sand, while eating sand-impregnated hamburgers and watching the remnants of someone's lunch of last week ooze up through the shingle must be one of life's most starkly negative pleasures. Always I've re-achieved civilization with relief.

In Cambridge I took up residence on the top floor of a large wooden house inhabited by two elderly ladies named Bradford. I arranged also to have my breakfast and dinner with my hostesses. The night of my arrival I told them at length of the wonders of Washington and my accomplishments in retrieving our landed heritage. They were not interested and early next morning invited me to leave. To soften the blow they said they were distressed by the way I rushed up the stairs. A few blocks away on Irving Terrace I found an Irish landlady of ferocious aspect. She tolerated me for the academic year, and the Boston Irish have ever since been deep in my affection. By the time of my arrival, many, like my landlady, were of the property-owning class. None doubted their position as the ruling class. The Cambridge city government was an Irish fief; so was that of Boston; so, with James Michael Curley as Governor, was that of the Commonwealth. Soon, with the arrival of the Kennedys and their friends, the social position of the Irish would be secure. Yet they would remain a bruised and exploited people, nature's eternal underdogs, as an ample and sometimes excellent literature would affirm. No other race withstands success so well.

After finding living quarters, I was shown to my office, a large, gloomy room on the top floor of Widener Library, from which I moved a few years later to the rooms in the newly built Littauer Center that I still occupy. Although there were interim tenants, there is also some stability in this world. My Widener quarters were later taken over by Archibald MacLeish, and I thought he caught my look of revulsion when once or twice I visited him there.

The city of Berkeley, in the days before Messrs. Jarvis and Gann and Professor Milton Friedman made the spending of money on urban sanitation an infringement of personal liberty, was sparkling clean and covered with geraniums. The California campus, as I have told, was a thing of grandeur. Especially in the filthy snows of winter, Cambridge was in dismal contrast. Harvard's random architecture, drifting incoherently into the city, did little for one's soul. Old Harvard men are known to love it. There is no accounting for taste.

*   *   *

In the late forties and fifties the Harvard economists gained a reputation for dangerous liberalism, and this became a source of grave concern to numerous graduates and to the Board of Overseers. Since I was a major cause of the anxiety, it is a matter to which I will return. In 1934, there was little occasion for worry.

Frank W. Taussig, then in his mid-seventies and of fine presence and aristocratic bearing — the Taussigs were among the first citizens of St. Louis — was the acknowledged center of the economics constellation. His two-volume textbook instructed the freshmen; he personally instructed the graduate students in basic economic theory and edited the *Quarterly Journal of Economics*. In the latter capacity, always sympathetic to the efforts of the young, he was notably helpful to my belief that the volume of one's publication was the basis of upward mobility in economics. Taussig was the American counterpart of Alfred Marshall. The world he described was also one of many firms competing in each and every market, the flawing exception of monopoly aside. Production provided the income to buy what was produced. There were cyclical rhythms that brought occasional bad times, but these were self-corrective. Trade was best when free, although measures to arrest the exploitation of consumers or workers commended themselves to men of good will.

Frank Taussig was one of the greatly civilized men who find the world mostly good as it is but who are immensely tolerant of those who believe it could be better. During World War I, he had been in charge of the rather elementary price-fixing that was undertaken during that conflict, and later he was Chairman of the Tariff Commission. He continued to think and speak much of these experiences. His basic graduate course was Economics 11, and it was taught in the kindly exchange with the students that is called the Socratic Method. The grade he achieved in the course settled a student's quality for life. When Harry Dexter White, who by the late forties had risen to be a highly effective Assistant Secretary of the Treasury, came under massive assault as an alleged subversive (an assault which continued after his death in 1948), one of the older professors commented that he had always had some doubts about the man; he had not done too well in Ec. 11.

Taussig was what was soon to be called an old-fashioned liberal. Charles J. Bullock, a conservative, managed to give the department at least a minimal polarization. He lectured on the history of economic thought in a course that was known to the students as the history of economics from Adam to Adam Smith. Lectures on this subject and on public finance frequently got stalled when Bullock suddenly remembered some Bolshevist aberration, as he saw it, of Herbert Hoover. He did not denounce Roosevelt; Roosevelt was beyond the pale. "Hoover," he once said, invoking a limited gift for metaphor, "had a buzz saw but didn't know how to use it. Roosevelt doesn't even know that he has a buzz saw." Bullock never said what he thought right, but he left no one in doubt as to what he believed wrong. William L. Crum taught statistics, and he examined Ph.D. candidates by asking how one scholar or another had misused figures. In my adult life I have occasionally been criticized for inadequacy in statistical or econometric method. Crum is responsible; from him I early formed the impression that no figure and no calculation was really valid and that it was foolish to expose one's self by citing one. In 1936, Crum had a brief moment of glory. That year the *Literary Digest*, at the height of its distinction, sent out 10,000,000 ballots to American voters and received back one in roughly every five. These showed that Alf Landon would be elected by a margin reflective of the return — 1,294,000 to 973,000.[1] Crum corrected the *Digest* figures for sampling error and wrote a series of articles showing that it would be an even bigger Landon landslide.

Landon himself, I found out much later, was under no such illusions. In 1971, I responded to a request from him that I give the annual Landon Lecture at Kansas State University. Richard Nixon had given it previously, and I learned to my pleasure from Landon that I was needed to correct the moral balance of the endowment. A gallant, amused and amusing man, then eighty-four, he told me of campaigning in 1936 just before Election Day in New Jersey and prior to a big evening rally in Madison Square Garden. At the end of the long day he sat down with Governor Harold G. Hoffman of New Jersey in the latter's suite in a hotel in Newark and said to Hoffman, "What chance in New Jersey, Governor?"

Hoffman replied, "None. What chance in the country, Governor?"

"None, Governor."

At this point they noticed that a man Landon had thought was a member of Hoffman's staff was taking down the conversation.

"Does he work for you, Governor?"

"No, I thought he worked for you, Governor."

The man was a reporter for the Newark *Evening News*. Hoffman said not to worry, he knew the publisher.

Landon said, "No, I think he knows that if he publishes this conversation, we won't need an election." The reporter agreed.

The chairman of the Harvard department of economics when I arrived, as he had been for some years before and would be for many years after, was Harold Hitchings Burbank. A native-born New Englander, a rarity in the department, Burbie was of medium height, chubby figure and bluish complexion. He was engaged in a failing struggle to protect Harvard from alien intellectual influences, although he didn't much care for the domestic sort either. Foreign scholars were frequently Jews, and that was another ground for rejection. In an exceptional exercise of determination, Burbie man-

---

[1] Actually there was a slightly worried tone. "The Poll represents the most extensive straw ballot in the field . . . the most experienced . . . the most unbiased . . . a Poll that has always previously been correct." *Literary Digest*, vol. 72 (October 31, 1936), p. 6.

aged, after World War II, to prevent the promotion to a professor-ship of Paul A. Samuelson, an eventual Nobel laureate and on the way to becoming the best-regarded of all American economists. In 1950, as his last act at the last meeting of the department at which he presided, he offered a motion to fund, meaning to add to capital, "some miscellaneous monies available to the department." Someone wearily said, "So moved." Someone else said, "Second the motion." There was no dissent.

On the way out afterward, I asked one of my colleagues what the motion meant. He didn't know. Nor did anyone else. When I investigated the next day, I discovered that over the years Burbie had been resisting, on a plea of poverty, the spending of endowment funds for bringing visiting lecturers to Harvard. Again the alien influence. Now, as his term came to a close, he was faced with something unprecedented in the annals of official misfeasance: exposure as a reverse spendthrift.

Withal, Burbie had many virtues. His door, unlike mine over the years, was always open. He listened to the troubles of students or young instructors with sympathy, though not with unduly taxing thought of alleviating them. And better than any person I have known, he solved the problem of how to combine research with teaching in an untaxing way. His field was public finance; his special interest was the financing of Massachusetts town governments. When he finished the study of the finances of one negligible town, he went on to check his conclusions by studying those of another. This work lasted him for all his life.

It was known in the department of economics that it had been some years since Burbank had read a book. This, shortly before my arrival, had somber consequences. The members of the department then lunched together each week. A young teacher named Redvers Opie, then the son-in-law of the great Taussig, later a fellow of Magdalen College, Oxford, and later still Counsellor and Economic Adviser to the British Embassy in Washington during World War II, engaged Burbie in discussion:

"I've just finished Austin Olney's book on the corporate income tax. How did you react to it, Burbie?"

"Olney is competent but really not first-rate. Judged strictly as a work of scholarship, there are some pretty serious flaws."

The following week Opie resumed:

"Burbie, how did you react to Richard McAdoo on the incidence of the property tax?"

"Interesting but mediocre. From a scholarly and scientific standpoint not first-rate."

"What would you say, then, about the new Andre Deutsch study?"

"I thought it of some interest. But as a scholar Andre Deutsch is not really first-rate."

Eventually someone told Professor Burbank that these scholars and several others were figments of the Opie imagination, and Opie later attributed his own departure from Harvard to this entertainment.

My personal feeling toward Harold Hitchings Burbank was affectionate as opposed to admiring and became more so when, in 1977, under the Freedom of Information Act, I gained access to my FBI file. In 1940, agents had asked Burbank about my fitness for Washington responsibilities, and he (his name was blotted out, but his identity was easily established) "advised" the agent that:

> . . . Galbraith was an excellent teacher; that he gave a commanding appearance due to his height of 5′6″ [sic] and his dignified bearing. It was [Burbank's] emphatic statement that Galbraith was absolutely loyal and patriotic. He said that though the subject leaned as far to the left as President Roosevelt, he was completely in sympathy with a democratic form of government . . .

More or less simultaneously with my arrival at Harvard, Joseph A. Schumpeter took up permanent residence at the university. There were many, and with reason, who thought him the most interesting economist of his time. Then in his early fifties, he had already lived several lives. As the Austrian Finance Minister, he had presided over the great postwar inflation and the ensuing collapse. He had been a principal in a disastrous business venture, a junior partner in a law firm in Cairo and a highly visible and popular professor at Bonn in Germany. His political and business misfortunes had left him with a deep distaste for practical affairs, and he condemned as intellectually debased economists who presumed to advise on practical questions. On the other hand, his theoretical work had been an unalloyed triumph. His *Theory of Economic Development,* published in German in 1912 when he was twenty-nine, celebrated the power of the entrepreneur as a force for social change. Seeing some hitherto unperceived need or some hitherto unperceived way of organizing to fill a need, the entrepreneur sets in motion a wave of change and imitation that renders existing plant and methods of production obsolete. It replaces them with something much superior; progress in capitalism proceeds in "a gale of creative destruction."[2]

Joseph Alois Schumpeter was a slightly swarthy man of solid frame and a little less than average height. He had an amused and expressive face and an unremitting love for company and conversation. That Cambridge lacked the style of Franz Josef's Vienna he never doubted, but he was determined to compensate as best he could. He held court each afternoon in a small coffee shop across Massachusetts Avenue from Widener Library; to his classes he recurrently pictured himself as a man of sophisticated knowledge and worldly interests and also of frustrated ambition. He had intended as a young man, he said, to be the greatest scholar, the greatest lover and the greatest general of his generation, but, sadly, the circumstances of postwar Austria had denied him the possibility of a military career. A gentleman, he once told his impecunious graduate students — the figure is firm in my memory — could not live on less than $50,000 a year. That, taxes and prices considered, would be the approximate present equivalent of $300,000. Given the choice between being right and being memorable, Schumpeter never hesitated.

No economist of this century so effectively articulated the case for capitalism. The other motivated conservatives of the age, Ludwig von Mises and Friedrich von Hayek — like the Chicagoans, as they are called, of the present day — defended the system by assimilating it to the competitive, neoclassical faith. Big corporations and big unions did not exist and big government need not and should not exist. This defense has the damaging flaw that the leaders of the large corporation, the most characteristic furniture of modern capitalism, exist in grievous inconsistency with the theory by which they are defended. Called before a congressional committee, the head of Exxon must confess a power over prices, customers, suppliers and the government that is wholly at odds with the vision of economic society advanced by the prophets on whose defense he depends.

[2] This, one of Schumpeter's famous phrases, is from a much later work, *Capitalism, Socialism and Democracy*, 2nd ed. (New York: Harper & Brothers, 1947), p. 83.

With Schumpeter there was no such problem; he accepted capitalism as it is and made it a force for progress and change. Even monopoly could be tolerated, for it allowed its possessors the rewards of their innovation as the competitive model did not.

All this notwithstanding, Schumpeter never became a cult figure of American conservatism as did von Hayek, von Mises and the other exponents of the traditional irrelevancy. This was partly because he lacked solemnity and loved to shock his own natural supporters. He praised Marx as a genius, a prophet and "a very learned man."[3] Contemplating the future, he asked, "Can capitalism survive?" And replied, "No, I do not think it can."[4] Men of property and high corporate position do not rally to such friends. Better someone who articulates emphatically and lugubriously what has been said before. At Harvard Schumpeter was sought out principally by students who wished to dispute his views. His assistant in those years and his most admiring friend was Paul M. Sweezy, who was later to be the best-known of American Marxist scholars and, I might add, my own friend of a lifetime.

* * *

Within a year, I was invited to become a resident tutor in Winthrop House. After my Irving Terrace lodgings, these accommodations — living room, fireplace, bedroom, bathroom, respectable furniture — were a great luxury. I even had a telephone. One sat down to excellent meals, which were served in those affluent days by competitively energetic waitresses from the self-confessed lower classes. As were the lodgings, these meals were free. I met each morning with the other resident tutors, often to hear from B. F. Skinner, who would become the most famous and innovative of social psychologists, of his imaginative exploits of the night before. Presently Fred fell in love, and we were enthralled no more. On the ceiling of my bedroom were the marks of bare feet. I was puzzled until I was told that my predecessor in the rooms, Glenn Millikan, one of the famous Millikan family of scientists and scholars, relaxed by walking around on the ceiling.

The Harvard houses, then numbering seven, comprised student rooms, dining rooms, common rooms, small libraries, suites for the

[3] Schumpeter, p. 21.
[4] Ibid., p. 61.

tutors, a certain number of athletic teams and an unconvincing effort to proclaim a special house style and tradition. In 1935, the houses were only about five years old. Winthrop House had been created from two adjacent dormitories of pleasant red brick, each filling three sides of a rectangle, the fourth side being open to the Charles River. It was now establishing itself as one of the less fashionable places of abode, with its position somewhat redeemed by the presence of an undue number of athletes. The Master was Ronald M. Ferry, a New Englander of warm heart and incoherent speech who was a permanent associate professor of biochemistry. That rank at the time was the uniquely brutal designation by which Harvard proclaimed to all his colleagues the alleged inadequacy of the holder for all his life. Ronald Ferry was aware of the low social position of his house and was committed to its improvement, as I discovered after a year when I was made a member of the admissions committee, the group of tutors who interviewed freshmen applying for admission. (Then, as still, students lived for their first year in somewhat depressing dormitories in Harvard Yard.) Ferry provided us with a ruled sheet at the top of which were the cabalistic letters: St. G. Ex.; E. & A.; O. P.; H. S.; and X. These referred to private schools in order of social precedence — St. G. Ex. being St. Paul's, St. Mark's, Groton and Middlesex; E. & A. were Exeter and Andover; O. P. was Other Private; H. S. was public high school and X. was Jewish, wherever educated. The precedence of the school established that of the student. We were told to accept automatically all the St. Grotlesex and, generally speaking, all the E. & A.'s. The O.P.'s were tolerated; the H.S.'s were definitely discouraged and the X.'s were subject to a quota that could never be exceeded.

Early in my service I admitted my best student, Theodore H. White. Later that day Dr. Ferry looked over the list, and his face became grim. Pointing to White, he told me that we were already up to our Jewish quota. I protested that White was not a Jewish name. He looked at me with a hopeless gesture and said that names meant nothing. Teddy was disaccepted over my objection. I was greatly distressed, and my relations with Ferry were strained for some time. As for White, he went to a more distinguished house and in more civilized times became a member of the Harvard Board of Overseers.

In my second year I was assigned to teach in the elementary course in economics, then called Economics A, and here I found anti-Semitism a blessing. A committee of instructors of which I became a member made up the small sections in which all the beginning teaching was then done. We were not allowed to see the grades or academic rank of the students, for then we would be tempted to assign the best students to ourselves. I accomplished the same result by putting in my sections the largest plausible number of truly Jewish names, judging that their owners had to be a lot better to get in. I had always, in consequence, an especially apt and articulate group of overachievers. My high grades came eventually to the attention of Burbie, who supervised the course. He advised me that he was taking my blue books with him to Maine to make sure that my marks were not inflated. He often said he was doing this; we knew, in fact, that the books, which were stored in a closet near his office in Holyoke House, were never disturbed.

Harvard undergraduates in the 1930s were also anti-intellectual but not as single-mindedly so as were those at Princeton. There were social clubs, but they had no great role. With one or two exceptions I've never known their names. I became aware of the distinction attaching to the Porcellian, which is said to be the most favored, only when Richard Whitney, former head of the New York Stock Exchange, was observed to be wearing its insignia, the Porcellian pig, on his watch chain when he passed into Sing Sing in 1938 for varied thefts and embezzlements.

Undergraduate prestige was associated with a secure and preferably established family — Cabots, Lowells, Whitneys, Roosevelts, Peabodys; a proper preparatory school, as mentioned; a sure sense of the current, usually rather casual, fashion in clothing; white shoes; a confident approach to sex; a reputable interest in athletics; and an adequate commitment to alcohol. The pursuit of high grades was damaging, for esteem went with a "gentleman's C," which could be achieved without undue difficulty by majoring in sociology and resorting, before examinations, to one or another of the tutoring bureaus around Harvard Square which maintained files of back exam questions, carefully predicted future ones and for a fee all but guaranteed a passing grade. There were, of course, exceptions to the socially tranquilized, and they were fairly numerous. Some opprobrium attached to them; they were called "greasy grinds" or "Manhattan Indians," but they enhanced the life of the community.

Winthrop House, though anti-Semitic, had so advanced by this time that it was no longer anti-Irish. This much affected my later life, for, in consequence, Ferry gave a less than adverse reception to the sons of Joseph P. Kennedy when they began to apply. It was the beginning of a long association.

The first was Joseph P. Kennedy, Jr., who came to Winthrop House in the autumn of 1935. We quickly became friends. Joe, Jr., was slender and handsome, with a heavy shock of hair and a serious, slightly humorless manner. He was much interested in politics and public affairs and was every faculty member's favorite. Some of their attention was in response to his father's concerns. Joseph P. Kennedy, Sr., had become Chairman of the Securities and Exchange Commission in 1934, and in 1937, he headed the U.S. Maritime Commission. But parentage was not everything. Franklin D., Jr., and John A. Roosevelt, sons of the President, were at Harvard at the time but attracted no equally solemn faculty interest, for they were not thought to be sufficiently serious. My principal memory of the Roosevelts is of an automobile contest one evening on Mt. Auburn Street in which one of them, I'm not sure which, was a participant. It involved driving two automobiles against each other from a stated distance at maximum speed to see which driver would succumb first.

Nor was great attention accorded John F. Kennedy when he arrived at Winthrop House in 1937. He too was handsome but, unlike Joe, was gregarious, given to varied amusements, much devoted to social life and affectionately and diversely to women. One did not cultivate such students.

Joe Kennedy was also critical of his younger brother. A few days before the election in 1936, he visited me in my rooms one evening. He had thought long and hard about the political prospect and had concluded that many people were allowing their hatred of Roosevelt and their hopes for Landon to destroy their good sense. This was a situation in which an intelligent businessman could make money. He would form a syndicate and bet on Roosevelt with any and all passionate Landon supporters.[5] He had learned that he could get odds.

---

[5] Earlier that autumn Harvard had celebrated its three-hundredth anniversary. One afternoon the Boston Symphony Orchestra played in the Yard, but through some mismanagement this was not made known. Students helping out on the great occasion were summoned to the gates to tell of the culture being wasted within. All were welcome; admission was free. A student working the gate by Widener added the further request: "Please do not wear your Landon buttons in the Yard." I stood and watched. Nearly all the graduates back for the occasion were wearing the sunflower buttons. Most took them off.

I encouraged the scheme but declined to invest. He went ahead, set up for business at the Business School and made enough money to buy a new car. After the election we drove in it together to have dinner with some friends in Wellesley. He was in a dark mood. Jack, a day or so earlier, without consulting his father, had bought a new car on the installment plan. Why should his brother have a new car when he hadn't earned it?

                         *   *   *

In 1927, in one of the more inadvertently portentous acts in its history, Harvard had brought John Donald Black, professor of agricultural economics, from the University of Minnesota to Cambridge. The result was to make Harvard a major center of agricultural instruction not alone in the United States but in the world. Students, many of mature years, came from all over the country and from Canada, Australia, Latin America and Europe to study agricultural economics under Black and, in later times, agricultural extension, home economics and agricultural conservation. Nominally they had to be accepted by an admissions committee. In practice they had only to apply, for Black's Harvard colleagues had learned not to resist his wishes. The students he wanted were admitted, for it was known that, in the end, he always got his way. Few if any of these scholars could afford Harvard tuition and living costs from their own resources so Black spent much of his time extracting money from foundations or from the government to finance research on which, ostensibly, they would be employed. He then spent more time making the half-literate, half-completed reports minimally acceptable to those who paid for them. If, at the last, one of "Black's people," as they were called, performed badly on his or her Ph.D. examinations, Black lowered the standard and allowed the student through. Better this than to brand a young person as a failure. Again the other professors had learned not to object. For all of Black's various enterprises I was his assistant. He had been influential in the early design of the agricultural legislation of the New Deal, and we thus shared a further close interest in what was going on in Washington.

Fifty-one when I met him, solid but not quite stout, John D., as he was called, viewed everyone with an expression of infinite benignity and kindness. With notable exceptions, Joseph Schumpeter whom he disliked being one, it was the way he really felt. He was one of a family of ten born on a small Wisconsin farm and one of seven who survived to adulthood. (One brother was killed leading his platoon against the Germans in 1918.) Of the seven, five achieved college or beyond. Black had taught rhetoric, as it was called, to engineers at the Michigan College of Mines on the Upper Peninsula, financed his own graduate work in economics and agricultural economics at the University of Wisconsin in the heyday of La Follette liberalism and had gone on to a professorship and department chairmanship in agricultural economics at the University of Minnesota. He had a substantial claim to being called the father of the subject.

Preeminently he was a teacher. Though he had never been known to prepare a lecture, his students listened with rapt attention to personal reminiscences, the rights and wrongs in the struggle for agricultural legislation, the personality and thoughts of the other agricultural economists and to his injunctions never, under any circumstances, to sacrifice what you perceived as the public interest to personal ambition or pecuniary return. Like Burbie's, his office door was always open to his students from shortly after dawn to dusk, and he had never been known to terminate a conversation. He assumed responsibility for his students' careers for life, and they brought him their intended wives for review. Their achievements were his. In later years, when I acquired a certain distinction in economics, he was, if possible, more pleased than was I.

*   *   *

All academic disciplines have their feuds — intense conflicts much cherished by the participants and regularly combining differences in scholarly method or conclusion with deep personal dislike. They are large in the minds of those involved and usually unknown to the world outside. Agricultural economists in those years were bitterly divided between a progressive faction led by John D. Black and a retarded faction headed by Professor George F. Warren of Cornell. (The terminology reflects Black's view.) The difference turned partly on the farm problem. Black greatly approved New Deal farm policies while Warren, anticipating the later faith of Professor Milton Friedman, thought all could be solved by the right monetary policy. Warren also thought the best way to improve farm management practices was to survey numerous farms to see which methods gave the lowest costs and the largest returns. Black's method consisted in building a budget of income and outgo for a particular farm and then calculating the effect on costs, income and profits of any plausible changes in crops, livestock, scale and methods.

My devotion to Black's view of farm policy and the budget method of farm management improvement, like my devotion to Black, was complete. In time I achieved a measure of prominence, although nothing approximating Black's eminence, as a member of the progressive school. When Warren retired, the nearly undisputed leader of the retarded school was Earl Butz at Purdue, who was joined by another distinguished member of the same school, Professor Joe Carroll Bottum. Butz and Bottum made a formidable team on the other side. Butz went on to be Secretary of Agriculture under Richard Nixon and to fall sadly afoul of John Dean, who told in the newspapers of hearing one of Earl's highly inappropriate stories.

*   *   *

As I have earlier noted, when I arrived at Harvard in 1934, I was given the undergraduate course in agricultural economics to teach. This was in succession not to Black but to Thomas Nixon Carver, who had just been retired at the earliest legal age. Professors were expected to be in Cambridge during term time, including the reading period. Abbott Lawrence Lowell one day asked his secretary to get Carver on the telephone, and when he came on the line, President Lowell asked him to step over to his office. Carver had to confess that he couldn't come; he was in Florida.

His class had been taught with a comparable lack of diligence, and because of its reputation only three students enrolled when I succeeded to it. One was a Japanese undergraduate who spoke almost no English and understood none at all. Another went promptly to sleep whenever I spoke. The third was rather good. It was a horrifying experience. By the end of the year I had, I believed, learned something about the Harvard system, and I asked those instructors and tutors whom I could trust to send into my course some of the students they were advising. To others I merely dropped a word that I was planning great things. The New Deal had made agricultural matters highly relevant. No fewer than forty joined up. This was far too many for a man of my junior rank, and the course was taken over by Black.

5

Revelation

I PROSPERED at Harvard, and after two years I was promoted to the rank of faculty instructor. This appointment was for three years instead of one and carried an annual salary of $2750. With room and board worth perhaps $1000 and at pre-World War II taxation, this was the current equivalent, given inflation, of around $18,000 or some two-thirds of my pay when I ceased teaching in 1975.[1] With their salaries thus slipping in value, economics professors often seek outside income, and one obvious place of resort is the big corporation. This is not good. When an economist argues for lower taxes on the affluent, people should be right in believing that he is speaking out of economic perception or compassion and not because he has been bought. Nor should he ever be inhibited in his speech by what a corporate client might think. These rules are now extensively honored in the breach. Numerous economists put their professional gloss on corporate propaganda, pressure for tax relief, resistance to regulation or varied efforts to subvert the antitrust laws. And most sell out for a shockingly low sum, not being aware that a reputation can be sold only once or twice. After it becomes known that a scholar can be had for money, his market value sharply declines.

* * *

My academic success somewhat lessened my need to be in Washington. But now in Cambridge I did need to make everyone aware of my eminence. The FBI files to which I earlier adverted cover numerous investigations of my character, credit standing, sobriety,

---

[1] Not a wholly accurate comparison, for in the early 1970s, being otherwise provided for, I had invited the university to forgo the usual annual increases in my favor. After I had been thanked profusely and received a further raise as the result of computer error, my pay had been stabilized.

marital fidelity, friends and associates. All reports were uniformly favorable. But nearly all of my colleagues and professional acquaintances, after conceding my affirmative qualifications, said that I had an unduly well-developed view of my own intellectual excellence. Many years later, in 1961, when I was about to go to India, the *New York Times* ran a profile of the new ambassador. At breakfast that day President Kennedy asked me how I liked it.

I said it was fine, but I didn't see why they had to call me arrogant. "I don't see why not," said the President, "everybody else does."[2]

During these years I began also to have my first experience in academic and political controversy and to consider the tactics and strategy of engagement. Later I gave this question more attention and wrote a small monograph on the subject.[3]

Both scholarly and political life require criticism of others and invite attack or reprisal. Anyone who is initiating combat should, as a matter of elementary caution, gauge the extent and severity of the probable reaction and consider his defense. If attacked, he should promptly and strongly respond. This is vital. In the past it has often been possible to attack academic people with impunity, for they are thought unlikely to react in any dangerous way. Their rule is to remain silent, "not stir up the animals." This is most unwise; a demonstrated capacity for reprisal serves valuably as a deterrent.

In late 1952 or early 1953, my neighbor and friend, a financial columnist and reporter for the *Boston Globe,* John Harriman, went to Washington to interview Joe McCarthy. He asked him if, in the aftermath of the great Republican victory, he wouldn't be opening a major campaign against the Cambridge subversives, a term that would now be enlarged to include all liberal Democrats. Joe said that such was his patriotic intention. Harriman asked if he had in mind such targets as Galbraith and Arthur Schlesinger. Joe replied, "No, I am going after people who aren't that politically sophisticated."

*   *   *

Before World War II, in English, other literature and the fine arts, Harvard still sheltered professors who owed their position to high Boston or New York social eminence. Some disdained salary. All

[2] As told in *Ambassador's Journal* (Boston: Houghton Mifflin, 1969), p. 52.
[3] *Economics and the Art of Controversy* (New Brunswick: Rutgers University Press, 1955).

professors believed that they had been summoned by their excellence to be among the favored few. That President Lowell's secretary once called the White House to say that the President wished to speak to Mr. Coolidge is, no doubt, an invention. But it owes its repetition to its apocryphal truth.

There was much justification for this inner but also visible glow. Harvard could then select scholars from anywhere in the world, for its salaries were far higher than those at any other university in the United States or abroad and around twice the level of those at the great state universities. Widener Library was beyond any rival, as it remains; the science laboratories were generally good. In the economics department when appointments were under consideration, there was never discussion as to whether the individual would come. The reference was to whether he "should be called."

The modern Harvard professor, allowing always for difference in perspective, is much less grand, much less affluent, much less secure and, I would judge, much less happy. A new academic style, emphasizing a measure of shabbiness in housing, attire and, on occasion, outlook, is legitimized by financial necessity. Travel, the most precious of academic perquisites, has not for a generation been at personal expense. Professors go where lecture invitations, conferences, colloquia, research grants or consulting assignments specify or provide an intellectually plausible justification. A few professors, of whom I am one, have managed to survive in the spacious, often unkempt professorial mansions of an earlier Cambridge. Mostly these houses can now be afforded only by physicians, psychiatrists, lawyers and executives of Polaroid. Harvard professors disappear at night into the distant Boston outskirts, there to engage in the suburban middle-class struggle with teen-age delinquency and crabgrass. At professional meetings to say that one is a Harvard professor no longer forestalls disagreement.

Once Harvard professors were selected and promoted by higher authority. As late as the reign (1909–33) of Abbott Lawrence Lowell, the president of the university had a large, sometimes exclusive part in this process. Personal strategy, accordingly, was to impress authority, but in its physical absence a scholar could relax. Now a professor is judged by his or (in rare instances) her peers. These are omnipresent, always looking for evidence of scholarly competence and perception or, more poignantly, their absence. So even a full professor who hopes to be an even grander university professor must always stand at attention. Institutional elitism has declined at Harvard. Authority has weakened. Democracy has advanced. But there has been a price. From this heightened sensitivity to scrutinizing peers comes a certain dulling of personality. No one can now afford to seem eccentric. Nor is the judgment above reproach. Professors considering and selecting others for promotion define excellence, perhaps inevitably, as that quality of mind and work that most resembles their own.

*   *   *

When the Agricultural Adjustment Administration was launched in 1933, the Brookings Institution in Washington decided to make a concurrent study of its operations. John D. Black was drafted into the task, and he then acquired funds for a similar study of another of the New Deal agencies, the Farm Credit Administration, a study which he put in my charge. My interest in the subject was minimal, but I did not suppose this to be a relevant consideration. Also almost everything there was to know about the Farm Credit Administration — a holding company for Federal Land Banks, Federal Intermediate Credit Banks, Banks for Cooperatives, the Production Credit Corporations and Associations — could have been learned in a couple of months and reported on in literate and detailed fashion in a couple more. But then, as now, any such dispatch would have been considered a grave defect in scholarly behavior and performance. Scholarship in the social sciences is assessed by its depth and precision but also by the length of time it has required. A quickly completed job, regardless of quality, is bad. A five-year effort is good *per se*. A lifetime work, not quite finished at death, is superb.

There is a practical reason here. Modern university teaching requires a large number of people. All, by stern academic convention, are required to do research both to qualify for their degrees and to prove their worth thereafter. Were large expenditures of time not an independent factor in judging the result, the aggregate of scholarly output would be excessive.

The new study took me back to Washington and for the first time to the rural South where I examined the operations of the Federal Land Bank at Columbia, South Carolina. I viewed the legislature of that state in bucolic session and inspected the state capitol with its honorable scars from Sherman's guns and its statue of Pitchfork Ben Tillman. But in the early summer of 1936, I was diverted to a quite different enterprise. Henry Sturgis Dennison entered my life. Or, more precisely, I was brought into his.

*   *   *

In 1936, Henry Dennison, then fifty-nine, was, arguably, the most interesting businessman in the United States. The plants of Dennison Manufacturing in Framingham, Massachusetts, and at one or two other locations in New England and in England made gummed labels, tags, a wide range of other paper products and crepe paper, for which Dennison and others in the company had discovered a new and vastly successful process of manufacture in 1914. The company had also, to Dennison's design, pioneered in unemployment compensation for its workers, in employee ownership and profit-sharing and, as it was then called, scientific management. Dennison was at one time president of the Taylor Society for the Advancement of Management and of the International Management Institute in Geneva.

Along with his business, Dennison had been an accomplished violinist from the age of eight or nine and was otherwise devoted to music. When his piano went out of tune, he taught himself to put it back. He was also a naturalist, inventor, part-time scientist, and his curiosity extended on to psychiatry and public affairs. Nor was he a dilettante; when some new subject captured his imagination, he regularly hired someone of professional competence to give him instruction.

A small man with a bald head, his need to attend to his numerous interests caused him to dart rather than to walk and to begin all sentences in the middle. After practice it was possible to make much sense out of what he was saying. The Dennison house, a large, low-slung structure with deep sleeping porches, stood on a high wooded hill a few miles from Framingham. Surrounded by forest and with a view all the way to Boston and the Bay, it was the most civilized place of abode in all New England.

Dennison, though a certified Yankee, had a deep suspicion of his kind. "Didn't you think well of *any* of your Harvard classmates?" his son James, who was more congenial than he, once asked.

"Not one," his father replied. The Boston business leaders —

bankers, investment bankers, merchants — he thought bores. Their confident comments on the needs of the Republic he dismissed with either amusement or disdain; their business misfortunes, a common feature of the time, he thought deserved. Most other of his colleagues, he believed, allowed their commitment to personal dignity, popular cliché and the Republican Party and their hatred of unions to override any residual intelligence. His view of his fellow businessmen had not been improved when, in earlier years, some had boycotted Dennison products because of his radical tendencies. He was thought to be spoiling the working classes.

There were exceptions to Dennison's disapproval. Any up-from-zero entrepreneur without cant or inhibition he admired. The Filene brothers of the great Boston department store; Beardsley Ruml, a businessman become a University of Chicago economics professor and a businessman again; and Henry P. Kendall of the Kendall Company were, with Professors Felix Frankfurter and Edwin F. Gay of Harvard, his friends. And Franklin D. Roosevelt, whom he had served in NRA and was now serving in lesser advisory roles, he adored. It was his service on a government advisory body that stimulated his interest in economics and brought us together.

Dennison was a member of the Administration's Business Advisory Council of the Department of Commerce. This was a convocation of high corporate executives that assembled at intervals, invariably, as Dennison saw it, to protest over the way the New Deal was rescuing the country from the depression. While not averse to help for themselves when this was needed, they did not think it necessary that farmers and the unemployed be rescued too. In time Dennison found some kindred spirits who agreed with him. One was Lincoln Filene. Another was his brother E. A. Filene, founder of the Twentieth Century Fund, on whose board Dennison served.[4] Filene was widely regarded as a Bolshevist, although Lenin once paid him the honor of disavowing him. (Filene had said that eventually workers and employers would realize that they had interests in common and this Lenin could not allow.) Also in agreement with Dennison were Morris E. Leeds, a Quaker manufacturer in Philadelphia of great conscience, and Ralph E. Flanders, a machine tool manufacturer in Springfield, Vermont, who later, while in the Senate, was the neme-

[4] As did I in later times. It was created "to study and advance the next steps forward in the social and economic life of the people."

sis of Joe McCarthy. It was Flanders who introduced the resolution of censure that reduced Joe to despair and his final immersion in alcohol. "I got to the top in my business," Flanders once said, "by getting up earlier than anyone else, working harder than anyone else, inventing a machine that made a great deal of money, having a keen eye for the interests of the company, and by marrying the daughter of the owner."

In early 1936, Dennison and Lincoln Filene, Morris Leeds and Ralph Flanders decided to write a book that would prove that businessmen could have affirmative thoughts on Franklin D. Roosevelt. And it would tell what Washington should do. I was hired for the summer and part-time thereafter to teach Dennison economics and to help on the manuscript. I moved out to the lovely house on Juniper Hill and was lodged back of one of the porches in a room that I continued to occupy at intervals for several years. My working space was in Dennison's excellent library, although he considered the word pretentious and called it the bookroom. My instruction took place under a pine tree just west of the house. It was frequently interrupted as Dennison shifted suddenly to some other topic, and I tried to discern meaning without the help of subjects or sometimes verbs. Soon a major difficulty arose.

It was that Dennison already had a firm idea as to what was wrong with the economy. And so had I. My view derived from the hitherto described classical orthodoxy of Alfred Marshall as modified by the recently published work of two young economists, Edward H. Chamberlin of Harvard and the wonderfully independent and formidable Joan Robinson of the University of Cambridge, who in later years has been my much admired friend.[5]

Economists had long conceded that monopoly was a flawing exception to the benign role of the market. The monopolist's output was smaller, his prices higher, than the competitive ideal. But a monopoly, one firm with the entire output of a recognizably distinct product, was hard to find. Apart from those supplying electricity, gas and telephone service and thus subject to government regulation, the Aluminum Company of America, ALCOA, singled itself

---

[5] Visiting her in Cambridge — the English Cambridge — in the early fifties, after I had been diverted for a number of years from academic matters, I asked her who the good young economists were at the university. She looked at me sternly, which in her case could be very stern indeed, and said, "My dear Ken, we were the last good generation."

out in those days as the major example. Accordingly, one recurred to it in instruction *ad nauseam.* Monopoly, if bad, was very rare.

Chamberlin and Robinson showed that a few firms, an oligopoly, could produce the same (or a similar) result as monopoly — prices too high, production too small. The firms did not need to communicate, only reflect rationally on the price and production that was best for all. And Chamberlin went on to argue that almost any producer of a consumer product, by advertising or by otherwise urging the unique features of his product, his location or even his own personality as a seller, could establish a partial monopoly. This was monopolistic competition.

Both monopolistic competition and oligopoly established themselves with astonishing speed in the economic orthodoxy. And unlike monopoly, oligopoly and monopolistic competition were not exceptional. One had only to look about to see them almost everywhere — in automobiles, steel, oil, chemicals, rubber, copper, toothpaste, even the monopoly that the neighborhood pharmacy exercised over its shopping area. Oligopolistic and monopolistic competition dominated modern markets.

Also, and unduly, my mind. Addressing Dennison's need to know what was wrong with the economy, I told him that free competition had given way to oligopoly and monopolistic competition, and because of the latter too many resources were being wasted on advertising and salesmanship. The shortfall in production from these defects caused the depression from which the United States and the world then suffered. The remedy was more competition. I wrote a lengthy paper explaining and affirming this revelation.

Dennison's view was very different. He saw income moving out from the production of goods in two broad streams. One stream went to people of modest income and was likely to be spent. The other went to the more affluent or to the business enterprise, and this was likely to be saved. There was a spendings stream and a savings stream, and these terms, used without cluttering verbs or predicates, were Dennison's own. Depression, he believed, was caused by the nonspending of the income in the savings stream. The remedy or partial remedy was to shift taxation from income that was being spent or was on its way to be spent to income that was on its way to be saved — from a sales tax, as one example, to the corporate or personal income tax.

To anyone properly learned in economics, it would be hard to imagine a more horrifying idea. Well over a century earlier Jean-Baptiste Say, the great French economist, had formulated Say's Law of Markets, which established that all production created the purchasing power by which it could be bought. All of the income from the sale of a product accrued to someone, somewhere, in wages, payments for raw materials, interest or profits. And in doing so, it provided the purchasing power to buy what was produced. Were some of these receipts saved, it made no difference; someone else would borrow and spend the savings, and if they didn't, the price of the product would automatically adjust itself downward so the reduced expenditure would still be sufficient to clear the market. In 1936, it was not only wrong but professionally unwise to reject Say's Law. It was a litmus by which the reputable economist was separated from the crackpot. The crackpot failed to pursue income from the sale of a product on to its use; thus his simplistic conclusion that there could be a shortage of purchasing power in the economy. Since I took seriously my reputation as well as my commitment to economic truth, my dilemma, given Dennison's heretical vision, was a difficult one.

Presently it became more difficult. Earlier that year *The General Theory of Employment Interest and Money* by John Maynard Keynes had been published in the United States. In the very same weeks that I was writing my brief for my views on competition and thus refuting the errors of Dennison, I was reading *The General Theory*. As I did, I discovered that Keynes was with Dennison and not with me. His explanation of oversaving was much more sophisticated than Dennison's but in practical consequences precisely the same. There could be unspent savings; when they appeared, prices did not adjust smoothly down to ensure that the same volume of goods would be bought by the reduced (after-saving) purchasing power. Instead output and employment fell until reduced profits, increased losses and the need to spend from past savings ensured that all income from current production or its equivalent was spent. A new economic equilibrium was thus established, one with a lot of people out of work — the underemployment equilibrium. I was shaken. This was not the primitive instinct of a businessman; this was the sophisticated case of a greatly renowned economist. I decided that I should tell Dennison, and one night over old-fashioneds, a Dennison specialty, in the long, beautifully windowed Juniper Hill living room, I explained how Keynes supported him and not me. Dennison replied that he was not surprised; Keynes had always made more sense than most economists.

Another and further difficulty then intruded. Dennison had by now read my manuscript. He wondered if there might not be something in my position and took my paper into Cambridge to get Felix Frankfurter's view. For Dennison, as for many others in that time, Frankfurter, still a Harvard Law School professor but soon to become a Supreme Court Justice, was the final arbiter of social truth. Frankfurter left my paper on his desk unread and presently came to assume that it was a book manuscript in search of a publisher. When an editor of the Oxford University Press happened into his office, he passed it along to him. We became aware of this when Dennison got a letter from Oxford accepting the manuscript for publication. Dennison was delighted, and I did not resist. So we collaborated on a revision that appeared in 1938 as *Modern Competition and Business Policy.* It is a bad book that should never have been printed; I have not ventured to look inside it for nearly forty years. But being an expression in slightly novel form of a superbly orthodox position, it attracted favorable attention. This extended to remote precincts. When I visited China in 1972 as President of the American Economic Association, it was, I discovered, the only one of my books in the library of the University of Peking. A year earlier a Soviet scholar who reviewed my work along with that of Gunnar Myrdal and Ludwig Erhard gave about a third of the space devoted to me to this volume.[6]

Along with *Modern Competition,* I also put the newly reputable heresies of Dennison into a manuscript, together with the views of Leeds and Flanders. The result, *Toward Full Employment,* was also published in 1938.[7] It was remarkable that so soon after the appearance of Keynes's *General Theory* a group of successful businessmen should have endorsed ideas that so many others would hold so rad-

[6] I. N. Dvorkin, *Critique of the Theories of Contemporary Bourgeois Economists* (*J. Galbraith, G. Myrdal, L. Erhard*) (Moscow, 1971).
[7] Henry S. Dennison, Lincoln Filene, Ralph E. Flanders and Morris E. Leeds (New York and London: Whittlesey House, McGraw-Hill). Filene listened and encouraged but did not contribute appreciably.

ical. This, however, remained unnoticed, for the book went un-
bought and unread.

* * *

We celebrated Dennison's seventieth birthday on March 4, 1947, and
the theme was the debate it occasioned in Heaven:

> The time has come, the Good Lord said,
> To knock our Henry on the head.
> He's lived his full three score and ten
> And should make way for better men.

The debate was good-tempered and resolved by a speech from a
new arrival:

> There are many worse bastards down below,
> I was F.D.R., and I should know.

Dennison was duly granted an extension. Only on February 29,
1952, did he arrive back on the hill from "the shop" in Framingham
to announce that he felt a trifle unwell. He died a few hours later.

* * *

By the autumn of 1936, Keynes had reached Harvard with tidal
force. There had been no such excitement among the younger economists before; there has been none such since. Here was a solution
to depression and unemployment, the most urgent problems of the
time. It was also a conservative one. Keynes showed that the government, by offsetting the excess of savings — the shortfall in purchasing power — could prop up the economy so that it functioned at or
near full employment instead of at some painful and socially demoralizing level down below. Markets, the subject of a totemic worship
by economists, continued to function as before. Private property, the
focal point of conservative passion, remained undisturbed except
perhaps as taxes might, on some later occasion, be higher. Corporations and banks as well as trade unions were as before. And
Keynes even made legitimate what the governments of all the industrial countries, including the United States, were already doing.
Depression had reduced government revenues and forced increases
in spending for welfare. The result was a deficit, and out of force of

circumstance this was being covered by borrowing, exactly as Keynes urged.

Yet the Keynesian proposals also produced a wonderfully choleric reaction from the right. In consequence, you could be concerned with saving capitalism, be in the ultimate sense a conservative, and still be thought a vigorously innovative radical. Never was radicalism so safe. Keynes himself had made his career by attacking men in high position who join comfortably to reassure each other in their mutual commitment to error. Thus his onslaught on the great men at Versailles for their belief that Germany could somehow be made to bear the cost of World War I; and on Winston Churchill for yielding[8] to the bankers and the high civil servants and returning the pound to gold at its old parity in 1925, with the resulting painful deflation in British prices and wages; and on the British and American financial and economic establishments for their failure to see that an active program of employing people on borrowed money would relieve the deprivation and suffering after 1929. Though young and unimportant, by following the master we could feel superior to the great men of Morgan's, Chase, National City and the New York Federal Reserve Bank.

Through 1936 and 1937, everyone was reading Keynes, the older faculty members mostly with disdain, the younger with joy. As the university was about to reassemble for the autumn of 1936, it celebrated its Tercentenary, to which I have already adverted. Roosevelt came and reminded his unadmiring audience of the sadness to which Harvard men were doomed. "[At the time of the two-hundredth anniversary] many of the alumni of Harvard were sorely troubled concerning the state of the nation. Andrew Jackson was President. On the two-hundred-and-fiftieth anniversary of the founding of Harvard College, alumni were again sorely troubled. Grover Cleveland was President. Now, on the three-hundredth anniversary, I am President."[9] Earlier the university had asked the various departments for recommendations of scholars who should receive honorary degrees. The senior professors invited suggestions from their younger colleagues. Junior members of the government department led by Rupert Emerson, a much beloved teacher of greatly independent mind, proposed Leon Trotsky. Not wishing to

[8] As his published papers show, reluctantly and with misgivings.
[9] *New York Times*, September 19, 1936.

be outdone, younger economists suggested the name of Keynes. Neither suggestion was thought to merit discussion. Perhaps to emphasize a point, D. H. Robertson, Keynes's principal rival at Cambridge, was honored instead. There were others who are now forgotten.[10]

What counted, however, was that Keynes's ideas be influential in Washington. We looked avidly for those in the capital who had experienced a similar revelation, and soon we found some. One was Marriner S. Eccles, who, as a banker in Utah viewing the broken farmers and businessmen of his community, had, like Dennison, anticipated the ideas of Keynes. He was now head of the Federal Reserve Board. Another was Lauchlin Currie, Eccles's assistant director of research and statistics and later the first professional economist at the White House. Soon a division developed between New Deal liberals in Washington, one that reflected precisely the difference that had so wonderfully confused my early education of Dennison. One group, the largest and for the rest of the thirties the most influential, continued to see as the cause of the economic problem the decline of competition, the ever more pervasive power of monopoly. Their remedy was a greatly invigorated enforcement of the antitrust laws. And there was such enforcement under Thurman Arnold down from Yale to head the antitrust operations of the Department of Justice. This was supplemented by a massive investigation of industrial structure under the joint auspices of the Congress and the Executive, the Temporary National Economic Committee. The second, smaller and, as to conviction, more tightly knit group saw the economic problem as did Keynes. We thought ourselves decidedly more modern and otherwise superior, and it was our inestimable advantage that we had Currie on our side. The White House had a natural influence on appointments; when economists were needed, Currie saw that reliable Keynesians were urged. My own reliability in this regard led later to my being placed in charge of wartime price control.

At Harvard the seminars on Keynes were frequent and intense, and they resulted in an effort by many of the younger economists to translate his ideas into simple American terms.[11] Before then, how-

[10] Wesley C. Mitchell of Columbia University, a friend and, on some matters, follower of Thorstein Veblen's, was one and is less fully forgotten than the rest.

[11] Richard F. Gilbert, George H. Hildebrand, Jr., Arthur W. Stuart, Maxine Yaple Sweezy, Paul M. Sweezy, Lorie Tarshis and John D. Wilson, *An Economic Program for American Democracy* (New York: Vanguard, 1938).

ever, I had resolved to go to the temple. In the spring of 1937, I applied to the Social Science Research Council, a Rockefeller benefaction, for a fellowship allowing me a year's study under Keynes at the University of Cambridge. Two other developments of that year were of personal importance.

In the election of 1936, I was a willing volunteer for minor political chores on behalf of F.D.R. One or two fellow Democrats suggested that were this contribution to continue, I had better become a citizen and vote as well. Earlier in California I had started the long process to do so. Now, in the autumn of 1937, I was examined on the Constitution by a man who said that, since I taught at Harvard, I surely knew more about it than he did. And with several hundred deeply impoverished aspirants whose Americanism had been strengthened by a recent regulation making citizenship a requisite for WPA employment, I took the oath of allegiance. No one in history has done so with so small a sense of emotion, so slight a feeling of trauma.

A few days later I married Catherine Merriam Atwater, the daughter of Alice Merriam and Charles Atwater, the latter a New York lawyer and accomplished sailor who once took his tiny craft, without radio or engine, all the way to Iceland. Kitty had been a graduate student at Radcliffe and a little earlier in Munich, an undergraduate at Smith and at the Sorbonne. She is a wise and affectionate woman of singular beauty, intensely loyal to family and friends, a superb manager of our personal affairs, a brilliant linguist and student of comparative literature, with no known enemy anywhere in the world, and we lived happily ever after.

6

In Innocence Abroad

OF THE DELIGHTS of an earlier time few were more celebrated than boarding a ship and going to Europe. Those who know only of Pan Am and Sir Freddie Laker do not know what they missed. However, they are fortunate in being spared the resulting conversation, for the merits of various vessels, their distinctive personalities and patronage were once extensively debated in academic and social circles. Informed participation in the debate also proved conclusively that one had been to Europe. In the better university communities it was thought that the *Statendam* of the Holland-America Line lent itself best to impressive reminiscence on return. The obligation that friends felt to come and see one off with flowers was as great as now for a memorial service. No one has ever been known to go to Kennedy or Dulles to dispatch a friend with like ceremony.

I recall my own sailings with a reminiscent or nostalgic pleasure that is stirred otherwise only by the remembrance of lovely women. Even the departures of others were sometimes impressed on my mind. Thus on the morning of March 7, 1947, when I was an editor at *Fortune,* I got word that Eric Roll, later Sir Eric Roll and later yet Lord Roll of Ipsden, a friend, historian of economic thought and one of the most diversely talented of British civil servants, was taking ship that noon. He had been in Washington with John Strachey, then Food Minister, to plead for more nutrients for the British people. I got a bottle of whiskey and some new books, both scarce commodities in England in those days, and took a taxi to the Hudson River piers to see him away. As I passed down 51st Street, great clouds of smoke rolled up ahead. The driver turned to tell me with forthright pleasure that the *Queen Elizabeth* was burning up "just like the *Normandie."*

The smoke was, in fact, coming from a U.S. Maritime Commission motor ship, the *John Ericsson,* on the other side of the pier. But the confusion among the Cunard passengers was appalling; they arrived and were disgorged on the street with their baggage, and the taxis or chauffeurs were sent away to make room for more. No one could go on the pier or the ship. The aspect was of a uniquely affluent refugee camp.

Using my Newspaper Guild membership card as a press pass, I got through the police lines and aboard, only to find the cabins of the British party empty so I left the bottle and books and started back to work. By now it had begun to rain, and Navy fire-fighter equipment was moving in. The huddling passengers and piled-up baggage had advanced appreciably in wretchedness. As I headed away to a taxi, I was hailed. Strachey, Roll and an aide, surrounded by bags and official cases, had been off-loaded in the rain. I greeted them and we talked, and presently I suggested that New York should do better by a visiting cabinet minister. The police, if asked, would surely let the party go on board. Eric Roll pointed to the policeman whom they had just petitioned; he had told them to get back where they belonged, saying a bit crudely that the last man asking to pass through the barriers had claimed to be Jesus.

I went over, told the policeman that I worked for *Time,* which was corporately true and more intimidating than *Fortune,* and urged the claims of hospitality and high protocol. The cop was unimpressed but said that I could speak to his superior, Inspector Ryan. He pointed to a huge man in civilian blue serge with a gold watch chain across an expanse of vest, who was watching over the scene of horror from a little distance. I pled my case to Ryan with eloquence and no particular exaggeration — a high official of a great and friendly nation being kept there in the rain. Mr. Ryan walked carefully to a point a few feet in front of Strachey and examined him minutely. I followed. Although John was wearing a ministerial homburg, his hair was in a disorderly fringe below. His suit was also shabby from the war, his shirt and tie bedraggled, and, like his companions, he was otherwise shapeless from the damp.

Ryan turned to me and said, "*What* did you say he was?"

Within the hearing of the party, I tried to explain again. Ryan shook his head in disbelief but then decided to play it safe. He motioned to his equally disbelieving subordinate to take them through the barrier and onto the ship. It was the first of my many encounters with John Strachey, a friendship, indeed, that ended only with his death in 1963, word of which reached me when I was returning from India.

*   *   *

At more orderly departures a kind of husky throat-clearing preceded a commanding blast from the whistle. A voice in carefully polished English intoned, "All ashore that's going ashore." The last drunk was poured onto the pier. The ship pulled away, and passengers looked down from the decks at the tugs so astonishingly far below. The river was left behind, the water boiled under the stern rail, and soon it stretched in a flattened, slightly disordered path to the horizon. This was never far distant, for only on rare Atlantic voyages did the sun ever shine.

"How was your crossing?"

"It was the worst in memory. Even the captain said so."

You walked the deck, exchanged glances of careful cordiality with the other passengers resting in their blanketed deck chairs and went to entertainments of inspired banality. A very large part of the pleasure for Americans was the attention they received from cabin stewards, deck stewards and waiters, for they did for the traveler what before in life he had always had to do for himself. The great ships were the last manifestation of the servile servant class. Anyone who had been at Harvard was reminded of another of Joseph Schumpeter's reactionary truths: one servant is worth a thousand gadgets.[1]

In those days the recently married were the objects of mild interest, for no one then assumed that they would almost immediately be divorced. So, sailing for Southampton on September 18 of 1937, we combined the ecstasy of travel on a great ocean liner with the more routine rewards of love and marriage. Our passage was on H.M.S. *Britannic,* a ship sadly devoid of value for future conversations; it happened only that she left New York on the day after our wedding. For around $150 in those times one could take along an automobile, and no American then willingly entrusted himself to an inferior European equipage. Our Ford convertible was swung off at Southampton, and we traveled to London by way of Winchester and Salisbury.

[1] Schumpeter also observed that thousands of devoutly democratic Americans went to Europe each summer to spend their time viewing the monuments of past despotism.

Then at the Carlton Mansions in Gordon Square in Bloomsbury we were awakened gloriously in the early morning by three pipers in the street outside who, on further scrutiny, were seen to be looking appealingly to the windows above. They were MacDonalds, my own proud clan; alas, that we had been reduced to this. It was while we were in London that I learned that it was unlikely I would see Keynes at Cambridge; he was still recovering from a heart attack.

*   *   *

We went on nonetheless to the university, and Keynes's absence was not as damaging as I had supposed. It was partly that he had never been there very much even when well. An insurance company in London, a farm at Tilton, Firle, Sussex, his friends in Bloomsbury, had always absorbed far more of his time. And his friends, students and acolytes in Cambridge — R. F. (later Professor Lord) Kahn, Joan (later Professor) Robinson, and the inimitably brilliant and lovable Italian economist Piero Sraffa — were as deeply into the ideas of the master as was Keynes himself. Indeed, they discussed little else, and neither, in the months ahead, did I.

Sraffa, by means that I never understood, had it made known that I was to be considered welcome at Trinity College, an association legitimized with a Fellowship many years later by my friend R. A. (Rab) Butler after he became Master. In 1945, I repaid my debt to Sraffa in an irregular way. He showed up in London one day asking that I find him passage to Italy, a military airplane being the only possibility. He thought a revolution imminent and didn't want to miss it. I was then a director of the U.S. Strategic Bombing Survey, in close association with the Air Force. Though my memory is uncertain, I believe a passage was arranged. Had Sraffa been the Lenin of an Italian Communist takeover — his sympathies were in this direction — I would have had an interesting time explaining it all. But no one who knew Piero Sraffa would have worried. He was one of the most leisured men who ever lived; a Communist revolution led by him would have shown no perceptible movement. And yet by serious present-day students of economics he is thought a prodigious scholar. That was because at frequent intervals he spent a few minutes to a few hours assembling, editing and annotating the papers of David Ricardo. So, for posterity, he has left a shelf of exquisitely and meticulously arranged volumes on the work of the early nineteenth-century stockbroker to whom both Marxists and classical conservatives render homage. All encountering these books in the library imagine Sraffa to have been a man of surpassing diligence.

An enduring reward from my year at Cambridge was friendship with Michał Kalecki, then in self-imposed exile from Poland.[2] A small, often irritable, independent, intense man, Kalecki was the most innovative figure in economics I have known, not excluding Keynes. His specialty was to bring the obvious into view and cause one to wonder why it had not been noticed before. This ordinarily happened in conversation; only rarely did Kalecki get around to writing his discoveries down. He did put in print the thought that the lower a man's income, the greater, were he rational, his aversion to risk. That is because the pain of loss is far greater for the poor man than for the rich, and the most cautious or conservative of all will be the peasant who lives at the margin of subsistence. If his gamble on something new turns out badly, he goes hungry, perhaps dies. A more affluent farmer, in contrast, risks only some income. Nothing more poignantly explains the reluctance of the poor villager to try some agricultural innovation. The age-old methods have proven themselves by the fact that he is still alive. New seed stock, tillage methods or crops have not so proven themselves and could fail. In later years in India, as I will tell, I often heard American agriculturalists inveighing against the unwillingness of the Indian farmer to accept American methods. Kalecki was always in my mind. If the innovation did not work out, the Indian farmer, as he himself well knew, would starve. The American, in contrast, would be safely home at Kansas State.

In 1958, I rode with Kalecki in a questionable plane flown by the Polish airline LOT from Warsaw by way of Budapest to Belgrade. He had returned to Poland after the war and a tour at the United Nations; his uncompromising integrity had brought him into conflict with organization men at the UN, as eventually it would in Poland. He asked me as we flew south if it had ever occurred to me that all the people in the world might be classified in accordance with the maximum length of time their thoughts were diverted from them-

[2] In 1935, Kalecki received a grant from the Rockefeller Foundation for work in economics. He traveled to Sweden, the London School of Economics and to Cambridge for study. Then, in 1936, his colleagues at the Institute for Research on Business Cycles in Poland were discharged in a disciplinary action for a wrong-minded report on the Polish economic condition. Kalecki decided to stay on in England.

selves. Two-hour men; ten-minute men; millisecond men like Richard Nixon. I had not previously thought about this matter, but in 1962, while recovering from hepatitis at my friend Ruth Field's house on Long Island, I invented a "psychometricist" by the name of Herschel McLandress who had come up with this measure — "the McLandress Dimension." This and his other scientific efforts of the same nature became a book by that title which I published, with a satisfactory response, under the pseudonym of Mark Epernay, the Mark from Mark Twain, Epernay from an old wine crate in the stable where I was working. The pseudonym was necessary because I was then an ambassador, and the State Department required its people to submit their writing for review while forbidding them to take compensation for it. Both requirements were defensible; the publishability of State Department prose and the resulting compensation would ordinarily depend far more on the individual's official eminence than on any literary or other quality. However, it did not seem that this rule need apply to anything written in true anonymity under a false name. Accordingly, I wrote to the then Attorney General, Mr. Robert Kennedy, proposing that I forgo the clearance and asking if I might keep the money. So difficult was the question or so grave the precedent that my letter was never answered.

Thus the long arm of Michał Kalecki. A few weeks before his death in 1970, I wrote him in Warsaw where he was now in retirement, confessing to this and numerous other debts and telling him of other writers who were similarly indentured. His widow told me that it was one of his last communications from the West and that Michał had allowed himself, however briefly, to be pleased.

*   *   *

Cambridge lectures before the war — D. H. Robertson on money and banking, G. F. Shove on the history of economic ideas, J. H. Clapham on economic history — were not memorable, although spiced on occasion with a certain innovative meanness. Robertson, a gentle man, was deeply pained by the errors of Keynes and possibly also by his notoriety. Notoriety in a university is always, often justly, seen by those so spared as proof of inferior scholarship. Keynes, in turn, was not fond of Clapham. He once said that after the age of fifty (or perhaps sixty) he would spend his time writing history; Clapham had shown that this required neither effort nor intelligence. I listened to the lectures without according them serious attention; for most of that year I read. I penetrated the thicket of technical controversy surrounding Keynes's work and became one of the acknowledged oracles. I also learned that this accomplishment, though it served indispensably for gaining the respect and attention of other economists, served negligibly as a guide to practical action. This is true of nearly all sophisticated elaboration in economics. A suitably complex exposition of some theoretical point in one of the professional journals — the *American Economic Review,* the *Quarterly Journal of Economics,* the *Journal of Political Economy, The Economic Journal (The Quarterly Journal of The Royal Economic Society)* of which Keynes himself was long the editor — serves to establish the credentials of a learned and priestly circle and to exclude the unwashed. It will rarely provide guidance on any question of practical policy, and, in fact, this is not expected.

Along with reading, I wrote some articles and reviews — again the lurking thought of scholarly advancement. One piece in *The Economic Journal* was entitled "Rational and Irrational Consumer Preference" and attracted some erudite attention. The conclusion was neither succinct, breathtaking, nor entirely comprehensible. "The problem (now defined in a somewhat narrower sense) is how the equilibrium, with small-scale production and a redundancy of entrepreneurs, is maintained when consumers would choose the economies of large-scale production and fewer entrepreneurs were they actually given the opportunity of doing so."[3]

In coming years I would review hundreds of volumes. After reading a book, it takes small extra effort to write down your view of it, and to do so is to impress anything that was worthy on your memory. Also, to be known as a book reviewer causes other reviewers, contemplating the reception of their own books, to be marginally more judicious. Literary survival is a multifaceted thing, and its weapons are rarely confessed.

Once a week that year I went to London to attend seminars at the London School of Economics. The LSE, as all perhaps know, was founded to serve the progressive vision of Beatrice and Sidney Webb and to be the staff college of British social democracy. By the 1930s, a common tendency in such design, it was intensely conservative in economic mood, although this conservatism was somewhat obscured

[3]*The Economic Journal,* vol. XLVIII, no. 190 (June 1938), p. 342.

by the presence, though not in economics, of Britain's best-known socialist scholar, Harold J. Laski. In notoriety Laski was easily the equivalent of a dozen or so less ostentatious conservatives. The University of Cambridge, anciently synonymous with aristocracy and privilege, was, in contrast, far more radical than the London School.

At the LSE I attended the seminars of Friedrich von Hayek and Lionel Robbins, both men of classical faith — seminar in each case being a conventional term that described a convocation of some seventy-five or a hundred contentiously articulate and deeply dissenting participants from all over the globe. Most notably present were the recent migrants from the repressive regimes in Germany, Austria, Hungary and Poland.

So competitive was the effort to be heard that Professor Hayek, a gentle man of comprehensively archaic views — all efforts by the state to protect or advance well-being he held to be on the downward road to serfdom — was only rarely able to speak. On one memorable evening he arrived, took his seat, bowed and in his polished accent said, "Now gentlemen, as I proposed to you at our last meeting, we will on this evening discuss the rate of interest." Nicholas Kaldor saw the opportunity and said, "Professor Hayek, I really must beg to disagree."

Although not given naturally to reticence, I did not during that year say anything whatever. Nor, as I recall, did my most distinguished compatriot in that learned throng, David Rockefeller. David came to visit us in Cambridge, and we played poker, but carefully for matches.

Our house in Cambridge was in an unpleasant area of semidetached dwellings near the northern edge of town — No. 21 Leys Road. Our next-door neighbor was unemployed and did not expect ever again to be otherwise. I greeted him each morning, commenting cheerfully if possible on the weather. He would give the matter some thought and say, "It's all right now, but it's going to rain." For part of the year we shared the house with John and Dorothy Dunlop. John Dunlop, later Chairman of the Department of Economics and Dean of the Faculty of Arts and Sciences at Harvard, a labor negotiator of prodigious energy and talent, Director of the Cost of Living Council under President Nixon and Secretary of Labor for a year under President Ford, gave every evidence of future eminence. He approached all household tasks with a single-minded competence that caused me to yield and relax. During this year he showed Keynes to be wrong on a matter concerning the relative movements of real and money wages. Keynes not only conceded his error but thanked Dunlop for the correction. One thought of a graduate student in physics who successfully amended Einstein.

Life in the Oxford and Cambridge colleges between the wars retained virtually all of its original style. Servants still attended the needs of students, although Cambridge had weakened to the point of allowing women so to serve. Proctors in their gowns and their assisting bulldogs in full regalia patrolled the streets to keep order and enforce the curfew. The menu at the better High Tables was far above the British average, as also the wine, and especially so at the numerous feasts. Much store was set by the quality of the after-dinner conversation among Fellows and guests in the Combination Rooms. I liked it very much and withstood admirably the kindly condescension with which any young American was regarded.

My wife, who on these occasions remained at Leys Road studying Italian, was less enamored of the Cambridge academic scene. She was also less impressed by the never-ending discussions of economics, for she had not in earlier life or study encountered the name of Keynes or that of any other economist. She had, however, a prodigious commitment to travel, inherited from highly peripatetic ancestors whose ancient Baedekers to the number of a dozen or more we had brought with us in a box from home. These years, 1937 and 1938, were the last that one could travel easily over all of Europe as far as the Russian border, and much of what I know of that continent goes back to that time. Naples, Siena, Ravenna, Ferrara, Prague, Leipzig, Poznan, Danzig now Gdánsk, Königsberg now Kaliningrad, I have not seen since. Dresden would disappear entirely in an action less of deliberate criminality than of casual military ignorance and irresponsibility.

*　　*　　*

From Cambridge we covered the English countryside on weekends and over long ones extended our journeys to Devon and Cornwall or the North. During the long Christmas holiday we traveled across Belgium from Bruges to Ghent to Brussels and Liège, then to Aachen and the tomb of Charlemagne, on across Germany to Cologne, Göttingen, Hamburg, Flensburg and then across Denmark to

Copenhagen. It was a severe winter in Europe; the roads almost everywhere were covered with ice, and sometimes, as in the Hartz Mountains, the snow was high beside the road. We had time to stop and see whatever was to be seen, and my wife placed a neat check mark against each monument, birthplace, museum, church and castle listed in the Baedeker. She would not willingly abandon a town while any sight remained unmarked. Before leaving Cambridge that winter, we acceded to the plea of two American friends, Ralph Emerson, later a notable botanist, and Edward Miller, later a prominent New York divine, that they accompany us in the rumble seat. That would help to pay for the gasoline. Before we had crossed Belgium, the outdoor seat had proved untenable so we made the journey to Copenhagen all four in the small space of a prewar Ford convertible. My wife, being the smallest, was forced to curl up on the shelf behind the front seat. She had to be told of the view. At the Danish border post we were asked to dismount and go into the customs shack to have our passports and car papers approved. The three of us in the front left the car, and the guard accompanied us inside. After a few minutes Kitty came in. The officer reacted with astonishment and suspicion and went out to have a further look inside the car.

Our passengers left us in Denmark; on Christmas Day we examined Hamlet's castle at Elsinore and then crossed over to Sweden and drove through the short afternoon and the night toward Stockholm. We put the top down and felt close to the deep snow. The moon was above and the black forests solidly on either side. We were alone on the road. No journey was ever more magically silent, mysterious or wonderful. In the early hours of the morning we came to the Swedish match town of Jonköping on the southern end of Lake Vättern. The streets were empty, dead. We made our way to the largest hotel, which the sign over the entrance proclaimed to be the Hotel Stängt. The door was locked; we rang for many minutes without result. We learned later that *stängt* in Swedish means closed.

It was one of the few occasions ever when my wife's linguistic aptitude failed. To acquire another European language was for her only a matter of weeks. By the time we left India in 1963, she had sufficiently mastered Hindi so that she could make a wholly adequate speech in that language. At a large farewell dinner given for us by T. T. Krishnamachari, then the Finance Minister, she so spoke. It was not as graceful an act as we imagined, for T.T.K., a Madrasi who had been reared speaking a wholly different family of languages, had to have an interpreter.

Many years later, in summer, we again journeyed by car across Sweden and again stopped, this time only for lunch, at Jönköping. A few days before in Switzerland I had been presented with a tiny gold-plated music box attached to a key ring on which I put the car keys. I went into the hotel washroom and stood at the urinal beside a blond, rather sad-faced Swede. As I began to pee, I jingled the keys in my trouser pocket and accidentally set off the music box. It played "Tales from the Vienna Woods." My neighbor heard the music, looked down at its apparent source and dashed wildly from the room. My wife saw him emerge, look back in alarm at the door and in even more alarm at me as I appeared. A musical gift beyond belief.

*   *   *

Among liberal economists in the 1930s, Sweden was regarded with the utmost approval. In Washington, as also in Britain, there was the already noted intense debate over the cause of the current economic despair. Was it, in the later terminology, the microeconomic effect of monopoly or the macroeconomic consequence of oversaving, underinvestment and the resulting shortage of demand? The achievement of Sweden, as it then seemed, was to have attacked both disorders. The huge consumers' cooperative movement — everywhere manifest in the stores of the *Kooperative Forbundet* — took on the monopolies and bought in huge quantities, thus bargaining down the prices. And it produced the goods itself where this served. That you best dealt with a position of exploitive power in the economy not by dissolving it as through the antitrust laws but by creating another position of countervailing power was a thought that was to remain strongly with me.

On oversaving, underinvestment and unemployment — the macroeconomic disorder — the economists of the Stockholm school had substantially anticipated Keynes. They had urged with success that the government budget be balanced only with the revenues that accrued at full employment and high levels of output. When employment and output fell and therewith tax revenues, the excess of public expenditures over receipts was a useful and necessary stimulant.

That the state should provide the purchasing power needed to keep people employed was common ground. Keynes, accordingly, was a source of very little excitement in Sweden.

In a fair world what has been called the Keynesian Revolution would have been called the Swedish or Stockholm Revolution. The Swedes failed of the honor partly because Sweden is a small country and more because the policy was put in effect far too peacefully. Revolutions require the signature of violence, at least in language. This the British and American critics of Keynes were good enough to provide.

*   *   *

In Stockholm I made the acquaintance of Bertil Ohlin, a later Nobel Prize winner and for long the leader of the Liberal Party; of the young Dag Hammarskjöld, then Undersecretary for Finance; of Karin Kock, later a government minister; and of Professor Gösta Bagge, then the head of the Conservative Party.

One evening I drove out from Stockholm through snowbanks higher than the car on either side to visit Gustav Cassel, a tall, patriarchal figure, by then retired from his professorship in economics, who, in his time, had a reputation of unchallenged eminence in the European financial world. He came down the stairs, greeted me warmly and said, "I expect you have been seeing all my Red students in Stockholm." He had Gunnar Myrdal principally in mind. He then questioned me at length about Roosevelt. I did not conceal my fealty. His disapproval was courtly and mild.

I began in those weeks a friendship that continues to this day with Gunnar and Alva Myrdal, both of whom would come to hold cabinet positions. And I would still later encounter Alva when she was Swedish ambassador in India.

Gunnar is a man of many achievements, and of his greatest I had an early knowledge, although for a while a faulty memory. Over lunch in Stockholm in late December 1937, he told me that he had just received a most curious invitation from Frederick P. Keppel, then the president of the Carnegie Corporation in New York: would Myrdal come to the United States and, as a civilized and learned outsider, take a look at the Negro problem, as it was then called? Thus there might be a break with the entrenched American prejudices and stereotypes. Myrdal thought it too romantic to be real. My reaction was rather different; no one, I believed, should turn down free money and travel from a foundation. A few days later we met again, and he told me he had changed his mind and accepted. He and Alva had gone to a movie and seen a film on Yellowstone Park. While studying the American race problem, there would be a chance to see all the American national parks.

Such is memory and its flaws. Forty years later I told this story at a dinner in New York celebrating the Myrdals. Alva told me afterward that the decisive film was not on Yellowstone Park but on yellow fever and how it had been cured. Perhaps they could help do the same for racial oppression.

From their research came *An American Dilemma,* a powerful document on racial injustice and the remedies, on which Myrdal was assisted by Ralph Bunche among others. It was a vital early step up in the struggle for civil rights.

In 1940, the American Economic Association met in New Orleans. This was almost, though not quite, the last time a major academic organization could assemble and have its few black members accept the nasty hotels reserved for their race. In 1971, the Association met in New Orleans again. By then hotel segregation had come to an end; black members and their white colleagues could rent the same acrylic rooms. I was president-elect in that year and in charge of the program. I invited Myrdal to New Orleans to accept the thanks and congratulations of the Association as the economist who, more than any other or all combined, had contributed to the change.

*   *   *

In Sweden, apart from meeting the economists and studying the cooperative movement, we began a lifelong commitment to winter exercise. My wife acquired skates to match my inevitable proficiency as a Canadian. I don't remember when I achieved my first pair; it is possible that, like many other of my countrymen, I was born so equipped. From the Nordiska Trading Company I now bought a handsome pair of hickory skis to match those of my wife. We tried out in the Stockholm parks and neighboring hills and on the way back across Sweden stopped for two days of crosscountry skiing. One went out at dawn and returned three or four hours later after dusk.

As we drove across Denmark, Germany, Holland and Belgium,

we managed to visit almost everything prescribed by Baedeker and presently were back in Cambridge for another term.

*   *   *

However, our travels had only just begun. In the spring Henry A. Wallace, at the behest of John D. Black, invited me to join a delegation from the United States to a meeting of the governing body of the International Institute of Agriculture, the predecessor of the Food and Agriculture Organization (FAO). Like its successor its headquarters was in Rome. It was only necessary that I pay my own way to Italy and my expenses while there; government junkets were not yet what they would one day become. So in May we departed Cambridge, visited Compiègne and Chartres and went on to Paris, where, with much else, I was taken to visit the family of the aged professor with whom Kitty had lived on the Rue Madame while studying at the Sorbonne. After a deeply anatomical discussion, which I did not follow, they concluded that she should not have married me. I was too tall and ungainly and, additionally, did not speak French. Neither this nor anything since has altered my feeling for the wonders of Paris. From there we went north and east to Amiens, Rheims and Verdun, the countryside immediately around Verdun being then, as it still is today, a dismal wasteland from World War I. In Geneva I watched the Council of the League of Nations seek words to condemn, while seeming not to condemn, Italian and Nazi intervention in Spain. Thence we went to the Riviera, Genoa, Pisa, Siena and on to Rome.

The International Institute of Agriculture, founded in 1905, operated from a small acreage in the Villa Borghese. Never a serious organization, it by now had degenerated into a minor embellishment of Mussolini's international image. The American delegation led by Undersecretary of Agriculture Milburn L. Wilson had no business being there, as some, at least, reluctantly admitted to themselves. I attended the opening and closing sessions and, after a brief exposure to the other parts of the program, went only to the receptions and dinners in between. At a certain moment, as the receptions came to a close, there would be a rush to the buffets, and these would be stripped down to the peonies by the more needful or greedy guests. A large woman once walked out before us in triumphant possession of a bunch of bananas. From Rome we went to

Naples, Pompeii, Herculaneum, Sorrento and Amalfi, back to Orvieto and Florence, across the Apennines to Ravenna, Ferrara and Venice, across the Dolomites and the Grossglockner to Austria and Vienna, on to Prague and Berlin. Later we went to Munich, to the castles of Ludwig II in southern Bavaria, over Switzerland to Lucerne, Interlaken, Montreux and Geneva, down across the Massif Central to Marseilles and back across central France to Paris.

*   *   *

Many have written of that last summer of peace in Europe, of the sense of foreboding, fear, despair. We did, indeed, feel it but under a surface that was often almost ostentatiously calm. There was also much difference as between countries. Thus Italian fascism was evident mostly in the public graffiti blazoned on every empty wall calling on Italians to Believe, Obey, Fight — Credere, Obbedire, Combattere. These words were principally striking for their contrast with the casual, skeptical reality of everyday Italian life and conversation and the several million who were committed to daylong indolence by the massive absence of jobs. In Verona we saw the Italian army deployed along the streets to welcome one of Mussolini's acolytes, and in the next years when I read of the Italian disasters in Greece and North Africa, I thought of the unpressed, indifferent and untidy crew which lined the Verona streets, their bayonet tips dangerously at my eye level, with the blade of one warrior clipping that of the next as they turned in sequence to marvel at my height.

We arrived in Vienna shortly after the Anschluss. Swastika flags hung over almost every façade — great rectangles of red cloth. But German and Austrian brownshirts were not much in evidence, and otherwise there was little from the recent invasion to attract attention. The terror was behind closed doors. We went to see the great socialist housing developments, Schönbrunn and the opera house as might any tourist at the time. We did observe that when we crossed the border into Czechoslovakia, our passports were checked not only by the customary Austrian border guard but more thoughtfully by an SS man.

Prague seemed wholly engaged in those early summer days with the Sokol games, a great extravaganza in youthful physical exercise. The Nazis had made their first threatening move only days before, but these the average citizen was trying resolutely to ignore. We drove one day from Prague to Carlsbad (now Karlovy Vary) and at night across the Sudeten Mountains into Germany. Before leaving, we bought an American flag to fly, if it seemed necessary, from the fender of the Ford, for such insignia was then the preeminent symbol of innocence and noninvolvement. Along the forest roads that night we encountered Czech army detachments. On the German side all was peaceful.

As were nearly all of my academic generation, I was eloquently adverse in my views of Hitler and National Socialism, passionately with the Loyalists in Spain. Kitty, who for a graduate year, 1934–35, had studied German literature in Munich and shared space in the *Studentinnenheim* with the tragic friend of Hitler, Unity Mitford of the Mitfords, was, though more quietly, equally hostile. Yet there seemed little against spending a few weeks in Germany, ostensibly on academic studies. Again the American sense of detachment, a feeling that was to dissolve in 1940 almost within days of the fall of France.

To justify the German summer, I had come up with a somewhat questionable piece of scholarly prestidigitation; I would make a study of the Nazi legislation that prevented the alienation of land that had been long in the possession of peasant families, the so-called *Reichserbhofgesetz*. This required a stay in Berlin to consult with professors and agricultural officials and a field trip to see the law in operation at first hand. We selected East Prussia for the field study because it was the most distant part of the Reich and the only part my wife had never seen. Later I published a paper in the *Quarterly Journal of Economics* on the land law, one that I am certain was never cited and was, very possibly, never read.

Berlin was also calm. Occasionally one encountered soldiers moving along the roads; one did not doubt that they were more lethal than the Italians. Each day at noon a jackbooted column came down Unter den Linden to the war memorial and, on leaving, did a virtuoso goose step. One drill sergeant with a stentorian voice performed as though both legs were attached to his body by universal joints. However, he seemed more ridiculous than menacing.

My wife had numerous college friends in Germany, but none was a Nazi. All without exception were quietly, sadly critical of the crushing power by which they had been captured. A friend and former companion, Edgar von Schmidt-Pauli, was doing military service as an officer in an army unit stationed north of Berlin. He came down to see us and promptly, in disregard of regulations, discarded his uniform. He wished to separate himself from the terrible context, and this wish extended into the ranks of officialdom.

In Berlin, as in nearly all foreign cities at the time, there was a Professional Harvard Man, a figure of vacuous grace and charm who made his career out of having been at Harvard. In Berlin the P.H.M. worked for the *Reichsnährstand,* the government body concerned with making Germany self-sufficient and otherwise efficient in its food supply. When we were planning our East Prussian junket, he told the provincial bureaucrats to give us a regal tour of the great Junker estates. They responded enthusiastically because, as we later learned, the telegram telling of our arrival promoted me, through a misprint, from being a leading young American economist to being *the* leading young American agronomist.

We went from one great estate to another. On one occasion there was champagne on the lawn in the morning. On another there was lunch in the great house in a dining room of unrelieved gloom hung about with the portraits of fiercely mustached ancestors, all in spiked helmets and full uniform, each seeking to look more dangerous than his neighbor. Horses and open carriages took us out over the vast acreage. There was near disaster when, at the very first of our stops, my wife, who had created an initially favorable impression by taking the reins and driving the horses, asked what was the difference between wheat and barley. My reputation as an agronomist hung in the balance.

At one of our stops one morning I sat next to a handsome woman of middle years, who commented on the social dialectic surrounding us. Her uncle, an imperial figure and the owner of the property, was contemptuous of both the officials who accompanied us and their politics. But he could not afford to show it. So he was being unnaturally gracious, and the officials, in turn, were rejoicing in the glow. Our tour continued to the great stud farm whence came the Trakehner horses and on to the Masurian Lakes. We looked at the World War I battlefield near (and officially at) Tannenberg and at the great war memorial there, reflecting in its architecture the combined inspiration of a Roman stadium and an American brickyard. On the last night before we were to start back across Poland, our accompanying host told us, though in the strictest confidence, that he too was not a Nazi. He did not wish us to carry away a false impression. However, our chauffeur, whose coat lapel sagged under the weight of Nazi insignia, seemed not to be subject to doubts.

Coming back into Germany from East Prussia through Poland on a little-traveled road, we found the barriers down, the border closed for the night. There was no place near to stay. The Polish border guard, whom we dug out of his cottage, was a towering figure, an inch or two taller than I. He affirmed that we could not cross. When Kitty asked where we could sleep, he pointed vaguely to a nearby field. To gain time she admired his stature. He informed her that, before the war — World War I — *he* had served in the Prussian Guard. Regimental pride transcended Polish patriotism. My wife asked if I could have made it; he thought my length adequate but expressed doubts as to my general physique and posture. Perhaps the latter, though, could be corrected. His thoughts were now wholly back in Germany; once again he was on parade at Potsdam. Awakening to the present, he concluded that we too should be allowed to journey into the world of his youth. If we could wake the German beyond the barrier, we could be on our way.

*   *   *

As the summer of 1938 neared its end, we returned to France, and one thought was heavy on my mind: in the preceding months there had been little to distinguish our activities from those of an everyday tourist. I was required by the terms of my Social Science Research Council fellowship to report, when in Paris, to the resident officer of the Rockefeller Foundation, the ultimate source of my money. This was to ensure that a serious effort at scholarly self-improvement was being made. The Rockefeller representative was a pleasant, graying man of good philanthropic aspect named Tracy B. Kittridge. He received me in his sunny, comfortable office. For my report I had collected the name of every economist, however marginal his credentials, with whom I had talked in the previous months. I told of meetings in Rome and of looking into agricultural matters in Berlin and East Prussia. And of visits to the League economists in Geneva. A few days before, a few hours south of Paris we had passed a small agricultural experiment station. We had turned back, met the man in charge and looked it over. I dealt with that. Eventually there was no more. It would be wrong, I felt, to improvise.

Mr. Kittridge looked at me sternly.

"Young man, I have some instructions for you."

I nodded and braced myself.

"You are now to take a good vacation."

So we did. We went down the Loire, around the coast of Brittany to Mont-Saint-Michel and across Belgium and Holland to Rotterdam and then home on the conversationally valuable *Statendam*. On the ship we had news of the meeting at Munich. From my fellowship of $2400 for the year, we still had a little money to spare.

7

Interlude

I RESUMED TEACHING and writing at Harvard in the autumn, and one now had the feeling that life was an interlude. Something more and larger awaited. For the moment, however, one's work and enjoyments were as before.

From 1935 through 1937, a young Canadian, Robert Bryce, fresh from Keynes's seminar in England, had been at Harvard, and he more than any other had been able to say with final authority what Keynes really meant. "Keynes is Allah," Schumpeter once observed, "and Bryce is his prophet." By 1938, however, Bryce had left to start his thirty-year career as senior arbiter of economic policy in Ottawa, a record unique among these perils. More than anyone else he made Canada the first country (allowing for the independent case of Sweden) to commit itself fully to the Keynesian compensatory faith. Now as the most recent arrival from the other Cambridge, I succeeded to the Bryce mantle. I was firm in my new authority.

There was an admirable forum. Alvin Harvey Hansen had come from the University of Minnesota to join the new school of public administration. He was thought to be a man of acceptably orthodox views, much devoted to the case for liberal trade. His textbook with Frederic B. Garver was an eminently respectable volume. But in the immediately preceding years, in the course of criticizing and correcting the Keynesian heresy, he had become a convert. Harvard, perhaps unwittingly, had hired the man who would become the leading American advocate of Keynes.

Hansen was a teacher of unpretentious honesty and kindness to whom students and younger faculty alike turned with admiration and affection. For his Monday afternoon seminar on fiscal policy — really on Keynesian economics — in the new Littauer Center, students filled the classroom and spread out into the hall. And communicants came regularly from Washington to hear and discuss the word. Seymour E. Harris, another latter-day convert who was also a full professor, joined the congregation. So did Paul Samuelson. The three would do much to make the Keynesian system the foundation of American economic thought, policy and instruction. As I've observed elsewhere,[1] the Keynesian Revolution entered the United States and went on to Washington by way of Harvard.

My free and comfortable rooms and the free food of a resident tutor were now gone; Harvard in those days put a heavy penalty on marriage. But there was redemption. On the evening of the great hurricane in the autumn of 1938, noting only that it seemed a high wind, we found a comfortable apartment on Concord Avenue just beyond the Radcliffe quadrangle. My wife then got a job at Widener Library, and Harold Hitchings Burbank gave me, at extra pay, a section of the elementary economics course to teach at Radcliffe.

This latter patronage, reserved for the relief of married instructors, mirrored the rigorous social and sexual mores of that unbelievably recent time. It was then unthinkable that Radcliffe undergraduates — women — should sit in the same classroom with Harvard men. This was less because they were an erotic distraction than that their presence would be an insult to masculine dignity and supremacy, although the reasons for the segregation were never given. Some things could be taken for granted. Accordingly, all courses of appreciable interest to women had to be repeated for their benefit, sometimes for only one student. I learned that a subject that took an hour to cover at Harvard required only forty-five minutes at Longfellow Hall in the Radcliffe Yard. I never discovered why.

As with the nonpresence of blacks, I did not then reflect on this expensive indecency. What existed must be right. During the war as an economy measure women were allowed to sit with men, but their second-class citizenship — inferior rooms, cheaper food, separate degrees, denial of teaching positions — continued. In the 1950s, as a trustee of Radcliffe, I began to reflect for the first time on Harvard's mistreatment of women. I started in a halting way to raise the issue, only to find that among the most fearsome enemies of change were some at least of the women trustees. They had prospered in this world of men; why should the present generation of young

---

[1] In "How Keynes Came to America" in *Economics, Peace and Laughter* (Boston: Houghton Mifflin, 1971), p. 43.

women be accorded special favors? Once I asked if we didn't have some higher purpose than preparing our graduates to be attentive wives and competent mothers. Maybe professional careers. Or achievements of the mind. One of my fellow trustees turned on me and said, "Professor Galbraith, let me just ask you this question. What else is as important as being a good wife and mother?" I was too frightened to reply.

In the planning of a new graduate center and residence, I urged that the rooms be considered as apartments to which students might invite and entertain their friends — in their own quarters instead of in the large ceremonial common rooms downstairs where all encounters were chastely in the public eye. "At some point in life a woman has to become the guardian of her own virtue." It was evident to me that I had come dangerously close to pornography.

I had more success in getting women appointed to the teaching staff. Harvard graduate students finance their own instruction by teaching undergraduates, but in the fifties most departments, including economics, denied women this opportunity. In the middle of the decade a brilliant Vassar graduate led all of her male competitors in grades and general competence, and I proposed that she be given an instructorship. Reluctantly, for no good case could be made against it, my colleagues agreed. She was told of her appointment by a devout male chauvinist and told also, in firm and certain tones, that she would never have got the job if Galbraith hadn't "bulldozed" the department into it. (Bulldozing my colleagues was a talent for which I yearned but never had.) My candidate broke down, cried and refused the offer.

However, the next year the story was different. For many decades until 1957 when she retired, the best instruction in economics in the United States was at Vassar by Mabel Newcomer and a coterie of talented colleagues, and now another of her students appeared at Harvard. She was both more determined and more beautiful than the first. I am persuaded that lovely women are rarely without intelligence and that women of labored mind rarely succeed in being physically attractive. The department yielded once again to my persuasion. I asked that this time the candidate be notified by mail. Years passed; moods changed; affirmative action arrived and a compelling young woman from New Orleans with a special competence in money and banking came up for promotion, this time to a tenured position. She shared with one of my earlier opponents a passionate interest in physical exercise, especially rowing, and he made a powerful plea for her promotion, which I supported. We were both defeated.

*   *   *

Soon after returning to Harvard, I received a call from Charles W. Eliot II, now the director of the National Resources Planning Board, a staff research body for the White House. Eliot wanted me to take charge from Cambridge of a major review of the experience with public works employment and spending from the earliest days of the New Deal to the present.

The job meant that I could again be regularly in Washington. The subject would also lend itself admirably to the Keynesian evangelism to which I was firmly committed. The Keynesian economists in the various government departments, including the Federal Reserve and the White House, had by now fully identified each other. They were also meeting regularly under the auspices of the National Planning Association, a private organization of liberal scholars, businessmen, labor leaders and farm organization people that still survives.

As often happens, their arguments were greatly reinforced by the actions of their opponents. From 1933 on, the American economy gradually — very gradually — recovered. Unemployment, which had reached a peak of 25 percent of the civilian labor force in 1933, was down to a towering 17 percent in 1936. It was only an appalling 14.3 percent the following year.[2] In 1936, production — Gross National Product in real terms — reached the 1929 level for the first time in the depression years.[3] The sound men in the Roosevelt Administration, those of accredited financial acumen, said it was now time to assert the ancient principles and truths. Conservative finance should again be the order of the day. Accordingly, the Federal Reserve raised bank reserve requirements, tightened up on bank lending and allowed interest rates to rise. Steps were taken to reduce the federal deficit — from $4.4 billion in the fiscal year end-

---

[2] U.S. Department of Commerce, Bureau of the Census, *Historical Statistics of the United States, Colonial Times to 1957* (Washington, D.C., 1960), p. 73.
[3] Ibid., p. 139.

ing June 30, 1936, to $2.8 billion the following year and to $1.2 billion in fiscal 1938.[4] It was a conservative and anti-Keynesian triumph, and would have been so celebrated except that the economy went into another ghastly slump. Within the depression there was now a recession — a new term. My study was meant to guide the support to the economy that would now be required.

G. Griffith Johnson, Jr., a young Treasury economist, my partner later in the Office of Price Administration and in the U.S. Strategic Bombing Survey in Germany and for many years an unpublicized force in the Motion Picture Association of America, took effective charge of the enterprise. I worked on the broad outline and put the economic case into intelligible language. I also ran interference with the cautious men from the Departments of Labor and Commerce who had been given a watching brief to counter any serious unsoundness of view. As is frequently the case, these were not conservatives but liberals who were impressed by the extreme political danger in their own faith and who were willing, accordingly, to become conservatives to avoid controversy. Pride in professional political aptitude always strongly supports such political abdication. Liberals especially yearn to show that they are not above pragmatic concession. American conservatives are much firmer in their faith. Some will even accept political immolation in support of their convictions.

I won most of my points. That is the advantage of the draftsman: he can concede points without conceding substance, and he can also draft the concessions. When Paul Porter was serving as an aide to Henry Wallace in the early New Deal years, he said, "I care not who is Secretary of Agriculture. Let me only draft the press release announcing the action."

Our eventual report conceded that "the view that depressions will correct themselves if left alone is by no means dead." But it went boldly on to express "grave doubt . . . [that this view] is likely to become again the basis of public policy."[5] It affirmed that under "conditions of general unemployment the provision of public works is a useful alternative to idleness . . . [and] so are other types of governmental activity: education, conservation, pest and disease con-

[4] Ibid., p. 711.
[5] *The Economic Effects of the Federal Public Works Expenditures, 1933–1938*. National Resources Planning Board, Washington, D.C., November 1940, p. 4.

trol, and a host of other things."[6] These careful words were perhaps the first unambiguous commitment to Keynesian policy by an official arm of the United States government. They attracted none of the attention for which I hoped and none of the outrage that my censors so greatly feared. We noted in the report that in resorting to public expenditure to reduce unemployment and mitigate the depression's effects, the experience of the United States was in only one respect unique: we had spent for peaceful works while other countries had been spending for arms. By the time our study was published, not long after the fall of France, we too were spending for arms. That, needless to say, made deficits that previously had been viewed with the utmost anxiety entirely sound.

The National Resources Planning Board was headed by Frederic A. (Uncle Fred) Delano, the uncle of the President. It consisted of three members and two advisers, one of whom was Henry S. Dennison. One day in 1939, while the board was getting a progress report on the public works study, word came that its members were wanted by the President. Dennison took me by the arm; he could not go to the President without suitable support. We filed into the Oval Office and were greeted each in turn by F.D.R. Thus encouraged in our efforts, we were discharged without recourse to any substantive business. It was my first meeting with the President; thereafter I was able to advert to him in personal terms.

*   *   *

As the late 1930s passed, the pressure of exterior depression and deprivation on our comfortable life at Harvard continued. Something clearly was wrong. The mood of younger faculty members moved appreciably to the left. Keynes was now widely embraced. The CIO, recently brought into existence by John L. Lewis, created a new interest in the trade union movement, and a union was organized by junior members of the Harvard faculty for purposes that were indistinct. However, the meetings that I attended were, as current trade union practice required, adequately militant in tone.

Beyond Keynes in these years there was a reviving interest in Marx, and a few Communists or followers made their presence felt. One of the latter — presumptively, for he took the Fifth Amend-

[6] Ibid., p. 3.

ment when formally asked — was Russell A. Nixon, a handsome, intelligent man who numbered among his students in beginning economics and later in labor economics the young John F. Kennedy. Whenever, as President, Kennedy encountered an arcane economic term or concept, it was his pleasure, were he in some trustworthy Harvard presence, to put his hand to the side of his mouth and say, "Why do you suppose Russ Nixon didn't teach me that?"

The leftward movement led to the great Harvard explosion of the late thirties, the equivalent of the strike and student/faculty revolt of thirty years later. The absence of alternative employment along with the comforts of Cambridge life had caused younger untenured faculty members to linger on at Harvard. The senior faculty came to fear that this would be more or less forever. Something must be done. J. Raymond Walsh, who was the first president of the Teachers' Union, and Alan R. Sweezy, an active member of the union but not to be confused with his younger brother Paul who was also at Harvard at the time,[7] were singled out for termination. The Walsh-Sweezy case broke in the spring of 1937. It seemed possible that the two were chosen because of their political activities and views, but this the university and departmental authorities denied. Presently an investigatory committee of professors, including Felix Frankfurter until he went to the Supreme Court, was impaneled. It reported a year later that the termination had been an innocent act. Some of the accumulated talent really had to go; two men of more formidable scholarship had been selected to stay; the more formidable scholars were, in fact, more conservative and far more restrained in political expression and action, but that was an accident. It is the kind of accident to which universities are prone.

I was not involved in the competition that deleted Walsh and Sweezy, for my appointment still had a year to run. Nor was I greatly concerned about my chances for promotion. My view of my own ability had advanced rapidly, more rapidly it developed than that held by my seniors. In the spring of 1939, Princeton invited me to come down to discuss an assistant professorship; one dissonant voice in an otherwise harmonious choir would add interest. I thought it wise to make the visit, for competition from another university would ensure my promotion at Harvard. At Princeton I pre-

[7] See Chapter 4.

sented a number of unreasonable demands; in particular I wished to be mostly concerned with graduate students. While discussing these details at a dinner at the house of the chairman of the Princeton economics department, a stoutish, exceptionally amiable man named Stanley Howard who taught corporation finance and who was said during the war to have taught geography to the Navy using the same notes, I was handed a telegram from Harold Hitchings Burbank. He had just come from a meeting with James Bryant Conant, and he advised me to take any post that was offered at Princeton. My Harvard prospects, the wire said, were very dim. My bargaining position went into a severe slump as did my morale. I recall that evening with distaste.

* * *

In the autumn of 1939, we took up pleasant quarters in a new apartment building on Palmer Square in the center of Princeton. New York was nearby. I continued to be much in Washington. For the rest I faced the indifference of the Princeton undergraduates and, in time, learned to reciprocate.

One of my colleagues and friends at the university was James A. Perkins, later the vice president of the Carnegie Corporation and later still a not uncontroversial president of Cornell. We shared the same discontent. The war had come to Europe. (It had come, indeed, while my wife and I were bicycling over Bermuda, and we had been hurried aboard the *Queen of Bermuda* for a blacked-out journey to New York, the vessel having been summoned to war duty in Britain.) Great events were in train, and we were on the sidelines.

At Princeton the Gothic was presentable; the grounds were well-maintained; the golf course stretched away from the Princeton Inn to the graduate school, and the more modish professors talked of their golf scores; of an evening, out for a walk, one met Albert Einstein. One or two students crept into our apartment after classes to talk about economics, politics or the war, but they risked being thought eccentric. Perkins and I concluded that we had been caught in one of the great cul-de-sacs of history.

We made a bargain that whoever first escaped would rescue the other. That promise was kept. As I will later tell, on April 29, 1941, in the early morning, I was put in charge of all prices in the United

States. After first calling Kitty, I sent a telegram to Jim, who arrived in Washington the same afternoon.

*   *   *

On two or three occasions during 1938 and 1939, I was invited to make a full-time commitment to Washington and the New Deal. The requests came from Lauchlin Currie, who wanted to place a reliable Keynesian in this agency or that. I resisted. But in the spring of 1940, I succumbed in a peculiar way. The American Farm Bureau Federation had decided that it needed an economist and an economic research department. It appealed for suggestions to Howard Tolley, my old California teacher, who was by now the chief of the Bureau of Agricultural Economics in the United States Department of Agriculture. Tolley saw a chance for infiltrating a friendly ally into the most powerful of the farm organizations, one that hung perilously at the time between support of the administration for its agricultural programs and rejection of it for its liberalism. The pay by university standards — $7500 a year — was handsome. I negotiated a leave of absence from my Princeton colleagues with an ease that was not at all surprising and in May of 1940 made my way to Chicago. The AFBF there functioned from dingy rooms at 58 East Washington Street, a short distance from Michigan Boulevard and the lake. Not many would have guessed from viewing our headquarters that, for its purposes, it was one of the most powerful political forces in the nation. It was an article of the Farm Bureau faith that only by keeping its base of operations out of Washington could it avoid political contamination or co-option by the federal government.

The Farm Bureau owes its origin to the establishment early in this century of the county agent system and the feeling that before farmers could be given the help of such a specialist, they should prove their interest by organizing a bureau or committee to sponsor him. Presently from the union of these local bureaus came state federations, which, in their turn, united for national political needs. The Farm Bureau was, in effect, a government-originated lobby on behalf of government services for agriculture. To its political purposes, a number of the states had added cooperative purchasing and insurance companies, and by 1940 some of these had become very large business enterprises.

Outside the South the Farm Bureau was the organization of the substantial farm families; in the South it was the voice of the big cotton producers. Small farmers only rarely were members, share-croppers never. The Farm Bureau was nominally extant in all states, but Illinois, Iowa, Mississippi, Alabama and Arkansas were then the solid pillars of its power. In Alabama in 1940, the local farm bureaus were guided by county agents who, under Walter Randolph, the state president, were the mainstay of the Bankhead political machine. This, impregnable at the time, sustained John H. Bankhead II, as senator and member of the Senate Committee on Agriculture and William B. Bankhead, father of Tallulah, as Speaker of the House of Representatives. Once in 1942, I received a compliment from John Bankhead, with whom I was negotiating a wholly irreconcilable difference of view as to the proper price of cotton. He said, "Doctor, you've learned a lot in this last year, and I congratulate you. You used to pretend you knew something about cotton. Now you admit your ignorance. That, sir, is progress."

Its power divided between North and South, corn and cotton, the Farm Bureau was similarly divided in its politics. The southerners were Democrats and cosmopolitan, secular and generally liberal in outlook. All were firm supporters of Roosevelt and the New Deal. However, the liberalism did not extend to civil rights for their black field hands and tenants; such thoughts in those days did not even fleetingly arise. The midwestern Bureau members were Republican, parochial, isolationist and (those from Ohio and Missouri apart) conservative. They accepted F.D.R. and the New Deal reluctantly and with a sense of self-abasement. As a practical matter, they could not afford the luxury of their ancient Republican faith; that might mean forgoing government benefits and price supports. But they did not cease to be sorry. Presiding over this coalition was Edward A. O'Neal of Alabama. Only rarely in my life have I encountered a man I liked as much.

Then sixty-four, Ed O'Neal was tall and ample, greatly resembling in build, face, speech and manner Senator Sam Ervin of Watergate reputation. He had been educated at Washington and Lee and had traveled abroad after graduation in the best tradition of the well-born southerner. He wore impeccably tailored suits from Savile Row and delighted in telling his farm audiences what they cost and of his belief that every farmer should be able to afford one as good. His style, income and Anglophile instincts were the legacy of an aristocratic family that had contributed a colonel to the War Between the States. Their fortune had survived at their plantation near Florence, Alabama, not far from Muscle Shoals and Wilson Dam.

Ed O'Neal called everyone laddie, whatever his age, and he was relentlessly and artistically profane. He was eventually banned for a year or two from the radio networks for telling an interlocutor that he should have learned the answer to his question at his mother's teat. On one occasion Ed took me with him when he went to lobby on Capitol Hill. He commandeered a committee room and called the relevant farm-state legislators to a session, which he chaired. His instructions were friendly but firm. They were heard with respect and obeyed.

At the Farm Bureau I never got to any research deeper than looking in the USDA Yearbook of Agriculture. That was because Ed (and his associates) soon discovered my ability to express myself in writing, and others as well. Since they had an insatiable need for speeches, resolutions, memoranda, demands and denunciations, I was soon fully occupied and much admired. They had never had anything approaching my talent at my speed before.

One of my tasks was to rewrite the resolutions after they had been formally passed by the directorate of the federation at their regular meetings in order to make these declarations accord more closely with Ed's needs and views. *Ex post* revision, he had learned, saved time and voice as compared with efforts to get things right before the voting. The task involved a useful clue as to how New Deal legislation had been enacted. Farmers in those days were numerous and powerful but not powerful enough to get what they needed from the Congress on their own. They had to have the support of urban Democrats. Similarly the unions for their needs — public works, social security or the National Labor Relations (Wagner) Act — required the support or, at a minimum, the acquiescence of farmstate legislators. Ed O'Neal had accommodated to this reality by making a discreet alliance with the emergent union leaders, principally with Sidney Hillman, head of the Amalgamated Clothing Workers. Each undertook to understand and respect the needs of the other.

This arrangement caused O'Neal no trouble at all in the South.

Unions were a purely theoretical concept to southern farmers; they might be bad, but there was no firsthand experience of them. In the Midwest, however, unions were a clear and present wickedness. In Minnesota a creamery strike only a few years before had backed milk up on the farms, and the residual bitterness was deep. The big farm cooperatives didn't want unions. And for numerous farmers unions in the neighboring cities were obvious threats to law, order, property rights, religion, the flag and the sanctity of the American home. It is not easy now to appreciate the depths of the antipathy.

This dislike led the midwestern Farm Bureau members to offer inflammatory resolutions condemning the unions, supporting anti-union legislation, opposing legislation being sought by the labor leaders and denouncing the tendency of the Roosevelt Administration to favor union demands. This was, or would have been, damaging to Ed O'Neal's discreet alliances. So he would acquiesce and then pass the resolutions over to me to improve the English. I made them innocuous except for just enough innocently inflammatory language to satisfy the original author if he happened to read it. This talent greatly pleased Ed; he could not do it easily himself.

*   *   *

The Farm Bureau provided admirable exposure to an American culture little encountered in Cambridge and Princeton and now largely lost to the American scene. The Farm Bureau wives were solemn, functional of form and deeply religious and seemed always to be expecting a challenge to some profoundly held belief. In their presence I usually felt the impulse to explain that I was neither an adulterer nor an anti-Christ. The men were not so ostentatiously devout. They were also open to argument as long as it did not involve the divine rights of agriculture, the sanctity of property or any need to change their minds. The American farmer, they did not doubt, was the most important person in the Republic; it was unforgivable and also sad that others did not see this. On ceremonial occasions they and their wives sang in lugubrious tones:

> When the farmer comes to town
> With his wagon broken down
> The farmer is the man that feeds them all.

If you'll only look and see
I think you will agree
That the farmer is the man that feeds them all.

The farmer is the man
The farmer is the man
Lives on credit 'til the fall.
With the interest rate so high
It's a wonder he don't die
And the mortgage man's the one that gets it all.

At noon on June 25, 1940, I was walking down State Street in Chicago on an errand and saw the headlines proclaiming the final fall of France. It was the last in the terrible sequence — the invasion and fall of Poland, the invasion of Denmark and Norway, then of Holland, Belgium and France, the evacuation at Dunkirk and now the end. Between 1914 and 1918 in Canada, as I've told, my family, like many of the Scotch, took a detached view of the Great War; it was for Englishmen, Frenchmen and the Canadian Tory acolytes of the English ruling classes to get themselves slaughtered. In the 1960s and 1970s, I was to be deeply suspicious of the cold warriors and opposed to our intervention in Indochina. But the events of 1938, 1939 and 1940 lent themselves to no doubts. Hitler and the Nazis were there and real; so were their venomous intentions. I was one of the many who, for those years, put their pacifism away.

A day or two after France surrendered, I received a summons from Currie, this one peremptory: I must now come to Washington. So, as the next chapter tells, for the rest of 1940, I divided my time between Chicago and the new defense tasks in the capital.

While at the Farm Bureau and rather to the surprise of my employers, I gave firm economic authority to the policy of providing substantial — they were then called high — support prices for corn, cotton, wheat and other "basic" commodities. The government would set the price and buy or provide nonrecourse loans to ensure that no farmer would sell for less. There had long been sentiment among farmers for this forthright way of supporting farm income, but it ran into strong objections from the U.S. Department of Agriculture and from economists — from the former for the added production it would stimulate, from the latter for its assault on the sanctity of the free market. When I encountered Henry Wallace in those years, he expressed horror at my advocacy.

General Motors could not function without some assurance that its prices would be adequate. Price stability is necessary for its planning. The ability to support its prices is given to GM by its size and the small number of other firms in the automobile market. As with GM so with oil, rubber, chemical, electrical, computer and most other manufacturing as well as much other enterprise. By 1940, it had become my view that what was good for General Motors was good for the farmer. To support farm prices was efficient. The losses from what economists call allocative inefficiency — from the distortions in production because of prices that are no longer a precise reflection of need — were more than made up from the added investment in fertilizer, machinery, irrigation and hybrid seed stock when farmers had the assurance of a reasonably secure return on their outlay.

My employers, Ed O'Neal in particular, were delighted to learn that there was a firm economic reason for what they longed to believe. The trend in agricultural policy not only in the United States but in other industrial countries has ever since been in our direction. And the gains in productivity have been great — in the United States far greater in output per farm worker than in output per worker in industry. Numerous economists, though recognizing the gains, have not ceased to protest.

* * *

My other effort in those years, one strongly supported by Ed O'Neal who was sympathetic to the British, was to try to counter the isolationist inclinations of the Farm Bureau. The voice of the great farm belt was almost uniquely influential in its opposition to international involvement. In the autumn of 1940, I hit upon a seemingly spectacular design for advancing the cause. England now stood alone, and Roosevelt was doing his best to rally American opinion. Why not give the President a major indication of moral support? The convention of the American Farm Bureau Federation would be in Baltimore in December; farm congressmen, public officials and the press would be there in force. Let us invite Lord Lothian, the British Ambassador, to give the banquet speech. Let him appear in this very heartland of the opposition. Although the step for Ed O'Neal was not without risk, he was enthusiastic. He softened up the state presidents, Earl Smith of Illinois in particular. After all, the speech would win attention as nothing in the Bureau's history, and the chance for such publicity surely outweighed deeper scruple. I drafted the invitation and sent it off.

There was no reply. We had reckoned without one major fact: the British Embassy had never heard of the American Farm Bureau Federation. Days passed. I suggested a follow-up letter or call; this Ed forbade. If the British did not know about his organization and recognize the importance of its invitation, to hell with them. Perhaps they were not worth saving.

While we were waiting for a reply, I had lunch one day at the Cosmos Club in Washington with Leonard K. Elmhirst of Dartington Hall, England, and second husband of the notable Dorothy Whitney Straight. A graduate in agriculture of Cornell, he knew the American farm scene well, and after our meeting it occurred to me that he could save the day. I reached him in Montreal as he was en route home and outlined the situation. His response was, "The silly, stupid *baastads*." Later, as my experience in diplomacy matured, I ceased to be quite so surprised when diplomats were thus described.

A few hours later calls began coming in from the British Embassy. The invitation had been mislaid; the invitation was so important that it had required special consideration; the acceptance had been delayed because the Ambassador was in England. So urgent was the reaction that there was no time to coordinate the lies.

Lord Lothian accepted. As we had hoped, the interest among the Farm Bureau members was intense. A special committee designated by Ed O'Neal went to meet him at the train, but while they were waiting, a telegram came from the embassy. Because of a "slight illness," the Ambassador could not make it. A diplomatic excuse. Ed's anger was nearly beyond control. I was depressed. Our isolationists could now say that the British did not even stoop to care.

Neville Butler, counselor of the embassy, was given the task of delivering the speech. Alone, Britain could not be sure of the result; victory or defeat "now depends largely" on help from the United States. He read with the manuscript nestled on one arm; his voice was far from strong; he was not otherwise an impressive figure. Ed O'Neal became, if possible, more angry. When the speeches were over and the tables were cleared, there was — an unnaturally festive touch — some dancing. The gloom was unrelieved until a further message came saying that Lord Lothian was desperately ill. And then in the early hours of the morning came yet another. The Ambassador was dead.

In diplomacy there is nothing like a good sense of timing. At a meeting of the directors, at the suggestion of Earl Smith of Illinois no less, a previously drafted resolution on help to Britain was given a solidly affirmative tone. That the path was thus a little smoothed for Lend-Lease a few weeks later cannot be doubted.

8

Washington, 1940

LEON HENDERSON was slightly under average height, of rather more than average width, and he seemed always to be adjusting his pants, pulling a little on his belt as though this would reduce his waistline. Perhaps because they had to be so large at his stomach, his trousers were always very loose below. They flopped when he walked or the wind blew. The rest of Leon's attire was somewhat more disorderly. He shaved regularly but without precision. His face alternated between an expression of unconvincing belligerence and one of shocked, unbelieving innocence, and sometimes he affected both at the same time. Mostly, however, he favored the belligerent expression, and this he sought to reinforce with a sharply jutting cigar that he rolled in his mouth but rarely smoked. He was highly intelligent, with a strongly retentive mind. After a few minutes' study of a paper on any subject, however complex, he not only had absorbed it for all needed use but could give convincingly the impression that he had written it himself.

The Hemingway syndrome was strong in the upper ranks of the New Deal in those years, as also, one later discovered, among the Air Force generals. It befitted a man to drink heavily, speak always with unvarnished directness, be unadornedly profane, play poker, enjoy the races, frequent the sporting restaurants and bars and, with exceptions, be dominant and successful with women. Henderson, with Harry Hopkins and other close friends, were all in the Hemingway mode. The Stork Club in New York was much favored, and J. Edgar Hoover, a member of this consortium, was called by Representative Vito Marcantonio the Stork Club detective.

Henderson had a constant companion — there is no other way to describe this vivid, living presence in his life. It was the public interest, and his days were spent, early morning until late night, in continuous reaction to the needs of his beleaguered friend. Along with the public interest, he also saw himself as the personally anointed protector of F.D.R., whom he adored.

Henderson came into the New Deal as an economist and Director of Research and Planning with the NRA (the National Recovery Administration), and he had served variously elsewhere, including as a utility man in the 1936 election campaign. By 1940 when he was 45, he was a certified member of the inner Roosevelt circle and a Commissioner on the Securities and Exchange Commission. On May 29, the day after the King of Belgium surrendered to the Germans and the day the British began the retreat to Dunkirk, Roosevelt appointed Henderson to the National Defense Advisory Commission, a body answerable to the President and authorized to prepare the American economy for war or, at a minimum, give the appearance of doing so. Henderson's task was to watch prices and, as necessary, prevent inflation, and I was to become his deputy.

The other members of the NDAC were William Knudsen, recently of General Motors, for production; Edward R. Stettinius, Jr., recently of U.S. Steel, for war materials; Ralph Budd from the Chicago, Burlington and Quincy Railroad, a businessman given to liberal aberration, for transportation; Sidney Hillman, a vice president of the CIO and, as already noted, president of the Amalgamated Clothing Workers, for labor supply; Chester C. Davis, until recently Administrator of the Agricultural Adjustment Administration and now a Governor of the Federal Reserve, for agriculture; and Harriet Elliott, Dean of the North Carolina College for Women, as it then was, to protect the consumer.

Knudsen and Stettinius led into Washington the wartime business executives, who, after long years of hating Roosevelt, the New Deal and all their works, now found themselves at the very center of the government action. Few men in history have been driven by conscience and the expectations of friends to such conflicting goals. There was, on the one hand, the undoubted need to prepare to fight Hitler. But on the other there was the need to retrieve the United States from the yet more immediate Roosevelt subversion, to reaffirm in Washington the essential principles and accustomed power of free enterprise. War or no war, one had responsibilities to one's beliefs, and, as noted, this was what one's fellow executives and Westchester neighbors were expecting. The stage was set for a major battle between the new arrivals and the entrenched New Dealers. The conflict developed quickly and continued throughout the war.

It did not equally engage the attention of all. William Knudsen, a dour, independent, elderly Dane still speaking in the accents of his native land, was above the battle. Stettinius did not quite know what was going on, an innocence that was not shared by the business executives he brought with him.

Ed Stettinius was, in fact, one of those far from exceptional people who give everyone else a glow of satisfaction from feelings of undeniable superiority. In later years he went on to be Lend-Lease Administrator, Undersecretary and then Secretary of State. Each promotion was urged and applauded by people who wanted an appointee who was free from encumbering thoughts of his own. Roosevelt, after contending for many years with the limited but stubborn convictions of Cordell Hull, was especially happy to have Stettinius as Secretary of State. Ed was an historic example of what we now call upward failure.

As the defender of the public and New Deal interest, Henderson saw himself in natural opposition to the businessmen. And he was also the powerful proponent of an activist view of government. This, needless to say, effective mobilization required, and it was something that even under the pressure of the times many of the business executives resisted. More than anyone else, Leon Henderson would lead and dominate the civilian side of the wartime administration. Rather more than Albert Speer, the man who managed German mobilization, he should be known as one of the greatly innovative figures of World War II.

A natural selection operated among those businessmen going to wartime Washington, which strongly favored the ones who had been most effective for their public relations or those who could best be spared. In consequence, once in the capital they were far better at communicating their fears than in initiating action. So on most matters it was the New Dealers such as Henderson, aided by having Roosevelt in support, who dominated the scene. The conflict was, nonetheless, enduring. My memory of wartime Washington by no means excludes the menace of Hitler and the Japanese. But almost as poignantly it is of the New Dealers' battle with the reluctant business spokesmen, for the tactics and strategies of this conflict preoccupied us day by day.

*   *   *

Responding to the call from Lauchlin Currie after the fall of France, I caught the Capitol Limited, the gleaming B&O train that was then the approved passage from Chicago to Washington, and went to Currie's office in what would become the Executive Office Building, then still the Department of State. I was excited, and my excitement deepened when Currie told me that my presence in Washington with Leon Henderson was essential. Control of inflation in the months ahead would be a task for Keynesian sophistication. We must keep limits on the aggregate spending for goods and services by taxation and back this up with the necessary wage and price policy. Henderson, Currie said, was wholly alive to these requirements. But he was fatally susceptible to the older liberal thought that almost any tendency for prices to rise unduly could be met by trust-busting — unleashing the power perpetually latent in the antitrust laws — and otherwise launching an anti-corporation crusade. Henderson had been active as a member of the Temporary National Economic Committee studying the depredations of big business. It was my job to keep policy in line with a rational Keynesian faith. I agreed wholly as to the need.

I went on to see Henderson at his office, was warmly welcomed and very soon became aware of a major problem. A small staff had already assembled — C. David Ginsburg, later a noted Washington lawyer; Edwin M. Martin, later to have a distinguished career in diplomacy; a few professional Henderson acolytes. And for the moment there was absolutely nothing for anyone to do. The prices we were to watch were stable. The price series and indexes to be watched were assembled in admirable fashion by the Bureau of Labor Statistics; looking at the results took no time. After the long years of deflation, most producers and all farmers were desperately hoping that prices *would* rise. Perhaps for a little they should. Our offices were adjacent to Henderson's in the building near the White House occupied by the SEC. There were as yet not even desks at which one could sit down and read the newspaper.

After death and dismemberment, idleness was the nightmare of World War II and much the greater threat in Washington. Men and an occasional woman received the call to serve their government, bade farewell to coworkers, friends and relatives, heard themselves congratulated for the service they were to perform, sensed joyously the envy of those left behind and arrived in the capital to find themselves unexpected, often unwanted and with little whatever to occupy their time. Few experiences could be so chilling. Nothing in wartime Washington was so feared by so many as having space in an office, a shared secretary and no function at all. The most ruthless and most frequent of jurisdictional battles in those years were waged not by people who wanted power but by people who wanted something to do. In the Pentagon in years to come there was even a word for it; it was called Pentagonorrhea.

*   *   *

I couldn't return to Chicago — not immediately anyway. Just short of desperation I was rescued by a call from Paul Porter, who had been made assistant and deputy to Chester Davis, the National Defense Advisory Commissioner for Agriculture. Davis in turn had a job for me. The NDAC had been given power to clear all important contracts for defense facilities. Some forty-eight new chemical, explosives, ammunition and other ordnance plants were scheduled for immediate construction, and Davis feared that they would be concentrated in the already industrialized Northeast as was the industry of World War I. Better that they be scattered over the South, Southwest and West where they would draw on the excess labor of the farms, be a lodestone for other industry and encourage a more rationally distributed economic growth. It was the chance of a lifetime; I would represent Davis's view. I accepted and moved into a small office in the new marble mausoleum of the Federal Reserve Board on Constitution Avenue, part of which had been taken over by the National Defense Advisory Commission. To give me ballast, Davis invited James McDonald Comer of Birmingham, Alabama, to come part-time to Washington. The son of Braxton Bragg Comer, a former Governor of Alabama, Donald was a stately, principled industrialist, the head and a major owner of Comer-Avondale Mills, Inc.

His reputation was that of a liberal, although, like many others at the time, this did not extend either to unions or minority civil rights. We became and remained close friends.

Comer's first step was to award me honorary citizenship in Alabama. I still voted in New Jersey, and he thought New Jersey legislators notoriously negligent of their constituents in Washington. Alabama congressmen were far more attentive. He notified all members of the Alabama congressional delegation of my new standing in the Old Confederacy. It was a nice and, in ensuing months, a highly serviceable gesture.

As the weeks passed, it became evident that Wilmington, Delaware, Pittsburgh, Pennsylvania, Cleveland, Ohio, and other such formidable industrial centers would, indeed, be the preferred locations for the new plants. Neighbors, schools, golf courses and a powerful homing instinct, I was to learn, are a significant force in plant location. The Army, rightly anxious to expedite action, was inclined to go along. I received congressional delegations and representatives of chambers of commerce; they praised Davis's and my enlightened policy and my own public personality with a warmth I have only rarely since experienced. No one was worried about the environmental effects; industry and jobs in those uncomplicated days were an absolute good. But it remained that most of the plants were scheduled for Delaware, Pennsylvania, Ohio and their neighbors.

Chester Davis, originally from Montana, was a slender, handsome man, a Roosevelt supporter on the more conservative wing and a long-established spokesman for the farmers on Capitol Hill. He had an unparalleled capacity for making his way through the bureaucratic thickets. He now instructed me in the art of getting one's way in Washington. I should go and see all of the commissioners of potentially favorable view — Hillman, Elliott, Henderson and Budd — and get them to join Davis in vetoing the next plant that came up for clearance at an already industrialized location. This I did, and almost immediately one such appeared, a TNT manufactory slated for Sandusky, Ohio. It was turned down. That same afternoon representatives of the Army-Navy Munitions Board, the operative agency in the War Department, came to *my* office to discuss a new list of locations, all in admirably bucolic settings. They reported that teams were being dispatched to assess other similarly remote precincts.

* * *

The most important of the new sites, although not by any corrupt design, served my new citizenship. It was a huge shell-machining plant at Gadsden, Alabama. When it came before the Commission for approval, my coalition collapsed in deep anger. Sidney Hillman,[1] a firm, civilized, intense man of unshakable liberal and trade union commitment, announced with emphasis that he would not allow any plant to go to a town that he could not visit himself. It had been to Gadsden in the 1930s that the rubber companies had expanded their operations when the rubber workers began organizing in Akron. The union had sought to follow the firms south; in consequence of the ensuing hostilities Sherman Dalrymple, the head of the United Rubber Workers of America, spent several weeks recovering from his wounds. A complaint of the new National Labor Relations Board noted that Goodyear foremen, supervisors and "flying squadron" members were encouraged by the company to deal violently with Dalrymple and union workers and that "eleven union members [had been] trapped in a Gadsden office building by a mob which smashed down the door and beat the unarmed men."[2] The location which had seemed to me so admirable was perhaps the most effectively anti-union town in the country.

Hillman was adamant and Davis was away. I called Donald Comer in Birmingham, and he was immediately sympathetic. He would phone Joe (as he called himself) Starnes, the congressman from the district, and Joe would persuade the city council to pass a resolution promising to protect the health and civil rights of all who might come to Gadsden, including even union organizers.

Joe Starnes was, in all respects, a faithful representative of his community. Voluble, charming and reactionary, he was ranking

---

[1] Many years later, for *The Affluent Society*, I was given the Sidney Hillman Award, along with some prize money, commemorating this notable figure. No other such solemnity has pleased me more. Accepting it on my behalf, for I was in Europe, Kitty enchanted the gathering by reciting from Omar:

> Some for the Glories of This World; and some
> Sigh for the Prophet's Paradise to come;
> Ah, take the Cash, and let the Credit go . . .

[2] *New York Times*, July 12, 1936.

Democratic member of the House Un-American Activities Committee, then called the Dies Committee and in its earliest days as a pre-McCarthyite innovation. It was not greatly feared by liberals, for Martin Dies, the chairman, was a rather primitive Roosevelt-hater, and anyone called for inquisition knew he had the sympathy and support of the President, something that was not to be true in later times under Truman and Eisenhower. I called Starnes and added my explanation of the need. The conversation remains in my mind:

"Doctor, how many people did y'all say that mill would be hiring?"

"It's very big, Congressman. Ten, twenty thousand, maybe."[3]

"Well, Doctor, with something like that at sta-ake, a man jest can't ever stand on principle."

The Gadsden fathers convened at Joe's behest and passed a resolution promising complete safety and freedom of speech and action to all persons coming to Gadsden, although it is quite possible that the concept of civil liberty was not then fully understood there. They added as an effusive touch that Sidney Hillman, if he visited Gadsden, would be treated with true Southern hospitality. I took the telegram with these assurances to Isador Lubin, who was then serving as Hillman's assistant, and together we went to see Sidney; all was well until he came to the last sentence about Southern hospitality. That, he said, was their escape clause; it would have to be deleted.

After some persuasion he relented, and the plant went to Gadsden. It was very big; it did open up the town. By the 1944 elections, Gadsden labor had a large and effective political organization that strongly supported Roosevelt, strongly opposed Joe Starnes and threw him out. He was not again in public life. A public man should stand on principle.

Before Starnes was discarded, I was lunching one day in the restaurant of the House of Representatives with Thomas H. Eliot, a close friend, later a professor of political science and later still the Chancellor of Washington University in St. Louis. He was then the congressman from Cambridge, Massachusetts, and an opponent of the Dies Committee. Joe Starnes assumed from across the room that he and Dies were the subject of our conversation, and he didn't want to have me, as an honorary citizen and a practical benefactor of Alabama, subject to adverse impressions. He joined us to ask that I not

---

[3] The original employment estimates have escaped me, and the surviving records do not show them.

believe the bad things that "friend Tom" might be saying about the Dies Committee. And he went on to urge that I not get put off by a noisy row that Leon Henderson was then having with Congressman E. Eugene Cox of Georgia, a man currently famous for his venomous personality.

Joe's defense was memorable:

"Friend Ken, I ask y'all just to remember that mah friend Gene Cox is the nice-est mean man in the *en*-tire Congress of the *U*nited States."

*   *   *

Were evidence needed of the repetitive tendency of history, the autumn of 1940 would offer a superb example. This was the second battle over Muscle Shoals, which turned out to be the first public controversy in which I had a major, even decisive, role. None is stronger in my memory, and my memory is readily refreshed, for this dispute is preserved as a small classic of bureaucratic infighting in what was once a standard text in public administration.[4]

In World War I, at Muscle Shoals, Alabama, two plants were built to fix atmospheric nitrogen for explosives — Nitrate No. 1, using a process that didn't work, and Nitrate No. 2, which was never quite finished and which was equipped also to make ammonium nitrate, an explosive. With the plants went Wilson Dam across the Tennessee River to provide the considerable amount of power that the process then required. For the next fifteen years, Nitrate 2 and the dam were the focus of ardent controversy — the sharpest of the time. American farmers wanted to have the dam and plant produce cheap fertilizer and thus break the hold of the so-called fertilizer trust on the price of plant nutrients. The chemical and fertilizer companies, the latter a powerful lobby, wanted this not at all. Much confusion was added in 1921 when Henry Ford offered to lease Wilson Dam for a hundred years and take over the nitrate plants and land for $5,000,000, all to do good. A liberal in the 1920s and early 1930s was one who wished to have the government operate Muscle Shoals. Conservatives were as easily identified by their antipathy. In 1933, the issue at long last was resolved in a manner far more devastating

[4] Harold Stein, *Public Administration and Policy Development. A Case Book* (New York: Harcourt, Brace, 1952).

than the most ardent defender of free enterprise could ever have imagined. Out of Muscle Shoals and the need to use the dam and the nitrogen plant, by way of Senator George W. Norris of Nebraska and F.D.R., came the whole enormous idea of the Tennessee Valley Authority. By 1940, the nitrogen fixation part of plant 2 — by the cyanamid process — was obsolete, but the ammonium nitrate trains, i.e., the explosive end, were still workable. The Army, in its planning, now proposed to establish a brand-new synthetic ammonia plant at the Shoals, which the TVA would build and operate to supply nitrogen for the ammonium nitrate.

The TVA was particularly anxious to be so involved. Here was a wartime role, and after the war the nitrogen would be available for its legally mandated program to develop farm fertilizer and its use. The reaction of the chemical and fertilizer industry was paranoiac. If TVA had come from that earlier aberration, what might come from this!

Yet nitrogen plants had to be built; men could not then get slaughtered *en masse* without their product. And Muscle Shoals, adjacent to an existing explosives plant, with land, ancillary shop, transportation and other facilities all available as well as the more modest amounts of power now required, was an ideal site. At an estimated $4,153,000 with completion in eleven months, no other location was within millions of dollars of being so economical or so prompt.[5] (The eventual cost, $7,669,000, was still highly advantageous.) From mid-July to mid-October the NDAC struggled with the issue. The industry men on the staffs of Stettinius and Knudsen, led by Edward R. Weidlein of the Mellon Institute of Industrial Research in Pittsburgh, resisted the TVA proposal. Davis, helped by Henderson, led the battle in its favor. I handled the day-to-day strategy. Ed O'Neal watched with attention, for, as earlier noted, his plantation at Florence, Alabama, was close to the Shoals, and he had long thought that these plants should be used.

Many issues of high public importance are decided by a test of bureaucratic skill. The sources of success in this arena are worth a word.[6] One must have high confidence in one's purpose, and each step must be so taken as to enhance the confidence of others. Any

[5] Stein, p. 401.
[6] In Chapter 26, I return to this subject as it is perceived when one is an ambassador.

mistake of the opposition must be exploited so as to weaken its credibility and support. One should remember that most Washington battles are won not out of one's own strength but from loss of confidence in others and the resulting rush to cover. One should never threaten to resign; that only tells one's allies that one might abandon the field. One should never, never accept as final the word of an expert. He can be wrong, careless or politically motivated. Finally one should, if possible, have the President on one's side. It was in the Muscle Shoals battle that I first learned these guiding rules, mostly from Chester Davis.

Two other nitrogen plants were scheduled to be built, one to be operated by the DuPont Powder Company, the other by the Allied Chemical Company. Davis opened the action in July by asking that the Knudsen/Stettinius industry men keep him informed on all developments in the nitrogen program, and I proceeded to inform myself on all aspects of the industry. Then in mid-September we had our first break. The industry men assured us that all was still under study, and simultaneously letters of intent, the equivalent of a decision, went out to Allied and DuPont. The TVA plant was being left in limbo, presumably for the duration. Sneaky behavior is always a confession of weakness; all experienced operators avoid it. Davis now put an eloquent letter telling what had happened into the pouch to Hyde Park where President Roosevelt was staying, along with a more forthright communication to Steve Early, the President's press secretary and general utility man. "Today's White House pouch contains a letter from me to the President which I consider important . . . Will you please see that my letter is brought to the President's attention at once?"[7]

Roosevelt did not fail us. He told the Secretary of War to suspend all negotiations and hinted that he might want all three plants built by the TVA. Now we were ahead. However, presidential intervention is almost always a onetime thing.

The industry men, out of their claim to superior expertise, next had recourse to technical objections. This kind of strategy is designed to exclude lay opposition, but as noted, no layman should succumb. He should understand the case and search for flaws.

[7] Stein, p. 408.

They first held that a nitrogen plant plus an aluminum plant that had recently been located in the Tennessee Valley area made for a dangerous concentration of war industry. The flaw was that the Tennessee Valley is rather long. The aluminum and nitrogen plants were around a hundred miles apart; our opponents had neglected to look at the map. Then it was held that there was a shortage of coke in the Birmingham area, coke being required by the process. A quick investigation showed that, with Michigan, this was, in fact, one of the two industrial areas with surplus coke capacity. And for the DuPont and Allied plants we discovered that coke ovens would have to be built in any case. I circulated and celebrated these and like corrections with much pleasure. The technical objections disappeared.

Next we suffered a reverse. Davis, meeting with Stettinius, agreed to have an outside expert brought in to review and resolve the whole controversy. It would be one of the most impressive engineering figures of the time, one Gano Dunn, the President of the great J. G. White Engineering Corporation. This kind of offer is difficult to resist; there is in all such warfare the ever-lurking, often dangerous obligation to seem reasonable. Yet Dunn was certain to be adverse.

We were saved again by our opposition. Gano Dunn turned out to be a man of magnificent presence but too much dignity to inform himself on his task. His report began, "I have gone thoroughly into the questions which . . . [were] put into my hands as referee." [8] He then resolved the dispute with towering incompetence. The TVA, he decided, should not be given a full-scale plant; that would ". . . not only represent the beginning of Government entry into a new field of private enterprise, but would constitute a menace to the market of the private companies after the emergency has passed . . ." [9] Instead TVA would be given a 37½-ton token plant, too small to be a threat and also far too small to supply the ammonium nitrate plant which was to be used with the nitrogen it needed. This solution conceded that politics — the TVA — was the real issue. Then Dunn produced a new battery of engineering objections. With my burgeoning technical confidence I managed to counter them all. The TVA, he said, was not up to the task of operating the plant; the

[8] Stein, p. 430.
[9] Ibid.

Authority's consulting engineers, a reputable private firm, said flatly that it was. Tank cars would not be available for the product. Dunn, it turned out, had the wrong product. "Mr. Dunn speaks of shipping ammonia rather than ammonium nitrate direct to the powder plants. He is mixed up on his chemistry. The ammonium nitrate manufactured at the Shoals will not go to the powder plants but to the loading plants to be combined with TNT for the manufacture of Amatol." [10]

Dunn could not be defended — not if he didn't know his chemistry. On October 18, the NDAC voted first five to two, then unanimously, to approve the TVA plant along with the ones for DuPont and Allied Chemical. Stettinius then heard angrily from his troops, as did Knudsen, and the vote was put back to five to two. I went to Hershey, Pennsylvania, for a short holiday and to reflect on this war within a war. There would be many more.

In the great expansion of nitrogen demand for fertilizer after the war — some spoke of the nitrogen revolution — the TVA plant went all but unnoticed.

*   *   *

The 1940 election was approaching in those autumn days, and my reputation for verbal agility and versimilitude now received a further boost. The White House asked Davis that I be loaned to President Roosevelt's speechwriting staff. To my delight, Davis agreed. We worked in a small suite of rooms in the then seemingly vast edifice of the Commerce Department on Fourteenth Street, a building that, until surpassed by the Pentagon, was thought the final achievement in architectural elephantiasis.

Richard V. Gilbert, a brilliant economist from my Harvard years, led our group, supported by his talented cousin, Milton Gilbert. Dick went on to direct research at the Office of Price Administration and then, a man of diverse talent, to assemble a modest fortune in whiskey. Milton was for many years the senior economic intelligence of the Bank of International Settlement in Basel. In the McCarthy era he was charged with unduly liberal views. I came to his defense with an affidavit, and later when I obtained my FBI file, I discovered that

[10] Ibid., p. 442.

this was evidence that I too was subversive. Also present in the group was G. Griffith Johnson, Jr., of whom I have told.[11] His was the enduring contribution.

Roosevelt did not make many speeches by present standards, and great attention was lavished on each draft, along with much supporting research. Then it all went over to the White House to be put in final eloquence by Robert E. Sherwood, the playwright, with guidance from Harry Hopkins and Samuel Rosenman.

It was Johnson's job to dig up the record of the Republican leaders in the Congress to show, among other things, that they had contributed with their votes to the flawed performance of which they now complained. One such shortcoming was the poor state of the nation's defenses — preparedness, as it was called. But the Republican congressional leaders had been among the stoutest opponents of higher defense appropriations. In establishing this opposition, Johnson noticed that the names of three Republican leaders recurred: Joseph W. Martin, Jr., of Massachusetts, the House Minority Leader; Bruce Barton, the advertising man turned statesman from New York who had won national prominence with the thought that Jesus was a pioneer in modern business enterprise[12] and thus, perhaps, a distant precursor of the great advertising firm of Batten, Barton, Durstine and Osborn; and Hamilton Fish, Roosevelt's own congressman from up the Hudson, the sole member of an early presidential enemies list. Word had been passed to us from the White House that we should not struggle to return his telephone calls. It was Griff Johnson who singled out the votes of Martin, Barton and Fish and saw how marvelously they sounded when put in that order. So with even greater delight did F.D.R.

We gathered at a radio whenever the President spoke to find out which, if any, of our phrases or lines had survived. After forty years I can still hear him from Madison Square Garden carefully exempting the average intelligent Republican from any obstructionist tendencies and then turning to the party leaders. "And who voted against the appropriations for an adequate national defense?" Roo-

[11] See Chapter 7.
[12] "He picked up twelve men from the bottom ranks of business and forged them into an organization that conquered the world." Bruce Barton, *The Man Nobody Knows: A discovery of the real Jesus* (Indianapolis: Bobbs-Merrill, 1924), p. iv.

sevelt paused, chuckled and put the names together, rolling out his answer — "MARTIN, BARTON and FISH."

It was too good to waste. A night or two later in Boston Garden he asked those assembled who had opposed adequate appropriations for agriculture. It was not a rural audience, but it never hesitated. Back came the mighty roar: "MARTIN, BARTON and FISH."

If any of my own words survived and were used, they were not memorable.

*   *   *

On election day that year Kitty and I drove to Princeton to vote and returned to Chester Davis's house to listen to the returns. By this time Paul Porter and I had become close friends as we were to remain until his death in 1975. Paul asked me where I had been, and why, following his own practice in Kentucky, I hadn't found a New Jersey Republican with whom I could pair, thus sparing myself the trip.

I said I didn't know a New Jersey Republican whom I could trust.

Paul replied, "Well, I certainly didn't trust my bastard either. I sent in an absentee ballot to be sure."

That wasn't true. But of the truth of a story told at his memorial service in Washington there is no doubt. He was returning to the capital with a colleague from some legal business in the West. As they neared National Airport, the pilot came on in a voice of deliberate calm. There was trouble with the landing gear; either the instruments were wrong or it wouldn't come down. So emergency procedures were invoked. Pens were removed from pockets; seat belts were tightly buckled; heads were put down between the knees. A silence fell over the cabin as the plane reached the ground between lines of fire engines and emergency vehicles. And it deepened as the motors were cut back and the plane came to a stop, only to be broken by Paul intoning, "Mutual of Omaha wins again."

Toward midnight on that election night there was a commotion on the street outside. Singing and shouting. We went out to see Steve Early and George Allen (a figure of the times who made a career out of knowing and entertaining Presidents) coming toward the house. Steve's pant leg was rolled up above his knee. They swayed to the sound of their own music as they came down the street. "Happy days are here again."

A few nights before, while getting the presidential party aboard a train in New York, Steve had accidentally stuck his knee into the groin of a New York policeman. Republicans had seized upon the incident, and it made headlines. The New Dealers were as arrogant as ever; they cared nothing for the average man or for law and order. Already the Imperial Presidency. Things cooled a bit when the policeman was sought out and said that of course he was voting for Roosevelt. But enough was made of the incident so that Steve had offered to quit. Thus the celebration. Others might believe that the election returns affirmed support for Roosevelt's policies and countenanced the Third Term. For Steve Early the American public had exonerated his knee.

*   *   *

Through that autumn and the following winter we lived in Washington in a pleasant furnished apartment in the Marlyn, not far from the intersection of Wisconsin and Massachusetts Avenues. Kitty worked on her doctoral thesis on Novalis (Friedrich von Hardenberg) at the Library of Congress. A very strong-willed and exceptionally short, exceptionally clear-headed young woman arrived to arrange meals and otherwise to facilitate our existence. Her name was Emily Gloria Wilson, and she remained a member of the family for the next forty years, managing our household affairs, rearing our children, accompanying us to India and eventually giving attention to our grandchildren. Her character and devotion were illustrated one afternoon in the mid-sixties. It had been a wearying day, and we had to go on to a dinner. I asked Emily to hold all telephone messages while I had a nap. Shortly thereafter the phone rang. Lyndon Johnson was calling from the White House, and he came on the line himself.

"Get me Ken Galbraith. This is Lyndon Johnson."

"He is sleeping, Mr. President. He said not to disturb him."

"Well, wake him up. I want to talk to him."

"No, Mr. President. I work for him, not you."

When I called the President back, he could scarcely control his pleasure. "Tell that woman I want her here in the White House."

*   *   *

On one lovely evening in the autumn of 1940, the President and Mrs. Roosevelt invited all responsibly concerned with defense matters, young as well as old, to a reception. Our excitement was extreme. My wife considered her attire for some days. The Griffith Johnsons parked their automobile a few blocks from the White House and took a cab so that they might arrive in appropriate dignity. I decided to take the President an apple from a basket of choice Northern Spies that my family had sent me from Canada. In the receiving line I lost my courage and passed it back to Robert Horton, later the uncompromising press officer of the Office of Price Administration — his rule was truth as he saw it, whatever the consequences — who munched it as we moved along.

As I greeted and then passed F.D.R., who, for such occasions, was seated on something resembling a tall kitchen stool, Eleanor stopped the person in front of me for a chat, momentarily holding up the line. The man behind Kitty came to a halt with his feet on her dress. F.D.R. noticed and continued to hold her hand. The effect lasted for some weeks.

Later the Roosevelts retired upstairs, and everyone danced. We all noticed that the son of William L. Batt of Stettinius's staff danced with the daughter of Sidney Hillman. It was then suspected and later known that the Batts had New Deal tendencies.

During those months I was commuting to Chicago for additional work there. At the end of the year my combined enterprises lodged me for a few days in the Johns Hopkins Hospital, where the diagnosis, not surprisingly, was fatigue. I detached myself from the Farm Bureau, and we went to Mexico City and Taxco to restore. Meanwhile the National Defense Advisory Commission had come under deep criticism for its general futility. Roosevelt kept it in existence but gave executive responsibility to the newly created Office of Production Management (OPM), headed coequally by William Knudsen and Sidney Hillman. It was a not uncharacteristic Roosevelt compromise: he couldn't give all power to a businessman or credibly then to a union leader so he appointed both.

The immediate effect was to reduce Davis's functions and therewith mine. The threat of idleness again. Accordingly, I turned my attention back to prices and economic policy. I had been riding to work with David Ginsburg, Leon Henderson's counsel, and John Hamm, Leon's cousin-in-law and general assistant. They spoke much of their plans for managing the economy and of eliciting from the White House the requisite executive order according them the authority to do so. I outlined a design for such management that had consequences beyond even my most optimistic thoughts. It took me back to Leon Henderson with whom this chapter began.

9

Price Czar Novitiate

Inflation clearly is undesirable; we should try if possible to avoid the inequitable distribution of burden, the demoralizing effects of unstable profit expansion, the arbitrary shifts in income distribution, and (so far as anyone knows) the increased difficulties of post-war readjustment, which are likely to be associated with rapid price advances.

J.K.G., 1941

WITH HIS SMALL STAFF in the newly created Office of Price Administration and Civilian Supply (OPACS), Leon Henderson had by now taken up residence in the Blaine Mansion, a large, gloomy, undistinguished red brick structure that once housed James G. Blaine, celebrated in his time, perhaps partly by the accident of rhyme, as the Continental Liar from the State of Maine. The house is immediately on your left as you continue out Massachusetts Avenue beyond Dupont Circle. In the course of the next twelve months we were moved to larger quarters in an apartment house in Georgetown and then to yet larger in Tempo D, a hastily built shelter on the Mall. This last and the other impermanent wartime structures followed the architectural prescription of F.D.R.: every effort must be made to ensure that, unlike the World War I temporaries, they not outlast their period of service. In practice, they hardly outlasted their completion. Our final move was to a huge permanent building of warehouse design and finish south of the Mall from which the Census had been evicted and which was later occupied by the FBI.

It was to the Blaine Mansion and to his office, a depressing parlor on the second floor, that Henderson summoned me early on the morning of April 29, 1941. Would I be in charge of the control of prices in the United States? It was an admirably casual offer of the most powerful civilian post in the management of the wartime economy (as it would soon be called), Henderson's own job alone excepted. In time, my more comprehensive and detailed involvement in the policy, the knowledge that went therewith and my somewhat greater confidence as an economist would give me even more power over price policy than Henderson. This is a common occurrence; in any large organization with varied and complex tasks, power passes down to those who are in daily touch with the action and have the resulting knowledge. Later I would see my own authority pass on to others more immediately participant and thus better informed. In all large organizations the crude perception of hierarchy and the wish to nourish vanity attribute far more power to the men at the top than in practice they exercise.

I accepted. I was not the first choice; Henderson told me he would have preferred Isador Lubin, a more senior figure in the New Deal pantheon and then the Commissioner of Labor Statistics. It was my good fortune that Lube, my friend from those years until his death in 1978, was not available. I have always felt grateful to him.

Perhaps, also, it was good for the country. Truth is not always coordinate with modesty. The job required one to envisage the structure of the wartime economy in the largest terms and then to translate this into extremely specific lines of action. That, better than most economists, I could do. It also required a truly extraordinary capacity to adjust one's views and actions when the initial conception or some details were shown to be inadequate or wrong. Economics is not durable truth; it requires continuous revision and accommodation. Nearly all its error is from those who cannot change. This too I had begun to see. Finally, as the other side of confidence, one had to believe that one's critics were ill-motivated, uninformed, unintelligent or instinctively wrong. This also was my tendency. These qualities are not wholly endearing. To the sensitive they could suggest an insufferable sense of superiority. But, on balance, they were probably right for the job.

After leaving Henderson, I went to the former bedroom that had been assigned as my office, phoned my wife and wired Jim Perkins, as I've previously told. Then I made the rounds of my newly inherited staff.

They numbered fewer than twenty. Later the Office of Price Administration would employ 64,000 across the country, along with numerous volunteer workers. However, most of those would administer rationing and rent control. The prices staff nationwide was much smaller — about 4300.

One of those already aboard was Donald H. Wallace. We had been fellow teachers and friends at Harvard. Slight of build, capable of great devotion, admirably informed and a prodigious worker, in the years ahead he was my wisest and closest counselor. He was also deeply subject to the tensions of the task and not very long after the war ended, succumbed to a series of heart attacks.

During the nitrogen battle of the previous autumn, I had been much impressed by the professional quality of the management at the TVA. Accordingly, I recruited Robert E. Sessions, the assistant to the general manager of that great and diverse enterprise, to be my deputy and to have charge of daily operations. It could not have been an easy task, for I continued to wish to be in charge myself. The dreary details of hiring, delegating and organizing the flow of instructions and response became his province.

A day or two after I took up the job, I was sought out by Mary Jones, a small, slight, brightly lovely, dark-haired woman once on the secretarial staff of Chester Davis. She was one of a sisterhood in Washington at the time which strongly shared the political convictions of the New Dealers, managed their offices, guided them on policy, disciplined them as necessary on dress, manners and personal deportment and maintained among themselves an intelligence service of invaluable scope and accuracy. In the next two years no instruction of mine, no major price regulation or amendment was unread by Mary Jones. Hundreds of mistakes, large, small or merely absurd, were caught by her unfailing eye. If she believed me to be acting hastily or unwisely, she told me so. Another Davis staff member, a tall, graceful, self-confident woman named Carol Piper, became my general assistant. By Mary Jones and Carol Piper more than all others I was sustained in the years to come.

*   *   *

In the weeks immediately preceding my appointment, David Ginsburg and John Hamm had intensified their efforts to obtain an executive order giving force to Henderson's tasks. And on April 11, 1941, President Roosevelt had yielded and established the Office of Price Administration and Civilian Supply. The Lend-Lease Act of early March was expected to add to the pressures on the civilian economy; OPACS, paralleling the OPM, was directed to ensure an adequate supply of essential civilian commodities, dispense with non-essentials and keep prices stable. On prices its administrator was "to take all lawful steps necessary or appropriate in order to prevent price spiralling, rising cost of living, profiteering and inflation."[1] A purist might suggest that price spiraling, rising living costs and inflation had much in common; the redundancy was intended only to emphasize the urgency of the task. The "lawful steps necessary or appropriate" for preventing price increases authorized the placing of ceilings over individual prices. This legitimized actions that had already been taken by Henderson as a member of the predecessor National Defense Advisory Commission to stabilize the prices of items coming under heavy rearmament demand. On February 17, 1941, a ceiling had been placed over the prices of used machine tools to keep them below the prices of new ones, and this had been followed by a few similar actions. The new lawful or appropriate penalties for violators amounted only to public denunciation, and, indeed, it was at this time that the word jawboning entered the language, an invention, I believe, of Leon Henderson. It then had a more ominous connotation, for to be jawboned was to be called a war profiteer.

To my design for a wartime economy I must now turn, and in some detail. A wartime economy is only a great acceleration of economic life; a good deal can therefore be learned from such experience that is perceived only more gradually in more leisurely peacetime existence. Some of the lessons of those distant years are still being learned.

*   *   *

A generation that has become accustomed to steadily rising prices, though it may not like them, will have difficulty appreciating the grave, almost paranoiac concern in 1940 and 1941 over inflation. This was the legacy of World War I, when between 1915 and 1920 in the United States wholesale prices more than doubled, and there followed a ghastly and, most supposed, counterpart slump.[2] Fear of

---

[1] Office of Price Administration. *First Quarterly Report* (Washington, D.C.: U.S. Government Printing Office, 1942), p. 7.

[2] "Doubtless the best-remembered lesson of our World War experience concerns inflation. The various discomforts of rapidly advancing prices made a deep impression on people; and largely by Newtonian analogy, the post-war deflation was associ-

repetition and attendant deprivation lasted through the depression years. It was intensified by knowledge of the total collapse of currency values in Germany, Austria and elsewhere in Central Europe following the war, a collapse that traumatically affected the thinking of German, Austrian and Hungarian economists, some of the most distinguished of whom later found positions and influence in the United States. So it was axiomatic that, in the coming conflict, inflation must, above all, be prevented. It was also axiomatic that to prevent much inflation one must prevent a little. It was probably Henderson who first voiced the thought that having a little inflation was like being a little pregnant. In any case, no one else made so much use of this metaphor.

*　　*　　*

In 1939, in a series of articles in *The Times* (of London) later published as a small book, John Maynard Keynes laid down the basic strategy for preventing wartime inflation. It was "to withdraw from the market, either by taxation or deferment, an adequate proportion of the consumer's purchasing power, so there is no longer an irresistible force impelling prices upward."[3] Total demand in the economy would thus be kept equal to the value of the total supply of goods and services available for purchase. As war demand increased and civilian supply diminished, which presumably both would, taxes would be increased or personal saving compelled in order to keep total demand in continuing balance with supply. Rationing and price control would be necessary in instances of special demand or shortage; they would be "a valuable adjunct," Keynes said, "to our main proposal."[4] But they would be only an adjunct. Finally Keynes emphasized the special importance of keeping the prices of basic necessaries stable — what were then known as wage goods, being the things wage earners of the day bought. Unions, in return, would be asked to forgo wage increases for the duration.

In early 1941, Alvin Hansen took up the discussion at Harvard.

---

ated closely with the previous advance." John Kenneth Galbraith, "The Selection and Timing of Inflation Controls," *The Review of Economic Statistics,* vol. XXIII, no. 2 (May 1941), p. 82.

[3] *How to Pay for the War* (New York: Harcourt, Brace, 1940), p. 51. By deferment Keynes had reference to forced savings — savings that would be collected like taxes but returned with interest after the war. It was an innovation that he strongly urged.

[4] Ibid.

Where shortages or bottlenecks developed, special efforts should be made to cure them. This localized inflation should be sharply distinguished from the general price increases that would occur as the economy reached the capacity of its plant and labor force and a general excess of demand forced up all prices. Then but only then, by taxation or forced savings, the growth in total demand occasioned by war expenditure should be arrested and held in balance with total supply. Hansen's position, a modification and reinterpretation, was well within the limits of the larger Keynesian orthodoxy.

In these same early months of 1941, I produced a somewhat different thesis, a trifle more heretical than Hansen's. I held that there would be no nice point at which demand in general would exceed supply in general. After years of depression, underinvestment and undertraining of workers, the productive plant of the United States was askew — surplus capacity here, shortages there. This and the uneven impact of war demands meant that capacity operations and full employment would come in a very irregular fashion as between different industries. There would, accordingly, be much inflation before there was, overall, full employment. I accepted that inflation must ultimately be controlled by keeping limits on aggregate demand, and I proposed a close watch on prices of products unaffected by war demand, for here would be the best clue as to when general restraint would be required. Because price increases came unevenly and well in advance of full employment, my design required many more controls — selective controls over the areas of shortage as they developed — than did that of Keynes or Hansen.

My manuscript, "The Selection and Timing of Inflation Controls," was widely circulated in Washington. I have written far longer, far more formidable treatises, but none had such an effect on either national policy or my own life. The official history of the wartime stabilization effort calls it "almost a prospectus" for "selective and rationally timed controls."[5] However this may be, it was this paper that led to my being put in charge of price control.

All of these proposals, with some refinements, put the Keynesian depression policies in reverse. Public spending in excess of taxes expanded demand and employment. Now taxation and compulsory

---

[5] William Jerome Wilson, *The Beginnings of OPA. Part I: The Price Control Act of 1942.* Historical Reports on War Administration (Washington, D.C.: U.S. Government Printing Office, 1947), p. 29.

saving would seek to reduce demand — the enlarged demand from the increased public spending for the war. Price control and rationing would be confined to the areas of special shortage — the pressure points where, despite an overall balance between demand and supply, the demands of war, the loss of overseas supply and inadequate past investment would cause shortages and force up prices. This, to repeat, was the rational design; it reflected the accepted best in modern economic thought. The legislation we would request would serve this end. There were two difficulties. There was a major and influential dissent. And however rational the design, we would come to learn that it would not work.

The dissent proceeded from the magnificent, some then said omnipotent, person of Bernard Mannes Baruch.

*   *   *

On all matters having to do with the management of a war economy Bernard Baruch had been, ever since World War I, the accredited, more precisely the self-accredited, sage. It is not easy now to convey an impression of his influence. Public deference was universal. At the same time private skepticism was also nearly obligatory. A number of New Dealers held that he was a highly accomplished fraud, but none ever said so in public.

Many notable men are physically disappointing on first encounter. Churchill, whom I saw only twice, was short, round and otherwise unimpressive, the scowl and cigar apart. Harold Wilson and Harry Truman would never have been noticed in a crowd. No one was ever disappointed by Baruch.

He was seventy-one in 1941, well over six feet tall, handsomely tailored, with glowing white hair that was impressively arranged on each side of a spectacular part, revealing a pinkly shining streak of skull. His face was patrician, commanding and yet rather benign. It gained something from the pince-nez and more from the wire that ran down from his ear to the hearing aid which, on frequent occasion, he turned off to discourage interruption. The impression of vigor he then conveyed was not contrived; it would sustain him for almost another quarter of a century.

During World War I, Baruch, under Woodrow Wilson, had been Chairman of the War Industries Board. It was the belief of many who had been there — Henry Dennison was eloquent on the subject — that he had been a figurehead, although of the very best in this vocation. The real boss was the less spectacular but more reliable Alexander Legge of the International Harvester Company. It is certain that Baruch never forgot his days of glory. He wrote of them, and, as the thirties passed and the new war approached, he was unrelenting on how the economy should now be managed. It was only one of the many issues on which he volunteered advice, but it was by far the most important.

While admiring his past, Baruch did not neglect his present sources of influence. Indeed, had he given the same thought to substance as to self-promotion, he would have been wholly invulnerable. To each of some twenty southern senators, men of assured tenure so that no money was wasted and no hard feelings were engendered by support to unsuccessful opponents, he made contributions of a thousand dollars, a noble sum in those days, in every election campaign. And to James F. Byrnes of South Carolina he gave five thousand to marshal and lead the troops. The statesmen so subsidized were then required only to speak at regular intervals on the wisdom of Baruch and to propose in any moment of crisis or controversy that Baruch be called upon to advise and resolve. All performed faithfully. Given a difficult problem, some well-tenured political figure would arise to general applause to say that in this situation the administration would do well to call on the nation's elder statesman, Bernard Baruch. He alone could say what should be done. The cost to Baruch, averaging out over nonelection years to some $4000 or $5000 annually, was insignificant.[6]

Baruch's further source of influence was the White House. This he visited on all possible occasions, partly to advise the President of the United States, partly to show the rest of the government (and the country) that he was the kind of man who visited the President.

---

[6] The amounts reflect common belief and discussion at the time. Here is Dean Acheson's account in *Present at the Creation*: "Mr. Baruch was undoubtedly a money maker through shrewd stock market speculations, as he himself has claimed. He made equally shrewd political use of his fortune, rarely squandering it on large party contributions, but dispensing it judiciously — and often nonpartisanly — in small individual contributions to senatorial and congressional primary or election campaigns. This practice multiplied his admirers in the Congress while his gifted friend, Herbert Bayard Swope, polished his public 'image.' " (New York: Norton, 1969), p. 154.

Anyone with such access to the White House, who, according to the legend, kept himself available on a bench in Lafayette Square outside, could not be ignored by lesser officials and politicians. Baruch's comments to the press on emerging from the Oval Office — his use of the presidency for echo and amplification — was the highest development of a notable art.

It was something that not all Presidents appreciated. Harry Truman wondered aloud why Baruch described himself as an adviser to Presidents; surely he knew that all Presidents had far more advice than they could use. Toward the end of his life, President Roosevelt concluded that the political rewards from keeping Baruch content and in the public eye no longer justified the effort. He sought to detach, although not, in the end, with success. This I learned from Eleanor Roosevelt.

One day in the early autumn of 1960, with the Kennedy campaign under way, I received a call from Mrs. Roosevelt. She was fresh from a meeting with J.F.K. and asked me, at Kennedy's request, to visit Baruch and solicit a campaign contribution. The money, though not unimportant, was not the primary reason. Only if Bernie, as she called him, invested could one be sure he would not defect. I was midway, more or less, between the Kennedy generation and the period of Baruch's greatest eminence and the only Kennedy lieutenant who knew him well.

I called on Baruch in his handsome Fifth Avenue apartment; now ninety, he was as erect and handsome as ever. The threat from the opposition was nil; Nixon, with characteristic untaste, had asked him to head a "Senior Citizens Committee" in his campaign. Baruch was greatly indignant. Was his only distinction being old — a *senior* citizen? We talked through the afternoon, and he pledged a contribution, which must have been modest, for I've forgotten the amount.[7] As had countless others, I listened to his persistent and imaginative name-dropping, which he had raised to the level of high art: "I told Josephus Daniels right there in front of Woodrow that his man Franklin was the one to watch." A few days later Mrs. Roosevelt was

[7] I arranged for Baruch to call on President Kennedy in the summer of 1961, noting in a letter to the President at the time that "this liquidates a campaign promise" that Baruch would be consulted. I also suggested to Kennedy that he would be enchanted by a level of vanity for which not even his service in the Senate would fully have prepared him.

in Cambridge for a television program she was conducting at Brandeis University, and I reported on my mission, mentioning this magnificent and characteristic accomplishment.

She told me, her voice slightly high-pitched, her words sharply edged, of how her husband in the last years had tired of Baruch and his use of the White House as a personal sounding board and of how he had made it known. "But that sort of thing didn't stop Bernie. When he heard on the radio of the President's death, he came right over to Warm Springs. And he stayed with us there and rode with us on the train back to Washington. And he remained with us through the state funeral and went with us on the train up to Hyde Park, and he stayed with us right through the family funeral, and there were several times when I thought he was going to get into the coffin with Franklin."

*   *   *

Bernard Baruch had a plan for war management that was far better known than ours and which had been presented "with the devotion and single-mindedness of a Cato. For twenty years, in lectures . . . in testimony before congressional committees, in magazine articles, and in books, he [had] expounded its merits . . ."[8] In 1941, he summarized it for a congressional committee: "I do not believe in piecemeal price fixing. I think you have first to put a ceiling over the whole price structure, including wages, rents and farm prices up to the parity level — and no higher — and then adjust separate price schedules upward or downward, if necessary, where justice or governmental policy so requires."[9]

[8] Wilson, p. 7.
[9] Testimony before the House Banking and Currency Committee, September 19, 1941. Also in Bernard Baruch, *Baruch: The Public Years* (New York: Holt, Rinehart and Winston, 1960), p. 287. The history of this book amplifies in a minor way the Baruch instinct for self-enhancement. His official biography was to have been that written by Margaret L. Coit, the Pulitzer Prize–winning biographer of John C. Calhoun (*Mr. Baruch* [Boston: Houghton Mifflin, 1957]). Though competent, sympathetic and interesting, it was not ecstatic and veered dangerously toward truth. So Baruch detached himself from it and proceeded, with cooperative help, to produce his autobiography. Prior to the appearance of each of these books, I received several friendly calls asking my advice on a range of economic and financial matters, the only such calls I ever got from him. Baruch's discovery of the value of my advice coincided with his discovery that it was books such as these that I was often called upon to review.

The Baruch plan blandly set aside the whole structure of capitalist markets for the duration of the war; it held, in effect, that in wartime prices, or in any case price changes, had no function whatever. We were horrified. All economists were horrified. An economist without a price system is a priest without a divine being. We had spent our lives learning about prices and teaching others how they rose to encourage needed production; how they fell to discourage unneeded production; how they rose to cut back on consumption in excess of supply; how they fell to encourage the use of abundant or surplus supplies. Under the Baruch plan all of this admirable mechanism would be in limbo. There would be economic *rigor mortis*. Except as materials and products were deliberately allocated by the government to wartime use and the remaining consumer supplies rationed, the war economy would be without a regulatory mechanism.

We could not accept the Baruch system.[10] Or so it seemed. Yet it was the recommendation of the single most influential voice on this subject in the country and, the political compensation considered, by far the most influential voice in the Congress. We, young and without any comparable experience, were required to challenge the advice of the man who, in the popular view reinforced by his own conviction, had all but won the First World War. This was the setting for the great dilemma and, in the fullness of time, the great comedy of 1941–42.

*   *   *

When I took over in those spring days of 1941, the first need was to get legislation authorizing our activities and imposing penalties for noncompliance, and the second was to keep prices as stable as possible under the authority of our executive order until the legislation was passed. It was to the legislation that Baruch posed the greatest threat, but it was to holding down prices that I turned my immediate attention.

What does one do when one is put in charge of all prices in the United States? On my first Sunday in office I went to the Blaine Mansion and sat down by myself with the Census classification of American industry. From this I derived the subdivisions of my of-

----

[10] And, as the official history points out, almost no one did. Wilson, p. 7.

fice — nonferrous metals; fuel; steel and iron and steel products; textiles, leather and apparel; and so forth.[11] It seemed almost too simple.

Then I invented a title for those who would be in charge of the various industry groupings, one that would last through the war. They would be called Price Executives. The title was to give an air of authority to a few individuals who made decisions granting or denying millions of dollars while being paid themselves $6500 a year before taxes.

After so dividing up the economy, I put by each division the name of a plausible head. Most were economists of my acquaintance; the rest were civil servants from peacetime agencies. In the next days I telephoned or telegraphed these nominees asking them to come to Washington. War tension was now high. Everyone I asked came. One whom I called was Merle Fainsod, later a noted Harvard professor of government, Harvard librarian, friend and perhaps the most selfless man ever to survive the contrary temptations of academic life. He was on Cape Cod; but later that same day he was waiting for me when I came back from an appointment. He too, like Jim Perkins, could move with dispatch.

While I recruited economists, David Ginsburg recruited lawyers, as talented a legal assemblage as Washington had yet seen. To each of the price units a lawyer was assigned with coequal authority. It was an arrangement admirably designed to induce friction, but it had elements of genius that I did not, at the time, appreciate. The lawyers had a far better sense of procedure — how you moved in government to get things done — than the economists. And they had a high sense of what was ethically or professionally legitimate. Their required attendance at every important meeting meant that every decision was taken in the presence of at least two people. Mil-

---

[11] In time, these subdivisions were further divided and subdivided so that under textiles and apparel was clothing, and under clothing was footwear, and under footwear there was a microcosm for soles and (reclaimed) rubber heels. Of little of this had I knowledge. At Harvard a decade later I was enchanted to receive for reading and later oral examination a Ph.D. thesis of excessive length on wartime price-making for soles and heels by the man who had been in charge in that area. It was impressive in the initiative described, the sense of high responsibility conveyed. Soles were graded and priced in accordance with their longevity as this was revealed by tests on the feet of Washington postmen. My office was pictured convincingly in the thesis as a distant and unsympathetic bottleneck. The doctoral candidate, discovering that I was to examine him, was visibly relieved to find me unnaturally tolerant of rebuke.

lions and tens of millions of dollars were at issue in these decisions. The virtue of the Ginsburg design was that any careless or corrupt tendency would always be arrested by the presence of a second man; any real corruption would have to be a conspiracy. In consequence of these precautions and possibly also our care in recruitment, price control survived for five full years without a breath of scandal. The OPA lawyers included men whose later careers kept them in the public eye: Harold Leventhal, a distinguished federal judge; Henry S. Reuss, as head of the House Committee on Banking and Currency and later the Joint Economic Committee, the principal economic power in the Congress; Henry M. Hart, Jr., a legendary figure at the Harvard Law School; Richard H. Field, another; David F. Cavers, yet a third; Nathaniel L. Nathanson, a noted Northwestern law professor; Ben Heineman and Sol M. Linowitz, major industrial tycoons; and Richard M. Nixon.

*   *   *

By the summer of 1941, prices of lumber, scrap metal, some textiles and quite a few other products — those not set by a few large-scale producers — were under the pressure of rising military and civilian demand. As the prices rose, we published schedules setting out the maximum permissible levels. Though unbacked by penalties — for these, as noted, we needed the legislation — these ceiling prices were taken seriously. In the interim, until enforcement procedures became available, they were surprisingly well observed.

The work in establishing ceilings, understanding issues in dispute, according hearing and appeal to interested and aggrieved parties, staffing and otherwise managing the enterprise and answering to the Congress, press and public was to be the most intense effort of my life. Conceivably I crammed more into those two years than into the following forty as I write. In 1961, when I went to India as ambassador, I was thought to be taking on a large and heavy task. I did nothing to dispel the illusion, and such was my reputation for diligence that President Kennedy singled it out for agreeable mention. By comparison with the regimen of a price-fixer, it was a life of appalling idleness.

*   *   *

We moved in the summer of 1941 to a house on the grounds of the Virginia Theological Seminary in Alexandria, Virginia, from which we went later to our wartime residence at 3207 P Street in Georgetown. On the morning of July 3, I took my wife to the Columbia Hospital in Washington, and an hour after I left her there, our first child, John Alan,[12] was born. I did not get back to the hospital until late that evening and not again for several days. That first night when I arrived, the telephone was ringing; it was Robert Ten Broeck Stevens of the socially archaic J. P. Stevens and Company, with whom, along with other textile manufacturers, I had been in session most of the day. Bob wished to continue his plea for a more lenient ruling against the excessive prices that the industry was charging for combed cotton yarn and the resulting cloth, the basic component of summer uniforms. My wife listened without interest for nearly an hour before Stevens became persuaded that I wouldn't relent. When work ended very late one evening a few days later,[13] I determined that I must see my wife and child, but visiting hours were long over. In the entrance hall of the hospital, silent and empty, a formidable woman peered at me from over the desk. "Yessir?"

"I'm Dr. Galbraith."

"Go right ahead, Doctor."

*   *   *

The textile industry was the archetype of the admixture of politics and economics that one encountered in the setting of prices. For years it had been depressed, even starved. Now suddenly it was wonderfully prosperous. The mills scattered across the South had ties bordering on incest with Democratic congressmen and senators whose support we would need for our legislation. We learned, when meeting with the industry, to schedule sessions morning, afternoon and evening to minimize the time available to the participants for causing trouble on Capitol Hill.

---

[12] Now a trial lawyer of distinction in Washington in partnership with Edward Bennett Williams.

[13] Before World War II, when women were still supposed to be weak, a normal hospital stay for childbirth was around two weeks.

Additionally we had no control over raw cotton prices; for ten years they had been a prime manifestation of the depression, a major objective of government price-*raising* efforts. Any action now to arrest the upward movement of prices would have reversed Appomattox, restored the Confederacy.

The leadership of the cotton textile industry was divided, the division reflecting a difference of view as to who could do the most for the mills in Washington. Robert Stevens believed he was the man. He was interested in both the personal prestige and the money. He was also omnipresent. One Scott Russell, the head of the great Bibb Manufacturing Company of Georgia, was the industry's authorized representative; he thought that he could be the most effective, but he was pleasant about it. As the summer of 1941 passed, we worked out an incredibly complex price schedule showing for each different cotton construction, i.e., kind of cloth, the permissible price, given all foreseeable spot or current prices for cotton. When promulgated on October 21, 1941, it took several pages in the Federal Register. Prices of cloth would go up as cotton went up. This was soft price control, and there was stiff opposition to the order from my staff. As men and women became committed to controlling prices, they became suspicious of anything that suggested a concession. Since normally I urged firmness, I now had difficulty urging anything less.

On October 26, when the regulation became effective, the price of raw cotton, incredibly, tumbled. It was a contingency of which we had not dreamed. The regulation showed the allowable increases in cloth prices as cotton went up; it did not specify the reduction if it went down. I resolved that things worked both ways, that the prices of cotton goods should now go down. Had I decided otherwise, I would have been held to have sold out to the industry.

Scott Russell protested with routine vehemence and went home in full appreciation of my problem. Bob Stevens, on the other hand, took up permanent residence outside my office to get the decision reversed. Escalation should be up, never down. Anything else was unfair to the industry, unjust to J. P. Stevens and Company. He was eloquent, aggressive, pleading and, as he deemed wise, ingratiating. Whenever my door opened, he almost literally fell in. Eventually I offered to call a press conference, explain my position and state plainly that he was a profiteer. Alternatively he could leave town. He protested but departed. Not long after, he was back in the office in a colonel's uniform and concerned with textile procurement.

More than a decade later, now the Secretary of the Army, Robert Stevens faced Joseph R. McCarthy in the great Army/McCarthy hearings. He did not do well. McCarthy was contemptuous of his intelligence, and others condemned him for ill-considered appeasement, selling out his subordinates. In the middle of the hearings, which were televised and held my fascinated attention, I received a telephone call from Paul M. O'Leary, the dean of the faculty of Cornell University. In 1941, he had been in charge of textile, leather and apparel pricing. (Later, as I will tell, he was the resourceful administrator of wartime rationing.) He was calling to find out if I was watching the show. I said I was. He asked if it had occurred to me that we were the only two professors in the entire Republic that day who were cheering for Joe McCarthy.

*   *   *

There were occasions in those years one did not forget. On June 22, 1941, out at our house on the Theological Seminary grounds, I turned on the radio at breakfast to hear that Hitler had attacked the Soviet Union. It was a luminous moment. For the first time the enemy force no longer seemed overpowering. There were other great moments to come, but that morning was the first on which I went to the office with hope. So, I believe, did most of the others immediately involved. Ever since, when I've needed to forgive the Soviets some inconvenient action, memory of that day on Seminary Hill helps.

*   *   *

The legislation we needed for wartime price control was, by a wide margin, the most discussed and the most controversial of World War II. There was a sharp debate over renewing the draft in the days just before the attack on Pearl Harbor, but the draft involved only the life and liberty of the subject. Price control involved money and property and thus had to be taken more seriously.

As early as February 1941, David Ginsburg had outlined the necessary laws, and in the next months successive versions of the Emergency Price Control Act of 1941 were circulated, the work, in the main, of Harold Leventhal. Then and later Leventhal proved himself a superb legal draftsman; given the need, he would produce in a few hours the requisite law. This talent was combined, in turn, with clear-headed economic judgment on which increasingly I came to rely. He also deserves to be counted one of the decisive men of World War II.

By summer extensive briefs had been prepared on various aspects of the legislation — the price prospect, what controls would accomplish, why labor was excluded, the special position of farm prices. These were forwarded to the White House, and President Roosevelt called a meeting to consider all the proposals. In response to each of his questions — the effect on labor, on the farmers, on the courts — Henderson was able to say, "We've sent you a memorandum on that, Mr. President." After the third or fourth mention of our toil, the President looked thoughtfully at him and said, "Leon, are you under the impression that I read those documents of yours? I couldn't even lift them."

The President sent a message to Congress on July 30 asking for the legislation, and Henderson, Ginsburg and I went to the Hill to explain it to Congressman Henry B. Steagall of Alabama, the Chairman of the House Banking and Currency Committee. A single administrator was authorized to set prices that were "generally fair and equitable" and that would effectuate the purpose of the Act, namely to keep prices down. Rents were included. Recourse, were we unfair or inequitable, could be had to an Emergency Court of Appeals, this to be appointed by the President. (Eventually the right of selection was given to the Chief Justice of the Supreme Court.) For violations there could be fines of up to $10,000 and jail sentences of up to two years, these rebukes each later being cut in half. None of this much interested Steagall, but farm prices did concern him very much. He was an old friend, fellow Alabaman and faithful servant of my friend Edward O'Neal.

We had accepted that we could not set the prices of farm products below parity. This was the sacred and semimystical goal of all farm legislation, a price for basic, i.e., corn, wheat, cotton, tobacco and other principal, products that stood in the same relationship to farm costs as the price in the ever-remembered time before the wars and before the depressions, the half-decade 1909–14. Steagall now suggested improving on parity by adding the law of averages. When some farm prices reached parity, some would still be below. So no ceiling should be set until a price had reached 110 percent of parity. That would allow them to average out at a hundred.

Farm prices that July stood at 95 percent of parity so Steagall's proposal effectively exempted them all and thus all living costs from control. Henderson, conscious of Steagall's power and, like most urban liberals, disposed to believe that the farm bloc was impregnable, agreed. Ginsburg and I were appalled, and so, when he thought about it later, was Henderson. On the way back to the office we were first silent, but then, with a gracelessness that could be characteristic, I reproached Henderson for the giveaway. Already regretting his action, he reacted with volcanic force, stopped the cab and invited me out. With difficulty I managed to negotiate continued passage. A few hours later he told me in the most pleasant possible way that I was right. My near-expulsion onto the Mall was a minor legend of those years.

The House hearings on the bill were a marathon; they lasted from August 5 to October 23. Nearly the whole committee turned out day after day. For most of the time the witness was Henderson, but Ginsburg rose to occasional points and so, once or twice, did I. The concern was over the vast powers we were asking. And the effect on farmers. And also, although not to the extent that might have been expected, on other producers. There were questions as well on the role of alleged subversives on our staff. I was brought to the defense of Robert A. Brady, who, a mere seven years before, had been my professor at California. A book of Brady's, *The Spirit and the Structure of German Fascism,* had been published by the Left Book Club in England, and a copy had fallen into the hands of a committee member. It said on the cover that it was "not for sale to the public." Obviously a clandestine document. I explained, incorrectly, that the Left Book Club was like the Book-of-the-Month Club. This was not true, and Martin Dies and the Committee on Un-American Activities picked me up on the evasion. A lie at a congressional hearing gets you by for the moment at the cost of worse trouble later on.

Henderson was more forthright. Asked if he would accept the judgment of the Treasury on the reliability of his employees, Henderson said yes.

"Would you accept the records of the FBI?"

"Right."

"Would you accept the records of the Dies Committee?"

"Absolutely not."[14]

Soon it was discovered that Henderson himself had been chairman of the Washington Friends of Spanish Democracy, which had supported Loyalist Spain against Franco. This, at the time, was hideously suspect. Henderson found the speech that he had given on accepting office and, despite many efforts to arrest the flow, read it to the committee from beginning to end. It was a prescient document detailing the intentions of Hitler and Mussolini. A committee member observed when he had finished that Henderson "exercised a little foresight there that some of the rest of us did not exercise."[15]

There was much discussion of what would now seem an inconceivable omission from our bill — the absence of any provision for formal control of wages. This was partly because, as liberals, we were avoiding political resistance from the unions, although in 1941 the CIO was only six years old and the AFL was somnambulant. But mostly the concept of wage-push inflation — wages shoving up prices — was not part of our economic thought, just as to this day it remains outside the system of the siege-resistant economists of the old school. Inflation, we believed, came when an excess of demand pulled up prices. And when prices were fixed, you would fix, *pari passu*, what could be offered as wages. Price control was an indirect form of wage control. The Congress, as it turned out, would have been delighted to accord us the one power we did not seek.

*   *   *

When Henderson finished, there came the witness we most feared, Baruch. In preceding weeks we had paid him great attention — careful trips to his suite in the Carlton to seek advice and to listen. Baruch, we said, was right in principle; it was only that we could not, as a practical matter, go so far. We continued to worry. Before the committee Baruch strongly affirmed his belief in his own plan — we should put a cap on all prices once and for all. The legislators were obviously impressed. But he also affirmed his faith in Henderson;

[14] Wilson, p. 64.

[15] U.S., Congress, House, Committee on Banking and Currency, *Price Control Bill: Hearing on H.R. 5479*, 77th Cong., 1st sess., August 14, 1941, p. 572.

no man "was better able" to do the job ahead. This came close to being an endorsement of our design. For the moment we were spared Baruch's, as it so seemed, monstrous aberration.

After Baruch there was another witness, the Honorable Tom Linder, Commissioner of Agriculture for the State of Georgia. His revelation was that the whole price control effort was a Jewish plot. Henderson was secretly Jewish. He was getting his job out of his friendship for "Baruch, Morgenthau, Straus, Ginsburg and the Guggenheim interests." Tom would have liked the Nuremberg Laws had he heard of them.

The committee could have questioned the considerable authority I was assuming after having been a citizen of the Republic for rather less than four years. There was no such query then and only one later. At a subsequent hearing Joseph F. Guffey, a New Deal senator from Pennsylvania of handsome white-haired aspect and modest moral tone, asked if I was foreign-born. I replied that, like so many others, including many of his constituents, I was. Joe relented and said, "Doctor, we are glad to have you here."

*　*　*

Among my tasks in those long weeks was to use my newly acquired identification with Alabama to cultivate the support of Henry B. Steagall. Then sixty-eight, Steagall was one of the authors, with Carter Glass, of the Glass-Steagall Act, a minor landmark in the development of American banking. He had never overcome the belief that he was specially endowed with knowledge in monetary matters. In the extreme form this conviction makes a man a money crank.

Once in those weeks, to be helpful, Donald Comer summoned Steagall, my wife and me to dinner at the Mayflower Hotel. One of Comer's mills was in Anniston in the congressional district adjacent to Steagall's. Conversation that night went back to the Confederacy and, reflecting the attitudes at the time, to one of Steagall's first cases as co-solicitor — prosecuting attorney — for Dale County. There was an angry battle and knifing one night in, as it was then called, the colored quarter of Anniston. A relative of the victim went out to the cotton fields the next day to take revenge and shot dead the man who had used the knife. The leading witness for the prosecution was a farm hand who had been driving a load of freshly picked cotton along the road.

"Did you see the accused, Jeb here, coming across the field with his gun?"

"Yes, sah."

"Did you see him shoot Jim Wilson?"

"Yes, sah."

"What did you do then?"

"I say to him, white man give you hell fo' shooting 'cross the road."

My wife, having listened negligently to the conversation on the subject, asked Steagall that night if he didn't think 110 percent *above* parity was a higher price than even the farmers needed.

On November 28, 1941, the House of Representatives, having rejected the substitute bill embodying the Baruch plan introduced by a young and exceptionally able congressman from Tennessee, Albert Gore, passed the Emergency Price Control Act. It was nine days before the attack on Pearl Harbor.

10

The Inner Face of War

We, by the grace of heaven, Emperor of Japan, seated on the Throne of a line unbroken for ages eternal, enjoin upon ye, Our loyal and brave subjects:

We hereby declare war on the United States of America and the British Empire. The men and officers of Our army and navy shall do their utmost in prosecuting the war.

Imperial Rescript
December 7, 1941

To ALL IN LIFE, there must be a supreme moment, the summit to which all ascends. If such a moment has not existed, it is frequently contrived in the telling. For me the obvious temptation is December 7, 1941. I was asleep at our house in Georgetown that Sunday afternoon, a minor circumstance that tells something of life at the time. Alfred Marshall thought no one should be forced to such toil that he did not recover his strength in the twenty-four-hour cycle of work and sleep. At a minimum the process should be accomplished in the weekly cycle, and it was over the weekly cycle in those years that I sought restoration. The resilience of relative youth notwithstanding, my work days were ones of accumulating strain and fatigue, and I tried on Sundays to rid myself of weariness in order to start the new week with renewed enthusiasm.

Dick Gilbert called me at three o'clock that afternoon to tell me that something had happened in Hawaii. I rushed, as did millions of others, to turn on the radio. I heard the news. Then almost immediately I was called by David Ginsburg. The senior defense officials were assembling in emergency session within the hour. Leon Henderson was in New York; we were to attend and speak for the management on the home front in the war that was now upon us. I drove to the Social Security Building south of the Mall which had been taken over by the Office of Production Management and the more recently created Supply Priorities and Allocations Board. I went with a sense of awe. The war had come, and of all the people in all the land, I was of the chosen. The fates had been kind or maybe just precise.

The meeting that late afternoon assembled irregularly. Men arrived when they heard the news or got the summons. Some were in tennis shoes, golf pants, pullovers, other athletic or casual garb. William Knudsen was there, along with William Batt. So was Donald M. Nelson, who, in a few weeks, would become head of the new, presumptively all-powerful War Production Board displacing Knudsen, whose feelings would be protected by his being made a nonbelligerent lieutenant-general. Blackwell Smith, later a notable Establishment lawyer, arrived. And others. It was soon evident that the gathering would be a major disaster.

That was because there was nothing to decide, and, in any case, so important were the people attending that none could speak firmly about a needed course of action lest it be a decision. So there was reference only to the news, and of this no one had heard more than was on the radio. A man did go out to telephone the office of Secretary Frank Knox at the Navy Department, and presently he came back with the notes of a message. But the word was only that everything was worse than expected. We didn't even know what had been expected.

Bill Batt saw how things were going and attempted a rescue. Turning to Knudsen and getting the attention of the others, he said, "Bill, what are the marching orders for tomorrow?"

Knudsen was sitting on a couch with his hat on. He didn't stir. He only looked at Batt with every evidence of having heard a foolish question and replied, "I expect we will be worrying about copper shortages just as we are today."

Someone then asked Nelson, who was in charge of purchasing and procurement planning, what we might lose "from east of Singapore." Those lands and oceans would presumably soon be Japanese. The question sounded good; another subordinate went out and brought back a huge stock book detailing alphabetically the inventories and sources of all essential materials.

David Ginsburg asked me to step out in the hall. He had just remembered that Henderson was to make an appearance that evening on the radio—"Edgar Bergen, Charlie McCarthy, Judy Garland and guest," it had read in the newspaper. David wondered if Henderson should be warned that at this grim moment it was not the thing to do. On the other hand, if he had already decided against it, he would certainly be angry at our thinking he needed such advice. I suggested to Dave that he call; he preferred that I do so. Jointly we tracked Henderson down at the Stork Club. He *had* heard the news and was shocked that we thought it necessary to caution him.

We went back to the meeting where the discussion had bogged down in the "Ks" on kapok. Kapok came from the now-threatened world, but there was a serious difference of opinion over whether it was essential. The debate was going nowhere. On that greatest of all evenings I decided to go home.

In front of the White House and also before the Japanese Embassy out on Massachusetts Avenue, small crowds had assembled. They too were seeking a rendezvous with destiny. For them too, disappointment.

That evening remained with me. Years later I drew on the experience to describe the meetings that Herbert Hoover had with business leaders in the aftermath of the Great Crash of 1929. My name for those sessions achieved a certain currency — the no-business meeting.

> Meetings are held because men seek companionship or, at a minimum, wish to escape the tedium of solitary duties. They yearn for the prestige which accrues to the man who presides over meetings, and this leads them to convoke assemblages over which they can preside. Finally, there is the meeting which is called not because there is business to be done, but because it is necessary to create the impression that business is being done. Such meetings are more than a substitute for action. They are widely regarded as action.[1]

*　　*　　*

The history of the military operations in Europe, the Pacific and in Asia during World War II has been amply written. Much less has been told of the war in Washington and almost nothing of its absurdities.

[1]*The Great Crash, 1929*, 50th Anniversary Ed. (Boston: Houghton Mifflin, 1979), p. 139.

In the autumn of 1940, as I've noted, there was conflict between the New Dealers and the businessmen, between those who feared that war mobilization and the influx of business executives would mean the end of the Roosevelt era and those who hoped both to save the Republic and to rescue it from Roosevelt as well. By the time of the Pearl Harbor attack this conflict had become triangular in form. The New Dealers and the business executives were still vying for control, but now the military was making its influence felt as a third force. It was a power of which, earlier on, few had been aware.

The New Dealers, following the leadership and indeed the explicit directions of F.D.R., had now converted to the war — to the belief that domestic economic mobilization should be prosecuted as urgently as possible with as much use of government authority as was necessary. When more production was needed, as of steel, it should be obtained by whatever means. Earlier that year, Leon Henderson had met with Tom Girdler, head of Republic Steel, the archenemy of the New Deal and the archfiend of the CIO, to discuss an expansion of steel capacity that the United States Steel Corporation was resisting. So formidable was Girdler's reputation as a reactionary that Henderson did not want to meet with him alone, and I was present as a witness. What Girdler had come to tell him was that, with government help, Republic would go for increased capacity and output. Nothing would be gained, he averred, in waiting for the "stuffed shirts and bureaucrats" at U.S. Steel. Henderson, overcoming all political scruple, was sympathetic.

Similarly, when much of a material such as aluminum, copper, steel or neoprene was needed for military production, we took the position that it should be assigned by government order — allocated — to that use. And when the production of civilian goods, the most notable case being that of automobiles, preempted plant, materials or labor that could be used for military purposes, it was now the New Deal position that that production should be curtailed or stopped.

The businessmen still took a far more leisurely view. Their reputation was for decision; their practice was delay. A few were forthright defenders of corporate interest or they wanted the profits from the now excellent civilian sales. But self-interest or outright profiteering were not major problems in World War II. On matters concerning production and procurement, as with price control, the war was notable for the absence of major scandal.

The greater difficulty, as I've already indicated, was the inferior quality of business talent that the war brought to Washington, and after Pearl Harbor the effective operators could be spared even less at home. There was also the dollar-a-year syndrome. Many executives remained on their company payrolls and received only a token dollar a year from the government. It was strongly suspected at the time that their policies followed their major pay. Far more serious, in fact, was the individual's feeling that, since he wasn't costing the taxpayer anything, his contribution could be in keeping with his compensation.

This lassitude was sustained by the deep suspicion of firm, affirmative exercise of government authority. Let allocation of scarce materials to military use be proposed or orders for the conservation of such materials or for restrictions on civilian production, and the response would be "I think the industry can be trusted to see to the need." By the end of 1941, the fears of the New Dealers as to what the businessmen would do to their reforms had given way to the fear that, in the language of the time, they would never get off their asses.

Meanwhile the military was emerging. In 1940, on economic, industrial and procurement matters, the military power was derisory — it was exercised by a handful of lieutenant colonels and colonels and a failed general or two. Now it was brought strongly to bear on decisions. The most obvious manifestation of the new force was its ability to build from scarce materials and with scarce labor a wholly new, wholly permanent headquarters, the 34-acre Pentagon, which, in time, would become the enduring symbol of military power. That scarce labor and materials should have been so used in the middle of a war was scandalous. But the soldiers were determined that they would not ever again be condemned to a peacetime lived out in cement bivouacs flanking the reflecting pool on the Mall.

As the military influence grew, numerous liberals, attracted by the style or persuaded that the soldiers were neutral or indifferent on domestic policy and fully committed on the war, joined them. This was the beginning of the partnership that was to have such significance in the Cold War and Vietnam years to come. Others remained apart, and a few expressed concern. We would defeat Hitler at the price of becoming a durably militarized state. My duties did not require a decision on the matter, and they so occupied my mind that I didn't dwell on the issue.

The ablest and most perceptive of the businessmen, Charles E. (Electric) Wilson, the former President of General Electric, also moved toward the military. Many more of them subsided into inconsequence, although with some continuing capacity for delay. By the end of the war the Pentagon had assumed full responsibility for its own procurement. The idea that it might need the support of a large civilian organization such as that of World War II would thereafter seem distinctly odd.

*   *   *

Dissatisfaction with the casual tendencies of the management of wartime production had mounted steadily through 1941; as it did so, one of our more powerful public traditions took over. That is to attribute to defective organization what should be attributed to poor leadership, inadequate people or lack of clarity of purpose. The remedy, in turn, is thought to lie in reorganization. In a major such reorganization in the summer of 1941, we had lost authority for civilian supply and thus over rationing when it became necessary.

The precipitating factor was a jurisdictional row over a proposal to limit automobile production between Joseph L. Weiner, a New Dealer, lawyer and old Washington hand whom Henderson had put in charge of civilian industry at OPACS, and the industry men of the Office of Production Management. By mid-1941, the automobile industry, in the midst of a nearly unprecedented boom, was gobbling an intolerable share of scarce war materials. The formidable Weiner believed that both the prospective war economy and more pressing civilian needs required curtailment of the number of cars produced. Henderson supported him. The reaction of the industry and the Washington executives ranged from disbelief to outrage. An order calling for less production than the market demanded; what next! The battle was extremely bitter, and the solution was to bury the conflict in a yet larger organization. In August of 1941, a new umbrella organization, SPAB — the Supply Priorities and Allocations Board already mentioned — was created, with Donald Nelson as executive director. Henderson was given an additional hat as a member of OPM-SPAB, and Weiner and civilian supply went with him to this new authority. The Office of Price Administration and Civilian Supply became the Office of Price Administration. With the change the responsibility for civilian rationing went to SPAB, the responsibility which I believed and had urged was absolutely essential for successful control of prices.

A further consequence of the reorganization was to take Henderson away from price control and draw him increasingly, under his second hat, into the struggles over the diversion of materials and plant capacity to war use. My authority over prices, as shared with David Ginsburg and his lawyers, became nearly plenary.

*   *   *

In the days following the attack on Pearl Harbor the Senate quickly passed the Emergency Price Control Act. Agricultural products and thus living costs were still effectively excluded, for no prices on farm commodities could be set below 110 percent of parity. I urged a veto and a prompt request for remedial action. The President, Henderson and Ginsburg believed that the bill should be signed, after which remedial action could be requested. There is little doubt that I was wrong. My energetic use of my authority also produced a design for lessening my power. Several separate price divisions would be created that would report directly to Henderson. I would function as a chief of staff. But Henderson, burdened with his other duties and lacking my unduly confident view of what should be done, quickly relented. After a short interruption I was again in charge.

The prices of nearly all uncontrolled items went up in the first days of the war. I had the commodity exchanges put limits on daily increases in wheat, soybeans, butter, eggs and other products. And price schedules setting ceiling prices were issued on some dozens of other products that were under pressure. The latter included cottonseed oil. This in those December days produced an explosion that all but washed Oahu from mind. Southern senators and congressmen marshaled by John Bankhead called us to Capitol Hill and made it clear that we must not open up hostilities against the Japanese Empire and the cotton kingdom at the same time. Henderson wisely ordered a retreat. However, our energetic actions had broken the immediate eruption in prices. In its place came a slower but more sustained rise.

Hawaii, because of its frontline position, had passed under military rule, and our authority over prices there was assumed by the armed forces. This was the cause of a more exotic crisis. A conscientious general was aroused over a sudden and unjustified increase in the amounts charged by the Honolulu whorehouses after the outbreak of hostilities. Sailors in from the sea especially needed protection from outrageous exploitation. He used his delegated authority to set tariffs. When the news reached Washington, some were deeply amused; I reflected only on the reaction in Congress and throughout the land were it learned how our powers were being employed. I sent Ben W. Lewis, a much respected professor at Oberlin College, out to Hawaii to supervise the military and to detach us from all forms of vice. And I also urged total reticence on the matter.[2] Then as in later official life when, directly or indirectly, I have found myself responsible for, or associated with, something indefensible or merely foolish, I have had the same sequence of thought. First: can the action be reversed? Second: can it be kept a secret? During World War II, secrecy was never possible. As a matter of high principle, OPA was never given access to classification or censorship.

More important, in the days after Pearl Harbor we were able to retrieve control over rationing. It was the result of a sanguinary action involving automobile tires. By mid-December it was evident that the natural rubber supply essential for all military and civilian transportation was in jeopardy. Access to Malaya and Indonesia would soon be interrupted; most likely those countries would be lost. With an optimism that now seems feckless, it was presumed that synthetic rubber could be had in usable quantities. But these supplies were months away. The Germans were using buna but had thoughtfully refrained from giving Standard Oil, their American partner, the requisite technical knowledge. Our people, more generous, had entered agreements to give the Germans information on butyl rubber,

[2] Professor Lewis remembers the assignment to Hawaii but not my anxiety over the ceilings on the cost of love. My memory, however, is firm. The military men were tackling in an innovative way what historically has been man's most costly indulgence.

which seemed to be our best alternative.[3] Until synthetic rubber became available, we would have to make do with the inventories of natural rubber on hand and the tires awaiting sale. The tires must, above all, be conserved. At that sad night meeting on December 7, it would possibly have been better had rubber, not kapok, come first in the alphabet.

The first impulse of the leisured business statesmen, we knew, would be either to inaction or to a plea for voluntary restraint[4] — retailers would be asked to sell only to those who really needed tires or those who were engaged in war work. Even this would involve time-consuming discussion and labored clearance, and meanwhile there would be an exuberant rush for tires. All would soon be gone. Gone too would be our first chance for rationing; one cannot ration what has already disappeared.

These concerns, like all others of those days, I associate with my large, sullen office in dark, dysenteric yellow in Tempo D on the Mall. It was just above Henderson's looking out on Independence Avenue. The rest of the building consisted of open bays with a partially enclosed space at each end for whoever was in charge. Desks were so jammed together that often there was no space to walk between. And even then there was not enough room for our whole staff; on occasion, we had to send new hands to sit in the reading room of the Library of Congress until desk space could be found.

Harold Leventhal, increasingly my ally on all matters large and small, came in one day just before Christmas to talk of the consequences of inaction. Neither of us was in the line of authority,[5] but we decided to act on our own.

Harold drafted an order of draconian simplicity, forbidding the sale of all new tires to anyone for any purpose anywhere in the Republic. Dealers were instructed to make and file an inventory of their present stock. This was my contribution; once so on record,

[3] The oil company executives responsible for this arrangement, William S. Farish and Walter C. Teagle, did not survive. Farish died of a heart attack; Teagle was sacked.

[4] Thomas Robert Malthus, the great economist, thought ministers, when performing the marriage ceremony, might urge voluntary restraint as a way of limiting the increase in population. The likely effectiveness in that case and this were roughly the same.

[5] Henderson had ultimate responsibility because, as earlier noted, he was in charge of civilian supply in OPM/SPAB.

they would fear that someone would come to check. We then obtained a list numbering around a dozen of all those in OPM/SPAB whose initials were required on such a directive. Harold made the rounds saying, "Here is the rubber order. It has to go out tonight." No one knew or reflected that he didn't belong to the agency; it was enough that his manner was firm and that anyone could surely see the need for such an action.[6] By the time his circuit was complete, Donald Nelson, custodian of the ultimate signature, had gone to a cocktail party — life in Washington did go on. But power of attorney had been left with his counsel, Milton Katz, later ambassador to the Marshall Plan and later and still a greatly distinguished professor at the Harvard Law School. A good lawyer knows when procedure defeats purpose. Katz signed for Nelson. Our guerrilla raid ended in total success.

The order became effective that very evening, December 26, 1941, and we then set our minds to how it could be made known across the land. The news wire services were notified and the leading papers. The broadcasting networks were asked to announce it at fifteen-minute intervals, and later that night, listening attentively, I learned that they did. We sent a telegram to each of the forty-eight governors requesting them to use all available radio and press to announce the ban on tire sales and to use the state highway patrol to enforce it. We notified the big retail chains.

The next morning on the way to work from Georgetown, I stopped at a large service station just off Rock Creek Parkway. I was depressed to discover that there were still new tires on sale, and the owner reacted in astonishment and disbelief when I told him this was illegal. I stopped again on the way home that night. The racks held only some old used tires.

Having stopped the sale of all new tires, we had now to find some way of selling them again but only to the necessary and needful. OPM/SPAB, cum War Production Board, had no useful regional organization and no stomach for the task. For price control we would have regional and local offices so the task was ceded to us. Rationing powers, having been lost in August, were now returned to OPA in January. A large, confident, articulate man named Frank Bane, who had been long associated with the Council of State Governments,

---

[6] This was Judge Leventhal's own interpretation of how it was accomplished, for which I am most grateful.

came aboard. He telephoned every governor asking him to appoint a good man to have charge of tire rationing in his state. Later that official would go on to appoint local price and rationing boards.[7] Meanwhile Harold Leventhal produced a further order telling who would be entitled to buy tires and how such entitlement would be checked and controlled. The ordinary motorist would have to make do for the war with what he had. By early January a full-scale rationing organization was in operation.

We had feared that during the freeze truck and bus transportation would be curtailed as old tires wore out and replacements were unavailable. There were a few desperate requests for rescue, but generally the problem did not arise.

For the next few weeks I was in charge of both price control and rationing. One of my lesser decisions brought a highly distinguished rebuke from President Roosevelt. Physicians, public officials and others rendering essential services were made eligible in case of need to buy tires, but ministers of the gospel were not. In truth I didn't think about the distinction at all. There was an immediate explosion, especially from the rural South. F.D.R. was outraged that anyone should be so casual about both fundamentalist religion and the fundamentals of American politics. Ministers were promptly proclaimed essential.

As the days passed, Henderson decided that I had enough to do, and the ablest of my subordinates, Paul O'Leary, of whom I've spoken, was subtracted from my staff and put in charge of rationing. I resisted the transfer, but I was wrong. The close coordination between price control and rationing that had seemed so important in theory was not important in practice. O'Leary accomplished the enormous administrative task of rationing sugar, shoes, canned goods, meat, gasoline and heating oil with the greatest ingenuity and skill. There were flaws, but they arose, as in the case of meat rationing, from divided responsibility. Authority for this was shared with the Department of Agriculture, but the USDA compulsively overestimated the supply that would be available, which meant that for some ration stamps there was no meat. When this happened, the

[7] It was an arrangement admirably designed to make political enemies in Washington; Democratic congressmen and especially senators saw Republicans or rival Democrats back home distributing the patronage and glorying in war appointments that rightfully, they thought, belonged to them.

entire purpose of rationing was defeated, for rationing is meant to assure a supply — a smaller supply but a certain one. If the assured amount is not forthcoming, all the bother is for nothing.

In the early months of 1942, concern for the rubber and tire supply reached the proportions of a small panic.[8] Bernard Baruch, along with James B. Conant of Harvard, was called in to study and report on conservation measures. Speed limits, tire inspection, provision for recapping and other precautionary procedures were all put into effect. No one noticed the sanguinary raid by which the stock of finished tires had been saved. Certainly no one criticized it. My share in that operation could have been one of my better contributions to the war.

Thirty years later I remembered the technique. In 1972, as the current president of the American Economic Association, I was invited, along with my two predecessors in office, to visit China. My passport went up to Ottawa for a visa, as was necessary in those days. There the Chinese refused to stamp it, for the passport banned travel in Communist China. The prohibition had been lifted, but the words remained. I asked the American Embassy for help; it said that protocol forbade their personnel crossing the threshold of the chancery of a country we did not recognize. I then thought of the rubber tire order. The handsome sister-in-law of one of my assistants was then living in Ottawa. She went to the Chinese Embassy, asked for my passport and struck out the offending words with heavy black ink. The visa was immediately stamped in.

*   *   *

A young lawyer who was a participant in the early rationing effort was Richard Milhous Nixon. He had come to Washington from his law practice at Wingert, Bewley & Nixon in Whittier, California, and

---

[8] Although it took some time to overcome traditional attitudes. Months earlier the government had taken possession of all stocks of raw rubber and placed title in the Rubber Reserve Corporation, an arm of the Reconstruction Finance Corporation. The RFC was then headed, as for many earlier years, by Jesse Holman Jones of Houston, Texas. One day in October 1941, a warehouse full of rubber in Fall River, Massachusetts, burned down. Between 15,850 and 20,000 tons were lost. Jesse created a small sensation with the extreme calm with which he took the news. "The rubber," he said, "was fully insured." *The Nation* (January 10, 1942), p. 28.

was hired by David Cavers, Associate General Counsel of OPA who was on leave from Duke University where Nixon had studied law. Nixon had first sought a job at the FBI. Not qualification but an appropriations cut, he later held, caused his rejection by J. Edgar Hoover, although some have wondered if the FBI ever had its budget cut. The OPA was notoriously a New Deal agency, and in later years Nixon did not want to risk guilt by past association so when congressman, senator and Vice President he said he had worked for the Office of Emergency Management. The latter was the administrative shell for all the war agencies. It was much as though a Marine had said that he worked in the public sector. In his memoirs Nixon tells that in 1942, he went bravely off to the war, although others of draft age in his office remained comfortably behind. It was, in fact, the policy of the OPA after Pearl Harbor not to request draft deferments, an occasional delay of a few days to complete a price regulation apart.

*   *   *

The tire stocks — how existing vehicles could be kept rolling — were my immediate concern in the early days of the war. The larger drama concerned the production of new automobiles. The industry's appetite for scarce materials, including rubber, could no longer be sustained. But the auto companies were still adamant. They wanted to prosper for just a little longer.

In late December Henderson cut a deal. The automobile manufacturers, the urgencies of war notwithstanding, would be allowed a few more weeks of production. Then it would stop; there would be no confrontation; the firms would not be accused of resisting the war effort. The reason was profit. The excuse was that this delay would allow the using up of components that would otherwise be wasted.

The decision being indefensible, Henderson went over his defense in detail. Such care in drafting is why a bad decision very often sounds more appealing than a good one. At a staff meeting on January 2 before the action was to be announced, David Ginsburg told him his explanation wouldn't wash. Henderson exploded in anger but later in the morning called us to another conference. He had

gone over his case again. It still wasn't persuasive, and at noon we
had a third rehearsal. By then he was both imaginative and eloquent. Staff cars were needed for the military; passenger cars were
needed for defense workers; the components would otherwise be
piled up in the factories for the duration. The weeks until the order
went into effect would be used to plan the production of tanks and
military vehicles and ensure that Detroit would truly be an arsenal
of democracy.

That afternoon we went over to the auditorium of the Social Security Building. It was nearly filled with reporters; stopping all automobile production in the United States was not a trivial thing.
Henderson was detailed, voluble, persuasive. There was silence
when he had finished, and the newsmen continued to scribble. I. F.
Stone, then as for generations the most intractably independent of
reporters, was sitting in the front row. Henderson tried not to see
him, tried again and failed.

Stone asked, "Mr. Henderson, may we assume that this was a
deal?"

*   *   *

Operating now with a firm mandate of law, I added rapidly to our
staff in the winter and spring of 1942. And the staff pursued prices
vigorously to bring them under control. There was a large lesson
from those months and numerous smaller ones. The large one was
that our design for economic stabilization — mine, in major measure — was a disaster. In modern times the standards by which economists in public office are judged have become very relaxed: Mr.
Nixon's, Mr. Ford's and Mr. Carter's economists have all presided
over grave misfortune and emerged from public service with enhanced reputations. In accordance with our system of upward failure
all have gone on to distinguished and better-paying jobs. Then it was
not known that public attitudes were so benign. I will return in the
next chapter to the failure I faced in those months. The smaller
lessons were more personal and, on balance, are more pleasant to
recall.

Early in our operations we froze gasoline prices, and in doing so,
we froze a price war in Kansas, Oklahoma and Texas. Phillips Petroleum Company, in particular, was caught with its station prices well

below cost. A day came when relief to Phillips could no longer be postponed, and it was allowed a price increase.

The same afternoon I received a letter from C. Tyler Wood, a broker in New York, a longtime friend of my wife's family and the custodian of their and our small financial affairs. (Later he entered government service, and by an improbable coincidence I inherited him as my AID director in India.) Wood had decided that Phillips looked good as an investment, and he was writing to tell me that a few days before he had bought some for my wife's account.

This too was a coincidence but one that never could be so explained. I went to the lawyer in charge of petroleum prices, Michael Quinn Shaughnessy. Quinn, an amiable Celt of casual and accommodating mind, told me not to worry. He took my guilt for granted. Everyone, he said, did it. Possibly then he was partly right.

My anxiety was not allayed. H. L. Mencken said of a conscience that it is the inner voice that warns you someone may be looking. Such is mine but with the further sense of that inevitable telephone call from a reporter, half accusing, half ingratiating, and then the glaring headline when all is exposed. I went to New York, gathered up the family assets (in fact, my wife's) from a custodian account in the Chemical Bank and took them to the United States Trust Company along with a letter resigning all authority over all questions of purchase or sale. If I did not invent the blind trust of later fame, I did reinvent it that day.

*　　*　　*

I learned also of the dangers from conscientious subordinates. Two such in those days went to Tarpon Springs in Florida to hold hearings on the price of sponges. When frustrated by a local gangster, they threatened him with major evil consequences in my name. A few days later he stepped on the starter of his automobile and, along with the car, was destroyed by an enormous blast of dynamite. Until reassured by J. Edgar Hoover, my people thought me in line for a murder charge.[9]

On another morning, to my surprise, a congressman from Indiana

[9] I have told of this in "My Forty Years with the FBI" in *Annals of an Abiding Liberal* (Boston: Houghton Mifflin, 1979), pp. 159–160.

called me to say that one of his constituents, Emerson Balmer, as I seem to remember the name, was the best undertaker in the state of Indiana. Also a loyal Democrat. Em Balmer, as he was called, should be our state funeral director, and if not that, he certainly was the man for county director. Marion County, embracing Indianapolis, he said, was an absolutely key area. I responded with seeming knowledge and was still pondering the request when another congressman came on the line. He wanted me to understand that "this undertaker business of yours is the god-damnedest nonsense I ever heard of." He was going on the floor of the House with a one-minute speech denouncing it and me and was allowing me the courtesy of notice. I asked him for a delay until I could investigate. I called around to see if anyone knew what was going on, and a division chief said he had a clue. A paper had just come to his desk mentioning a proposed meeting on the control of funeral prices.

This was, indeed, the clue. A new man in our now large consumers' goods division had turned his mind to the lines of business that would be especially under pressure from the war. Undertaking, he had concluded, would be a growth industry. A representative of the funeral directors' trade association whom he sought out said that he was on target. But funerals, he learned, were a highly unstandardized commodity. The price varied with the elegance of the casket. And the location, spaciousness and appointments of the funeral home. And also with the deftness and subtlety of the undertaker and the comfort he accorded to the bereft. Even how an undertaker walked at the funeral — quietly and gracefully or flatfootedly, heel and sole — could be a factor in the price. It followed that no two funerals could be under the same price ceiling.

The problem was resolved. In each state a distinguished and trusted mortician would be appointed State Funeral Director. He would then appoint a respected and experienced counterpart in each county. The county man would attend every funeral, assess comprehensively its quality and set the appropriate maximum price. The work of this local official would be kept under review by the State Funeral Director, who also would coordinate prices as between county directors to ensure that none got out of line. Word of this design had gone out to the profession. Undertakers, eager as were all in those days to serve, had petitioned their congressmen for the jobs. Thus my calls. In words later made memorable by our own Richard Nixon, we cut this effort off at the pass.

*   *   *

Finally, I became aware that spring of how the great executives kept the war machine rolling.

The man in charge of aircraft production for the War Production Board in 1942 was Merrill Church (Babe) Meigs, a longtime Hearst publisher in Chicago. His early interest in aviation is commemorated in Meigs Field, the landing strip on the Chicago waterfront. By the spring of 1942, the growing power of the military had seriously eroded Babe's responsibilities, which had never been perceptible in any case. He was reduced to going early to the executive dining room that the OPA shared with the War Production Board and lunching in turn with his fellow war mobilizers as they passed through. He was an excellent companion. And, on occasion, he went out on an inspection trip.

One day he asked me to go with him to inspect the Lycoming airplane engine plant at Williamsport, Pennsylvania. After first declining, I canceled my appointments for the afternoon and called up Babe to tell him I would go. I thought it time that I got out and saw the reality of our mobilization effort. We flew in Babe's two-seater gull-wing monoplane from National Airport; it was early spring, and I watched the mauve and green of the Maryland and Pennsylvania countryside below. Nowhere in the world, Henry Adams said, does spring come with such beauty. Presently we circled, and I noticed that Babe was wiping away tears. I had not previously thought him a sentimental man. He pointed to a huge winged structure down below, mopped his eyes again and said:

"My old friend Moe Annenberg is down there. I always circle a few times here for Moe."

It was Lewisburg Penitentiary. Moses L. Annenberg was an old friend of Babe's from the days in Chicago when space on the newsstands was won and maintained by armed force. He had been very helpful in this regard to Babe when he was a publisher. A few months before, Annenberg had gone to jail for income tax evasion, regretting that because of his advanced age he had only a few years to give to his country.

At Williamsport we visited the executive offices, looked at an engine on a test bed and were asked to avoid the factory proper because such visits disrupted production. On the way back to the airport with a senior executive, Babe said:

"Any labor trouble, Jack?"

"No, none at all."

"You aren't treating the bastards too good, are you?"

11

The Dynamics of Error

THE EXPERIENCE of being disastrously wrong is salutary; no economist should be denied it, and not many are. The best, most elegant and most applauded designs can fail, and greatly to your surprise if, in persuading others of their excellence, you have persuaded yourself. By early spring of 1942, as I've already indicated, the extraordinarily logical model of wartime economic management that had brought me my considerable and welcome power was proving itself a disaster. That it had invited the support of the most sophisticated economists of the time would not mitigate the disaster; it would only provide me with excellent company in the debacle.

Spending for the war was now outrunning tax revenues, even though taxes were being (though still moderately) increased. It would continue to do so even when the economy reached the unexpectedly elastic upper limits of its plant and labor force. There was no chance that tax revenues would keep pace with military and civilian spending. The beautiful Keynesian balance between total purchasing power and the aggregate of the goods and services to be purchased was like a rainbow, seen but never approached. Instead excess demand would persist and drive up all prices — relentlessly. It was already beginning to do so.

Once during these weeks I went to the Treasury to have lunch with Henry Morgenthau, Jr., the Secretary, and Harry Dexter White, then his blunt, unpleasant and able Director of Monetary Research. We went over the figures and the prospect. White was abruptly insistent. Some help might come from a massive program of forced savings — as urged by Keynes. Taxes could go up. Neither would serve. Were inflation to be avoided, it would be up to us. White, with Morgenthau agreeing, said we weren't doing very well. "It's getting away from you. You must get moving."

Meanwhile, and more immediately, we faced a hitherto unforeseen problem, one that should have been foreseen, with the selective controls. Those prices that we caught and fixed were, for the moment, holding. But each price-fixing action took time; costs had to be obtained, meetings held and the results deliberated. Some divisions, units and subunits of our now considerable organization were more deliberate than others. Since one firm's prices could be another's costs, the uncontrolled or later-controlled prices were beginning to unhinge those under earlier control. And the profits of the later-controlled producers were a point of comparison for those we had attended to earlier. Also very often we found ourselves moving decisively on less important prices while more important ones awaited action — vigorously on pepper, not at all on bread. Finally we began to realize for the first time what an unreasonably large number of products and prices there were in the American economy.

These were the days of the great military disasters in the Pacific — Bataan, Corregidor, Singapore, Java, and at sea the sinking of the *Prince of Wales* and the *Repulse*. Now came the failing effort to chase the prices and the evident failure of my design. Maybe nothing worked.

I began to accept that I had been very wrong. We needed, somehow, to move on all prices at once — place a general ceiling over all. My eloquent speeches against Baruch became increasingly painful to recall. There was also the troubling fact that the previous autumn the Canadians had done what he recommended. I had been up to Ottawa; it was obvious that they were doing a better job of price stabilization than we were.[1]

In March I confessed error, though discreetly to myself, and asked Donald Wallace to join me in heading a special group of our most inventive members to devise ways and means of putting a ceiling over all prices.

Harold Leventhal, assisted by another young lawyer, David Cobb,

[1] In the early days of the war, Canadian price control was under the general direction of a board of senior civil servants — the Wartime Prices & Trade Board — headed by James Coyne whose grandfather had been a sometime political ally and rival of my father's in Elgin County in Ontario. Later it was under Donald Gordon, a hard-living and sometimes hard-drinking public servant of great ability who accepted fully my feeling that price control and the sorrow often thereby inflicted on would-be profiteers was a job for which the ethnic tendency and religious training of the Scotch were admirable qualifications.

was as always the draftsman. Our group met late every afternoon, first to consider what to do, then how to do it, then to anticipate the problems that would arise in so doing. The first two steps were easy. A single general order would be issued stating that no price that legally was within our purview could rise above the highest level reached in a period immediately prior to the issuance of the order. That decision taken, we considered draft after draft and how, then and thereafter, we would answer the questions and anticipate or deal with the problems that would arise from this wholly uncharted action. It was a completely fascinating exercise. I took the issues home at night, woke up with them in the small hours of the morning, brought possible solutions back to the office.

I thought also of the personal implications of this change of direction. How could I retain confidence after such a massive admission of error? How could I explain this reversal to myself and others?

It was a somber prospect and one that I never had to face. No one — not a single soul — ever asked me to explain my 180-degree change of course. There was no notable comment from Baruch. He assumed, I'm sure, that, sooner or later, we would see the light.

*   *   *

April 28, 1942 was, perhaps, the most important date in the history of wartime economic policy. On that day, by the General Maximum Price Regulation, all prices legally within reach were effectively fixed for the duration of the war. The ceiling price was the highest charged in March by that seller for the same item to purchasers of the same class. In 1942, the government of the United States could still keep secrets. Until well into April, i.e., until the March base period was safely in the past, there was no press or radio mention of our meetings or our plans.

The GMPR or General Max was not related by careful rational forethought to the admirable results that it achieved. It was far less elegant in conception than the ideas that it replaced. As with much economic legislation, its rationale was only the total absence of an alternative.

Historians have seen this as the response to a stentorian demand from President Roosevelt in those days that inflation be brought under effective control. F.D.R., in fact, made his demand at our request; it was to give the necessary sense of urgency to our action.

Otherwise he was not involved. He had much else on his mind at the time, and no White House meeting preceded this massive step.

On April 27, the day before the General Maximum Price Regulation was issued, Congress was asked for more taxes, for authority to control consumer credit, for the repeal of the exemption of farm prices and, in a general way, for support for a wage-stabilization policy. Steps would be taken to stabilize the remuneration received by individuals for their work. And on April 28, also a busy day, rents were fixed. Ceilings were proclaimed in 302 urban centers across the country, adding to the 21 where action had already been taken.

Rent control, which initially had been under my authority, was now administered by Paul Porter. Later when complaints mounted over the complexity of our price regulations, he came to my assistance with the Porter Plan for price control. The Porter Plan, holding that extreme simplicity was the key to success, proposed that there be one price, $5.00, for everything.

*   *   *

Apart from his innovative approach to economics, Paul Porter was an extraordinarily competent administrator, and he became head of the Office of Price Administration in its latter days. His selection as deputy administrator for rent control was in consequence of the kind of bureaucratic maneuver that only rarely works and that only with the passage of time does one confess. In the weeks following Pearl Harbor, temporarily back at the Columbia Broadcasting System for which he was Washington counsel, he was increasingly anxious to be occupied with the war. John Hamm and I proposed him for rent administrator. Henderson, who was recurrently and rightly conscious of the youth of his subordinates, wanted Chester Davis, now the head of the St. Louis Federal Reserve Bank, to return to government service for this post. I suggested to Henderson that the only chance of getting Davis was to have F.D.R. ask him. This was arranged, and meanwhile by calling Davis I ascertained that he was not interested. I then asked him to propose Porter to the President. He did, and the President passed the suggestion on to Henderson. Coming from the White House, it had, as I hoped, the force of a command.

It was Porter's claim, not especially related to the reality, that his standard for allowing rent increases was precise and firm: no upward adjustment would be allowed during the war until after the second bankruptcy. Rent control was the least controversial aspect of OPA operations and the only control that lingered long after.

* * * ＇

In the intense planning that preceded the issuance of the General Maximum Price Regulation, many and perhaps even most of the ensuing problems were foreseen. Not all were solved. As often in public and private administration, a formula had frequently to serve as a solution.

Thus a seller might not have sold or offered the item in March 1942. His maximum price then became the price that was charged for the most nearly similar item. If none such existed, it was the price charged by the "most closely competitive seller of the same class." Who this might be could be debated. There were other dilemmas. Goods do not distinguish themselves sharply; one product often grades by infinitely small degrees into the next. No known exercise in legal incantation could speak to the difference in price appropriate to the difference in the number of buttons on two dresses. Also the regulation gave different people different prices for the same product depending on the price they had charged in March, with an indecent advantage to the person who had charged the most.

Many of these problems diminished as one moved back from retailers to wholesalers and manufacturers. The latter were certain to have sold some of every item in March. Product lines also acquired a more distinct identity. It was evident, nonetheless, that the General Maximum Price Regulation could be only a holding action. As quickly as possible it would have to be replaced by specific schedules, industry by industry and product by product. These would spell out in specific and unmistakable form the prices that would be allowed — and with random differences between sellers erased. Where necessary, these prices would also need to be tied to objective grades and standards. The ratio of peas to water would otherwise be gradually but infinitely widened against the peas and in favor of the water. The association of prices with specific grades and standards, including a reliable ratio of peas to water, would be our most controversial action. However, there was now a more immediate crisis.

* * *

In public administration good sense would seem to require that public expectation be kept at the lowest possible level in order to minimize eventual disappointment. The compulsion, however, is always to promise more than can be achieved. The General Maximum Price Regulation was issued with the usual excess of promises. The Office of Price Administration would be relentlessly firm in resisting all price increases. And in consequence prices would now be stable and the threat of a great wartime inflation would be in the past. Meanwhile an unperceived event was in train that would require a massive increase in prices of coal and electricity over a large area with further consequences for other prices.

The menacing event was the German submarine activity along the eastern seaboard. It meant that all coal shipments out of Hampton Roads had to be moved from the ocean-going colliers to the railroads. The increased cost was slightly over a dollar a ton. As one consequence of the higher cost of coal the whole utility rate structure of the area would be unhinged and likewise the cost of heating. Against our promise of no more price increases this was the immediate reality.

Our only hope was to have the government pay the added cost of the freight — a subsidy. For this we had no money. Only one man in Washington had large discretionary funds outside the budget — Jesse Jones as head of the Reconstruction Finance Corporation. He had been accorded them to rescue failing enterprises and now for war emergencies partly because he was thought adequately tight-fisted, the needs of congressional allies and admirers apart. I proposed to Henderson that we ask Uncle Jesse for money to keep delivered coal costs where they were; Henderson dismissed the idea as impossible.

It was, however, within my personal authority to make the request. Howard Tolley, my California teacher, an old Washington hand and now on my staff, pressed me to do so. I did not go directly to Jesse Jones but to his fellow Texan William L. Clayton, the great Houston cotton merchant, with whom in the past months I had formed a warm association, one which would continue in the years to come. Then sixty-two, Will Clayton was tall, strikingly handsome, beautifully attired, articulate, affable, assured and stubbornly his own man to the extent that he was not controlled by his always stubbornly liberal wife. In 1934, he had helped found the American

Liberty League to preserve American values, these being those of free enterprise as understood by Pierre S. Du Pont, numerous other Du Ponts, Winthrop Aldrich and John W. Davis. By the time of the election in 1936, impressed by the fact that his wife was matching dollar for dollar for the Democrats all of his contributions to conservatives, he was with F.D.R. He had now joined Jones, who did not feel that any business tycoon from Houston could be all bad.

Jesse Jones should have worried, for Will Clayton was now coming into close association with the young New Dealers. I had learned to call him to check any important action having to do with cotton. He would give his answer the same careful and detached thought that he would apply to his own decisions, often calling back with a further amendment. At four one afternoon we met in his spacious office in the Lafayette Building.[2] George W. Stocking, a liberal professor then from the University of Texas who was in charge of fuel prices, and Dexter M. Keezer, former president of Reed College in Portland, Oregon, were with me. Will listened to our truly passionate plea, took notes as always, studied them when we had finished and then excused himself. In fifteen minutes or less he was back; he had persuaded Jesse Jones to give us upwards of ten million dollars to pay the extra transportation costs and hold the line on New York and New England fuel prices and utility rates. We thanked Clayton to the extent that our astonishment allowed and made our way out in silent awe. In the elevator either Stocking or Keezer broke the silence to wonder what three college professors were doing in a job like this. That night Henderson was having a party for friends and members of his staff. He reacted to my proud announcement of our coup in total disbelief.

By the end of June 1946, $5.6 billion had been spent to offset exceptional wartime costs such as the loss of the colliers or to compensate for politically indispensable increases in farm prices.[3] Jesse Jones, who had provided much of the largesse, had come deeply to regret his role. In 1943, I went one day to the White House to discuss food subsidies with James F. Byrnes, who meanwhile had been

---

[2] A structure on the corner of I and 15th streets that Jesse Jones, in a narcissistic operation, had financed with a loan to a private builder against the security of a lease from the Reconstruction Finance Corporation.

[3] Seymour E. Harris, *Problems in Price Control, Part I. Stabilization Subsidies 1942–46*, Office of Price Administration, Office of Temporary Controls (Washington, D.C.: U.S. Government Printing Office, 1947), p. 14.

put in charge of the domestic aspects of the war effort. Jesse, who was being called on for the money — ordered, in fact, to supply it by F.D.R. — was sitting, a huge, aging, utterly forlorn lump, in Byrnes's anteroom in the new East Wing. After we had gone into his office, Byrnes asked me if I had observed the Jones grief over the money he was being forced to spend. "He's been out there crying all day," he said with obvious pleasure.

*   *   *

Those April days of 1942 were, as noted, the turning point in wartime economic management. Prices of products protected from control continued, not surprisingly, to rise after the General Maximum Price Regulation — the Consumer's Price Index for food went from 122 in May to 130 in October (1935–1939 = 100).[4] But the index as a whole in those same months went up from only 116 to 119, and the prices of fully controlled products were almost flat. Then in October Congress relented and allowed us to place ceilings on most farm products. And it instructed existing agencies to stabilize wages. Thereafter for the rest of the war and during the first year of peace prices were, for all practical purposes, unchanged. In 1943, the Consumer's Price Index averaged 124 for the year; for 1944, it was 125.5; through 1945, it was 128.[5] There was a slight upward drift, a gain of three or four points, in the first half of 1946. But even in that first peacetime year there was no substantial bulge until late summer when the controls and subsidies were brought to an end.

*   *   *

There is difficulty in praising convincingly an achievement with which one has been associated. Architects are not thought best for reviewing their own buildings, poets their own verse. However, the figures on the wartime accomplishment are objective. From 1941 to 1944, Gross National Product increased (in constant 1958 prices) from $264 billion to $360 billion and was only slightly lower in 1945.[6] By 1944, industrial production was *two and a half* times the prewar level. The output of durable manufactures was *three and a*

[4] Ibid., p. 238.
[5] Ibid.
[6] *Economic Report of the President, 1959,* p. 140.

half times.[7] Of the $360 billion of production in 1944, the federal government took $160 billion for the war or not much less than half.[8] And about half was used the following year. Unemployment, for all practical purposes, was at zero. This vast expansion, transfer, even convulsion, was accomplished without inflation. Inflation is part of the memory of World War I; also of the Ford and Nixon years; also, alas, of the Carter years. Inflation is not part of the memory of World War II. This stabilization of prices was not at cost to output or efficiency. The expansion in output itself belies that.

The theologically committed have sought, not without success, to minimize the role of this effort. That so much could be accomplished with the market, totem of totems, in partial suspense was deeply damaging to the established faith. So it has been argued that quality diminished and the black market expanded and there were disguised price increases. And also that the inflation was only postponed until the war was over, the controls lifted, the subsidies brought to an end. None of these objections can be entertained for a moment by the person of secular mind.

Quality deterioration occurred, but it is technically possible and economically feasible only for a limited number of goods. For steel, aluminum, gasoline, wheat, cotton, coal, it isn't technically possible, as a moment's thought will establish. For other products firmly identified with a seller or brand it isn't economically wise. People remember.

There was a black market for a limited number of items — whiskey, some meat, some gasoline. It was not something to which the ordinary citizen had recourse nor was it ever much a part of the American wartime memory.

When controls were lifted, there was, as noted, a bulge. In 1946, the Consumer's Price Index rose by a little over 8 percent; the following year it was up slightly above 14 percent.[9] It then leveled off. In 1978, it rose by 9.0 percent; in 1979 by 13.3 percent;[10] as this is written in mid-1980, it has increased in the last six months at an annual rate of 14.8 percent. In these years we have been at peace;

---

[7] Harris, p. 239.
[8] *Economic Report of the President, 1959*, p. 141.
[9] *Economic Report of the President, 1958*, p. 160.
[10] *Economic Report of the President, 1980*, p. 263.

the percentage increase in national product has been minuscule as compared with the war years. Unemployment has been greater by tenfold. No previous controls penned up the recent inflation.

*   *   *

Thus the achievement. But as earlier failure was unforeseen, so was success. Economics humbles its practitioners both in their optimism and in their doubts.

We were saved partly by the fact that the supply of civilian goods, while it did not keep pace with demand, increased beyond any pre-war calculation. Never in the long history of human combat have so many talked so much about sacrifice with so little deprivation as in the United States in World War II. In 1938, the last year of peace in the world, $140 billion worth of goods and services were available for personal consumption. In 1940, the last year of peace in the United States, $156 billion worth were so available at comparable prices. After four years of what were called wartime sacrifices, $173 billion worth were to be had in 1944 and were had.[11] More goods still were available the next year. Munitions, manpower and other military needs in World War II were supplied out of the increase in production with this further increase for civilian use. An unsuspected and mighty resource of the Republic was the idle plant and idle men of the depression by whose re-employment the war was sustained. A war that required a *pro rata* cutback in civilian consumption would be a new and disenchanting experience for Americans.

There was, to be sure, a change in the composition of the supply of civilian goods that became available. The supply of nondurable goods — clothing and other ephemeral products — increased. The supply of durable goods fell by about half, and some, such as new automobiles, ceased to be available at all. But here also there was a pleasant and unforeseen surprise. People did not pursue the dwindling supply, bid for it, run up its price in a black market. They saved their money for the cars and refrigerators and houses that would, they knew, become available after the war. And, less optimistically, they saved against the unemployment which, reflecting the depression experience, nearly all expected to recur.

Personal savings during the war years rose to unprecedented lev-

[11]*Economic Report of the President, 1959,* p. 140. These are at 1958 prices.

els, far outstripping business savings, which normally account for the greater share. By 1944, around a quarter of all disposable income going to individuals was being saved as compared with less than five percent in the last of the peacetime years, from five to eight percent in the years after the war.[12] Americans worked during the war not for current consumption but for the promise of future goods. Or simply for money. It was an extraordinarily deft way of getting current effort without any drain on currently scarce plant, scarce materials and scarce goods: much effort now in return for goods when the war was won and things were again abundant. One sorrows that such a superb design was not the product of foresight and planning.[13]

It owed much to the confidence of people in their money, confidence that dollars could be held without risk for later use. Had prices been allowed to run away, that confidence would have been dissipated, and therewith an absolutely indispensable wartime advantage would have been lost. Whatever else, our sense of the unwisdom of inflation was prescient.

*   *   *

We were successful also because, even in those days, concentration in American industry had gone far beyond the current estimate or appreciation of the textbooks. Oligopoly, the monopoly of the few, which had impressed itself on my classical thoughts at Harvard, was no longer the exception by 1941. For around half of the economic system it was the rule. Where a few large firms dominated an industry, as they did steel, aluminum, oil, chemicals, pharmaceuticals and many others, prices were already controlled by the seller. The supervening government control, however different in purpose, was not different in kind from what had been done under private auspices before. The administrative task was also greatly simplified. It is far easier to deal with a handful of large firms than with a plethora of small ones.

Compliance was also facilitated by industrial concentration. Surveillance was easier. The organization men of the great corporations,

[12] In absolute amounts individual savings were $2.9 billion in 1940, $38.4 billion in 1944. *Economic Report of the President, 1968*, p. 231.
[13] To this design I later gave the name "the disequilibrium system." The designation had a limited vogue. "The Disequilibrium System," *The American Economic Review*, vol. XXXVII, no. 3 (June 1947), pp. 287–302.

though they might dislike the controls, did not think it good personal or corporate strategy to violate them. Also a violation required the knowledge and participation of several or many executives, in short a conspiracy. There was always the chance that some excessively patriotic employee would squeal. Small entrepreneurs had far less reason to expect discovery.[14]

Far more manpower was required to control farm and food prices, cotton textile prices or rents than those of steel, copper or chemicals. It was in the smaller-scale industries too that political objection was encountered. In 1947, at the meetings of the American Economic Association in Atlantic City, I reviewed the wartime experience with price control before a sizable audience consisting mainly of my former colleagues in the enterprise,[15] and I later assembled these and other reflections on the experience in a small book, *A Theory of Price Control*.[16] After noting that producers and handlers of farm products "complained with especial bitterness of OPA regulations, perhaps partly because it is their nature to complain, but partly because, as participants in competitive markets, their difficulties were greater,"[17] I went on to a theorem "all too evident in this discussion" and rivaling in tautological truth the Coolidge dictum that when many people are out of work, unemployment results. The theorem is that "it is relatively easy to fix prices that are already fixed."[18]

Thus the reasons for the success. I have always thought *A Theory of Price Control* one of my more important books. No other combines such technical competence as I possess in economics with such experience in the subject. It was so regarded by its reviewers. But there were few of these and, initially, few readers of any kind. The experience persuaded me that one could spend one's life producing professionally well-regarded books that would go extensively un-

[14]The pristine capitalist entrepreneurs were harder to deal with than the good organization men. In the summer of 1941, in the course of some early negotiations with the automobile companies, I met with two Ford executives in Washington. They asked me to keep their visit confidential. Henry Ford (the elder) was not, at the time, according recognition to Roosevelt and the New Deal. Accordingly, he had forbidden members of the firm to meet with Washington agencies to discuss such matters as car prices.

[15]In a paper entitled "The Disequilibrium System."

[16]*A Theory of Price Control* (Cambridge: Harvard University Press, 1952; reissued in 1980.)

[17]Ibid., pp. 16–17.

[18]Ibid., p. 17.

read. And one could be even less fortunate. In the natural course of events, one's books come to those reviewers, the established specialists in the field, who are the strongest defenders of the established view. It is a system that selects an adverse jury for all inclined to innovation. I decided that henceforth I would submit myself to a wider audience, a decision that, in contrast with some others, I have not regretted.

* * *

In the 1950s, as the Cold War deepened, the government, through the Rand Corporation, commissioned a major study of economic mobilization — of the appropriate procedures in the awful event of another conflict. The best in acceptable thought was brought to bear. The recommendations followed faithfully the design that brought us so near to disaster in the dark winter of 1942.[19]

[19] "In principle, our program is very simple — to remove a generalized excess of demand for resources and output by direct limitations on the spending budgets of consumers, business firms, and the armed forces, and, once this inflationary potential is removed, to rely wherever possible on the price-income mechanism to allocate resources and distribute output. So-called direct controls over allocation and distribution would not be substituted for the price-income mechanism, but instead would be designed to stimulate or supplement it when it does not work quickly enough or aggressively enough to expand or divert output and when it actually obstructs the defense effort." Tibor Scitovsky, Edward Shaw and Lorie Tarshis, *Mobilizing Resources for War* (New York: McGraw-Hill, 1951), pp. 232–233. The authors proposed a system of expenditure rationing instead of taxation to resist demand. This is a distinction without an economic difference.

12

The Rough Game

IN THE LATE SUMMER of 1942, I went to Havana for a few days to visit my friend Carlos Hevia, a noted Cuban democrat and once for 72 hours (January 16–18, 1934) the President of the Republic. Hevia was now in charge of Cuban price control and rationing. He had taken the General Maximum Price Regulation and replaced the references to the United States with ones to the Republic of Cuba, but in the absence of either fear or enforcement, the effect was not noteworthy. My principal discovery in Havana was how great was my accumulation of fatigue; for the first two or three days I couldn't sleep and thereafter I could do nothing else. I then went on to Puerto Rico to address the problems being faced there in applying regulations designed for the mainland to goods that were subject to high, rising and uncertain shipping costs along with the additional uncertainty as to whether the goods would survive the submarines and arrive at all. I solved the problem by conceding extensive autonomy to the local officials; they could set prices at whatever level they deemed best.

This journey was the beginning of an association of many years with that beautiful island — with Luis Muñoz Marín, the first elected governor; Jaime Benítez, the Chancellor of the University; and Teodoro Moscoso, Jr., the originator of "Operation Bootstrap," which transformed the one-crop sugar economy into one with a substantially diversified light industry. Bootstrap did not make Puerto Rico a paradise. But no one who knew of old this neglected, exploited and overcrowded island, its worst slum lucidly named El Fanguito (The Mudhole), could doubt thereafter that progress is possible.

I sat one night during this visit talking with Rexford and Grace Tugwell — the great New Deal brain truster was now governor of Puerto Rico — on a terrace of La Fortaleza, the graceful old residence once of the Spanish and now of the American governors. An occasional ship passed below on its way into the harbor, the crews lining the rails to see the beautiful façades that masked the squalor behind. We were joined by Rupert Emerson, before and for many years after a Harvard professor of government, who in 1940 and 1941 had been in charge in the Department of the Interior of the American colonial world — Puerto Rico, Alaska, Hawaii, the Canal Zone. Now, after clashing with Secretary Harold Ickes, he had become head of OPA operations in the dominions beyond the seas. The effective government of Puerto Rico was then by the great sugar companies, by the port merchants of San Juan whose appalling markup on all merchandise was an expression of both their natural rapacity and the strength of their monopoly, and by the newspapers which reported only what was favorable to those in power. Elections were held at regular intervals, but they did not challenge the true rulers; votes were purchased by the power structure for compliant statesmen, who then behaved as required and rewarded themselves as needed.

It was Rex Tugwell's view that evening that were the Puerto Ricans encouraged to use their franchise honestly, great resources for self-improvement would become evident. I found this hard to believe. The world owes much to men and women who are undiscouraged by the voices of realism; in the next years Tugwell brought the United States government to the support of Muñoz Marín, who, in turn, proved himself one of the talented political leaders of the century. The grip of the old oligarchy was broken; democracy, it was shown, could be both humane and economically efficient.

I returned to Washington to the bitterest and in a perverse way the most interesting months of the war.

*   *   *

On September 7, 1942, F.D.R. requested an end to the effective exemption from control of farm prices: "I ask the Congress to take this action by the first of October . . . In the event that the Congress shall fail to act, and act adequately, I shall accept the responsibility, and I will act."[1] The Senate promptly responded by enlarging the

---

[1] Harvey C. Mansfield and Associates, *A Short History of OPA: Office of Temporary Controls*. Office of Price Administration (Washington, D.C.: U.S. Government Printing Office, 1947), p. 52.

exemption, this by an engaging exercise in statistical legerdemain. In the depression years the wages of farm labor were negligible; accordingly, when these wages were included in the index of prices paid by farmers, the index was brought down. And this in turn lowered the price to which the farmers were entitled under the so-called parity formula — the price that reflected the pre-1914 purchasing power of farm products. When the low depression wages lowered the parity price, their exclusion from the index of prices paid was righteously defended by the farm organizations. However, by now farm wages had risen sharply. To include them in the index would now raise the parity or just price. Accordingly, to include farm wages had become an elementary act of social justice. This also raised substantially the level below which no ceiling on farm prices could be set. Never had the subject of statistics been so serviceable. However, in conference, this concession was foregone, and, as I have told, on October 2, the day after F.D.R.'s deadline, we finally got full authority to fix farm prices. Three days later the General Maximum Price Regulation was extended to almost everything except fresh fruits and vegetables. And on October 3, James F. Byrnes was given general authority from the White House over all of the price- and wage-stabilization efforts and other domestic wartime programs of the administration. In December when, as I will tell, Henderson resigned, he became, effectively, my superior.

For controlling inflation I now had all the power I could possibly need. And as that power was deployed, the fear of inflation receded. But precisely as the fear of inflation disappeared, the fear of those controlling inflation took its place.

The politically most influential fear was that felt by the farmers as now their prices passed under control. In 1942, they were, I would remind, still numerous and (as still) very articulate. So were their defenders in the Congress. I collided regularly with commodity groups — the cattlemen, the dairymen and the wool growers, people that Ed O'Neal himself had once told me were too single-mindedly selfish to be tolerable companions in the farm movement. One meeting on cattle prices in those days turned into a three-day shouting match in which congressmen and senators from the range country joined. If higher prices could not be obtained by argument, then perhaps by intimidation. I resolved after this meeting to be forever a vegetarian. I didn't keep that resolution, but in spite of what the cigarette ads affirm I have never ceased to doubt that pursuit of cattle across a desert is uniquely in conflict with human values. Likewise the pursuit of sheep. One day that fall the Australian Minister came to see me about our price on wool. He was under frightful pressure and pled for understanding. "It's not only that these chaps are farmers; they also live out there with their rams."

Rationing was now being extended rapidly — to sugar, coffee, gasoline, shoes, some ten products in all in 1942. This added to our political difficulties. To forestall hoarding, all planning had to be done in careful secrecy. Then would come the sudden announcement without prior explanation or justification; inevitably it had a highly arbitrary resonance. Surely we were asking for sacrifice for the sake of the soul or to remind people that there was a war going on.

The political defense of price control was now increasingly in my hands, and I was, I cannot doubt, unduly self-righteous. I could not conceal my dislike for the lobbyists, trade association representatives, professional business spokesmen and hireling Establishment lawyers who sought to associate patriotism with the need for even more money than they were already making.

*   *   *

In the midterm elections in November, the Democrats lost heavily — 43 seats in the House and 9 in the Senate. The casualties were especially severe in the Middle West and included a number of firm supporters of the administration and the OPA. I was not thought to have helped, but the instant wisdom attributed most of the blame to coffee rationing. Scandinavian and German voters, among whom coffee use reaches addiction, were thought to have voted their indignation. The Office of Price Administration, as pioneer public opinion polls showed, remained overwhelmingly popular with the people until it was wound up in 1946. But this did not prevent our becoming a profitable object for political attack. Our liberal allies elsewhere in the administration, once concerned that we were doing too little, now believed we were doing too much too unfeelingly. Inflation had to be controlled. But surely it could be done in a politically more deft and conciliatory way. In Washington all alliances are kept subject to the exigencies of personal advantage.

Those in charge of the various OPA operations — rent, rationing, price control — together with the top lawyers and the inevitable mendicant advisers, men who are entrusted with speech but not authority, met each morning in Henderson's office to consider the state of our affairs. I there followed a most important bureaucratic rule: never enlarge unnecessarily on either your own problems or your own achievements. To do so is to involve others and dilute your authority. My first real sense of the adverse tide came one morning that autumn when Dexter Keezer reported that a couple of his senior subordinates were leaving the agency.

"It's now the mice," Leon Henderson observed, "who are leaving the sinking ship."

Then a few weeks later in December the intercom box on my desk barked, and Henderson summoned me down to his office on the floor below. Such calls were usually to hear the complaints of some senator, governor or senior business statesman. A visit to Henderson allowed the petitioner to tell others that he had got word through to those immediately responsible — that he had done all he could. This call, however, was to a meeting to tell us of Henderson's intended resignation. His health, his eyesight in particular, would not permit him to continue. Since he did not expect anyone to believe this, he repeated it several times with increasing emphasis and indignation. In fact, he was persuaded that there would be ever more severe attacks on our efforts and that he could blunt them by removing himself from the scene.

Leon Henderson was, I believe, never completely happy again. Divorced from public concerns, he did not wholly exist. He turned to a variety of advisory and business activities, none of which succeeded. Neither did a brief career as a radio commentator. As I write, he has been long in retirement in San Diego. The debt owed to Henderson for preparing the civilian economy for World War II has never been even partially recognized. Had it not been for his bold, intelligent actions and those he authorized, civilians would have suffered. And so assuredly would those who did the fighting.

*   *   *

Henderson was replaced by Prentiss Brown, a liberal former senator from Michigan, whose recent defeat had been generally attributed to his role in the handling of OPA legislation in the Senate. An agreeable man, there was little about the job that he understood and less that he wished to understand. The responsibility for price control now devolved even more fully on me. The attack that Henderson sought to defuse abated for only a few days. Then it was discovered that as long as I remained, the reform was incomplete.

The instruments of immediate pressure were press, radio and the congressional committees. Washington, and especially the White House in recent times, have developed a siege mentality toward what is now called the media. Our habit and, indeed, our instruction in those days was to take attack in stride. Chester Davis, my mentor on this, instructed me firmly as to the rule: if you hear your name mentioned on the radio, turn it off. If you encounter it in the *Congressional Record,* stop reading. Similarly if in a column. Whether favorable or unfavorable, the effect on you is equally adverse. I tried without success to follow his advice.

The *Washington Times-Herald,* then the erratic right-wing voice of Cissy Patterson, was the first to give attention to my efforts to subvert and undermine the American system. It was almost immediately joined by the *Chicago Tribune.* Only if one was attacked by the *Tribune* in its great aboriginal era under Colonel Robert R. McCormick (or while his influence remained) could one know the depths of the political depravity to which one could descend.[2]

In late 1942 and 1943, I was also increasingly and adversely on the minds of the trade journals. One, the *Food Field Reporter,* known as the bible of the food trades, amended its masthead to recognize my role. There, more or less permanently, was the slogan: GAL-BRAITH MUST GO.

On the radio, with a national audience and accessible to all with a

[2] I was still being instructed a decade later. One morning in 1956, traveling with Adlai Stevenson in the presidential campaign of that year, I stumbled awake in a depressing motel in the Quad cities on the Mississippi. The *Tribune* was outside the door. Across several columns went the headline: "THE MAN WHO THINKS FOR ADLAI." As usual, I ignored Davis's injunction. The article left nothing unfavorable unsaid. "Galbraith is Stevenson's specialist on economic and financial affairs . . . He used his powers [in World War II] to attempt to foist grade labeling on all canned goods in order to break down trademarks and brand names . . . The issue is now in the open, and it is simply this: Do Americans want to sacrifice their personal and economic liberty for a mess of socialist pottage?"

The inference was that they did not. It occurred to me in the next grim moments that from being a minor (or, as I thought, major) asset in the Stevenson campaign, I had become a grave liability. Later in the morning I encountered Stevenson and learned of his delight in discovering that the intellectual deficiencies which the *Tribune* had so often attributed to him were, in its new view, really mine.

complaint, was Fulton Lewis, Jr. Lewis was more vicious than mean. His theme was irresponsible, radical, reform-impelled youth. *Young* J. K. Galbraith, *young* David Ginsburg, others of the very young. And he was a pioneer in the technique later perfected by the noted columnists Messrs. Evans and Novak of maintaining an open line to any aggrieved politician, public official or lobbyist with an adverse interest and then reporting his grievance as accepted truth.

My wife during these years worked for the Department of Justice, where she was concerned with the activities of various foreign groups and associations of a possibly damaging nature.[3] One of her fellow workers listened faithfully to Fulton Lewis, and so regularly, on returning home, I heard what had been said about me the night before. Lewis would have been pleased that I did not escape.

However, the most effective attack on me was through the congressional committees, and this proved an education of lasting value.

*   *   *

Eight or ten committees had authorized access to our operations, and they provided a superior opportunity to both those seeking a change in our policies and those resisting change. The two appropriations committees had the most obvious leverage, for in order to obtain appropriations and then supplementary and deficiency appropriations our appearance before them had to be nearly continuous. The ranking Republican member of the House Appropriations Committee was an unforgettable upstate New Yorker, John Taber, who strongly opposed all of our activities, as he opposed all of the twentieth century. Dexter Keezer believed that so cosmic was John's hatred that he even hated himself. In later years, in files made available under the Freedom of Information Act, I learned that Taber had described me as an enthusiastic Communist and, among other

---

[3] One of her special concerns was Otto von Hapsburg, who was seeking at the time to form an Austrian battalion to fight with the U.S. Army. The question was whether as the last of the line he had sufficiently abandoned his claim to the old Empire of the Hapsburgs. If he had not, Czechs, Hungarians, Croats, Slovenes and others of the former subject peoples would be greatly repelled and lose interest in the war. After much unsuccessful FBI effort, Kitty resolved the case adversely for Otto by discovering in the Washington phone book that his personal telephone number and the number listed for the Austro-Hungarian Chancery were the same. Many years later we were invited to dinner with this pleasant, scholarly man in Davos, Switzerland. After some thought, we decided not to tell him who had done him in.

depraved tendencies, as being deeply doctrinaire. The latter condemnation was heard by the FBI agent as Doctor Ware, and for the next several years anyone checking into my file learned that I was heavily under the influence of this Dr. Ware. Eventually the FBI went back to Taber to recheck his view. He denied being the source of the accusation and said he had gotten the information secondhand from an operative of the Republican National Committee. There was some decency in the man.

The Senate and House small business committees, the two agricultural committees, the House Committee on Interstate and Foreign Commerce and, in later times, a committee on the abuse of executive power (the Special Committee to Investigate Executive Agencies), of which abuse I was considered virtually the sole source, all now became vehicles for attack on our regulations and, more especially, on my interpretation of my duties. It would be pleasant to see in the congressional committee the means by which a democracy, even under the stress of war, protected the rights of the citizen, but, alas, I was never called by a committee to answer the complaints of any individual voter. Even businessmen made their case directly to us. The congressional committees were the recourse of the lobbyists and the great law firms serving their interests. Some of the latter were voicing the fears and grievances of their clients; more were showing that they were vigilant in earning their pay. By the late winter of 1943, I arrived at the office each morning to ascertain what committee was investigating me that day. On occasion there was more than one. A year and a half earlier, the fear of inflation had brought out a concerned and friendly audience. Now people were reassured; one had only the exponents of the hostile view. Once or twice I persuaded representatives of consumer organizations to come and lend moral support. More often, some staff members apart, I was alone. Always there was the low theater — sad or angry denunciation, righteous or aggrieved response — which, if not enjoyable, was at least not boring.

Sometimes there was no audience at all. The hearing was a gesture to the lobbyists, a way of allowing them to prove they were doing their job. Such were the hearings of the Senate Committee on Agriculture and Forestry, the occasion for my most frequent trips to Capitol Hill.

*   *   *

The committee was then headed by Ellison DuRant Smith of South Carolina, known to the world as Cotton Ed Smith. He was supported in his outer office by his son, known to a smaller circle as Boll Weevil Smith. Any farm lobbyist or group with seeming grounds for a complaint about prices or merely in need of self-expression called Cotton Ed. Cotton Ed passed the complaint to Boll Weevil. Boll Weevil scheduled a hearing and summoned me.

Then seventy-nine, Cotton Ed was of massive build with large, slightly sagging jowls, sparse gray hair, used gray complexion and a flowing mustache, gray in the middle, a deep tobacco brown at the two ends. There was at the time a walrus in the Washington zoo that Paul Porter took his daughters to visit of a Sunday. They were very fond of it, and because of the resemblance they called it Cotton Ed.

Smith sat at one end of a long green-topped table, I around the corner on his immediate left. The lobbyist sat on his right and, by special courtesy of the chairman, was allowed to question me and find adversely on my actions, personality and motives as though he were a committee member. Occasionally a Republican would come in to sit morosely on the other side of the table. More rarely a newspaperman or two would be behind me in the room, chair tipped back against the wall, eyes vacantly on the ceiling.

Proceedings would begin when Cotton Ed fished a plug of tobacco from his pocket and took a large bite, although some always averred that it was the plug he put in his mouth and the bite that went back in his pocket. So provided, Cotton Ed's jaw then began a rhythmic three-phase movement, up, then forward, then far down to begin the round again. A small ooze appeared at the corners of his mouth, adding insignificantly to the pigment that was already on his mustache.

Cotton Ed's jaw and mouth were distracting. So was the result. Charles Dickens, when he visited the Capitol in 1842, was distressed that the cuspidor was everywhere the most conspicuous piece of furniture. Perhaps in consequence, by 1943, the spittoons had been withdrawn, and, accordingly, Cotton Ed was obliged to use the floor. Presently when you looked down, you saw brown rivulets approaching from under and beside the table, inching steadily across the marble floor. They were, you knew, quite harmless; yet as you concentrated on the committee's questions and your answers, you couldn't avoid moving your feet lest they be caught in the tiny flood.

One day while I was so concerned, I was also defending our ceilings on pork and pork products from attack by the representative of a swine-producers' association. It was a dreary show; the product has long been believed to lack charisma. Suddenly Cotton Ed rose to his feet, looked at me, looked at the farm representative, looked at a Republican senator dozing by the table and said, "Hogs! Hogs! Hogs!" Then he left the room. We were surprised.

*   *   *

Other committee assaults as the weeks passed were more serious. One, unforeseen, involved rayon hose. With silk gone and cotton déclassé, rayon stockings were the principal alternative. The surging demand could most easily be met by a fugitive product that would not last a washing or a week. We proposed standards specifying various levels of durability, with different prices attached to each. The explosion was nearly deafening. A parade of witnesses told the congressional small business committees that it was a clear case of consumer reform under the cover of war necessity. We owed it to the boys fighting in Tunisia and the Pacific that they come back to an economic system unsullied by such improvement. My answers were a lonely exercise in ineffectuality.

*   *   *

More violent was the great grade-labeling controversy. As canned goods came under the ration, we were, as I've noted, concerned lest a week's ration stamps for a family go for some thickened water and a few isolated vegetables. The solution was a moderate one. The armed forces bought canned products in accordance with United States government grades; this grading would now be extended to civilian sales. The grade would be stamped on the can, and the price, as for the stockings, would be according to the grade.

Nothing in Washington is more nauseous than the doctrine that a prestigious law firm may, with complete propriety, mount in Congress a paid political assault on the public interest, holding in defense that everyone is entitled to counsel. The suborning of legislative or administrative process for pay enjoys no high legal justification, and no one should concede it. The assault on prices and standards for canned products was orchestrated for the National Canners' Association by the great Washington law firm of (as it then was) Covington, Burling, Rublee, Acheson and Schorb. The press was alerted to the thought that grades and labeling might eliminate the often hypothetical differences between cans of tomatoes that were featured in the advertising. The farm organizations were told that, somehow, our prices and standards would reduce their prices so they should make common cause with their old enemies, the canners. The General Maximum Price Regulation had frozen different canners at different levels of prices. Our regulations eliminated these differences, which did not, needless to say, commend itself to those with the higher prices. Such flat pricing, it was contended, was especially ominous, for it was held to reflect some malign prewar design for reform on my part. A solitary embattled position, mine at the time, is not pleasant and certainly not persuasive. Grade-labeling had to be abandoned. It was not a decisive loss, but had wartime shortages and deprivation been greater, it would have been missed, and the service of the great lawyers to the war would have been understood more clearly.

A grave danger in such a battle is defection from your own ranks. Great pressure was brought to bear on the men recruited from industry to give guidance on the regulations. If they could be persuaded to say that their practical advice was ignored, as often for good reason it was, it would count heavily against us. It would prove that professors, including assistant professors, were playing impractical, purely theoretical games with free enterprise. During the grade-labeling fight two of our business hands were persuaded to bail out. One of them, a major manufacturer of baby food, was, however, forced to be restrained in his criticism. This restraint reflected his fear that, were he unduly outspoken, someone might publish a recent government report telling of the presence of assorted worms in the family product.

*   *   *

At other times that spring life fell yet further short of being good clean fun. The chairman of the committee to investigate my abuse of executive power was Howard W. Smith, a powerful senior figure in the Congress and the representative of nearby Virginia. He had been the principal sponsor of the Smith Act, which required the finger printing of all aliens and the punishment of all who advocated or taught the overthrow of any American government by force or violence or who organized or belonged to an organization so dedicated. He would not during their lifetimes have tolerated Washington, Jefferson, Jefferson Davis or Robert E. Lee, though in 1940 he did introduce legislation to celebrate the 200th anniversary of Thomas Jefferson's birth. Smith turned over the investigatory task to one Harold L. Allen, who had been brought down from New York for the purpose. Allen combined prosecutorial meanness with extreme incompetence and, it developed, a vulnerable record.

His thought was to prove that our plans for reform were not only sinister but long predated the war. To this end he had a survey made of the Ph.D. theses that had been submitted by various members of the OPA staff, an undoubted breakthrough in the search for subversive intent. Mine on the expenditures of California counties did not serve. However, he assumed that my treatise *Modern Competition and Business Policy* with Henry S. Dennison had somehow earned me my degree. His manner in pursuing the questioning, including his confident presumption of my guilt, would have been thought distasteful even if directed at someone given to child abuse.

Mr. Allen: So, Doctor, what you had in mind here in drafting this order was the correction of competitive inequities between manufacturers?

Mr. Galbraith: That was one of the factors.

Mr. Allen: That was the subject of your doctor's thesis, wasn't it out at, where was it, California or Harvard — *Modern Competition and Business Policy,* by Dennison and Galbraith — was that your doctor's thesis?

Mr. Galbraith: No, sir.

Mr. Allen: That is one of your supplementary works?

Mr. Galbraith: That is a book I participated in the writing of.

Mr. Allen: And the inequities subsisting in competition between efficient and inefficient producers was one of the subjects dealt with here, was it not?

Mr. Galbraith: It is some 4 or 5 years since I have looked at the book. Your familiarity with it is somewhat greater than mine, apparently. I do not know.

Mr. Allen: Well, the elimination of inequities among competitors has long been a subject near to your heart, has it not?

Mr. Galbraith: I shouldn't say so; no.

Mr. Allen: It has been a subject to which you have devoted considerable study?

Mr. Galbraith: If you are trying to develop the point that I am, by seeking to establish dollars and cents or flat prices here, plugging some personal theory of my own, the answer is "no; I am not."

Mr. Allen: Well, I will bear that in mind, thank you.[4]

It is essential for good democratic process that adversary, even hostile proceedings have an overlay of civility, however transparent. Of this Allen was unaware. After the first morning, I returned to my office in a precarious balance between fury and contempt. I faced many more such sessions, including another one that afternoon.

But there wasn't to be another session. Awaiting me at the office was a lawyer on our public-utility-pricing staff, an old New York political hand, and he had a story.

Ten years earlier Harold Allen had been Second Deputy Commissioner of Police in New York City and a great activist in the suppression of crime. A major and, some thought, necessary form of lawbreaking in those days was the sale of unstamped and thus untaxed beverages that were on hand in quantity in bars, saloons and speakeasies when the prohibition laws were repealed.

A popular watering place under suspicion for the sale of such stocks was the bar of the St. Regis Hotel. One night Allen led a posse of policemen to the hotel and, stationing the uniformed men outside, went in to examine the goods. He bought a drink and, the evidence of its illegality being perhaps unclear, bought several more. Untaxed or not, the booze was indubitably intoxicating. Allen became troublesome and had to be restrained by a couple of newspapermen who were drinking in the bar. At this point he remembered his duty, blew his whistle, and the police came in and closed the place. His procedure came under criticism from the newspapers. Mayor Fiorello La Guardia did not approve. There was a public investigation, and Allen was sacked.

I faced a moral dilemma. Allen was investigating the abuse of power, and these were his credentials. I could advert to them in the next session, which would put the press on his trail. Or I could warn him that I planned to do so. That would be close to blackmail. I followed the obviously decent course and sent him word of my intention. Soon I got a call that the hearing for that afternoon was

---

[4] U.S., Congress, House, Special Committee to Investigate Executive Agencies, H.R. 102, 78th Cong., 1st sess., April 14, 1943, p. 157.

canceled. A few days later Allen returned to New York, and the investigation petered out. Two wrongs do not make a right, but as to two abuses of power it is not so clear.

*   *   *

As the spring of 1943 passed, many of my original colleagues — John Hamm, David Ginsburg, Harold Leventhal, Ben Heineman, Henry Reuss — departed. Mostly it was the draft, but there was also the feeling that a few more men thrown to the wolves would ease the attack. During those weeks my wife had our second son.[5] In 1941, her hospital room had been so filled with flowers that it reminded us of the recent last rites in Chicago of Greasy Thumb Gusick. Now there was only one rose from our garden. I was no longer worth the price. A minor episode triggered my departure.

Prentiss Brown had brought from Michigan an advertising man named Lou Maxon to improve, as it would now be said, the image of the agency. Lou told the press that it was my image that was most in need of repair. And, less wisely, he said he would intervene in policy so as to ensure it. When queried, I told the papers that Lou could mind his own damn business. The exchange then became acrimonious. F.D.R. was once believed to enjoy squabbles between his subordinates. Now he had tired of them and thought they were diverting attention from the larger war abroad. He sent word that we both could go, though I was to be given another major post. Harry Hopkins told Ed Stettinius, who had been put in charge of Lend-Lease, to employ me, and Ed offered me the job of Lend-Lease Administrator in South Africa. Prentiss Brown, when he broke the news on the morning of May 31, 1943, invited me to say that my health was a factor in leaving OPA, but this I declined to do. The applause on my departure was brief but intense; not often have I so succeeded in pleasing conservatives. In the next OPA appropriations bill, a bill of attainder was attached — the anti-professor amendment it was called — prohibiting professors from setting prices. The amendment, obviously unconstitutional, was ignored.

*   *   *

[5] Douglas Galbraith, who died of leukemia seven years later.

On the next few months I do not find it altogether pleasant to dwell. The sudden loss of power leaves you suddenly, unimaginably empty, facing decompression and a psychic case of the bends. You are assailed, however unnaturally, by self-doubt. And by continuous thought of the decisions that now lack your guiding hand. Worst of all, and least expected, you are now naked to your enemies. You are attacked and you no longer have the accustomed means — secretaries and typists, press officers, readily assembled newsmen — with which to make the needed reply. The months of accumulating fatigue also flowed over me like an oily stream.

After catching my breath, I spent a few summer weeks at the Lend-Lease offices in an apartment building near the present site of the State Department. For the beautiful Edward Stettinius I was a terrible affliction, politically damaging but, because of the White House, to be suffered. Soon I discovered that his agency as a whole had few identifiable functions and now, with the Mediterranean newly open and ships no longer going around the Cape, none at all in South Africa. I abandoned thought of going there and joined a task force consisting of the kind of executives who believed Ed Stettinius a leader and which was considering whether machine tools bought by Britain with Lend-Lease should be reclaimed after the war. Such retrieval would keep British industry from having an unfair competitive advantage because of the free capital and advanced technology so provided. I thought the idea silly, as it was, and discovered with joy that George Ball, who, as associate general counsel, had the New Deal watching brief on Stettinius, wholly agreed. It was the beginning of a friendship that united us on many political and public adventures.

Herbert H. Lehman then asked me to join him in planning for the agency that was later to become the United Nations Relief and Rehabilitation Administration (UNRRA). My new job was mildly useful, but there are grave limits to the amount of time that one can spend on such planning. Indeed, at the end of the first week I had suggested everything that could be suggested. Again I faced the most terrible of all public experiences, a job and an office and no visible work.

I had not yet been called by the draft. After securing the requisite signature from my wife, I went over to my draft board to volunteer. Previously I had been told that this would be an idle gesture; my height was two and a half inches more than the services could clothe or otherwise assimilate. In what may have been a somewhat irregular procedure, someone at the draft board telephoned over to (as I recall) Fort Myers and ascertained that this was still true. I would like to say that I was disappointed. I was not. As a youngster in Canada I had been required to train with the high school cadet corps. Military choreography, it developed, was beyond me. On inspection days I was made to fake illness and remain in uniform on a bench. The school thus got paid for my training, and I didn't ruin the parade. Now, though I was relieved, my conscience was not entirely clear. Months later I would greatly welcome a chance arranged by George Ball to associate myself with military matters, without any marching, and go to Europe and the Pacific. But meanwhile, in the absence of any occupation in Washington, I called Ralph Delahaye Paine, Jr., the extraordinarily civilized managing editor of *Fortune,* and accepted a standing invitation to join his editorial staff. There, though I had not previously written for profit, I was an immediate success. *Time, Life, Fortune* and Henry Robinson Luce are a story in themselves, one that belongs mostly to the postwar years. I must first finish the war. I've told of the incomparable banality of the beginning — the night of Pearl Harbor. The days preceding total victory were, for me, more satisfactory.

13

Germany, 1945

As the war began at that feckless meeting of the men in hasty dress, I think of it as ending in a resort hotel in Luxembourg. The hotel, once modestly fashionable, was long, low, white, with a veranda running full length along the front. Before it was a waterless fountain and pool with a sun-baked water nymph in the middle. All around was a high barbed-wire fence covered top to bottom with a greenish-yellow camouflage cloth. There were guards and machine guns. A sergeant at the gate told an applicant for admission one day that he had to have "a pass from God, and someone to verify the signature." It was, indeed, that rarity among jails, one far easier to leave than to enter.[1]

It had been the principal hotel of Mondorf-les-Bains in Luxembourg, a few miles southeast of Luxembourg City on the French border. One evening in the early summer of 1945, we had finished interrogating the inmates for the day and were waiting inside on the central stairway for our transport. On one side below was the main lounge of the hotel, on the other to the left the dining room. A heavy thunderstorm was lighting the rooms from outside — great vivid flashes that were followed almost instantly by the crashing thunder. The faces of the men now waiting for dinner, some reading, some chatting, some standing alone, some sitting quietly on the lounge chairs, were all familiar. Angry, expostulive, barbaric, fearsome, they had dominated the newspapers for fifteen years. Julius Streicher, after Himmler the most appalling of the Hitler acolytes, was there. Also Dr. Robert Ley, the head of the *Arbeitsfront;* Joachim von Ribbentrop, the foreign minister; and Walther Funk, the head of the Reichsbank. Present in slightly dismantled uniforms were Hit-

[1] I wrote of this hotel and its occupants in "The 'Cure' at Mondorf Spa," *Life,* October 22, 1945, pp. 17–24.

ler's immediate military staff — Field Marshal Wilhelm Keitel and Colonel General Alfred Jodl, men whom Albert Speer a little earlier had called the nodding donkeys. Grand Admiral Karl Doenitz was also there and Field Marshal Albrecht Kesselring, the last commander on the western front. As we waited for our car and they waited for their dinner, the lightning and thunder continued, and a colonel standing with me had a sudden, astonishing and valid thought: "Imagine anyone back in 1940 risking a play — *A Hotel in Luxembourg in 1945* — with this cast and setting. It would have been laughed out of town."

The hotel at Mondorf was the place of detention for the highest Nazis. Code names in those days had acquired a certain archness, and the spa was called Ashcan. It was under U.S. Army direction; a British counterpart near Frankfurt for more technical prisoners, including Speer and the alleged financial genius Hjalmar Horace Greeley Schacht,[2] was called Dustbin.

Hermann Goering was not with the men awaiting dinner but in a bedroom upstairs. A large mattress had been spread on a narrow army cot to make him more comfortable, and it hung out over the sides. Goering, his vast, loose bulk collapsed on the bed, gave the impression of sagging farther over the mattress edges. He was suffering from drug withdrawal, my only encounter with this torture or, indeed, in a sheltered life, with drug addiction. His commitment, like that of Howard Hughes, had been to codeine, and he had an ample stock when taken prisoner. The U.S. Army cure had involved only abrupt confiscation.

Others also were undergoing rehabilitation. Ribbentrop, Funk and Ley had been continuously drunk for months, a natural enough recourse for shallow, even primitive men who still, when sober, were able to see the inevitable. Drink was escape. Albert Speer in earlier interrogations had said, "In the last months one had always to deal with drunken men." He went on to guess that when the history of the Third Reich was written, it would be said that it drowned in a sea of alcohol.[3] Ribbentrop had on his person when taken prisoner two last-minute appeals to the British for peace that were of his own

[2] Our interrogations of Schacht showed him to be a man by then impervious except to financial cliché and with almost no knowledge of what had been going on.

[3] It wasn't, in fact, ever said; the convention that protects the political and military lush and his inebriated actions and decisions extended to the Nazis. Even Speer's memoirs omitted mention of the drunkenness.

composition and reflected the general Nazi hope for common action against the Russians. They were addressed to the Honorable *Vincent* Churchill. One thought of a letter to *Albert* Hitler.

The guests at Mondorf were not a terribly useful source of information. Goering, heaped pathetically on his mattress, knew little of Luftwaffe operations for which, nominally, he had been responsible and even less of economic and military matters in general. He gave whatever answers he thought would most likely please his four interrogators or would foreclose the subject and get us away. The air attacks, he said, had devastated German war production, which was not so, but it was what he thought Americans would wish to hear. Others were uneasily sensitive to the darker corners of their past, a matter which came up because we had been asked to get them on the record, to the extent possible, on war crimes. Field Marshal Keitel had been head of the army honor court that had hung those officers with complicity, real or suspected, in the July 20, 1944, attempt on Hitler's life. When first questioned, he couldn't remember that anyone at all had been sent to the meathooks. The penalties for lying to his captors, possibly exaggerated for the occasion, were then made known to him, and his memory improved. He sought us out not once but twice with upward revisions. Ribbentrop had no knowledge at all of the concentration camps until his memory was similarly assisted. Then he told of hearing of them while ambassador to London and warning Berlin of their adverse diplomatic effect.

As a matter of much interest, Ribbentrop was pressed on why Hitler had declared war on the United States after Pearl Harbor, an act with such an electric and unifying effect. He told of Hitler's belief that for all practical purposes the United States was already at war with Germany, an incredible thought for anyone who had been in Washington in those days. And he cited Germany's treaty obligations to Japan. A Lieutenant Stein who was handling translations then asked a further question on his own: "Why was that particular treaty the first one you decided to keep?"

                    *   *   *

In those sunny early summer days, the inmates, not a bookish group, spent most of their time walking up and back on the long veranda. Julius Streicher always walked alone. Once we saw him turn to the dry hole in front of the hotel and come to attention, his arm raised in the Nazi salute. We judged that he was back at Nuremberg, and a battalion of brownshirts was marching by. After a few minutes he relaxed, lowered his arm and resumed his solitary walk. The others seemed uneasy. The nymph in the dry pool showed no response.

The generals at Mondorf had remnants of bearing and dignity. General Jodl had gone so far as to rebuke one of his early interrogators, Major General Orvil Anderson, and my notes have his exact words: "You are trying to kill Germany; we want to fight wars in the old way and give up a province or two when we lose." Why now an unsporting animosity? In contrast with the soldiers, the civilian Nazis looked shabby, depressed and wholly repellent. Stripped of neckties and belts to deter suicide and extensively unshaven, they would have fitted easily into the daily scene at Leavenworth.

When we were finished at Ashcan, I flew back down the Moselle to Frankfurt and on to my headquarters at Bad Nauheim. Our work was important enough for airplanes but not in my case for a safe one. So I had a Canadian C-64, underpowered by its one engine for the six passengers it was meant to carry. That day I was alone with the pilot, an Americanized Belgian who had wanted to fly fighters and who did the best with what he had. (A few days later he survived a crash, and so did I from not being with him.) On the morning of our flight he had, with my help, persuaded Colonel Burton C. Andrus, the jailer at Mondorf as later at Nuremberg, to take him on early rounds through the hotel. The effect had been deeply depressing. He had always supposed from the vast scale of the conflict that our opponents were heroes. A few weeks later I was to write of his disillusion: "Who'd have thought that we were fighting this war against a bunch of jerks?"[4]

* * *

My passage to Mondorf and Bad Nauheim had begun in the winter of 1945. The yet earlier and deeper origins were in the nature of aerial warfare, now forever to me a hideous thing. All of the wartime bombing, accidents apart, being on the far side of enemy lines,

[4]"The 'Cure' at Mondorf Spa," p. 24.

knowledge of the destruction depended on the reports of those in the bombers or later aerial reconnaissance. Neither source was given to understatement; neither air crew nor photographs minimized the admittedly ghastly consequences. Accordingly, in the autumn of 1944, George Ball was asked to assess, *ex post,* the support given by the Air Force to the Normandy landings and the success of the airmen in denying the Germans access to the front. He went on to propose a much more ambitious assessment of the results of the strategic bombing of Germany. Similar suggestions came from the Air Force itself, and President Roosevelt, reflecting on the claims of the air generals, also urged such a study on Secretary of War Stimson. Out of the several proposals in November 1944 came the United States Strategic Bombing Survey. It was to be independent of the Air Force, although advised and supported by it, and independent and accurate in its findings. Accuracy to many of the Air Force generals had a somewhat specialized connotation; it meant establishing with some clarity that the bombers won the war.

The head of the USSBS was Franklin D'Olier, a colonel from World War I and thereafter the first national commander of the American Legion. He was now chairman of the board of the Prudential Insurance Company. An amiable figurehead, D'Olier was nonetheless concerned to ensure independence of judgment and appropriate standing vis-à-vis the Air Force; to this end he had asked that the directive establishing the USSBS be signed personally by President Roosevelt. D'Olier accorded general direction to Henry C. Alexander, a handsome and intelligent lawyer upwardly mobile from Murfreesboro, Tennessee, to a partnership in J. P. Morgan and Company. Alexander, in turn, saw his task as one of clearing the way for those who would conduct the actual investigations; this he did with energy and resource, and also grave fear that as a Morgan partner he would be discovered serving in the wartime New Deal. That would make the sky fall in. Former Communists are not the only Americans who have experienced paranoia in past times.

The Survey was organized in directorates — transportation, aviation, weaponry, the cities — each corresponding to a target or target system of the bombers. A special division headed by Dr. Rensis Likert, a pioneer in public opinion research, examined the morale of the German civilians under the bombing. For this task Likert recruited, among other unlikely warriors, W. H. Auden, the poet, and Nicolas Nabokov, the composer. "It was bad enough," a German woman in Cologne was said, perhaps apocryphally, to have complained, "to have your house destroyed and your family buried in the rubble. But then we were asked how we liked it."

A secretariat of three Boston lawyers — Associate Justice of the Superior Court of Massachusetts Charles C. Cabot of the Cabots, Colonel Guido R. Perera and my long-time Cambridge neighbor and friend, then-Colonel James Barr Ames — was to have the task of assembling the work of all the investigating groups and writing the ultimate report. Perera, an articulate and forceful man,[5] had played an important role in getting the Survey organized, as earlier, alas, he had been influential in selecting the targets for the bombers. Like the Air Force generals, he had some tendency to identify ultimate truth with earlier design. And neither he nor Charles Cabot, a trim-figured, trimly mustached, handsome man, was accustomed, as a member of the most revered Boston legal establishment, to having conclusions challenged, as they would be, in a brash, uncouth way. Both also believed, perhaps rightly, that a decent respect should be shown the air generals — Henry H. Arnold, James E. Doolittle, Carl A. Spaatz and Ira C. Eaker — who had carried the burden of the war.

Colonel Perera had been a powerful advocate of the great attacks on the German ball-bearing plants in Schweinfurt on August 17 and October 14, 1943, the most disastrous operations in the history of aerial warfare.[6]

*   *   *

For our task we were thought to need military advice, and for this we had Major General Orvil A. Anderson. Orvil Anderson was a large-boned man with a roughly carved face and a badly weathered complexion. In World War II, Air Force officers affected a casual as

[5] Who graciously made his literate, privately published autobiography available to me.
[6] Nearly one-third of the planes participating were lost or disabled beyond repair; unescorted attacks had to be abandoned; the Eighth Air Force did not operate usefully again for some months; and no identifiable harm was done to German war production. *Summary Report (European War)*, United States Strategic Bombing Survey, September 30, 1945, p. 5.

distinct from a spit-and-polish style. Orvil went further and managed to look as though he had slept in his uniform. His personal assistant and constant companion was a WAC captain of pleasant, rather stately aspect. Henry Alexander disapproved of such associations.

Anderson had served his Air Force apprenticeship under Brigadier General William (Billy) Mitchell whom he revered. He had once set an altitude record as a balloonist and had flown the civilian mails when F.D.R., following the discovery of corruption in the civilian air mail contracts, gave this job to the Army, with numerous crashes and serious casualties as a consequence. He was highly intelligent, without tact, believed in air power as others believed in the Holy Spirit and was compulsively articulate. His brilliant and youthful colleague, Colonel (later Major General) Ramsey D. Potts, once told me how one of the greatest upward swings in Orvil's career was accomplished. In Washington one day early in the war when Anderson was a staff officer, his mastery of nonstop conversation exhausted the patience of Henry Harley Arnold, the head of the Air Force, and also the limits of the sunny disposition that caused Arnold to be called Hap. He told Anderson to proceed to Bolling Field and place himself aboard whatever airplane was that day going the greatest distance from Washington. Anderson asked if that was an order; Arnold replied that it was from the heart. So Anderson went to London and out to Eighth Air Force headquarters at High Wycombe, where, in accordance with custom, he again occupied himself in nonstop talking. Then one day when the planes had gone out on a mission and General James Doolittle, the commander, had gone into London to get a uniform fitted, the meteorologists called to say that fog would soon close in and all the fields in southern England would be inaccessible. Earlier, the RAF had experienced such a turn of weather; fields and hillsides were splashed with planes. Although not in the line of command, Orvil moved in and called back the mission. The aircraft made it just in time. His reward was to be put in charge of operations, and from this job he had come to the Survey.[7]

* 			* 			*

[7]Orvil Anderson's military career came to an abrupt end in 1950 when he was sacked as Commander of the Air War College by General Hoyt S. Vandenberg for saying that he would willingly lead a bomber force against the Soviet atomic energy and weapons centers.

George Ball brought me into the Survey in the very early spring of 1945 to have charge of the overall economic assessment of the German mobilization effort and the effect thereon of the air attacks. Our first planning sessions were in the partners' room at 23 Wall Street, in Henry Alexander's private office and in the Morgan private dining room. I thereafter took leave from *Fortune* and went down to Washington to recruit a staff. Then and later in London with the assistance of Burton H. Klein, an Air Force captain and later and still a professor at California Institute of Technology, I assembled one of the more diversely talented groups of scholars ever brought together for a single research task. It was not difficult. As the war came to an end, many highly qualified people were becoming available in civilian Washington. More could be combed out of the armed services and were full of joy at their rescue from the now besetting idleness. The British, more cautious or xenophobic than we, had not used fully the scholarly talent that had taken refuge on their shores from Germany, Austria and elsewhere in central Europe. These men we also hired; they knew German and Germany well and had a highly motivated desire to serve.

My subordinates, in a manner of speaking, for in the long history of human conflict few in any military formation were so little given to any form of obedience, were a roster of the famous of the next economic generation. Nicholas Kaldor, later Lord Kaldor; E. F. Schumacher of *Small is Beautiful*; my old partner Griffith Johnson; Paul A. Baran, with Paul Sweezy to become the most distinguished and by far the most entertaining of American Marxists; Tibor Scitovsky, another noted economist; Edward Dennison, later to become one of the leaders in modern statistical analysis; and many more. Everyone — American, British, erstwhile German or Hungarian — was given a rank theoretically reflecting his previous civilian station in life and told to provide himself with an officer's uniform, which he then wore without insignia of rank. Some tried to sustain a slightly military bearing.

*   *   *

On April 12, 1945, I was ready to leave for London where we were to be based and went back to New York for a small farewell celebration. Toward evening one of the guests, Letty Hamm, wife of my OPA colleague John Hamm, called to tell us between sobs that the radio had just reported that President Roosevelt was dead. We assembled that night less in gloom than in shock. We had come to suppose that F.D.R. was forever. He had been so for twelve years, nearly all of our adult lives. The following morning I went to Washington on the train with another committed Roosevelt man, Nelson Rockefeller. We speculated on the effect on our future, politically and otherwise. Nelson guessed — as it turned out, rightly — that he would survive.

The next day before dawn George Ball and I left for London from Patuxent, Maryland, by NATS (Naval Air Transport Service). Those who have flown only in the modern jet cannot know how unpleasant was an ocean crossing in those primitive bucket-seat planes. It was not the discomfort but the tedium. The better part of three days was required; it was too dark to read, too noisy and too cold to sleep. Endless hours up to Stephenville in Newfoundland; endless hours down to the Azores; a long, long day to Prestwick near Glasgow; a final flight to London. Never did life so nearly stand still as on those journeys. Before departure one had a movie that depicted the procedures to be followed when the plane ditched and filled up with water. If all other recourse failed, one could always turn one's mind back to that film.

Our London headquarters was in Grosvenor Square, in the offices lately abandoned by Dwight D. Eisenhower and SHAEF.[8] Many who now visit London must wonder how so much of the eighteenth- and nineteenth-century city survived the Blitz. The explanation is partly that tourists tend to go to the West End, and it was the City and the dreary proletarian wastelands to the east that got the bombs. But also the destruction was selective, a building or part of a street here and there. Not until one got to Cologne, Hamburg, Frankfurt or Berlin did one see cities in which every building was an empty, roofless shell. For me they remained an utterly sickening sight. When I first went to India, to Calcutta, I was similarly appalled by the poverty, but after living there a few weeks, I found that my eyes had developed an impermeable glaze; I no longer reacted to the deprivation. The devastation of the German, and later and especially of the Japanese, cities is with me still.

In Germany as in London the bombing had a nasty class aspect.

_____
[8] Supreme Headquarters, the Allied Expeditionary Forces.

The densely populated working-class districts got the full force of the bombs; often the affluent outer suburbs escaped.

*   *   *

In London I assembled my economics faculty and divided them into industrial sections corresponding roughly with those of the Gross National Product. (In coming months our statisticians would calculate the first GNP figures ever for Germany.) The wartime production or performance of each sector — capital equipment, construction, basic materials, weapons, labor supply — was to be established, as also that of the important industries therein. Special attention was to be given to the production of weaponry. The effect of the air attacks both on aggregate output and on the individual industries was then to be assessed. All of this arranged, my economic warriors were dispatched to Germany to follow the armies in the final days and look for the figures and the people who could interpret them.

In the original plan other teams would inspect the burned and battered factories. And specialists were deployed to do so. They learned only that the factories were very burned and battered. Such inspection did not show when or by how much production had been curtailed. For this the production records were needed, and even these told little of the effect on the output of the industry as a whole or of the ultimate effect on weapons production or, beyond that, on military operations. Did oil shortages ground the airplanes or only civilian transport? Did the destruction of the factories eliminate the German Air Force or was it lost in combat? For the full answer only the overall statistics and the interpretation of the statisticians, officials and generals would suffice. That interesting task was ours. So, accordingly, was the resulting influence on findings. As ever, it was not to my regret.

*   *   *

With the end of the war with Hitler only weeks away, Washington was planning the final attack on Japan. Information was wanted on what the bombers had accomplished over Germany, and this we were being pressed urgently to supply. I now followed my teams to the scene both to see what useful information they were procuring and to satisfy my nearly uncontrollable curiosity as to the effects of the war.

On that first trip to Germany we billeted ourselves at a temporary headquarters outside Cologne. Immediately adjacent were acres upon acres of tulip fields in full bloom. They were a wonderful relief from the devastation. I clambered across the ruins of one of the great bridges over the Rhine to examine the remains of an engine plant on the east bank; it was in very poor condition, and it was there that I realized how little could be learned from inspection alone.

I was back in London on V-E night, a curiously passive scene. Everyone was in the streets and looking for the behavior of someone else that would make the evening memorable. There was none of the wild emotion that, one knew, had marked the ends, false and real, of World War I. At Buckingham Palace the King and Queen did appear on the balcony along with Winston Churchill. He, a small, distant, indistinct figure, gave a V-for-victory sign; it wasn't very impressive. Next morning early I went to Biggin Hill Airfield and back to Germany.

*   *   *

George Ball and I made our headquarters that spring and summer in Bad Nauheim, the pleasant spa town on the autobahn 20 miles north of Frankfurt. We occupied a small private hotel, Villa Grünewald, on the outskirts; our economists and the supporting military staff were in the much larger Park Hotel in the town center. The Germans, accustomed to Prussian standards of military attire and decorum, viewed us with wonder. D'Olier, the secretariat and various others of the higher command remained in London while George Ball developed deeply unflattering theories as to their occupation there. George concentrated his attention on the effect of the bombing of the cities and with Paul Nitze, another director, on the meaning of our findings for the Pacific war. I remained with the economics.

That allowed me to visit the various teams and guide or participate in the interrogation of senior German military and civilian figures, who were now becoming available in volume. One traveled along highways and autobahns through two nearly continuous lines of foot-travelers, one line going in one direction, the other in the opposite. It was hard to suppose that the end of the war had found any European at home. As word passed that there were Americans in the neighborhood, soldiers came out of the woods to surrender. Military prison meant regular meals. On May 11 in Augsburg I stopped at army headquarters while my driver found out the way to a high-level prison camp where we were to interrogate Wehrmacht generals. An American sergeant asked me to take along a German SS general who had just arrived in a reconnaissance vehicle and was trying to surrender. I told him to follow me to the jail. On our arrival, I found that I was turning in Hitler's greatest military favorite, Sepp Dietrich.

A section of the autobahn between Munich and Augsburg had been converted to an airstrip, the center concrete being painted green to disguise the change. In cul-de-sacs along the road were curious-looking aircraft, sleek and without propellers. One wondered if they had been delivered without them. They were, in fact, the Me-262s, the first jet fighters, and a full technological generation more fearsome than anything we or the British possessed. Only a monumental error — Hitler's demand that they be redesigned as a light attack bomber — had kept them from being used with disastrous effect.

In Munich one of our teams came upon an impressive breakthrough in the art of economic warfare — a printing plant and some 130 millions in five-pound bills.[9] They were to be dropped on Britain. Polish engravers had been brought out of the concentration camps for the work and shot when it was finished; the Germans did not wish such accomplished counterfeiters to survive. At Garmisch we interrogated the crew of a radio-directed repair train that moved out on call to replace rails and ties destroyed by bombs. The repairs, they said, could be quickly accomplished. But eventually they were prevented from reaching the breaks that most needed repair by the need to repair the numerous breaks in the track that allowed them to get there. A difficult problem.

On another afternoon I stopped to visit the fathers at Kloster Ettal and to join them over glasses of their liqueur, which I had first consumed in an adjacent bistro seven years before. For the moment there was a lack of comity within the Church. The fathers spoke with the utmost bitterness of the Franciscans and their cautious relations with the Nazis. In Munich that same evening the Stars and

[9] My notes say dollars, but that seems implausible.

Stripes were flying over Adolf Hitler Platz. An American Army band, with great gusto and marvelous sound effects, was rolling out *Right in der Führer's Face.* The crowd thronging the square looked relieved and appreciative. It was much better than London a week earlier. A few hours later I got orders to go to Flensburg on the Danish border for the most important interrogations of that year.

*   *   *

Already there were indications that we might have to change our view of German economic management during the war. People have believed for four hundred years that the Armada was defeated by God and a tiny British force when, in fact, it was outgunned by ships of greatly superior range, greater size and only slightly inferior aggregate tonnage. The myth of ruthless Nazi competence established during the war years still endures. In reality, German war management was for a long time halfhearted and incompetent.

In both the American and British views at the time the German war economy was effectively and powerfully mobilized. In the American metaphor it was the "tightly stretched drum"; in British intelligence it was a "taut string." It followed that any production of almost any kind that was denied by air attack was serious. It could not be replaced by reduced civilian consumption, for that was at a minimum. It could not be compensated for by increased overall production, for that was at the maximum. There was no slack.

Between British and American air-power strategists there was an historic disagreement as to how the taut German economy should be attacked, necessity being as ever the parent of belief. The Lancasters and Halifaxes of the RAF (and also the unarmed all-wood Mosquitoes) could fly only at night; by day they were hopelessly vulnerable. In the dark they could find only the cities, and from this technological imperative came the conclusion. The cities were the ideal target; by destroying them, one would inflict irreparable damage on German war production and also, perhaps, on the German will to fight. The heavily armed American planes could go by day and find specific industrial targets, although it was early discovered and at heavy cost that they needed fighter escorts. (It was learned more gradually that to find a target was not necessarily to hit it. Nothing in World War II air operations was subject to such assault as open agricultural land.) But however bitter the disagreement between the USAAF and the RAF and their supporting staffs, and also among the Americans on which industrial targets to hit, there was total agreement that much damage was being done to the German war economy. This we in the Survey also assumed.

Our first indication that something was wrong came in London before the fighting stopped. It was a superb statistical find, the *Statistische Schnellberichte zur Kriegsproduktion* or the German statistical overview of war production.[10] The factories producing tanks, self-propelled guns and assault guns — Panzer in the German military designation — were not a primary target. But they drew on labor, coal, steel, ferroalloys, machine tools, transportation and all the lesser resources and fabrics of industrial life. A general disruption of the German economy could not be meaningful if it did not affect the production of these items. In 1940, the first full year of war, the average monthly production of Panzer vehicles was 136; in 1941, it was 316; in 1942, 516. In 1943, after the bombing began in earnest, average monthly production was 1005, and in 1944, it was 1583. Peak monthly production was not reached until December 1944, and it was only slightly down in early 1945.[11] For aircraft (as I shall later tell) and other weaponry the figures were similar.

Very soon George Ball's investigations of the attacks on the cities would produce some equally disturbing conclusions. Thus, for example, on three summer nights at the end of July and the beginning of August 1943, the RAF came in from the North Sea and destroyed the center of Hamburg and adjacent Harburg. A terrible firestorm sweeping air and people into the maelstrom caused thousands of casualties. Destroyed also were restaurants, cabarets, specialty shops, department stores, banks and other civilian enterprises. The factories and shipyards away from the center escaped. Before the holocaust these had been short of labor. Now waiters, bank clerks, shop-

[10] It carried the highest German security classification, and this was rendered in English as "top secret." The translated documents remained on my desk one night and there attracted the attention of night prowlers on the lookout for security violations. I spent an hour or so next morning urging that because something was a German secret, it did not automatically become an American secret, not at least at that stage in the war.

[11] *The Effects of Strategic Bombing on the German War Economy,* United States Strategic Bombing Survey, October 31, 1945, pp. 278–279. These figures are from the *Statistische Schnellberichte zur Kriegsproduktion,* supplemented and checked by other documents from the German Ministry of Armaments and War Production (the Speer Ministry). They are not necessarily the exact series that I saw in the initially captured document, but the effect is wholly the same.

keepers and entertainers forcibly unemployed by the bombers flocked to the war plants to find work and also to get the ration cards that the Nazis thoughtfully distributed to workers there. The bombers had eased the labor shortage.

We were beginning to see that we were encountering one of the greatest, perhaps the greatest miscalculation of the war.

14

Albert Speer and After

ALBERT SPEER, forty in 1945, was tall, slender, with dark, slightly sparse hair and a mobile, sometimes amused face. In all respects, including the touch of humor, he was strikingly in contrast with the other Nazis, as he himself was fully aware. And it was evident by his behavior that he had every intention of putting the greatest additional distance between himself and the primitives, as he regarded them. Guessing rightly that, when faced with the Nazi abominations, they would plead ignorance, the guilt of others, their own inability to exercise corrective influence or even their personal righteousness, he had decided that he would accept his share of the responsibility. That would accentuate the difference.

In earlier years, in contrast with that of Goering, Goebbels, Himmler or even Julius Streicher, Speer's name had attracted little public notice in the United States or Britain. However, in the intelligence agencies, notably in the OSS in the United States, he had become a major figure, the German miracle man. He had worked wonders with German war production. On the effect of the air attacks in particular, no one else would be his equal in authority so, as an intelligence target, a phrase then coming into use, he was at the top of the list.

In Germany in 1945, there was no civilian government, no newspaper apart from *The Stars & Stripes*, no trains, no post, no radio. Information came irregularly through army communications or unreliably by word of mouth. On even the most important matters one stumbled in ignorance, and this included the movements of the high Nazis. In consequence of the talk of an Alpine redoubt, the first search for them was in Bavaria, and it was there that Goering was found. But the more important movement had been from Berlin to Flensburg on the Danish border, and this, initially, we did not know.

However, shortly after the surrender, two of our junior staff members, Wolfgang Sklarz, a second lieutenant, and Harold E. Fassberg, a technical sergeant, were poking through some scratch office buildings in Flensburg, and they came upon Speer's name on an office door. In his testament of April 29, specifying the succession and signed the day before his suicide, Hitler had excluded Albert Speer from office, but the Führer's authority, not surprisingly, had dwindled. Speer was now head of the theoretical Ministry of Economics and Production in the equally theoretical government of Admiral Doenitz.

It remains a mystery as to why this government was allowed to function, so to speak, through most of May 1945. It had an army, one that was so packed into the city of Flensburg that there was, quite literally, almost no pedestrian space on the streets. German soldiers moved in one direction or the other all day in two dense field-gray waves. But the city and the army apart, the government had neither territory nor function. It was said at the time that SHAEF had a conceptual problem: how did one take the surrender of a government that had ceased to exist in consequence of its unconditional surrender? Some Germans believed that the Americans and British were seeking to preserve a Nazi nucleus to keep the Soviets in line. Against this explanation, which was nonsense in any case, was the presence of a sizable Russian mission in Flensburg.

On May 19, I flew there in our Survey C-47 to join the interrogation of Speer. We circled the airfield until we had assured ourselves that other Allied planes were on the ground and thus had survived the mines. Colonel D. E. Smith, who was with me and who was what the British in India once called a very pukka soldier, gave an arm-breaking salute to two uniformed officers who marched forward to greet us. They turned out to be of the Luftwaffe. We learned that we had billets on the *Patria,* a Hamburg-America Line vessel that had waited out the war in the harbor of the mostly undamaged city. The waiters, who had also been overlooked, served us breakfast and lunch in the sparkling spring sun on the veranda deck.

Speer had taken living quarters in Schloss Glücksburg, the castle of the Dukes of Holstein a few miles from town, a handsome structure with a moat of lakelike proportions. We reached it in jeeps and requisitioned transport; a Jewish lieutenant of German origin, telling George Ball and me that he was settling old scores, persisted in driving through the pedestrian masses at breakneck speed. At the castle the captain of the SS guard, a small, unfearsome-looking, rat-faced man greeted us each day and bowed us into the great hall, a vast rectangular room with a low vaulted ceiling. For the interrogations we used a small room on one side at the far end.

These were conducted brilliantly by George Ball, who, with almost no help, proceeded with confidence on topics on which he was manifestly uninformed. American clerical talent being as usual in the Army of that time unavailable, Speer's secretary was recruited to transcribe the proceedings. These lasted for three days. We met at noon, for, as a superb example of the power of organized inertia, the German cabinet continued to meet each morning at eleven to consider the nonexistent tasks of its nonexistent state. Speer himself was far from enchanted. At our first session he proposed that we arrest him and so spare him this *opera bouffe,* which with some pride in his mastery of the American idiom he called "Grade B Warner Brothers."

On the second day when we arrived at the castle for the afternoon's business, Speer had disappeared. His secretary was in tears; the little SS officer was wringing his hands in deeply unmilitary distress. We learned that a party of men had come to the castle at five that morning, arrested Speer and taken him away. The secretary and the SS man both thought that it had been the Gestapo. Speer had been talking very freely, and Himmler was known to have been in the vicinity. While we considered these improbabilities, Speer came in, smiling agreeably. An OSS team had arrived in Flensburg the night before, heard of his presence and moved to arrest him first thing in the morning. They took him to a headquarters they had requisitioned in the town, where toward noon Speer told them he had an appointment. They replied that he would not be keeping appointments for some years, but when he explained that it was with some Americans whose names by now he knew — a Mr. Ball and a *Dr.* Galbraith — it was decided that his capture had been ill-considered. He was driven back to the castle and deposited outside the moat. There had been a mixup between two unduly eager intelligence teams. Speer assured us that this kind of thing "was always happening under Hitler."

*   *   *

No defeated government looks good. Had the Germans or the Japanese come to Washington, they would have been appalled by the inept nontalent that had been unloaded on the wartime administration or that had found shelter there. But after all allowance, the story of defective planning, bad judgment and incoherent administration that Speer added to our earlier assessment was impressive. It was supported by an armful of documents from his ministry which, thoughtfully, he had brought out of Berlin to a bank vault in Hamburg and which we promptly sent people to retrieve.

The first and most sweeping defect was inherent in the German conception of mobilization planning. Earlier at a meeting in Bavaria, Nicholas Kaldor, in a mood of tense excitement, had outlined a preliminary and, as it developed, accurate hypothesis. All knew of the acceptance by Germany of the Blitzkrieg as military doctrine — the commitment to the all-powerful, quickly completed military thrust that had destroyed Poland in 1939, the Low Countries and France the following spring and which, in the summer and autumn of 1941, had carried the German armies to within sight of Moscow with the intention of ending the Russian campaign in that year. What had not been recognized was the counterpart application of the Blitzkrieg doctrine to war production. This held that from a modest weapons-producing capacity, stocks of tanks, other vehicles, aircraft, ordnance and ammunition could be accumulated. These stocks would then be expended in a great, rapid, ruthless, victorious push. In the next pause before the next push, stocks would be built up again. The thrust being fast and successful and the pauses between adequate, the continuing output of weapons and the requisite factory capacity did not need to be very great, and there did not, accordingly, need to be much sacrifice of civilian consumption. So it was in the early years of the war.

The American and British belief, as noted, was of a highly organized Germany — the taut string. And equally in the early years, of a dilatory, uncommitted Britain. In 1940, from an economy with a total output some 30 percent smaller than that of Germany, the British produced more military aircraft than Germany, nearly as many tanks and many more of other kinds of armored vehicles. In 1941, a year for which more complete comparisons can be made, British war production far surpassed that of Germany in almost all categories.[1] "The general picture of the German war economy . . . is not that of a nation geared to total war. It is rather of an economy initially mobilized for fighting relatively small and localized wars, and subsequently responding to the pressure of military events only after they became harsh facts . . . For the war against Russia, fuller preparations were made, but preparations which hardly strained the capacity of the economy . . . Soon after the attack began some important types of munitions output were allowed to decline on the premise that the war would soon be over . . . [T]he Germans did a far from distinguished job in managing their wartime economy. Both Britain and the United States moved much faster . . ."[2]

As the production objectives in Germany were low, so were the standards of performance. This was Speer's first point of emphasis. The Nazi cabinet members and the *Gauleiters* were men thrust suddenly into high position and great power. Few were technically or intellectually up to wartime tasks. Nearly all responded to their new income and authority with unabashed hedonism. They did not generally see the need for sacrifice in civilian consumption, and, in any case, they were stoutly unwilling to set an example. "If a *Gauleiter* won't give up his servants, he cannot tell others to do so."[3] In September 1944, Germany had 1.3 million domestic servants as compared with 1.6 million in May 1939.[4] As late as 1943, 50,000[5] Ukrainian women were imported for household service. Meanwhile German women were not mobilized for factory work in any appreciable numbers. Speer, an ardent reader of *Life* magazine, told of his

[1] There were 20,100 military aircraft produced in Britain to 10,775 in Germany; 4845 tanks to 3790; 16,700 guns of 20mm and over to 11,200. Burton H. Klein, *Germany's Economic Preparation for War.* Harvard Economic Studies (Cambridge: Harvard University Press, 1959), p. 99. Only in small infantry arms and torpedoes was German production in 1941 appreciably larger than that of Britain. Colin Clark, the British-Australian statistician, estimated Britain's prewar national income at around 70 percent of Germany's (Klein, p. 96). Klein, to remind, was my deputy in the direction of the economic studies of the U.S. Strategic Bombing Survey.

[2] Klein, pp. 235–236. Perhaps this modest early effort reflected also aversion to the thought of another war of economic and human attrition, an aversion which remained in Germany, and also France and Britain, as a legacy from World War I.

[3] The quotations from Speer are as in my notes, but it is possible that I then paraphrased his statements or answers.

[4] *The Effects of Strategic Bombing on the German War Economy,* United States Strategic Bombing Survey, October 31, 1945, p. 204.

[5] Speer said or was understood to say 250,000, and this figure gained some currency.

discontent at seeing pictures of American war plants full of seemingly eager women workers. Nazi doctrine held that the proper concern of women was with *Küche, Kirche, Kinder* — kitchen, church and children.

More incredibly, few industries, continuous process operations apart, had a night shift in Germany during the war. Nor was the workweek much lengthened. Foreign workers, voluntary and compelled, seemed in limitless supply, but the slave workers, needless to say, were not highly motivated. Expansion was by adding more plant capacity and more day shifts.

Speer was eloquent on his efforts to have French workers produce weaponry in French factories for the Germans, this instead of bringing them to Germany. But as the war progressed, Frenchmen, not retarded in such matters, learned that being at work in one place made them vulnerable to the agents of Fritz Sauckel, the German plenipotentiary for labor. They could be seized *en masse* or in the needed skills. Accordingly, absenteeism became a matter of elementary caution. Speer then had especially important French factories placed under the protection of his ministry with the promise that their workers would not be carried off. Sauckel responded with plans for raiding these establishments, although this roundup did not, it appears, come off. Nonetheless the vigor with which Sauckel pursued Frenchmen earned him the title in Berlin of "Father of the Maquis."[6]

Surrender did not end the animosity between Speer and Sauckel. In Flensburg Speer left us with the impression, without ever quite saying so, that Sauckel should rank high on any war criminal list. Sauckel, under interrogation in the same days in South Germany, was more forthright: of Speer he said, "There is a man you should hang." Sauckel was hanged.

*   *   *

Speer gave other less persuasive reasons for Germany's casual performance. Britain by Dunkirk, the United States by Pearl Harbor, had, he thought, been shocked into great effort; no similar disasters had shaken Germany out of her accustomed bureaucratic and administrative habits. Not even Stalingrad had wholly served. "The

[6] See my article "Germany Was Badly Run," *Fortune*, vol. XXXII, no. 6 (December 1945), pp. 173–200.

soft men and the weak were never sorted out and discarded as they were in Britain and the U.S. The weak remained in positions of responsibility to the last."[7] In his journals published thirty-three years later, he observed, as had Goebbels, that the German wartime slogan was wrong. It was, repetitiously, "Victory is certain"; "Blood, Sweat and Tears" would have been better. George Ball, Paul Nitze and I, veterans of wartime Washington and the frequently easygoing or delaying tendencies there, were not so greatly impressed.

More impressive was the effect of Hitler's persistent intrusion on technical decisions, especially those involving ordnance and aircraft. Of such matters the Führer knew a good deal and in all cases enough to be damaging. Nor was he the only source of trouble. The Luftwaffe under Goering was a special administrative disaster. Until the winter of 1944, it controlled its own plane production, and air generals back from the front could order modifications that they deemed desirable without knowledge of the effect on production, and they often did.

Hitler also dismissed unwelcome information as irrelevant. Thus from late 1942 on, American war production figures were sufficiently satisfactory so that they ceased to be secret. It was also thought that they would have an adverse effect on German and Japanese morale. Instead Hitler made light of them, calling them propaganda. Nor were others perturbed, for he forbade their circulation.

Other intelligence, Speer noted, presented a different problem. The German intelligence agencies, as later investigation established, had information of the utmost accuracy on the exact day and the particular beaches on which the Normandy landings would take place. There had been, however, no good way of choosing between the report that was right and some twenty or thirty others on the same subject that were wrong. It's a difficulty that often recurs in the intelligence business.

*   *   *

From the relatively superficial mobilization of the German economy in the early years came the paradox of the German war performance. As sources of raw materials were lost, territory diminished

---

[7] United States Strategic Bombing Survey Special Document, *Speer on the Last Days of the Third Reich*, p. 2.

and, most of all, as bombing intensified, war production increased. And it increased enormously. Not until the autumn of 1944, when the Western Allies were on the frontiers of the Reich, did German war production reach its peak. It was then three times greater than it had been in early 1942, when Speer had taken charge after Fritz Todt, his predecessor, was killed in an airplane crash. It remained high into 1945.[8] Speer's success was the result not of getting more out of a tightly organized economy but of improving belatedly and substantially on a nearly trivial early performance.

There were, however, some singular accomplishments. The Germans showed great energy and resource in dispersing, reorganizing and repairing plants and facilities after the air raids. The most damaging of the strategic air attacks were on rail transport and the synthetic oil plants. These did not immobilize the German Army or Air Force, although they did increase the time required for troop movements, and the availability of gasoline became a consideration in planning military operations. (In the planning of the winter attack in the Ardennes in 1944–45, for example, some of the fuel was to come from captured stocks.)[9] At the peak, 350,000 men were engaged in the repair of the huge synthetic oil plants, in their dispersal and in building new underground facilities, which, however, were still unfinished when the war ended.[10] A spectacularly successful effort was made to retrieve aircraft production after attacks on the airframe plants, those producing all of the airplane except the engine.

This last achievement, a matter of much controversy, first came to our attention in Flensburg. In the last week in February 1944, every known airframe plant in Germany was attacked; 3636 tons of bombs were dropped.[11] Losses of the attacking American bombers, though they were under escort, were heavy. In January, before the attacks, 2077 combat aircraft — fighters and bombers — were produced by the Germans. In March, the month after the attacks, production was up to 2243. By September 1944, when the peak was reached, production was nearly twice what it was before the raids.[12] There was

[8] As shown by the index of all munitions production. *The Effects of Strategic Bombing on the German War Economy*, p. 283.

[9] This was later confirmed by Speer in his own book *Inside the Third Reich* (New York: Macmillan, 1970), p. 417.

[10] *Summary Report (European War)*, United States Strategic Bombing Survey, September 30, 1945, p. 8.

[11] Ibid., p. 6.

[12] *The Effects of Strategic Bombing on the German War Economy*, p. 277.

some shift after the attacks from making bombers to making fighters, but in the immediate aftermath there was an increase in both. The Germans managed to retrieve by proceeding with great energy to get the machinery, mostly undamaged, out from under the rubble, and they then got it going again in neighboring schools, halls, churches or wherever space was available. Meanwhile management of the industry was shifted from the incompetent Goering and the Luftwaffe to the more effective Speer ministry. It could be argued that the effect of the air attacks was to increase German airplane output.

On the evening when we first discussed these figures on the deck of the *Patria,* Orvil Anderson's voice broke, and he asked, "Did I send those boys to do that?" However, he soon recovered his poise and gave his attention initially to faulting the German statistics and, when that proved impossible, to seeking to have them overlooked.

The Luftwaffe was, indeed, ineffective by the time of the Normandy landings. But this was because it had been defeated as a combat force; it was not that it was short of planes.

* * *

In the mornings in Flensburg, we brought lesser Nazis to the *Patria* for questioning — I made special note of the interrogation of Franz Seldte, a minister of labor under Hitler. Using our license to inquire into war crimes, we asked him for his views on the concentration camps. He told us with some passion that he had advised Himmler that they were an "unauthorized cruelty." Offered a chance to visit them by Himmler, he had declined. He then asked us to consider the figures on the population of the camps and the deaths there in relation to the total population of the Reich. Statistically they weren't so bad.

On another day, after the interrogation of Speer had ended, we drove across the border to Denmark and on to Fredericia, the old fortress city that was besieged and occupied by Bismarck. For miles above the frontier the German army was in an unbroken line as it made its way down from Norway and northern Denmark. Some pulled their gear on children's wagons; some pushed it in baby carriages. Some officers were on bicycles. Since quite possibly we were the first Americans seen on that road, we were, *pro tanto,* heroes and liberators to the Danes. Housewives reached into their baskets for flowers, and one, despairing, threw a cabbage. Orvil Anderson, against orders, had flown over Germany with his airmen; none of the rest of us had heard any shots fired in anger and only the odd ones in drunken glee. Yet our fraud was strangely pleasant.

As we strolled through the town that night, a large crowd assembled behind us, and the neighborhood barber identified himself as the head of the local resistance. Almost forcibly he turned us into his shop for a celebratory drink of Danish whiskey. Paul Nitze questioned him on German atrocities and his own resistance role, but on neither was he completely satisfactory. As to atrocities, the Germans had cut off his supply of condoms, a major item of barbershop revenue, and he suspected them of feeding their troops saltpeter as a substitute. As to resistance he told us firmly that he had not shaved a single German officer since the surrender. That was now nearly two weeks before. No one should generalize from so small a sample.

*   *   *

On May 22, the interrogation of Albert Speer at Glücksburg lasted through the afternoon. And, word having come that the future of the Doenitz government had finally been resolved, it lasted all night, though for some reason it was moved to a nondescript house in the town. I kept the notes.[13] Rightly anticipating that this would make one of the more dramatic stories of the war, our questions turned much on the last days in Berlin and in the Führerbunker. It is a story that would be retold, first by Hugh Trevor-Roper in his classic *The Last Days of Hitler,* later by John Toland and others and in his memoirs by Speer himself. Then, as in the retelling, it was the story of Hitler's flight from reality; of divisions being moved and committed when they were down to 600–800 men; of largely imaginary forces coming to the rescue of Berlin; of the moment of total joy when word came of President Roosevelt's death with the thought that Harry Truman would see the light and move on to fight the Russians.

Speer told also of his own conviction in the last weeks that the war was lost; of Hitler's increasing sense of Speer's highly rational de-

[13] These were written up, and the resulting report was lost in intelligence archives for thirty-four years. While she was checking documents for these memoirs, it was discovered by Londa Schiebinger, my friend and assistant, and published in *The Atlantic* in July 1979 under the title "The Speer Interrogation: Last Days of the Third Reich."

featism; and of a meeting on March 27 in Berlin when Hitler told Speer that it was "impossible" for one in his position "to deny the hope of victory" and that he was to go on leave, using ill health as the excuse, the same excuse that had been used three days earlier to dismiss General Heinz Guderian. Speer refused to dissemble and said he would resign instead. Hitler explained that he could not afford such a resignation, adding to Speer, "Were you an officer, I would have no choice about what to do with you. But you are my old artist, and I feel differently."[14] A little later Speer, as did so many others, yielded to the Hitler presence and told the Führer, "I stand unreservedly behind you."

We heard also that night of how, by failing to make available the requisite explosives, Speer had subverted the scorched-earth policy that Hitler had ordered in the final weeks. And he told also of his thought of bringing Hitler and the war to an end by introducing tabun, an exceptionally deadly nerve gas, into the air intake of Hitler's bunker in the Chancellery garden. There were major elements of fantasy in both of these accounts. A scorched-earth policy is not easily carried out in a highly industrialized country under any circumstances; there is much too much to scorch. By a disorganized army in rapid retreat it would have added only marginally to the previous destruction. When withdrawal becomes urgent, bridges can be blown, but there cannot be a pause to destroy factories, power plants, railway yards and the rest. Speer's belief, which others have shared, that he saved the German people's livelihood is nonsense. As to his plan for giving all in the bunker terminal neuralgia, it was but one of several enterprises that crossed his mind for ending the war, including the kidnapping of individuals in Hitler's immediate entourage and their delivery by plane to the Western Allies. He code-named these proposals the Winitou cases for an American Indian hero in German children's literature. The gassing was aborted when the air intake pipe was suddenly lengthened and he couldn't reach up to drop in the tabun. None of the other plans were acted upon. None would have been. They acquired a more serious aspect only with the later retelling.

Speer also told of his eleventh-hour visit to the bunker over the night of April 23–24 after recording a last-minute broadcast in

[14] The language here is from my notes. In the document based on these notes and in Speer's memoirs, the wording is slightly different.

Hamburg against the scorched-earth policy. It was a perilous passage from Rechlin airfield, first in a Focke-Wulf 190 to Gatow, the western aerodrome of Berlin, then in a reconnaissance plane to land on the East-West Axis, the great avenue through the Tiergarten, where he narrowly avoided collision with a truck. By now the Russian troops were only a few hundred yards away. Hitler was much touched by Speer's thoughtfulness in dropping by. Earlier at his birthday celebrations on April 20, he had announced his intention of staying in Berlin until the last moment, then flying south to the Bavarian Alps as Goering would do that same night.[15] In the three days since his birthday celebration, Hitler had changed his mind and become "almost" reconciled to seeing it out in Berlin. He told Speer that at the end he would shoot himself, and he was concerned lest his body fall into the hands of the Russians. Martin Bormann, "the Mephisto to Hitler's Faust," was still urging flight to Bavaria. Keitel, Jodl and their staff had by now departed the vicinity — Speer noted with contempt that Keitel had succeeded in passing through the entire war without ever coming within the most distant range of the guns. Now remaining with Hitler on the night of April 23 were only Bormann, the Goebbels family, Eva Braun (who Speer said would always be a disappointment to historians as a mistress because she was such a comfortable, agreeable hausfrau type), Generals Hans Krebs and Wilhelm Burgdorf and a few others of lesser rank. Hitler had been greatly depressed by the mass exodus — by the sudden discovery by so many, as Speer put it, that they had urgent business elsewhere. "[He] was always convinced that his followers [whatever their reliability or devotion] were unquestionably men of courage. He was, Speer observed, quite wrong."[16]

At four in the morning of April 24, after offering his place on the plane to Magda Goebbels who declined, Speer flew out to Rechlin where he encountered Himmler. Himmler told Speer of his peace negotiations through Count Bernadotte of Sweden and of his conclusion that he was the only man on whom the Allies could rely to keep order in the defeated Reich. Thus he would be found indispensable to them. Speer now offered Himmler his plane to go and

---

[15] Goering believed that he would be well received by the Americans. It was Speer's view, strongly expressed in Flensburg, that because of his incompetence Goering had, indeed, been our best friend.

[16] *Speer on the Last Days of the Third Reich,* p. 10.

see Hitler and urged him also to make himself available, by surrender, to Montgomery. Himmler declined both offers.[17]

*   *   *

My notes tell with quite exceptional precision that on the morning of May 23, after the Speer interrogation was over, I got back to the *Patria* at 7:15 A.M. and slept until 8:15 A.M. Then, with Drew Middleton of the *New York Times,* I watched from an upper deck while Admirals Doenitz and von Friedeburg came smartly along the quay, saluted the ship and flag and marched up the gangplank. The Third Reich at that moment came finally to an end. Admiral von Friedeburg, who had participated in the earlier surrenders in Rheims and Berlin and was perhaps becoming distressed by the repetition, asked to be excused to go to the washroom. There he shot himself. As we went to the airfield to fly back to Bad Nauheim, thousands of German officers were being marched away.

*   *   *

In Bad Nauheim my life had only the excitement enjoyed by any administrator of a large-scale statistical enterprise. In a small office off the terrace of the Park Hotel I read preliminary reports of the effect of the attacks on diverse German industries, conferred tediously on the meaning and reliability of our masses of figures and considered where more information might be unearthed and who might be found among the German officials to interpret it. I struggled also to keep our people on the job; with the European part of the war over, travel over Germany in pursuit of fugitive information seemed much preferable to work at a desk. And not all such enjoyment could be denied. I issued an order: "Junkets are herewith prohibited except on Sundays. A junket is any business trip which if taken by anyone but yourself would be considered unnecessary."

*   *   *

Not quite all was routine. There was the problem of the care and management of Paul Baran. A technical sergeant in rank, Baran was one of the most brilliant and, by a wide margin, the most interesting

[17] In the days preceding this meeting with Speer, Himmler had been roaming aimlessly in the vicinity of Flensburg. Later he was taken into custody by the British and, while being given a routine examination, bit a cyanide pill.

economist I have ever known. He was currently celebrating the end of the war with the Germans by intensifying his ongoing war with the United States Army. Then thirty-five, Baran had a background that brought all security officers who looked into it to the edge of nervous collapse. His parents were Polish Jews of some means at Nikolaev on the Black Sea, his father a distinguished specialist on tuberculosis and an active Menshevik in his younger days. According to Paul, the elder Baran was on good terms, political differences notwithstanding, with Lenin and the other old Bolsheviks. After first welcoming the October Revolution, he moved away from it to Poland and then to Germany but returned to Russia in 1925 where he remained until his death. Paul stayed behind in Germany to complete his education, returned to Russia in 1926 to enroll in the Plekhanov Institute of Economics at Moscow and then, after a couple of years, went back to study again at the University of Berlin. In the mid-thirties, again in Russia, he got word that he would have to be over the border by January 19, 1935. That was because, though a Communist, his acceptance of Communist discipline was very like his response to the discipline of the United States Army. In the presence of any pressure to conform, Baran's mind turned compulsively to the most annoying possible expression of dissent.[18]

In his Berlin years Baran, along with his own studies, wrote Ph.D. theses for solvent, ambitious but otherwise inadequate colleagues and worked for an advertising agency where he gained distinction for a memorable advertisement for a male contraceptive. It showed a gravestone on which were engraved the words: "Here lies no one. His father used NIMS."[19]

In the late thirties, Baran arrived at Harvard, impressed all with his amused intelligence and went on to serve brilliantly during the war in the OSS. This latter service was to the despair of the House Un-American Activities Committee, which, more or less simultaneously with his appearance on our rolls in 1945, exposed him as a certain subversive. How could anyone with such a background be otherwise?

[18] This history relies heavily on a memoir by Paul M. Sweezy, "Paul Alexander Baran: A Personal Memoir" in *Paul A. Baran 1910–1964: A Collective Portrait,* Paul M. Sweezy and Leo Huberman, eds. (New York: Monthly Review Press, 1965), pp. 28–80.

[19] My recollection of the brand name is impressionistic.

Baran's war with the Army was tactically diverse. His uniform attracted immediate attention, for his stomach bulged over his belt, his pants were always being hitched up and his shirt was only episodically inside. His hair, like his uniform, was in a constant state of disorder, and once, he said absent-mindedly, he appeared on parade in carpet slippers. He couldn't or wouldn't remember to call an officer "Sir" or to salute except as he might encounter one before a urinal. Least supportable of all, the average officer could not ordinarily understand what Baran was saying but could guess that the extravagantly convoluted sentences reflected adversely on his intelligence.

After the war Baran became an immensely popular professor at Stanford. Following his death in 1964 from a variety of self-destructive enjoyments, a politically motivated employee in the university administrative offices collected and released a whole packet of letters from alumni protesting Baran's existence, along with the replies of Stanford officials expressing their honest regret that tenure and the principles of academic freedom made it impractical to fire him. In Germany that summer I followed a more discreet procedure. As recommendations from the military flowed in for punitive action on Baran — reprimand, condign punishment, release to combat duty in the Pacific, reduction to private no-class — I put them under my office blotter. At the end of the summer the blotter was raised appreciably from the desk. I then tore them all up.

That autumn Baran and I were on the same plane from Prestwick in Scotland back to the United States. In accordance with accepted practice, the ranking officer, a major, was entrusted with the personnel files of the enlisted men moving with him. A man of courage and compassion and a great admirer of Baran, he called him to his side, and using a safety razor blade on the binding that held the papers together, he removed all the condemnatory material from Baran's file and squeezed it out a crack in the door into the Atlantic. (Planes were not then pressurized.) Baran arrived in New York with a perfect military record.[20]

---

[20] Of this operation I have a totally clear recollection. Checking recently with the officer in question, now a distinguished professor, I found that he had no memory of the incident and was disposed rather indignantly to deny ever engaging in such enlightened malfeasance. For that reason I do not identify him.

However, managing Baran had its anxious moments. One German we much needed for work that summer was Dr. Rolf Wagenfuehr, the senior economist and statistician of the Speer ministry. Exceptionally among the high staff of such departments he had remained behind in Berlin. Other German officials brought to Bad Nauheim claimed to have known him as a roast beef Nazi, brown outside, red inside. He was finally located in West Berlin from which he was engaged in rehabilitating the German statistical services for the Soviets in East Berlin. A diligent man, he had spent the days immediately following the surrender completing the manuscript of a book on the history of German war production. Although we had the right of summary arrest, I was uneasy as to its use and had specified that for professors, scientists, officials and the like, notice should be given. On being told of our desire that he go to Bad Nauheim, Wagenfuehr removed himself to a house in Neukoeln in the Russian sector. Baran led a posse there and, quite literally, lifted Wagenfuehr out of bed from beside his wife. He was flown to Bad Nauheim, and the Soviets, very properly, were outraged. A strong protest went up to Marshal Zhukov and across to General Eisenhower; I was, of course, the person responsible and in line for Ike's anger. The matter was resolved when Jurgen Kuczynski, a German Communist on our staff, advised me that he much wanted to go to Berlin to see if his house and library had survived the war. Were he allowed to go, he could, as a practicing comrade, square things with his fellow Communists. So, a fortnight or so after the kidnapping, as the Soviets called it, and after Wagenfuehr had given us much useful guidance on the German war production statistics, Kuczynski took him back to Berlin. I asked James Barr Ames to go along and keep an eye on the operation. And sure enough, Kuczynski was warmly welcomed by the Soviet officials, our well-rehearsed explanation of our aberration was accepted, Wagenfuehr was reinserted in the Soviet statistical operations and Ike's fury was averted.[21] In

[21]This story is in a memoir on Berlin in *Annals of an Abiding Liberal* (Boston: Houghton Mifflin, 1979), pp. 197–198. I repeat it here partly because in 1980, Kuczynski was reported in the press as saying that in these months he and his sister were working for Soviet intelligence. This could not have been a very significant assignment, for in the German phase of our operations with which he was associated there were no secrets. Our material all came from German sources available also to the Soviets and, in any case, was all eventually published.

later years Wagenfuehr moved to the West. Kuczynski, released
from service on completion of our German work, went to live and
work in the German Democratic Republic.[22]

On other matters Baran was equally resourceful. In Flensburg he
interrogated a senior steel magnate who, taking note of Baran's
rank, barely supportable military bearing and possibly also his recognizably Jewish aspect, said, "I am accustomed to talking only with
vice presidents and leaders of industry. Who are you?"[23] Baran replied that such was his official position that he could keep the tycoon
in jail for one day for each question he failed to answer, and that
was his intention. The answers were thereafter fluent and detailed.
Later in the summer in Wiesbaden, Baran uncovered General Franz
Halder, the commander in the early campaigns on the eastern front
who was fired by Hitler in disagreements over strategy at the time of
Stalingrad and arrested after the July 20 attempt on Hitler's life. He
had expected on the day of the surrender to be taken promptly to
see General Eisenhower and maybe then to General Marshall. Instead, not uncharacteristically, he had been left in total neglect for
several weeks by American soldiers who had never heard his name.
Baran, who had specialized on these matters for the OSS, interrogated him for many hours on the details of German operations on

[22] Teams operating on behalf of the Survey were required to keep logs of these
operations, this being usually the task of the most literate NCO in the enterprise.
Checking my memory of the Wagenfuehr episode against these logs I was struck by
the description, possibly by Baran, conceivably by another NCO, of the Berlin scene
in those days. "[We passed] . . . through the Brandenburg Gate, still relatively intact,
but looking the worse for wear, and into the Tiergarten. All of this section of the city
is an utter shambles. Those buildings that have not been turned into a heap of rubble
stand roofless, partially wall-less, gutted by fire, beyond possible repair. The Tiergarten looks like a no man's land. Its trees have been stripped of all but the largest
branches, and are leafing from the trunks. As elsewhere in the city the grassplots now
contain the bodies of many Russian and German soldiers who fell in the street fighting. Perhaps more grotesque than anything is the remains of Berlin's statuary, of
which there was a plethora; horses without former riders, figures without heads or
limbs." And here of a storm: "In the later afternoon a savage windstorm sprang up,
lifting half the dust and rubble of the city and distributing it around indiscriminately.
The remaining pieces of glass in windowless Berlin were flying through the air; documents and papers which had been tossed outside in an effort to clean up buildings
soared heavenwards; the walls of some gutted buildings collapsed; the atmosphere
was opaque. Later in the evening the wind died, in order to give the mosquitoes,
breeding in the stagnant canals and static water pools, a chance to come out for their
usual night life, while the team observed the ten-thirty curfew." *Daily record of USSBS
Spearhead Team,* United States Strategic Bombing Survey, July 16, 1945, pp. 3 and 5.
[23] Again as in my notes.

the Russian front. When finally Baran showed signs of being satisfied, Halder begged with great respect to have a turn: "Could I now ask my interrogator a question?"

Baran: "Yes."

Halder: "Has the American Army many intelligence officers like you?"

Baran, in an unprecedented sacrifice of truth to modesty: "I wouldn't know, General."

Halder: "If it has, it explains much about this war. I may tell you that your knowledge of the problems facing the Wehrmacht on the eastern front is markedly greater than was that of the Führer."[24]

The stories could continue. One night in a normal breach of military regulations, Paul Baran was dining with George Ball, some others and me at the Villa Grünewald, the officers' billet where we lived. The military commander at Bad Nauheim, a lieutenant colonel of deeply offensive personality — in civilian life a car dealer from Ohio — arrived and loudly demanded that Baran, as an enlisted man, be sent back to his quarters. George and I protested; the colonel became violent and obscene. We surrendered Baran but intimated to the colonel that he would somehow be made to suffer for his intrusion and insolence. Then we considered how this might be accomplished. A few days later a military police detachment arrived in Bad Nauheim, arrested the colonel and took him away. Thereafter, high-ranking officers stepped into the street and saluted on our approach.

In truth, a little earlier we had brought a high official of the Auto Union automobile company to Bad Nauheim for interrogation. As the Russians were about to occupy the part of Germany where he lived, he had asked our colonel for an army vehicle to move his more valuable possessions into the American zone on the promise of a division of the salvaged goods. The colonel had then shown his loot to a visiting officer who, in civilian life, had worked for Fiorello La Guardia in New York City and was thus a ferocious enemy of graft. It was he who had sent in the military police. We never saw our man again.

* * *

[24] As remembered and retold at the time. I again repeat from *Annals of an Abiding Liberal*.

As the Big Three meeting approached in Potsdam, couriers came to Bad Nauheim looking for information and guidance on the German economy. We obliged, and George Ball decided that we should attend. When, as I've often told, I pointed out that we had not been invited, George said that if we allowed hurt feelings to govern our actions, we would only compound the error. With Paul Nitze we went to Berlin, out to Babelsberg, the site of the conference, were admitted to the compound without question when we explained that we had come to attend the meeting and began operations with an excellent lunch at the senior officials' mess. I joined Isador Lubin, who was developing the position on reparations and whose people we had previously provided with information on the surviving plant. History was not altered by our brief presence. But it was something to attend a Summit on one's own invitation.

George Ball had told me in earlier weeks of the existence of the atomic bomb. Surveying the old-fashioned destruction in Germany, I had deeply hoped it would not work. Now it came and also the end of the Japanese war. The effect on the morale of the men I had sought out from the Army for the Survey was immediate. Until then hard, diligent work meant avoiding combat in the Pacific. Now the same hard work could mean going with us to Japan. But by now our overall economic report, a large, competent and literate document, was nearing completion. When it was finished, we closed the headquarters in Bad Nauheim and went to London and, after reviewing it further there, returned home. George Ball slept all the way from Prestwick to Iceland to Newfoundland to New York. This he did by combining a large amount of whiskey with a substantial dose of sleeping pills. Contrary to all medical expectation, he arrived greatly refreshed. A much decorated sergeant shared a seat with me and asked if I would like to hear of his war adventures. I told him I would not. He made several more attempts at conversation, which I rejected. Finally he asked me who I thought would win the World Series. I asked him what leagues were playing that year.

*   *   *

Back in Washington in Army Air Forces Annex #1 at Gravelly Point, Virginia, not far from National Airport, we found that the Secretariat of the Survey had written a short summary report that was as the Air Force would have wished it. Our patiently gathered data on the disastrous failures of strategic bombing were extensively ignored. There were no serious failures mentioned. Even the successes were lost in a story of general success. The question had political importance, for part of the claim of the Air Force to independence from the Army was thought to depend on the wartime achievement of the bombers. Ball and I prepared to contest the report and somehow to get it rewritten. It would be dreary work — piecemeal change, word by word.

Then Henry Alexander intervened. He was distressed less by the content of the summary than by its abysmal level of literacy. He asked me to prepare a new and readable draft — once more the awesome power from being the one who can write. I took a typewriter to the Cosmos Club in Washington and wrote exactly what we wanted said with something more for bargaining thrown in.

My manuscript, in turn, led to a war of attrition, one that lasted for days in the dreary buildings by the airport. But now the basic draft was mine; it fell to the opposition to struggle, sentence by sentence, for modification and retraction. General Anderson, supported by Guido Perera and Charles Cabot, led the attack. I defended it with, as I only later came to reflect, a maximum of arrogance and a minimum of tact. George Ball, who had resumed his law practice as counsel for Jean Monnet, nonetheless came over to help. Henry Alexander, not concealing his distress at the conflict, presided and sought to mediate. At some point I said to Orvil Anderson, "General, this is just a matter of intellectual honesty."

He replied, "Goddam it, Ken, you carry intellectual honesty to extremes."

By giving way on nonessentials, we kept the basic case. German war production had, indeed, expanded under the bombing. The greatly heralded efforts, those on the ball-bearing and aircraft plants for example, emerged as costly failures. Other operations, those against oil and the railroads, did have military effect. But strategic bombing had not won the war. At most, it had eased somewhat the task of the ground troops who did. The aircraft, manpower and bombs used in the campaign had cost the American economy far more in output than they had cost Germany. However, our economy being much larger, we could afford it. A final paragraph or two written by Henry Alexander somewhat overstated the contribution of air power to the outcome without altering the basic facts. The purposes of both history and future policy would have been served by a more dramatic finding of failure, for this would have better prepared us for the costly ineffectiveness of the bombers in Korea and Vietnam, and we might have been spared the reproach of civilized opinion. Still, no essential information was concealed or seriously compromised. Our large economic report, *The Effects of Strategic Bombing on the German War Economy,* which made all the basic points, was published without censorship of any kind.

My conduct of the argument made lasting and influential enemies, not, however, including Orvil Anderson. Once my text had been accepted, he urged that I not consider the war over and come to Japan. There the Navy and Naval Air arm had been playing the leading role. He wanted their claims to accomplishment now made subject to a similar excess of intellectual honesty.

15

Japan, 1945

THE GREAT YEAR, the one into which so much history was com-
pressed, was not yet over, and the rest was not without instruction.
As the enormous struggle in Europe had come to an end, so eventually did the smaller one in the Army Air Forces Annex #1 over
how it had been won. After the final summary report was agreed
upon, there was a further skirmish over a bomber that had become
separated from its group over Germany in the autumn of 1944. It
had dropped its bombs through thick cloud cover on what the primitive radar (H2S) of the time told it was Cologne. It had been, in fact,
over the Rhine, and the bombs hit one of the great bridges. The
bombs were too light to damage the bridge much, but they were
wholly adequate for setting off the demolition charges that the Germans had put in place in the event of an Allied breakthrough. The
span had come down across the stream, a devastating barrier to the
dense river traffic. By the autumn of 1945, further thought and
analysis had made the operation one of the best-planned and executed of the war. After some discussion it was now agreed that the
planning, at least, would not be featured.

Then or perhaps earlier there was also a minor struggle over the
B-17, the Flying Fortress itself. A rugged vehicle that brought its
occupants home if anything could, it was much respected by all concerned. But it had been designed to fly without escort and to protect
itself and its neighbors in the same flight with its own weapons. This
meant a heavy load of gunners, guns and ammunition, and, in consequence, it could carry no great weight of bombs. After the
Schweinfurt debacle it became clear that the Fortress could not, in
fact, defend itself, that escort aircraft would be required. It was still
arranged for its great load of men and weaponry; thus it was now a

bad design. General Anderson met my efforts to make this point with massive indignation. His exact words are still with me: "You are insulting a great airplane." On this he won.

Back in New York, I wrote the article already mentioned called "Germany Was Badly Run." It was published by my *Fortune* colleagues with some misgivings, for the thesis seemed to them too drastically at odds with accepted truth. Here are the concluding paragraphs:

> If German war management was poor how did the German armies manage to fight so well and so long? The Wehrmacht, in the days of its great successes, occupied all Europe except for a few odd corners. It reached the Volga and almost reached the Nile. When it was finally thrown on the defensive it stood off the armed millions of Russia, the U.S., and the British Empire for two and a half years.
>
> The simple fact is that Germany should never have lost the war it started; the undermobilization and overconfidence of the early years help solve the very real mystery of why it did. In the early years Germany's advantages were enormous: it had a large margin over its enemies in preparation, it held the initiative, and it had the moral advantage of being the only country that wanted to fight. Had the Nazi leaders applied their own formula of total war from the beginning they could hardly have avoided overwhelming the opposition they met before 1942.
>
> Even after the tide turned at Moscow and Stalingrad, Germany's position was strong. There was the well-publicized advantage of internal lines of communication that grew shorter and thicker as the communications of all Germany's enemies became longer and more tenuous. German weapons were of good quality, German scientists and technologists were ingenious, and because of the short pipelines new weapons could be quickly put into use. Most important of all, there is little doubt that Germans are durable and skillful fighters with a well-disciplined acceptance of the idea of getting killed. Except in the east they were well moated by the ocean and the Mediterranean. They should have been hard to defeat. That they were defeated is conclusive testimony to the inherent inefficiencies of dictatorship, the inherent efficiencies of freedom.[1]

As I wrote this piece, I came under the pressure that I earlier mentioned to go to Japan. It was now my duty to help tell the truth about the Navy and Douglas MacArthur. So, on October 20, I flew to San Francisco where I was issued orders of incomparable secrecy. That was because in Washington I had been put in charge of a party of British scientists who were proceeding to Japan to look at the effects of the air attacks, including the awful aftermath of the atomic

---

[1] "Germany Was Badly Run," *Fortune*, vol. XXXII, no. 6 (December 1945), p. 200.

bomb. Anything even remotely having to do with the Bomb was subject to awesome restrictions.

These orders produced a memorable Catch-22 in Honolulu. Arriving there of an early, fresh and sunny morning, I felt extremely unwell, and I didn't think to associate my ill health with the mass of shots required for the Pacific that had been plunged into my arms the day before. Nor was any connection made by the doctor I consulted, who uncovered a fever just short of ignition. He sent me to Tripler General Hospital, now Tripler Army Medical Center, where forms were filled out. Then I was ordered into bed. My British scientists in their ill-fitting RAF uniforms were waiting for me at Hickam Field. I tried to tell the doctor I was doing something very secret and very important, but he was unimpressed. With my fever I was a menace to the health of others, if not to myself. I could not explain, but I could not stay.

He left, and a little later I noticed that an army vehicle was about to move away from the nearby gate. On inquiry I learned that it was going to Hickam Field, and I went along. At the field I bought several cans of pineapple juice to slake my thirst and took off with my unkempt warriors for Kwajalein in the Marshall Islands. On arriving there the next day, I felt much better. When I was hospitalized in Tripler again in early 1962 with hepatitis that I had contracted in India, I told the doctors of my earlier visit. One went down to the files and got my card; it listed me as still AWOL or some civilian equivalent.

Over the Pacific, even more than over the Atlantic, one despaired in those days that an airplane journey would ever end. Eventually this one did; we reached Tokyo late one afternoon and came into town on the back of a truck. I took billets in Frank Lloyd Wright's Imperial Hotel, an appalling hostelry built and furnished for occupants half my length, and I became aware that very evening of Japan's eventual commercial preeminence. A small man knocked on my door to sell me a bottle of whiskey. The label said *"Genuine Suntory Scotch Whisky."* Added was the note: *"Bottled Especially for the Visiting* (sic) *Occupation Forces."*

*   *   *

The cities of Japan in those dark autumn days were a manifestation of unspeakable gloom. Here a burnt-out bank, there the walls of a community bathhouse, otherwise only ashes and gaunt, free-standing chimneys. In Europe, as I've told, the USAAF and the RAF, because of different equipment, had chosen different targets for their bombing attacks, but military doctrine then proclaimed that what had been feasible was in fact strategic. Now the same thing happened in Japan. There the B-29s, operating at maximum range, could best hit the cities so it was the attacks on the urban centers, mainly with incendiaries, that became the approved design for victory. Sixty-six Japanese cities were so attacked and leveled in a range from 25 to 90 percent. Only the personal intervention of Secretary of War Henry Stimson saved the still pristine and beautiful former imperial capital of Kyoto. Industrial targets, including the aircraft plants, were taken up only as operations across the Pacific brought them within range or, as actually happened, the supply of incendiary bombs ran out.

The Japanese economy was far less resilient under the air attacks than that of Germany had been. When plants were hit, they were not so soon put back in production. But no more than in Germany was it the bombing that won the war. Japan's defeat began with the luminous insanity of its own military leadership — of men who, already extensively engaged on the Chinese mainland, took their country into conflict with the vastly greater industrial power of the United States, and by an attack on Hawaii that was superbly designed to resolve all American doubts as to the need or justice of the war. There can be few better warnings from history of the limitless perversity and danger of what is called the military mind.

At its greatest, Japan's production of munitions was only about one-tenth that of the United States.[2] The bombing did reduce it, though on frequent occasion the industrial plants so hit were already down in consequence of the naval blockade. "Blockade and bombing together," we concluded, "deprived Japanese forces of about four months' munitions production. That production could have made a substantial difference in Japan's ability to cause us losses had we invaded but could not have affected the outcome of the war."[3] In Japan as in Europe the war was won, in the larger sense, by the greater weight of industrial power and of manpower and immediately by

[2] *The Effects of Strategic Bombing on Japan's War Economy*, United States Strategic Bombing Survey, December 1946, p. 2.
[3] Ibid., pp. 2–3.

troops and ships and aircraft in direct and dangerous combat. ". . . [T]he outcome of the war was decided in the waters of the Pacific and on the landing beaches of invaded islands . . ."[4]

The ghastly leveling of the cities may well have weakened Japanese morale and caused people to think even more favorably of surrender. And while Japanese decisions were not then being taken in response to public opinion polls, this may, indeed, have had some effect on the leadership. However, men of practical thought were still available in Japan. Far more powerful in forcing the surrender than the bombing was the knowledge that, after the defeat of Germany and after Russia's entry into the war, Japan, a small country, faced all the effective military power of all the rest of the world entirely alone.

Nor were the atomic bombs decisive. It has long been held in justification that they made unnecessary an invasion of the Japanese mainland and thus saved the resulting fighting and thousands, possibly hundreds of thousands, of casualties on both sides. On few matters is the adverse evidence so strong. The bombs fell after the decision had been taken by the Japanese government to surrender. That the war had to be ended was agreed at a meeting of key members of the Supreme War Direction Council with the Emperor on June 20, 1945, a full six weeks before the devastation of Hiroshima.[5] The next steps took time. The Japanese government had the usual bureaucratic lags as between decision and action. The means for approaching the Allies had also to be agreed. And there was need to ensure the acquiescence or neutralization of recalcitrant and suicidal officers and military units. At the most the atomic bombs only advanced the decision.

The effect of the bombs on the Japanese surrender was the subject of especially careful study by the Survey. The conclusion was as follows:

> Based on a detailed investigation of all the facts, and supported by the testimony of the surviving Japanese leaders involved, it is the Survey's opinion that certainly prior to 31 December 1945, and in all probability prior to 1 November 1945, Japan would have surrendered even if the

[4] Ibid., p. 59.
[5] *Summary Report (Pacific War)*, United States Strategic Bombing Survey, Chairman's Office, July 1, 1946, p. 26.

atomic bombs had not been dropped, even if Russia had not entered the war, and even if no invasion had been planned or contemplated.[6]

I had no part in writing this conclusion. By the time it appeared in the summer of 1946, I had moved on to other duties, which included, in a remote sense, the government of Japan.

Paul Nitze had replaced Henry Alexander as the effective head of operations for our work in the Far East. An attractive, self-possessed man, he devoted the rest of his life to studying the theory and practice of aerial destruction, emerging in the end as a devout partisan of the art. The effect on my mind and mood was different. I had none of the sense of discovery and excitement that had pervaded our earlier work in Germany. All I felt was the vast suffering visited on innocent people by their disastrous leaders and by unnecessary actions on our side. About Hitler and the Nazis one still had feelings of fear and relief that they were vanquished. For Japan one had only sympathy and sorrow. In later years an historian of our efforts came across a first draft of my comments on the bombing of Japan in the National Archives. I had described it as "this appalling business," which was how anyone of any sensitivity would have felt.

*   *   *

Yet not all was grim. Predictably, some lighter moments were provided by Paul Baran, now released from the Army and working for the Survey as a civilian. One day in Tokyo he met on the street a senior executive in one of the great *zaibatsu* or industrial, commercial and banking combines.[7] It was a pleasant encounter, for Baran had known the man in Berlin and had written a Ph.D. thesis for him. This was a distinguished piece of work on the position of Japan in the world economy and, by Baran's account, had won its nonauthor an honorary professorship on his return home. He invited Paul to join him for lunch the following Saturday at his house near Tokyo, and Paul asked if I might go along. Baran suggested that I procure a staff car instead of a jeep for the journey because he had told his friend that he was bringing his general with him, and a staff car then signified that rank in Tokyo.

[6] Ibid. See also *Japan's Struggle to End the War,* United States Strategic Bombing Survey, Chairman's Office, July 1, 1946, p. 13.
[7] The Yasuda group, if my memory serves.

At a Japanese-style lunch in an undamaged house of great charm in the suburbs, Paul's friend asked if I would speak to MacArthur and arrange permission for him to get back into business — the manufacture of radios. I said this might be difficult and asked him how, in any case, he would get the necessary materials. He said that he had put some supplies aside from those allocated for war production.

"Does that mean you foresaw the defeat of Japan?"

"No, but we did observe that the victories of our glorious Army and Navy were occurring ever closer to our home islands."

After lunch he took us to visit what he called his "reconversion enterprise." This was a former factory canteen, recreation hall and dormitory that with the peace he had turned into the Radio City Music Hall of whorehouses to serve an adjacent American air base. In the huge main room GIs were dancing with Japanese girls, some of the latter in western dress; some in kimonos; some in Girl Scout uniforms because they alone were available. Each girl wore an embroidered letter A or B on her blouse or dress. The manager joined us and explained that this was his inspiration: it indicated the extent of the woman's commitment. Some wished to restrict themselves only to dancing, and the letter saved fruitless effort and eventual frustration. Our soldiers, he said, thought the system would one day be adopted in the United States. We then were taken on a brief tour of the dormitories. Over a wicket inside the door was a sign:

SHORT VISIT	10 yen
LONG VISIT	40 yen
WITH TEA	45 yen [8]

I asked our host as we emerged in the sun how he found his transitional enterprise. There were, he said, unsolved problems. Because of the hard seats in the jeeps, the soldiers took the bedding with them. He was very anxious to get back to electronics.

*   *   *

After an early lunch one day I joined the throng outside the Dai-Ichi Building, Headquarters for the Supreme Commander of Allied

[8] The prices are notional, the real ones having long since faded from memory.

Powers (SCAP), to see the ceremony staged there each day — the Departure of Douglas MacArthur. It had become a matter of much admiring comment. Precisely at the scheduled moment, he would make his appearance — pressed, impeccable, with the rich metal foliage on his cap, yet with his open collar striking a different, slightly casual note. His pace, like that of a young actress entering the restaurant of the synthetic Romanoff in the great days of Hollywood, was always just a shade faster than normal. This focuses attention and adds a spirited, dynamic note to personality. With MacArthur in conversation would be an aide; waiting was a large black car with two tall, white-gloved, white-helmeted military policemen protecting the open door. Just before getting in, MacArthur would turn and accept the crowd with a casual but well-considered salute.

Or such was the accepted choreography. That day things were different. During the period of waiting my towering disproportion attracted the attention of a Japanese photographer. He turned his camera up toward my face. Others were similarly attracted. Necks were craned; two or three more cameras were focused. By the time Doug arrived, I had become a competing attraction. Not quite all had turned back before he reached his car. Perhaps it was egocentric, but I thought I detected a slightly sour glance along with his salute.

It was my only encounter with the great man, although in 1956 during the presidential campaign of that year I was participating in an intense political session in Washington when word came by way of Chester Bowles that MacArthur wished to endorse Adlai Stevenson for President. He required only that Adlai call on him and ask. Not love of Stevenson but a deep resentment of Eisenhower was the reason. We debated the matter and thought with pleasure of the resulting brief commotion, but we did not pursue the offer either with MacArthur or, so far as I know, with Stevenson. It did not seem likely that many of MacArthur's admirers would go with him on this switch.

*   *   *

On one occasion we flew from Tokyo in small planes to an airfield and aircraft factory seventy-five miles or so to the north. Lining the field were rows of single-engined fighters already coated with orange-yellow rust. Aluminum having been unavailable, the fuselages had been covered with light tinplate. The landing gear was not re-tractable but detachable — a single pull of a lever after take-off sent the wheels back to earth. The planes were designed specifically for suicide missions. I thought them out of a bad dream.

Suicide was not a novelty in Japan in 1945. Through one long afternoon on the USS *Ancon,* the Navy command ship now tied up in Tokyo harbor, we interrogated Prince Fumimaro Konoye, the last civilian head of the Japanese government before the outbreak of war. Paul Baran carefully addressed the prince as *Mr.* Konoye and didn't give the impression of believing all that he heard. But the occasion was not wholly unpleasant; Franklin D'Olier, who was visiting Japan, was concerned to ask Konoye about his son Fumitaka, who had been at Princeton and who had been captured by the Soviets in Manchuria. That night Prince Konoye committed suicide.

*   *   *

Orvil Anderson told me one day that he was planning a trip to the island battlegrounds of the South Pacific. Orvil, as I have told, had been a close disciple of Brigadier General Billy Mitchell, the great exponent of air warfare on whose court-martial for insubordination Douglas MacArthur had served in 1925. Anderson felt toward MacArthur as MacArthur did toward Eisenhower but rather more so. The trip would have the principal purpose of proving that the distance between Guadalcanal and the Philippines, which it had taken MacArthur three years and more to traverse with his anti-quated conceptions of warfare, could be covered in a B-17 in one day. I was asked along to help confirm the fact. Other and deeply fraudulent reasons having to do with the need for a firsthand view of the scene of South Pacific air operations were adduced and sol-emnly accepted. Unnecessary travel is always more ingeniously as well as more indignantly defended than that which is useful.

At two o'clock one autumn morning, we took off from Atsugi Air-field and passed Mount Fuji, huge, white, perfect of line, gleaming under the full moon. At 7 A.M., after going up the river nearly to Nanking to await the clearing of fog, we came down for reasons that were never disclosed to me at the Shanghai airport. As we disem-barked, a GI, under arrest, was being hustled aboard a MATS (Mil-itary Air Transport Service) plane for return home. Paul Nitze and

I sauntered over to ask as to his crime. The military policeman said, "We found this $100,000 on him going through security, and we don't think he got it honest."

It could, in fact, have been honest, the legality of using public aircraft for private arbitrage apart. In different Chinese cities the Chinese yuan had a radically different purchasing power and, therewith, a very different exchange rate in relation to the American dollar. In Chungking, where in consequence of the government presence there was much paper and few goods, purchasing power was low and also the rate of exchange with the dollar. Both were higher in Shanghai where, though paper was plentiful, the stores were richly stocked with goods. The rate in relation to the dollar was highest of all in Peking, which had not been touched by the war.

Meanwhile the only regular communication between these cities was by military plane. Crew members buying Chinese currency in Chungking and selling in Shanghai or buying in Shanghai and selling in Peking could profit beyond the wildest dreams of avarice. And since they were the only ones making the journey, they had no competition in this profitable and utterly riskless enterprise. Peace back home and the rigors of the competitive system must have been a severe shock for these entrepreneurs.

After the devastation of Tokyo or the German cities, the Shanghai shops seemed extraordinarily rich. There were silks and satins in abundance and numerous other items that had long been unavailable in New York. Paul Nitze and I immediately had an urge to go shopping. But having lived for many months in the planned, rationed and moneyless economies of Germany and the U.S. Army, we had no dollars. Nor would anyone cash our checks.

In Shanghai we picked up a businessman who needed a ride to Manila. Through the night, in competition with the motors, which were separated from us by only a thin skin of metal, Orvil Anderson recounted for him the history of the air war in Europe, lingering with pleasure on the thinking behind each of the many missions. The businessman was deeply pleased by the attention; Anderson was delighted to have a listener who did not, as we had learned to do, take evasive action. The consequence was that Orvil totally lost his voice. The rest of our voyage was in blessed peace.

The center of Manila was a congeries of half-demolished, drunkenly leaning structures, the result of some hasty efforts at demolition. Corregidor, which we inspected by C-47, looked benign; Bataan had already been reclaimed by the jungle. An admiral who accompanied us told of the need to modernize the defenses of Manila Bay. He was not a radical in such matters. The famous concrete battleship which before the war had been part of the defenses would have to be replaced by a concrete aircraft carrier. To see the effect on Anderson, I endorsed the concept. His outrage was extreme, and he couldn't make it known.

A day or so later, with extra fuel tanks, we left before dawn to start the MacArthur journey and flew all day — over Cebu, over Mindanao, over much ocean, over Morotai, over yet more stretches of ocean to the city of Hollandia (now Jayapura) and along the coast of New Guinea (now Papua New Guinea) and long after dark that night to a landing at Manus in the Admiralty Islands. It was not quite Guadalcanal; that we reached the next day. But in the few sentences he could manage, Orvil persuaded us that we had gone the basic distance in a day. It persuaded me only of how far MacArthur had gone. I would have given him ten years.

I was even more persuaded next morning when, with Nitze, I arrived a little late at the airfield. Anderson's personal pilot, a talented young musician in private life, was receiving a horribly croaked lecture from his boss. On refilling the fuel tanks, it had been learned that we had landed the night before with only some fifteen minutes' worth of fuel left. Some carelessness with the gauges. Another turn or two, and we would have gone into the ocean.

At Guadalcanal, as on Bataan and also the other islands where men had fought, the jungle had by now erased the scars of battle, and its detritus had sunk beneath the foliage. Guadalcanal, with its regular and stately rows of coconut palms, impressed one primarily with its beauty. An officer who had fought there said that even during the fighting he had thought of its tourist possibilities. Only at Truk in the Caroline Islands, the great Japanese naval and air base, where the beautiful lagoon was spotted with wrecked ships and the coral perimeter was covered with desperately scratched-out gardens for growing food, did the war still seem real.

*　　*　　*

I arrived back in Washington late that year. After completing formalities at Army Air Forces Annex #1, I took the train back to New

York. The long, incredibly boring flights were all behind me. So were the ears attuned always to the roar of the motors, the mind to the thought that they might in the next moment stop — a small matter as compared with the lot of those who had risked combat but nonetheless for me exigent. Sitting in the parlor car, I resolved happily never to fly in an airplane again.

16

Cold Breath

AT THE END of 1945, it is possible that I knew more about the drained and shattered economies of both Germany and Japan than anyone alive. In any case, no one had had a more privileged and compelling exposure. Remarkably it was not a thought that occurred to me, but it did to Clair Wilcox, a much admired Swarthmore professor and during the war the price executive for steel and other heavy industry in the Office of Price Administration. He was now in the State Department advancing the cause of lower tariffs and an international organization to promote and defend liberal trade that became the General Agreement on Tariffs & Trade or GATT. Pressure to use my knowledge of the defeated lands came also from Will Clayton, now Undersecretary of State for Economic Affairs, and in lesser measure from Willard L. Thorp, an early New Dealer, Amherst College professor and now Clayton's deputy.

In those days one did not easily resist such efforts. The prestige of public service was very high; so was the sense of obligation it aroused. (On both of these matters the Vietnam war and Richard Nixon were to change much for the worse.) Accordingly, in 1946, I won the agreement of Harry Luce and my *Fortune* colleagues to yet another leave of absence and returned to Washington to have charge of economic affairs in Germany and Japan and, rather as an afterthought, in Austria and South Korea.

In those days the State Department was divided into a dozen or so regional or functional offices. An office director was a person of power and distinction. With time, in the ineluctable way of bureaucracy, new strata were laid on above; the head of a State Department office is now barely qualified to oversee relations with the Seychelles or Monaco or maintain liaison with the Interstate Commerce Commission. My domain was called the Office of Economic

Security Policy. Already the word *security* was thought to confer cachet.

Among my fellow office directors and presiding over the meetings of the Coordinating Committee in which we regularly assembled was Loy Henderson, a stern and vigilant warrior against Communists, idealists and the notion of a Jewish homeland. One of the members was Alger Hiss, who headed the office charged with United Nations affairs and whose past position on Communism and espionage would presently become a matter for all-consuming debate. Slender, handsome, quiet-spoken, scarcely a presence in the Coordinating Committee, Hiss made no impression on me whatever. By my liberal colleagues he was thought excessively cautious, strongly oriented to Establishment positions and a bit of a stuffed shirt.

At the Department I inherited a strong young staff, including Seymour J. Rubin, who was engaged in extracting the funds of the erstwhile Nazis from the Swiss; Charles P. Kindleberger II, on his way to becoming a noted economist and economic historian at MIT; and Walt Whitman Rostow, later, in the Vietnam years, the intensely controversial National Security Adviser to Lyndon Johnson. Rostow was then one of the most effective young officers in the Department but was thought to be too favorably disposed to trying to work things out with the Soviets.

I took up quarters in a building a little down Pennsylvania Avenue from the Department proper, and in the spring we moved our children into an unattractive house with an unkempt yard in the Cleveland Park area out Connecticut Avenue. One day one of our sons, playing with matches, came close to burning it down. It was a premature and doubtless excessive manifestation of good taste.

*   *   *

My arrival at the Department was not an occasion for unrestrained joy. Echoes of the controversy over my administration of price control were still being heard, especially on Capitol Hill. Though I did not then know it, my FBI dossier was replete with the objections of outraged citizens whose prices I had declined to raise. With Roosevelt gone, the Washington bureaucratic mood was cautious; individuals whose sanguinary social views had once attracted only admiration were now regarded with caution. I was investigated for my new post, and, not surprisingly, the Security Screening Committee of the

Security Office of the Department of State on January 25, 1946 formally disapproved my appointment. I would "draw sharp criticism to the Department . . . [and] jeopardize certain programs and appropriations." And, "It cannot be conceived that this applicant possesses qualifications which will in any way offset or compensate for the resulting damage to the Department's prestige." I was then appointed and didn't know of this depressing view until I received my file under the Freedom of Information Act. I judge that neither Will Clayton nor Jimmy Byrnes, now Secretary of State, was impressed by such attainder, for I had worked in the closest association with both. Byrnes, when I reported for duty, did, I thought wisely, ask me to avoid being too much of a presence on Capitol Hill.

*   *   *

No one still young will be easily persuaded as to the type of men who ran the State Department in the years before World War II or who were now seeking to retrieve their earlier eminence. One must begin with a vital and much misunderstood institution in modern democracy. This is the Secular Priesthood. As its sacerdotal counterpart mediates between God and man, so the secular priesthood mediates between man and the unknown.

There are important areas of the public polity where the people at large and their legislators agree that so complex or abstruse are the problems that no one can hope to understand them. So there must be delegation to those who, out of knowledge, experience, ignorance or self-assurance, have led themselves and others to believe they do understand. They are the secular priesthood. Since perpetuation of a sense of mystery is a source of power for the priestly group, its members regularly resort to arcane communication that no outsider can penetrate. The operations of the Federal Reserve System and the Pentagon, as all should fear and regret, and the conduct of foreign policy are the great strongholds of the secular priesthood. In these areas the public and its representatives are most readily persuaded of their ignorance. Hence the delegation.

It is not necessary or even usual that members of the priestly group know the ultimate consequences of any decision — of some military intervention or innovation, a change in central-bank lending rates or American support or nonsupport of some dictator. No one else knows either, and, as with heavenly justice, there is comfort in assuming that there is someone somewhere who does. A well-cultivated aspect of assurance on the part of the particular priestly group, combined with an absence of introspection by the members on their own limitations, adds greatly to public confidence.

Only when the decisions of the secular priesthood are shown to be catastrophically wrong — as on the vulnerability of Fidel Castro's regime to a few thousand irregulars landing at the Bay of Pigs, the timeless unity of the Communist world just prior to the break between Moscow and Peking or the omnipotence of American fire and air power in the Vietnam jungle — does popular confidence have a tendency temporarily to dissolve.

The secular priesthood, it should be observed, naturally associates class interest with valid policy. Decisions of central bankers are in keeping with the interests of the banking community; those by the military on weaponry are never damaging to the military establishment or the weapons industry; those by our diplomats reflect the economic, social and political preferences of the general social class with which the priestly group associates or from which it is drawn.

* * *

As noted, the secular priesthood has always considered foreign policy its special domain, and before World War II its members were a very small, very select body in the State Department. Secretaries of State came and went with some frequency, although a few, like Cordell Hull, were durable. Politicians and New York or Boston socialites turned up on occasion as ambassadors. But primary responsibility was exercised, even monopolized, by a small group of well-connected, upper-income Americans selected for their task by family membership and attendance at Groton, Exeter, Andover or St. Paul's and Princeton, Harvard or Yale. They were attracted to the State Department because manner there was as important as knowledge and more easily acquired and because it was the one government department where a true-blue gentleman could work. No Groton man could serve in the General Accounting Office, the Bureau of Labor Statistics or the Department of Agriculture. Earlier travel and family background meant that these men were at home, as most Americans were not, in European society. They often heard themselves described as "not typical" Americans. Most, although by no means all, had some money of their own or from their wives.

Most were WASPs, as they would eventually be called, although a few others, occasional Catholics such as Robert Murphy, were assimilated to the priesthood and even wholly equaled their colleagues in social ease and political conformity. All "felt that they belonged to a pretty good club," Hugh Wilson, a revered member, said in 1927, adding, inaccurately, that this "feeling . . . fostered a healthy *esprit de corps.*"[1]

It was to this *esprit de corps* that anyone joining the Department after World War II was exposed. I was better prepared than most. The class-consciousness of Hugh Wilson's club was not a great shock to anyone who had known Harvard before democracy. One had there encountered personal assurance combined with an unchallengeable sense of moral and social superiority. This last was especially stressed. Among prewar Harvard men, it was not important that an individual be intelligent, but he did have to be superior.

As viewed by the State Department priesthood, American democracy brought decidedly vulgar people to the Congress and to other parts of the Executive. This, however, was inevitable; the farm and back country and even the working classes did exist. The prestige structure that accorded the priestly members *their* position remained unchallenged. Other countries, however, had every need to keep unions, socialists, Communists, reforming politicians and divers forces of disorder in their place. Dictators were inevitable and, except in principle, desirable, and this was especially true in Latin America. Once, after the war, I called on a senior, wholly assimilated member of the club who was American ambassador to Guatemala. In response to some feckless observation about democracy, he reminded me sternly that Jorge Ubico, the long-time Guatemalan dictator, "had run a very tidy government down here." His sort, he said firmly, would always be needed.

As to all generalizations, there were exceptions. The secular priesthood at State abhorred Communism, the Soviet Union and the Jews, and for many the three were roughly identical. Stalin invited no special opprobrium for his purges; it was sufficient that he was a Communist. But in the years after the war one small group of young officers — Charles E. Bohlen, George F. Kennan and Llewellyn E.

[1]Quoted in Martin Weil, *A Pretty Good Club: The Founding Fathers of the U.S. Foreign Service* (New York: Norton, 1978), p. 47.

Thompson, Jr. — were fascinated students of the Soviet experiment as also of the Russian language, character and culture. And for China there were the China hands — John Carter Vincent, John Stewart Service, John Paton Davies and O. Edmund Clubb. All had concluded that Chiang Kai-shek and his evanescent, predatory and combat-resistant armies were not on the wave of the future. So it would be, or might be, the Communists. For being right the China hands were called severely to account in the fifties by John Foster Dulles and the McCarthyites on Capitol Hill. Their colleagues in the secular priesthood accepted, on the whole gracefully, the need to sacrifice them to the general good. The China officers were not the real custodians of American foreign policy.

The war years had not been easy ones for the old diplomats. They were neither mentally nor operationally prepared for an effective role. A crusade for democracy did not stir them deeply; in a relaxed moment not long after the attack on Pearl Harbor, Roosevelt said he had hopes for at least neutrality in the State Department during the war.[2] But more important, leisurely management of an embassy and reflection on the incoming telegrams were no preparation for the active tasks of the time. The agencies with direct operational responsibilities — the Army, the Navy, the Lend-Lease Administration, the Board of Economic Warfare, the Office of War Information, the Office of Strategic Services — came along and moved the secular priesthood relentlessly to the sidelines.

Now in 1946 the time had come, if ever, for a comeback. F.D.R., a nemesis, was dead. Harry Truman, from a different culture, was less sensitive than Roosevelt to their class aspirations and was more impressed by their superb assurance. His principal adverse encounter was with the unyielding opposition of the priestly group to a Jewish state, an opposition which was assumed to be pro-Arab but which was not for that reason any less anti-Semitic.[3] The war being

[2] Ibid., p. 103.

[3] During the summer of 1946, although I had no formal responsibilities in the matter, I was drawn into meetings on Palestine and the Jewish homeland, as was then the reference. The White House was searching for people who were sympathetic. John H. Hilldring, a general recently from the Pentagon, and I were among the few available. One incidental consequence was that, sometime later, I was approached, somewhat tentatively I believe, to go to Palestine as head of the mission of peace and conciliation that eventually was led by Count Folke Bernadotte of Sweden. I begged off. Bernadotte, on September 18, 1948, was assassinated.

over, Communism could again be an enemy. So could the impractical idealists who held that people turned to socialism out of exploitation or despair.

In Upper Canada (now Ontario) in the last century, as I have elsewhere told, there was a moral and political cleavage between the
rural Scotch and the prestigious Toryism of the English-oriented
ruling class. The resulting attitudes were far from dead in my youth;
they required that one be compulsively against any self-satisfied elite.
One never joined, and one never overlooked any righteous opportunity to oppose or, if opportunity presented, to infuriate. No
psychic disorder could be more useful. It forces one automatically to
question the most pompously exchanged clichés of the corporate executives, the most confidently vacuous voices on military adventure
and the most generally admired triteness on foreign policy. To me
it has been valuable, I believe, on matters as diverse as the deeply
sanctioned obsolescence of neoclassical economics and the greatly
self-approving commitment in Vietnam.

                              *   *   *

The consequence of my less than affectionate relationship with the
renascent diplomats was less that I was unpopular than that I had
very little to do. My staff handled all routine matters; all questions
of policy, signaled by the so-called action copies of the telegrams,
went to the priestly members, who often failed to advise me of their
operations. I was left with what remained, which was largely nothing
at all. My idleness was accentuated by an exceptionally spacious office, a very big desk, some expensive leather chairs and an uncomfortable leather sofa.

I exaggerate slightly. Far Eastern political affairs were in the
hands of John Carter Vincent. Though a high foreign service officer, he too had a pronounced instinct against the automatic wisdom
of the secular priesthood. In ensuing years he was first detached
from Chinese affairs where his knowledge led him to truths in conflict with needed belief, and then he was purged by John Foster
Dulles. John Carter and I either saw eye to eye on Japanese policy
or if we differed, such was my admiration for him that I didn't venture to make my doubts seriously known. Management of European
affairs, in contrast, was rigidly monastic. German matters were immediately in the hands of James W. Riddleberger, later Ambassador

to Yugoslavia and an amiable man with whom one could have conversation though often to no particular effect. European policy as a whole, to which most issues gravitated, was in the possession of one H. Freeman Matthews, a banner member of the old club and a man of substantially inaccessible mind or, to be fair, one into whose mind few found the effort at penetration rewarding.

There was a yet further difficulty. The power that my priestly friends sought to monopolize was itself slight. The chain of command to the occupied countries ran through various coordinating committees in Washington by way of the Chiefs of Staff to the great proconsuls, Lucius Clay in Germany and Douglas MacArthur in Japan and Korea. Austria was yet another fief. With Germany there were weak and exiguous links of authority; with Japan there were virtually none. The Korean War was to show that even on great and dangerous decisions MacArthur's power was nearly plenary. Once that summer John Carter Vincent and I considered, not entirely seriously, what our policy should be were MacArthur formally to break off relations with the United States. I am certain that the general didn't know of my existence as an ultimate source of guidance, and it is quite possible that he had never heard of John Carter Vincent.

Policy differences also contributed to my isolation as well as that of my staff. I was not attracted by the thought of conflict, military or even political, with the Soviets. I believed that the divisive issues — reparations, Berlin, how Germany would be governed — could be negotiated. Patient effort was needed, effort that recognized that many Soviet attitudes were a cover for insecurity occasioned by the terrors of the recent past. And it was idle for us to ask the impossible. Communism in Russia was there to stay; it was unlikely that it would long be resisted on her borders.

All this the old guard dismissed. They were experienced, knew Moscow at first hand and had served in Warsaw or Bucharest before the war. The only thing the Soviets would understand was an adamant no. In 1946, the Cold War as a concept had yet to be born. For the old diplomats it had always existed.

But there was also a problem with one's allies. The wars, east and west, were then only a few months over. That the Germans and the Japanese must first be made to pay and then be made economically innocuous was still a test of faith on the liberal left. The Morgenthau

Plan for the pastoralization of Germany, though in decline, was not yet dead. An upper limit on German industrial output was still accepted.

Partly from those grim weeks in Japan I had come to the conclusion that the only humane policy in either Japan or Germany was to restore economic life as quickly as possible. Limits on production were academic; for the foreseeable future the only economic policy was to produce the most possible.

I had yet more serious doubts about the reparations policy. After the experience of World War I, payments in money had come to be seen as a great unsettling factor in world economic relations. Keynes, more than anyone, had made the point. So compensation would now be had by dismantling and shipping out the plant and equipment. This, I came to believe, was worse. Workers in the towns affected saw the source of their livelihood go, they could only believe forever. And it was not altogether certain how valuable was this secondhand plant in the places at which it arrived.

On reparations I had a measurable influence. For setting reparations policy in both Germany and Japan, Harry Truman, in a substantial failure of judgment, had selected Edwin W. Pauley, an independent oilman from Los Angeles who was seeking to exorcise by public service a not wholly supportable reputation in the oil business. We were friends, in a manner of speaking. Lacking any independent opinions, Ed Pauley had been subject to the strongly punitive mood of his subordinates. This included a very stiff line on reparations from Japan. His draft report called for massive dismantling and removal of Japanese industrial plant. For the devastated and desolate cities I had seen, this added action seemed to me intolerable.

As some had persuaded Ed Pauley one way, it occurred to me that I might persuade him the other. So every few days as his report took final form, I called on him, sometimes with Edwin Martin, my assistant on these matters, who was at the beginning of a long and distinguished public career. On each visit we would urge that an additional industry be excluded. The Japanese would need cloth. And oil. And fertilizer. The aggregate of our attrition was very satisfactory. The Ed Pauleys of the world sometimes serve better than they know in high office.

*   *   *

One way to escape bureaucratic confinement (and exclusion) in those months was to carry one's ideas directly to Berlin and to General Clay. Lucius Clay was one of the most intelligent, adept and, as necessary, politically resourceful administrators of his time. An engineer officer whose father had been a senator from Georgia, Clay, along with his fellow general Brehon B. Somervell, had been principally responsible for organizing wartime military supply and transport. The business civilians like Donald Nelson of Sears and Charles E. Wilson of General Electric got the attention; Clay and Somervell got the results. Intense, attenuated, a chain smoker who paid for it horribly in his last years with emphysema, Clay did not welcome interference from Washington intruders. But neither could he resist any idea that seemed worthwhile.

I was in Berlin for two tours that year, the first for negotiations with the British in London and Jean Monnet in Paris, and then with Clay on means for reviving European coal production, without which little else could then be produced or transported. The answer to the German coal problem with which I was principally concerned was depressingly simple; it was to find some way of giving the miners of the Ruhr and the Saar the food they needed for their heavy work so that their output would be greater.

The British, on the narrowest of rations themselves and following a policy of equal shares for all, were opposed to any solution that gave more calories to German miners than their own ration provided to Englishmen at home. And more for the German miners might not mean more for those who actually dug the coal; miners would share with their families, who were also hungry. So some of the men would come to the mines as weak as before. Our solution was to arrange a big ladled serving of suitably liquid stew in the mines. Such canteen feeding did not count against the ration in Britain so the British were reconciled. And the Germans couldn't take it home to their children. War is disgusting and so is its aftermath.

Around the first of September, with Edward S. Mason, my longtime friend and Harvard colleague, I went back to Germany to clear with Clay a series of proposals for reviving German industry and agriculture, restoring substantial government authority to the Germans and affirming Polish administration (though not Polish title) to the erstwhile German lands east of the Oder-Neisse.[4] All of this was in anticipation of a trip to Germany by Secretary of State Byrnes to announce the new policy.

The policy he proclaimed on September 6 in the Stuttgart Opera House, after a United States Army band, innocently guided on its selections, had finished playing "Stormy Weather," retained a stern warning against a revival of German militarism. It would not be "in the interest of the German people or in the interest of world peace that Germany should become a pawn or a partner in a military struggle for power between the East and the West."[5] And limits on German industry would continue; only output sufficient for a European-style standard of living and necessary exports would be allowed. However, since production was still far below these levels, their proclamation was empty rhetoric.

*   *   *

In Washington that year food for our former enemies had been a major preoccupation. During the summer of 1946, the world, quite literally, ran out of bread grains. In difficult Washington bargaining the British negotiators, Herbert S. Morrison and Christopher Mayhew, had been persuaded to surrender to the Germans some of their perilously thin reserves. Corn was shipped, along with wheat, to keep them going. Only good organization and an astonishingly effective rationing system, considering what it had survived, got the Germans through. The supply of corn combined with the efforts to revive German industry helped launch one of the more notable of postwar politicians, Ludwig Erhard. I am not sure that these aspects of the story have ever been told.

From late 1947 to early 1948, the head of economic affairs in the British and American bizone was one Dr. Johannes Semler. Wheat was still in short supply, we were still shipping in corn, and, in January 1948, he made a speech in which he noted that what we were sending our former enemies was "Hühnerfutter." He probably

[4] I had worried about affirming Polish administration. The transferred lands, perpetuating the World War I experience with the Saar and the demilitarized Rhineland, would be a continuing source of tension. There would be a struggle to get them back. The ultimate effect of foreign policy decisions is, however, uniformly hidden from all; no one could foresee the good sense with which postwar Germany would accommodate to the inevitable.

[5] James F. Byrnes, *Speaking Frankly* (New York: Harper & Brothers, 1947), p. 189.

didn't intend to be pejorative, but translation can change and not always improve meaning. In English his phrase came out, "The Americans are sending us chicken feed."[6] Semler was fired, and General Clay ordered a search for a more tractable man. He was told that Ludwig Erhard had no Nazi taint, was very good-natured and was given to making speeches on free enterprise. Erhard was appointed. His speeches continued winning him much reputable applause. And he arrived just in time to be credited with the effects of a highly successful currency reform.

Along with getting more coal, a revival of the German economy required that something be done to get less money. For twelve years prices had been rigorously controlled. With food and all other goods now scarce and with wages, salaries and most other payments continuing as before, there was much money and little that it could buy. In consequence, the entitlement to goods was not from having cash but from having the requisite ration cards or coupons. Only German diligence and discipline kept people working for the redundant Reichsmarks. As for the shopkeeper, when he punched a ration card and delivered some food, he did not get anything in return he could use. So he and other sellers had come increasingly to demand some further *quid pro quo* with negotiable value. The best generally available item was cigarettes. In their various denominations — singles, packs, cartons — they were not a bad form of currency, and unlike gold, silver or paper they had inherent use. But something better as well as healthier was needed.

The amount of money that people had in hand or in bank accounts had somehow to be reduced equitably. What was left would then find acceptance at the stores and would be worth producing goods to obtain. The design of this reform was undertaken during 1946 by two exceptionally resourceful American economists of German origin and Jewish antecedents, Raymond Goldsmith, later and long of Yale University, and Gerhard Colm, a highly effective official of the Bureau of the Budget. To their product, for ballast, was added the name of Joseph M. Dodge, a Detroit banker of liberal views who was General Clay's financial adviser. Thus the Colm-Dodge-Goldsmith Plan.

[6] *The Papers of General Lucius D. Clay*, vol. II, Jean Edward Smith, ed. (Bloomington: Indiana University Press, 1974), p. 528. It is only fair to say that after looking carefully at the speech, General Clay continued to feel that Semler's statement was ill-intentioned.

At first glance a currency reform seems a simple, straightforward thing; you ask people to bring in the old currency, in this case the Reichsmarks, and you give them one of the new, the Deutsche Mark, for ten of the old. As an incidental advantage, currency hoards that cannot easily be explained — those of profiteers, black marketeers, important thieves — are left in limbo to become worthless, for their owners will prefer not to come forward to make the exchange.

So much is easy, but then come the complications. A simple exchange involves an egregious discrimination against the individual or family that happens to have its assets in cash or bank deposits.[7] All such take a bath. In contrast, those, usually the more affluent, who have their assets in real estate, stocks, paintings or personal property emerge unscathed.

Colm and Goldsmith sought to equalize the impact (and also partly to compensate those whose houses or other property had been destroyed in the war) by a capital levy on the wealth that would otherwise have been untouched. This was fair, but the horror of American conservatives was extreme. If a capital levy could be sanctioned by Americans in Germany, might it not be a precedent for similar action one day in the United States? This would be a terrible thing not only for the capital but also for capitalism. At meetings that summer in the Pentagon, Howard C. Petersen, a man of conservative instincts who was then serving as Assistant Secretary of War and who would later become a leading Philadelphia banker, could not control his alarm. In the end, in June 1948, the currency reform went through but without the inimical levy. Behind the mystifying shroud that protects monetary action from public scrutiny, the poor, as usual, were made to pay.

But that was a lesser failure in a larger success. Knowing that the reform was coming, shopkeepers and other traders had for some time been thoughtfully setting goods aside, avoiding their sale for the soon-to-be nearly worthless Reichsmarks. When the new money came along, the shelves were suddenly full. There being things to buy, the Deutsche Mark was worth working for, so production also increased. It all seemed a miracle, and perhaps it was. But for this miracle not Gerhard Colm, not Raymond Goldsmith, not even Joe Dodge got the credit. The applause went to Ludwig Erhard. Only

[7] Or government bonds if they are included in the exchange.

later, when far from successfully he succeeded Konrad Adenauer as Chancellor, did the extent of his accidental eminence become partly clear.

Erhard was, withal, a fat and pleasant man. The last of my few encounters with him was in Mexico City a year or two before his death. We were both giving lectures; he asked me why I thought it necessary to come to Mexico to counter his truths.

*   *   *

Berlin during the summer of 1946 had altogether a more pleasant aspect than it had had a year earlier. That was partly because no one longer lived with the desolation. The focus of life had moved to the tree-lined streets and large villas of Zehlendorf and on out to Havel Lake. Here the houses of the affluent, reflecting the already-noted class discrimination of the bombs, had been almost completely spared. However, there was now some compensatory tendency, for after the war these houses became the target of American officers and civilians looking for comfortable, not to say luxurious, quarters.

The infinite capacity of Americans for adjustment was never better affirmed than by the ease with which inhabitants of meager apartments in Alexandria and Arlington accommodated to mansions near the Havel and how quickly they made the comparative performance of cooks and servants a staple of conversation. It was, in fact, repellent. A friend of mine from agricultural days, by then a high foreign service officer on the staff of Robert Murphy and in Berlin with a new wife, devoted nearly his full time to organizing his household and servant corps on a scale to which he was not accustomed. When I dined with him, he spoke of nothing else. During our September visit, Edward Mason and I were housed on Am Hirschsprungstrasse in the house of Bernhard Rust, the former Nazi education minister. Of vast scale, it featured, with much other vulgarity, lascivious beds, gilt plumbing and sunken baths of synthetic malachite. One day I traveled to the British zone to collect Barbara Ward, later Baroness Jackson, then on the staff of *The Economist,* a diverse and talented writer, a woman of rare and slender beauty with a gift for effective and often devastating expression. In the car on the way back she eloquently denounced the unaccustomed luxury in which officers of the British occupation forces were living in Hamburg and Berlin. Then she came to our house.

The extreme availability of servants and also of mistresses was a by-product, inevitably, of the availability of food in the American dwellings. Service or sexual liaison meant added rations not only for the person so recruited but for an extended family as well. Thus did poverty restore the subservient social and sexual values of earlier times. In 1947, following a celebration of this hedonism in *The Saturday Evening Post,* General Clay placed all servants "except one per house for maintenance purposes and one outside employee for large lawns" on a "personal employment basis." He wrote sadly to Dwight D. Eisenhower, then his superior in Washington, that he did not think he would "ever be free of the type and kind of personnel who abuse the privileges which are made available to them and therefore draw adverse press comment."[8]

Efforts were also being made in 1946 to restrain the more routine opportunities of the enlisted men. Even a private's pay in dollars had a huge purchasing power either directly or when exchanged into cigarettes, coffee or other items available to the privileged Americans. That summer a large recreation center, Truman Hall, was opened for the soldiers just across the street from American military government headquarters in Zehlendorf. At the same time, a new policy was adopted designed to limit the commercial operations of the soldiers. Instead of paying them in full in the greatly cherished dollars, they were given the equivalent in chits usable in modest quantity only in American bars, PXs and like facilities, of which Truman Hall had a full range. The rest of their pay was held for later release. In honor of the new and unpopular medium of exchange, Truman Hall promptly became known as Harry's Chit House.

*   *   *

My more depressing memory of Berlin in 1946 was of the conversations that turned on the menace of the Soviet Union. Clay and such of his staff as the highly intelligent William H. Draper, Jr., were contemptuous of such fears. That Russia, recovering from by far the worst devastation of World War II, was physically or even emotionally in a position to begin a new war was dismissed by Clay as fantasy. Against this was the professedly deeper insight of the old

[8]*The Papers of General Lucius D. Clay,* vol. II, p. 325.

priesthood, including Robert Murphy. There was an audience for the latter view among wartime officers for whom, after the excitements of the war, a return to civilian life was a promise of unspeakable tedium. And there was a response also from the business executives who agreed that, although free enterprise was in all respects superior to Communism, only constant vigilance would save it from superior Communist wile. Already, to enter an opposing argument in evening conversation was often to be in the minority. Much later there would be a further consequence. A persistent expression of a minority view caused you to lose your effectiveness. Your dissent being predictable, it was not thought to add usefully to the discussion or deliberation. There was a patient pause while you spoke; then everyone got down to the real business. Eventually it came to be thought more efficient to leave dissenters out. Why waste the time?[9]

In the autumn of 1946, I didn't feel that I was losing my effectiveness. Rather, reflecting on the preceding months, I could not feel that I had any to lose. However rich in instruction, these months had been very low in accomplishment — and especially in comparison with my awesome authority at the Office of Price Administration. Perhaps I should have remained in the State Department and done battle. Instead I resigned and went back to *Fortune.*

[9] My Cambridge neighbor James C. Thompson, Jr., who was later to become Curator of the Neiman Foundation, brought this tendency to general attention as the fate of those in Washington who opposed the Vietnam intervention.

17

Time — Fortune — Life — Luce

Now I MUST RETRACE my steps; chronology has no unique claim over convenience. In 1943, as I've said, when my time at the Office of Price Administration came to an end and the alternatives dissolved into the vacuum that for so many has followed power, my mind turned to a suggestion of a few months earlier from Ralph D. Paine, then the managing editor of *Fortune.* I had been dining with his editorial board, telling of my concerns and achievements as a price-fixer, and he had proposed that when my service in Washington was over, I join the staff of the magazine. I took the train to New York, visited Paine and accepted his offer. It is possible that he had forgotten making it.

I was at *Fortune* from the autumn of 1943 through 1944, left in 1945 to serve with the Bombing Survey and was away again in 1946, as just noted, for the feeble months in the State Department.

For the New York years we took an apartment belonging to Columbia University on Riverside Drive a little above 116th Street. Our windows looked out spaciously at Riverside Park and the Hudson. This was then a calm and even enchanting territory. Streets were clean, fear unknown, and our children Alan and Douglas were exposed every afternoon in the facing park to the sunlight and somewhat fresher air from New Jersey. Naval convoys assembled in the river below, ships being added several a day for a week, and then of a morning all would be gone.

My wife taught German at Columbia, and I was treated courteously at university receptions as a faculty husband. Just above us in the apartment house lived Corliss Lamont and his handsome and interesting family. Corliss, a socialist, civil libertarian, philosopher and agnostic, albeit the son of Thomas W. Lamont of J. P. Morgan

& Company, was regarded with the greatest possible interest by the FBI. So, from our close, if initially accidental juxtaposition, was I. My file, when it became available, was replete with well-considered doubt; no good American could have such a neighbor.

Before going to *Fortune*, I had never written for a living; my total earnings from such art could not have amounted to as much as a thousand dollars. So I was starting at the top. *Fortune* was then, as was intended, one of the best-written magazines in the English language. It proudly eschewed the adamantly vulgar *Time*-style used by its sister publication; its roster included some of the best-known writers of those days. To move abruptly without preparation into this company involved a certain risk. More precisely, it involved a nearly insane self-assurance, one on which I later looked back with astonishment.

As my initial task I proposed a series of articles on the postwar American economy and its prospect. The first, one of the first of its kind, would be an estimate of the postwar Gross National Product and its components. With this would go a consideration of the policies that would prevent a relapse into the kind of depression which the 1930s had taught almost everyone to believe was normal. The statistics I worked out with the assistance of friends in the Department of Commerce; the policies were a cautious infusion of Keynesian measures that would ensure the spending or investment of all that might be saved at a high level of income, output and employment. These required a deficit in the federal budget, something that still had to be mentioned with caution. Massive charts helped make the point.

The result was an occasion for celebration. Paine came down to my stark office, manuscript in hand, to tell me that it was the best thing of the year. The January 1944 New Year's number would be torn apart to give me the lead and featured position. My future as a *Fortune* writer was secure. As I relaxed, I became fully aware for the first time that I had had some misgivings over my gamble.

I did not thereafter have difficulty in persuading editors to accept my prose. When one has demurred, usually because of a too improbable or politically too inconvenient thesis, another has always proven eager. In 1963, I was vacationing on Majorca. One day, after visiting Robert Graves in Deyá, I stopped for a cup of coffee in the vine-covered café on the road at the top of the little hillside town. One of the many literary men thereabouts, bearded and sad of eye, came by and said:

"You're Galbraith?"

I agreed and invited him to have a drink.

He accepted and we chatted. He said, "You know, you have no idea what it's like to be a writer. Your stuff sells."

*   *   *

Fortune, in 1943 a little more than ten years old, was written almost entirely by its own staff, each story normally by a writer/researcher team. Only rarely did one receive a byline. This not everyone regretted, for, as on all the Time, Inc. publications, there was often a dichotomy between personal belief and what got published so identification with the result was not always sought.

The difference between what was believed and what was written, rewritten and published was the great psychological hurdle at the Time, Inc. publications; it was resolved by writers in one of three ways. One group accommodated their writing but not their convictions to what would appear in the magazine. This they did without concealing the act from themselves or even from their colleagues. They were assisted by the ample pay, and, on the whole, they found contentment in their work. A second group tried to believe what they felt they needed to write. Their life was much more difficult, and alcohol and psychiatry were regularly required to facilitate the adjustment. A third, yet smaller number believed what they wrote, and their adjustment was excellent. Many of them occupied senior editorial posts. Others were of lesser rank and trying hard. What they wrote was frequently a bore, and they were poorly regarded by their colleagues.

The gap between belief and expression was much less wide at *Fortune* and *Life* than at *Time.* On the weekly newsmagazine writers had to tell of the devious economic and political designs of F.D.R. and the even more damaging intentions of the New Dealers. Also those of the Russians, so far as distinguishable. And there had to be regular affirmations of the spiritual integrity, moral superiority and military efficiency of Chiang Kai-shek. The sensitive suffered further, for this had to be in the syntax that *Time* then favored. In that arcane English form, as Wolcott Gibbs observed in *The New Yorker* in those days, "backward ran sentences until reeled the mind" and "where it will all end, knows God."

On *Life* the pictures involved no similar conflict with either political conviction or responsible sentence structure, and on *Fortune* we were committed to good English. It had also been Harry Luce's reluctant discovery that, with rare exceptions, good writers on business were either liberals or socialists. To this he was reconciled. Better someone with questionable ideas who wrote interesting and readable English than a man of sound view who could not be read at all. Also when Harry encountered a good conservative affirmation in economics, even if readable, he did not much care for it. He had heard it before.

Prior to my arrival at *Fortune* Archibald MacLeish and John Chamberlain had been the star performers. Both, by the standards of the time, were far to the left. I joined Eric Hodgins and Wilder Hobson, two richly hilarious observers of the American business scene and both diligent connoisseurs of corporate absurdity. Also Herbert Solow, a recently recusant Communist, and Gilbert Burck, a prodigious writer of no overpowering political convictions but with a notable capacity for finding amusement among the folk types of the business world. Once Burck stopped in Minneapolis to interview an entrepreneur who, Luce had been told, was establishing a reputation as a business sage. Harry Luce was always on the lookout for such people; his day-to-day encounters were with very routine businessmen, and somewhere, he felt, there must be a mentally deeper kind. Otherwise how could the American business system be as good as it was? The Minnesota Bentham was a grave disappointment to everyone but Burck. He came back to report that his man had told him, not without emphasis, that "what the American businessman needs today is some new platitudes."

*   *   *

There was recurrent tension from the difference in the political attitudes of *Fortune* writers and those of the executives and firms described with awe on our pages. Just prior to my arrival there was a superior crisis in connection with a several-part article on the United States Steel Corporation. Dwight Macdonald, the writer, had recently adopted Leon Trotsky; he was, he averred, confirmed in his faith by his exposure to the corporation and its executives. As the series progressed, it became deeply subversive. Only by major surgery was the Marxian specter excised.

If the political views of *Fortune* writers were sometimes disconcerting, so more often was their physical appearance. As a general routine, someone of low literary ability but impeccable dress would be sent to corporate headquarters to "open up" a story. Then a writer and researcher of normal attire, manner, laundry and hair style would go in to do the work, often to the alarm of the company concerned. Once we heard that the *Chicago Tribune* might let us do an article on the business side of its operations. Little was known of its corporate affairs, which all thought would make a good story. It would also be something of a coup, for Luce and Colonel Mc-Cormick were less than friends. We dispatched our most carefully pin-striped staff member, a man of slow mind but reassuring aspect, to see the Colonel and close the deal. McCormick's secretary told our emissary when he reached the *Tribune* tower that the Colonel "never saw anyone personally for the first time." Our staffer struggled with that concept, but then it was explained. The Colonel would first study a picture and decide. A *Trib* photographer materialized with a Graflex; several pictures were snapped, and, after an interval, a messenger came back with an envelope containing the proofs. These the secretary took in to Colonel McCormick; after a further interval she came out and told our man the Colonel would not see him.

*   *   *

Our freedom at *Fortune* was also somewhat enhanced by location. *Time, Life* and the corporate offices in those days were in the first Time-Life Building just off Fifth Avenue in Rockefeller Center. A few months after my arrival, *Fortune* moved to a couple of floors halfway up the Empire State Building. To be out of sight was to be slightly out of mind. The Empire State was not densely populated in those days, and Burck discovered, to his delight, that one lonesome proletarian had the job of going, hour after hour, day after day, over the empty floors with the sole task of flushing the toilets. Gil thought it was to keep mosquitoes from breeding in the stagnant pools.

There was a strong feeling that *Fortune,* which cost a stiff dollar a copy in those days, was kept around business offices and better homes as a prestige item and was not read. Surveys always showed otherwise, but the neglect was certainly considerable. I rarely encountered anyone who had read anything I had written. The mails brought little comment except from those directly, praised or condemned in our articles. It occurred to me, as it would again, that one could spend a lifetime writing well for a minuscule audience, and this had much to do with my eventual departure. A writer gradually accumulates reputation and associated capital from his writing, but at *Fortune,* as at *Time,* this didn't happen. Even when an article was signed, the great institutional overburden caused those who read it to attribute it not to Hodgins, Hobson or Galbraith but to *Fortune.* This also I came to think unrewarding.

*   *   *

By far the most important influence on our liberty of expression or the lack of it was Henry Robinson Luce. Forty-five years old in 1943, he was a rather slender man of medium height, with heavy eyebrows, strong features and restless, searching, somewhat nervous eyes. In speech he had an unparalleled talent for parentheses. When he spoke at company gatherings, there would sometimes be bets as to whether he could unravel a particular sentence and come back to his original subject and verb. Often he could.

Such were the complexity of Harry's speech and the generating thought that he rarely noticed what he was eating, drinking or smoking. He met for lunch in those days with his senior editors and writers in a dining room on top of the RCA Building in Rockefeller Center. Present always were one or two well-paid sycophants of confident manner who tried with little success to anticipate his line of thought and guide him to his food. He paid no attention to them. (These functionaries were regarded with cautious disdain by their editorial and working colleagues; the one closest to Luce at the moment was known as "the current Jesus." None ever lasted very long.) Harry would look distractedly at the menu, be diverted and eventually point helplessly to whatever was first on the list. Through the meal he would listen to others only as some seemingly new idea might be voiced. That would rivet his attention, and it didn't matter greatly (China apart) if it was wholly contrary to his beliefs. Luce was conservative, Republican, establishmentarian and romantically chauvinist. But all these were secondary to the Luce curiosity.

This last, properly exploited, accorded one several additional de-

grees of freedom. One might have to go to Harry's office to justify
something one had written or had passed as an editor. But his political or other objections were always secondary to his interest in the
novelty of the case. This one learned to emphasize. He would protest, affirm disbelief and then, with a gesture of regret, say to go
ahead.

No one could confuse this with full freedom of expression. In any
large organization there are only differing degrees of restraint. And
the fact that it is often self-restraint or self-censorship does not make
it any less confining. Self-censorship at *Fortune,* I learned, involved
a constant calculation as to whether a particular statement — sometimes a sentence or a paragraph — was worth the predictable argument, perhaps with Luce, possibly with some frightened or zealous
surrogate. Often one decided that it was not the day for a fight. Or
if your conscience was compelling, you couched the favorable reference to Roosevelt or the CIO in such careful language that it would
slip by, overlooking the near-certainty that it would slip by all your
readers as well.

Still, self-censorship at Time, Inc. was not a new experience to
anyone who had been in public office. In the preceding years I had
learned its use in the Office of Price Administration and studied it
further in the State Department; later still as an ambassador I would
become accomplished in the craft. A subliminal process of the mind
measures all the diverse public consequences of any word, phrase,
assertion or piece of previously undisclosed or unemphasized information. What other public officials, politicians, columnists, business
groups, newspapers, will be aroused? With what public or personal
damage? The various responses run through the mind so rapidly
that information is offered or suppressed, as at a press conference,
without visible hesitation. After a lifetime in public office, self-
censorship becomes not only automatic but a part of one's personality. Only in the most infrequent cases can there be escape for autobiography or memoir. And what there passes for candor is only a
minor loosening of the chains; it cannot be more, for the individual
is rarely aware of his manacles.

Even a short term in office is dangerously addictive. On leaving
Washington, I had always to persuade myself very deliberately that
it was no longer necessary, or so necessary, to assess the effect of my
words. While in India in the Kennedy years, I achieved a minor

reputation for the easy openness of my ambassadorial expression. Indian and American newspapermen expressed admiration and State Department colleagues surprise and, on occasion, concern. A diplomat who spoke his mind. It was a pleasant fraud. Understanding the process of self-censorship, I simply applied it more consciously than others, thereby allowing myself a greater but still harmless degree of freedom.

The extreme practitioner of self-censorship in our time, it should be noted, is not the writer, public figure or even the diplomat. It is the great business executive. He assesses all public and most private expression against corporate need and policy, and the most common consequence is deep, dignified or righteous silence. Mentally the executive raises the art of self-censorship to a further dimension; the corporate truth becomes truth, and any expression or thought in conflict is excluded not because of caution but as error. Few men in history have ever been so circumscribed in their freedom of expression and have regretted it less. It was why, more than incidentally, Harry Luce, with his searching, indefatigable curiosity, found his business friends so tedious. He liked the economic system, but without ever quite conceding it, he found its principals a trial.

*   *   *

Harry Luce was himself an exceptionally informed and competent businessman. Around him were men, including the current Jesus, who spoke learnedly of circulation and its promotion; advertising and its sales; advertising agencies and their quirks and preferences; new magazine ventures and their prospects; competitors and *their* prospects. Luce almost always knew more than they and was far less inclined to make wordy optimism and trade cliché a substitute for thought.

Luce was also a superb editor. Once or twice a year he would come to *Fortune* and take personal charge of an issue, appearances that we called The Comings. His passion was for information as opposed to interpretation or theory. The latter in those days — an article on the success of the capitalist system or its prospective downfall at the hands of ill-intentioned government — carried the derogatory designation of "think piece." First-rate writing meant facts, however they might be arranged or misarranged for effect.

Luce's further and yet greater editorial passion, as I've elsewhere told,[1] was for economy. Nothing so troubled him as wasted words. In 1944, talent being then scarce, I was put in charge of what was called the middle of the book. These were the principal stories, in the main somewhat breathless voyages of discovery into one or another of the large corporations. By then I had learned to drain out excess verbiage. But it was a marvel to see how much more Harry, with a few sweeps of a soft black pencil, could remove and how little in consequence would be lost.

Once a fulsome draft on the West Coast clothing industry came to him by accident and, a few hours later, my greatly condensed version. He remarked with warm approval on the way I had mastered the requisite surgery. It was the praise of a master. Not since working for Harry Luce have I gone over a manuscript without the feeling that he was looking over my shoulder, that his pencil would presently pass through my paragraphs as he said, "This can go."

Harry Luce did not doubt the effect of his editorial instruction. In 1960, at a luncheon at *Time*, he remarked to John F. Kennedy, to the latter's frequently expressed delight, "I taught Kenneth Galbraith to write. And I tell you I've certainly regretted it."

Finally the curiosity that gave us our degree of freedom also made Luce a notable editor. That was because his curiosity was one's own (and that of his readers), with the difference that it was uninhibited. Often you didn't discover you wanted to know until Luce asked the question. One evening I walked with him from Rockefeller Center to the Waldorf Towers where he lived while in town. On the way he saw the sign of a private detective agency in a second-floor window. He asked for whom private detectives mostly worked, how they operated, if they were licensed, what they got paid. I didn't know, but by the time we reached the Waldorf, I wanted to know.

In the autumn of 1961, Harry Luce came to India to attend a great conclave of Christians. His father had, of course, been a missionary, but ecumenical communication, not the rescue of alien souls, was the purpose of this convocation. When the meetings were over, I invited him to join us on a trip to Rajasthan, and in Jaipur I became sick and had to be flown back to Delhi. He returned by embassy car with my wife. There was no feature of Indian social, cultural, marital, hygienic or agricultural life on which he didn't seek

[1] In "Writing and Typing" in *Annals of an Abiding Liberal* (Boston: Houghton Mifflin, 1979), p. 289.

information. They made numerous detours to investigate villages, temples and wells that caught his eye. When they got back to Delhi, Kitty was exhausted. Harry was still asking questions. I could have warned her. In the outlying bureaus and branches of his publishing empire, thoughtful and aspiring residents sometimes prepared for a Luce visit by reading up conscientiously on everything that would be seen on the roads to be traversed.

It will be gathered that, political differences notwithstanding, Harry Luce and I maintained a friendship and a certain reciprocal respect. That is so. I was his guest at a large dinner given for the greater glory of *Life* magazine — its twenty-fifth birthday — just before I left for India. The occasion was made mildly memorable by my dinner companions, the Duke and Duchess of Windsor, who in those days could be purchased for an appropriate subsidy to grace such occasions. I made a note of my conversation with the Duke:

"I hear you are going to In-jea."

This I affirmed.

"I had a very good time there in my early youth. You must do the pig-sticking in Rajasthan."

I murmured unconvincingly that I had heard very good things about it.

"Oh, it is excellent. And you will find the people most agreeable in their own way. They have been most uncommonly decent to my niece."[2]

*   *   *

Luce was a pervading but by no means a preemptive presence at *Fortune.* Two relaxed and civilized gentlemen, Ralph Paine, of whom I have spoken, and the executive editor, Albert L. Furth, provided overall direction. Both were open to ideas and, more remarkably, to fantasy — a reaction, perhaps, to the relative solemnity of Luce and the total gloom of his housecarls. I was allowed to explore the advantages to New Englanders of forming a separate sovereign state complete with its own money, tariffs, foreign loans and balance of payments deficit. Wilder Hobson and I consulted for weeks on a classification of American businessmen by their dress: "The plumage of the American businessman reveals, after considerable study, a

[2] Elizabeth II had just visited India.

good deal of information concerning his habitat and allied subjects."[3] Our categories — Vestments, investments; Anglo-Park Avenue dash; Southern comfort; Genuine Harvard — did not, to our sorrow, take hold.

For much of my time at *Fortune* my office adjoined that of Eric Hodgins, and we shared the same aggressively indifferent secretary. Only the fact that he spent most of his life in the institutional anonymity of Time, Inc. kept Eric Hodgins from being remembered, even as Sinclair Lewis, as a connoisseur of the folk habits of the American entrepreneur. Hodgins had graduated from MIT with a degree conditional, he said, on a promise never actively to practice any form of engineering. After lesser editorial and writing tasks, including a stint as editor of the *Technology Review*, the MIT alumni magazine, he became successively a writer at *Fortune*, the managing editor, a corporate vice president without useful function and then, by his own choice, a much-valued writer again. Along the way he won a hard battle with alcohol and in the days of our friendship was a devout communicant of Alcoholics Anonymous.

A big man, in clothes that seemed rarely to have been changed, with a deeply marked face and an explosive laugh, he suffered from a chronic oversupply of information. All Hodgins's stories, though in fact tightly written, came in at twice the publishable length. We got the originals from the typing room to read. Editing not only took out valuable material (as distinct from the usual dross) but also sharp changes of pace and recurrent descents into hilarious vulgarity, the latter exquisitely designed to stir the reader out of his normal somnambulance.

"If Mr. Dascomb," he said of an advertising man he celebrated in a venture into near-fiction, "had chosen the Church as his career he would have been a bishop, and a bishop among bishops . . . [H]e had a bishop's overwhelming advantage that although his human frailties might be intermittently evident, it was obvious that he was nevertheless in constant two-way communication with the Holy Ghost. Where others had to rely on feeling, or, at best, on facts, Mr. Dascomb had the higher advantage of Revelation . . . There was, however, a widespread opinion throughout advertising circles in the United States that Mr. Dascomb was a bastard."[4]

[3] "The Business Suit," *Fortune*, vol. XXXVIII, no. 1 (July 1948), p. 104.
[4] *Blandings' Way* (New York: Simon & Schuster, 1950), p. 39.

Eric's examination of the woes of an urban innocent who built a house in the wilds of Connecticut — *Mr. Blandings Builds His Dream House* — grew out of a shorter piece in *Fortune* and became a notable movie with Cary Grant and Myrna Loy. He followed this with *Blandings' Way,* another semi-novel on Connecticut exurbia and the New York advertising business, from which the quotation above on Mr. Dascomb is taken. In the last years of his life he wrote a moving account of his efforts to contend — in the end successfully — with a stroke (*Episode: Report on the Accident inside My Skull*) that initially rendered him incapable of such elementary tasks as tying up his shoelaces. When he died in 1971, Eric was at work on his autobiography, an infinitely amusing document, and I patched it up for publication. Alas, the best had still to be written.

As was true of Thorstein Veblen, Eric surveyed and occasionally destroyed without being subject to the greatest source of banality in economic and business writing, which is the obligation to be constructive. One should be permitted to identify absurdity or error without being required to correct it. Hodgins also knew, as do depressingly few business writers and editors, what businessmen like to read. That is not of the brilliant achievements of other business executives but of their mishaps, moral lapses, mistakes and, as occasion offers, their disasters. These are both more varied and more interesting than the success stories, and they give the business reader a greatly rewarding sense of his own superiority.

Hodgins had a high view of Time, Inc. as a source of imaginative corporate aberration, and, under his instruction, I came partly to share it. One glowing example remains in my mind.

During the war years and again during the Eisenhower administrations, the principal emissary of Time, Inc. in Washington was Charles D. (C.D.) Jackson. A large, effluent man, C.D. exuded a confidence in his own abilities that, manifestly, he thought justified. After the war Harry Luce put him in charge of one of his rare setbacks, Time-Life International. According to Luce, with World War II we had entered upon the American Century. Harry was susceptible to the thought that the principal, indeed inevitable, manifestation of this epoch would be round-the-world coverage of the news by *Time* and *Life* in a large convoy of local English and foreign-language editions. The Luce sycophants were predictably enthusiastic. The initial consequence, at a time when few currencies could be converted into dollars and no one needed to advertise goods, these being everywhere in appallingly short supply, was losses that were an impressive subtraction even from Time, Inc.'s earnings. Luce didn't like losses, and Jackson was determined to retrieve. The losses continued. One of C.D.'s explanations brought Eric roaring into my office, for it was a truly magnificent example of triple-reverse conditional free enterprise prose, turning a bad deficit into a substantial achievement. It was in a circular to members of the "senior group" at *Time,* a privileged community of old hands who participated in profits. In it C.D. advised (and here I paraphrase) that if business conditions in the second half of the year had been as favorable as in the first half, Time-Life International would have been within shooting distance of the break-even point.

*   *   *

My years at Time, Inc. were instructive. I did not fully accept C.D. Jackson's lesson that, with proper prose resource, any delinquency or shortcoming could be explained. But, as I've indicated, Harry Luce's instruction in writing was a lifetime gift. And there was another professional dividend. The early *Fortune,* more than any other journal anywhere in the industrial world, saw the modern large corporation as a primary economic and social force. My years there as writer and editor provided a diversity and intimacy of exposure to its structure, operating goals and economic, social and political influence that could not have been had in any other way. From those years came a lasting immunity to the mythology of the neoclassical textbook economics and its image of a world of competitive firms with authority and ownership united in a single personality and guided by a single mind. To them I owe in part the notion of the technostructure[5] as the decisive managerial and innovative instrument in the modern large enterprise and much else that became part of my Harvard teaching and of *The New Industrial State.* My debt to Harry Luce and *Fortune,* or as some would prefer their responsibility, is not slight.

*   *   *

To have continued forever at *Fortune* was tempting. The pay was good — by far the highest for any similar group of journalists in

[5] See Chapter 32.

New York. The company was congenial and generally free from the cutthroat competitiveness that characterizes many such enterprises. As I've noted, the subordination of political conviction could have been managed, although in time it might have become dangerously habitual. Nonetheless I continued to believe that I should be at a university, teaching as necessary and writing on my own. The example of Hodgins, superb but nearly unknown, was not wholly out of my mind. Also I had come to feel that I was no sooner started on a subject — an important postwar series on the congenital inadequacies of the housing industry, for example — than I had to stop learning and thinking and go to press. Finally it was all too evident that Time, Inc. paid its people well and discarded them insouciantly as over the hill at around fifty. The Galbraiths, as I've told, were thought to be rather long-lived. This disparity could be corrected if I accommodated to the brief period of professional utility in the usual Time, Inc. way — heavy smoking, heavy drinking and a high-tension response to the everyday exigencies of life. This cut one's actual life expectancy down to corporate need. But I enjoyed life.

One day in the summer of 1948, John D. Black called me to urge that I come back to Harvard. He had received a large endowment of funds from the United States Department of Agriculture to study the marketing of agricultural products, primarily in New England. The Congress had been caught up that year in the notion that by more efficient marketing of their products farmers might be made more prosperous without costly subsidy. I would be a lecturer, a second-class citizen, but at the pay of a professor. Kitty and I drove up to Cambridge; we concluded that this was where we felt at home. In the autumn of 1948, after an absence of nine years, I went back to academic life.

18

Academia Redux

FOR THE SUMMER of 1947, while I was still at *Fortune,* we borrowed the house of friends, Janey and Charles Siepmann, in Brookline, not far from Brattleboro in southeastern Vermont, and there I settled down to survey the current state of the economics of industrial organization — roughly of the great corporations — in an article for a volume to be published for the American Economic Association.[1] The town of Brookline is in a valley between long, forested hills (called mountains) which ends at Newfane, architecturally the most nearly perfect village in all the land. I joined Kitty in love of this tranquil and lovely countryside, and we resolved to be a part of it. For the next third of a century southeastern Vermont would be an epicenter of our lives and those of our children.

This is an area of sometimes fertile valleys accommodating rather leisurely streams and a few surviving farms. Above the steep hillsides is a high, irregular tableland with rocky outcroppings and much loose stone. Once this land too was farmed, a major mistake. Now it is covered again with hardwood forest. Farther above and to the west are the Green Mountains. These resisted even the most optimistic settler.

Beginning in 1765, after the end of the French and Indian War, people from already well-populated Connecticut and then from Massachusetts and Rhode Island moved into this countryside — into the hills and later the more densely forested valleys. The movement does not sustain any heroic myth: ". . . religious and political considerations were distinctly secondary. 'It was the old land hunger that drove men and women and little children into the Vermont

---

[1] "Monopoly and the Concentration of Economic Power," in *A Survey of Contemporary Economics,* Howard S. Ellis, ed. (Homewood, Illinois: Richard D. Irwin, 1948), vol. I. Published for the American Economic Association.

wilderness.' "[2] This hunger, however, was not slight. For thousands of years land, any land, had been the symbol and source of economic independence and, in amount, an index of power and prestige. So it remained. The new arrivals cleared off the trees and moved the stones off the fields and arranged them into the neat walls that still run through the woods. By repressing their own innovative tendencies, which would have been disastrous, and following instead the handsome designs available in the books on architecture, they built beautifully proportioned houses. However, very soon, in the high country, they discovered the extent of their error or that of their parents.

The land was execrable. And the climate, however satisfactory it might later be for summer dwellers and winter skiers, was also inhospitable and eccentric — in 1811, a great deal of property was swept away by rain and floods, and in 1816, there was much snow and ice in early June. Meanwhile word was spreading that good, deep, black soil mercifully free of stones was to be had in upstate New York, in Ohio and beyond. And in 1825, the Erie Canal made farm products from this rich land available to — and competitive with the produce of — the East. So those who had moved into Vermont, or more often their children, began to move on. Agriculture in the high country went into a decline. Field by field and farm by farm, the rocky landscape went to trees.[3] The houses fell into ruin or burned down except where an occasional family more stubborn or more obtuse than the rest stayed on.

In Townshend on the border of Newfane we bought the house of one such family in a burst of extravagance, as it then seemed, in the autumn of 1947. It had started as a Cape Cod cottage. The rooms encircled, intelligently, a massive central chimney, with one large fireplace for the kitchen and living room, smaller ones for the bedrooms. The house had then been gracefully lengthened and was eventually made to border two sides of a shaded, pleasantly irregular lawn. The wide pine floorboards had been worn and polished to a rich silken sheen. With the house came 235 acres of meadow and forest, together with streams, small lakes and a flour-

[2] Lewis D. Stillwell, *Migration from Vermont* (Montpelier: Vermont Historical Society, 1948), p. 77. He quotes Walter H. Crockett, *Vermont: The Green Mountain State* (New York: Century History Company, 1921), vol. I, p. 258.

[3] The meadows nurtured pine seedlings. These grew, were harvested and were replaced by hardwoods.

ishing population of deer and beaver. Not all in nature succumbs to progress; far better to be a deer, beaver, porcupine, raccoon or game bird in Vermont today and far more numerous your company than a century ago.

From the house what was once a public thoroughfare runs for a half mile through the deep woods to the mailbox on what is now the nearest road. Up that road a few yards is the graveyard, only half-filled, that once served the adjacent farms and the long deserted village. From beyond the grave one of the dead continues a salutary warning:

> My flesh lies slumbering in this ground
> While friends and neighbors sleep around
> And you, kind reader, pause and view
> The sod that soon may cover you.

For the house and land, the more remote acres of which we have not yet seen, we paid $6750.

*   *   *

We spent the summer of 1948 in Vermont, and that September I went down to Cambridge to resume teaching at Harvard. The journey was for me not without misgivings. There would be need, after nine intense and at times powerful years, to accommodate to the relative serenity of the scholarly life. And I was not happy about the ambiguity of my academic rank. In American universities a lecturer, as noted, is proclaimed not quite first class. This, after warning myself against puerile vanity, I still found disagreeable.

Less had changed at Harvard than one might have imagined. Harold Hitchings Burbank was still the chairman of the department of economics. Graduate students still swarmed, although not with quite the earlier excitement, to the seminar on fiscal policy of Alvin H. Hansen, which he now shared with his congenial but much more conservative colleague John H. Williams. I moved into the offices in Littauer Center which I had abandoned in 1939 and which I still occupy. Very soon my academic dignity was by way of being rescued.

Howard R. Bowen, later the president of Grinnell College in Iowa and thereafter of the University of Iowa, was then dean of the college of commerce and business administration of the University of

Illinois. He invited me to become the chairman of his economics department. (In a major explosion on behalf of free enterprise though not free speech, Howard would soon be charged, among other misdemeanors, with showing insufficient enthusiasm for instruction in advertising. Teaching better forms of advertising, he said, was like teaching a woman to be a better prostitute.) Kitty and I went out to Urbana-Champaign to investigate, and when the offer became known in Cambridge, the Harvard department met and voted me a full professorship.

The vote was unanimous that day because of the absence of Gottfried Haberler, one of the numerous and highly civilized Austrians who had migrated to the United States in the 1930s with a commitment to preserving here without compromise the competitive and laissez-faire economy that, through its failures, had been lost in Austria and Germany. In the decades following World War II, Austrian economic policy has been a model of successful, undogmatic pragmatism. None can doubt that it benefited greatly from the emigration of these distinguished scholars to the United States; addressing the Austrian Social Democrats in 1971, I enjoyed making this point in a polite way. Like many others, Haberler associated unthinking commitment to the market and automatic resistance to government intervention with scientific competence. Feeling this way, he dutifully went to University Hall on his return and registered the lone dissenting vote. None of this greatly affected our relations over the next thirty years.

*   *   *

To describe the developments that now followed my recommendation to a professorship, I must resort to metaphor. On a winter day in the mid-seventies I went with my wife to the University of Louvain to receive an honorary degree. The ceremonies over, we were taken to the nearby Brussels airport by our Belgian hosts to catch our plane. We stood in one of two lines leading up to the counter, and opposite us in the other was a homburg-hatted, fur-collared man, a picture of solid, bourgeois accomplishment. He was, in fact, a connoisseur of literature if not of fine writing. He looked across at me and in a highly effective voice said, "You are Professor Galbraith."

I bowed.

"You have written the most expressive words in the English language."

I bowed more deeply, even gratefully, and asked him what they were.

"They are in your journal of an ambassador. It is where you say, 'The shit hit the fan.' "

All within earshot were, I believe, impressed.

I had used this phrase to describe the effect when, during my Senate confirmation hearings before going to India as ambassador in 1961, two conservative senators — Alexander Wiley of Wisconsin and Frank J. Lausche of Ohio — came up with the discovery that I had urged the recognition of Red China. (In fact, I had urged the more cautious two-China policy of the time — let us recognize mainland China whenever there is assurance that we can continue diplomatic relations with Taiwan.) For a time this put my confirmation in doubt, but I was saved by the strenuous advocacy of, among others, Hubert Humphrey. That I should be a Harvard professor hit the members of the Reverend and Honorable, the Board of Overseers of Harvard College with an even more resonant splash.

This liturgically august body numbering thirty members is elected by the Harvard alumni and, with the smaller Corporation, comprises the bicameral government of the university. Not for some decades prior to 1948 had the Overseers risen above ceremony, and, to their credit, they have not done so since. Nor have they done much of anything else. Dignity, shared presence and generously shared self-esteem are often a substitute for function. But no pattern of behavior is wholly predictable; my proposed appointment turned gentlemanly contentment and torpor into ardent and eloquent indignation. For only the second time in modern memory the Board of Overseers blocked a professorial selection.

Partly it was an accident. Charles Cabot, who had stood with the Air Force in the climactic row over bombing and from whose hands I had taken the writing of the basic Survey report, was now on the Executive Committee of the Board of Overseers. He was not a mean man nor one to carry a grudge. But he had seen me behaving in an admittedly uncouth way and, as he saw it, on the wrong side. No brash civilian should have placed himself in opposition to the experienced wisdom of the Air Force or shown such a lack of respect for the acknowledged heroes of the Republic. This Charles Cabot knew, and therewith he knew his duty as a Cabot.

Almost immediately there developed a second and more serious objection. Sinclair Weeks, another member of the Board of Overseers, now between service as a United States senator and as Eisenhower's Secretary of Commerce and the most resolutely regressive influence in the Commonwealth of Massachusetts, was appalled by my liberalism. He was joined in concern by Clarence B. Randall, the head of Inland Steel, and Thomas S. Lamont of J. P. Morgan, who, differing with his brother Corliss, thought that I had an excessive commitment to the economics of the late New Deal and, more alarming, that of John Maynard Keynes. There were already too many Keynesians in the department.

A committee of the Overseers was constituted to investigate the appointment, and its finding was deeply adverse. Then friendly members led by Charles E. Wyzanski, Jr., an old New Dealer and now a federal judge, and stimulated from the outside by Thomas Eliot, rallied to my side, as did President James Bryant Conant and the university provost, Paul H. Buck. Though deeply confidential, particulars of the battle were made known to me immediately. And while officially in ignorance I submitted a brief on my own behalf, concentrating righteously on my having told the truth about the Air Force's achievements. This was strong ground. George Ball took an active hand in my support; so, with some qualification, did Paul Nitze, with whom in later years I was to have sharp differences on the merits of military thought. Ball sought out Stuart Symington, then Secretary of the Air Force, who in a highly cooperative gesture declared that the Air Force had nothing against me.

The battle lasted for a full year; this was partly because my supporters, guided by Wyzanski, had, on occasion, to get a postponement to avoid certain defeat. To be so in limbo was not pleasant; in truth, it was very disagreeable. Then one afternoon in 1949, after a meeting of the full Board of Overseers, Paul Buck called me up to say in an admirably direct way that right had prevailed. It had required a threat of resignation by James Conant.

There was for me a lasting effect. Often in academic and public life one wonders whether one must speak out on some issue where the emotions or pecuniary interests of the reputable are in opposition to the public good. Perhaps this time one can pass and accept the pleasures of a tranquil life. Always when faced with this decision, I have thought of Sinclair Weeks, Clarence Randall and Thomas Lamont. Surely I must do whatever might be possible to justify their forebodings.

Charles Cabot, as noted, was a decent man impaled on an issue that he didn't fully understand. I wondered if he might not sometime seize an opportunity to express regret. And a year or two later the opportunity arose. Dwight D. Eisenhower, at the time President of Columbia University, accepted from W. Averell and E. Roland Harriman the gift of Arden House, the great French-style chateau achieved by their father, E. H. Harriman, in the Ramapo Mountains forty-eight miles north of New York City. The Columbia trustees, when they had recovered from their distress, agreed that Arden House would be allowed to serve one of Ike's more cherished academic visions, perhaps his only one. Americans of compelling corporate or other public reputation would gather periodically in these Arcadian surroundings to resolve the major issues of the time. After the American Assembly, as it would be called, had met, legislative and executive decision in Washington would be inevitable and supremely intelligent.

The first such convocation was held in May 1951. At Averell Harriman's insistence some trade union leaders were added to the list of participants. So, rather to my surprise, was I. Quickly it was decided that conclusions would not be reached. This is in accordance with the basic ethic of such gatherings; it is sufficient for the success of a conference that ideas be exchanged. Since it is very hard to have a conference at which ideas are not exchanged, it is difficult to have one that is not a success.

The exchange of ideas at Arden House lasted for several days, and one problem was not foreseen. More were present than the considerable number once entertained by the Harrimans, and there was a shortage of bathrooms. So acute was this deprivation that one formed the practice of trying every bathroom door as it was encountered. Were one not responding to need, one sought to forestall it.

Attending the conference, among others, was Charles Cabot. I had not seen him during the great struggle of 1948 or after, and for the first two or three days at Arden House, having been assigned to different discussion groups, we passed only at a distance. Then one morning I was making my way along the impressive gallery that joins the main house to the part that was later built for Averell Harriman. Along this gallery are bedrooms and bathrooms, and, as I passed the latter, I conscientiously tried the doors. At one, as my hand turned the knob, another hand turned it from within. Out, with clipped mustache, well-cut hair, lean figure, quiet, good suiting, stepped Cabot. I had previously decided as to my demeanor when we met and especially if he expressed regret. I would be no less gracious, nowise less a Cabot.

He said, "Good morning, Kenneth."

I bowed and replied, "Good morning, Charles."

He then moved on a step or two and hesitated; it was obvious that there was something on his mind. So I too paused. He started down the hall again, and again he hesitated. I remained with my hand on the bathroom door. Then, his mind made up, he squared his shoulders, came to a full stop and said, "Kenneth, there is something I must tell you."

I smiled in a friendly, encouraging way.

He said, "It won't flush."

*   *   *

At Harvard I set out to repair my academic reputation and show that despite the occupational peripeteia of the previous nine years, I could be a safe and somber scholar. Edward S. Mason, now dean of the school of public administration, asked me to take over his course in industrial organization — the economics and regulation, roughly, of the modern large firm. This took me from the agriculture on which I had been expected to concentrate my mind to the economics of a society dominated by the big corporations. It was a subject with which I would be durably involved.

On January 4, 1947, I had joined with the archons of the contemporary liberal faith — Eleanor Roosevelt, Hubert Humphrey, Chester Bowles, Joseph Rauh, Jr., Reinhold Niebuhr, David Dubinsky and Arthur M. Schlesinger, Jr. (Ronald Reagan being also an early communicant) — to found Americans for Democratic Action. At the launching session in the Willard Hotel in Washington I had confined myself to urging that the organization be called the Liberal Union. I was defeated. There was fear at Harvard, not wholly illegitimate, that I might concern myself unduly with political activity of this general sort at the expense of the students, scholarly writing and decent academic reticence. Accordingly, in 1948, I eschewed all connection with politics, apart from voting, and united with others in assuming that Thomas E. Dewey — whose careful ambiguity had caused Harold Ickes, Roosevelt's Secretary of the Interior, to speak of Thomas Elusive Dewey, the Candidate in Sneakers — would be the next President. I listened at home to the very early returns that election night and began to wonder. Later at Arthur Schlesinger's house I was joined beside the radio by Barbara Kerr, a talented and amusing woman who was then writing editorials for the impeccably Republican *Boston Traveler.* The other members of the party, in the tradition of Cambridge liberalism, were listening to their own analyses of the Dewey prospect or adhering closely to the bar. The news coming over the radio was still at variance with expectation. Improbable areas were showing Truman strength; in all probable ones he was leading. Presently Barbara disappeared and returned in her coat to listen for another minute. I asked her where she was going.

"That editorial on 'Return to Sanity' isn't going to run. I've got to do a 'No Mandate for Socialism.' "

*　　*　　*

In the spring of 1950, our younger son Douglas, just seven and intelligent, determined and variously accomplished beyond his years, developed leukemia. His steady decline, accepted with unfrightened calm, is something on which after thirty years I do not care to dwell. What relief there was came from Dr. Dorothea Moore, who gave day-to-day guidance and care, from the superb staff of Children's Hospital in Boston, from its truly pleasant wards, from Dr. Sidney Farber, the great pioneer in cancer research who never allowed us to give up hope, from Dr. Charles A. Janeway also of Children's Hospital, who became a lifelong friend, and from numerous neighbors, friends and graduate students at Harvard who organized themselves into relays to provide replacement blood. One day the students in their enthusiasm even swept along a young tourist who was peering into Littauer Library.

Soon the ordeal was over. We went to Montreal and by Canadian Pacific steamer to Europe for the summer. In the next two years two more sons, Peter Woodard and James Kenneth, were born. Our three sons are now highly self-sufficient and richly rewarding adults, and I leave their further history to them.

*   *   *

In Paris that summer, I got word that President Truman, perhaps without his knowledge, had established a joint commission of Germans and Americans to form a policy for relief of the great refugee population — then estimated at between eight and nine millions — in West Germany. It would be headed by Hans Christian Sonne, a New York financial entrepreneur of Danish origin and strongly compassionate instinct. A message asked if I would join the commission and proceed to Germany as soon as cleared for loyalty and general respectability to make the initial arrangements for its work.

Clearance came after some delay, which was later explained as resulting from the weight of my FBI file and the reassignment of the first man who was reading it when only halfway through. Meanwhile Kitty and I had gone walking by and up the Jungfrau out of Grindelwald in Switzerland. I went to the American Embassy in Bern to pick up the permit then required for entering Germany, and, this in hand, I called on my old friend John Carter Vincent, now the chief of mission. He took me into his staff meeting for a discussion of various confidential and commonplace matters and afterward, when I bade him goodbye, seemed greatly surprised; he thought that I had come to join his staff.

I went on to Frankfurt, returned to Boston for a minor but disagreeable operation to remove a polyp from my throat, and joined the commission briefly late that autumn in the dark and nervous days following MacArthur's defeat at the Yalu. Then as on my earlier visit I lived with Shepard Stone, a former assistant Sunday editor of the *New York Times* and subsequently, as a resolute proponent of collective good works, associated with the Ford Foundation, the International Association for Cultural Freedom and the Aspen-Berlin Institute for Humanistic Studies. He was then handling press and other public information matters for John J. McCloy, who was at the time the American Occupation head in succession to Lucius Clay. For McCloy, a man with an undeviating commitment to the Establishment view, of which he was on occasion the author, Shepard Stone had a possibly excessive respect.

I was with Shep when word came that Truman had hazarded the ill-considered thought that it might be necessary to use the Bomb to restore the position in Korea, a threat that in the next days led Clement Attlee to fly in alarm to Washington. Without hesitation Shep got on the telephone to instruct his staff and all others concerned to use every possible means to downplay, ignore or otherwise reduce comment on the President's aberration. A good man can help his President a lot.

The Sonne commission was, perhaps, the least useful in all the long history of organized government cerebration, a hard competition to win. We were studying a problem that had nearly solved itself. Blue-collar workers from what was now Polish Silesia were working a sixty-hour week in the Ruhr. Small manufacturers and makers of diverse handicrafts from the Czech Sudetenland were now back in production in Bavaria. Lawyers, doctors, accountants and professors from Eastern Europe had by now found employment. Only the old feudal classes and those isolated in rural communities, most notably in Schleswig-Holstein, were still excluded from the economic and social life of West Germany. One day at a hearing in the Ruhr I asked a witness who was speaking eloquently of "the burden of the refugees" if everything wouldn't be worse if all these industrious immigrants suddenly went home. An honest man, he agreed after some thought that it would.

On few matters are we so determinedly obscurantist as on attitudes toward migration. The practical evidence on its effects is overwhelming: West Germany, Israel, Singapore, Hong Kong, Taiwan, Miami and the Punjab in India have all had a large inflow of migrants since World War II. These areas are the economic success stories of this era. That such migrants, extensively selected by themselves for their initiative and by disaster for their strength, resource and ability to survive, should make a powerful contribution to economic development is hardly surprising. Many are made strong by the very act of migration itself. Had they remained at home in peace, they would have lived out their lives in the comfortable mental and physical lassitude that is praised as happiness and contentment.

Migrants want to come; employers are eager to have them. The economic development to which they contribute is desirable. But instead there is the perversity of the present attitudes: the governments of the receiving countries seek to prevent the influx, those of the supplying countries deplore the exodus. Fortunately the power of government in this matter is small so the movement continues.

In Germany in 1950, this conclusion began to obtrude on my mind, and in 1978, I returned to the subject in lectures at the Graduate Institute of International Studies of the University of Geneva and at Radcliffe College. Most reviewers of the small book that came from these lectures[4] criticized my endorsement of the social and economic values of migration.

*   *   *

My principal preoccupation in the early fifties was with the idea of countervailing power, which led to a book on the subject published in 1952.[5] In the economics of the textbooks, to remind once more, the power to enhance one's prices and income at the expense of others is held in check by the market. The business firm is prevented from raising its prices and enhancing its profits at the expense of the consumer by the presence of competitors who, seeing their chance, will sell more for less. And similarly if the buyer of labor, farm products or raw materials seeks to depress the wages of workers or prices of farm producers below the market rate, he too invites them to go elsewhere. If there is a higher market rate, there is an elsewhere — someone is paying the higher wage or price because he can do so and still make money.

The critical requirement for both the buyer and the seller is that there be an eager alternative — a firm that will sell at the lower price, an employer who will buy at the higher one. Power is held in check by competition and only by competition.

Few of undogmatic mind can now doubt that, as capitalism develops, so also does the concentration of production. Fewer firms of ever greater size produce an ever greater share of all goods and services. With this industrial concentration the supply of alternative sellers and buyers diminishes or ceases to exist. Or there is a tacit understanding between the great firms as to what prices will be asked or paid. That the individual worker, needing regularly to eat,

[4] *The Nature of Mass Poverty* (Cambridge: Harvard University Press, 1979).
[5] *American Capitalism: The Concept of Countervailing Power* (Boston: Houghton Mifflin, 1952; rev. ed., 1956; and also White Plains: M. E. Sharpe, 1980).

often committed to a mortgage and in doubt as to alternatives, can deal on equal terms with the large corporate buyer of labor can be believed only after much careful training.

Where competition failed, the neoclassical response was to say that the market concentration that allowed of control of prices should be reversed and competition re-established. Monopoly and oligopoly, where they could not be overlooked, were impermissible.

Liturgically this remains the response. The paper sword of neoclassical economics in the United States, derived from a day when monopoly could be thought exceptional and agreement on prices overt not tacit, was and remains the antitrust laws. They are the ultimate triumph of hope over experience. In the near century of their existence they have not dissolved economic power and have not perceptibly arrested the great thrust, massive and ineluctable, to greater concentration that is the history of capitalism in all the industrial countries. That concentration and the associated accession of market power have not been perceptibly less in the United States than they have been in the other industrial countries, which have had no similar antitrust laws or have made no similar effort.

To look at the world as it exists is often an informative thing. From trying to do so, I had come to believe that the problem of corporate power was solved in practice not by dispersing it but by creating another, opposing and thus annulling position of power. Contending with strong corporate buyers of their products, farmers had formed marketing cooperatives to sell their crops and livestock. This was a far more practical course than seeking the dissolution of Swift, Armour or General Mills. Contending with high prices uncertainly related to quantity or quality, consumers had formed buying cooperatives. This was also better than waiting for the big food companies to be broken up. And this process had extended into the corporate fabric itself. The check on the market power of the big canners was the buying power of the big chains; of the big appliance manufacturers, that of Sears and Montgomery Ward. And one observed that where the organization necessary for the requisite annulling of economic power was too difficult to achieve, the assistance of the government was invoked. Thus farm support prices and the minimum wage.

The supreme manifestation of countervailing power was the trade union:

The operation of countervailing power is to be seen with the greatest clarity in the labor market where it is also most fully developed. Because of his comparative immobility, the individual worker has long been highly vulnerable to private economic power . . . Normally he could not move and he had to have work. Not often has the power of one man over another been used more callously than in the American labor market after the rise of the large corporation. As late as the early twenties, the steel industry worked a twelve-hour day and seventy-two-hour week with an incredible twenty-four-hour stint every fortnight when the shift changed.

No such power is exercised today and for the reason that its earlier exercise stimulated the counteraction that brought it to an end. In the ultimate sense it was the power of the steel industry, not the organizing abilities of John L. Lewis and Philip Murray, that brought the United Steel Workers into being . . .

As a general though not invariable rule one finds the strongest unions in the United States where markets are served by strong corporations.[6]

My oral outline of the magic and mysteries of countervailing power sufficiently impressed Craig Wylie, then a senior editor of Houghton Mifflin, that he forthwith invested an advance of a thousand dollars in the prospect. It seemed to me a handsome, even reckless, gesture. The book, when published, did attract a fair number of readers and went through two further editions and into French, German, Spanish, Italian and Japanese translations. At the end of 1953, the American Economic Association scheduled a special session to consider it. A newspaper reporter covering the meeting heard one young scholar tell another, "It's time to go and hear them destroy Galbraith." The effort was undertaken with enthusiasm and competence by David McCord Wright, then of the University of Virginia, and George Stigler of the University of Chicago. Neither approved new thought, however plausible. I survived. Professor Wright caused me some subsequent travail by noting, quite justly, that the notion of countervailing power sanctioned the continued existence of monopoly. He then proceeded to say, with possible exaggeration, that, "albeit quite possibly unconsciously, I should judge Dr. Galbraith one of the most effective enemies of both capitalism and democracy."[7] This, a year and a half later, was taken by Senator

---

[6]*American Capitalism: The Concept of Countervailing Power*, rev. ed., pp. 114–115.

[7]*Papers and Proceedings* of the Sixty-sixth Annual Meeting of the American Economic Association in Washington, D.C., December 28–30, 1953, published in *The American Economic Review*, vol. XLIV, no. 2 (May 1954), p. 30.

Homer E. Capehart of Indiana as indication of deeply subversive motivation in connection with some testimony I had given on the stock market, testimony that had, it was alleged, caused the market to take a nasty plunge. I will return to this misfeasance.

The critics faulted me for not conforming to textbook truth. In doing so, they missed, alas, the major flaws in my case. That a countervailing assertion of economic power is the normal answer to original economic power, I still wholly believe. But in 1952, carried away by the idea, I made it far more inevitable and rather more equalizing than, in practice, it ever is. Countervailing power often does not emerge. Numerous groups — the ghetto young, the rural poor, textile workers, women clerical workers, many consumers — remain weak or helpless.

There was also an erroneous implication in the title and a euphoric tendency in the text. Countervailing power is not peculiar to American capitalism; elsewhere there was an impression that American capitalism, in contrast with other national versions, was uniquely viable.

I did note that countervailing power "does not function . . . when there is inflation or inflationary pressure on markets."[8] Then the trade union does not confront the power of the corporation. Rather, the corporation concedes to union demands and passes the cost of the settlement on to the public. And when there is inflation, no organization of consumers and no supermarket chain bargaining on their behalf is effective in contending with the upward thrust of prices. Thus does inflation nullify countervailing power. Also from inflation come pressures for price guidelines and price controls. More than social welfare measures or Keynesian action to ensure adequate purchasing power, employment and production, these could alter the character of the market and, indeed, of capitalism itself. Such being the case, "Boom and inflation, in our time, are the proper focus of conservative fears."[9]

But on economic foresight one must be content with modest claims. I did not at all foresee that inflation would become a seemingly permanent condition. Nor did I fully see that the organizations created to express countervailing power — farm organizations, trade

[8] *American Capitalism: The Concept of Countervailing Power*, rev. ed., p. 128.
[9] *American Capitalism: The Concept of Countervailing Power*, rev. ed., p. 201. This is the book's closing line.

unions — would, in conjunction with the corporations whose power they answered, become a cause of that inflation. One can survive orthodox criticism without harm; the great march of history is a more relentless thing.

* * *

In 1952, I published a second book of which I have already made mention, this one on the wartime experience of price control, the more general economic management of the war and the resulting lessons.[10] Then I set to work on the volume that, after considerable change of course, would be called *The Affluent Society*. But into its preparation were spliced the two presidential campaigns of Adlai E. Stevenson.

[10]*A Theory of Price Control* (Cambridge: Harvard University Press, 1952; reissued 1980).

19

Adlai Stevenson

THE ESTEEM or relative disesteem in which the American people hold their leaders and its precise nuance are rather exactly indicated in speech (though not in prose) by the way they are designated in everyday reference. This politicians themselves rarely understand.

At the very highest level of respect, political leaders are referred to by their initials. The three Presidents who, beyond all others, have been accorded the greatest admiration in this century have been, proceeding back in time, J.F.K., F.D.R. and T.R., the latter proving that a three-letter resonance is not essential. It was not for this reason that H.H., C.C. or even W.W. failed to be loved.

At only a slightly lower level is the use of the full name — Harry Truman, Lyndon Johnson and Woodrow Wilson. Harry Truman came within an eyebrow of achieving H.S.T., perhaps did, and Lyndon Johnson was L.B.J. until the Vietnam war put him back to his full name.

Down the scale, indicating affection, sometimes amusement but no awe, is the nickname. Ike, Jimmy or Gerry. President Carter, on taking office, insisted on being Jimmy. A mistake.

Irretrievably at the bottom are those who rate only the last name — Hoover, Harding, Coolidge and the most firmly so confined, Nixon. A reference even to *Richard* Nixon suggests that one is being ceremoniously polite. Characteristically in his memoirs Nixon tried thoughtful self-enhancement: he called them *RN*.

In this peerage Adlai Stevenson, for one who did not make it to the presidency, stood very high. At the time of his death there was a general reference to A.E.S.; he never fell below the level of his full name. On his right to this distinction the American public understood him completely.

People who were close to F.D.R. or J.F.K. found much pleasure in explaining their President to outsiders. Those of us around Stevenson spent much of our time explaining him to each other. On one characteristic there was no need to dwell: Stevenson's supreme sensitivity to the feelings, including the vanity, of others. To everyone he encountered he gave the impression that that very person of all people was the one whom at that precise moment he most wanted to see. His brightening glance on entering a room suggested that all there were those he most cherished. This instinct for others owed much to its being genuine. There were a great many people whom he truly liked. He liked being with them and disliked being alone. In later life, day or night, he rarely was. But, characteristically, Stevenson was not content to be considered a companionable, gregarious man. On this, as on many other matters, he felt compelled to picture himself and to believe that he was something he was not. So, though loving company, he sought to convey the impression of a lonely, slightly withdrawn figure most at home when by himself with his own thoughts. And the more susceptible of commentators and biographers have so described him.

Many people seek to alter, mostly to enhance, their own personalities, and in politics as also in academic life the impulse is endemic. The politician tells how he captured a particular audience, persuaded a recalcitrant legislator, devastated an opponent. Thus he redeems a repellent mumble, a humiliating compromise, a bad reverse. Regularly he places this enhancement in the general flow of conversation so adeptly that he is able to believe that listeners will think it purely incidental. And perhaps there are audiences so obtuse that they are thus fooled.

In modern academic life scholars owe their distinction and in early years their promotion to the judgment of their peers. Self-enhancing conversation is, accordingly, an art form. At Harvard the man who has commented diffidently on an obscure paper by an even more diffident scholar at the Modern Language Association returns to the faculty club to tell, *en passant,* of the devastation he wrought on the truly great man from Antioch. Incoherent testimony at a legislative hearing attended only by the subcommittee chairman can, in the subsequent recounting by an economist, become a polemical triumph of historic proportions.

John F. Kennedy, as I've often told, was one of the few public men who was wholly satisfied with his own personality. It allowed him to be a constant and much-amused student of the art of self-enhancement and its consequences. In the summer of 1960, on the Sunday after his nomination, Arthur and Marian Schlesinger and I drove to Hyannis Port to have lunch with him. The conversation turned inevitably to the campaign, and Kennedy said it was one of his advantages over Nixon that he would not be tired. "Nixon must always be thinking about who he is. That is a strain. I can be myself."

More perhaps than any political figure of our time, Adlai Stevenson was committed to personality modification for public purposes. But here is why he was often misunderstood; the alteration was to an end that was hard to imagine. Stevenson was committed to picturing not his strength in contending with harsh circumstance but his frailty, not his certainty but his doubts, not his wisdom but the immeasurable extent of what he needed to know. So habitual had this posturing become that he was largely unaware of it himself. It was an impulse in a politician for which no one was in the slightest prepared.

Outwardly it was very convincing, but it was also denied by fact and behavior. In the war years Stevenson had held a senior position in the bureaucracy as assistant to Secretary of the Navy Frank Knox. He then went on to a founding role in the United Nations, to a gubernatorial nomination and election and, in 1952, with only the slightest and most discreet of effort, to a presidential nomination. To all of these positions he had moved with certainty of purpose and in all he had served with precision of knowledge and thought. He preferred, nonetheless, to see it all as a largely accidental triumph over pathogenic indecision and despair.

Stevenson practiced this amiable fraud in a dozen different forms. He was believed to have difficulty in making up his mind. One soon discovered that his views on nearly all matters were exceedingly firm and, when wrong, inconveniently so. The world saw him as a bookish intellectual. There could be doubt as to whether, after becoming governor of Illinois, he ever read a serious book. He recurred often to the works of Barbara Ward Jackson, but their substance he had most likely gotten in conversation. No one was so relentlessly admiring of mine; he was always about to read them. Stevenson's conversation, as also his letters, tell of the vulgar horrors of his political campaigns; survival to the end was always in doubt. With some others I came to believe that he loved every parade, every rally, every cheer, every band, every other moment of the great show. He was regarded as a liberal and perhaps is rightly so described. But he was also a committed elitist. He ran for President not to rescue the downtrodden but to assume the responsibilities properly belonging to the privileged.

* * *

I did not know Adlai Stevenson during the war years[1] or those immediately following. We first met at a gathering of politicians one warm evening in early August of 1952 on the grounds of the Governor's Mansion in Springfield. In the preceding four years I had continued to keep aloof from politics; I was still proving myself to be a serious professor. Also in those, the salad days of Joe McCarthy, I caused worry in a bureaucracy that was committed to reducing its own risks. Nervous and cowardly officeholders, concerned to protect their own flanks, were the greatest allies of the witch-hunters.

Nor was I at the Democratic Convention that July in Chicago for Stevenson's nomination. But in the days following, while speaking at a conference on rural development problems in Berkeley organized by Thomas C. Blaisdell, Jr., an old New Deal hand, I was called by George Ball and Arthur Schlesinger at the Durant Hotel. Would I come urgently to Springfield to write speeches — the fatal fluency again. Kitty and I detoured for a day to look at the Grand Canyon, my only ground-level view of that massive scar, and one early morning a day or so later I left the Santa Fe Chief at a depressing siding some distance from Springfield and made my way to the Illinois capital by bus. On arriving at the hotel, I received word from Arthur that I should remain in my room until further notice. This was disconcerting.

The reason was that at a press conference a day before, Stevenson had been asked if his campaign wasn't being taken over by radicals — specifically by dangerous figures from Americans for Democratic Action. Of ADA, Schlesinger and I, as noted, had been founding members. Also, another deeply sensitive point, the gathering-in of speech writers at Springfield seemed to proclaim that the candidate could not write his own. Stevenson's tendency to self-denigration did not extend to his oratory; of this he was openly

---

[1] He had helped George Ball in the earliest study of the effects of the bombing but had departed before I arrived.

proud. My arrival, along with my negligible talent for invisibility, was not opportune.

But after a few hours Stevenson was persuaded that most of his recruits were in the mainstream, and I was released. To protect his reputation for doing his own work, we would be careful to call ourselves researchers, not speech writers, a nomenclature by which not even Stevenson could have expected very many would be fooled. The gathering on the Governor's lawn which now occurred was to welcome John Sparkman of Alabama, the vice-presidential candidate, to the campaign. Stevenson emerged a little late from the Mansion, a large structure of early Charles Addams design, to greet the guests. He was shorter than I had imagined and already a trifle stouter than his earlier pictures had proclaimed. The latter tendency he would resist unsuccessfully for the rest of his life. His hair was even then getting sparse, and, as ever, he gave the impression that the thirty or forty politicians present were all precisely the people he most wanted to see.

John Sparkman had not been the choice of northern liberals for the second place on the ticket. An eminently decent and good-humored man, a veteran of the New Deal battles — when still in the House of Representatives he once described himself to me as a TVA-liberal — he, of course, acquiesced in the southern opposition to civil rights. Four years earlier, at the 1948 convention, there had been an explosion when Hubert Humphrey and his allies had pressed for a civil rights plank, and southern delegates had walked out. The selection of Sparkman was now intended to heal those wounds. Some thought it a backward step and one that could also be costly in black votes in the North. The most interesting thing that happened that pleasant evening was a conversation between Sparkman and Arthur Schlesinger in which Arthur stressed the service Sparkman could render by concentrating on foreign policy.

*   *   *

In the American culture there is no institution with such a high potential for pure comedy as a presidential campaign staff. It is recruited hurriedly, *ad hoc,* and extensively by self-selection. Many are prima donnas; more are self-identified saviors of the Republic. This convocation must then undertake a vast range of tasks — deciding with the candidate as to the stand on issues, putting the results into speeches, raising money, arranging travel, planning the candidate's reception wherever he appears, staging his television, moving the press, ordering bumper stickers, deciding who among the hundreds the candidate will see or must see. In accomplishing all of these matters the participants are profoundly inexperienced. That is because only the morbidly committed and the pathologically unemployable ever wish to go through more than one campaign. And power in a campaign organization passes not to the most competent but to the most self-confident — to the man who can say with the greatest show of banal conviction, "I'll tell you what the American voter really wants."

Such an individual, if he can speak with special vehemence on how the citizenry is to be aroused and can otherwise outline convincingly a nonexistent rationale for the candidate's travel and use of television time, will greatly impress the reporters covering the campaign, especially those to whom he will reveal the ultimate strategy in the strictest confidence. He will then see or hear himself described as a "real pro," an "accomplished tactician," and the praise will continue until just before the candidate's concession speech.

The Stevenson campaign staff of 1952 was better than most, for, exceptionally, there was a general realization of our newness to the task and the associated incompetence. We also, even more exceptionally, got along well together. Unfortunately these admirable qualities were combined with the belief that the professional politicians in the cities and states knew what *they* were doing. We listened to them with excessive respect, on occasion tried to follow their relentlessly self-serving advice and wished we had someone of high professional competence in charge of our own operations. Instead we had Wilson W. Wyatt, a former and much-celebrated mayor of Louisville who had served in Washington in the immediate postwar years. A most intelligent and able man, he was nonetheless held to be an amateur, and he so regarded himself. It was a mistake that was not repeated in 1956. Then James A. Finnegan of Philadelphia, a certified Irish politician of much charm and great white-maned beauty and a true professional, was in charge. Under Jim the confusion was somewhat worse.

*   *   *

Immediately after the convention Stevenson had decided that the campaign would be run from Springfield. This was his response to current and, by subsequent standards, exceedingly minor scandals in Washington, mostly involving free iceboxes. A Springfield headquarters would put a salutary moral distance between Adlai Stevenson and Harry Truman and identify Stevenson with the honest heartland of the Republic. This move away from the capital was neither necessary nor wise and reflected Stevenson's feeling, never fully concealed, that Harry Truman was a slightly off-color, somewhat vulgar politician.

Office space was not abundant in Springfield, and for the researchers *cum* speech writers a large room and some adjacent bedrooms were found on the top floor of the Springfield Elks Club. Soon we were known to all not as the researchers but as the Elks. Arthur Schlesinger took leave from Harvard that autumn to be the principal coordinator of our efforts and Stevenson's most accomplished draftsman. Alone among all I've ever observed in this craft he could remove his coat, address his typewriter and without resort to reference books, documents or pause for thought produce an entire speech at one sitting. Within weeks he had achieved a perfect mastery of Stevenson's balanced sentences and could play perfectly to his delight in antonyms and his frequent willingness to subordinate meaning to euphony. I also mastered the Stevenson style, and the effect was not slight; I have never since written a speech for myself or someone else that did not have something of the Stevenson tone. On a few occasions I produced a draft on some subject or other for John Kennedy, but he rarely used them. Once he looked at one with a grimace and said, "It sounds like Adlai."

The Elks membership included John (called Jack) Fischer, for long thereafter the editor of *Harper's*; W. Willard Wirtz, then a law professor at Northwestern University and later Secretary of Labor under Kennedy and Johnson; and David E. Bell, a former assistant to Harry Truman, subsequently Kennedy's Director of the Budget and head of AID and thereafter executive vice president of the Ford Foundation. Also present were Robert Tufts, a young Oberlin professor; Sidney Hyman, then a young Washington journalist; and John Bartlow Martin, a talented *Saturday Evening Post* writer, a recognized authority on the more depraved tendencies of Chicago crime and politics, later Ambassador to the Dominican Republic and later still Stevenson's biographer.

At the Governor's Mansion, Carl McGowan (with William Mc-Cormick Blair, Jr.,[2] one of Stevenson's two most trusted assistants and later a federal judge) relayed our speech drafts to the candidate and, infrequently, the candidate's thoughts back to the Elks. At great moments we assembled in Stevenson's office to get the word direct. As Adlai's eloquence became evident, volunteers sought to contribute; speech drafts came in from different parts of the country, and, on occasion, the authors brought them to Springfield in person. One so to show up was Herbert S. Agar, a former editor of the Louisville *Courier-Journal* and a writer of books prolifically, mystically and exhaustively evocative of the American dream. Agar brought a script of stunning resonance, what Henry James once described as an unaided flow of sound. "So we are marked men, we Americans at the mid-century point. We have been tapped by fate . . . What a flowering of the work and the faith of our fathers!"[3] Arthur Schlesinger and I read the document with horror and consigned it to the files. This, as experience had by now shown, meant that it would never be retrieved. Unknown to us, however, Herbert had taken a copy direct to Stevenson who thought it wonderful. It was the main text for his address in the Mormon Tabernacle in Salt Lake City on October 14 and was generally thought the most successful of the entire campaign.

Our best-regarded outside contribution came from James Wechsler, then, and as of this writing, of the *New York Post*. Given on August 28, the speech was to accept the nomination of the New York Liberal Party, a rather more impressive power at the time than it has since become. Wechsler produced a marvelously funny polemic. "This [the autumn of election years] is the time when even the most obsolete Republican becomes momentarily reconciled to the machine age . . . a truly remarkable interval, a sort of pause in the Republican occupation and I've often thought that it might well be called

---

[2] Blair kept intact the record of this group for upward mobility into and in the federal service by becoming an ambassador to Denmark and to the Philippines in later years.

[3] *Major Campaign Speeches of Adlai E. Stevenson, 1952* (New York: Random House, 1953), p. 248.

the liberal hour."[4] Out in Springfield we met each evening in the bar of the Elks Club to review the day's activities and have a drink; after late August, we called it the Liberal Hour. On one memorable occasion we were joined for this interlude by Woodrow L. Wyatt, a British journalist and parliamentarian who was covering the campaign and who was fresh from an interview with Colonel McCormick of the *Chicago Tribune*. The British Consul in Chicago had expressed horror when Woodrow had said that he was asking to see McCormick. "The Colonel detests us, don't you know." But the Colonel had granted the interview and explained in a kindly way his willingness to do so: "The British are no longer important enough for me to dislike."

One of my contributions to the campaign was Eric Hodgins. I called him from Springfield soon after my arrival and only hours before C.D. Jackson, who had taken leave from *Time* to work for the Republicans, asked him to join Eisenhower's staff. Arriving in Springfield, Eric told with much pleasure of his response to his old friend: "Piss on you, C.D., I'm going to work for the right man." The experience for Eric was utterly depressing, and part of the problem was the prolixity that had made him so famous at *Fortune*. As he could not write a short article, so he could not write a speech that could be rendered in less than two hours. Nor did he find it easy, as a ghostwriter must, to accommodate style and content to his principal.

In contrast, John Bartlow Martin, another writer with an uncontrollable commitment to detail — his two-volume biography of Stevenson[5] gives day-by-day and sometimes hour-by-hour occurrences — proved a master of the whistle-stop speech. No one else could say so much on two pages of triple-spaced typescript.

*   *   *

In the Agar speech and its reception lay a political lesson that Stevenson had learned and that members of his staff — Schlesinger, Martin, Galbraith — pridefully refused to accept. Political communication, we believed, should be deeply matter-of-fact. A good

[4]*Major Campaign Speeches of Adlai E. Stevenson, 1952*, pp. 31–32. From this I took the title *The Liberal Hour* for a collection of essays published a few years later (Boston: Houghton Mifflin, 1960).

[5]*Adlai Stevenson of Illinois* (New York: Doubleday, 1976) and *Adlai Stevenson and the World* (New York: Doubleday, 1977).

speech was one that dealt lucidly with issues — unemployment, labor law reform, health insurance, defense. The language, however embellished, should remain subordinate to the ideas. Stevenson, in contrast, had sensed that political oratory is, in part, a form of poetry. It takes the audience into realms of the imagination where they yearn to go. It offers a vision of past achievement, an escape from harsh prospect that is pleasurable to contemplate. We thought this vacuous; words without meaning. Adlai Stevenson knew better; and it is more for the poetry than for the substance that he is remembered.

Substance could not, of course, be elided, and on this there was tension between Stevenson and his ghosts. The tension concerned domestic, not foreign, policy; it would have been better, though a miracle at the time, had it been the other way around.

Stevenson continued to worry a little lest he had been taken over by radicals. We felt that he was insufficiently committed to the constituency and the policies that had brought the magnificent string of Democratic victories all the way from 1932 through 1948. Carl McGowan was the man in the middle. Repeatedly he sought to assure us that Stevenson was not a conservative, that he needed only to be persuaded. Stevenson's fear, he held, was that he would be thought automatic in his political responses, a predictable voice for the liberal clichés of the New Deal and Fair Deal years.

He did not stress another restraining force, namely Stevenson's affluent Chicago friends and Libertyville neighbors. With them he had lived on terms of reciprocal esteem and affection. They were not enamored of the Roosevelt or especially the Truman oratory, and they didn't wish to see their friend seduced. This, with some effect, they made clear. Stevenson never fully escaped their hand.

In the end he could be persuaded, although only on occasion, to elaborate ambiguity. For several days in late August Willard Wirtz and I worked on a speech to be given on Labor Day in Cadillac Square, Detroit, to the massed forces of the United Automobile Workers, then as now the liberal political spearhead of the labor movement. Their prime concern, as was that of all the labor movement, was the Taft-Hartley Act, which had been passed in 1947 by the Republican Congress over a Truman veto and which outlawed jurisdictional strikes, secondary boycotts, the closed shop and much else. By 1952, the Act had developed a symbolic power that was independent of its practical effect, a frequent development in politics. The test of a politician's worth to the labor movement was where he stood on the "slave labor law." Stevenson could not be persuaded to call for repeal; he astonished and depressed us by saying that if this cost him the support of the unions, so be it. Better to "tell them what I really think than to deceive them in order to get their endorsement."[6]

In the compromise, the speech urged not repeal of Taft-Hartley but its replacement. The law should be withdrawn and another substituted that did not include the more objectionable features. Stevenson then inserted a sentence affirming his inconvenient belief that it was not a slave labor act.

No one was pleased. However, that day in Detroit was very hot, the bars around the square were open and few in the audience were in a mood or condition to pay attention. So not much harm was done, at least to those on hand. In saying that slavery was not involved, Stevenson preserved his reputation for simple truth against the contrary effort of his staff, something not all candidates have been able to do.

I wrote the speeches on farm policy. This is the most privileged task of a presidential speech writer, for no colleague and no candidate feels sufficiently informed to tamper with the result. Should one try, you have only to look at him in a sympathetic and condescending way, and he will then subside and perhaps apologize. On nothing is the intellectual inferiority of the urban American so easily exploited as on anything having to do with agriculture. Later in India, as I will tell, American agriculturalists assisting the Indians were greatly depressed at having an ambassador who could not be so subdued.

I also wrote speeches on economics, a more contentious matter. By 1952, the enthusiasm for the Keynesian revolution was at its peak; it was the magic that had made for Democratic economic success. I regarded myself as one of its prime protagonists; it was partly why, at the behest of George Ball and Arthur Schlesinger, I was in Springfield. Our candidate had heard of Keynes but largely from people who supposed him subversive. Stevenson's own views on economic policy, to the extent that they existed, had been formed at

[6] Martin, *Adlai Stevenson of Illinois*, p. 677. The quotation reflects closely my own recollection of Stevenson's words.

Princeton thirty years before in an economic atmosphere dominated by a stalwart resistance to the twentieth century. It was his uneasy suspicion that Keynesian economics as reflected in the Employment Act of 1946 was a dubious excuse for the budget deficits of the Roosevelt and later Truman years. It being convenient to tax less than you spent, liberals, with the help of Keynes, had made this intellectually respectable. He would not be gulled; at most he would be silent. All close to Stevenson on economic matters were distressed. When the election was over and in light of our hope and intention that he would be the candidate again in 1956, we set about bringing his knowledge of economics abreast of the times. It was an imaginative experiment in adult education to which I will also return.

*   *   *

There was, unfortunately, no similar tension in the thinking behind the foreign policy speeches. These were written by Robert Tufts, whose Cold War instincts were moderated by Arthur Schlesinger and then amended further, sometimes while Stevenson was sitting on the platform listening to the introductory speeches, by the candidate himself.[7] They gave full sanction to the fears and tensions of the time. "What we know . . . is that the enemy is implacable, sullen, determined, and dangerous . . . The grimmest knowledge of all is the certainty of the enemy's relentless ambition to rule our lives . . ."[8] It was accepted that the Communist chain of command reached down from Moscow to Peking and on to P'yongyang and that the latter capital was wholly subject to the authority of the first.

No one should assume that American election campaigns are conducted in a context that allows candidates any inconvenient freedom of speech. To have departed from official Cold War belief in 1952 would have brought charges of naiveté if not of outright disloyalty. Joseph McCarthy was then attributing to Roosevelt and Truman the "twenty years of treason." Stevenson was under direct Republican attack for having attested favorably in a sworn deposition in 1949 to the veracity, loyalty and integrity of Alger Hiss. Nixon, as the vice-presidential candidate, was charging Stevenson with guilt by his as-

[7] Then as now these preliminary speeches provided ample leisure for such task. At a great rally in New York on October 28, John Cashmore, the senatorial candidate, got such a grip on the microphone that only physical force saved some of the television time for Stevenson.

[8] *Major Campaign Speeches of Adlai E. Stevenson, 1952*, pp. 35–36.

sociation with the "spineless" diplomacy of Dean Acheson. Eisenhower was accepting the political rewards of the anti-Communist crusade, though being careful not to embrace McCarthy too closely. An early television address on the Sino-Soviet threat was supposed to be given by Joe but was shifted to Clare Boothe Luce. She delivered it while dressed in a rhinestone evening gown against a stark black studio backdrop. We watched it from the basement of the Mansion in Springfield as though through a bad snowstorm, for Springfield television then came at maximum distance from St. Louis. The American surrender to Bolshevism was rendered in taut, high-pitched, frantic tones. So awful was the effect that there was a full minute of silence at the end of the broadcast, silence which was only broken when Eric Hodgins addressed the wife of his old friend on the television screen in terms that I am still reluctant to put in print. Campaigning in Wisconsin, Eisenhower allowed McCarthy to introduce him in the latter's hometown of Appleton, but a flying wedge of reputable men then quickly crowded Joe to one side of the vestibule of the railroad car. There, while Ike spoke, he occupied himself, as Murray Kempton told the next day in the *New York Post,* by shaking hands with his friends and waving agreeably to his creditors. In time, however, Joe had his success. Eisenhower deleted from a speech a defense of George Marshall that, it was feared, would annoy McCarthy, and toward the end of the campaign Joe was unleashed on national television. In a well-contrived slip of the tongue he referred to "Alger" Stevenson, and he accused Arthur Schlesinger, and also Bernard DeVoto[9] and Archibald MacLeish who had contributed speech drafts, of Communist tendencies. I was the only one of the Cambridge contingent with Stevenson who was omitted, and I said that I felt neglected. It was a very shallow pretense.

The effect of the Nixon/McCarthy attack, as noted, was to lock Stevenson into the Cold War orthodoxy. He could not warn of the warlike tendencies of the Republicans or promise to work for the peace in Korea for which all yearned. That would show that he was, indeed, soft on Communism.

"The finest [election] strategies," John F. Kennedy remarked after

[9]The noted essayist and historian whom I counted one of my closest Cambridge friends and who was known to us as Benny. McCarthy that night called him Richard DeVoto.

the 1960 campaign, "are usually the result of accidents."[10] One further consequence of the Nixon/McCarthy attack could not have been
more brilliant had it all been planned. On October 24, in a speech
written with imagination by Emmet John Hughes, Eisenhower said
that if elected, he would "go to Korea." Implicit therein was the
promise to seek a negotiated end to the Korean War. It was electri-
fying. As always in the United States there was a real difference between the vocal commitment to the heroic and warlike stance and
the deeper commitment to peace. Meanwhile so frozen was the
Democratic position by now that we did not even recognize the
power of the Eisenhower initiative. And the response, when it came,
was pathetic in its stereotype. "The General has announced his intention to go to Korea. But the root of the Korean problem does not
lie in Korea. It lies in Moscow . . . The Korean War must end and
will end, as we all know, only when Moscow is convinced that the
people of this country . . . are united in unshakable determination
to stand firm . . ."[11]

After the election Eisenhower did make peace — and with the
North Koreans, not the Soviet Union. The bargain to which he
agreed, roughly the line on which the armies then stood, could have
been had months earlier by the Democrats — as was promptly
pointed out by Harry Truman. The charge that Eisenhower had accepted what the Democrats rejected may have been the least damaging attack to which any politician was ever subject.

Peace in Korea has now survived for more than a quarter of a
century, and peace, however fragile, is better than any war. Its
achievement by Eisenhower followed one of the stable patterns in
the interweaving of American domestic politics and foreign policy,
one that would again be manifest in the detachment from Vietnam,
in the opening of relations with China and in the earliest steps toward detente with the Soviet Union. It is worth repeating. American
conservatives, because no one doubts their hatred of Communism,

---

[10] A comment made in Palm Beach on December 23, 1960. During the campaign
that year Martin Luther King had been jailed in Georgia, and there was much favorable reaction when John Kennedy promptly telephoned Mrs. King and Robert Kennedy as promptly telephoned the judge. Neither brother knew what the other was
doing. (John Kenneth Galbraith, *Ambassador's Journal* [Boston: Houghton Mifflin,
1969], p. 6.)
[11] Martin, *Adlai Stevenson of Illinois,* p. 743.

have more easily come to terms with reality and made more sensible bargains with the Soviets and the Chinese than American liberals, who, as ever, have lived in the fear of being thought soft on Communism.

The Korean War, apart from the casualties and the cost, had, like the Vietnam conflict later, a poisonous effect on American politics. The witch hunts, the Cold War psychosis, the diplomatic blunders and clandestine disasters of the Dulles brothers, were all nurtured by the hostilities. All would have been worse had the war continued. So in 1952, peace in Korea was, indeed, the transcendent issue. For getting peace, not even the most affectionate Stevenson supporter can doubt, Eisenhower was the better bet.

There is one reservation, however. In 1956, Adlai Stevenson became a voice for negotiation with the Soviets on the then new H-bomb and against the men who, enhancing their reputations for tough and thus impermeable minds, urged its production and accepted the risk of its use. During the Cuban missile crisis in 1961, he urged keeping open the lines of communication with the Soviets and proposed the removal of obsolete nuclear missiles from Turkey in return for a similar withdrawal from Cuba. Even in those more rational times he was bitterly criticized for wanting "some kind of Munich." Reacting as he then did, one wonders if he might not have had misgivings earlier. Perhaps he was the captive of a staff which feared to be thought soft and which protected and immobilized itself with an armor plate of anti-Communism. In doing so, it immobilized Adlai Stevenson as well.

*   *   *

The best remembered if not necessarily the most important incident of the 1952 campaign was the discovery in September of the Nixon slush fund and Nixon's frightful television ode thereafter to Pat, Republican cloth coats, Checkers and Uriah Heep. Its impact on the inner Stevenson campaign community was very different from that on the country at large.

For several days in mid-September there were rumors that wealthy Nixon supporters had established a fund to serve his more sinister purposes. Money for Nixon could hardly be for a righteous use. Then, on September 18, the story was broken by Peter Edson, the columnist, and the *New York Post* gave it a major splash. Other reporters moved in on Nixon, who was campaigning in northern California and Oregon. He admitted the existence of the fund and said that it was for the most innocent of office purposes. At almost the same moment the principal sponsor of the philanthropy, one Dana C. Smith, delightedly proclaimed from Los Angeles that the fund was to reward and keep in office an admirably conservative and effective friend of big business. This, Smith, reflecting his own undoubted view, thought the highest virtue. Thus victimized by his supporters, Nixon resorted to form: "You folks know the work that I did investigating Communists in the United States . . . and the left-wingers have been fighting me with every possible smear . . . And believe me, you can expect that they will continue to do so. They started it yesterday." [12]

For once it didn't work; even in those days not everything could be attributed to Bolshevist conspiracy. Eisenhower asked for a better explanation, and the Checkers speech was the result.

My reaction to the initial rumors was the normal one, that of saints apart. How wonderful! But then I encountered George Ball (or possibly it was Carl McGowan), and all my pleasure evaporated. There were also Stevenson funds, and it was inevitable that news of these would come out. Some of the Stevenson money was surplus left over from his gubernatorial campaign, and some had been contributed by friends and would-be friends. It was used for necessary but unbillable entertainment and most of all to supplement the salaries of the people who had been brought down to Springfield at a personal loss. All this was more righteous than the Nixon operation, but such distinctions are not easily made in an election campaign. And there had been individual outlays, as for a Christmas party for the Stevenson offspring, which, if trifling, were not easy to justify. Worst of all, although this was perhaps a blessing, the campaign staff accounting of receipts and expenditures was chaotic.

In the end Nixon was damaged by the episode and Stevenson was not. Something can be attributed to what someone reaching for profound scholarly effect could call the differential time dimension in American politics. This is an important and much-neglected thing. Nixon's Checkers speech with its deeply synthetic bathos produced an instant emotional response. The telegrams and letters flowed in.

[12] Martin, *Adlai Stevenson of Illinois,* p. 687.

But these were from the kind of people who are immediately susceptible to what the unscholarly call bullshit. Being thus susceptible,
they are open to a new and different assault the very next day.
Those who do not so respond, the invulnerable, think it awful, and
they are the ones who remember. Remembering, they render the
durable judgment and write the history.

*   *   *

I spent August and most of September in Springfield.[13] When Harvard reopened, I resumed teaching and went to Illinois for long
weekends or joined the campaign party when it came within range.
My memory recaptures especially one sublime autumn day when our
plane landed in early morning at Bridgeport, Connecticut, where we
were greeted by William Benton of *Encyclopaedia Britannica,* philanthropic and courageously liberal fame, who was in a losing race for
reelection to the Senate, and by Abraham Ribicoff. We were met
also by a long line of red convertibles provided by a local Packard
dealer. Willard Wirtz and I shared one for the day with a Connecticut woman political leader of mature years, and when the motorcade
slowed, we listened to the comments of the bystanders: "How much
mileage do you think she gets?" "They have a pretty good turn-in
value." "Which one is Stevenson?" The crowds were sparse, and
once when they were especially so, our Connecticut companion allowed herself a few tears. Sixteen years before, she had ridden behind F.D.R. in a motorcade through the state; the lines of people,
she remembered, were then several deep even when the highway
passed through the woods.

The first speech was by the railroad station in Bridgeport. Then
we swung back to another on the New Haven green and then to
Derby, Ansonia, and through one shabby mill town after another up

---

[13] When I returned to Cambridge, I found my wife in possession of a letter that no
other presidential candidate in all history would have sent or had sent:

"I address you as the real victim of Ken's participation in this campaign enterprise.
I know with what disappointment you must have watched him vanish — just at vaca-
tiontime — into the wastes of the Illinois prairies, and I want you to know how much
I value your willingness to view the loss with good temper.

"It does not help you much to know how effective and useful I have found Ken's
presence here to be, but it is a point I wish to make for whatever worth it may be to
you.

"Thanks again, and I hope I shall one day have the opportunity to speak my gratitude in person."

the Naugatuck Valley. Stevenson couldn't bear to look down at the familiar faces of the clustering reporters and give the same speech twice so there had to be a different one for each stop. I had helped John Bartlow Martin with the drafts, and on the plane out of Springfield, Stevenson told me how good he thought the writing was. This was sheer pleasure, and it was even greater pleasure to stand in the crowd and hear your own words in lovely cadence and emphasis. My joy diminished only slightly in the late afternoon when we reached Waterbury, where the address was on the common. The crowd was excellent and attentive but reacted adversely when Stevenson spoke warmly of his pleasure at being "here in Watertown." There is a Watertown only a few miles down the road.

There was another adverse effect as the day passed, for eventually all were in a terrible need to pee. And there was no way this could be managed. A motorcade cannot pull up to a service station. The American ethic does not allow a stop while everyone gets out and goes into the bushes beside the road. No car can break away, however desperate the occupants. The pain must be accepted; for some problems there is no solution.

* * *

My friendship with Adlai Stevenson, not appreciably cooled by my support of John F. Kennedy in the late fifties, continued for the next thirteen years until his death. There would be another Stevenson campaign in 1956. But for all who joined and loved Adlai Stevenson, the 1952 campaign was the crest. With only slight embarrassment we mentioned St. Crispin's Day — alas, an optimistic metaphor.

It would be hard for the young to understand not only our surprise but our shock at the outcome. For twenty years liberal Democrats had won; Harry Truman in 1948 had shown that whatever the portents, they would still do so. It had become the natural order of things. At Arthur Schlesinger's house on election night in 1952, we learned that the natural order had come to an end.

20

Depression, Crash, Communism and the Canadian Pacific Railway

ON THE MORNING after the election I awoke with the feeling that some cord — something vitally connecting my past with the present — had snapped. I struggled through a Ph.D. examination for Burton Klein, my wartime assistant — the barely supportable ceremony at which a candidate who has written an acceptable thesis (in this case a fine one on Germany's wartime economic performance)[1] is told that he may have his degree. His surprise, were he told otherwise, would be extreme. Burt, who was suffering from acute disappointment over the election results combined, I judged, with a terminal hangover, added to my depression by observing at the end of the examination that he felt like a fellow who had picked up a dime on the way to a funeral.

In succeeding days my depression deepened. For two decades Washington had seemed an accessible and friendly place, the recent loyalty investigations apart, where one went easily to argue, protest, persuade; it would now be a closed, forbidden city. There certainly would be no dropping in on Ezra Taft Benson, the new Secretary of Agriculture. And definitely not on John Foster Dulles. I had come, without ever realizing it, to think of myself as part of a permanent government. I too was now out of office.

My depression got worse. Whiskey brought a brief moment of relief before dinner. Increasingly massive doses of Seconal were necessary for sleep. Classes became a struggle. In the growing darkness of the late Cambridge autumn I turned to a neighbor and friend who was also a brilliant psychiatrist. My visits were a beautifully

[1] This became the already-mentioned (see Chapter 14) *Germany's Economic Preparation for War,* Harvard Economic Studies (Cambridge: Harvard University Press, 1959).

guarded secret. I feared that my credibility as an economist would suffer were it rumored that I was receiving such attention. I learned to my surprise that I had long been subject to cycles of euphoria and depression. These had been relatively mild — not far out of the plausible range of a normal reaction to good news and bad. The election campaign and its aftermath had merely increased the amplitude of the cycle. The excitements of travel and the hope of victory had enhanced the euphoric tendency; the defeat and its morbid prospect had taken depression to the depths. I doubt that I was the first person involved in politics so to suffer. Or the last.[2] On discovery of my disorder, I turned my mind to tracing previous cycles. Presently the cloud lifted. Thereafter when it returned, save for one occasion in India when it was evidently accentuated by hepatitis, I could recognize it for what it was. This brief darkness I came to consider one of the more useful experiences of a lifetime, and I have not since minimized the services of psychiatrists.

*   *   *

I continued teaching about agriculture and industrial organization. In the latter course I was still dwelling thoughtfully on the antitrust laws, the public design for maintaining competition that my thesis on countervailing power had held to be nugatory. Economic instruction has a dynamic that can be quite independent of both evidence or personal belief. My mind, however, was now much engaged with the problems and the possibilities of economic development. This then led on to speculation on its natural counterpart, the causes of the poverty that made economic improvement so urgent. I resolved, if I could learn the causes, to write a book on this indubitably vital subject; it would be called by its natural title, *Why People are Poor*. But before going abroad to consider the poverty of India, Egypt or Mexico, it seemed appropriate first to treat of the domestic deprivation. There was an adequate manifestation scattered in individual cases over all the country. And poverty existed in great concentrations on the Southern Appalachian Plateau, elsewhere in the rural South as well as in the urban slums. The rural poverty — an existence based on meager shelter, simple repetitive food, negligible

[2] Thomas Francis Eagleton, in some small measure by my efforts briefly the vice-presidential candidate in 1972, had a similar, if more painful, episode. See Chapter 32.

schooling, no health care and in the South no right of protest or other expression — had attracted attention through the New Deal years. But, as always with poverty in the countryside, it was far less on the public mind and conscience than urban unemployment and economic despair. Nothing is so firmly established in Puritan and Presbyterian belief as that people cannot be suffering very much if they are out in healthy fresh air — and also safely out of sight.

All New Deal and subsequent efforts, it might be noted, assumed that the blight of rural poverty would be solved within the rural community itself. Thus the early Subsistence Homesteads of the New Deal, the later Resettlement and Farmers Home Administration efforts and the rural community development projects of the Johnson Administration. All took capital and enlightenment out to the country where the people lived. When it was finally achieved, the remedy for rural poverty, which for the black, nonurban population has been sweeping, was complete and very different: it was accomplished by the people moving out. The urban poverty which they then entered was far from pleasant but also somewhat less easy to ignore.

James Perkins, whom I had rescued from Princeton during the war, had by now done a stint as an administrator at Swarthmore College and gone on to be a vice president of the Carnegie Corporation. No one should imagine that reciprocity in patronage is confined to politics: Perkins promptly provided me with a grant — $8000 — for research and secretarial help. Eventually the books resulting from this and a later beneficence earned some hundreds of thousands of dollars in royalties. That philanthropic investment should produce such large personal returns seemed to me open to justifiable criticism. But to return money to a foundation would violate all the canons of academic decency — rather like returning unused drinking water to a well. So I shared my returns with the department of economics at Harvard. This, to the eventual extent of nearly $200,000, was used for scholarships and to relieve the sudden anxieties of graduate students beset by pregnancy, illness or other unexpected need. My colleagues attributed my largesse to generosity instead of troubled thought, and this I didn't seek seriously to correct.

In 1969, I might here note, after what I judged to be a decent interval, I published *Ambassador's Journal,* my day-to-day account of my years in India. It was greeted favorably by Houghton Mifflin with a guarantee, in the end mostly earned, of $250,000. On this the federal taxes were sufficient to cover my ambassadorial salary of $27,500 annually with around a hundred percent additional return. Both as a professor and as a diplomat I have managed to return a profit to my employers. However, much should be expected of an economist.

* * *

Why People are Poor, despite much background reading and some painful thought, encountered difficulty. I did not have a convincing explanation as to why in either individual cases or in large rural and urban communities poverty persisted under conditions of general and improving well-being. Lacking such an explanation, my preliminary chapters on the subject were so devoid that I couldn't bear to read them myself. It was certain no one else would.

The reason I came only later to understand. In the established or neoclassical tradition of economics to which I was still subject, poverty or something very like it remained for most people the normal condition. Labor, as also capital and other resources, were committed to production up to the point where any further contribution — input it has always been called in economics — served no longer to cover its cost. In nineteenth-century economics labor was assumed to be intrinsically, indeed biologically, abundant, and this abundance in competition for jobs kept wages at the minimum that would sustain life. Higher wages would enhance reproduction and therewith the abundance of toilers that would bring real wages back down.

Nothing quite so Malthusian was believed by the 1950s. But deprivation was still the norm. Trade unions could sustain incomes, but they still had only a fugitive role in economic theory — they were an *imperfection* in the labor market. And the long and dreary experience of the depression years with their vast unemployment had nowise lessened the impression that workers in the modern capitalist society were meant to be abundant, redundant and poor. In setting out to explain poverty, I was explaining what economics had always explained. My enterprise lacked novelty.

From this perception, as gradually it emerged, came the solution. What needed explanation was the nature of a society in which most people were at a level of comfortable well-being, in which such well-being had become the norm. One then inquired into the reasons for the exceptions — why quite a number, individually and collectively, nonetheless remained poor.

All this, however, was in the future. Meanwhile I was stalled — I saw myself again as one of those articulate scholars whose seminal work of social comment remains forever incomplete except in conversations at the faculty club. Soon an alternative presented itself.

In the spring of 1954, at the behest of Jack Fischer, I wrote for *Harper's* a commemorative piece for the twenty-fifth anniversary that October of the great stock market crash of 1929. At the same time Arthur Schlesinger, engaged in those years on his mammoth and superb history of the New Deal, complained to me that no one had ever written a minimally competent history of the Great Depression, an event at least as important for its effect on the American psyche as the Civil War. And I discovered that no one, Frederick Lewis Allen in his classic *Only Yesterday* possibly apart, had ever tackled the great stock market debacle that ushered in the depression. I resolved to set poverty aside and write a book about it.

With *The Great Crash,*[3] my frustration turned to joy. Of this and my effect on the stock market and the Senate Republicans in the spring of 1955, I have told in the prefaces to its later editions. I allow myself a little repetition.

One pleasure was in the discovery in one of its manifold forms that the emperor had no clothes. Or, in more precise terms, it came from learning how the fashionable, smug, secure and pompous could arrange their own demise. This, after 1929, was the fate of the very greatest men of the financial world — of Richard Whitney, the vice president, later president, of the New York Stock Exchange whose brother George was a greatly eminent partner at Morgan's; of Albert H. Wiggin, the head of the Chase National Bank; of Charles E. Mitchell, the head of the National City Bank of New York; and of the great men of the investment house of Goldman Sachs, including, among others, their counsel and ally John Foster Dulles. All were riding the boom, as were the less pretentious speculators. All, with the exception of Wiggin, who was short in the stock of his own bank, were firm in their belief that the values they were helping create by their own mindless optimism were real. Every sug-

---

[3] Boston: Houghton Mifflin, 1955; 50th anniversary rev. ed., 1979.

gestion to the contrary was dismissed as subversive negativism. The Crash was a violent collision with reality from which none escaped. Mitchell only unexpectedly stayed out of jail. Whitney, the most intransigent defender of the Stock Exchange against any and all government regulation, was, as I have said, sent to Sing Sing. Wiggin was sacked. By investing in their own beliefs, all except Wiggin had ruthlessly defrauded themselves. The threat to men of great dignity, privilege and pretense is not from the radicals they revile; it is from accepting their own myth.

Exposure to reality remains the nemesis of the great — a little-understood thing. The steel executive who condemns all government intervention discovers almost immediately that he needs protection against Japanese imports. On the day that nuclear reactors are proclaimed safe, one threatens to spill radiation over the countryside. All who articulate the convenient belief should never worry about their critics, only revelation of the truth.

*   *   *

The Great Crash was published on April 21, 1955. Six weeks earlier on March 8, I went to Washington to testify on the current state of the stock market before the Senate Committee on Banking and Currency. In preceding months there had been a mild upward flurry, and so strong was the memory of those autumn days of 1929 that Senator J. William Fulbright, the committee chairman, thought it well to see if any similar trouble portended.

The hearing that morning was in the large Senate caucus chamber; like most hearings on economic matters, odd as this may seem, it was well attended. But on this day senators arrived and, in contrast with normal practice, did not, after assuming an aspect of furrowed preoccupation easily confused with the need for a bathroom, quickly depart. As the proceedings continued, cameramen and television crews arrived.

My testimony was benign; I told what had happened in 1929, carefully avoided any prediction of a similar disaster and suggested only some mildly precautionary tightening of margin requirements. But the reminder itself was mortal; as I testified, the stock market took a major dive, one of the largest in years. Some $7 billions in values, a large sum in those days, were lost. Almost alone among the participants I did not know what was happening. Fulbright, perhaps the most diversely intelligent and amusing legislator of the last forty years, thought to protect his flank. If as the result of our hearings that morning the stock market should "fall out of bed," would we not, he asked, be severely blamed? And surely, he implied, this would be deeply unfair. I replied that, were the market so weak, historians would relieve those conducting the hearing of responsibility. Fulbright responded that he, not the historians, would shortly be up for reelection in Arkansas. When my testimony was over at noon, I was advised as to what had happened.

And I was even more strenuously advised in the next days. A flood of mail, by far the heaviest of my lifetime, descended on Cambridge. It was denunciatory, defamatory, physically menacing or pious, the latter being from correspondents who said they were praying for my death or dismemberment. The financial press hovered on guard for any further word with similar implications. At the end of the week, to get away from it all, we went skiing at Mt. Snow in Vermont where I broke my leg. This being reported, I then learned that I had done something for religion; the pious read the news and wrote to tell me their prayers had been answered.

A few days later, wearing a cast, I hobbled down to a meeting in New York. Averell Harriman, newly the Governor of the state, inquired as to my accident and said, not uncharacteristically, "You probably don't know how to ski." Later that night at the Plaza, where I then stayed, I was called from Washington by a staff assistant to Senator Homer E. Capehart, Republican of Indiana, who read me lines from a small pamphlet I had written a few years earlier on the design for European economic recovery. It said, with no pretense to novelty, that the Communists had a better reputation than their opponents for addressing social grievances and rising above parochial and self-defeating nationalism. Thus their appeal. My caller was prosecutorial, even threatening. Would I admit to being the author? Did I believe what I had said? I told him to be aware of the context, a defense of democracy no less. I sensed that he believed he was on to something big.

The next Sunday Senator Capehart came on television to cite my praise of Communism. He concluded, in effect, that my committed Communist activism took the very practical form of destroying stock market values.

I had been put on guard by my nighttime call and also by Senator

Mike Monroney of Oklahoma, a sterling New Dealer and good friend, who had shared the television program with Capehart, which had been filmed a day or so earlier. I was perhaps unduly prepared.

I've told earlier of my advice to anyone so attacked. Always counterattack strongly; that may discourage your enemy and it will surely please both you and your natural allies. And by now I had formulated three supplementary rules, to wit: (1) Act promptly so as to get the same press attention as the original onslaught; (2) Do not say anything that is even marginally short of truth, for that, when exposed, undermines your whole case. Better all the damaging details; (3) Never lean to understatement.

On that same Sunday I put these principles into effect in telegrams to the wire services and the networks. The cost, about $50, was appalling. What statesman, I asked, would hold it subversive to speak candidly to a congressional committee about the stock market? Or edit my prose, as Capehart had done, to make it sound a little more like Lenin? And, borrowing from a response by Bernard DeVoto when similarly attacked, I suggested that anyone who was unacquainted with my views was for that reason unqualified as a senator. Not only were they in the American tradition, they were an operative part of it more or less. Then I got to the most luminous fact of all. The offending pamphlet had first been given as a lecture at the University of Notre Dame. By clear implication Capehart was attacking a monument to education, enlightened Catholicism and intercollegiate football in his own state of Indiana. By one of those coincidences that fiction writing does not allow, I was shortly able to enlarge on these themes while keeping a previously scheduled lecture engagement at another Indiana monument, Purdue University. All politicians are impressed by what they read in their home-state papers.

Capehart was now on the defensive, but he had the help of my old opponent Sinclair Weeks, now the Secretary of Commerce. Having seen my testimony and being reminded of my iniquity in the Harvard controversy of six years before, Weeks forthrightly asked the FBI for an investigation. J. Edgar Hoover thereupon dispatched an urgent handwritten release: "What Do Our Files Show on Galbraith?" The principal conclusion, as eventually revealed by the Freedom of Information Act, was not agreeable, but it must have been a grave disappointment to both the Secretary and the Senator:

"Investigation favorable except conceited, egotistical and snobbish."[4]

Capehart now came as close to an apology as senatorial dignity allowed. The only enduring pain from the episode was suffered by an impeccable conservative, David McCord Wright. Wright, it may be recalled, had thought me an enemy of capitalism from being dangerously soft on monopoly.[5] This conclusion Capehart, no man for small distinctions, had included in his indictment. Wright was spending the year at Oxford and wrote to Capehart, "I would be willing to fly home and testify if it is not too expensive and you feel that it would do any good," adding also the paranoiac thought that, unless so put down, "Galbraith may try a general smear of my character and politics." Even if morally justifiable, this was an enterprise I would not have thought worthwhile. Capehart, no man to cover for his friends, blithely published Wright's letter in the hearings.[6]

*   *   *

For some time in my casual writing I had been experimenting not only with clarity but also with cadence and rhythm. There is no mystery here; you test the words and sentences until the result rewards the ear. If your ear is right, then so is the rhythm. *The Great Crash* made the *New York Times* best-seller list for a week, which gave me great pleasure, but more came from Mark Van Doren's review, which said that it brought the language of poetry to history. Any writer who says that he is negligent of such praise is almost certainly lying.

Nor, I think, is any writer unaffected by his adverse reviews. The only convincing case to the contrary, as I've also previously told, was John Steinbeck. In January of 1954, Kitty and I went for a holiday to St. John in the Virgin Islands. The only other guests at the then modest hotel of Laurance Rockefeller's at Caneel Bay were the Steinbecks. He and I toured the island together and considered how effectively the slaves, when their revolt of 1733 was righteously suppressed by enlightened international action, assured themselves of the last word. They destroyed the plantation economy by rushing like lemmings from a high promontory into the sea, a singularly de-

---

[4] Office Memorandum, United States Government, March 23, 1955. Reproduced in FBI file on J.K.G.

[5] See Chapter 18.

[6] U.S., Congress, Senate, Committee on Banking and Currency, *Stock Market Study*, 84th Cong., 1st sess., 1955, p. 298.

finitive form of what the British call industrial action. With Elaine Steinbeck and Kitty we met each evening for drinks — I still called it the Liberal Hour and John called it Milking Time — and we remained friends thereafter. In 1958, I returned to London from a journey to Poland and Yugoslavia on the day that *The Affluent Society* was published in the United States. As I stood at the newsstand in the Dorchester Hotel reading a frightful rebuke in *Time* magazine — "a well-written but vague essay with the air of worried dinner-table conversation" — I became aware that someone was looking over my shoulder. I had no wish for anyone to see what I was reading or my gloomy response. But John's observation lifted my spirits: "Unless the bastards have the courage to give you unqualified praise, I say ignore them."

*   *   *

In those years, 1953 to 1955, my attention was also on the enterprise to which I earlier adverted, the economic education of Adlai Stevenson. As I've said, all who were with him in 1952 took for granted that he would again be the candidate in 1956. We thought it important that he be at home with the ideas he was espousing. We could not have another campaign during which, on Social Security, trade unions, Keynesian economics and other elements of the contemporary liberal creed, he could feel himself the instrument and perhaps the victim of his staff, the helpless receptacle for whatever they poured in.

We had another purpose, one that served usefully to conceal some part of our educational designs from our student. Our years in office had been intellectually stimulating; the need to react to new circumstances and newly created problems forced thought, which politicians no less than others so struggle to avoid. Now we were out of office. Would we not lapse into political and mental desuetude — and personal boredom? In September 1953 in New York I talked of this with Averell Harriman at a long meeting at which we also agreed we were both smoking too much.[7] I sent out conclusions to Stevenson:

> How can we do the most to keep the Democratic Party intellectually alert and positive during these years in the wilderness? We have all told our-

[7] I stopped abruptly a few months later on encountering the very first statistical reports relating cigarette smoking to lung cancer. Harriman also stopped.

selves that mere opposition is not enough. Yet it would be hard at the moment to say what the Democratic Party is for. On domestic matters we are for good and against evil and for tidying up the unfinished business of the New Deal. We want an expanding economy but there are few who could be pressed into any great detail as to what this means or takes. We are solidly opposed to Hooverism and depression, but there wouldn't be much agreement and fewer new ideas as to what prevention or cure might require. In fact, we are still trading on the imagination and intellectual vigor of the Roosevelt era and that capital is running thin. You will remember yourself the number of times during the last campaign when you found yourself rejecting (or on occasion reciting) ancient and flea-bitten clichés in the absence of anything involving thought. . .

[Intellectual torpor is] the disease of opposition parties, for initiative and imagination ordinarily lie with responsibility for action.[8]

Stevenson responded with interest, and Thomas K. Finletter led in organizing what came to be called the Finletter Group. Finletter, a former Secretary of the Air Force, later an ambassador to NATO and a man of intelligence, public sense and great charm, provided the setting and raised the money for travel expenses. Acting as dean of the faculty, I recruited the talent. Averell Harriman, Arthur Schlesinger, George Ball, Roy Blough (a member of the Council of Economic Advisers under Harry Truman) and Clayton Fritchey, who, with unexampled enthusiasm, honesty and skill, handled Stevenson's relations with the press in the 1952 and 1956 campaigns and who was later a widely known columnist, were among the regular participants. Our first meeting was on October 31, 1953, at Finletter's apartment on East 66th Street; the subject, agricultural policy, was not calculated to arouse undue passion in midtown New York. I had written the required paper. In further meetings full employment, fiscal policy, monetary policy, tax policy, arms policy, Indochina, wiretapping and numerous other subjects were explored. Seymour Harris of Harvard, a prodigious contributor, produced some ten papers on education, medical care, health insurance, income distribution, old-age insurance and one entitled "An Economist Examines the Promises and Performances of the Republican Administration."

Most of the further meetings were at Finletter's apartment and lasted through dinner and deep into the night. Once or twice we

[8] This letter is quoted in John Bartlow Martin, *Adlai Stevenson and the World* (New York: Doubleday, 1977), pp. 83–84.

met at our house in Cambridge and once in Chicago. Stevenson was a less than faithful attendant, but we were much comforted by his assertion that he was an avid student of the papers we debated, amended and approved. On one notable evening in New York Paul Samuelson, fresh from his classes at MIT, lectured Stevenson for several hours as he might a beginning economics student on the meaning of National Income and Gross National Product, the reasons why they might be less than the optimum, the unemployment that would result from their decline and the nature of the fiscal and monetary cures. Stevenson, we agreed, showed encouraging evidence not only of interest but of understanding.

The Finletter Group, if it did not fully inform Stevenson, did greatly mitigate his anxieties. In the 1956 campaign he responded warmly on ideas ranging from full employment policy to the virtue of unions to health insurance that had filled him with worry four years before. Even a Princeton economics education could be retrieved. For the rest of us the pleasure in the company and the discussion was, as ever, taken as proof of profound social value. The Finletter Group was the forerunner of a yet more ambitious educational effort, that of the Democratic Advisory Council which was brought into being after our second defeat in 1956.

* * *

In those years I was also concerned with Puerto Rico. To this day few mainlanders viewing only the appalling hotels in Santurce east from San Juan can know how compellingly remote and romantic are the inner valleys and mountainsides of this lovely island and also how poor its people once were and often still are. As Luis Muñoz Marín and his colleagues set out to provide an industrial alternative to the deadening deprivation of the cane fields, I was asked, through the University of Puerto Rico, to organize a study and report on various of the economic and social problems of the island. This in turn gave content to our work at Harvard on economic development and employment to younger colleagues and older graduate students. Our principal investigation was of a superbly commonplace problem.

As the industrialization of Puerto Rico showed promise of succeeding, attention turned to the way goods were being made available to the population. There, as earlier told and as elsewhere in the

Caribbean and Central America, a powerfully exploitive role was played by the port merchants. They divided among themselves the franchises for all branded products that came from the mainland from Camel cigarettes to Campbell soup. Each had a small monopoly in one of these brands, and the margins were in keeping. With the resulting income went the effective political power.[9] Then in the country hamlets and in substantial measure in the towns, these goods were retailed by keepers of tiny stores who again divided the market among themselves and scrupulously avoided anything as mutually damaging as price competition. By mainland standards, the ultimate prices were frightful.

The result of our efforts was *Marketing Efficiency in Puerto Rico*,[10] by a substantial margin the least known of my books on economics. Much of the work was, in fact, done by Richard Holton, later and still a professor at the University of California at Berkeley and one-time dean of the school of business administration there, and by various assistants.

A further result of our study was the establishment by the Puerto Rican government of a commission of chain-store executives and marketing experts to recommend and encourage practical reforms. On this I served. We urged port improvements to weaken the position of the importers by providing more physical space for competition. And following recommendations in Holton's and my study, we urged the encouragement of modern chains and supermarkets, including consumer cooperatives, a proposal we had originally made with some unease. "In one sense the marketing system has become a form of unemployment relief — it returns a small income to people who would not otherwise find a livelihood . . . Puerto Rican retailers have developed a live and let live attitude which allows for the business survival of the large number of people found in the industry. Profits that could be made are foregone in order to allow others to make a living."[11] Holton, in earlier conversation, had put the problem more directly: "We must teach these people to get the Christianity out of their system."

[9] See Chapter 12.
[10] By John Kenneth Galbraith and Richard H. Holton (Cambridge: Harvard University Press, 1955).
[11] *Marketing Efficiency in Puerto Rico*, p. 3.

In time and perhaps partly as the result of our urging, modern supermarkets and merchandising arrived in Puerto Rico, and the Christianity, if not wholly removed, was greatly mitigated. Economists in pursuit of efficiency are righteously cruel to those who must be sacrificed. However, there is no doubt that high prices for the poor are also cruel.

*   *   *

As noted, *Marketing Efficiency* was published by the Harvard University Press. The good fortune of this worthy institution was related to another of my current concerns. In the last century David A. Wells, a distinguished Harvard benefactor, established a fund for the publication of prize essays, specifying that no prize might go to any publication that advocated debasement of the currency or related fallacies. The resulting books were to be given free to libraries or serious readers. However, President Eliot refused to allow the books to be so distributed on the grounds that no free book would ever be thought worth reading. Therefore the books were sold, and the receipts were then made available for printing yet other books in a series that became the Harvard Economic Studies. Presently the Harvard department of economics became possessed of the most securely profitable publishing enterprise since Caxton. Costs were paid out of the endowment; gross receipts were net profit.

On returning to Harvard from *Fortune,* I was thought especially qualified as a publisher. So I became chairman of the departmental publishing committee, a position I occupied for nearly ten years. It was not noticed until near the end of my tenure that while I always spoke in meetings of the decisions of my committee, it was a committee of one, myself. This greatly simplified choosing and approving manuscripts; when books had been so passed, they went more or less automatically through the remaining editorial machinery of the Press. I published very nearly as many books in those years as were published in all the previous history of the series combined. Many were far from readable. There was some minor power in my position. In the American university, promotion depends on publication. Thus to be in control of publication was to have some influence on the academic prospects of my younger colleagues. This small authority I enjoyed and deployed with impartiality and justice.

It was perhaps not surprising that I found *Marketing Efficiency in Puerto Rico* worthy to be put out by the Harvard Press.

*   *   *

My attention during those years was also, perhaps surprisingly, diverted to railroading. The Canadian Pacific Railway was then headed by Norris R. Crump, and it occurred to him that it would be useful to have some outsiders look at his highly stereotyped operations. Instead of a consulting firm, perhaps a number of young academic economists would be better and also cheaper. I was invited to assemble a team from among my younger Harvard faculty colleagues to study whatever might seem worthwhile or interesting. The CPR would pay; we would be free to publish the results. A newly installed computer at CPR headquarters would be available.

I brought together a talented group — Holton again, Richard E. Caves, John R. Meyer, Merton J. Peck and Charles Zwick — all to become leading economists of the next generation. John D. Black lent an advisory hand. Beginning in 1954, my colleagues used the CPR as a lens through which to see the problems of the railroads, of government transportation policy and the Canadian economy. I used my more limited participation for further instruction on the nature of corporate management.

The CPR, as no Canadian needs to be reminded, is a very large part of Canadian history. Its tracks and trains, promised to British Columbia in 1871 to bring that province into the national federation, served quite literally to tie Canada together. And the company was, and remains, an estate of national scale in itself. Farm land, forests, minerals, oil and scenery were included in its rich endowment, and these remain even today. Beside rail lines that extend into the United States, it then operated hotels, ships, mines, telegraphs, metal refineries and, reluctantly, an airline. The railway men did not look with favor on such passing fads as airplanes.

By the mid-fifties most of the Canadian Pacific operations had gone rather grandly to seed. Aged hierarchs presided over freight, passenger and other departments with a rigid attention to past practice and a lofty indifference to patronage, cost or profit. Among the many contributions of the railroad to Canadian culture was its unique architecture, known then and still as CPR Gothic, and the company was run from the culminating example, the cavernous

Windsor Station in Montreal. Once with my young colleagues I attended a meeting of the senior management in the boardroom of this fortress. Except by Crump and one or two others, we were regarded with indignation verging on hostility. One reason was some calculations by my associates that had shown that a clutch of parlor cars then on order would not, under the best of circumstances, pay the cost of pulling them around, much less return a profit. We took considerable pride in this finding as also the generally unpromising prospect for most passenger travel; it was the pleasure of a doctor who reports to the family that his diagnosis can be trusted, for it will soon be evident that the patient is dying. The aged railroaders, most of them up from the ranks, did not like it at all. They saw our report as a juvenile intrusion, at odds with tradition and what a good railroad man really knew.

The most rewarding ten days of our whole CPR enterprise were given over to a tour of the company lines in the late spring of 1955. Not before or since have I had a journey that combined such interest and such scenery with such elegance. Richard Holton accompanied me; our host was Robert A. Emerson, vice president for operations and maintenance and one of the progressive forces in the firm. We traveled in the private car that had taken Sir Edward Beatty, the most awesome of all company presidents, over the line in the greatest days of the system. With us was a male secretary, for Canadian virtue did not permit of a woman riding alone with men in this splendid vehicle. Our journey took us from Montreal and Ottawa through the pre-Cambrian Ontario wilderness, past the head of the lakes, over the endless prairies and through the spiral tunnels that, in the manner of a circular staircase, take the railroad down the far side of the Rockies. And then we went on through more mountains of much grandeur and along the Thompson and Fraser rivers to Vancouver and the Strait of Georgia. We stopped in the major cities to talk with local railroad officials. When we continued, we sometimes were attached to a passenger train, and sometimes we rode placidly behind a freight. Not until this trip did I fully appreciate the scale of my native land. This no one now traveling over it by air can possibly know. Doubtless it would be yet more revealing to walk.

During the journey I formed some thoughts on the future of the company. In those days its forests and its lands and their subsoil wealth were seen only as sources of traffic to be developed for its rail lines. The railroad and in much lesser measure some operating mines and a metal refinery were truly all that mattered. I urged that the future would be with the natural endowment. There were sympathetic ears, but I was told also that no such concept could ever be sold to the *real* railroad men, and they were the decisive locus of entrenched bureaucratic power. Time, aided by death and retirement, has since turned the CPR into a company that is, indeed, centered on its vast natural wealth.

The railroad men were not wholly perfect even in their deeply committed role. In those days the first units of the Canadian, the gleaming bubble-top express from Montreal to Vancouver, were delivered to Windsor Station. It was a beautiful train. My colleagues went down with officials of the company to view this marvel; Robert Emerson came back to his offices in the station to get out various blueprints and memorabilia of the right of way. The bubbles on the train, he learned, ran slightly higher than the minimum height of the tunnels. In economics there has long been debate over the significance of, as they are called, marginal effects. Here there could be none.

Two books, one on the Canadian economy and one more generally on rail transportation and its competitors, emerged from this enterprise. They were also found acceptable by the Harvard University Press.[12]

The years at *Fortune* had involved a certain experience with innovative and otherwise successful corporate organizations; it was such companies that suggested themselves for celebration in the magazine. The CPR was far from being the worst of North American railroads; conceivably, with all of its sclerosis, it was one of the least bad. But it was a valuable reminder that corporate stultification is also a feature of modern enterprise and is self-perpetuating. Mediocrity clones as does excellence. One was prepared by the CPR for Penn Central and Chrysler.

---

[12] *The Economics of Competition in the Transportation Industries* by John R. Meyer, Merton J. Peck, John Stenason and Charles Zwick, and *The Canadian Economy* by Richard E. Caves and Richard H. Holton. Both books were published in 1959. Caves and Meyer are now professors at Harvard and Peck at Yale. Holton, as previously noted, is a professor at the University of California at Berkeley. Zwick, later a Director of the Budget, is now a banker, and Stenason, who had originally been with the CPR, is Executive Vice-President and Director of Canadian Pacific Investments, Ltd.

There remained, among these diverse fascinations, the nagging knowledge that my book on poverty in the midst of well-being was making little progress. The needed answers were still unrevealed and seemed important. Early in 1955, I resolved that come summer I would take a year off and think of nothing else.

21

First View of India and
The Affluent Society

MY INSTINCT was eventually to prove sound. Painful though it is, the best way to think and write is to do nothing else. One is then forced into effort as an escape from boredom and one's own personality. The discovery was, however, delayed.

When school was out in the summer of 1955, having arranged a year's leave from Harvard and been given a Guggenheim fellowship, I loaded our three children and Emily Wilson on a German freighter laden with Canadian wheat at Trois Rivières on the St. Lawrence River and went thence to Hamburg. My thought was to settle down to writing in Switzerland.

From tales told of the cattle boats on which students went to Europe in my extreme youth, I had long wanted to cross the Atlantic on a freighter. My wife, afflicted with no such desire, went by plane. She was fortunate. The journey was placid, cramped and, reading apart, infinitely boring. The only relief from tedium came in mid-ocean when we met a sister ship of the same German line, and the two vessels celebrated frivolously, each rushing to circle the other in a kind of maritime waltz. On our arrival we watched the relatives of the crew swarm aboard; so abbreviated was the turn-around time that many who lived at a distance could not go home. Thus the conjugal visits.

In the next summer months in Switzerland — on the Lake of Lucerne at Sils-Maria, down at Brissago on Lago Maggiore (where Hemingway's lovers came ashore after rowing up the lake) and at Saas Fee — I read and struggled to write on the causes of poverty. In the autumn we settled into a pleasant flat on Chemin Krieg near the Route de Florissant in Geneva, and I embarked on a further course of reading in what had been the library of the League of Nations and was now part of the United Nations.

There were occasional flashes of hope. In Saas Fee working by myself, a few ideas emerged full and round, and I wrote furiously. In Geneva I was pressed to give some lectures at the Graduate Institute of International Studies at its lovely place of learning on the shores of the lake.[1] The Institute, the creation of William E. Rappard, was now headed by the diverse, thoughtful, amused and amusing Jacques Freymond, who was to become a close friend. Lectures are also a good way of forcing thought. The day and hour approach inexorably; you cannot stand silent before even the most exiguous audience. So you force yourself into substance and conclusions, confident in the knowledge that no one present will remember enough to be damaging. But I was still at a loss. The encasing orthodoxy had still to be escaped: people were poor because economics intended them to be so. There did not seem to be much more to be explained. Then there came an autumn evening of greater personal portent than we could have guessed.

We dined with Richard Kahn of King's College, Cambridge, who was by now, as college bursar after Keynes, in recognized succession to the master. The other guest, a tall, slender, deeply featured and powerfully self-assured Indian, was Prasanta Chandra Mahalanobis. Mahalanobis, then sixty-two, had been a prize scholar in physics at Cambridge during the First World War. He and Rani, his sharply perceptive and singularly independent wife, were intimates of Rabindranath Tagore, the Bengali poet, writer and painter. From being a professor of physics at the University of Calcutta, Mahalanobis had made his way via meteorology to economic statistics and on to economics and economic planning. He was now the head of the government-supported but largely independent Indian Statistical Institute, a source through innovative sampling techniques of much statistical intelligence, not all of it precise, on Indian industrial and agricultural production, incomes and prices, population and manpower. Mahalanobis was also a member of the Planning Commission of the Government of India of which Jawaharlal Nehru, to whom Mahalanobis was adviser, friend and confidant, was chairman.

As did Nehru, Mahalanobis belonged to the world of Sidney and

[1] For some years, as I write, I have been an honorary professor and lecturer each winter at the Institute.

Beatrice Webb, George Bernard Shaw, R. H. Tawney, G. D. H. Cole, Harold Laski and the Fabian Society. It was a world in which decency, compassion and wide-ranging intelligence were combined with the belief that the nature of the economic order is, above all, a matter of moral commitment. Socialism involves no decisively difficult administrative problems, no really serious questions of organization or motivation. Even the weight of population on land resources, seemingly so inescapable in India, is not centrally important. These barriers to economic development were inherent in capitalist culture, mentality and experience. With socialism all would diminish or disappear. To cite the difficulties in the path of socialist development was to invite the suspicion of being secretly in the service of capitalism or, at a minimum, innocently a victim of its doctrine. Such optimism as to the prospect in India came more easily in the 1950s than a quarter century on. I continue to believe that men and women of such decency deserved to be right.

Mahalanobis spoke that evening in Geneva of India's Second — and the first politically and intellectually serious — Five-Year Plan. And more particularly he told of his generally successful efforts to bring scholars to his Institute from both the socialist countries and the West to counsel on the Plan and India's development in general. He had gone to the Eisenhower Administration for help, and it had offered him Professor Milton Friedman, then of the University of Chicago. I responded thoughtfully to the news, noting that to ask Friedman to advise on economic planning was like asking the Holy Father to counsel on the operations of a birth control clinic. Mahalanobis was pleased by my metaphor and proposed that I come to India instead. He carefully included my wife in the invitation. She had been suffering from my literary anguish and saw India as an escape. We agreed to go early the following year.

One weekend that autumn we journeyed to the Berner Oberland and went walking from the village of Gstaad, of which, until that time, neither of us had heard. This too was to have a durable effect. I was soon to find there a tranquil climate for writing which I have used ever since. It is a lovely village midway between Montreux and Interlaken in a valley where three mountain streams come together. The sun shines in; the low mountains around are shelter from the winds. Once, along with its cattle, Gstaad lived on its sawmills, and these still operate. For many years its sedentary population of around 1500 has been seasonally doubled and then trebled by an influx of the fashionable rich. They have brought shops, restaurants, a swimming pool, ski-lifts and every other amenity. They also make excellent neighbors for a writer of liberal instinct. Half are functionally illiterate and thus have no tendency to intrude on one's time. Those who can read are also deterred: "I've heard of Galbraith — some kind of Bolshevist." Often in Gstaad I have looked at the telephone and wished it would ring.

We returned to Gstaad for the 1955 Christmas holidays and left Emily Wilson and our two younger sons, now turning four and five, while we went to India. Emily enrolled them in the village school where, by their account, they taught their classmates English. In January I had first to return to Canada on CPR business and to Toronto to testify in the legislative chamber at Queen's Park on the longer-term Canadian prospect before the Royal Commission on Canada's Economic Prospects headed by Walter L. Gordon.[2] As do lectures and solitude, the need to give such testimony also usefully forces thought. With somewhat less confidence than I sought to display, I held that sooner rather than later our concern with the quantity of goods produced — the rate of increase in Gross National Product — would have to give way to the larger question of the quality of the life that it provided. That would mean better protection of the environment, greater need for public and social services.

After meeting Kitty in Zurich and waiting out a great winter storm, we went to Beirut where I lectured at the American University. We then took the road to Damascus, visited Ba'albek, turned north to the ancient towns of Homs and Hamā, saw Krak des Chevaliers and returned to Beirut by way of Byblos.

Had one but a single week in a lifetime for seeing the great sights of antiquity, Athens, Peking and the Nile would have a claim. But the temples of Jupiter and Bacchus at Ba'albek, proof of what prodigious builders were the Romans, are in competition as also Damascus, plausibly the oldest continuously inhabited city in the world. In Damascus one can view the Great Mosque, the labyrinthian souks filled with merchandise of the most dubious quality and the surrounding wall where one can see the high window from which Paul escaped in the basket. Then in the same week one can visit Krak des

---

[2] Gordon, the most diligent, versatile and intellectually independent of Canadian leaders, would become my lifelong ally in varied liberal enterprises.

Chevaliers, the vast creation of the crusading Order of the Hospital of St. John of Jerusalem, called by Julian Huxley the most nearly perfect castle ever built. The curtain wall of Krak surrounds an entire mountain top, and through its angled gate a whole company of the armed monks, several abreast, could pass to safety at a full gallop. The surrender of its depleted garrison to the forces of Sultan Al-Malik az-Zāhir Rukn ad-Din Baybars on April 8, 1271, was perhaps the strongest signal that the Frankish era in Outremer was at an end.

From Lebanon we went to Bombay and on to Calcutta, arriving there on February 9.

* * *

Few can forget their first sight of India, and certainly not if they come in through Calcutta. We passed in the late evening shadows from Dum Dum Airport to Barrackpore Trunk Road. Our way was through two peering, silent processions, white-clad with dark bare shoulders and dark bare legs, which moved endlessly, where one wondered, on each side of the road. Beyond the pedestrian chain, deeper in the shadows, were the hovels of those lucky enough to have a roof, here mostly refugees from East Bengal. Visible too were the charpoys or rope cots of those who lived and slept without shelter of any kind. Cattle, also silent, turned to view us as we passed. Heaps of refuse were everywhere. Soon it all became almost commonplace. A few days later driving into the center of Calcutta, my wife and I saw a baby, emaciated, half-prostrate, venting a long white stool beside the road. The infant was obviously very sick, but not until later did we react to what we had seen. Elsewhere, even in the South Bronx, one would have rushed to call an ambulance. Thus do one's eyes glaze on exposure to India.

The Indian Statistical Institute occupied a cluster of buildings out from Calcutta on the road to Barrackpore, and a notable convocation awaited us there. Norbert Wiener, the father of cybernetics (roughly the logic of the computer), a silent, tense man, was a visitor at the time. Also Oskar R. Lange with his rather younger wife Irene Oderfeld, she a magistrate back in Poland. Lange, an economist and active member of the Socialist Party in Poland in the thirties, had moved to the United States to escape the primitive prewar fascism of his homeland. He had become a professor at the University of

Chicago, which was not so alien an environment as might be imagined, for Lange's socialism took as its ideal the distribution of productive resources that would be achieved in the classically competitive market. Absent only would be the economic distortions and the abused power inherent in monopoly or the private ownership of land or capital. Thus at Chicago he could live companionably with Frank H. Knight, Henry C. Simons and others for whom the competitive market was a totem.

In the closing months of World War II, Lange had gone to Russia, made his peace with the Soviet government and doffed his Chicago professorship to become the first Polish ambassador in Washington and thereafter at the United Nations. From there he returned to Warsaw. By 1956, he was in disfavor with the Stalinist regime of the time, and in later years he told Paul Sweezy (who told me) that for months he never went to bed without the compelling thought that he might be arrested before dawn.[3] No word of this came from him in India; he was far more reserved than I remembered him in prewar days.

While we were in Calcutta, the Khrushchev Twentieth Party Congress speech on "The Personality Cult and its Consequences" — the excesses of Stalinism — became known to the world press. We discussed it. After first expressing some doubts as to its authenticity, Lange came around to accepting its bona fides. He did not, however, think it portended any very great change. What it did portend was the end of the Stalinist regime in Poland and his return to a position of prestige and influence. I was to be his guest in Warsaw two years later.

Also at the Institute was Paul Baran, fresh from visiting his parents in Moscow. Now at the near-zenith of the Cold War he was, as ever, in pursuit of the most unpopular available political position and thus more pro-Communist than ever. His health, abused by heavy smoking, negligent eating and a great abhorrence of exercise, was in sad repair. Mahalanobis's socialist views were generally in line with Baran's, but since neither could brook agreement, they clashed bitterly. Nicholas Kaldor, who was not only one of the most noted but also one of the most absent-minded of British economists, arrived soon after we did with his wife Clarisse and two of his talented

---

[3] This did not imply death. The Polish government in this oppressive time was not bloodthirsty, something of which one was later told with some pride.

daughters. It was the time in China when the hundred flowers were about to bloom; Nicky and Clarisse, to the openly expressed envy of everyone at the Institute, were on their way to Peking. Then he would return to India. After a bountiful dinner and warm farewells, the Kaldors departed one night for Dum Dum Airport and China. Two hours later they were back; Nicky had forgotten the passports.

Others came to the Institute, as did local visitors from Calcutta. Meals were with the Mahalanobises in the great house where Kitty and I inhabited a small flat on the top floor. The conversation turned back to British times, to the great Bengal famine of the war years and always, in the end, to the Indian economic prospect. More seemed then to be possible than one could now imagine.

At no other place in the world at the time was there such easy and intense exchange between people of the socialist and the nonsocialist worlds and of the rich countries and the poor.

It was not an exchange that I found wholly comfortable. John Foster Dulles was Secretary of State, and he regarded the reputation of the American Republic, then so high, as his personal possession to be dissipated at will. No man could have been more successful. He was particularly anxious to prove that capitalism was all that socialists believed it to be. American foreign policy was dominated by a single ruling passion, which was to defeat Communism. Christianity, Jesus himself, sanctioned this crusade. Any despot who was an anti-Communist was an ally; our policy everywhere was to enter military alliances and arm the indigent. Neutrality, called neutralism, was immoral, and the Indians were the outstanding case. With all else the policy was pompous, self-satisfied and sanctimonious. One had difficulty imagining a more damaging figure for the poor lands than John Foster Dulles, although this was partly because the work of his brother Allen in the CIA was still unknown.

Yet in India in those days I didn't find it comfortable to lead or join in the adverse comment on the Secretary of State; it seemed too easy a way of cultivating applause. I thought of Churchill's adjuration: do not criticize your government when out of the country, never cease to do so when at home. So, like Oskar Lange, I became unnaturally silent when the policies of my own government came up for discussion.

*   *   *

A few days after our arrival there appeared the most interesting of our visitors, the Rt. Honorable Evelyn John St. Loe Strachey.[4] Then fifty-five, of a family with roots in India going back almost to Warren Hastings, John Strachey was tall, big without being bulky, a superbly entertaining conversationalist with a gift for absorbing and inducing laughter. In the thirties he had been a Communist, although for tactical reasons (what Washington would come to call the need for deniability) he was never, as he once told me, issued a card. He left the party at the time of the German-Soviet nonaggression pact. Though he described the break to me one day as the most wrenching experience of his life, he did not compensate on leaving with bitter anti-Communist passion.

In Clement Attlee's cabinets Strachey had been Food Minister and then Secretary of State for War. The appearance of a former Communist in this latter position, as John was amusingly aware, caused tremors in the Pentagon that the building itself was but barely able to withstand.

Mahalanobis wanted his visitors to travel over India and see at first hand the problems with which independence and the Five-Year Plans were contending. Nothing could have been for us more welcome. We joined with John Strachey for our journey. This covered India from Madras and Mahabalipuram in the south to the Himalayas in the north, some by air, some by train, shorter distances by car. It was a lively, wonderful time. North from Puri on the Bay of Bengal, we visited the Black Pagoda (now called the Surya Deula) of Konarak, the great temple of black stone, which is around a hundred feet high. Built to represent a chariot, it is mounted on large carved stone wheels and is pulled by a team of highly improbable beasts. The pagoda itself is covered from bottom nearly to the top with superbly carved statues showing a variety and resource in their approach to sexual intercourse that would be impressive to Dr. Comfort. Strachey was enchanted first by two missionaries who felt obliged to view it from a safe distance; then by one stone couple locked for centuries in an especially intense embrace — "what a jolly good fuck!"; and finally by an Indian professor of archeology who accompanied us and who excused it all by saying somewhat formally that, after all, "it is essential for the continuation of the human race."

---

[4]See Chapter 6.

I was less enchanted six years later when Mrs. John F. Kennedy, while visiting India, expressed a desire to see Konarak. With only the mildest exercise of imagination one could see her being photographed while looking at some notably expressive sexual achievement, possibly at one accomplished woman who makes love to two violently tumescent men at the same time. And it was equally certain what ambassador would be blamed for the resulting pictures, however edited for publication. Why, the bureaucracy and the press would ask, had not this "photo opportunity" been more carefully analyzed? I warned Jackie of the danger, and she was obdurate. So, sheepishly, I went to her husband. It could have been the least satisfactory interview any official ever had with a President. Kennedy said only, "Don't you think she is old enough?" In the end for reasons of time and a sinus attack, Konarak had to be dropped from the schedule.

Strachey's family background, political eminence, his books and his exceptional credentials on the left made his arrival in any town a major event and required, inevitably, a speech. I was also asked, partly out of courtesy but also because, of all the races on the earth, the Indians have the most nearly inexhaustible appetite for oratory. In Hyderabad in the Deccan one day we viewed the vast palaces of the Nizams, some inspired architecturally by Waterloo Station and already in deep decay. Then we were entertained at lunch by the Rotary Club. Before the meal the Rotarians were introduced to us with the usual Indian attention to ceremony (the names are notional):

"This, Mr. Strachey and Professor Galbraith, is Rotarian Ram Singh! Rotarian Singh is the head of our Water Board here in Hyderabad!"

"This, Mr. Strachey and Professor Galbraith, is Rotarian Ahmed Kahn! Rotarian Kahn is our leading jeweler here in Hyderabad!"

Then along the line came a small man with a pleasant smile. His introduction sent Strachey perceptibly into shock.

"This, Mr. Strachey and Professor Galbraith, is Rotarian Krishna Mehta! Rotarian Mehta is the chairman of our Communist Party here in Hyderabad."

Going to Delhi from a suburban station north of Calcutta by train, we learned that elementary courtesy survives in a busy and uncouth world. After we were settled in our compartment — luggage, coconuts for thirst, overstuffed chairs on which to relax — the station-master appeared, saluted and said, "Sirs, may I have your permission to start the train?"

*   *   *

In Delhi I became acquainted with Jawaharlal Nehru. Our first encounter was at a garden party for John Foster Dulles at the American Embassy Residence. Nehru was standing a little apart from the throng on the spacious, very green lawn — a handsome, lean, rather small man with nicely carved features, light of complexion as befits a Kashmiri and wearing the white jodhpurs that were his special style. His expression was one of evident distaste for the proceedings. Later we met and talked about economics. It was a subject in which he had little interest. One was a socialist, at least in principle, and that was sufficient. For a time he regarded me with suspicion. Surely I was engaged in some peculiarly intricate proselytizing for American capitalism.

In New Delhi the Indian Statistical Institute had a commodious house and garden on King George's Avenue, which was presided over by another physicist turned economist, a luminous and charming man named Pitamber Pant. To King George's Avenue, Indians and foreign visitors also came. One evening in the garden Strachey, with an eloquence that far exceeded his own convictions, set out to persuade Charles Bettelheim, the noted French sociologist and ardent socialist, of the unwisdom of making India a test case for socialism. Indian economic life was on too small a scale, too diffuse and its problems too intractable. Before socialism, first capitalism. Bettelheim was appalled. Listening, I thought with amusement, was Indira Gandhi.

One day, with Nicholas Kaldor and Wilfred Malenbaum, a former student of mine in economic development, Strachey went with a large party of Indian officials to see a village that was being improved by the Community Development and Cooperation Plan. There was then great hope — which I largely shared — that Community Development would change the face of rural India. Its leader, Surendra Kumar Dey, was everyone's hero.

The village selected for display, in keeping with established practice, had been wonderfully cleaned up for the visit. The mud streets had been swept; women, ordinarily more usefully occupied, were for that morning engaged in handicrafts; the children had been rounded up from the fields and various youthful enjoyments and put in school. The high point of the afternoon was a colloquy between Malenbaum and a tall, handsome, very ancient Sikh.

"Old man, you have seen great changes here in Harapur." (Another notional name.)

"Yes, I have indeed seen great changes!"

"And great improvements too?"

"No, I have seen no improvements. Things were far better under the British."

*   *   *

To justify the manifold delights of our visit I wrote a number of papers on the Second Five-Year Plan. None was memorable and some were misguided. The exception was a memorandum on the organization of the new public enterprises.

This, a matter of prime importance in India and a theme to which I was often to return, dealt with the relation of the new public corporations to the government. The ultimate ownership of the very large industrial corporation, public or private, matters little. What is important is the autonomy that the management is accorded for operations and the rigor of the tests of performance to which management is made subject. Operating decisions or those on personnel and other such matters must never be second-guessed by civil servants or politicians. A corporate personality, like that of an individual, is impaired and distorted by paternal supervision. And the delay inherent in seeking ministerial or other higher approval is uniquely damaging. A wrong decision isn't forever; it can always be reversed. The losses from a delayed decision *are* forever; they can never be retrieved.

The management of the public enterprise must also be subject firmly to the test of earnings. That is because there is no other test — none that so comprehensively measures effectiveness in getting the most return for the least cost. Leadership should be undisturbed so long as it succeeds. When earnings fail, it should be changed and the new one left on its own to do better.

In India these rules were not followed. The public enterprises were being seen as an extension of its government departments. Accordingly, the corporations sought decisions from the relevant civil servant or minister on a wide range of matters. They were not subject to the harsh test of earnings; it was not clear how performance was measured. I called this relaxed system "post office socialism." On various occasions, "conventional wisdom" and "convenient social virtue" being examples, I have invented phrases that were intended to survive. "Post office socialism" was taken up and eventually became a byword in India without any such intention.

When I had finished my paper on the public enterprises, I gave a copy to S. S. Khera, the senior civil servant most concerned. Further to ensure attention, I also gave a copy to Asoka Mehta, a friend and one of the leading members of the Praja (popular) Socialist Party, then in opposition in the Parliament.

Mehta was much impressed by my thesis. He rose in the Parliament to read from the paper and to urge the government to consult with its author, Galbraith, who, he noted, was currently in India. Though he was an American, Galbraith's views on the public sector were worth hearing. The minister involved, Pandit Gouind Ballabh Pant, who had been rapidly briefed by Khera, was unimpressed. Entering the debate, he said that Galbraith was no doubt a worthy man. But his officials were in touch with another and much more useful man, also an American as it happened. His name was Braithwaite.[5] Braithwaite, as compared with Galbraith, was a man of much sounder thought. Pant then read some extracts from the same paper, the one which Khera had given him; these paragraphs, he said, showed the superior insights of Braithwaite. Mehta intervened to urge the merits of Galbraith. The minister stood firm for Braithwaite. The debate that ensued on the relative managerial wisdom of the two men was inconclusive.

All was reported next day in the Indian papers. Kitty and I had meanwhile flown back to Calcutta and with Strachey were on our way to Darjeeling, the lovely hill station which in British times was the retreat from the damp summer heat of Bengal. Strachey and I pieced together, as it happened correctly, the events that had produced this most improbable of parliamentary disputes. When we got

[5] Braithwaite is a familiar name in India, that of a long-established Anglo-Indian business firm.

off the plane at Baghdogra, the airport on the plain below Darjeeling, two stalwart policemen came forward to greet us.

Looking up first at John and then yet farther up at me, one said, "My, you gentlemen are very, very tall."

John replied, "Ah, but you should see Braithwaite."

*   *   *

One day in Benares I saw in the Bharat Kala Bhavan, a fine museum with its treasures beautifully displayed, its collection of Indian paintings of the sixteenth to eighteenth centuries. The magic of these small, beautifully contrived works, their aspect of amused mystery, their sometimes sophisticated, sometimes naive themes, their exquisite portraiture, never thereafter left me. I assembled the available books on the subject and read them all. And I went to the museums in India, Britain and the United States to see more. From all of this came some of my most pleasant hours. One day I awoke to discover that I had both an extensive knowledge of Indian painting and excellent judgment; indeed, I was an authority on the subject. The eventual result was a book, *Indian Painting: The Scene, Themes and Legends*,[6] of which I was co-author with Mohinder Singh Randhawa, the greatest of Indian authorities on the subject.[7] It is my only writing to which, to my knowledge, no one has ever taken serious exception.

During our stay in New Delhi we went one day to have lunch with John Sherman Cooper and his wife Lorraine at the Embassy Residence. Cooper, as I was later to learn, was one of the few diplomats who made an impression on Jawaharlal Nehru. Nehru thought him a man of perception and style; a phrase recurred in his conversation, "Ambassador Cooper once told me . . ." Lorraine Cooper liked being an ambassador's wife more than anything in the world and made no effort to conceal the fact. As afterward we made our way back to King George's Avenue, I confided a secret to Kitty: "When the Democrats get back in, I think I will get myself made ambassador to India." She didn't believe me nor did I, but so it came to pass.

After New Delhi we spent a few spring days in Kashmir, the first

[6] Boston: Houghton Mifflin, 1968.
[7] I also, in later years, made purchases, and the result, a well-regarded collection, is in the Fogg Art Museum at Harvard, with some to go also to Smith College.

of many in that loveliest of valleys. It was the season when the sod rooftops and the Moslem cemeteries are thick with daffodils, the terraced paddies a fresh vivid green from the rice coming through the water, with the Himalayas as always reaching to their unbelievable white-clad heights in the near distance. The Alps, the Rockies and all other mountains are related to the earth, the Himalayas to the heavens, a thought to which I will recur. Then we went to Rome. The Hotel Majestic on the Via Veneto was unprepared for our arrival so we were lodged in an enormous suite, much of which we didn't explore. In the quiet of the night, after we were in bed, a toilet in one of our distant bathrooms flushed. We both had the same thought: Braithwaite again.

*   *   *

I had planned to seclude myself in King's College, Cambridge, and spend the summer on another effort with the book. Nicholas Kaldor had suggested it but had forgotten to tell the college.[8] Richard Kahn seemed surprised when I called him from London and doubted that there was any space available. So I went instead to Switzerland and joined Kitty, Emily and the children in Gstaad.

In that summer of 1956, in a handsome chalet apartment a little off the main street — our sons and Emily were in another, which belonged to the excellent local carpenter just across the garden — the book suddenly took form. Often I almost thought it was writing itself.

*   *   *

Much was now clear in my mind. The rich society was the new and interesting case; poverty was the still common but aberrant situation. However, since poverty had until now been the norm, it was affluence that had never been fully understood or examined. The United States, the preeminent example of well-being, continued to make the increased output of privately produced goods the *summum bonum* of all social achievement. All progress was measured by the percentage

[8] This might have been foreseen, for there had been further evidence of his forgetfulness. A few weeks earlier we had met the Kaldors to travel together in northern India. Nicky had become an enthusiastic photographer, but his work was impaired because, as his daughter explained, he never remembered to remove the cap from the lens.

rate of increase in output. At the gates of heaven, as I later suggested, Saint Peter asked American applicants only what they had done to increase the Gross National Product.

In a poor society, where the need for food, clothing and shelter has preeminent urgency, the relationship between the increased production of these serviceable items and increased happiness (or decreased pain) is not in doubt. As the quantity of goods increases and their variety proliferates, their urgency for other than the poor declines, a proposition viewed by economists of stable mind as heresy. Preoccupation with the production of goods thus gives way to concern for ensuring their purchase and use, for these are necessary to maintain employment. The enjoyment of goods becomes subordinate to the need for ensuring the employment and income that comes from producing them.

Because needs are less urgent in a society of abundance, they are also more mobile. No one can persuade a hungry man to a more compelling after-shave lotion or a socially more distinguished style of footwear. With well-being this becomes possible. Wants, it was long assumed in economics, emerged from instincts wholly internal to the consumer. With lessened urgency, their source becomes external; they are the product of salesmanship, advertising and fashion.

As production and consumption increase, it becomes possible also to consider the effect of increased output on physical surroundings. Is the added production or the added efficiency in production worth its effect on ambient air, water and space — the countryside? If not, with increasing production should come a balancing concern for environment. That case seems trite now. It had novelty in 1956 — not least to me.

Increased production, by implication, meant increased production of private goods. Reflection on this suggested that there should be concern that the supply of public services be kept in phase. There is, after all, an inescapable relationship between the supply of packaged goods and the tasks of the garbage-collection service that removes the detritus. Otherwise, as in contemporary New York, movement is impeded by the filth. And, if less mathematically, there is need to maintain a proper relationship between education by private television and education by public schools. And also, a point on which not even the prophets of private affluence and minimal government dissent, there is an association between outlays for private air travel and the needed expenditures for public air traffic control.

I called this needed relationship between the production of private goods and outlays for public services the social balance. The greatest error in the eventual book was here. I didn't realize how enormous would be the public costs of congested existence in the modern metropolis, costs made greater by the migration of the socially unprepared from the poor rural areas. I didn't see that a minimally tolerable social balance in New York City would require public outlays far beyond any imagined at that time.

From the fact of general well-being came the new position of the poor. They were now in most communities a minority. The voice of the people was now the voice of relative affluence. Politicians in pursuit of votes could be expected to have a diminishing concern for the very poor. Compassion would have to serve instead — an uncertain substitute.

I identified also the case of what I called insular poverty, that of the Southern Appalachians and much of the deep South, where an instinct to remain within driving distance of one's birthplace supported by negligible or incompetent education and poor health care kept people in an equilibrium of poverty. Remedies, one noted, were usually addressed to those remaining in the community; the most effective remedy, in fact, was to escape. This was an idea of the utmost importance that I did not then adequately develop but to which I later returned.[9] It was one of the few weaknesses that my motivated critics overlooked.

* * *

As with the novelty of concern for the environment at the time, it is now difficult after twenty-five years to give an impression of the commitment of economists and the official intellectual establishment in the 1950s to the absolute importance of maximizing the output of goods — of the increase in the GNP as a measure of social excellence. A case to the contrary had a deeply eccentric tone. I rightly foresaw condemnation reinforced by righteous indignation over the argument that the urgency of goods declines with increased supply. Interpersonal and intertemporal comparisons of the satisfactions from increased consumption had long been held invalid by econo-

[9] In lectures and writing in the late 1970s published as the already-mentioned *The Nature of Mass Poverty* (Cambridge: Harvard University Press, 1979).

mists, a manifestation of unprofessional thought. Cosmetics could give quite as much joy to one woman as bread to another; this was elementary, and, anyhow, who could deny it? Equally a brass-buttoned vest could be as big a source of pleasure later in a man's life as a sandwich had been earlier. One must assume, accordingly, that satisfactions did not diminish with an increased supply of goods and that a given increment of consumption was as rewarding for the rich person as for the poor. It followed that the increased production of goods retained all of its social urgency, whatever the increase in wealth and however great the wealth of the individual.

Equally it was important to resist the thought that wants are in any way contrived by those who produced the goods. Were this possible, it would mean that production was, in part, a closed cycle; production was in response to the wants that were stimulated in their turn by the producers of goods. The greater the production, the greater the stimulation and thus the greater the resulting needs to be served. If allowed, this brought the traditional economic tests of performance to the edge of absurdity. The greater the success in increasing output and the greater the *need* to stimulate more wants, the greater the *need* for more output. If orthodox economic modalities were to survive, the consumer must be the ultimate and sovereign source of wants.

My colleagues rightly recognized that my case that wants were at least partly contrived by those who produce the goods was deeply subversive of the established orthodoxy. As a matter of vested interest if not of truth, they were compelled to resist.

*   *   *

In time and with much persuasive assistance from pollution, my argument that production should be tested for its environmental effects was accepted. So by some has been the concept of social balance. That the consumer is in part the instrument of the producer, his wants the result of the process by which they are satisfied, is still strongly resisted by all with an instinct for the safe view. Scholars no less than generals know when there is no further room for retreat. Far better to ignore the $38 billion[10] that goes annually in the United States for advertising than sacrifice the concept of consumer

[10] *Statistical Abstract of the United States, 1978.* United States Department of Commerce, Bureau of the Census, p. 854.

initiative and sovereignty. That, as noted, cannot be allowed. So, in the accepted liturgy of economics, advertising still remains a way by which General Motors advises the retarded that it has automobiles or else it is a purely frivolous outlay that does nothing for cars, cosmetics or detergents. One firm's advertising outlays are canceled out by those of others. All are left as before.

*   *   *

One small part of the book would win general acclaim for its aptness and sense of spontaneity. That was the title. This was, in fact, the product of desperation, and I did not perceive its virtue until after the book was published. For a long time my working title was "The Opulent Society," and this I had used for an anticipatory essay. But opulent has a greasy, obese sound; I needed an adjective that was descriptive but neither wholly neutral nor pejorative. *Rich* or *wealthy* was too strong, and they carried a suggestion of inherent (or inherited) bias. One morning in Gstaad, as I have elsewhere told, I thought to look in the dictionary. There was *affluent*.

Other invention was more deliberate. For the beliefs that are at any time assiduously, solemnly and mindlessly traded between the pretentiously wise, I needed a phrase that was overtly respectful but with an undertone of disdain, even amusement. Something nicely balanced between approval and ridicule. For months I experimented. Finally one day at Winthrop House I tried out my most recent idea — "the conventional wisdom" — on Carl Kaysen, then my fellow economics professor at Harvard, later an ally against military aberration or adventurism in the Kennedy years, later still the successor to Robert Oppenheimer at the Institute for Advanced Study at Princeton, and now at MIT. He told me to search no further. Conventional wisdom was right. I accepted his judgment, and I am indebted. So possibly should be others, for the phrase has long since passed out of my possession and into general use.

In arguing the combined importance of care of the environment and a balance between public and private outlays, I observed that:

> The family which takes its mauve and cerise, air-conditioned, power-steered, and power-braked car out for a tour passes through cities that are badly paved, made hideous by litter, blighted buildings, billboards, and posts for wires that should long since have been put underground. They pass on into a countryside that has been rendered largely invisible

by commercial art . . . They picnic on exquisitely packaged food from a portable icebox by a polluted stream and go on to spend the night at a park which is a menace to public health and morals. Just before dozing off on an air-mattress, beneath a nylon tent, amid the stench of decaying refuse, they may reflect vaguely on the curious unevenness of their blessings. Is this, indeed, the American genius?[11]

I lingered long over this paragraph. I thought it too patently contrived, too ripe, but in the end I let it stay. It was to be the most quoted passage in the book.

As the summer of 1956 passed, we left Gstaad for England and Nicholas Kaldor's house in Cambridge where I could use Nicky's library. I worked there while John Foster Dulles engineered the Suez debacle. Then we went home, and after the Labor Day weekend I went to Chicago to join the new Stevenson campaign. This time not even Stevenson could pretend to reluctance; after being defeated in the Minnesota primary on March 20, he had been forced to fight hard for the nomination. This he achieved, and Estes Kefauver, one of my best friends ever in politics, was given the second place on the ticket.[12]

As I entered the campaign, I felt pleased with the book, of which I now had a full draft. The election break proved to be a God-given pause. When I returned to the manuscript a few months later, the faults — half-developed argument, imprecise language, unqualified generalization, unsupported statement, awkward English — obtruded from every page. To put it right, or as nearly so as I could make it, took me nearly another year.

---

[11]*The Affluent Society* (Boston: Houghton Mifflin, 1958), p. 253.

[12]During the 1956 campaign Estes was never less than an hour behind his speaking schedule and sometimes three or four. One of his California admirers attributed this to his need to shake hands with every man he encountered and pay court, as it were, to every woman.

22

A.E.S. Redux

THE CHALLENGE to Adlai Stevenson from Estes Kefauver in the 1956 primaries had been stronger than anyone had expected, and he had to mount a major effort in California to retrieve earlier losses. Through the campaign that autumn he complained of a residual weariness from this earlier struggle, and it could have been real. But it was not outwardly evident in early September when, on the first campaign trip, we flew from Chicago to Springfield, Illinois, for what was called, imaginatively, a homecoming celebration and then on to Columbus, Ohio, and New York. The scholars who had made up the Elks Club were mostly back again. That individuals so intimately associated with the defeat in 1952 should have assembled so confidently a second time will strike the politically uninformed as odd. It was not a thought that occurred; politics doesn't favor such introspection. But also Stevenson's speeches had been considered the most distinguished and elevated feature of the earlier campaign, and they had been promptly assembled into a book that had a very satisfactory sale. So we were thought, not exclusively by ourselves, to have done well.

There was a strong feeling that the 1956 campaign needed to be run with more professional acuity than the great 1952 adventure so, as I've earlier said, it was put in the hands of Jim Finnegan of Pennsylvania, a solid organization man. Jim's Irish name suggested professional competence as did the solemnity with which he pondered the simplest question and the firmness with which he enunciated the most obvious decision.

On our journey east, Adlai spoke at the Ohio State Democratic Convention and sought the endorsement of Frank Lausche, then governor and later senator from Ohio. The new professionalism required that we ignore Lausche's political views, which were marginally, although not thoughtfully, to the right of Herbert Hoover. On the flight to La Guardia on a smallish two-engined Convair, professionalism was also manifest in an intense and extended debate over who should first greet Stevenson as the door of the plane swung open in New York and who should ride with him in the limousine into town. The problem was that New York — city and state — had almost as many Democratic chiefs as tribesmen: there was Averell Harriman, the governor; Herbert Lehman, the former governor and greatest of the elder statesmen; Robert F. Wagner, Jr., the mayor; Thomas Finletter, co-head of the Independents for Stevenson; and Eleanor Roosevelt, the den mother (as she was then called) of all Democrats. Everyone had a greater or lesser claim. The decision was further complicated by uncertainty as to who would actually be there. Eventually instructions were radioed ahead but without any indication of how they were to be carried out.

It did not matter; on our landing and drawing up to the terminal, the race as ever was to the swift. Mrs. Anna M. Rosenberg, Truman's Assistant Secretary of Defense and the cochair of the Independents, was first away from the gate, and, carrying far less weight than the rest, she led at the steps by several lengths. For the trip into town the question of precedence did not arise. The New York Democrats had provided a limousine so long that it was later said, though untruthfully, that when the front end came off the Triboro Bridge into Manhattan, the back bumper was still in Queens. In any case, all with a claim could go with the candidate. Members of the staff had to be distributed one to each of the following automobiles, and our number being insufficient, two or three cooperative newspaper reporters were recruited from the press bus to ride in the extra vehicles.

*   *   *

In the 1956 campaign Stevenson was much less troubled by the liberal heresies than he had been four years before. As I have indicated, time and our instruction had removed the sense of novelty and dissipated the anxiety. Seymour Harris of Harvard again produced a whole armful of position papers which, though not read by the candidate, did not leave any doubt as to the stalwart liberalism of his stand. It was far easier then to urge better health care, better pensions for the aged and a better deal for the poor when there was no appreciable offsetting concern about inflation or enhanced bureaucracy, only the principled opposition of those who saw these policies as personally expensive or socially debilitating for the poor.

Harris made another contribution during the campaign with marked personal effect for me. At a political meeting one evening in Cambridge, he said, genially, that I had told him it was my ambition, were we successful, to be ambassador to India. I was distressed, for I had assumed my confession was in strict confidence. Seymour understood better than I the advantage of having these things known.

The headquarters for the 1956 campaign was in Washington, to which, after Harvard opened, I repaired for several days each week to write speeches. Or I joined the caravan on the road. With hindsight it is hard to suppose that any Democrat could have expected that Stevenson would win against Eisenhower in 1956. But politics is energized by false optimism, and, at least in the early days of the campaign, we had much hope. My doubts began to develop one day in Iowa.

It was on September 22. I had gone with Stevenson to Des Moines, and we then drove through the cornfields to a farm between Newton and Colfax, the setting of the National Plowing Matches. This agrarian festival regularly provided presidential candidates with an audience for the obligatory farm speech. I listened with attention to the one Stevenson delivered, having written it myself.

Ike had been firm in his promise of more income to farmers four years before; since then, farm costs had risen considerably more than farm prices. In consequence, farmers were restless, and this mood I had undertaken, as best I could, to exploit. "I am not going to attack President Eisenhower's motives . . . I am even willing to believe that he did not fully understand what he was saying to America's farmers in 1952. He had been in the Army and living in New York and Europe . . ."[1] Then, after observing that corn, wheat, cotton and rice had all receded in relative (parity) price, the speech continued, "But there is one success in the record. Four years ago peanuts were 82 percent of parity; now they have gone up to 88

[1] Quoted in Adlai E. Stevenson, *The New America* (New York: Harper and Brothers, 1957), p. 180.

percent. This administration has a fine record on peanuts! It almost made me wonder if General Motors had gone into the peanut-oil business!"[2]

This appeal to agrarian economics, humor and populist sentiment was well received. Stevenson was happy. When the campaign party moved on to Denver, I remained behind with Donald R. Murphy, a greatly civilized man who was then editor of *Wallaces' Farmer.* We walked over the fields and talked with as many of those attending as possible. Murphy's acquaintance was wide; one inevitably lost touch on agricultural matters in Cambridge, and this was a chance for me to retrieve. The responses to our questions were, if not a sample, certainly a metaphor of the political feeling of the time. All agreed that the businessmen — the big boys — had taken over after the twenty Roosevelt/Truman years. Treasury Secretary George M. Humphrey was openly and unapologetically on the side of the rich who wished to become richer, a community that included himself. Charles E. (Engine Charlie) Wilson, Secretary of Defense and former head of General Motors, had admirably, if too candidly, emphasized the point when he linked what was good for General Motors with what was good for the country, later noting, somewhat ruefully, that the automatic transmission had been designed so that he could drive with one foot in his mouth.

That the populist suspicion of big business was still on our side was not in doubt. But everyone we talked to that afternoon, almost without exception, made another point: they were not going to vote for the Democrats because they didn't want another war. After World War II and the Korean conflict, we were seen, indubitably, as the war party. "I might vote Democrat," one slightly encouraging citizen told us, "but my old lady won't. Not if I kicked the hell out of her. She doesn't want our boy going off to any new war."

By the end of the afternoon I was in a very reflective mood and so was Murphy. I went on to Denver to rejoin Stevenson and to tell of my unease. In 1956, even more than in 1952, Eisenhower was the man of peace.

Secretary of State Dulles was not. His brinkmanship aroused justifiable fear. He was engaged that very autumn on his supreme exercise in ineptitude with Nasser over Suez. Stevenson did manage to

[2] Ibid.

gain attention for this and for two major initiatives toward peace, both soon to be accepted as commonplace. He proposed that we stop the open-air testing of hydrogen weapons and that we make plans for the ending of the draft. However, Ike remained the pacific figure. And on nuclear testing and the draft Stevenson came under heavy criticism from members of the foreign policy establishment — from those who rally without thought against any new departure in foreign policy especially if too moderate.

The lesson, I believe, is clear. There is a huge constituency for peaceful resolution of conflict in the United States; it is silent, amorphous, independent of party, intractable of view and ultimately decisive. But the peaceful do not react to the details of foreign policy. Their reaction is to who gets the country into war and who brings the war to an end. This forthright calculation worked for the Republicans on Korea as it did for them again on Vietnam. Specific issues such as nuclear testing and the draft serve only to arouse the articulate and visible convocation of the bellicose.

A further lesson is that even when popular opinion is moving ineluctably your way, as it was on the draft and the Bomb, it is a risk, as a matter of pure and dismal political calculation, to get too far out in front. The enduring word comes from the not quite immortal Alexandre-Auguste Ledru-Rollin, the Paris revolutionary of 1848. Looking from his window and seeing a crowd pass by, he said, "I must follow them, for I am their leader."

And there is a third lesson. In raising issues before they are politically mature, losing politicians may render their greatest service. So it was then. Had not Stevenson (and others), aware of the political consequences, stepped out in front on the testing of nuclear weapons, we would still be cowering under the radioactive fallout, accepting it and the associated cancer, as was then urged by the architects of strategic thought, as "one of the inevitable costs of freedom in a world beset by Communist menace."

*   *   *

On Saturday, October 27, as Election Day neared, Stevenson was speaking in San Francisco and the East Bay. The wisdom of campaign managers had triumphed that day; he had been scheduled into the district of almost every needful aspirant to the California legislature, to which was added a major address in Washington

Square. And for the night there remained a large rally in Gilmore Stadium in Los Angeles. With help from Clayton Fritchey, I had written the Los Angeles speech. It dealt sternly with Ike's tendency to be absent and golfing during all the great moments of recent crisis. And it went forcefully into the shortcomings of Richard Nixon. On the latter I had let myself go; Stevenson had once paid me a notable compliment: "Ken, I want you to write the speeches against Nixon. You have no tendency to be fair."

I had, nonetheless, been scrupulously truthful: "Our nation stands at a fork in the political road. In one direction lies a land of slander and scare; the land of sly innuendo, the poison pen, the anonymous phone call and hustling, pushing, shoving; the land of smash and grab and anything to win.

"This is Nixonland. America is something different." [3,4]

It became known as the Nixonland speech.

It was late afternoon before I could get to Stevenson at the old Claremont Hotel on the Oakland-Berkeley line to get his changes and clear the speech. Deadlines for the next day's Sunday papers in the East, given the difference in time, were dangerously close — or past. Stevenson read my words and recoiled. They were far too tough: "This is the kind of speech that can only lose us votes." Then wearily and after looking at his watch, he approved it: "I suppose we might as well tell the truth."

The stadium that night was packed, thanks in part to requisitions issued by the United Automobile Workers and other responsive unions. The lights played on the platform and unmercifully on a row of ancient motion picture actresses who, in accordance with the local folkrites, had been recruited for the front row. Stevenson, his fatigue unrevealed, was in excellent form. The crowd responded boisterously and from the heart to the probing of the Nixon character. I watched and listened from just behind the film stars. It was a good time.

In the spring of 1959, I was in Moscow after a visit to India. Also in the city was P. C. Mahalanobis of whom I told in the last chapter; he was there to be inducted as an honorary member of the Soviet Academy of Sciences. One night I visited him at his hotel, and

---

[3] Quoted in Stevenson, pp. 248–249.
[4] During the Watergate years these lines were unearthed in Washington to show how prescient was Adlai Stevenson on the character of the 37th President.

Modest Iosifovich Rubinstein, an economist member of the Academy and an agreeable man, told me that in 1956 he had been part of the Soviet delegation that had been invited by President Eisenhower to view the presidential elections. It had been thought good that Communists should see Americans electing their highest officials.

I asked what had been the high spot of his tour.

"I think it was that great meeting of Governor Stevenson in that football stadium in Los Angeles."

It was a baseball field, but the difference seemed immaterial. I saw the chance for collecting a major personal credit.

"What did you think of the speech that Mr. Stevenson gave that night?"

Rubinstein's expression changed, and he winced. "That was not a speech that you would hear in a cultured country like ours."

*   *   *

In Pittsburgh a few days later I listened to a long discussion over whether Stevenson should cancel some of the next day's schedule in upstate New York and go on television instead to answer an Eisenhower speech on the Middle East. France, Britain and Israel had just moved against Nasser and to the Suez Canal. The discussion continued, and I went to my room to try to sleep. My stomach had recently ceased to absorb food; now I discovered that I was bleeding from some undiscovered internal lesion. I was declared a casualty of the campaign and put on a plane to the Peter Bent Brigham Hospital in Boston. I was still undergoing varied indignities there on Election Day, and I didn't turn on the television in my hospital room to learn how badly we had lost. Next day the doctors confessed their inability to find anything wrong. It was not surprising, for already, the campaign over, I was feeling appreciably better.

*   *   *

Instead of returning immediately to *The Affluent Society,* I now addressed myself to an instrument of economic management on which the Eisenhower Administration, with the approval of conservative economists, was coming increasingly to rely — monetary policy. Their use of it was modest as compared with what we have since experienced and suffered.

Nothing in economics so lends itself to mystification as money. In consequence monetary policy can be used with very little complaint as to its discriminatory, even reactionary effect. Nowadays this is at least partly understood. Then monetary policy was presumed to be a technical exercise, uncertain perhaps as to its effect but socially neutral in its impact on different groups.

The facts are simple and different. Monetary policy works as it encourages or discourages the spending and respending of borrowed money. It is that spending, nothing else, that has a practical effect on the economy — on prices, production and employment. To bring monetary policy to bear against inflation, the Federal Reserve discourages the lending of money by the banks. This it accomplishes by raising interest rates and by increasing the banks' reserve requirements — the cash they must hold in reserve — so that they have less money to lend. That is all there is to the policy.

The effect of this action is very different as between small firms and large. House builders, other construction firms, smaller retailers, other small traders and, in appreciable measure, farmers depend for their operations on borrowed money, and they cannot, in the normal case, pass along the higher interest charges. Their prices are still determined, in greater or less measure, by competition in the market.

The position of the large, strong corporation is almost exactly the reverse. It finances its operations extensively from retained earnings. Having substantial control over its prices, it can pass the higher interest charges along to its customers. Or, as I then argued, it will have "unliquidated monopoly profits" by which the higher interest can be absorbed. So when monetary policy is invoked against inflation, the primary effect is on the small man, not the large corporation. The approval of the policy by the rich and powerful is thus an accurate reflection of their own self-interest. The applause by those so favored that has long been accorded Professor Milton Friedman, its most distinguished advocate, has been greatly deserved. My case to this general effect, published in mid-1957,[5] was challenged but not, I believe, effectively rebutted. I count it one of my less celebrated but most useful contributions to economics that I helped

[5] "Market Structure and Stabilization Policy," *Review of Economics and Statistics,* vol. XXXIX, no. 2 (May 1957), pp. 124–133.

make clear the pecuniary nexus between an undue reliance on monetary policy and the people who so ardently approve its use.

* * *

I returned to *The Affluent Society* at the beginning of 1957, and soon my shock at discovering that what had seemed so good was, in fact, so bad gave way again to the normal euphoria of creation. The book went to the publisher late that autumn and came out at the end of May 1958. Meanwhile it rendered a highly questionable service to my Harvard teaching. For my principal course, Social Sciences 134, I used for each day's lecture one of the chapters of the book in its current version. I was to continue the practice through the two later volumes, *The New Industrial State* and *Economics and the Public Purpose.* Students came in large numbers and seemed not to mind. Those who heard earlier versions, subsequently revised, have presumably lived ever since in error.

In one respect I improved on precedent. At Cambridge when Keynes was completing his masterwork *The General Theory of Employment Interest and Money,* he read to his lecture audiences from the printer's proofs. On occasion a proof would slip from the sequence to the floor. It was said he never noticed. 1 watched my papers with care.

* * *

In early May of 1958, the book about to appear, I left for a lecture tour in Poland and Yugoslavia. In Poland I was sponsored by the Polish Economic Society and Oskar Lange, in Yugoslavia by the Institute of International Politics and Economics and Janez Stanovnik, later the Executive Secretary of the United Nations Economic Commission for Europe.

Such a tour was no casual thing at the time. A little earlier, Shepard Stone, then of the Ford Foundation, had made funds available to Polish and other Eastern European scholars for visits to, and study in, the United States. It was an admirably useful, even somewhat courageous step away from the Cold War and one much welcomed in the recipient countries after the twenty-year separation enforced by Hitler and Stalin. My visit to Poland was a reciprocal gesture made possible by the disappearance on August 5, 1956, of the Stalinist government of Bolesław Beirut and its replacement by that of Władysław Gomulka. When my invitation to Poland became known, an emissary came from Washington to tell me that the Yugoslavs did not wish to be thought less liberal than the Poles. Although by then various natural scientists had penetrated the Iron Curtain, economists were more dangerous. I was, I believe, the first non-Marxist to lecture on economics there. The ideas in *The Affluent Society* seemed too *recherché* for the grim socialist world so I recurred to countervailing power and *American Capitalism*.[6]

The journey to Le Havre and eventually Eastern Europe on *La Liberté* of the French Line was to be my last experience of this kind of luxury. Among others my companions were John and Jane Gunther and a handsome and intelligent woman named Barbara Adams who was experiencing the excitement of a first journey abroad. I saw her again on a later trip to Paris and then our paths diverged until one day in Katmandu, Nepal, in April 1964, when I was giving a commencement speech at the local and somewhat hypothetical university. As I finished, she approached, elegantly clad in a sari, and took my arm. In the interval she had married and discarded a husband and become a valued member of the extended royal family of Nepal. An attractive and intelligent American can go far.

Thirteen years after the war, Warsaw was still stark. Barren, grass-grown heaps of rubble separated the shabby apartment houses scattered cabbage-patch fashion across the landscape. Cracow, undamaged and suffused at that season with lilacs, was in lovely contrast. So in less measure was Lublin, where I lectured, equal time for each, at the Catholic and local state universities.

This was my first serious exposure to a socialist and planned economy. Meetings with senior economists and planning officials in both countries made it a distinctly instructive one. I saw in practice what I had already come to believe — that modern socialism is overwhelmingly an exercise in administration and that the administrative task is very different as between the great firm and the small.

Large-scale enterprise is highly organized and bureaucratic, whether in the socialist or nonsocialist world. Performance in both cases depends less on market incentives and discipline than on the

[6]The Harvard University Press published my notes on the journey along with my basic lecture, "Economic Power in the American Setting." (*Journey to Poland and Yugoslavia* [Cambridge, 1958].)

peer pressure to which participants are subject, the instinct to excel, the hope for promotion and the general enthusiasm inspired by the leadership. For agriculture and small enterprise there is no ready substitute for the market — for its rewards to useful achievement and its counterpart penalties imposed on incompetence and sloth. These also, a deeply neglected point, cause the individual entrepreneur, through long hours commanded by his own need or avarice, to exploit himself. For small-scale enterprise any sort of planned substitute for the market must replace its system of rewards and penalties and this impulse to self-exploitation with a heavy, costly and and ineffective overburden of supervision and administration.

These distinctions between large and small enterprises were already being accepted in both Poland and Yugoslavia. Agriculture in both countries had been kept in or returned to the market. In Yugoslavia, under the cachet of market socialism, public or cooperative ownership of other enterprises was being made subject to the test of profit and loss. The effort at a more comprehensive exercise of state authority had already passed into history and was being referred to as the bureaucratic period.

* * *

In a Communist country one is naturally eager for indications of surveillance or, even better, of sinister intrigue. Feeling myself a pioneer, I was naturally thus alert. As I dined by myself one night in the dimly lit, slightly overstuffed restaurant of the Grand Hotel ORBIS in Warsaw, I became aware of two men of deeply conspiratorial aspect at the immediately adjacent table. They were talking in low intimate tones in English, and, by moving my chair slightly, I discovered I could hear some of what they were saying. My recollection is notional:

"He has real courage."

"Yes, but he has made enemies."

"Nonetheless he would speak out against them."

"You really think he would?"

I was now deeply engaged, my imagination fully at work. Presently I learned that they were both chiropractors from Cleveland, Ohio, who were discussing the chances of getting fair treatment from the medical establishment and legislature in the state.

Trial and deprivation, as so often in Polish history, had nurtured the national humor. At my welcoming dinner given by the Polish Economic Society, one of my hosts said I would discover that "No country has done so much for the theory of planning as Poland — and so little for its practice." Later I was asked (as I believe many have been since) if I knew the difference between capitalism and Communism.

"Well, I will tell you. Under capitalism man exploits man. And under Communism it is just the reverse."

One Sunday I drove into the country to Łowicz with an old Bolshevist who was a long-time agricultural expert. We visited farms, a church service and one of the numerous chateaus of the Radziwill family. In later years, through his wife Lee and sister-in-law Jacqueline Kennedy Onassis, I was to become well acquainted with Stanislas, or Stash, one of the most prominent of the clan. Though the family was the oldest of feudal exploiters, two others in the Radziwill line, Stash's father and brother, were surviving safely and not without honor in Communist Poland. The patriarch attracted an approving crowd when he walked through the streets of Warsaw, and his son was in the foreign office.

The churches we passed that Sunday had communicants spilling out the doors. "It is a form of protest," said my radical friend, who took the precaution of crossing himself when we went into one church to listen to the powerfully resonant voices of the organ, choir and congregation. He told me how he had gotten the peasants to use commercial fertilizer of which initially they were suspicious. He went out at night to the fields and spread the nutrient in the form of a cross. By harvest time, the cross was strongly visible in its greater and greener abundance. He then explained to the God-fearing that this was the work not of the Deity but of an appropriate combination of nitrogen, superphosphates and potash.

I learned also of the common tendencies of parliaments and politicians, whatever their circumstances:

. . . [With] a charming woman economist from the university, I called on Lange at the Parliament. The Chamber was in session, and we listened to a speech or two while Lange — who sits on the ministerial bench — was being told of our arrival. About half the seats were filled. In reassuring parallel with Western democracy no one was paying the slightest attention. The position here is an interesting one and not well understood. In the democratic state the representative requirements of government take far more people than can, in fact, be employed in the business of governing. To avoid the disaster of their participation, but while also avoiding the appearance of idleness, we have speeches. Any number of people can be occupied in making speeches or, more particularly, in serving as an audience. While it is often supposed that speeches are for the purpose of communicating ideas, in fact they are primarily for the purpose of disguising the unemployment that is inevitable in the democratic process. I was glad to see that this great democratic invention is also useful in a Communist state.[7]

On arriving in Warsaw, I found that, through some negligence, I was without reading matter, and in even the busiest schedule there are empty hours or evenings. I went next morning to the bookstores; only Frank Norris's *The Octopus* was available in English. Its principal modern value is to celebrate the transitory character of social conflict. The exploited farmers of the Central Valley in California for whom he mourns are now rich and powerful. The Southern Pacific Railway — the Octopus — is a harmless weakling. The writing is also bad. I wired Barbara Adams in Paris, who went to Brentano's and bought me some Dickens. I had disliked him intensely when he was forced upon me in school; in Poland, with no alternative but *Dombey and Son,* I discovered how prodigious was my juvenile judgment.

In Warsaw I visited Michał Kalecki, who was now in charge of long-range, called perspective, planning. He expressed his strong disapproval of American economic and foreign policy and also much of what was being done in his own country. We traveled together to Belgrade. On the plane were two stylishly dressed young women whom Michał viewed with distaste. "They are probably Hungarians," he said. "That is the way they dress." We stopped in Budapest and there, indeed, they disembarked.

*   *   *

On May 30, 1958, I got back to London; *The Affluent Society* had been published earlier that week. *Time,* as I have told, accorded it a massive sneer. The rest of the reviews, which Kitty had assembled by the telephone for my call, ranged from fulsome to ecstatic. Kermit Gordon, soon to be Director of the Budget and then head of the Brookings Institution, thought it "the most brilliant essay in politico-

[7] *Journey to Poland and Yugoslavia,* pp. 67–68.

economic criticism in a decade." The *Chicago Tribune,* which two years earlier had accused me, as "the man who thinks for Adlai," of every currently unacceptable form of social and moral perversion except sodomy, was poetic: "Lo, what a man of wit has arisen to do biopsy on what Carlyle called 'the dismal science' of economics." Philip Graham, publisher of the *Washington Post,* devoted a full page to praise. A little later, Malcolm Muggeridge said, "I put it in the same category as Tawney's *The Acquisitive Society* and Keynes's *Economic Consequences of the Peace.* It is unique, witty and inescapable." Only a strong character can resist such praise. I made no effort.

A few weeks later Kitty and I began a summer-long trip to South America — Peru, Chile, Argentina, Brazil and then Guatemala and Costa Rica. In Rio, visiting the Embassy, my eyes lit on the familiar bulk of a recent Sunday *New York Times. The Affluent Society* was second on the best-seller list. This achievement is not, universally, a mark of academic or intellectual excellence, but I was able to persuade myself that there might be exceptions.

23

Kennedy, Democrats
and *The New Industrial State*

IN THE 1950s, John F. Kennedy, to all of us for some years still Jack Kennedy, became a presence in our lives. I had known him, as I have told, at Winthrop House in the thirties, the good-looking, popular, not quite serious younger brother. I saw more of him after the war when he was congressman for the Massachusetts 11th Congressional District, which he became in 1946. Popular myth to the contrary, many at Harvard have had difficulty in believing that the Kennedy brothers are in the very first league, wholly worthy of the Harvard badge and blessing. Perhaps as a consequence, Jack Kennedy, while in Congress, was a little remote from the university community. There was some justification for Harvard's view. Kennedy's congressional career was far from spectacular, and in those years he was neither physically nor politically prepossessing. He was thin and a trifle callow in appearance and bearing, unremarkable in liberal political expression and thought. In 1952, against the Eisenhower tide, he defeated Henry Cabot Lodge, Jr., for the Senate. But his victory reflected less any personal achievement than the natural advantage in Massachusetts of a Catholic and Irish aspirant over a too impeccably qualified member of the old Republican establishment. Kennedy's congressional performance did call for defense rather than celebration when running against Lodge. His casual attendance record on the Hill was held by some to be the result of an unduly active social life, and at a meeting one evening during the campaign then governor Paul A. Dever, a quintessential politician in manner and physical aspect and a very good man, faced the issue with righteous anger and slightly quivering jowls:

"I hear it being said that my young friend Jack Kennedy isn't working down there in Washington, that he's too fond of girls. Well, let me tell you, ladies and gentlemen, I've never heard it said of Jack Kennedy that he's too fond of boys."

*   *   *

From the Senate Kennedy called me at infrequent intervals for my views on economic legislation. On occasion I thought he seemed a little tired before I was through. However, one rather small matter established me firmly in his confidence.

I have spoken earlier of farm price supports. As I have told, the affection with which firm minimum prices were regarded by farmers was matched by the substantial service they rendered to agricultural efficiency. They made it possible for farmers to invest in fertilizer, machinery, hybrid seed stock and other technology with, weather apart, a solid assurance of return. Thus they enormously enhanced such investment and nourished an increase in output per farm worker that much exceeded the productivity gain in industry.

Nevertheless the support prices had never ceased to be a source of distress to economists, who preferred their free market faith to practical achievement. In the textbooks prices find their independent market equilibrium. Anything that interferes, however serviceably in practice, is, *pro tanto,* wrong. So the debate over farm policy continued, and in the early 1950s, there came a compromise — a proposal, in effect, for a halfway return to the market. Support prices would remain, but they would rise when supplies were short, fall when they were abundant. Thus, in their operation, they would resemble market behavior. These were called flexible supports, and they were applauded by those of adequately conventional view. Farmers didn't like them at all, especially the reduction in price when crops were good and when, to the forthright man of the soil, a strong support to prices seemed most needed. Why a lifeboat designed to sink a bit as the ship sinks?

On agricultural matters Kennedy was uninformed, sometimes, one thought, rather proudly so. "Where I grew up, we were taken out on a bus to see a cow." He now turned to me on the question; I urged him to oppose flexible supports and did so with the peculiar certainty that derives from being right. He listened but yielded in the end to the more prestigious advice of Clinton P. Anderson, senator from New Mexico and recently a Secretary of Agriculture. Anderson had been sold by the faithful on the flexible supports. A farm senator might possibly have been forgiven; in a senator from Massachusetts it showed a parochial consumer bias and a hopeless ignorance of real farm needs.

In 1956, after his nomination, Adlai Stevenson declared the vice-presidential selection open to a free vote of the convention. Kennedy was narrowly defeated by Estes Kefauver, and his position on agricultural policy and price supports was believed, and especially by Kennedy himself, to have made the difference. In consequence, he came to regard my advice on agricultural and, by inference, on various other practical issues as impeccable.

"I don't want to hear about agriculture from anyone but you, Ken. And I don't much want to hear about it from you either."

In those years, the late fifties, when Kennedy was home in Massachusetts, I would occasionally meet him for a discussion of economic matters. Or less frequently he would suggest a Saturday night dinner, usually with the Schlesingers, in an upstairs room at Locke-Ober Restaurant on Winter Place in Boston where, never varying, he always ordered lobster stew. His conversation was wide-ranging and informed; my respect and affection grew.

For its January 1960 issue, *Esquire* asked a total of fifty-four alleged public and literary figures for their preference among the possible presidential candidates. Adlai Stevenson led the field by a wide margin with sixteen supporters. Kennedy was fourth after Nixon and Humphrey with five votes. One of them was mine; another was that of Crane Brinton, the Harvard historian, who wanted a candidate who would not support "orthodox or 'classical' economics [but] what I call neo-Keynesian or Galbraithian economics." Kennedy, who took this poll more seriously than I did, called up in obvious pleasure to congratulate me on my good judgment and also my influence. He professed to believe that I had shown courage.

*   *   *

Much more of my time from 1956 on was devoted to a new instrument of political enlightenment and progress — the Democratic Advisory Council of the Democratic National Committee.

In the late fifties the leadership of the Democratic Party bore some resemblance to the membership of a club. The same faces were always to be found in the reading room or bar. Or the parallel could have been more with an Episcopalian vestry — men born comfortably to the faith, its accepted custodians. The faith was that the government, by innovative action on behalf of the old, unfortunate or poor, could ensure their employment, health and happiness at no great cost to the rich. Most or all of the needed revenue would come from the expanded output and income from the better management of the economy. This the liberal experience had shown to be possible. If there were doubts, one could put them aside; in politics, as in the vestry, one does not raise difficult questions involving divinity, the Trinity or even the personal dedication of fellow members to the Ten Commandments. Defeat, even as severe a one as in 1956, did not shake our commitment to our faith. To win is to be affirmed in truth by the voters; to lose means only that one's convictions are being tested by adversity.

The origins of the Democratic Advisory Council were in the Finletter Group. Many of the great vestrymen were out of office — Adlai Stevenson, Averell Harriman, who had just lost the New York governorship to Nelson Rockefeller, Dean Acheson, Herbert Lehman, Thomas Finletter, William Benton. The DAC would be their voice. We would assemble every few weeks to consider initiatives on foreign and domestic policy, a kind of cabinet in exile.

The foreign policy committee of the council was headed by Dean Acheson; after a gentlemanly contest I became head of the domestic policy committee. Paul M. Butler, the current chairman of the Democratic National Committee, gave the council strong support as did Charles Tyroler II, who became the executive director of the DAC. In Congress the Democrats had majorities in both houses, with Sam Rayburn of Texas as Speaker and Lyndon Johnson as Senate Majority Leader. It was part of our claim that we were taking the Texas image off the party, a service that Johnson and Rayburn both thought unnecessary. When the council was organized, Rayburn wired Butler to tell him that the Democratic program would emerge, as usual in a democracy, from those who had been elected by the people.

*   *   *

Our meetings were well attended and well designed to show that on domestic policy we were in a somewhat exhausted political tradition and on foreign policy one that would eventually bring us disaster. Thus the developing issue of civil rights, soon to become central, scarcely intruded on our discussions nor in any important way did blacks participate. Women, Mrs. Roosevelt apart, were not yet people. I persuaded Mabel Newcomer, the great Vassar economics teacher, to join our sessions. She did so but rarely spoke. Of inflation, which by now I was persuaded was our next great problem, there was no serious mention. All progress was still measured by the annual increase in Gross National Product. Many were surprised when at a meeting one day Arthur Schlesinger made a stirring speech saying that we should consider the qualitative as well as the quantitative side of life — the whole reward from existence rather than the simple increase in the output of goods.

However, our foreign policy discussions were the true portents. At each meeting Dean Acheson, aided by Paul Nitze, who was by now an unrelenting Cold Warrior and serving as Acheson's vice-chairman and amanuensis, produced a paper attacking whatever John Foster Dulles had done in the preceding weeks. The attack was always for being too lenient toward Communism and the Soviet Union. Lehman, Stevenson and Harriman would then take exception with a view to moderating the language. Harriman alone was abrupt: "You know, Dean," he said one day, "I don't agree with your declarations of war." Many, in fact, recognized the need for accommodation with the Soviets, but it was going too far to say this out loud. That the Soviets, either directly or through their Chinese puppets (as the latter were automatically regarded), were moving to dominate the former colonial world was not contested.

Here, early and in miniature, were the fatal politics of Vietnam. It was not that the issue was debated and the wrong decision taken; it was rather that there was no debate. The old liberal fear of being thought soft on Communism, the fear of being attacked by professional patriots and the knowledge of the political punishment that awaits any departure from the Establishment view (as manifested against Stevenson on the draft and the H-bomb) all united to eliminate discussion. Democracy has, as ever, its own forms of authoritarianism.

I was not wholly passive. With the others I sought to mute the Acheson calls to battle. Acheson would then respond with a stand on some domestic issue that was well to the right of the irretrievably conservative Ezra Taft Benson. But I was more worried than outspoken. My concern for the thought-denying process by which foreign policy issues were being resolved did remain and grow, and it served me as an early warning as we became ever more involved with Indochina and Vietnam.

*   *   *

The DAC proceedings were held without the press. Then when the meetings were over, Acheson and I would go out to make public our conclusions. His problem was not great; in those days the Washington press corps outdid even Dulles in Cold War orthodoxy. A successful question was one that exposed some suggestion of softness, some possible appeasement. Acheson was invulnerable. My task, which was to proclaim once more our passion for full employment, better health, education and welfare, a decent minimum wage and approximate parity for agriculture, was only tedious. There is an end to the novelty one can bring to even the best causes.

Not all, however, was grim in those gatherings. One afternoon — it was December 8, 1958 — Harry Truman joined our deliberations. Since the presence of a former President greatly enhanced our prestige, we invited the press in for the beginning of the meeting. Almost immediately there was trouble with one of our western-state representatives. After lunch he had remained at the bar to take advantage of the free liquor, an opportunity unparalleled in his past experience on the Great Plains. Coming back as the microphones and cameras were being put in place, he told Truman of a sinister plot in his state to have all farms first mortgaged to, and then expropriated by, Northwestern Mutual Life Insurance Company of Milwaukee. He wanted this stopped and the company taken over by the government. He implied, indeed he said, that Truman as President had failed the farmers by not doing so. I was presiding and moved to get things back on saner ground.

My best thought was to ask the President how things had gone in New Haven where, somewhat earlier, he had served as a Chubb Fellow at Yale. Truman first dismissed the man from the West, telling him that the way his farmers voted out there, they deserved to be expropriated. Then he turned to Yale.

"You know, Professor, every university is like every other. Students all Republicans, faculty all Democrats. People who talk about the differences remind me of once out in Independence when I went down to the courtroom to fill in the time.

"We had a prosecuting attorney in those days who was really pretty good. One day he had a fellow up for rape, and he opened up by saying, 'Your Honor, I intend to show that this man had sexual intercourse with this poor unwilling woman. And, Your Honor, I will show that he was also guilty of fornication with this reluctant young woman.'

"That kinda surprised the judge. Since we were pretty informal out there, he said, 'Bill, I don't understand. What's the difference between the two?' And Bill said, 'Judge, I have to admit I've tried them both, and they're pretty much the same!' That's how universities are in my experience. Different names, otherwise the same."

At this moment Charles S. Murphy, once counsel to Truman in the White House, later an Undersecretary of Agriculture and Chairman of the Civil Aeronautics Board, appeared in front of the table where we were sitting, which was now laden with electrical equipment. He held up a piece of paper which said, "THE MIKE IS LIVE."

Beads of perspiration came to my forehead. Not Truman the professional. He looked at the message and said, "They can't use that. It's too dirty."

*   *   *

I remained as chairman of the domestic policy committee of the DAC through the rest of the fifties, but after *The Affluent Society* was published, my participation somewhat diminished. I had begun to believe not that I had written the wrong book but that I had written only a small part of the right one.

With industrial development, I had shown, initiative in economic life moves from the consumer, the classical source of all economic decision, to the producing firm. Increasing affluence having released wants from the level of stark physical need, producers adjust consumer taste and behavior to *their* needs by advertising and salesmanship. The goals of the society become extensively those of the producers. The quality of the consumer's life becomes secondary to the producers' preoccupation with output.

So much was in *The Affluent Society*. But the obvious prior question concerned the institution that had produced this change. It was not the neoclassical or textbook firm, subordinate to the authority of the market and like any citizen to that of the state. It was the modern great corporation. With economic development the corporation achieved great size; its influence came to bear strongly on prices, costs, consumer responses and the policy of the state. On questions of economic and social policy the reputable public opinion became, in no small part, that which reflected the legislative and other public needs of the large corporation and its leadership. The voice of the corporation became, by its volume and reputability, the voice of the public. For a full half of the economy, the textbook image of the business firm was not only a parody of the reality, but, by describing the firm as subordinate in its decisions to the overriding authority of the market and the state, it concealed the reality in the exercise of economic and political power. Specifically it concealed it from all who studied economics. Perhaps this was convenient; perhaps it is good tactics for those who have influence to conceal their hand. Political attitudes might be adverse were young scholars told how they are governed. Student attitudes toward economics might be adverse were it known that its effect was to tranquilize them.

Since the 1930s, the innovative studies of Adolf A. Berle and Gardiner C. Means[1] and the later work of James Burnham[2] and Robert Aaron Gordon[3] had thrown much light on the changing character and the role of the corporation. Berle and Means and Gordon had shown with irrefutable statistics that as a large corporation grows larger and older, control passes from the owners to the managers. And Burnham had celebrated the power of the new managerial class. But this structural change, a thing of breathtaking importance, had never made much impression on economics as it is taught and practiced. Nor had the effect on motivation of the shift to managerial power been considered — a truly major lapse. The schools of business had long been concerned with such questions; their instinct as to what was important was better than that of my fellow econo-

[1] *The Modern Corporation and Private Property* (New York: Commerce Clearing House, 1932, and New York: Harcourt, Brace & World, 1968).

[2] *The Managerial Revolution: What is Happening in the World* (New York: John Day, 1941). James Burnham, partly because he was a stalwart right-winger well out of the political mainstream and partly because he was not a certified academician, never got full credit for his contribution. In my early editions of *The New Industrial State* I was among those in default.

[3] *Business Leadership in the Large Corporation* (Washington: Brookings Institution, 1945).

mists. *The Affluent Society* had dealt with some of the consequences of these changes. It would have been more logical had I dealt first with the institution — the great corporation — that was their cause. These are all matters that would long occupy me, and they are ones to which I will return.

* * *

McGeorge Bundy was the dean of the Faculty of Arts and Sciences at Harvard in those years, and, in consequence of the far from compelling rule of Nathan Marsh Pusey, he was the effective head of the university. In late 1958, I told Bundy of the further book that I felt I must write. His response was immediate: "If you have another book in you as good as *The Affluent Society,* I will certainly help you get it out." He arranged that Harvard give me leave for the next two winter terms, those of 1959 and 1960.

I now abandoned my residual teaching in agriculture, and Bundy moved Gottfried Haberler from the Paul M. Warburg chair in economics to one commemorating Galen L. Stone, which was represented as being even more honorable. I was installed in Haberler's place. Only an unconvincing sense of decency kept me from reflecting that I was replacing the man who had so righteously opposed my original appointment.

Paul M. Warburg was the principal architect of the Federal Reserve System, a member of its first board and, as a New York banker, almost the only voice of warning from that community on the disaster being prepared by the great stock market speculation of 1928 and 1929. The money for the chair had come from his son James P. Warburg, who had retrieved the failing family fortune by making a well-timed investment with an unknown Cambridge inventor Edwin Land, thus becoming an important owner of the Polaroid Corporation. More than occasionally in the past conservative Harvard graduates had endowed chairs only to find them occupied by liberal professors. The Warburg experience had been the exact reverse; a strongly liberal family found itself sustaining a highly conservative scholar. This Jim Warburg had observed with sorrow, but he was far too civilized to complain. With my appointment to the Warburg professorship he could, however, allow himself to show his pleasure. He came to Boston, called us to a dinner at the Ritz and offered as his toast: "May your bottom ever rest comfort-

ably in my Daddy's chair."[4] Soon thereafter he added handsomely
to the endowment. My only problem of conscience from these events
involved John D. Black, who had yearned to have me keep Harvard,
however improbably, as a center of agricultural instruction. He was,
I believe, a little sad.

                            *   *   *

At *Fortune,* as I have noted, I had seen a good deal of the interior of
the large corporation, and at OPA I had been exposed comprehensively to its leadership. In later years I sought help from the executives of DuPont and Westinghouse and from Robert McNamara
when he was at Ford. In 1958, I decided that I would look at industrial management in an entirely different context. A comparison of
managerial structure and motivation in the United States and the
Soviet Union would be instructive. One would see the common controlling requirements that applied to the organization of the great
enterprise, no matter what the political environment in which it existed. In the spring of 1959, I went to Russia by way of Sri Lanka —
Ceylon as it then was — and India.

I had been invited to Ceylon by the government of Solomon West
Ridgway Diaz Bandaranaike, who was soon to be assassinated by a
dissident Buddhist monk. My task was to review the economic plans
and planning in that lovely land, once described by a nuncio to Rome
as fifteen-and-a-half Italian leagues from Paradise,[5] where floral and
botanic extravagance nurtures the same tendencies in politics. In
those days industrial discipline there was associated by the dominant
Trotskyist mood with capitalist exploitation, and so, to some extent,
was serious work. Accordingly, and especially among the Sinhalese,
as distinct from the more diligent Tamil population, both discipline
and work were resisted, often with some vehemence and indignation. Ships were made to wait offshore to load or be unloaded; buses
and the railroad ran casually at a huge loss; even the elephants at
work in the forests and fields had conformed, one judged, to the
leisurely pace. I read reports and consulted at length with the planning board members. Since none of my advice was relevant either to
the politics or the lassitude and since these were the controlling factors in the economic development, none of it had appreciable value.

[4] As it did until I retired in 1975.
[5] This is my memory of the stated distance.

The Bandaranaikes lived with hospitably open doors in a modest bungalow. The Prime Minister was slight, intelligent and unimpressive. His wife, solid and substantial, seemed nonetheless to be in her husband's shadow. It didn't occur to me that later and durably she would be Prime Minister of this, at the time, exquisitely ungovernable land or that even later she would be consigned to the common gaol. I did learn of the breathtaking extent of the ruined cities of the north, the lush high beauty of Kandy and Nuwara Eliya and the charm of roadsides along which women, dressed as for a holiday, stroll and turn to inspect the passing cars.

*   *   *

In India three new publicly owned steel plants were being brought on line under British, West German and Soviet auspices. And at Jamshedpur the Tata Iron and Steel Company was completing, with American help, a major expansion of its mill, the original Indian steel enterprise. One could here compare the common features of large-scale industrial organization and management as they emerged from different national and ideological contexts. I spent a few days at each mill.

I had no difficulty in discovering that whatever the sponsorship, the problems and solutions were, for all practical purposes, the same. And so, broadly, were the organizations for accomplishing the task. So in mood and manner were the men in charge. Had the Soviet managers bringing the plant in Bhilai into being been moved to a similar task in Pittsburgh, they would, one felt sure, have been operational in a week, aided by a marked Ukrainian aspect and accent. Also impressive was the discovery that exposure to a blast furnace in India in late April, the most relentlessly scorching season, eliminates all fear of eternal punishment.

I was further enchanted to find the thin line that divides honesty from criminal culpability, at least in provincial India. One noon in Bhilai, returning to the rest house to escape the worst of the midday heat, I passed a Bank of India branch. An American Express sign was on display, and it occurred to me that I was nearly out of money. I went in to cash a traveler's check. I signed one and gave it to the branch manager, who examined it and said with stern emphasis, "This is an *obvious* forgery."

I heard myself explaining weakly that it wasn't. But he pointed to the two signatures, and it was clear they did not coincide. One had a very different flourish at the end.

He handed me a piece of coarse paper and told me to try again.

Contriving to sneak a glance at the original signature, I felt remarkably like a forger. This autograph, too, he declared false. But all turned out well. My third attempt he pronounced genuine, and he forthwith gave me my money.

*   *   *

In New Delhi I talked with Jawaharlal Nehru about *The Affluent Society*, which he had just finished reading. He told me he didn't care for the economic and social system I had described. I felt that I had helped him find a hitherto unrevealed virtue in the uncomplicated poverty over which he presided.

From New Delhi I went on to Tashkent in the U.S.S.R., to Alma Ata and back to Samarkand. In Tashkent I was invited by the provincial leaders to stand on the platform to review the local May Day parade. It was an innocent show, devoid of tanks, replete with flowers and banners celebrating the joy of work, real or alleged, in factories or farms and in numerous schools. All have seen the news photos of the substantial, mostly grim-faced men standing in a row watching this kind of procession. That day I was one of them. Our pictures were taken. I wondered if a print might find its way into my FBI file; that could require a rather eloquent explanation. I concluded that I would survive. My companion for the occasion was the leader of a delegation from the German Democratic Republic, a woman of mature years and efficient build whose clothes made no concession to style or fashion. She wanted to know if, by any chance, I had encountered her relatives in Connecticut.

Samarkand, not then on the tourist route, is one of the great delights of Asia. Since my years at *Fortune* I had been interested in photography and had raised my skill and eye to a subprofessional level. I spent two days photographing the tombs, mosques and minarets. Because of the study that camera work requires, something often more valuable than the prints themselves, these monuments remain brilliant in my eye. The actual pictures found their way into scholarly use in the Harvard School of Design.

At Alma Ata I could have been the first to learn of a rift between China and the Soviet Union. One day, with an Indian film producer of my acquaintance, I went walking in the Tien Shan mountains which, with gleaming white snowcaps, tower over the city and make the boundary with Sinkiang. Turning into a lonely and decrepit village by the roadside, again with my camera, I was attacked by a fierce and accurate dog. It tore a sizable chunk of flesh from the inside of my leg just a few inches below what in my youth were called one's private parts. I was transported quickly back to Alma Ata where a doctor disinfected and sewed up the wound and told me that I would have to have shots for rabies.

"The dog," he said, "could have come over from China."[6]

*　　*　　*

With Lloyd Reynolds, a professor of economics at Yale and a long-time friend, and John Michael Montias, a younger Russian-speaking economist, and joined on one occasion by Averell Harriman who was then in the country, I spent the next weeks visiting industrial establishments, state planning officials and university departments of economics in Russia. At a great automobile plant near Moscow as word passed that Harriman, the wartime source of arms and much other help, was touring the establishment, the production line came spontaneously to a halt. Workers came from all over the huge floor and massed around to hear a few words. It was a notable and deserved tribute, and I have rarely in my life seen a public man more pleased.

I learned much about the Soviet economy in those weeks and a little at least that served my immediate purpose. The managerial structure of the Soviet firm is much simpler than that of the American or western corporation. That is because sales, marketing, merchandising, dealer relations, as also personnel, legal and also consumer and public relations departments, are absent or exiguous. Soviet consumers can be counted upon to buy whatever is available. Also the planning apparatus that relates supply to demand stands above the enterprise in the state bureaucracy as the Depart-

---

[6] A young Russian from Leningrad, the local head of Intourist, had placed himself at my disposal, as he had, some time earlier, at that of Adlai Stevenson whom he, like so many others, greatly admired. The doctor told me that according to whether or not the dog (which they would send for) was rabid I must have eleven or twenty-two injections. I would give him my itinerary; he would send me a telegram saying either "The dog is sick" or "The dog is well." My guide, as he translated, added thoughtfully, "And that telegram to an American will occupy our secret service for at least six months so you will never receive it." Nor did I.

ment of Energy in Washington stands over the oil companies in the United States. But within the Soviet firm there is the same need for joint decision-making — for an arrangement by which specialists share the information or experience that is relevant to any important decision and of which no one person can be fully in command. As in the capitalist firm, these decisions and operations generally require autonomy; they must not be second-guessed from above or outside. If there is such intervention, it will be uninformed and thus damaging. Nor can anyone doubt that the great industrial enterprise stamps its culture — its hours, discipline, work attitudes and air pollution — on its community whether that be Russian, German or American. Out of this experience, but also out of the then emerging literature on Soviet management, I developed the case for a broad convergence in the industrial systems of the socialist and nonsocialist worlds. The difference is not between external control by owner-capitalists or control by the state. Neither, given the intricate and technical character of the managerial task in the great enterprise, is effectively and continuously possible; the required knowledge, whether by owner or politician, is lacking. What is common to the large enterprise in both systems is the inevitability of collective decision-making and guidance in which numerous specialized participants contribute the needed knowledge or experience.

Eventually my case for a convergence in the nature of the great enterprises in the capitalist and Communist worlds was published in both the United States and the Soviet Union. In both countries it was attacked, but in both it also gained a measure of acceptance. It is my devout hope that from this convergence — the fact and not my description of it — will come an eventual decline in the doctrine of inevitable conflict between the two economic systems.

*   *   *

Our meetings with academic economists, which we had in universities from that of Georgia in Tbilisi to Leningrad, were pleasant but not altogether informative. That is because the Soviet system draws the best economists into the institutes that are closely associated with state planning operations or into the state bureaucracy itself. Those remaining in the academic world have, with exceptions, a detachment from reality that is noticeable even to an American economist. The meetings with those directly involved in operations were far more interesting. At all of them there was the likelihood of an assertive case for the Soviet system and then an equally self-serving response. Our hosts would point to their achievements and to the failures of capitalism. Reynolds and I would then find ourselves defending capitalist accomplishments. Conversation with Soviet economists since that time has become much easier, perhaps partly because confidence in the perfectibility of both capitalism and socialism has markedly declined. And the ancient Russian tendency to find amusement in absurdity has asserted itself. A meeting with Soviet scholars can now, on occasion, become a relaxed exposition of comparative shortcomings.[7]

One morning as we were leaving the Hotel Ukrainia, the towering, unbeautiful monument to Stalinist architectural design where we were housed and where one could wait twenty minutes for an elevator, I told Reynolds that when the inevitable case for Soviet achievement was next made, I proposed to change my response. I would question the standard by which we both measured success.

Our session that day, a thoroughly pleasant one, was with members of the Institute for World Economics and International Relations, well-known to all visiting scholars for its hospitality. A senior member questioned me on *American Capitalism* and countervailing power. But he ended with the usual query: "Do American economists and scholars appreciate the scale of our planning? Do they realize that one day we will overtake you in the production of goods?"

I professed shock and said, "Surely you are not going to do that."

"You must take our intentions seriously."

---

[7] I've told in the past of a visit in the early 1970s in Cambridge from a Soviet editor who had worked on my books. Making conversation as we prepared to go to lunch at the faculty club, I pointed to the *New York Times,* which told on the front page that a Texas congressman had just been corralled for public misfeasance. I said, "Where everyone works for the state you must need a vast force of auditors."

My Russian friend replied, "It is not, in principle, a problem. As you know, Lenin said that with socialism all acquisitive instincts disappear."

"Surely there are exceptions even to such an impeccable Leninist law?"

"Yes, unfortunately. It was investigated a year or so ago. The Institute for Sociology of the Academy of Sciences made an audit of all the firms in one of our industrial towns. They wished to assess the state of honesty in our country."

"What did they learn?"

"They found that all of the senior management officials were enhancing their income in one irregular fashion or another."

"What happened?"

"The Party took it very seriously. They cracked down on sociology."

"That," I replied, "is what concerns me. Here in Moscow the streets are wide; the automobiles, by American standards, are few. Yet already it is as much as life is worth to pass from curb to curb. Have you thought what a tenfold increase to New York standards, a fifteenfold increase to the Los Angeles level, would do to your traffic, would mean in parking space, would require in repair services, would do to your good, clean air? I am appalled that a planned economy should have no goal except to rival the worst mistakes of an unplanned one."

There was a moment of rewarding silence. I glanced at Lloyd Reynolds, for I felt I had done well. My pleasure didn't last.

"Well, do you agree that we will catch up with you in everything but automobiles?"

*   *   *

We feasted for a few days on Leningrad — opera, circus, the Hermitage and more economists. Then I went back to Vermont to write. I worked on the book through the autumn, and then for the winter and spring of 1960 (after an unmemorable trip to Pakistan to lend support to Harvard efforts on behalf of development there) I went into retreat in Switzerland. Not before and not since have I been emotionally so involved with a task. At the end of each day, I felt physically as well as mentally drained. I wondered if I could possibly live long enough to finish this thing on which I was so deeply engaged and which seemed so important. I surrendered sex, alcohol and friends to my involvement.

In the summer and autumn of 1960, I finally broke away from the book to help with the nomination and election of John F. Kennedy. I had a severe sense of guilt in doing so. The choice later that year between finishing *The New Industrial State*,[8] as it was eventually to be called, and agreeing to go as ambassador to India caused me the greatest anguish. For a time I could not sleep, lost weight and one day sent word to Chester Bowles, who as Undersecretary of State and our former envoy there was much concerned with who would represent us in India, that I would not go. I would remain a professor and do what I was meant to do. Usually in life, when faced with desirable alternatives, I have managed to have both. For the

[8] Boston: Houghton Mifflin, 1967.

moment, this seemed not to be possible. However, I soon changed my mind again and accepted the appointment.

Four years later, though with less tension, I had to make the same kind of choice once more. In Washington one day, George D. Aiken, the senior senator from Vermont (accompanied on the occasion by Ernest W. Gibson, a federal judge and before that a much-respected governor), proposed that I run for the Senate from that state. Aiken was (as he remains) a Republican, but, in the best Vermont manner, he cared little about such details. And he didn't care for the Republican candidate. In the campaign it would be made known that I had his friendship, though not, of course, his endorsement. I gave the matter thought. Again the book on which I was at work stood in the way. Also, no doubt, natural caution. I did not run. In the Johnson landslide of that autumn, I might not have lost.[9]

---

[9] In 1972, urged by Edward Kennedy, I considered what amounted to an offer of the Democratic nomination for the Senate from Massachusetts. My competition would have been Edward W. Brooke, a friend and the only black in the upper house of the Congress. I canvassed friends, the Black Caucus in Washington (which was favorable) and the black establishment in Boston (which was adamantly opposed). A day or two before the convention, I took myself out of the race. I would have faced the comment, "Galbraith is a great friend of minorities except when he wants something for himself." I was also influenced by the thought that at the time I could not have beaten Ed Brooke.

24

J.F.K.: The Campaign

By 1960, John F. Kennedy had developed the personal and political style that would be his trademark. Some of it was thoughtfully designed, including, in particular, the dark, well-tailored, unobtrusive and, from the absence of vest or hat, slightly casual dress. Clothes on a politician, he believed, should not detract; perhaps, just a trifle, they could add; but above all, in his view, they should not obtrude. On occasion, one caught the quick twinkle in Kennedy's eye as he surveyed the iridescent sport jacket on some unreticent statesman fresh in from Grand Forks.

More of the Kennedy political style was instinctive or instinctively reactive. The Boston political fashion into which he had been born — and of which his maternal grandfather, John Francis "Honey Fitz" Fitzgerald, was the archetype — was baroque and effusive, where not flamboyant or florid. The crowd roared its greeting and possibly its approval; the candidate waved arms, clasped hands in a narcissistic handshake over his head, maybe shouted in responsive exuberance. All this Kennedy detested. You acknowledged applause with a bow, a smile, at most a half-raised hand. The cheering was a folk rite; only an idiot imagined that it indicated enduring affection. The face-wrenching effort by which Nixon acknowledged what he wished to believe was love was inane. Even Ike went too far. "If I have to wave both hands above my head in order to be President, I won't have the job."

Adlai Stevenson, as I have told, spent his adult life in a persuasive effort to present himself as he was not. The grace with which he pictured himself as a harried, wavering intellectual lost in the harsh, demanding, dogmatic world of politics was one of his most engaging qualities. Kennedy gained grace by precisely the opposite trait, by being himself, and some of the tension between the two men was occasioned by, as Kennedy saw it, Stevenson's instinct for pretense. More than any American politician since F.D.R., John F. Kennedy, as I've already noted, was completely content with his own personality. He never felt it necessary to say anything by way of self-enhancement.[1] The least attractive tendency of politicians is to imitate their own newspaper or television image. Here I am, the friendly, roughhewn, outspoken, outgoing man as so often described. Not this for Kennedy. He was openly amused by such posturing. However, he was not easily tempted on to denigrating comment about others. This he also rejected as a way of enhancing one's own public and self-esteem.

Against one personality trait Kennedy had struggled with a singular lack of success — impatience. Its principal manifestation was a marked unwillingness to hear at any length what he already knew or did not need to know. On numerous subjects, from agriculture to economics to Vietnam to the imponderables of Indian politics, I had occasion to inform him. The occupational hazard of any professor is didactic prolixity, and I early learned to look for the warning signs — a finger nervously rubbing his forehead, a quick word of interruption — that made it clear he had heard enough.

Chester Bowles, an admirable and kindly man, came a trifle too enthusiastically to ideas. Often he could not control this enthusiasm; one was informed at unnecessary length on what he had learned. One day when he was Undersecretary of State, I went into the Oval Office just after he came out. Kennedy said, "Chet tells me there are six revolutions going on in the world. One is the revolution of rising expectations. I lost track of the other five."

At least partly because of impatience Kennedy was not greatly effective as a legislator. He didn't relish the painstaking persuasion, concession and compromise on which legislative achievement depends. Nor was he deeply admiring of his colleagues as a class. During one long night session Kennedy dropped into a seat beside John

[1] He *was* concerned to minimize his health problems, and he particularly played down the trouble he suffered from his back. Once after the 1960 convention at lunch in Hyannis Port he mused at some length on the relative unimportance of Addison's disease from which he suffered and the effects of the required treatment. He would, he said, not mention it during the campaign, as his father had never mentioned that he occasionally went to the hospital to have some relatively harmless skin cancer scraped off. The immediate and effectively erroneous reaction would have been to say that Joe Kennedy had cancer. A similar exaggeration would be made of J.F.K.'s condition were it reported so better not to discuss it at all.

Sherman Cooper, then Republican senator from Kentucky, whose personal style he much admired. He surveyed the adjacent Republicans and said, "Terrible people you have to live with, John."

Cooper replied, "I could say things about some of your fellow Democrats."

"I know," said Kennedy. "Windbags and demagogues."[2]

*   *   *

For those whom he trusted, Kennedy's most rewarding characteristic was his breathtaking candor — the quick chop through to truth that one immediately recognized as something to be kept in confidence, a discretion for which I, at least, never heard him ask. Only rarely was he betrayed. On April 10, 1962, after Arthur Goldberg, his Secretary of Labor, had negotiated successfully with the unions for restraint in a steel wage settlement, Roger Blough, Chairman of the Board of U.S. Steel, called in on the President to say that the corporation was raising its prices $6 a ton. "My father always told me that all businessmen were sons-of-bitches," Kennedy later remarked to friends, "but I never believed it till now."[3] This generalization was repeated, and it reached the papers. Kennedy was distressed, though mostly because it condemned so many besides Blough.

In later years Carl Kaysen[4] and I exchanged our best examples of the Kennedy candor. Mine went back to the day after the Inaugural. Richard Cardinal Cushing had seized upon that happy occasion for an enduring prayer. Kennedy said, "I knew it would be long, but halfway through I was saved by the thought that here is Kennedy, the first Catholic President, being inaugurated, and Cardinal Spellman is having to watch it on television."[5]

Kaysen remembered a Kennedy comment about negotiations on the Panama Canal with President Roberto Francisco Chiari of Panama in June 1962. The two men had talked privately and then taken a break. Before they resumed, Carl brought in some more information that Kennedy had requested. The President looked up from his

---

[2] I was told of the incident by Cooper.

[3] Quoted in Arthur M. Schlesinger, Jr., *A Thousand Days* (Boston: Houghton Mifflin, 1965), p. 635.

[4] See Chapter 21.

[5] Francis Joseph Spellman, a Massachusetts native and then head of the archdiocese of New York, was the Church's major bridgehead to the conservative Republican establishment. He was no friend of the Kennedys.

desk and said, "I'm not doing very well in these negotiations, Carl."

Kaysen expressed concern and asked why.

"He says we've been screwing them all these years, and I agree."

One of Kennedy's candid remarks could have caused him some trouble at the time and would cause him more now. He believed there was an unperceived sex link in politics; how otherwise explain why so few women were successful in the field. Commenting on this one day in his office, he said, "Name me a woman who *really* has it in politics."

I promptly offered the name of Eleanor Roosevelt, and he said, "Sure, name another."

I added the name of the first Elizabeth, and he said delightedly, "Yes, and now you have left only Maggie Smith."[6]

*   *   *

Kennedy did greatly respect Eleanor Roosevelt and rather more her influence on the liberal wing of the Democratic Party. This influence, based on both her husband's reputation and her own, was enormous in the late fifties. Unfortunately until Kennedy became President, her suspicion of him was very deep; it derived from her belief that his father had been willingly defeatist as ambassador to Britain and was now hopelessly conservative. So no Kennedy could be trusted. A plan to bring Mrs. Roosevelt and J.F.K. together in early 1960 added another chapter to my considerable history of failed efforts at political maneuver.

Mrs. Roosevelt was then conducting a television interview program, which originated from Brandeis University. After I appeared on it one day, it occurred to me that an interview with Kennedy would be the ideal way of getting the two on better terms. It would reassure liberals and reassure Mrs. Roosevelt.

With some difficulty, I persuaded her to invite Kennedy; with less difficulty, although he had misgivings, I persuaded Kennedy to accept. All of this was arranged in the last days of 1959 as a good start for the new year. Their preliminary meeting, the show itself and the ancillary conversation went well. When it was over, the two went out to meet the press, and a reporter asked her if their exchange meant that she would now support Kennedy. She replied with emphasis

---

[6] Margaret Chase Smith, long a Republican senator from Maine.

and even indignation that it did not. It was this disavowal, not the show, that made the headlines.

We dined at Locke-Ober's that evening; Kennedy, who had also that day formally announced his candidacy, was disconcerted and depressed and confirmed in his doubts as to my political acuity. In succeeding months, without my help, he did win her confidence and even her affection.

* * *

In the winter of 1960, I departed for Switzerland to work on *The New Industrial State.* It remained for a closer circle of Kennedy workers — Theodore Sorensen, Kenneth O'Donnell, Lawrence O'Brien and Sargent Shriver — to pursue the convention delegates and serve in the primaries. In modern presidential politics there are two concentric rings, and the inner one consists of those who commit themselves fully to the early battles. The outer ring is of those who, from great public or Establishment prestige, gain office after all is won. Between the two rings there is always a measure of tension. Where, the insiders ask, were the latecomers when the risks were great and the going hard? My position was somewhere between the rings.

Thus I missed the Wisconsin primary when Kennedy challenged Hubert Humphrey on the latter's home ground. The result, by the arcane calculus applied to such contests, was unclear. Nor was I in West Virginia for that state's primary. There, though unknown, rich, a Catholic and needing to appeal to working-class and Protestant rural voters who had always been for Humphrey, but aided measurably by having more money and a better organization, Kennedy came from behind to take Humphrey out of the race.

Because I was not in West Virginia, I missed one of the great political orations of all time — one that retrieved the morale of the Kennedy workers in the early and gloomy days of the campaign. It was given by an ardent local supporter, the most eloquent of West Virginia Democrats and an historian of parts. The speech began with a stirring articulation of first principles:

"This campaign is being based on the source of all spiritual truth." To illustrate the point, the speaker, in a reverent gesture, placed a Bible on the podium before him.

"It is being based on the source of all historical truth." Even more reverently he then placed a copy of Kennedy's *Profiles in Courage* on top of the Bible.

Then silently he brought an American flag from his breast pocket and placed it over the two books.

The speech that followed was not remarkable until the concluding peroration. In this he adverted to his own standing as a student of history and the fact that other men long before John F. Kennedy had faced their moment of despair.

"I can tell you," he said, "that on the second day of the great battle of Waterloo, Napoleon was a discouraged man. He looked out over the battlefield and said to the drummer boy beside him, 'Drummer boy, the English are standing firm. The Old Guard is making no progress. We are defeated; sound the retreat.'

"The drummer boy looked at Napoleon and said, 'Master, in all our campaigns in Europe, I have never learned to sound the retreat.'

"Napoleon was touched — deeply touched. So he said, 'All right, drummer boy, SOUND THE ADVANCE.' And history tells us what happened. That drummer boy sounded the advance, Napoleon went on to win at Waterloo just as John F. Kennedy will go on to win in West Virginia."

And so, of course, he did.

*　　*　　*

Having avoided the primaries in 1960, my first thought was to omit the convention as well. These vast ceremonials are now a bloated corpse. Candidates, as we know, are selected in the primaries or in the local caucuses and state conventions. There cannot be two separate arrangements for performing the same task and so it is the pre-convention selection that counts. It follows that by the time the delegates assemble, the candidate has been chosen. Or the choice has been narrowed to, at most, a couple of contenders, and it is hard to have a deadlock or even much of a contest when two (or fewer) are in the running. But now fraud enters. A semblance of life is breathed into the corpse by delegates who, having been elected or selected and having traveled to the great event, wish to believe they are doing something. In this wish they are abetted by the press, which is enjoying an expense-paid reunion and a carnival untaxing to the mind, and above all by television commentators whose livelihood is involved, as also their reputation for raising banality to an art form:

"How would you rate the applause for that speech, John?"

"Average for this stage of convention proceedings I'd say, David."

Lester Markel, the long-time Sunday editor of the *New York Times*, once told me that he looked forward confidently to the day when the *Times* would send one man to a national convention and tell him not to file more than fifteen hundred words.

*   *   *

It is possible that the tedium of a convention can be relieved by the intrusion of a truly great issue as was the case in 1968. There was never any doubt that Hubert Humphrey would be nominated that year; there *was* question as to how clearly it could be shown that he had no mandate to continue the Vietnam war. This made the riotous Chicago gathering the only really important convention of my experience, and I will return to it in a later chapter.

In Los Angeles in 1960 no alternative to Kennedy — Lyndon Johnson, Stuart Symington or Adlai Stevenson — had a serious chance. This was evident before the convocation if one could count. However, the urge to be present was stronger than I supposed, and when one day in early July I heard on the radio in Vermont that, among other Democratic Party functionaries, I had just arrived in California, I forthwith got reservations and departed.

I reached Los Angeles a couple of days before the opening to a better welcome than I could easily have imagined. Word was waiting for me to repair at once to Room 8314, the Kennedy suite at the Biltmore and the epicenter of a barely supportable excitement. There I was asked by Robert Kennedy to join the convention organization and have general charge of Kennedy delegations west of the Mississippi and north of the Southwest. On California I would work with Jesse M. Unruh, then about to become Speaker of the California Assembly; Colorado would involve a similar liaison with Byron R. White, a local Kennedy leader, former athlete and future associate justice of the Supreme Court. The Kennedy allotment of floor credentials had all been dispersed so Bobby gave me his. He thought it unlikely that any guard would try to exclude him.

American politics, as previously noted, accords the most improbable promotions to the rank of political sage and even more rapid, as well as more deserved, demotions after defeat. Nonetheless I was puzzled at my sudden and unexpected ascent. It was later that I learned that, on arriving in Los Angeles, the Kennedys had discovered that there was no one in the entourage, apart from Theodore Sorensen who was indispensable as an assistant and speech writer, who was not Jewish, Catholic or Irish. For the great Protestant Northwest they needed someone who was ostentatiously either a WASP or a closely negotiable substitute.

Through those July mornings in a car driven by a Kennedy volunteer and decorated with large pictures of the candidate, I made the rounds of the hotels where my delegations were housed, attending caucuses at which no business was being done, speaking well of Kennedy and responding to questions as to his positions on Social Security and civil liberties and his policies toward the Russians, reclamation, the economy and the Vatican, responses that I had extensively to improvise. It was a great delight. When the convention assembled in the afternoons, I visited the various Kennedy delegations on the floor to make sure there had been no defections. There were none,[7] and when I so reported to Bob Kennedy, either on the floor or at a crowded morning staff meeting, he had difficulty believing it. Once, just before the first voting, I told him things were sewed up. He was outraged and warned me strongly against such overconfidence.

*　　*　　*

In delegate strength, Kennedy's closest, though distant, rival was Lyndon Johnson. In 1960, a southerner, even including a Texan, was still politically confined to the South. Johnson's white supremacy support, while solid there, was poisonous elsewhere. This L.B.J. knew as well as anyone. Combined with his own decent instincts, it had caused him as Senate Majority Leader during the Eisenhower Administration to back the first civil rights legislation since Reconstruction. Nor had he failed to tell northern liberals, myself included, of the skill and effort he had brought to the cause. It was not enough to lift the ban.

[7]Or virtually none. When Stevenson's name was entered, I lost a half vote in Iowa, that of Stephen Garst, son of Roswell Garst, the hybrid-corn king and a great Stevenson admirer. This was more than offset, however, by the withdrawal of the Iowa governor, Herschel Loveless, as a favorite son and the release of his delegates to Kennedy.

For a man so very much larger than life, Johnson was only dimly known north of the border states. I was always surprised at how frequently I was asked what he was like. In Los Angeles one evening as I was leaving the Biltmore, I met him coming from his car into the hotel. A crowd had gathered on the sidewalk outside to view the notables as they moved in and out. Johnson was greeting those assembled, bowing to the right and left; it was all too plain that most of the people didn't recognize him. He seized on me with unexampled pleasure as someone who did.

Among those who retained a lingering hope that conventions were not quite cut-and-dried was Adlai Stevenson, and, at least for the public record, so did his two gallant advocates and managers George Ball and Senator Mike Monroney of Oklahoma, perhaps the only legislator from that state ever to oppose a price increase for crude oil (as he did in World War II). Stevenson was greatly popular with the galleries, the crowds outside the convention hall and also, their commitment to vote otherwise notwithstanding, with many on the convention floor. In a rare misjudgment, on being pressed up to the platform when he arrived to take his seat with the Illinois delegation, he contented himself with saying that the nominee might well be the last survivor of the terrible crowds at the Biltmore. All had wanted a touch of the old oratory, not a wisecrack. But Eugene McCarthy retrieved with a resounding nomination speech, the best of the convention and quite possibly one of the few to be heard. Only when they came to vote were the delegates unmoved.

Since I had been with Stevenson through two campaigns, I was regarded by his more devoted supporters as an ingrate, a turncoat, a Kennedy opportunist and also morally and ethically leprous. All was made worse by my excessive visibility on the convention floor. It was, I thought, a trifle unfair; I had been supporting Kennedy publicly for a couple of years. Moreover, Stevenson had firmly taken himself out of the race earlier on. With Arthur Schlesinger who was also supporting Kennedy, I went to call on Adlai at the Ambassador soon after his arrival, and there was no suggestion from him that we were being politically recusant. But not everyone in politics is given to distinctions. On Saturday, July 9, before the convention opened, I journeyed happily to Pasadena in a Kennedy car to a garden party being given for selected delegates and visitors by Agnes Meyer, a devoted friend of Stevenson's and the strongly motivated mother and mother-in-law of the *Washington Post*. I strolled into the garden where I was immediately surrounded by eloquently critical friends of Adlai's — Agnes Meyer herself, Gay (Mrs. Thomas K.) Finletter and (I believe) Alicia Patterson of *Newsday*. They denounced my apostasy with a resourcefulness of language that left me not only silent but stunned. "The worst personal betrayal in American history" was one of the milder observations.[8] Feigning a sudden need for a bathroom, I passed into the house, out the front door and escaped.

*   *   *

Agriculture, Kennedy's nemesis in his vice-presidential effort in 1956, was still pursuing him, and on the day before the balloting, delegates from the farm states caucused to make known the needs of their industry. I was dispatched to represent and defend Kennedy and arrived in time to hear a stem-winding speech for Lyndon Johnson by William Robert (Bob) Poage of Waco, Texas, for twenty-three years a member of the House Committee on Agriculture and then its chairman. The rafters echoed with the danger to farmers from a President born in the urban and consumer-minded East. No one from that part of the country, he proclaimed not too inaccurately, could possibly understand the politics of American agriculture. As Poage wound up to his climax, Kennedy, having decided that he had better be present to speak for himself, moved into the chair next to mine. I urged the thought on which I had intended to dwell — that Franklin D. Roosevelt from New York, as eastern and urbanized a state as Massachusetts, was the best friend the farmers had ever had. One should be cautious in praising one's own acts of genius, but there are exceptions to every rule. In his talk to the caucus J.F.K. made election of a liberal easterner, Roosevelt or Kennedy being interchangeable, all but imperative for American agriculture.

Entering the car that day to ride back to the Biltmore, there was a characteristic Kennedy gesture. I started to get into the back seat, and Kennedy motioned me into the front beside him. "You should know enough by now about politics to know where to sit. It's more democratic to ride in front, and if you get in back, six politicians will climb in on top of you."

---

[8] The one I repeated to Arthur Schlesinger. See *A Thousand Days,* p. 34.

Kennedy and I covered some of the state caucuses together, and before both the Iowa and the Kansas delegations I heard him say how admirably each of their governors — Loveless of Iowa, George Docking of Kansas — was qualified to be Vice President. I asked him about this, for I guessed he had no intention of choosing either. "They would rather be mentioned and passed over," he said, "than not be mentioned at all."

* * *

There was further evidence one evening as to how extensively the convention drama must be contrived. Passing down the aisle as I "worked the floor," I met Edward R. Murrow equipped like a spaceman with his own antennae. He asked me what was new.

"Oh, everything's under control," I replied without thought.

Conventions are hard on the feet, and shortly thereafter I went into a television monitoring room off the floor to rest mine for a few minutes. As I watched, Murrow appeared on the screen and sat down opposite Walter Cronkite.

"Well, Ed, what's new?"

"I just talked with Ken Galbraith, Walter."

"That's interesting, Ed. Professor Galbraith, eh? He usually has something interesting to say."

"Well, he did. He said that everything is under control, Walter."

"That's pretty important, Ed. So the Kennedy people think that everything's under control?"

"That's the message, Walter. Under control."

"That's very interesting, Ed. As they see it, all under control?"

* * *

On Wednesday, July 13, at the morning staff meeting at the Biltmore, Robert Kennedy had his own last roll call of the states. Our lead after favorite-son withdrawals was now overwhelming — only twenty-one votes short of nomination. After promises or commitments had been duly honored, the desire to be with the winner would take over. We were in. But Bob allowed no such calculation. Caution and the belief that convention delegates could somehow be swayed required that we think our majority febrile, at any moment ready to dissolve. I rode out to the Sports Arena with Sargent Shriver and other members of the family. All were silent; it was as to a funeral. When the roll call reached Washington state, Kennedy became inevitable, and Wyoming (with the outlying possessions still to come) switched to clinch the vote. In a few minutes it was hard to find anyone who hadn't intended to come aboard.

I went to a press party held by the *New York Post,* gave various interviews along the lines of my communiqué to Edward R. Murrow and then toward midnight went to a dinner party being given by Joseph Alsop at an expensive local watering place called Perino's. (My friendship with Joe Alsop was a casualty of the Vietnam war, but it has since been somewhat repaired.) The restaurant, large and florid in the local manner, consists, or then consisted, of a central area surrounded by small enclaves shaped like wombs, each with a single table around which the customers slid in sequence. As I arrived, I was greeted in the central area by Bart Lytton, a local savings and loan magnate and Democrat who was later to fall on hard times. In tribute to my recent visibility among the delegates, he hailed me by my first name as an old friend, although I had encountered him only a couple of times before. Reluctantly, for I was very late, and only in deference to a prospective contribution to the Kennedy cause, I acceded to his request to come and meet some of his newspaper friends. I slid in front of him into one of the wombs; he introduced me to the couple opposite.

"Buffy, Norman, this is Kenneth Galbraith."

The man Norman, of mature years, put his hand to his ear.

"I didn't get the name." He was, I now realized, Norman Chandler, the publisher and principal owner of the *Los Angeles Times.* Buffy was his no less influential wife.

"Norman," Lytton repeated with prideful emphasis, "John Kenneth Galbraith."

"That must be an embarrassing name. Sounds like that SOB with Kennedy."

The Alsop dinner came to an end, and I drove with Jean Stein vanden Heuvel, a longtime friend, to her parents' house somewhere in the western wastes of the city for a swim. It was by then daylight, and after breakfast I came back to the Mayflower Hotel across from the Biltmore, where I was billeted. It was the first time in my memory, air travel apart, that I had not gone to bed all night. As I entered the room, the phone was ringing. It was Bob Kennedy to tell me that his brother had picked Lyndon Johnson as his running mate and that I should get out to the Sports Arena; I might, he said, have a revolt on my hands. It crossed my mind that Bobby didn't sound pleased, as by later account he was not. But I didn't inquire further into the selection nor did I ask Ted Sorensen, who, if memory serves, called me a little later.

On the way to the convention hall I put together my argument. It went back to Roosevelt again — "the same thing F.D.R. did in 1932 when he picked John Nance Garner." Even another Texan.

There was, indeed, objection. Joseph L. Rauh, Jr., before and later my ally in many liberal causes, grabbed a microphone and appealed to the candidate from wherever he was watching to correct this outrage. Several in my delegations were vocal. But out of weariness and the desire to be with the winner rather than because of my countering eloquence, the objection quickly collapsed. By this time, as I will tell, I had come sufficiently to appreciate Lyndon Johnson's qualities so that I had few qualms myself.

Some weeks after the convention, a group of ADA liberals visited Kennedy at Hyannis Port. John A. Roche, later a White House aide to L.B.J. and later still a professor at the Fletcher School of Law and Diplomacy, asked Kennedy why he had picked Johnson. Characteristically he numbered his reasons on his fingers:

"First. Somehow I had the feeling that Johnson takes more of the Catholic flavor off me than anyone else. A Southern Protestant.

"Second. He obviously helps in the South.

"Third. It wouldn't be worthwhile being President if Lyndon was the Majority Leader."

Kennedy, who didn't at all share my interest or pleasure in Johnson's scandalous characterizations and inventive scatology, then added, "But, as Bobby says, the man is a bore." It was not a view that many would share.

*   *   *

Early in the campaign I was back in Los Angeles to raise Hollywood money, as it is called in politics, at a party given by Henry and Afdera Fonda in a house they had rented from Linda Christian, which was greatly enhanced by nude portraits and statues of the former occupant. Edward Kennedy was the other attraction. When the money pitch began, Bart Lytton came forward with $5000. When no one else matched it, he did. I was back in California again that autumn to campaign with Henry (Scoop) Jackson, another friendship that was to suffer with Vietnam. We were speaking in San Diego on September 26, the day of the first Kennedy/Nixon debate, when I got a message from Kennedy asking me to "come over" for a pre-debate discussion. He thought I was in Chicago with him and his campaign staff. On October 13, the day of the third debate, I again got word to cancel my engagements and come to the Carlyle Hotel in New York for such a discussion. This time, happily, I was just down the street. Kennedy, Sorensen, Arthur Schlesinger and I lunched together. Kennedy was visibly ill at ease. Occasionally he would propose a likely question for discussion and then change the subject before the answer. Once he was distracted by where he had put a check handed to him a few minutes earlier by Mary Lasker, New York's most consistent supporter of good causes. "I must learn to be more careful with money." Finally he called off the session and proposed to Sorensen that they go and get the feel of the studio.

Kennedy and I rode down in the elevator together, and I remarked that he seemed a bit tense, not perhaps the most useful comment at the time. His reply in the full light of history was compelling: "I keep saying to myself, 'Kennedy, you're the only thing that stands between Nixon and the White House.' " [9]

My contributions as a Kennedy speech writer, on occasion celebrated by the press in later years, were negligible. Kennedy's speeches were written throughout the campaign by Sorensen and Richard Goodwin, and I helped, mostly on economic issues, by notes or telephone calls to Goodwin. Perhaps it was wise to remain at a slight distance. Nixon, in the South, was trumpeting his discovery that the Democratic Party had become "the party of Schlesinger, Galbraith and Bowles," a trinity he held to be the political equivalent of Lenin, Stalin and Mao Tse-tung.

I did draft the compulsory speech on economics, and my version, after some debate, was selected over another that, as things were then seen, was less radical. Joe Kennedy attended the meeting at which the speech was discussed and greatly to his son's astonishment came down solidly on my side. "I would like to know," Kennedy said to me afterward, "what hold you have on my old man." This particular speech was given to a meeting of business writers and editors in

[9] Arthur Schlesinger, who was in the elevator with us, also remembered the remark in slightly different form. *A Thousand Days*, p. 72.

New York. Kennedy hurried through it; some who were present thought he had difficulty in concealing his distaste for the subject: others suggested his aversion was to the audience.

My principal task during the campaign was to be a presence in those places where Kennedy stood no chance but where, as a matter of politeness and good politics, someone of minimal renown had to appear. And, with Averell Harriman and Arthur Schlesinger, it was to try to reassure Jewish audiences, particularly in New York state.[10] For explaining to a liberal Jewish audience that Kennedy was not a new Torquemada — that the Holy Father would not be a presence in the Oval Office — another Catholic would not do. Nor would another Jew; he would too easily be thought in the great tradition of assimilation. So once again ethnic affiliation proved more important than political aptitude. My coverage of Jewish or predominantly Jewish organizations in Manhattan, Brooklyn, the Bronx and extending out to Great Neck and into Westchester was comprehensive.

The apogee of this effort was on one elegant October morning when I got word from the Carlyle to cancel a speech to a Democratic club on the West Side and go instead to represent Kennedy before the Federation of Jewish Women's Organizations whose members were assembled in a theater off Broadway to hear the case for the two candidates. Kennedy had been scheduled to speak himself, but then it became known that Nixon would not be there and would be represented by Senator Jacob Javits instead. Campaign protocol forbade Kennedy's appearance with someone of secondary rank. So someone yet more secondary was sent.

Javits spoke first. There was no temple, B'nai B'rith, effort by the United Jewish Appeal or any other organization in New York or Israel however remotely Hebraic which did not receive mention in his introduction or speech. I contemplated my Highland name, my early but recusant association with the Covenanted Baptist Church and reached over to the folder of the confident, handsome woman who was presiding, extracted her introduction of me and where it said Professor of Economics at Harvard, wrote in *Paul M. Warburg* Professor of Economics. When this title was mentioned, there was,

---

[10]This was an effort we were to make again in a much more extensive way for Robert Kennedy in his senatorial campaign of 1964; he came to refer to it as the greatest Christian mission to the Jews since the New Testament.

from the audience, an audible sigh of relief. I told them in a conciliatory way that they would have no trouble voting for the man to
whom Javits had devoted his fulsome, merited and, indeed, all-but-
exclusive praise. But that man, unfortunately, was Javits himself, not
Nixon. And Javits was not running for President.

*   *   *

No one, however passionately he remembers the Kennedy years, will
think the campaign of 1960 memorable for its illumination of the
issues. As was the case from 1948 on, the Democrats were as much
for the people as was possible without frightening the comfortably
moderate voters into believing they would be unduly taxed or otherwise threatened. The Republicans were as much for private and
corporate wealth as was possible without hopelessly alienating those
who looked for succor to Social Security, farm price supports, trade
unions and the minimum wage. On foreign policy the Republicans
took a strong stand against Communism, and the Democrats showed
as ever that they weren't soft on Communism.

Kennedy promised in thoughtfully unspecific terms "to get this
country moving again." He was helped by Eisenhower's economists
who had chosen the election months to make a major drive for a
budget surplus and to affirm a tight money policy. In consequence,
farm prices were falling, unemployment was rising modestly and
Ike's advisers were showing that economists cannot be outdone even
by Cold Warriors in winning defeat for the politicians of their party.
Herbert Hoover, Gerald Ford and Jimmy Carter are their other
trophies.

On foreign policy Kennedy promised to close the missile gap,
which did not exist, and he affirmed his support for Cuban "fighters
for freedom," a damaging exercise in rhetoric which, when translated into action by the CIA a few months later, gave him the disaster at the Bay of Pigs. I was speaking at a rally in Brooklyn on the
late October evening when Kennedy's statement on Cuba appeared
in the headlines. It made me acutely uncomfortable, and more so
because my audience was sharply critical. There was another lesson
here, one that has yet to be fully learned. Because superpatriots
make far more noise than the calm people of peace and good sense,
they are assumed to be far more numerous and powerful than they

are in fact. So they are appeased. Only after defeat or at the brink of disaster (one prays not beyond) are they discovered to be the minority which, fortunately, they are.

Kennedy had not learned this lesson in 1960, but no leader ever learned more quickly from experience. The recklessness of the professional chauvinists became a recurring theme in his conversation. To this both their Bay of Pigs misadventure and their advice during the missile crisis contributed. In the late autumn of 1962, I was in Washington from India and went with the President and Jacqueline Kennedy to the National Theater.[11] To escape the autograph hunters — "Mr. President, I didn't vote for you, but I sure admire your stand on quite a few issues" — we went backstage during the intermission and sat on some stairs. He told me with much feeling and some anger of the recklessness of the professional advice he had received during the crisis just passed, in particular the proposal to bomb the missile sites. "I never had the slightest intention of doing so." The worst advice as always was from those who feared that to be sensible made them seem soft and unheroic.

*   *   *

The political rhetoric and maneuvers were soon over, and the election was won. It was not the excellence of the Kennedy effort but the weakness of Nixon's that served. Many of us thought Kennedy was better than his campaign, and on this we were right.

---

[11] I mention this evening in *Ambassador's Journal* (Boston: Houghton Mifflin, 1969), p. 520.

25

Diplomacy; Spooks

KENNEDY, I've always believed, was pleased to have me in his administration but at a suitable distance such as in India. This saved him from a too close identification with my now extensively articulated economic views. At his very first press conference in Los Angeles after his nomination he was asked if he and the Democratic Party could now be considered committed to the ideas in *The Affluent Society*. He evaded with skill and grace. A few days after the election he asked Arthur Schlesinger if I wanted to be Chairman of the Council of Economic Advisers. Schlesinger mentioned my interest in India. Kennedy, Arthur said afterward, seemed far from distressed.

On my side, I was little enchanted by the thought of doing with slight authority what I had done with vast power twenty years earlier. And equally I didn't wish to come every day to the same discussion of the same questions around the same oak table, mostly with the same people, not all of whom I much wished to see. Professors fresh from the relative squalor of academic offices are greatly attracted to Washington — to the leather chairs, expansive desks, thoughtfully wasted space, the framed presidential commissions and the other decor of high officialdom. I had had it before.

The White House, I also knew, is an excellent address but an occupationally unhealthy place to work. While it may not be safe to attack the President, it is always safe to impugn his subordinates. In consequence, the walking wounded from service in the Executive offices — Harry Vaughan, Sherman Adams, Walt Rostow, Bert Lance — would fill a small hospital or, as in the case of the Nixon men, a medium-sized minimum security jail. Given my exceptional visibility, there was little question as to who would become a lightning rod.[1]

[1] Immediately following the election Sargent Shriver, Arthur Schlesinger and I were made a committee to propose names for the economic posts in the administration —

My resistance was not, however, absolute. In December, while visiting Kennedy in Palm Beach, I agreed after a little persuasion to join the White House staff for the first months after the Inauguration. I took over Cordell Hull's old office in the onetime State, War and Navy Building, now the Executive Office Building, next door to the White House, and from there I served in support of Theodore Sorensen on the massive literary production, mostly messages to Congress, required or thought needed by a new administration. With some absences in Cambridge, I spent these weeks calling the black Mercury sedans to my service, eating in the White House mess and having my telephone calls returned with exemplary speed. It was pleasant. But I had no serious regrets when in April, after an investigation that sought out 106 informants, covered three decades of temptation and found nothing compellingly subversive, I was cleared by the FBI and the Senate and went off to India.

While I was ambassador, I kept a detailed journal with the intention of one day publishing it. This I did six years after leaving India[2] when I could no longer be accused of cashing in on my experience with the indecent haste that is now the norm. It is not my purpose to repeat what I there tell of the Kennedy era, and to ensure that I do not, my publisher is keeping *Ambassador's Journal* in print. In that volume I softened my views of some of my colleagues for reasons of compassion or tact. Some secret matters I omitted because of the feeling that I should abide by rules that I had promised to obey or, a more important matter, because an ambassador's responsibility for maintaining good relations with the people and officials of the country to which he is sent does not end on his leaving office. Also history rescues some actions from obscurity as it consigns others to oblivion. Thus our growing involvement in Vietnam by which I was then dis-

---

Treasury, Budget, Council of Economic Advisers and others. As Chairman of the Council Kennedy's first choice would, I believe, have been Paul Samuelson of the Massachusetts Institute of Technology, but Samuelson had always declined Washington service. With others I urged the name of Walter W. Heller, then a relatively unknown professor of economics at the University of Minnesota. So, no doubt more influentially, did Hubert Humphrey. I also urged another Minnesotan, Orville L. Freeman, for Secretary of Agriculture. In his autobiography (*Grassroots* [New York: Random House, 1977]) George McGovern mentions me as a partisan of his appointment to that post in preference to Freeman. At different stages, to the best of my recollection, I urged both.

[2] As mentioned earlier, *Ambassador's Journal* (Boston: Houghton Mifflin, 1969).

tressed but far from fully preoccupied has now a much greater stature. To the matters omitted from my day-to-day journal I now turn and, in the main, confine myself.

*   *   *

The job of an American ambassador is to maintain civil communication with the government to which he is accredited and, to the extent that personality allows, to personify the majesty and dignity of the United States. No one should suppose that this is either intellectually or physically taxing. It has long been a prime assumption of American politics that anyone, regardless of experience, education, political aptitude or knowledge of elementary English sentence structure, can be an American ambassador, and few such assumptions have been more thoroughly tested. The effects have not been uniformly happy, but the worst consequence has been little mentioned. That lies in the unfairness from having professional foreign service officers spend their lives working their way up the ladder and then, at the last, being denied the top post. Instead they end their career as a subordinate to a politically unbuttoned manufacturer of canned dog food, whose appointment may also rob the free enterprise system of a socially valuable entrepreneur.

In India during my time there were some fifty ambassadors, including the High Commissioners, as they are called, from the other Commonwealth countries. They were a spectacular example of what economists, following Joan Robinson of the University of Cambridge, call disguised unemployment. The ambassadors from Argentina or Brazil could not have had more than a day's serious work a month. The more deeply engaged diplomats from Scandinavia, Holland, Belgium or Spain could discharge their essential duties in one day a week. Others from some of the lesser Latin American or Levantine republics were more heavily engaged but in genteel operations in the black market — in particular, the importation under diplomatic cover of watches, gold, pharmaceuticals and other items of high value and small bulk, which were at a premium in India. Thus these envoys pieced out their inadequate official earnings.

All set much store by the routine of official entertainments as did my American colleagues. These festivities were said to build good will, and much useful information was held to be exchanged under

the impulse of food and alcohol. Good will that can thus be purchased has value, some parts of the press possibly apart, in keeping with the pay. During my years in India I never learned anything
at a cocktail party or dinner that I didn't already know, needed to
know or wouldn't soon have learned in the normal course of business. The emphasis that diplomats of all countries in all capitals accord to entertaining is the result of a conspiracy by which function
is found in pleasant social intercourse and controlled inebriation.

*   *   *

One of my urgent instructions on going to India was to spend as
much time as possible in travel.[3] This it was thought would put me
immediately in touch with the country and its people. Though it was
unclear as to whom or how the resulting benefit would accrue, it
would be great. With few instructions in my life have I so happily
complied. I was to see the infinitely varied landscape, urban areas
and culture of India, and it was a duty. Nor was this all. A brief and
easy negotiation with Robert McNamara, by then Secretary of Defense, during which I emphasized the great size of India, brought
my air attaché a handsome Convair to facilitate my movement. This
success also brought a rebuke from Kennedy, who thought my airplane would be attributed to our friendship and that all other ambassadors would wish to be similarly equipped. He professed to be
relieved when I proposed that Convairs be confined by general rule
to ambassadors to countries with a population of 400 million or
more.

It was necessary to make speeches as one traveled, but more easily
than I had expected, I learned that these could combine modest
grace with no content. Our travel did enhance the standing of local
politicians whom we visited and by whom we were displayed; unfortunately, this worked equally for the good ones and the bad. It also
added greatly to my knowledge of Indian architecture, agriculture,
geography and history but contributed little on questions of importance to Washington; such things are learned all but exclusively in

[3] ". . . [M]odern diplomacy requires a close understanding not only of governments
but of people . . . Therefore, I hope that you will plan your work so that you may
have time to travel extensively outside the nation's capital." President Kennedy to
Chiefs of Mission, May 29, 1961.

the capital. I saw people, but of the 440 million then in India, I saw only an infinitesimal fraction, and the benefits from so seeing (or from being seen) are deeply questionable. All this I came only reluctantly to admit. So compelling is a phrase about "getting out among the people" that even now it seems shameful to confess how little is thus achieved.

In New Delhi I concentrated diligently on those matters that I could do better than members of my staff — seeing Nehru (who doubled as Minister for External Affairs) and other senior government officials, responding to the occasional telegram that could be rendered into intelligible English and which raised a serious policy issue, making those social appearances at which only the Ambassador would serve. I sought to avoid administrative duties ranging from problems of personnel selection to crises in the sex lives of the Marine contingent and supervision of routine diplomatic, consular and reporting activities for which others were more qualified. The necessary tasks, I soon discovered, could be accomplished in around two hours of official work a day. Any more time involved ill-concealed idleness. I devoted the further hours to writing, reading and the study of Indian art. During these years I wrote a number of books, some of which I've already mentioned: a memoir on the Scottish community of my boyhood in southern Ontario,[4] a book on economic development derived from speeches on the subject, which I have always counseled those who have inquired to avoid;[5] my first experiment with fiction, *The McLandress Dimension*, published under the name of Mark Epernay;[6] and the daily diary that became *Ambassador's Journal*. Also, with M. S. Randhawa, I began the book on Indian painting of the sixteenth to eighteenth centuries that I've already described.[7] This should be proof that my ambassadorial duties did not totally engage me. However, in the press, among Indians and in Washington I acquired, with very little fraud, a reputation for exceptional diplomatic diligence.

On the other hand, as for those flying an airplane or guarding a

[4] *The Scotch* (Boston: Houghton Mifflin, 1964).
[5] *Economic Development* (Cambridge: Harvard University Press, 1962).
[6] Boston: Houghton Mifflin, 1963.
[7] *Indian Painting: The Scene, Themes and Legends* (Boston: Houghton Mifflin, 1968). See Chapter 21.

bank, there are for an ambassador moments of intense action. The first of these involved not the Indian government but the CIA.

*   *   *

On March 27, 1961, shortly before departing for India, I had lunch at the Metropolitan Club in Washington with G. Lewis Jones, a foreign service officer of conservative temperament, then the Assistant Secretary of State for Near East and South Asian Affairs. He told me that he considered past or intended CIA activities in India a blot on the democratic processes we praised and affirmed. He urged me to inform myself and bring them to an end. Lewis Jones was a good man.

Two mornings later I had a briefing on intelligence operations in India by the CIA. Richard M. Bissell, Jr., joined it and showed me a paper with the proposed budget for the coming year. Bissell was an economist of ability and intelligence and an early Keynesian, who, in the New Deal days, had held himself aloof from the political enthusiasms of the time. Keynes was one thing; liberal politics was something else. In consequence, his professional competence, combined with his inner conservatism, made him highly acceptable to the businessmen who were associated in later years with the Marshall Plan, and he was a particularly influential figure in its management and success. He went on to join Allen Dulles in the belief that Communism anywhere called for an automatic and often unthinking response and that a system so evil allowed of indecency in return.

Bissell that morning must have been taking time off from the final stages of the planning of the Bay of Pigs operation, if anything that anarchic could be said to have been planned. He was Deputy Director of the CIA for Plans, this being the euphemism for clandestine operations or what, optimistically, were assumed so to remain.

Bissell's list both appalled and depressed me. In one sense, as I then noted, what was proposed was unimportant; it wouldn't change anything. Indian politics has its own uncontrollable dynamic; as such, it proceeds independent of any possible external influence. Nothing could be less related to result than any effort of the CIA. But the certainty of disclosure of the enterprises being proposed and the consequent effect on our relations with the Indian government (and the effect also on myself as the American ambassador) could be very damaging. Since many Indians would be involved and subject to the changing pressures of politics and conscience, such disclosure was inevitable. A large sum, well into the millions, was to be made available to help non-Communist candidates in the elections twelve months hence. Smaller amounts were to be set aside to subsidize newspapers and a few key politicians and to sustain a magazine on public affairs of adequately anti-Communist temper. That night I wrote in my journal that I had been briefed "on various spooky activities, some of which I do not like. I shall stop them."[8] It was an optimism I did not at all feel; journals can be used, when all else fails, for personal reassurance.

A day or so later — almost my last in Washington — I learned from Chester Bowles of the intended operation against Cuba. I reflected morbidly on the activities with which I was becoming involved. I was unhappy for the country; I was even more unhappy, alas, for myself. I was accepting what I was meant to oppose; one day I would have to answer. But as have thousands before and many more since, I told myself that by keeping the job I might make a difference. Like most so persuaded, it was really that I now wanted to be ambassador. On Cuba I wrote a letter to the President urging the costs of what I called our past military and political "adventurism," as when MacArthur went to the Yalu River, the U-2 destroyed the Paris Summit or when, as in Guatemala, seeming success was at grave cost to our reputation elsewhere in Latin America. The letter was less to persuade the President than to appease my conscience.

I was especially disturbed by one particularly insane enterprise. Long flights were being made by the CIA from the neighborhood of Bangkok over India to the northern border of Nepal. There the planes dropped weapons, ammunition and other supplies for dissident and deeply unhygienic tribesmen who had once roamed over the neighboring Tibetan countryside and who now relieved boredom with raids back into the territory from which they had been extruded. This military action was thought to cause great distress in Peking or, as Dean Rusk still insisted, Peiping.[9] But the tribesmen had achieved the standing of a faithful ally; to a faithful ally, in

---

[8] *Ambassador's Journal*, p. 51.

[9] Once they did hold up a Chinese truck convoy and returned with what was held to be important military information on Chinese troop dispositions.

the ethic of the time, we had to be faithful regardless of the cost.

On arriving in New Delhi in April, I began a full investigation of CIA operations. I was not troubled by an open mind. I was convinced that most of the projects proposed would be useless for their own anti-Communist purposes and were capable, when known, of doing us great damage as well. The local CIA station chief, an intelligent former history teacher named Harry A. Rositzke[10], was not strong in their defense. Neither he nor others were disappointed to learn of my opposition.

Accordingly, in May 1961, I returned to Washington with the purpose of bringing all clandestine operations in India of all kinds to an end. No subsidies to parties, politicians or papers; no other unnecessary undercover activities. Only the normal reporting that is conducted with indifferent accuracy by all major states would remain.[11] I wrote a memorandum detailing my objections and circulated it to those I hoped would agree. And I took it, along with my stronger oral objections, to Kennedy, Robert Kennedy and McGeorge Bundy, who was now the President's Special Assistant for National Security. My major defense so prepared, I then tackled Richard Bissell, other senior-level CIA officials and finally Allen Dulles. In letting it be known that I had carried the matter to the White House, I encouraged the impression that the President had been sympathetic, as generally he was. They knew in any case that Kennedy had heard, without countering argument, that the operations were insane.

I was prepared for a sharp struggle; in fact, it was far easier than I could have hoped. My timing, if accidental, was superb. The Bay of Pigs fiasco had left the once dangerously confident architects of clandestine operations in a severely chastened mood. Dulles, when I approached him, was almost exclusively concerned with learning to whom my memorandum had gone so he could get the copies back. They were evidence against his administration; on some matters he was more acute than on others. One of Dulles's senior subordinates did tell me, at first angrily, then tearfully, that I was turning India over to the Communists. I thought to reply that given the individu-

---

[10] Author of the lucid and interesting *The CIA's Secret Operations*, on his CIA years (New York: Reader's Digest Press, 1977).

[11] This would also be subject to what, in those years, I called Galbraith's First Law of Intelligence: "You cannot know the intentions of a government that doesn't know them itself."

alist, not to say sometimes anarchic, tendencies of the Indian left, no one could wish Communism such a misfortune. I refrained, but it was a thought that would serve me well in the autumn of 1962 during the border war between China and India.

All *sub rosa* operations, with the exception of the overflights to Nepal, were scratched. Later, with the help of Robert Kennedy, I persuaded the President to bring these to an end.[12] In the years since I left India, there have been repeated explosions in the Indian press and Parliament over CIA intervention in Indian politics. None has seriously concerned activities during or subsequent to my service. Had the Dulles/Bissell proposals proceeded, they would have become known, and the Indian reaction would have been fierce. And the effect on our relations with India would have been poisonous. As a less important matter, except to me, I would have been deeply implicated. Aborting these activities was perhaps my single most useful service that spring.

Nor, needless to say, did Indian Communism flourish in consequence. In 1962, the Congress Party under Jawaharlal Nehru won a sweeping victory. Indian Communists, as the years passed, split into pro-Soviet, pro-Chinese and pro-Indian parties, with various fringes that considered all of the above too moderate. Given two Indian Communists, there is a certain likelihood that there will be two Communist parties. Communist governments have come to power in West Bengal and Kerala; there they have shown that the problem of too many people, too little land, too little industry and the resulting equilibrium of poverty is as intractable for Communists as for everyone else. In India as elsewhere in the poor lands there is no revolutionary salvation. Were it so, Communism would have triumphed long ago.

Back in Washington in the autumn of 1961, I encountered Richard Bissell one day at the Hay-Adams Hotel. He said he was leaving the government. The President had told him that after the Bay of Pigs any future mishaps would inevitably be blamed on him. He would be safer out. It was sad. A man of quietly courteous manner

[12] This case I made while the President was nursing his back with hot water in the bathtub, turning on the tap with his foot. Bob Kennedy joined us, and one of his sons, then around eight, listened to these deeply secret matters with obvious interest. It is quite possible, even likely, that others had made similar recommendations by then.

with a deeply intelligent face, his service as a principal architect and guide of the Marshall Plan had earned him the admiration of all so involved. As Dulles was in a post far above his intelligence, Bissell had involved himself in enterprises far below his worth. I have not, to my regret, seen him since.

26

The State Department, Jawaharlal Nehru and India

THE CANONS of bureaucratic achievement — how one moves in an organization and moves an organization — have been much discussed. I gave them a great deal of thought during the intense days of World War II; in the Kennedy years I found myself rediscovering them for the far lighter tasks of an ambassador.[1] I would suggest eight rules in all:

(1) Either have the President behind you or cultivate that impression in the greatest circumspect measure. By the same token, never suppose that you can fight the White House; if you are at odds, you must admit defeat and, if the issue requires it, resign.

(2) Use the press in a wholly forthright way. The official with good access to the press is respected, perhaps even feared. The one without such access, who avoids reporters and who is without voice on his own behalf, confesses to an insecurity or diffidence that others are invited to exploit. The man who relies on surreptitious leaks similarly admits to a lack of effectiveness. He must also spend much time covering his tracks and can be defeated not by judging the merits of his case but by exposure of his activity. Most bureaucratic leaks proceed not from strength but from weakness.

(3) Make your views widely and persuasively known through the relevant part of the government by means of the printed word. The modern bureaucracy is very large; one can see only a few people for direct persuasion. But there is no limit to the number of people who

---

[1] By 1961, the intensity of bureaucratic warfare had also, I thought, much mellowed since the time of the New Deal. Then one fought without mercy to win; if you lost, as I did in 1943, you were out. By the 1960s, all was more amenable and refined. I was amazed to discover how dangerous one could seem when playing by the old rules.

can be reached by a well-argued paper. And if it is readable, since reading is the principal occupation of bureaucrats, it will be read.

(4) Given the choice between keeping the confidence of your friends and appeasing your enemies, never hesitate. It is your friends who give you power. You can overcome opposition, but you cannot do it without allies.

(5) Anger and indignation may usefully be simulated but should never be real. They impair judgment.

(6) On foreign policy, as on economic policy, the essence of wisdom lies in not being too sure — no one can foresee for certain the outcome of a particular line of action. Nevertheless for bureaucratic success one must cultivate an outward air of assurance. Others who are themselves uncertain will make your confidence a substitute for their own doubts. If you lack assurance, they will substitute theirs.

(7) Adopt, where appropriate, a modest aspect of menace. Many public officials will go against their convictions to avoid a fight. And some are conveniently lacking in convictions.

(8) If at all possible, be mentally accommodated to catching the plane out of Washington on any given morning. Nothing so weakens the position of a senior public official as the knowledge that he so loves or is otherwise so committed to his job that he will always, in the end, come to terms.

*			*			*

In India I made agreeable use of these several procedures. Given my past association with J.F.K., I sought always to give the impression in the State Department that I was in close and constant touch with the Oval Office. I enhanced this feeling with frequent letters to the President, which I made interesting or vulgar enough to ensure his attention. His reference to them in conversation then made my access known.

The American press corps in New Delhi was always short of news with what its members inventively called an American angle. Two reporters in particular — Selig S. Harrison of the *Washington Post* and Philip Potter of the *Baltimore Sun* papers — could be counted on to get one's thoughts to Washington and the White House rather more rapidly and influentially than did the official communications. But the departmental telegrams, which are circulated in the hundreds and beyond the State Department to the White House, the

Pentagon and the CIA, are a superb avenue for personal persuasion. As with my letters to the President, I worked hard to make the important ones interesting or, on occasion, indecent or insulting, for I wanted to be sure they were read. I still encounter retired admirals who tell me of their pleasure in finding one of my cables in the morning mail.

In late 1961, I conducted a modest campaign by telegram against the Department's continued and undeviating support of the government of Premier Antonio de Oliveira Salazar of Portugal with our associated and obsolete commitment to colonial rule in Africa and India. I noted, among other exaggerations, that we were exchanging our whole position in that part of the world for a few acres of asphalt in the Azores. Dean Rusk asked McGeorge Bundy to ask the President to curb this use of telegrams to propagate my views. Kennedy sharply refused. Unlike the rest of his official literature, he said, my communications lightened even if they did not inform his day.[2] The ability to write so as to command attention is one of the most valuable of bureaucratic weapons.

Comment on my use of the other principles of bureaucratic achievement or aggression requires a word on the people at whom they were directed.

* * *

The Assistant Secretary of State for Near East and South Asian Affairs, my immediate point of contact in the State Department in those years, was Phillips Talbot, successor to the principled Lewis Jones of whom I have earlier told. Talbot was recruited to his post by Chester Bowles with my initial and rather hasty approval. He was a participant in the New York foreign policy guild, a scholarly convocation whose members, supported by charitable foundations, make their careers in the study or discussion of foreign policy and the promotion of international understanding or its converse. The requirements for admission are varied but depend above all on an instinct for the currently fashionable cliché. Talbot, then forty-six, was a man of slightly more than average height, adequate bulk, full face and strikingly soft, almost malleable complexion. He had headed, with evident adequacy, an organization called the American

---

[2] I learned of her husband's response from Jacqueline Kennedy, who happened to be present.

University Field Staff, which promoted international comity by stationing representatives of the American academic community in diverse foreign lands. On arriving in Washington, he moved comfortably into alliance with the surviving acolytes of the Dulles brothers. It was their belief that policy in the poor lands might include some compassionate help. But this would be subordinate to our system of military alliances with the indigent. However irrelevant Communism might be in an impoverished agricultural village, whatever the difficulty in telling a Communist from an anti-Communist jungle, anti-Communism was the ultimate basis of all policy. These were attitudes that many of us had hoped to change. It was disconcerting to discover that we had recruited a believer.

Presently, however, I learned that there was much to be said for Talbot. His delight in his unexpected emergence in the mainstream, as distinct from the philanthropic periphery, of foreign affairs was extreme. So also was his desire to avoid controversy. Thus by assuming a sufficiently menacing stance in accordance with rule seven above, I found I could get my way on all important matters. An aspect of extreme assurance also helped. In August 1961, after a meeting in New Delhi, I noted in my diary: "In the afternoon, Talbot held forth on the harmony in Washington, the many studies of foreign policy under way, and committed himself to nothing. He will, I think, always be controlled by the most disagreeable person around him. Perhaps I can qualify."[3] I still think of Talbot with gratitude, though not wholly with affection.[4]

*   *   *

An altogether more formidable and interesting figure was Dean Rusk, in many ways the epitome of the public organization man. In 1961 he was fifty-two, of pleasantly unathletic aspect, with a graceful trace of the South still in his speech; he was uniformly courteous and agreeable in personal manner and unwavering in his commitment to his own view of the public interest.

Dean Rusk also gave one the impression, even after a relaxing

[3] *Ambassador's Journal* (Boston: Houghton Mifflin, 1969), p. 183.
[4] In later years Talbot's adaptability stood him in good stead. He became ambassador to Greece and had to accommodate to the colonels when they seized power in 1967. Appealing to him for help, Mrs. Helen Vlachos, the brilliantly independent (and conservative) Greek newspaperwoman, was told she would do better seeking the protection of a smaller embassy. We could not give offense.

drink to which he was far from averse, of being relentlessly on guard. He heard views contrary to his own with patience and, one soon discovered, with no thought of changing his mind. His public faith called for perfect loyalty to the President whom currently he served. Of much of what he heard from Kennedy and more of what he heard from Bundy, Schlesinger, Richard Goodwin or the White House staff he disapproved. He did not resist or often debate. But neither did he change his mind.

On Dean Rusk far stronger influences[5] had come to bear to shape a far stronger character than in the case of the passive Talbot. From a secondary academic position in California as associate professor of government and dean of faculty at the small but reputable Mills College in Oakland, he had gone on to major staff responsibilities in the China-Burma-India theater in World War II. This transition from slight civilian to major military tasks left him with a deep respect for military men, their judgment of other men, their devotion to country and their ability to turn from words to action. After considering a military career at which, unquestionably, he would have excelled, he moved in 1946 to the State Department to deal with United Nations matters. From this he went on to become Assistant Secretary for Far Eastern Affairs with responsibility after 1950 for day-to-day political policy on the Korean War. This conflict, then assumed to be a surrogate enterprise of the Kremlin, gave Rusk a lasting commitment to the unity and comprehensiveness of the Communist design for world rule and the role of military force as the answer. So did another, less remarked influence. Like Richard Bissell, many senior State Department foreign service officers influential in the fifties and various key CIA figures, Rusk's general conservatism had protected him from McCarthy and the loyalty investigation traumas to which many liberals had been subject. This accorded him flank protection on the right and a marked assurance in personal manner and position. His views had been above attack in the fifties. So they were now.

[5] Much has been made of Rusk's staunch religious upbringing and his consequent susceptibility to deep moral judgments and canonical belief. Thus he was held to be the close counterpart of John Foster Dulles, both products of an early and inflexible Presbyterianism. This is pretentious nonsense. Rusk was governed by principle, however unwise or inconvenient. Dulles's commitment, on the other hand, was to whatever served his current need, interest or convenience; he was devious in accomplished degree. And no one ever suggested that his brother Allen, who came from the same religious background, was subject to any kind of moral imperative.

Dean Rusk had become Secretary of State because of a common
tendency in public affairs. We know the faults of friends; others,
whose faults are unknown, are assumed to be of purer stripe.
Though William Fulbright was the most plausible choice, both the
President-elect and Robert Kennedy knew him well, and they felt
that he was too closely tied to the white supremacy syndrome, which
had served his Senate survival. What would the emerging African
nations say? Kennedy was also well acquainted with Stevenson, another obvious choice. But, as I've noted, Kennedy was not comfortable with Stevenson's political style, and he knew that Stevenson had
an exceptionally loyal constituency of his own. Perhaps, aware of this
support, maybe appealing to it, Stevenson would be unduly independent. Kennedy also knew Chester Bowles; he thought him somewhat
romantic as regards the poor lands and unduly articulate. Because
he didn't know Dean Rusk, he didn't suppose him to have any drawbacks.

However, Rusk's drawbacks were, in fact, great. His excessive respect for military men and military power made him dangerously
sanguine about military accomplishment. And he had a strongly di-
chotomous view of the world. On the one hand, the free nations; on
the other, the comprehensively united Communists. China was not
a separate entity; it was, he averred, "a Soviet Manchukuo" without
any of the effective attributes of sovereignty. On this as on other
matters Rusk was not responsive to contrary argument or information. When, with the passage of time, the rifts began to appear between the Chinese and the Soviet Union, Rusk was unperturbed. He
merely adjusted the facts to his faith. Were the Communist states
divided, he insisted, it was only over how best to destroy the free
world.

*   *   *

Unlike Talbot, Rusk could be neither cowed nor ignored. In my
early months in India I made the mistake of contesting with him
head-on. In August 1961, anticipating the autumn meeting of the
U.N. General Assembly, ambassadors were instructed to go to the
governments to which they were accredited with a new design for
keeping the Chinese out of the United Nations. Since we could no
longer muster a majority to this end, we would have it voted an

Important Question. By this legerdemain, admission would require a two-thirds majority. A lengthy telegram told in tedious detail how this fraud was to be explained to the Indians. I regarded the effort with distaste. There was no chance of persuading Nehru, for the Indian government was then sponsoring the admission of the Chinese. Also Senate opposition to my confirmation as ambassador had turned on the belief that I favored the inclusion of the Chinese in the U.N. I couldn't have the adverse senators believe they had acted in vain. I kept the instructions on my desk for a day or two. Presently a telegram for the State Department came through New Delhi from my neighboring ambassador in Nepal, Henry E. Stebbins. Commenting on the tortured persuasion required, he noted that the only member of the Royal Nepalese government capable of following such illogic was currently in Calcutta having his teeth fixed. Stebbins was a career foreign service officer. Political ambassadors are the ones who are meant to take risks. I enlisted the help of our ambassador in Ceylon, Frances E. Willis, and produced a thoughtful case for reconciling ourselves to the inevitable. Let us, subject to protecting the position of Taiwan and some possible revision of the membership of the Security Council, accept the will of the majority. A cable came back from Rusk, composed, I later learned, by the Secretary himself: "To the extent that your position has any merit it has been fully considered and rejected."

I was similarly defeated when I said that we were no longer concerned with collecting military allies among the poor lands and that, accordingly, the Indians need not see in our friendship a cover for some military design. Rusk wired me sternly that the military alliances that he cherished were still our policy. In fact, they were not, but no one had yet disavowed them. On this I was redeemed by events. In the autumn of 1962, during the border conflict with China, the Indian government reacted in panic one night to bad reverses in the eastern Himalayas, and our military support was urgently sought. Washington was anything but happy about having a new and exceptionally expensive military ally. My restatement of my earlier heresy was much welcomed.

I didn't make the mistake of confronting Rusk again. Where possible I bypassed him, and numerous enterprises that seemed important to me were too small to achieve his attention. This was true in the early days of the efforts against our Vietnam involvement. On this, as on other matters, I could go direct to the White House. Thus Rusk could be survived.

Unchanging beliefs in a changing world are, however, dangerous. So is great certainty of moral purpose in pursuit of less than moral ends. By 1963, Kennedy had become disenchanted with Rusk; his character notwithstanding or because of it, he would have to go. On the last occasion that I saw Kennedy at leisure — it was on a Saturday afternoon cruise on the *Honey Fitz* off Hyannis Port on August 3, 1963 [6] — he told me that after the election he would replace the Secretary of State. He talked of the successor. "McNamara would be all right. But then if I don't have McNamara at Defense to control the generals, I won't have a foreign policy."

Kennedy's death was Rusk's special tragedy. With Johnson he came into his own. His military orientation and his commitment to a unified Communist crusade put him strongly in support of the Vietnam war. Lyndon Johnson, coming fresh to these seemingly complex and subjective issues, relied on him and was left, in consequence, without a civilian counterweight to the military mind and mystique. The result was a painful end to the public careers of both men. [7]

*   *   *

There is, as I've urged, much to be said in government for purely negative accomplishments. Thus in denying our restless spooks their opportunity in India, I excluded the inevitable later explosion. This would have been painful. We do not experience and thus we have no measure of the disasters we prevent. But in going to India, I had more affirmative ends in mind. The first was to cement a close friendship, based so far as possible on deserved respect and confi-

[6] This was the day Philip L. Graham, the talented, charming and deeply troubled publisher of the *Washington Post,* killed himself. He was a close friend of the President's and a long-time acquaintance of mine. Word of his death came to the boat by radio while we were talking.

[7] I wrote in those days, "The appearance of the State Department as a full-scale participant in the military power may have been the hopefully temporary achievement of Secretary Rusk. Apart from a high respect for military acumen and need, he in some degree regarded diplomacy as a subordinate to military purpose." *How to Control the Military* (New York: Doubleday, 1969), p. 24. The incorrect usage of "hopefully" is inexcusable.

dence, with Jawaharlal Nehru. The second was to make it clear to Nehru, the Indian press, the Indian intellectual community and as many other Indians as might spare time for the subject that the United States had something more interesting to offer than the parochial and endlessly reiterated anti-Communism of the Dulles era. I would show that it was my good fortune to represent a diverse, innovative and compassionate community which had a certain confidence in its achievements, which did not believe, numerous generals, ideologues and idolators apart, that the struggle against Communism was the only reality. We sought friendship with other countries for its own sake. We were not opposed to neutralism or nonalignment. That was India's decision, not ours. Kennedy in an amused moment had once said to me, "Find out from Nehru how this nonalignment works. I think I would like it." I was determined, finally, to direct our large economic assistance effort, now greatly increased by the new administration, so that it would have maximum effect.

In the event, I found myself engaged on a further task that I far from foresaw. That was the management of affairs with as little American involvement and Indian humiliation as possible during the war between India and China in 1962. It was a small war but the one in which I was to have an important, possibly even decisive, role. My reflections on this intense and illuminating experience are in the next chapter.

* * *

Friendship with Nehru came easily. My previous visits and my books had paved the way.[8] Brought together now in line of duty, our relations remained informal and infinitely agreeable. I looked forward to any call, whatever the business. So, I think, did he.

Nehru, then approaching seventy-two, was solidly in command of party and Parliament and without rival on the political scene. Sadashiv Kanoji Patil, his Minister for Food and Agriculture, a former mayor of Bombay and a quintessential politician who in the last century would have moved easily into authority in Boston, had been asked in an interview in London who would be Nehru's successor. He had replied with characteristic Indian intonation and emphasis,

[8] In addition to *The Affluent Society* another, the collection of essays called *The Liberal Hour* (Boston: Houghton Mifflin, 1960), had by now made its way to India.

"Who can say? The Prime Minister is like the great banyan tree. Thousands shelter beneath it, but nothing grows."[9] Nehru reacted angrily to this metaphor, partly because of its truth, and treated Patil to a special silence for some months.

Age notwithstanding, Nehru retained a prodigious capacity for work; it was his pride that no important paper remained untended on his desk overnight. But, withal, he was a lonesome man. His wife had been dead for many years. Many of his parliamentary and cabinet colleagues and fellow politicians bored him, as did most diplomats. In one respect he was curiously like Kennedy: political posturing, diplomatic pretense, rearticulation of the approved truths about freedom, democracy, economic progress, all these he had heard too often before. Encountering them again, and especially from someone who thought himself original, clever or profound, his eyes glazed and it was plain that his mind wandered. I came positively to dread the American visitor who had thoughts on the need for unity in the free world or for individual enterprise in economic development.

In the nostalgia of age Nehru's mind turned not to Gandhi and the struggle for independence; it reverted to his yet earlier experiences when, in England, he had been with or near men and women of compelling interest — the world, as I have told, of R. H. Tawney, the Webbs and of Trinity College and Cambridge. Once he said of himself that he would be the "last Englishman to rule in India." On another occasion I asked him if he had seen in a just-published volume of Churchill's memoirs a wartime minute demanding to know the prison conditions under which Gandhi and Nehru were being kept and reminding the recipient that it would one day be necessary to do business with them. Nehru hadn't seen it but said that he had always expected good treatment from Churchill: "We were both at Harrow." In another, lighter moment in 1961 in Washington after encountering Rusk and Fulbright, both Rhodes scholars, he wondered if there weren't an undue number of Oxford men in positions of power. He professed relief when I reminded him that the key posts in the world — Indian Prime Minister, U.S. Ambassador to India — were held by Cambridge men.

History in its great sweep had carried Nehru far away from the

[9] *Ambassador's Journal*, p. 175.

world of his youth. I knew it at first hand — knew Harold Laski, G. D. H. Cole, Hugh Dalton, John Strachey. So I was an avenue back, a better one, on balance, than the career men of the British High Commission. A late-afternoon invitation to call on the Prime Minister always meant some business, but this then gave way to general and reminiscent conversation.

Nehru was also greatly interested by John F. Kennedy, although he believed the President to be alarmingly young and inexperienced. Before Kennedy's Summit meeting with Khrushchev in Vienna in 1961, he asked me to warn the President of Khrushchev's tendency to unguarded and violent responses. These would be disturbing to the President but less so if he realized that they would also be disturbing to Khrushchev when he later had occasion to reflect on them. Nehru "told me to tell the President to have in mind that Khrushchev is a man of exceedingly fast responses. When Khrushchev first visited India, he confided to Nehru his feeling that he must improve British and U.S. attitudes toward the Soviets — in effect, clean up the image left by Stalin, although Nehru did not put it in these words. Then Khrushchev went to Burma. Reacting angrily to a question, he denounced British imperialism and all its filthy works. Back in Delhi, Nehru asked him if this were a wise way to make friends. Khrushchev replied, 'We react that way. We were surrounded and subject to siege for forty years.' "[10]

We talked also of books, and I kept Nehru supplied with ones I thought he would like, for I had arranged with various publishers to send me volumes of major current interest. The selection was far from enchanting, but Nehru thought my inadequate but still superior access a unique blessing. Once I gave him Edwin O'Connor's *The Last Hurrah*, the ultimate document on the folk rites and politics of the Boston Irish. He was enchanted. Thereafter, when leaving New Delhi with the prospect of time to spare, he would call to ask for something else as good.

More than books he liked handsome, intelligent and entertaining women. Barbara Ward Jackson, the author and economist; Angie Dickinson, the film actress; and members of the Robert Joffrey Ballet who danced for him at the new American Embassy Residence designed by Edward Durrell Stone all added greatly to my access

[10] *Ambassador's Journal*, pp. 127–128.

and reputation. So did my wife, whose beauty and resistance to any
form of political dissimulation Nehru greatly admired.

*   *   *

Since World War II, the visit by a head of state to his counterpart in
another capital has become our most relished form of international
intercourse. It wins an impressive if depressingly repetitive press
coverage, but its purpose is only slightly understood.

Such visits are not to do business; the principals are rarely in command of the detail that any genuine negotiation requires. Also — a
further handicap to any achievement — both disagreement and
agreement must be avoided. Disagreement signifies failure and reflects badly on the participants; agreement, as distinct from mere
ratification, is too dangerous. As noted, one or both of the principals
are certain to be insufficiently informed; a contract agreed to at their
level cannot easily be undone. State visits are almost entirely a pleasurable perquisite of high office. They are greatly enjoyed by those
making them and, on frequent occasion, evoke a display of enthusiasm and affection in the country visited that the visitor knows he will
never achieve or deserve at home.

New Delhi, next only to Washington, London and perhaps Paris,
was the best place to observe these ceremonials. The Indian scene
and tradition lend themselves well to pageantry; having no alternative occupation, thousands of Indians can be counted upon to turn
out for a visitor, although on occasion for the head of a very minor
principality a small subsidy had to be paid to those bringing bullock
carts to line the route. In my years the state visits averaged around
one every fortnight in the season of tolerable weather.[11]

[11] In Washington the dean of the diplomatic corps traditionally goes to the airport
to welcome an arriving ruler on behalf of all his diplomatic colleagues. In Delhi all
ambassadors mounted their cars, unfurled the national flag on the front fenders and
rode out to Palam, for it helped fill the day.

At the airport seats in order of precedence were arranged under a tent. Once,
through an error, there was no chair for the Argentine Ambassador who arrived late.
A short, chunky man with very short legs, he nonetheless managed a considerable
dignity. He said, "There is no seat for the Argentine Ambassador. I am insulted. My
government is insulted. I will leave. But I am a practical man so I will stay."

I initiated the practice of sending my deputy or another officer, along with a well-
phrased letter to the arriving potentate explaining the inescapable character of my
duties that day. It seemed to me in keeping with the dignity of the United States that
its Ambassador should seem to be deeply engaged. I could then read or write. Eventually my default became known in Washington and was the subject of analysis. The
result was a thoughtful telegram stressing the special importance of my being on

Yet to all generalizations, as always, there are exceptions. One visit during these years — that by Jacqueline Kennedy — if it did little for international understanding, did much to strengthen my association with Nehru.

Jacqueline Kennedy concerned herself excessively with dress and related artifacts of style. These only slightly enhanced her beauty; and they served if anything to disguise an alert and penetrating intelligence. She had always a sharper view than her husband of the people around the presidency, and while Kennedy leaned to charity, she leaned to truth. Her characterizations could be brief and devastating. The Chairman of the Joint Chiefs of Staff when the new administration came to power was General Lyman L. Lemnitzer, later described by Schlesinger as an "amiable" man.[12] Lem, as he was known, was a soldier of solid build, square, impressive face and good carriage. "We all thought well of him until he made the mistake," J.B.K. once said, "of coming into the White House one Saturday morning in a sport jacket."

When Mrs. Kennedy came to New Delhi in March of 1962, Nehru went to the airport to greet her and, at the earliest opportunity, moved her from the quarters we had contrived to his own house.[13] There she (and her sister) occupied the apartment once inhabited by Edwina Mountbatten, wife of Lord Louis Mountbatten, the last Viceroy of India, and a very great Nehru favorite. Nehru did not fail to tell of the earlier tenant, and he devoted himself fully to his guests' instruction and enjoyment. As the resident expert, I was commissioned to buy an eighteenth-century miniature to be presented to her by the Prime Minister. On her departure, Nehru reported favorably to Parliament on her passage. For the rest of my tour my access to him, already good, was fully affirmed. This visit, seen by the press as a far from solemn event, was the only one from which I derived visible benefit.

*   *   *

hand for the next visit, which was by Prince Norodom Sihanouk of Cambodia. I went and greeted the Prince warmly. He looked at me with suspicion. A little later I went in the early hours of a morning to meet my wife who was returning from a trip home. I had made a mistake on her flight; she was not aboard, but on it, instead, was the Prime Minister of Barbados. I greeted him enthusiastically and had thereafter a special reputation for diligent attention to protocol.

[12] Arthur M. Schlesinger, Jr., *A Thousand Days* (Boston: Houghton Mifflin, 1965), p. 200.

[13] In imperial times the spacious dwelling of the Commander-in-Chief.

Jawaharlal Nehru, as I have told, did not like economics. He had been taught that given a sufficient depth of socialist faith, economic success would result. So, following the frequent custom of American Presidents when beset by economic problems, he took refuge in international affairs.

His method of disposing of both unwanted ideas and unwelcome requests was effective — and deeply disconcerting. It was, simply, to remain totally silent. You urged some economic action or petitioned him for some acquiescent position on Pakistan or in the United Nations. He did not oppose; instead he said nothing. When the silence became unbearable, you repeated your thought or request and now heard your own words with despair. There would be further silence. You now yearned to hear him say no. When eventually he did, you gratefully escaped.

                    *   *   *

By 1961, Nehru was losing some of the political resiliency of his earlier years, and this was fully evident in the autumn of 1962 during the border war with China. The adjustment then required was very great. Nothing in life had prepared him for military decisions; he believed that a modern civilized statesman could remain above such barbarism. And especially he believed that his India could remain apart from the differences and the tension between the Communist and the non-Communist worlds. He could be the arbiter above the battle; on this his unique prestige in international affairs depended. So to some extent did mine, for it was because Nehru was important that being ambassador to India was thought significant.

The conflict with China destroyed this higher role for Nehru — literally within hours. He must have seen the pleasure that this brought to committed chauvinists the world around.

In 1963, as my time in India was coming to an end, I spent a day with the Prime Minister touring in the Punjab. People lined the streets of the villages and packed the halls to see and hear him. He seemed tired, and when he had occasion to speak, he said little — a gesture, a few words of greeting, his accustomed reminder that India was governed for the governed. But he did tell the principal audience of the day how much he liked having me in New Delhi, how much he would miss me, how faithfully, in his view, I had tried to help their country. It was music of the highest order. Perhaps I had gone beyond bureaucratic design to friendship itself; I hoped so. A year after I left India, he died. It was a moment of much sadness but not of great surprise. From the psychic wounds from that unnecessary war in the Himalayas, he never quite recovered. He once said to me of Lyndon Johnson, "He is the kind of politician I understand." He would have understood L.B.J.'s despair in the aftermath of Vietnam.

*   *   *

My effort to show that we were concerned with more in the world than the parochial anti-Communism of the Dulles era — that I represented a more interesting and eclectic society — was far more easily accomplished than I had expected. My early statements about not seeking Cold War allies, however it distressed Dean Rusk, greatly helped. And on this enterprise I soon found myself with the sterling support of Edward R. Murrow.

Murrow was a family friend — Kitty had been a lifetime friend of his wife Janet Brewster. When he was proposed as head of the United States Information Agency, however, Arthur Schlesinger and I had risen above friendship to urge against the appointment; we assumed that after his long years in radio and television, often passing along the Washington word, he would be another voice for the prevailing orthodoxy. We were deeply wrong. He promptly made clear his opposition to the traditional litany. And as to India, he quickly withdrew the existing heads of the United States Information Agency, men impeccably in the old tradition, and sent out William H. Weathersby and Barry Zorthian,[14] who were both solidly in support of my affirmative design.

In Washington itself, change as always came more slowly. For some months after Kennedy took office, the USIA continued to churn out barely literate warnings of the infinite scope and wickedness of the international Communist design and, though more

---

[14] Weathersby went on to become vice president for public affairs at Princeton. Zorthian, afterward a senior executive at Time, Inc., was the press officer in Saigon during the worst of the Vietnam war. He accomplished the approximately impossible feat of doing his job to the satisfaction of his superiors while retaining the respect of even the most obdurately suspicious of the reporters. He was unaided in this task by any pretense to personal beauty. He did not, it seems likely, make his own clothes, but he could not ever have thought to remove them when taking a shower.

rarely, of the virtues, some deeply improbable, of American competitive and corporate enterprise. All this material we now stockpiled. Previously it had been principally read by those who wished to condemn the myopic character of our cultural preoccupation or otherwise open an argument with us. The Soviet ambassador asked me one day why we had ceased to dwell on the menace of Soviet Communism; he missed it.

I did manage to make use of an imaginative article from Washington depicting the United States polity itself as the prototype of a great modern corporation. All in the U.S.A., it said, was consistent. The people of the Republic were the stockholders; the Congress was the board of directors; the Cabinet was the top management; the President was the company CEO (Chief Executive Officer). All, government and business, were united in the same democratic structure and instinct. I released this finding not to the Indians but, by way of the diplomatic pouch, to Kennedy, pointing out that the American people had made a mistake. Wanting a man with corporate experience as President, they had obviously intended to get his father. Perhaps it was not too late to switch. With much pleasure Kennedy got Murrow on the phone and read to him extensively from the article, giving the impression that he believed Murrow had written it himself. "What did you mean by this, Ed?" "Is this really true, Ed?" Murrow said afterward that it was the most painful phone call he ever received. The argument on behalf of corporate America was not reprinted.

Especially irrelevant as well as unreadable were the free presentation books on the Communist machinations; these in earlier years had been widely distributed to the influential or those thought particularly susceptible to the menace. The most revered example was J. Edgar Hoover's *Masters of Deceit.* I also arrested this flow. At the same time I removed *The Affluent Society* from a list of books disapproved by the USIA that were available to libraries and others only by special request to Washington. Rarely, as I have often told, have I had such a feeling of righteously exercised power.

*   *   *

There remained, as a Dulles legacy, the problem of Pakistan. Then abutting India on both sides, Pakistan had been seen by John Foster Dulles as a great military and moral bulwark against Soviet and

Chinese Communism. To this end it had been brought into the Southeast Asia Treaty Organization (SEATO) and further bilateral alliance with the United States. The operative consequence of these steps was a substantial flow of weapons to the Pakistan Army and Air Force.

That Pakistan could stand against the Red Army was the kind of fantasy to which only minds disciplined to avoid all practical thought could rise. The Pakistanis themselves were incapable of such an imaginative flight. Being more practical, they saw the arms and the alliance as a highly serviceable support to their claim on Kashmir against India. For this the arms were relevant. The anti-Communist crusade in Washington thus became in Asia a potentially lethal source of tension between two neighbors. The Communist powers were left quite outside. And by the time of my arrival in India, as a further complication, the Pakistanis were moving to establish close relations with Peking. They were winning support from the unified worldwide movement against which they were being armed. A full understanding of foreign policy requires a certain flexibility of mind.

The obvious course was to detach quietly from our military commitments to Pakistan and thus to lessen the tension between the two subcontinental countries. I set out to bring all possible persuasion to this policy, seeking Washington allies in the effort and, as necessary, invoking my other rules for bureaucratic achievement. Thus, in August 1961, news swept over New Delhi of a large shipment of supersonic F-104s to Pakistan. For reasons of secrecy they were being unloaded in Karachi in the dead of night. Asian cities being as they are, only the thousands without sheltered sleeping space would thus be able to penetrate the secret. Washington had also acceded to a Pakistani request that the number of planes be kept classified. This maximized the adverse effect, for Indian paranoia raised that number from the actual twelve to several hundreds. I requested that the relative insignificance of the gift be made known, but my request was denied.

At this moment Talbot came to New Delhi to a regional meeting of American ambassadors. I asked him who was in charge of such matters, and he assured me that he was. I then gave him the choice of having me tell the Indians of the insignificant scale of the shipment or holding him fully responsible for the predictable Indian appeal to the Soviets for a much larger number of MIGs. After some protest he surrendered. In time, although it took far too long, the arguments against arms for Pakistan had effect. The flow dwindled and ceased to be an issue.[15]

*   *   *

Our economic assistance program to India when I was there amounted to about $670 million a year, including food;[16] this approximately offset the ill-will that we incurred with our military hardware in Pakistan. My third and final effort as ambassador was to improve the effectiveness of our economic aid. Here I had much latitude. My prestige on economic matters and economic development was such that no one in Washington or on my staff in India risked correcting or even guiding me. And my reputation extended to the Indians; at our first meeting Nehru expressed the courtly hope that my being an ambassador would not end my earlier role as an economic adviser.

My AID[17] director was also amenable. As previously mentioned, he was C. Tyler Wood, a onetime partner of the Wall Street brokerage house of Gilbert Eliott & Company, who had been converted by World War II to public service. As a friend and counselor of my wife's family, he had been the counterweight to my father-in-law's somewhat romantic tendencies on personal finance: Mr. Atwater once invested in railroads, he said, out of a feeling of compassion. Wood had no damagingly preconceived ideas about our assistance effort, and he was a pleasant and able manager.

On industrial investment in these years I formulated what I called the mass consumption standard. This meant only that our investment should be strongly guided to those industries that directly or

---

[15] In 1980, following upon the Afghan crisis, a new offer was rejected by Pakistan. It was correctly seen as irrelevant to the defense of the country against the U.S.S.R.

This same F-104, the Lockheed Starfighter, later achieved fame in Germany for the casualties it inflicted on those who flew it. A Lockheed representative, an agreeable ex-general, was in New Delhi at the time seeking business with the Indian government. He petitioned the Embassy for help; I gave him none and thus conceivably saved both money and Indian lives.

[16] U.S., Congress, House, Committee on Appropriations, *Foreign Operations Appropriations for 1963*, 87th Cong., 2nd sess., 1961–62, 34, pt. 3, p. 389.

[17] Agency for International Development. This name and the acronym were adopted during the Kennedy years.

ultimately served the needs of the masses of the people.[18] There was thus a bar against giving money for projects serving national prestige or vanity or the elite and the affluent. I doubt that my formula made much difference. It largely codified what was the general Indian and American instinct. The relative merits of investment in steel or electric power were still debated, but that was because no one quite knew which served mass consumption better. And, in any case, it was best to leave such choices to the Indians, who would have to live with the result. My principal concern on industrial policy was to urge the operational autonomy for public (and private) enterprises on which competence so vitally depends. The Galbraith/ Braithwaite paper[19] on this subject and the draft chapters of *The New Industrial State* were strongly in my mind.

The most serious American mistakes were in agricultural assistance, not industrial investment. The right agricultural policy in a country where the supply of food makes the difference between survival and starvation or possible death, is, it need hardly be said, of the utmost importance. It was also a subject on which the Indians were willing to yield extensively to the great reputation and success of the United States. And what we urged was far from valid.

Neither the United States Department of Agriculture nor the great American centers of agricultural research, extension and instruction — Iowa, Michigan, California, Cornell, Wisconsin, Minnesota, Ohio State, Illinois[20] — have any counterpart anywhere else in the world. From the latter and other land grant universities men of high professional quality (if sometimes undue age) came to the AID mission, to special teams in the Indian states and to the Ford Foundation. They were devoted to their task; no suggestion of capitalist evangelism or subversion could be attached to their efforts even by the most imaginatively anti-American critic. Their mistake was in their commitment to a technical and institutional imperialism.

This was not subtle; they believed that what worked and worked brilliantly in the United States must surely work in India. So it fol-

[18] And the export industries, since they served the same ultimate end.
[19] See Chapter 21.
[20] Perhaps I might add Connecticut, where at Storrs my wife's grandfather Wilbur Olin Atwater was founder and first director of the nation's first agricultural experiment station. He was also a founding parent of the United States Department of Agriculture.

lowed that whatever was urged on farmers or taught to their wives, sons and daughters at home must similarly be urged or taught on the subcontinent. Home economics, poultry husbandry, animal science, veterinary medicine, farm management, agricultural economics, all subjects of college instruction and agricultural extension in the United States, should similarly be available in India.[21]

However, the need in India was not for a broad-scale effort but for the utmost concentration on essentials — on hybrid seed for grain production, supporting soil and water management and on pest control. It was grain that kept people alive, bountiful crops of wheat and rice that kept prices down. And it was important that as little as possible else be done, for, apart from using scarce funds for things of lesser urgency, efforts on a wide scale diverted the attention of the men on the land from what was most important. In much of India it meant that the small, usually illiterate cultivator had such a confusing range of sophisticated recommendations that all were ignored. An educator must sometimes seek to economize on the mental effort that he requires of his students. If too great, it invites hopelessness and rejection.

No American ambassador before had brought to his job more impressive agricultural credentials than did I. A degree in animal husbandry, advanced degrees in agricultural economics, service with the American Farm Bureau Federation, some years of teaching agricultural economics at Harvard, a working acquaintance with all the great men of the farm scene. My agriculturalists were impressed, but mostly they were dismayed. As I've already indicated, all earlier ambassadors had had a highly developed sense of their own inferiority on agricultural matters. It is a subject, indeed, on which a Princeton man can profess ignorance with a certain pride. This ignorance the agriculturalists habitually had cultivated and exploited; there are some things that no urban-minded dolt was ever meant to understand. Now all this was changed. An ambassador was invading their hitherto autonomous republic.

I made my case for a concentration of our agricultural efforts on the life-sustaining cereals with such eloquence as I could command. I was heard with respect, but when I came to specifics there was shock, even indignation. When I urged against bringing home econ-

---

[21] As also in Pakistan and the other densely populated agricultural countries.

omists to advise on the running of the exiguous Indian households, a former student of mine, a good man, noted forcefully that instruction in home economics was established practice in Kansas. One day in Bangalore I announced a policy of firm concentration on soil and water management, including fertilizer use and the production of grain hybrids. Policy it became. Nothing, I believe, was changed in consequence.

Wheat and rice production in India in the last two decades has increased prodigiously in the good monsoon years. It is this increase that has made the green revolution. Mostly this reflected the personal initiative of the good farmers of northern India, notably the Punjab. Some was the result of that part of the technical effort that was on behalf of water, fertilizer and grain hybrids. There have been no similarly visible gains from the effort that was diffused to all the other things.

I've been asked a hundred times if, as ambassador, I had control over the CIA. Always and truthfully I've replied that I did — that my local contingent, confined to benign reporting of widely available information, was a model of disciplined obedience. No one has ever asked about my agricultural experts. Never by any stretch of the imagination could such a claim be made about them.

27

Intimate Perception of a War

THE INDIAN PENINSULA, roughly a diamond in shape, is protected on the two lower sides by the sea and on the two upper by the world's highest mountains. No other civilization of such size has enjoyed such formidable natural fortifications, and there could be no greater monument to the ineffectiveness of such protection. First through the mountain passes and then in from the sea, invaders have been coming to India for two thousand years. All who made a serious effort succeeded. One consequence of this history is a sense of extreme vulnerability, especially as regards the mountains over which most of the intruders came. This unease powerfully afflicted the British; they never ceased to fear that the Russians would one day come down over the passes and claim the Indian plain for the czars. And some also warned of the eventual threat of a renascent China.

After independence, India inherited the British anxiety, a not surprising thing, for she also inherited civil servants and soldiers of Indian birth who in imperial times had been exposed occupationally to the British alarm. So India continued to look up at her mountains not with assurance but with concern.

The Himalayas cannot be assimilated to any of the other great mountain ranges. The Alps and the Rockies are related to the earth, the Himalayas, as I've said, to the heavens. One looks up to them as to another world, which, indeed, they are. The Indian plain is hot, if there is water, verdant, and where there is water, one is rarely beyond the sound of voices. The mountains and the high plateaus are cold and fearsome, and one encounters people with surprise. On the plain the people are Aryan and Hindu or Moslem in religion and culture. Those of the mountains immediately above the Indian plain combine Buddhist with Hindu traditions and have ethnic and cultural links with China and Mongolia. These links become stronger on the high plateau on the other side of the mountain crest.

British policy toward the mountain regions and the Tibetan plateau beyond varied both as to place and time. On the upper eastern slope of the diamond north from the valleys of the Ganges and the Brahmaputra the policy was to leave suitably subject principalities as a buffer; thus the continuing states of Nepal and Bhutan and for a time of Sikkim. Elsewhere it was sometimes their policy to advance and govern the frequently contentious tribes of the border; this particularly was the effort in the high country on the northwestern edge of the diamond. In other places and other times it was policy to pull back and, in the manner of the New York police with the Mafia, hope that these people would contain their energies and deter other intruders by the ferocity of their intramural strife.

* * *

At the very top of the Indian diamond lies the onetime princely state of Kashmir, and across a high mountain pass east from Srīnagar and the Vale of Kashmir, at a height of 17,400 feet, is the vast desert plateau of Ladakh. Ladakh is an extension of the Tibetan plateau,

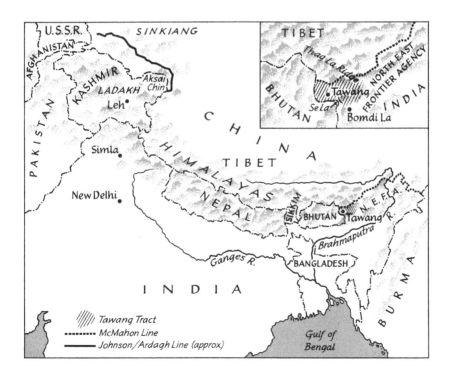

and culturally as well as geographically it is a bridge to Tibet, as Tibet is one on to China. A generation that knows something of the climate and landscape of the moon would not be unprepared for the climate and landscape of Ladakh.

In 1841, this desert — a no man's land but related by proximity and custom to Tibet and thus distantly to the now exiguous Chinese Empire — was invaded by an Indian force dispatched by Gulab Singh, the ruler of the Indian princely state of Jammu on the northern plains. The invaders crushed the Tibetan defenders, but then winter came. The plateau in winter is not a pleasant place. The sun can be strong and warm, but when you step into a shadow, you are suddenly very, very cold. The invaders, glorious in their victory, were nearly all frozen to death.

Gulab Singh retrieved the position the following year and signed (or anyhow inscribed) a peace treaty with the Tibetans requiring each side to respect the other's territorial rights, no effort being made to say what these were. In Asia at the time it was not usual to trouble over precise boundary designations; that was purely a European custom. A few years later Kashmir itself fell to the British, and Gulab Singh was installed there as ruler. The transmountain plateau that he had conquered thus became part of Kashmir and of the British Empire.

The line between British-Indian and Chinese-Tibetan territory was never settled. The Chinese government being impotent, it felt, reasonably, that anything to which it might agree would be adverse. The British were likewise uncertain, whenever they put their minds to it, as to what territory they thought it wise to have. Those close at hand generally favored having more — the forward policy. Those farther away favored leaving things as they were. In the 1860s, an adventuresome surveyor named W. H. Johnson made his way over the country and proposed a boundary far to the north and east of Kashmir. A rough approximation of this line was again urged in 1897 by the then Director of Military Intelligence of the British General Staff, Major General Sir John Ardagh, a man of decidedly forward instinct. Others more sensitive to the quality of the real estate involved demurred.

The Johnson/Ardagh Line encompassed the Aksai Chin, a waste of stone and sand more than a hundred miles across and some 17,000 feet high. Even by the severe standards of Ladakh, the Aksai

Chin is a frightful place. The more thoughtful alignments excluded this territory and ran near to the main range of the Karakorams well to the west.

Sovereign India inherited this unsettled and unmarked border but not, on the whole, the doubt as to where it should be. Though Nehru initially had reservations, his government came eventually to assert a claim to an approximation to the Johnson/Ardagh Line and thus to the Aksai Chin. This was far from being settled possession. Until well along in the 1950s, it seems unlikely that any responsible Indian ever saw the territory so claimed; certainly none seemed to have known that the Chinese were building a road across it. However unpleasant this landscape, it provided access for the Chinese to the distant province of Sinkiang.

Only in 1957 did rumors reach New Delhi of this construction project, and only in 1958 were patrols sent to confirm this impressive trespass, one of the patrols promptly disappearing into Chinese hands. The Indian government now protested the intrusion, and a little later the Indian Army began, so far as the formidable logistics allowed, to establish posts on or near the disputed terrain. Detachments then went out to confirm the claim. There can be few places in the world where hostile forces could more easily evade each other, but in October of 1959, there was a damaging encounter with the Chinese and nine Indians and one or two Chinese were killed.

*   *   *

Elsewhere on the border there was also an inherited disagreement between the Indians and the Chinese. At the several high mountain passes along the Indian-Tibetan (now Chinese) frontier the Chinese took the position generally that the passes and shadowing mountain peaks were theirs by ancient right. The Indians held that the top point in the road or, more precisely, track was theirs. This difference was usually resolved by seeing who could first get to the top of the pass when the snow melted in the spring, the question of ownership being singularly irrelevant during the winter. A far more serious dispute was over another large area a thousand miles to the east and south of Ladakh.

This was the great rectangle, now on the Indian map as the North East Frontier Agency (NEFA), to the east of the kingdom of Bhutan. As late as the 1960s, I was one of the few — perhaps the few

hundred — non-Asians ever to have visited both this area and Ladakh, although my view of NEFA was from an Alouette helicopter.
Even as compared with Ladakh, NEFA is an alarming sight. Valleys
of dense jungle give way to sudden great mountain ridges. The
passes are at 16,000 feet or more, which is to say that to cross the
ranges one must go higher than to the top of Mont Blanc, Europe's
highest peak. At the far north, a final range gives way to the Tibetan
plateau. For Indian soldiers coming from the hot, verdant plains
and valleys, their normal world, this Antarctic scene with its thin,
unsustaining air was a strange and frightening thing, made more so
by the fact that very few of their officers had ever had experience of
it either.

In the last century NEFA was occupied by scattered tribes who
made an exiguous living from herds and flocks and some patches of
agriculture and who found relief from their existence by slaughter-
ing each other in sanguinary fashion as opportunity arose. Effectively it too was a no man's land, and to keep it so was British
policy. To this end a line was drawn along the southern side, this
being the northern border of the Brahmaputra Valley, and no one
was allowed to cross this Outer Line, as it was known, without official
permission. While Chinese maps had long shown this territory to be
part of Tibet, the Chinese and Tibetans took an equally reserved
view of the tribesmen and their inhospitable terrain. With the exception of a wedge-shaped area of a couple of thousand square miles
narrowing down from Tibet along the eastern border of Bhutan and
encompassing a large Buddhist monastery at a settlement called Tawang, they too thought it more sensible to keep out. The Tawang
tract was under the administration, in a manner of speaking, of
Tibet.

*   *   *

In 1914, just weeks before the outbreak of the First World War, the
British met with the Tibetans and the Chinese in Simla, the British
summer capital on the edge of the Himalayas, to arrange various
matters — concessions and extraterritorial rights — in Tibet. The
British negotiators used the occasion to advance a claim to the eastern territory that they had previously regarded with such intelligent
reserve. They proposed that the border be along the crest of the
Himalayas on the edge of the Tibetan plateau. The map and the

line on which this claim was based were the achievement of a British military surveyor, one Captain Henry McMahon; its effect was to bring all of NEFA, including the Tawang tract, into India. However, even the competent McMahon had been set back by this landscape. His demarcation, as it approached Bhutan at its western end, did not follow the peaks but became, instead, a simple straight line. At Simla the Tibetans in their *de facto* independence from China at the time accepted the McMahon Line. They were in no position to resist. The equally weak Chinese delegation was not, it would appear, advised of the concession.

In the next thirty years the local people south of the McMahon Line were left to continue happily in their often lethal ways. Not until 1944 did the British get around to occupying the Tawang tract, which, in contrast with the tribal regions, was a settled and culturally relatively advanced area. In the years following independence, the Indian authority also remained both tenuous and somewhat perilous. In the early fifties a unit of the Indian border patrol, the Assam Rifles, moving through the tribal territories, was given a warm and festive welcome by the inhabitants, provided with food and shelter and then extirpated almost to a man.[1] However, by 1959, the Indians had made their way to the neighborhood of the McMahon Line. Here as on the Aksai Chin there were clashes with the Chinese. The quarrel was not over acceptance of the Line; this the Chinese, perhaps out of a continuing and sensible regard for the inhospitable tendencies of the tribal people, were disposed, it appears, to concede. Rather, the disagreement was over how the last few miles of the Line were to be construed.

In this area, as noted, McMahon had resorted to a straight line, and such a line on this countryside could be on the nearly vertical slope of a mountainside. To move or make camp a patrol had to go down to the partly level land of the valley below, which was to invade the next country. This often happened. Since elsewhere in India and also to the east in Burma McMahon's Line had followed the high ground, the Indians were persuaded reasonably enough that the intended border was along the top of the Thag La Ridge,[2] three or

---

[1] Some seventy soldiers and civilians died. Mention of the episode is in Neville Maxwell's competent, though in the Indian view somewhat pro-Chinese, history, *India's China War* (London: Jonathan Cape, 1970), p. 74.

[2] *La* means pass. In the case of Dhola, Simla, etc., place name and pass have been united.

four miles to the north of McMahon's straight line. Rival territorial claims deriving from the cartographic and topographic frontiers became a cause of war. Rarely in the long history of human conflict have so many been so aroused over such a few acres of such questionable terrain.

*   *   *

From the late 1950s, diplomatic notes, at first friendly, then acerbic and finally angry, were exchanged between Peking and New Delhi. Each side protested the intrusion of the other in the east or west. In early 1960, to a somewhat frigid welcome, Chou En-lai came to New Delhi to negotiate a settlement. As noted, the Chinese seem to have been willing to surrender their ancient claims to NEFA in the east and accept the McMahon Line as on the map. In return they would get the Aksai Chin and their road to Sinkiang. But by 1960, Indian democracy had intervened, as only democracy can, to limit the freedom of government for negotiation. The Indian government had not succeeded in persuading the Chinese that the Aksai Chin and the land between the two McMahon Lines belonged to India. But in making the case, the Indian leaders succeeded completely in persuading Indian politicians, the press and the articulate public that these lands were irrevocably Indian. Gulab Singh and the later travelers had established a claim to the Aksai Chin no less firm than that of Lewis and Clark to the Oregon territory. This was the sacred soil of India, and reference to such consecration now became standard in Indian parlance.

Additionally, Nehru's parliamentary and press opposition, though relatively insignificant in numbers, was fervently anti-Communist. And it slightly suspected Nehru and strongly suspected his Defense Minister and ambassador-at-large Krishna Menon of being susceptible to Communist persuasion, pressure or intrigue. Even in India at the time there was the oft-cited need for anyone left of center to show that he was not soft on Communism. After 1960, to show such firmness as well as to support their claim with a presence on the ground, the Indians began moving patrols and posts up toward the edge of the Aksai Chin and more circumspectly to the sliver of land between the two McMahon Lines.

The pressure for this forward policy was not military but civilian and political. The Indian Army knew very well the difficulties. Until late in 1960, troops in Ladakh had to be supplied by air — by American Fairchilds, the Flying Boxcars — or by mule track. Then a road was completed, but the round trip from the Indian plains by truck took a full month and allowed of a net load, in addition to fuel for the journey, of only around a ton. However, Ladakh was as accessible to India as Nevada to California as compared with the disputed corner east of Bhutan. That was eleven days' march north from the valley of the Brahmaputra over mountain passes that could be traversed only on foot and on occasion only with the help of ropes. On the Tibet side, both east and west, access for the Chinese across the plateau was relatively easy.

* * *

In December 1961, Leonid I. Brezhnev, then still the more or less ceremonial president of the U.S.S.R., had visited New Delhi. In conversation before the large state dinner in his honor he had said to me, "I hear that in your country you are considered a man of the left."

My response was relatively noncommittal, but it had prompted him to add, "I invite you to visit the Soviet Union so you will have the experience of being a reactionary."

I thanked him, and on October 20, 1962, my Soviet ambassadorial colleague Ivan Alexandrovitch Benediktov having renewed the invitation, I was in London intending, after a visit to Washington, to go to Moscow. On coming out of the theater that evening, I learned from headlines in a highly accessible intelligence source, the *Evening Standard,* of major fighting between the Indians and the Chinese in NEFA. Over the continuing protests of army officers immediately aware and involved, the Indian government had launched a campaign to shove the Chinese back over the Thag La Ridge and to establish the high peaks of the Himalayas as the boundary. Among the reasons given was the barely supportable thought that strategic considerations required that the border be along the crests of the mountains — crests that could not possibly be garrisoned.

Late on the night of October 20 or perhaps early next morning, I was awakened at the hotel to receive a message from President Kennedy telling me to return to India forthwith. It was not, as I immediately supposed, because of the outbreak of war between India and China. The message was occasioned by the Cuban missile crisis and the need that I be present to explain the American position to Nehru and through him to the nonaligned world. Thus had come one of the grim coincidental happenings of recent history. In the same week, on almost the same day that the two great western powers confronted each other over Cuba, the two huge Asian countries went to war in the Himalayas.[3]

In the next days, in consequence of the coincidence, I had more independent authority than any modern ambassador has enjoyed in another country in wartime. Washington was wholly occupied with the missile crisis. Regular diplomatic communication channels were almost completely preempted by its priority messages.[4] A day or two after my return from London, a sparse message from the White House confirmed that all attention was elsewhere and said that Carl Kaysen of the White House staff would be the highest official with time for my problems. Kaysen and I had long seen eye to eye on the need for a less adventuresome, less militarily oriented foreign policy so I could be sure that his support would be broadly sympathetic. Dean Rusk, most generously in light of our earlier acerbic correspondence and relations, confined himself throughout to expressions of warm confidence in my management.

As the war progressed, a series of massive defeats turned the Indians to the American Embassy for material help and therewith for moral support and military and political guidance.[5] Unlike other

---

[3] Secretary of State Dean Rusk was persuaded that the Chinese, anticipating our preoccupation with Cuba, had seized the occasion for their attack. This was nonsense. There was, however, a certain parallel in the position of the two democracies. Both Nehru and Kennedy were limited in their negotiating power by the political danger in seeming insufficiently stalwart. Both, in consequence, had to take actions or assume risks that were unwise. This has remained my reservation as regards those who see the missile crisis as a great Kennedy success. Domestic American political considerations — the need to be tough — intruded far too deeply on an issue that threatened the end for all time of civilized survival.

[4] Eventually a pair of emergency radio transmitters were flown out to New Delhi by the CIA, and work began on the huge backlog of communications that had by then accumulated. Something went wrong; for the first two days the messages went out and up into the troposphere and never came down.

[5] Neville Maxwell observed that "The American Ambassador . . . [became] in effect a privy councilor of the Indian government." He adds, if I may be allowed, that this was "a role Galbraith played with zest and tact." Maxwell, p. 420.

ambassadors, I had no independent military (or CIA) contingent with which to share power. When a sizable military advisory force eventually arrived, I was able to keep both it and its communications fully under my control.[6] It is my intention here to tell of the lessons learned in the exercise of such power. But first I must add a further word on the course of the war itself.

*   *   *

The eastern front, the cartographic conflict, was entrusted by the Indians to General Brij Mohan Kaul, a compact man of slightly less than average height, brisk military manner and singularly bad judgment. He owed his advancement in the Indian Army to a capacity for political accommodation, notably to Krishna Menon, rather than to experience of military command, of which he had almost none. His tendency in issuing orders was to ambiguity, compromise and, in misfortune, to whatever might transfer blame. He was also a man of no slight charm.

My own doubts as to Kaul's judgment were stirred, though not adequately, shortly before my October departure for London. He had just returned from a firsthand tour of the Thag La front, and he asked me to call on him late one evening at his house in New Delhi. There he told me that one day soon the Indians were going to evict the Chinese from the land claimed by India. Jawaharlal Nehru, Krishna Menon and the government did not sufficiently understand the difficulty of the task; it would only be possible with our help. Accordingly, he told me, he had advised the Indian government to abandon its commitment to nonalignment and seek our assistance. He took for granted that such was our antipathy to Communism we had only to be asked. I thought him a bit unstrung and said it would not be our wish to be so involved, while reflecting that, given the current view of China as an instrument of the world Communist conspiracy, there were some of my countrymen who had precisely this ambition. I was much less impressed by this conversation than I should have been. Like all of the World War II generation, I was inured to the idiosyncratic tendencies of generals.

The effort to throw the Chinese back over the Thag La Ridge in

---

[6] See Chapter 21.

mid-October never came close to the peaks. Instead, it ended on October 19–20 in a severe defeat in the valley below. The Indian units, all sparsely supplied and equipped,[7] were dispersed. Some were killed, more taken prisoner and the rest escaped over the border into Bhutan.[8] General Kaul, suffering physically from the high altitudes and nervously from the defeat, was flown back to New Delhi.

India proper was hardly at risk from this defeat — or skirmish. Some of the world's highest mountain ranges lay between the Chinese and the Brahmaputra Valley to the south. The Indians regrouped to defend the high passes over these mountains. Se La at 14,600 feet, about twenty miles south and west of the McMahon Line, was made the principal strong point; Bomdi La, another twenty miles farther south and west, was to be in support. These passes were formidable in defense. Not surprisingly they also involved equally difficult problems in access. However, in the lull that followed the Thag La defeat, the Indians were able to get several thousand troops up to this area along with some equipment, but there remained the question of sustaining them on these lofty sites.

It was a time of much excitement. In New Delhi the war fever was extreme. There were widespread demands that the Chinese be promptly expelled; all problems of terrain and military feasibility were ignored. War is always fatal to careful thought, and in one grave manifestation of this General Kaul was allowed to resume command.

In mid-November the Chinese proposed negotiation. Given the current state of Indian opinion and its nearly total divorce from military circumstance, this could not be considered, and I did not suggest it. To have done so in that excited atmosphere would have been to lose credibility as a friend. Perhaps I should have so urged.

The Chinese then resumed their advance. After some unconcealed road-building they turned into what were deemed to be largely impassable tracks which came around the mountains and passes on which the Indian forces were perched. It had been my view in New Delhi, based on staff discussions, that the Chinese had

---

[7] They were partly supplied by air, but on that vertical terrain it was nearly impossible to find sufficiently level drop areas where supplies could land and be retrieved.

[8] Disturbed by the Indian weakness, the Prime Minister of Bhutan, the King's brother-in-law, appealed to me for guidance. I advised that he proclaim neutrality, disarm the Indian troops and then allow them to make their way back to India.

not yet made their point and that their road-building had some purpose. So there would be a follow-up of their earlier attack. Washington disagreed. When the Chinese moved around the high passes, I was proven right. My further estimates of developments then went unchallenged, although, as it happened, the principal one was wrong.[9]

When the Chinese came around the main Indian force at Se La, the confusion of the defenders was extreme, and the defeat was total. Some Indian soldiers were killed; some died of exposure and starvation; more were taken prisoner; a large number made their way in small parties down to the plains. All equipment was lost. No Chinese was taken prisoner. Two or three years later General Kaul visited me in Cambridge and told me that he was writing a book that would show that the campaign was, all things considered, a success. It seemed a challenging literary exercise.

Meanwhile in Ladakh, over the strong resistance of the Indian troops scattered in their frigid posts, whose skill and determination went unremarked in the larger defeat, the Chinese forced the Indians away from the Aksai Chin. Then, on November 21, the war came wholly and abruptly to an end. I turn to the lessons learned from this improbable conflict.

*   *   *

My first discovery was of the physical problems with which one must contend. In ordinary times, as these pages have made clear, an ambassador is not overworked. Then, in the autumn months of 1962, at the moment when time for calm thought was most needed, I found myself with more decisions to make of more consequence than I had made in all the previous months combined. When sleep was most needed, the most news, usually adverse, came in to destroy it. In time my deputy Benson E. L. Timmons succumbed to fatigue, was hospitalized and left me with yet more to do. I discovered again, as I had when directing price control, that one's capacity for intense and sustained effort is greatly extensible. On ordinary days we function at a fraction of our capacity and relieve conscience by commenting on how hard we are working. But there are limits. Without

---

[9]On the basis of highly dubious information, I forecast another thrust down through Sikkim. It never materialized and, I judge, was never contemplated.

doubt, one of the perils of our time is that the gravest decisions must be made by tired people.

Also there is the further problem, rarely discussed, of sleeping pills. No doubt there are those who can shelve thought, relax from tension and go promptly to sleep after great, intricate, demanding or dangerous tasks. It is probably because they don't quite know what they are doing. For others there is no alternative to sedatives to interrupt thought and allow sleep. Such was then my case. I doubt that others similarly situated have had a different ability or experience. President Kennedy did not; in those days I used the same quick-acting barbiturate that Dr. Janet Travell prescribed for the President. One does, however, pay the penalty in dullness and, without doubt, impaired judgment the next morning. And also in the need for increasing the dosage as the weeks pass, with the tendency for weariness and tension not to be dissipated but to be suppressed and accumulated. Only not to sleep would be worse.

*   *   *

I discovered also, on my return from London, the urgent uses of history. I needed to know immediately the background and understand the causes of the conflict with which I was concerned. Since the troubles in those distant hills had been considerably in the news, it was unforgivable that I had not fully acquainted myself with the history of the area, but I had not. Nor had anyone on my staff. Nor, in any usable form, was there anything from Washington. The Indian government had a huge brief on its side of the case. It was, as F.D.R. had said of our briefs on price control, too heavy to lift. And it did not convey a wholly detached tone. One could not act rationally without a knowledge of the issues. My first unexpected task of the war was to understand its causes and the merits on both sides.

I concluded that there was much to be said for the Indian claim to NEFA, the detail of the precise border alignment apart. The issue was between the older imperialism of China and the newer imperialism which India had inherited from the British. No modern nation can assert ancient imperial rights. It would prove a hideous source of conflict; there would be overlapping claims by Iranians, Greeks, Italians, Mongols and Turks, and the successor states would all now be in hideous combat. The history also showed that for the Chinese this area was not the major issue in dispute. So, with Washington's slightly reluctant permission — these are matters over which no ambassador should expect to have plenary authority — I announced our support of India on her claim to the McMahon Line. Which line I did not say. A few hours after I released this assurance on October 27, there came a strong protest from Taiwan; as the still-recognized government of China, it was defending, somewhat imaginatively, all Chinese soil.

Having concluded that the Indians had a decent case in the east, I resolved to maintain silence on the west. For the Chinese the Aksai Chin was a passage, for the Indians a desert. The fact that the Indians had not discovered the Chinese road for two years seemed to suggest a tenuous claim. I then checked with the one detached authority available to me in New Delhi, Chester Ronning, the Canadian High Commissioner. Handsome, informed, confident and an old China hand, he did know the history. And he was wholly persuaded that the Indian case in the west was not strong.[10] I was still not completely happy. I continued through all of those weeks to be troubled by my lack of really adequate and secure knowledge of the background and thus of the merits of the conflict.

*　*　*

A more fundamental uncertainty concerned the nature of the war with which I was involved — and offering guidance and extending material help. Everything depended on Chinese intentions; these to a singular degree were unrevealed. Was this only a border dispute? If so, one should remain cool and do everything possible to prevent escalation into full-scale conflict. Or did the war reflect the aggressively expansionist tendencies attributed by all hard-nosed warriors to the international Communism in which China was assumed to be a full and assenting partner? Could those who used those vital phrases, which along with other liberals I had indignantly resisted, conceivably be right? The prophets of a relentless Communist expansion dominated the scene in Washington, although the attack on India was somewhat a test of their faith. Military allies, not neutralist India, had always been thought the endangered species. That India had to be protected from Communism was to some a new, troublesome and expensive line of thought.

---

[10]*Ambassador's Journal* (Boston: Houghton Mifflin, 1969), p. 435.

The conventional rule, in such matters, is clear: always assume the worst. Certainly after the Chinese had moved into NEFA and around the eagle's nest at Se La, one should do so. The Chinese would take Assam and go on to exploit for Communism the deeply justified discontents and diverse revolutionary enthusiasms of Calcutta and Bengal. The East is red or is meant to be. The lesson I now learned was that no glib assumption should ever be allowed to replace thought. To have assumed the worst case would have gone far to ensure the worst case. Were an invasion of Assam and Bengal intended, counteraction against bases and transport in Tibet would be in order. The enemy should be hit where it hurt. Our policy as friends would be to provide the Indians with the necessary aircraft and ordnance, come to the protection of their cities and begin movement of the other military supplies for a serious war.

To all this, and especially to the air attacks on Tibet, the Chinese would then have been forced to react. And meanwhile Indian public opinion, already clamorous, would reject as a transparent Communist trick any further proposals for negotiation. Additionally, decision would pass into the hands of the men, Indian and American, whose business it is to fight and often to like war. That, perhaps most of all, would ensure the worst.

The wise and safe policy was to assume not the worst but the least case. This was a dispute over the boundary, a major demonstration by the Chinese to force a settlement on favorable terms. It called for a limited and thus revocable response. Not without misgiving, I proceeded to act on this belief.

There was support. Past Chinese foreign policy, Cold War doctrine to the contrary, had been cautious. Hong Kong had continued to survive as a remnant of British imperialism. The Chinese had intervened in Korea only when MacArthur had made his feckless drive to the Yalu. They had protested much on Matsu and Quemoy, the Nationalist islands next to the mainland, but had never taken them over. Could responsible Communists wish for a war requiring supply lines over the Himalayas — over goat tracks and rope ways rather than roads? Or — a more subjective thought — for anything as disastrous as a Communist Bengal? The Chinese gift is for the organization that socialism requires; the Bengali instinct, never without charm, is for anarchy.

My mind was not as firmly made up as this sounds. Were I wrong, the consequences would be unpleasant for the Indians, the United States — and for Galbraith. A professor resisting elementary precepts had minimized the Communist threat. Let him be excoriated and then exorcised; let his error be forever an example for all. I would spend the rest of my life with as challenging a job of explanation as General Kaul's. After the fall of Tawang on October 26, I noted in my journal that the Chinese might be out to take all of NEFA and warned myself that ". . . I must keep my mind open to this. The worst course is to make an estimate and then be so proud of it that one cannot accommodate it to changing evidence."[11] However, I continued to resist the assumption that India or any appreciable part of it was the target. At issue was the dubious border acreage. This need to detach safety in personal reputation from wise public decision and the difficulty in doing so were visibly evident in later years in Washington. To many it seemed wise personal strategy to argue that Communist (and significantly Chinese) ambition in East Asia was unlimited. The dominoes would everywhere be pushed and fall. By so assuming the worst and acting accordingly in Vietnam, one could never be accused of underestimating the Communist threat.

*   *   *

I had also to enforce my least — or lesser — case assumption on my own staff. I would be badly undercut were my subordinates to urge a full-scale invasion and war on the Indians. Here I learned that Americans are disciplined and subject to sensible persuasion.

My deputy Lane Timmons was by experience an old Cold War hand. But like the other career officers he quickly accepted the arguments for the least case. The senior members of the embassy military staff, Colonel Clifford A. Curtis of the Army and Colonel George Hannah, Jr., the Air Attaché, were calm and thoughtful men. Both also saw that to act on the worst assumption would ensure that everything would be worse. Another senior member of my military staff — I see no reason at this late stage to cause him pain by giving his name — strongly disagreed. Indeed, he was appalled that the Indians should not be immediately and enthusiastically embraced as a new ally in the anti-Communist crusade. When he saw

[11] *Ambassador's Journal*, p. 436. The Chinese did, in effect, take NEFA before withdrawing.

his Indian counterparts, he talked of military supplies that would forestall the Chinese by land, air and notably by sea. These conversations then passed into the Indian armed forces and up through the Indian government. Word came back to me of wonderful things — destroyers, anti-submarine craft, ordnance — under discussion with the Indian military men. I resolved the matter by asking my subordinate not to commit himself to any official Indian on any matter having to do with the war. Discipline served here; he obeyed.

The New Delhi CIA staff was not only compliant but included W. Lowrie Campbell, an accomplished authority on the mountain peoples and on the terrain where the fighting was in progress. From him, as well as from my earlier visit, I had a better feeling for the country up by Bhutan than did some of my Indian counterparts. This, presumably, is what good intelligence is for.

As the war reached its climax, there was one moment, however, when I feared loss of control. Desmond FitzGerald appeared in New Delhi. FitzGerald was then near the zenith of his career as the most sanguinary, imaginative and personable architect of covert operations in CIA history. Also the most irresponsible. In his memoirs, William Colby, a later head of the Agency, tells of being asked about FitzGerald when he was under consideration to be in charge of all clandestine operations. "I urged that Des FitzGerald be chosen but I cautioned Helms [Richard Helms, then CIA director] that he would have to maintain tight control over him to keep him from charging off into some new Bay of Pigs. Helms did choose Fitz-Gerald . . ."[12] FitzGerald had a plan for companionate guerrilla mischief in association with like-minded adventurers among the Indians. I assigned a trusted subordinate to be with him as a guide and assistant with the further task of reporting fully to me on everything that took place. A spy to watch a spy. Fortunately, the war ended and FitzGerald went home before anything damaging got started.

*   *   *

As the Cuban crisis eased, the war in the Himalayas became the focus of Washington's attention. Soon we were overwhelmed with offers of help. There was another lesson here — the threat of num-

---

[12] William Colby, *Honorable Men: My Life in the CIA* (New York: Simon & Schuster, 1978), p. 242.

bers. Each new arrival of any importance diluted and endangered my own control. And also my policy of keeping the response to the minimum, for numerous of the volunteers were in search of heroic achievement. Timmons and I met each morning to draft cables declining proffered talent. The key to controlling those who came was, as always, to keep full control of communications. Then you know fully what is going on and can act as necessary against that of which you disapprove, including vetoing the transmission itself. After the Indian defeats, when we began replacing the lost weapons, a substantial military staff became inevitable. I was told that this mission would be subject to the authority of the Secretary of Defense. I returned a telegram saying that, in fact, all would be subject to my authority and "that all . . . communications would of course go through me." I commend this language to all ambassadors who serve in troubled lands.

* * *

In these weeks I learned also of the main temptation of such times; it is that one will come to enjoy war too much. Civilian administration is by discussion and consensus; military action is by information and command. The latter has a rewarding simplicity for all civilians and especially for anyone from the discursive tradition of academic life. This is why few men become as dangerously warlike as the academic figure who is plunged into military affairs.

Apart from the leverage accorded by our supply of weapons and other equipment to the Indians, I found it relatively easy to be effective on military matters. My generation of American civilians was steeped in the culture by World War II, the Korean War and the perilous peace between and after. The Indian political leaders, in contrast, were without similar experience, and they were given to exaggeration both on what might be accomplished by armed force and what was to be feared. When the Indians surrendered Se La, rumors swept New Delhi, one being of a great Chinese airborne assault. Jawaharlal Nehru would be replaced as head of the government by the recently discharged Krishna Menon. The serious problem that the Chinese would face in trying to drop paratroopers on New Delhi without a fleet of transport planes was ignored. Those who rejected the paratroop threat accepted that the Chinese would invade all of Assam and possibly Bengal. This too was to ignore

some exceptionally formidable obstacles in supply. I devoted urgent
and successful effort at the Ministry of External Affairs and directly
with the Indian Air Force to keeping the Indians from using their
aircraft. It was unlikely that they could hit Chinese troops moving
through the mountains. On this I was able to assert a highly professional knowledge from my service with the U.S. Strategic Bombing
Survey. But there was a yet more important reason for keeping the
planes on the ground. So long as the opposing forces are infantrymen crawling across the fields or, as in this case, over nearly impassable mountain trails, war has a manageable time dimension. There
is time for thought, negotiation. Once airplanes enter, escalation is
immediate and the conflict passes out of control. I had much satisfaction from these efforts; I still look back on them with possibly
undue self-approval. Not everyone has helped to limit or cool a
war.[13]

I learned further lessons, however, in the danger to one's equilibrium in such times. After the defeat below Thag La and at my behest, we sent rifles, mortars and ammunition by plane from Europe
to Calcutta to replace what had been lost. After the disaster at Se La,
I persuaded Washington to send C-130s to ferry replacement troops
from the Punjab and to fly supplies to Ladakh. Instead of the
month-long round trip by truck to bring a ton of supplies up from
the plains to Leh in Ladakh, a C-130 could of a morning pick up
several times that weight in Delhi and be back by noon. These modest contributions established me as a benefactor of unparalleled
benignity. And with no effort at all, an ambassador can, like a senator procuring a dam or a Ford Foundation executive dispensing a
grant, persuade himself that the largesse is really his own.

In diplomacy an ambassador regularly measures his success by
the warmth of the relations he establishes with the government and
people of the country in which he serves. History and the accident
of events, not personal capacity, are almost invariably the determin-
ing factors in such relationships. But it is ambassadors who get the
credit. The Chinese and the war made me a paragon of diplomatic
achievement overnight; the editor of the most relentlessly inventive
anti-American weekly, *Blitz* of Bombay, called in one afternoon to

[13] I had some leverage. The Indians asked our assurance that if they bombed the
Chinese, we would intervene to prevent retaliatory raids on their cities. This assurance I declined to give or support.

tell me that the United States had been given an entirely new image in his journal and that I would be pictured henceforth as the best-beloved figure since the Lord Krishna. Delegations waited for me with garlands when I came out of the Residence. On one occasion they hung flowers on my Cadillac as well. I went once to NEFA and twice to Ladakh to be received as a savior by the soldiers. Presently I found myself enjoying it far too much. To promise more, to encourage chauvinism, would have been to enlarge this dubious pleasure. It would have been too easy. The lesson is clear.

*   *   *

My military euphoria did not reach wholly dangerous dimensions. However imperfectly, I was aware of the danger. And I was rescued by the Chinese. By November 19, they had taken most of NEFA. That day the Indians, in two desperate messages to Washington, asked for large-scale American aid and air intervention to counter the accepted threat to Assam and Bengal. Plans of a sort were made to abandon Assam, and some civilian administrators, anticipating it, took off on their own.[14] Word came that General Kaul had been captured, and President Sarvepalli Radhakrishnan, on whom I was calling that evening with Senators Mike Mansfield of Montana and Claiborne Pell of Rhode Island, said quietly, "It is, unfortunately, untrue."[15] Though I still deeply doubted the Chinese intentions as regards Assam and Bengal, I had a serious failure of nerve; I asked that units of the Seventh Fleet steam into the Bay of Bengal, a request that I soon canceled. Then, early on the morning of November 21, word came that, the day before, the Chinese had proclaimed a ceasefire and an end to the war. Their troops would be withdrawn, unilaterally, to positions behind the lines from which it had begun. That would leave NEFA in Indian hands; the Chinese would have the unwholesome Aksai Chin and their road to Sinkiang.

---

[14] These were the days when the paratroop invasion was thought to impend and when I urged against resort to air attacks.

[15] *Ambassador's Journal,* p. 487. The worst of moments, I should note, still vouchsafe their modicum of humor. On another tense day, Bourke B. Hickenlooper, Republican senator from Iowa and a voice of grave concern on foreign policy matters in the United States Senate, also visited New Delhi. I took Hick, as he requested, to see the Prime Minister to whom he delivered a half-hour lecture on the dangers of aggressive Communism. I lingered afterward for a word with Nehru on more pressing matters, and he mused as to why the senator had thought he needed that particular lecture on that particular day.

On hearing the news, I was assailed by the thought that the Indian government might not accept the ceasefire. The Parliament and the press were still in a highly belligerent mood, the defeats notwithstanding; India's humiliation must be erased and redressed. The great psychological barrier to asking American help had already been breached; they could rely on our anti-Communist passion to ensure that all their military needs would be met. I was uninstructed, but I had no doubt as to what my instructions should be. I went to see Nehru, and with more passion than I have ever brought to any similar persuasion, I urged him to accept the ceasefire. And I then asked Paul Gore-Booth, the British High Commissioner and the Indians' other source of military support, to make the same case, which he did.

I met Nehru that day in his small, shabby office on the edge of the great circular Parliament chamber that the British built for Indian democracy. He looked old and very tired. He heard me in silence — as usual. I believe that he never heard an argument that was more welcome. I might have come to tell him — as shortly and vehemently he would be told in Parliament — that he should reject this overture and hold it to be fraudulent, a Chinese trick, a Communist ploy. India must fight on. It would have been a sad message for him.

Later still that long day, I had to meet the American press. It was now in New Delhi in force, and word of my persuasion on the ceasefire swiftly became known. The fault of the American press is not that it stands too intransigently in opposition to current policy; far more often it stands militant guard against any seeming retreat from such policy. Here, some now felt, was an example; soft appeasement instead of a firm stand, an invitation to further Chinese aggression. Also the reporters had come halfway around the world to find that their war had dissolved under their very noses. How could I so serve the Chinese and so damage them? Phil Potter, a close friend in the press corps and, as I've noted, the relentlessly diligent servant of the *Baltimore Sun* papers, proclaimed that I was another Kennedy, meaning Ambassador Joseph P. Kennedy, the President's father, who was held to be a man of Munich. I found, to my surprise, I didn't mind. Overall I was too pleased by the day's achievements.

The criticism did not last more than a day or two. Here was another small lesson. Criticism that is not sustained by events — the Chinese did not renew the conflict — has no enduring effect.

The parliamentary criticism of Nehru also dissolved in the deeper relief that the war was over. My own Indian nimbus remained undiminished. Nor was that all. Almost precisely a decade later, I visited Peking. Officials of the Chinese foreign office spoke warmly of my role in persuading Nehru on the ceasefire, for this had received prominent mention in their accounts of the conflict. With luck, one can succeed on both sides of the same war, but no one should count on it.

* * *

In the aftermath of the hostilities, Washington decided to press for a settlement between India and Pakistan on Kashmir, partly as the price of military aid. It was futile; Nehru, having absorbed a defeat in the Himalayas, could not accept another in Kashmir. The disputed territories of the world are usually those which, for good reason, civilization and national concern come to last. The Vale of Kashmir, almost uniquely, is worth quarreling over. I could not forestall the negotiation effort so I involved myself in it without hope or enthusiasm. Nothing came of it except for me a friendly acquaintance with Zulfikar Ali Bhutto, then the Pakistan Foreign Minister, a friendship which later extended warmly to his wife and especially his daughter Benazir and which left me deeply resentful of the evil way by which his political career was brought to an end.

In those months I indulged a dubious fantasy of my own. By now, as I will tell, Vietnam was much on my mind. As a *quid pro quo* for our help in the Himalayas, I proposed that the Indians join in some unspecified way in seeking stability in Indochina. Our role would thus be diluted. I believed we were incapable of guiding political development in countries geographically and culturally distant from our own. The Indians would compensate for our shortcomings. There were expressions of Indian interest, but Washington, the White House in particular, was deeply skeptical of the prospect. Carl Kaysen gave the effort the damaging, but not inappropriate, acronym of GATO — Galbraith's All-Purpose Treaty Organization. As the Chinese threat receded, Indian interest in my plan evaporated.

So did my dream. There was a final lesson here: hope is a poor substitute for substance.

The border between China and India remains unmarked, east and west, to this day. The Chinese still have their road across the Aksai Chin; the Indians have NEFA. There has been no shooting to speak of since the ceasefire. It is not a perfect peace, but it is far superior to any war, and I am pleased to have had a hand in its making.

28

Lyndon Johnson

AFTER THE CHINESE WAR the Embassy in New Delhi lapsed into its normal, synthetically busy, undemanding routine. The conflict had added a military mission to our staff; it came as always with the extraordinary amenities of the modern soldier, and these included an airplane capable of landing, as our existing pair could not, on small fields. During the winter months we took it to visit the dramatic desert capitals of Bikaner and Jodhpur, at the first going out in a jeep to pursue and view the herds of black buck and deer. These graceful beasts looked back with resentment at our vehicle. We also visited Simla, and with Mohinder Singh Randhawa I worked on our book on Indian painting. To this end we visited the ruined palaces in the Kangra Valley and the Punjab Hills, which in their time had nurtured superb painting, some of the most enchanting ever, and we looked at the breathtaking mountain vistas and lovely Dogra women which were its subjects. And we journeyed to Kishangarh in Rajasthan, a tiny fairy-book capital, where the most magical of all eighteenth-century painting was accomplished.[1]

---

[1] On the way to Kishangarh, Randhawa and I stopped in Jaipur; he, as befitted a civil servant, at the state guest house; I, by earlier invitation and perhaps less appropriately as the representative of a democratic state, at the princely palace of the Jaipurs. The Maharajah was away; I dined with Aisha Jaipur, the third in seniority of his wives, who was accurately accounted one of the most beautiful women in India and who was then by a wide margin the most comely member of the Indian Parliament. A night at the Jaipur palace did not imply intimacy; as much could be concluded from two people staying overnight at Windsor Castle or in Grand Central Station. A short time later, when I was back in Washington for a ceremonial visit of President Radhakrishnan, President Kennedy, with enormous pleasure, showed me a dispatch from the Indian secret service that had been relayed to the CIA and sent with Mach II speed to the White House, telling of my sojourn and stressing the incriminating absence of the Maharajah. Kennedy carefully wrote at the bottom, "Seen. J.F.K.," and asked that I sign my name in such fashion as to suggest a confession. He expressed the thought that the accusing paper going to the Kennedy Library would be a rewarding encounter for some historian and that it would do something for my otherwise unduly staid image.

Harvard allows its professors a leave of absence for a maximum of two years, the exception being times of war and national emergency. Since I had indubitably been involved in a war, albeit one with no great impact on Cambridge, Massachusetts, my leave had been extended. It was something of a temptation to remain in India. My wife had come to love both the country and the life. We were well regarded by the Indians if not exclusively for ourselves, then for our government-sponsored largesse. As I've noted, affection even if so purchased is pleasant. The large force of servants and the thoughtfully organized services of the Embassy swept up all of the ordinary cares and annoyances of life. "You know you are back in Washington," Mrs. Charles "Chip" Bohlen, a veteran of much embassy life, once said, "when you remember that the car must go for inspection and you realize you must take it yourself."

Perhaps the fear of enjoying this life too much intruded. A central instruction of our Covenanted (Old School) Baptist Church of Wallacetown, Ontario, was that man achieved grace by eschewing enjoyment for himself and so far as might be possible for others. In any case, I determined to resume teaching in the autumn of 1963 and, more particularly, to finish *The New Industrial State*.

Accordingly, in mid-July we left New Delhi. In November 1961, Chester Bowles had been removed as Undersecretary of State, ostensibly because of his unduly loquacious style, in fact because he was not in harmony with the brisk, sanguinary anti-Communist faith of Dean Rusk. Bowles had persuaded himself that beneath the evil of Communist design and supporting it were social discontents and political abuses that drove men and women to extreme solutions. That there were forthright military remedies he thought overly simple. And admittedly he was inclined to enlarge at length on these views as well as to be guided by them. The stern foreign-policy men of the time had responded with amused contempt but also with a firm determination to bring an end to such nonsense. In consequence, Bowles had been idling for many months in a face-saving White House post, that of presidential adviser on economic development. Now, to his great relief, he became my replacement. He had, of course, previously served as Ambassador to India (and Nepal) under Harry Truman.

Back in Washington on the way to Harvard I was diverted by Kennedy and Carl Kaysen to the matter of Canadian air routes of which

I have told[2] and to a special study of the balance of payments. The deficit, minuscule by later measure, was believed alarming. My study contributed further and, I later came to feel, unnecessarily to the alarm. I met with Kennedy on these and other matters, and on November 22, while I was at lunch at *Newsweek* in New York with Katharine Graham and Arthur Schlesinger, a staff member came in to say that the networks were carrying word of the shooting of the President. I have written elsewhere of this and the ensuing days and of the wretchedness of the time.[3] It is not my thought to punish myself or the reader more.

*   *   *

On the afternoon of November 23, I met Lyndon Johnson while crossing between the Executive Office Building and the White House West Wing. He gathered me back to what had been his vice-presidential office in the EOB to ask my help on the speech he was to give to a joint session of the Congress the following week and to talk of the tasks he would face in his administration. He was at pains to speak of his commitment to civil rights and the liberalism we had both inherited from Roosevelt. I was easily persuaded and emphasized another concern. For nearly three years I had been living in close proximity with our foreign policy. I **thought** it committed the President to ill-considered, unnecessary and **poten**tially ruinous adventures. The political damage would be suffered not by the architects of the policy but by the President. As the next chapter will tell, I had Indochina and especially Vietnam in mind. While I did not feel in need of L.B.J.'s assurance on domestic policy, I felt that he did not give much heed to my foreign policy concerns. Our exchange was a metaphor of the Johnson years. A man who was strong, innovative, confident and resourceful on domestic policy would be destroyed by a military effort which served no American purpose and which, in its political aspects, wholly misjudged the nature of power and the scope for influence in the post-colonial world.

*   *   *

Lyndon Johnson and John F. Kennedy had their political faith from the same source — the New Deal and the belief that government,

[2] See Chapter 1.
[3] *Ambassador's Journal* (Boston: Houghton Mifflin, 1969), pp. 588 ff.

the federal government in particular, could be a decisive force on behalf of the less privileged. They also believed that out of such effort would come assured political reward. The twenty years of power from 1933 to 1953 were the proof. Johnson's commitment was, however, stronger than Kennedy's. He was less detached, less cerebral, more anxious to show himself involved and successful. Roosevelt was a generation removed from J.F.K., and after Joseph P. Kennedy's break with him, F.D.R. was no household saint in the Kennedy family. Johnson, on the other hand, was truly a Roosevelt man; F.D.R. was ever in his mind as a model of what a good President should be. As with many of our generation when young, Johnson knew his political position only when the President had stated it. Nothing so endured in his memory as his appointment by F.D.R. in 1935, when he was twenty-seven, to head the National Youth Administration in Texas and his service from 1937 on as Roosevelt's favorite young congressman. There were many later occasions when Lyndon Johnson, deferring to Texas wealth, folk rites, oil or cupidity, thought it wise to subdue his liberal convictions. But he never abandoned them, and he was particularly concerned to prove to himself and to others that he had not. This need lay behind his oft-quoted comment on his onetime protégé John B. Connally: "That S.O.B. has forgotten he was ever poor."[4]

As compared with Kennedy, a less than novel point, Johnson had a much more effective appreciation of the uses of power. Partly because of Kennedy's relative youth, partly because of the narrow margin by which he was elected in 1960, yet more because his instinct was to avoid anything obtrusive, extravagant or threatening, J.F.K. was continuously circumspect in bringing the force of his office to bear on the Congress, the Executive, the press and the public. Once to my urging of some seemingly sensible action, Kennedy replied, "I agree, but I don't think the government will agree." It was not a remark that Johnson would have made.

We speak more often of presidential power than of the means by which it is exercised. These are not very subtle or impressive. Certainly Johnson's methods were not. He decided what he needed by

---

[4] For Johnson this expression was a gloss on language and carried no strong derogatory connotation. Huey Long once distinguished between the conversational and the opprobrious form. Reacting in anger to some action of a political associate, he said, "You're a son-of-a-bitch, and I'm not using profanity. I'm talking about your parent."

way of legislative, bureaucratic, press or public action or support. Then he himself asked those involved directly. He was not greatly given to threat, as was sometimes suggested. Nor to promise. The Johnson method played on the natural preference of people to say yes when asked by the President personally, especially if the request is in strong and urgent language with the presidential chair and face moved up very close. By agreeing, you could ingratiate yourself while believing that you were rendering a public service. Johnson reinforced his requests with appeals to vanity — the support of the individual being asked was always decisive — and, if it seemed useful, to pleas for sympathy or resort to something close to tears. Fear, if it was invoked, was the result of the individual's hearing, along with Johnson's inspired scatology, how ineffable, stupid or absurd were those who had refused to see the light and go along. You could easily imagine how you would be described if you managed to resist the Johnson persuasion.

* * *

I first came to know Lyndon Johnson in 1941. In later years and as President he seemed a large man, compelling of stature. In 1941, he was lean and gawky, a country boy, if not vulnerable, then certainly far from being the secure and solid figure the world later knew. With his contemporary Jerry Voorhis of California (who was defeated by Nixon in 1946), Lyndon Johnson was a liberal's liberal in the House, and our introduction was through money-raising efforts on Johnson's behalf by Clifford and Virginia Durr, transplants to Washington from Montgomery, Alabama, whose committed (and in Virginia's case, uninhibited) liberalism was eventually to arouse the gravest suspicion in the McCarthy era. Many years later Johnson told me that one of his proudest Senate accomplishments was in telling Joe McCarthy and another witch-hunter, William E. Jenner of Indiana, to lay off the Durrs or suffer the full if unspecified consequences of the Johnson wrath. McCarthy, he told me, "frightened good."

In the 1950s, while serving on the Democratic Advisory Council, I saw Lyndon Johnson with some frequency, for the Council existed, as I've indicated, partly to take the Texas image off the Democratic Party. This effort Johnson did not feel at all necessary, but we met, nonetheless, on amicable terms.

I have a particular memory of going, on September 19, 1957, to visit the Johnsons at the L.B.J. Ranch when he was Senate Majority Leader. I had been lecturing at the Air War College at Maxwell Air Force Base in Alabama — a mildly distressing occasion for me, for it was the first time I noticed that colonels looked young. I went on to Austin and from the airport was taken to meet Johnson and go dove hunting on the lovely upland country near his ranch. The hunting was a painful thing, for I had almost never before shot a gun. But as a New England intellectual I didn't feel I could let down my side so, at intervals, when a dove or something equally out of Audubon flew by, I shut my eyes and pulled the trigger. Jacqueline Kennedy once told me her husband had been similarly troubled but worse; he had been forced to shoot at a deer.

Arthur Schlesinger had been invited to visit Johnson in Washington a short time earlier — looking forward to the 1960 elections, Johnson was cultivating northern liberals. Schlesinger told of being treated to an explosion of conversation, one that he had found it both undesirable and impossible to interrupt. The politics, personal foibles, sex lives, abilities and absurdities of Johnson's Senate colleagues had been reviewed in detail in the course of a long morning. Arthur, by his own account, had remained silent and attentive throughout.

Johnson and I conversed that day over drinks at the ranch on which we had been hunting, in Johnson City, driving back to the Johnson ranch, at supper, after supper, on a walk by the Pedernales and into the early morning by the swimming pool. Once he spoke appreciatively of Schlesinger's visit, adding with a sigh, "The damn fellow does talk too much."

He had asked me as a special favor to bring him a speech on economic policy. I had produced an unexceptional exegesis of the current liberal faith with some of the thoughts I had just worked into *The Affluent Society.* For dinner the Johnsons gathered around a large table, L.B.J. at the end, the assemblage extending as far down each side as might be necessary. Were there too many, there would be, farm style as we called it in Canada, a second sitting. At dinner Johnson, with appreciative gestures, read my speech to the gathering.

Most of our conversation that evening was on economics. I doubt that Johnson had ever read a serious book on the subject. He was, nonetheless, confidently in command of the basic ideas, as economists who were later to serve with him in the White House were without exception to agree. He had had much oral instruction, which his attentive and receptive mind had preserved. And in the case of a good congressman or senator much economic knowledge, from daily exposure, comes in through the pores.

I heard that day and evening, as did every other visitor, of the dams and lakes L.B.J., aided by a wise and pliable government, had brought to his Texas constituents and neighbors. (Next day I saw some.) I heard too of his fears that his recent heart attack would set a limit on the effort he could apply to politics, and I was far from convinced. I heard finally, this as we drove from Johnson City to the ranch, of the hard struggle his parents had had to survive on this land. In fact, Lyndon Johnson's father, a state legislator and a leading citizen, was a man of comfortable means. In later years I came to know Sam Houston Johnson, Lyndon's amusing, liberal, intelligent and highly unmotivated brother. Sam Houston told me that Lyndon's estimate of the Johnson family income had gone down by around fifty percent for each year he was in public office.[5]

L.B.J. continued to find much value in my speech drafts, the last politician to express a need for them. After he became President, he still, on occasion, asked for help. The last time was in the mid-sixties when his request was relayed by my Cambridge neighbor and friend Francis M. Bator, then a Johnson assistant. The President had exhausted all of the local resources; I was in Vermont, and he would send a plane. One came to the nearest airport, in Keene, New Hampshire, and we stopped in New Jersey to pick up Joe Califano, then White House counsel, who was on some business there. By then my opposition to the Vietnam policy had opened a rift with the administration. Johnson asked me to keep my visit confidential; he said he didn't want to worry Dean Rusk.

I worked on two speeches all through that long afternoon in the West Wing office of Jack Valenti, Johnson's principal assistant for such matters. At the end of the day Johnson came in, put one foot up on Valenti's desk and proceeded to review what I had written.

One speech was ceremonial and unimportant. The other was on

[5] My last encounter with Sam Houston Johnson was during the Democratic Convention in Miami in 1972. He called me from Texas to say he wanted to endorse Frances "Sissy" Farenthold, the most liberal of candidates, for Vice President. I dictated a telegram which he dispatched back and which was read to the convention.

economics and the related purposes of the Great Society. I had combined various of my beliefs and what I knew of Johnson's with all permissible rhetoric. Watching the President, I could see that he approved. Presently he laid the typescript down on the desk.

"Ken, you've saved my life. It's exactly what I want to say. I'm not going to change a word."

Only a very secure man accepts a speech without change. Most feel they must assert their own literary competence and political personality, however negligible, by making some amendments of their own.

"I'm not going to change a word. It's great."

Then his face clouded, and he added, "But I can tell you something. Nobody else will think so." Then came the Johnson metaphor:

"Did y'ever think, Ken, that making a speech on ee-conomics is a lot like pissing down your leg? It seems hot to you, but it never does to anyone else."[6]

As people around Kennedy protected him from his candor, so all associated even distantly with L.B.J. protected him from his scatology. Perhaps because of a similar early association with farms and barnyard humor, I greatly admired it — in contrast with Kennedy who didn't like it at all. On occasion, much literary value was lost in the laundry for public use. Thus Johnson did not, as widely reported, say of Gerald Ford that he couldn't walk and chew gum at the same time. That would be weak and lacking in style. Johnson said, "That Gerald Ford. He can't fart and chew gum at the same time."[7]

*   *   *

In December 1963, to resume in chronological order, a few weeks after the death of President Kennedy, I made a speech in Washington on our need to become serious about the islands of poverty that remained a disgrace in the Republic and with which I had dealt in *The Affluent Society*:

[6]Jack Valenti remembered the metaphor and gives it in slightly different form in *A Very Human President* (New York: Norton, 1975), pp. 251–252. He also, a small detail, says that it was he who summoned me down. It was Francis Bator, as the latter has affirmed.

[7]I remind all again, including friends of President Ford, that Johnson's characterizations did not sacrifice vigor for mere truth.

. . . [O]n one elementary point there must be no doubt. If the head of a family is stranded deep on the Cumberland Plateau, or if he never went to school, or if he has no useful skill, or if his health is broken, or if he succumbed as a youngster to a slum environment, or if opportunity is denied to him because he is a Negro [still the accepted usage], then he will be poor and his family will be poor, and that will be true no matter how opulent everyone else becomes.

Equally there must be no doubt that the means for rescuing this man or his children — investment to conserve and develop resources, assistance in relocation of workers, assistance to new industries, vastly improved education, training and retraining, medical and mental care, youth employment, counselling, urban recreational facilities, housing, slum abatement and the assurance of full civic equality — will require public effort and public funds. Poverty can be made to disappear. It won't be accomplished simply by stepping up the growth rate any more than it will be accomplished by incantation or ritualistic washing of the feet.

I went on to urge, I believe, for the first time, the idea of a Teachers Corps:

To the best of knowledge there is no place in the world where well-educated people are really poor. Why don't we select, beginning next year, the hundred lowest-income counties (or in the case of urban slums more limited areas of equal population) and designate them as special educational districts. They would then be equipped (or re-equipped) with a truly excellent and comprehensive school plant, including both primary and secondary schools, transportation and the best in recreational facilities. The construction employment in this part of the task would not be unwelcome. Then, in the manner of the Peace Corps, but with ample pay, an elite body of young teachers would be assembled — ready to serve in the most remote areas, tough enough and well-trained enough to take on the worst slums, proud to go to Harlan County or to Harlem.[8]

Johnson read and greatly approved my comments. Similar ideas, I am sure, had been stirring in his mind and the thoughts of others. As he later told,[9] he was also impressed by my argument, developed in *The Affluent Society* and pressed in conversation, that the very poor in the United States slip easily from the attention of politicians, in-

[8] "Wealth and Poverty" before the National Policy Committee on Pockets of Poverty, December 13, 1963.
[9] In his memoirs, *The Vantage Point: Perspectives of the Presidency 1963–1969* (New York: Holt, Rinehart and Winston, 1971), p. 72.

cluding liberal politicians. They live in the voiceless anonymity of the urban ghettos and in the even greater silence of the Appalachians, the Ozarks and the rural South. Access to press, radio and television, as also to politicians, is itself correlated with income. A plea for public funds by the head of Lockheed, Chrysler or a deeply needful bank is instantly heard; the poor man doesn't ask, for he knows no one is listening.

During the Christmas holidays of 1963, economists on Johnson's staff proposed pilot programs to test what might be possible by way of remedial action on poverty. Nothing so assuages the liberal conscience at low cost as a pilot program. This Lyndon Johnson well understood. Instead he proposed a billion dollars for a serious effort and asked Sargent Shriver to come up with a full-scale design. And he asked me to lend a hand. Beginning in February, we went to work in the offices of the Peace Corps, of which Shriver was then the head.

It was a task rich in practical instruction but not one on which I look back with satisfaction. It should have had my attention full time. Instead I was teaching and writing and commuting to meetings in Washington. Worse, we had an excess of plausible suggestions: Job training. Money and talent to improve bad schools. Head start programs to make up for deficient family training. Medical help to overcome physical handicaps. The inevitable agricultural program, dimly conceived and trading on urban innocence, to help the poor small farmer. One possible remedy for poverty would be to give the poor income; this alone was excluded.

My preference was for letting unemployed youngsters have a chance to learn marketable skills — what became the Job Corps. And for the cadre of well-motivated teachers that became the Teachers Corps. For improving the schools these teachers could do what money, in face of a tradition of bad school administration and community ignorance and neglect, could never accomplish. Of the most popular of the proposals, providing funds to allow communities to develop their own programs of self-help — the Community Action Programs — I was less sure. No doubt we underestimate the capacity of the local community to organize for its own betterment. But there is also danger that men and women of idealism and good will, captured by the mystique of community self-realization, will be unduly optimistic as to the accomplishments from local initiative. The Community Action Programs proved very popular. I remained uncertain as to what was good and what was less good.

When the Office of Economic Opportunity was formally organized, I was appointed by the President to its supervisory board and served until my position on Vietnam became too difficult for Johnson. Like corporate boards of directors, supervisory bodies established by Presidents are, with the rarest exceptions, valuable principally for the education they accord their members. So in this case for me. One of the best of our meetings was at a Job Corps camp in New Jersey at the former Camp Kilmer U.S. Army base. I talked that day with numerous of the enrollees, most of them black. It was wonderful and a trifle embarrassing to hear their thanks for a chance to learn, among other things, the more arcane aspects of automobile repair.

That day, in an explicitly educational exercise, our board was given a lecture on alcohol and alcoholism as a cause of poverty. I sat next to James B. Conant, by now retired from Harvard and a fellow board member. During the talk he leaned over to tell me that in his more than adequate experience alcoholism was not uniquely a problem of the poor. The group most afflicted, he could affirm firsthand, presumably out of experience with their festivals, was the alumni of Harvard University.

The efforts of the Office of Economic Opportunity, however flawed; the great increase in federal aid to education; the provision of medical care for the old and the poor; and, most of all, the revolution in civil rights reflected the valid Johnson instinct. There are many strategies for the achievement of conservative — or reactionary — ends. Those who drew Lyndon Johnson away from these preoccupations into Vietnam and made that his fame were as skilled as any in all history.

*   *   *

In 1964, I watched L.B.J.'s nomination at Atlantic City, a convocation in which not even the television commentators could find a modicum of suspense. Johnson sought to help by trying with transparent fraud to give the impression that he was undecided about his Vice President. Perhaps instead of Hubert Humphrey it might be Eugene McCarthy or Thomas J. Dodd of Connecticut, who was soon to be censured by the Senate for uninspired larceny. And there was a brief struggle over the seating of the Freedom, as distinct from the routinely white, Mississippi delegation. None of this, and certainly not the oratory, relieved the tedium. I saw old friends, strolled on the decaying boardwalk with Arthur Schlesinger, made my way over the convention floor with an air of serious concern, and went home before the end.

That autumn, in a far from reluctant response to L.B.J.'s request, I campaigned in New England and New York, the Middle West and up the West Coast from Los Angeles to Seattle. By now, in the relentless course of political progress, I had passed on from writing campaign speeches and the stage following, which is speaking in hopeless precincts, to being a nearly sufficient attraction in mildly plausible Democratic territory. However, a shill was still deemed advisable. For one glorious autumn day I campaigned in a small plane across Ohio accompanied by Lucy Bird Johnson. At a succession of meetings ending with a large Cleveland rally, she spoke well of her parents, and I followed with a persuasive message on Barry Goldwater's warlike tendencies and his commitment to a revolt of the affluent against the poor. Goldwater was a man before his time.

In Wisconsin my supporting cast consisted of Suzanne Roosevelt, the handsome wife of Franklin D. Roosevelt, Jr., and the superbly articulate Scotty Fitzgerald Lanahan, later Smith. Scott Fitzgerald would have been fascinated but also a trifle disturbed by his daughter's speeches, for, as an artist, he remained always within the accepted modalities. His characters kissed but did not go to bed; their language, however compelling, was never vulgar. Not so Scotty. At a rally at the University of Wisconsin at Madison she rang a brilliant change on the Goldwater campaign slogan, "In your heart you know he's right." It was, "In your ass you know it's just gas." It brought down the house. With difficulty I persuaded her not to use it before a more responsible audience the next night in downstate Illinois.

At the White House one day in early January 1966, Sargent Shriver now being increasingly occupied with the war on poverty, Lyndon Johnson asked me to take over the Peace Corps. I was wholly unprepared, as almost certainly he intended. I escaped by saying that I would have to consult my wife. In her diary Lady Bird, who was present, observed that "he [Galbraith] sounded as if he really might do it but then said, 'I have to talk to my wife,' and that's

when a man wants to put on the brakes."[10] As usual, this shrewd
and multitalented woman had it right.

*   *   *

An earlier offer from Johnson, considered and abandoned or just
possibly only imagined, had larger consequences. On the evening of
July 15, 1965, Lyndon Johnson called me in Cambridge. I was out,
and later when I returned the call, the President was unavailable.
Very early the next morning Kitty and I left for Washington to
attend the funeral of Adlai Stevenson, who had collapsed and died
of a heart attack on Upper Grosvenor Street in London two days
before.

We assembled briefly at Arthur Schlesinger's house, a sad convocation that included Lauren Bacall, Marietta Tree and others of Adlai's devoted friends. At the cathedral I sat next to Arthur; Edward
Kennedy joined us just as the service began. During the first hymn,
in a scene direct from Evelyn Waugh, Schlesinger or Kennedy, perhaps both, began to pass me information:

> Oh God, our help in ages past
> Our hope for years to come
> You are the first on Lyndon's list
> In our eternal home.

The call of the previous evening came back powerfully to my
mind. The rest of the service escaped me. Then when we emerged
from the church, McGeorge Bundy, who was still National Security
Adviser, asked us to come over to the White House. So I was to be
offered Stevenson's job as Ambassador to the United Nations. Two
years almost to the day had elapsed since I had left the Embassy in
New Delhi. I was well regarded in the new countries — and by liberals at home. I was thought to have been a success in India. It
didn't seem possible, however, that Dean Rusk had been consulted.

It was a post I did not wish to take. One is tied by a telephone to
the Department of State and instructed in detail and often in conflict
with one's personal convictions by officials far down the line. Neither
the policy nor its defense is one's own. A lawyer, professionally a
mouthpiece, can defend the improbable, impalpable or criminal

---

[10]*A White House Diary* (New York: Holt, Rinehart and Winston, 1970), p. 349.

without being supposed to believe what he says. A professor cannot; he is expected to be sincere. If he says what he does not believe, he is a hypocrite. I was also by now deeply, even emotionally, committed to *The New Industrial State*. I could not again put the book aside.

Yet it was not an easy job to refuse. There would be Johnson's accomplished persuasion. When my refusal became known, a larger public would say that Galbraith had no interest in advancing the cause of peace. The United Nations is an organization but also an act of conscience. The only solution for me was to have a better suggestion: "Look, Mr. President, I know the right man for the job." Such, though less coherently, were the thoughts that passed through my mind that morning. I had a name.

A few weeks before, Arthur Goldberg, then newly an Associate Justice of the Supreme Court, had lectured at the Harvard Law School and, when it was over, had dropped by our house for a visit. He told me that after his intensely active years as a labor lawyer, politician and Secretary of Labor, the Court involved a severe case of decompression. Its much more deliberative pace was a great and by no means wholly welcome change. Goldberg's visit blossomed in my memory.

Bundy had, in fact, another matter in mind. But while we talked in his basement quarters, L.B.J. became aware of our presence and summoned us upstairs to the Oval Office. He was in the best Johnson form.

"That Stevenson. Why did he have to die right now? He was always off in his timing. Who am I going to get to take his place?"

By now Johnson may have had second thoughts. Or quite possibly there had been no first ones. Or he had talked with the Secretary of State. But I was intent on avoiding all risk; I told him of my meeting with Goldberg and that Goldberg was a little bored on the Court.[11] Johnson was immediately interested; he wondered if Goldberg could be persuaded, changed the subject and then returned.

"How would Arthur get along with the A-rabs?"

[11] There was no justification for my using the word bored, and Goldberg, when he later heard about it, was justifiably angry. Johnson, in his memoirs, tells that I also suggested Arthur for Secretary of HEW replacing Anthony Celebrezze (Lyndon Johnson, p. 543). I cannot think this likely.

I urged the obvious, that Goldberg was not only a highly experienced — and superbly durable — negotiator but far above prejudice in such matters. Once again we digressed, once again Johnson returned to Goldberg. My wife, who had been watching the President, remarked as we left the White House that I had made a sale. Knowing L.B.J.'s virtuoso tendencies, I expressed doubt. But — always assuming there had been danger — I was out clear.

That afternoon we flew to Hyannis Port to have dinner with the Robert Kennedys and numerous of the clan and went on to Cambridge. A day later Johnson called up to say that he had talked with Goldberg and he had accepted. It now occurred to me that I had told Robert Kennedy of my recommendation. This Johnson would not appreciate; he didn't care to have his decisions seem other than his own. I confessed. The response, though my memory is not exact, was also vintage Johnson: "Well, if anyone asks you if you made a recommendation, shut up, deny it."

It was a poisonous thing I did. Goldberg's resignation cost the Court a good and liberal jurist. Abe Fortas replaced him and became the focus of the violent anti-civil-rights antipathy. This, abetted by personal financial indiscretion, forced his resignation, and the way was then open at least indirectly for Warren Burger as Chief Justice. I did little for liberalism that morning.

* * *

As I've noted, it was on foreign policy that Lyndon Johnson was uncertain of his own judgment. Of this uncertainty I had more than an inkling. In mid-May of 1961, in the season when Kipling said of India that it was a pile of sand under a burning glass, Lyndon Johnson and Lady Bird had come on an official tour. He was my first important visitor at the Embassy, and he asked me to meet him in Bangkok to provide him with any useful information I might have. In Indian town and countryside during the next days, Johnson was the confident, articulate and eloquent man I knew so well. His rapport with the villagers was easy and complete. So also with the local officials and, needless to say, the engulfing Indian and American press. The official sessions were sadly in contrast. Though Nehru could not have differed more from Johnson in background, interests, culture, mood and manner, he was visibly attracted by him, as he later said. But in the discussions of foreign policy, even in the banalities to which men of high position are confined, Johnson was diffident, uncertain, insecure. He glanced repeatedly at me for reassurance. There were embarrassed silences that, characteristically, Nehru did nothing to fill and Johnson, most uncharacteristically, did not exploit. At the principal session the unease did not end until, by accident, the conversation happened onto rural electrification; this both men greatly favored.

Johnson sought to compensate for his uncertainty in foreign policy with an outward display of firmness, strength, decisiveness. This made him open to the advice of those who urged the seemingly strong as distinct from the restrained and considered course. Perhaps also his instinct was for an assertively masculine pose, as others have suggested. Combined, these qualities put him at the mercy of those who took pride not in their knowledge but in their will to act. Thus the disaster in Southeast Asia.

Through the 1960s, the menace of Vietnam grew steadily in my mind. At first I talked with Johnson of my concern; then it became impossible to talk. One listened instead to his impassioned, even angry, defense. I began to make speeches against the war and to help organize against it. This L.B.J. saw as infamous. The youngsters might defect on the war; I was of his age and generation. Support from old hands could surely be expected. An understandable thought.

One last time in 1966, he called me briefly to Washington. India had suffered a bad harvest and was threatened with famine. I had concluded, while ambassador, that easy supplies of grain from the United States were in some measure a substitute for a strong Indian policy on domestic cereal and fertilizer production. Thus the danger of eventual famine was increased. Once, when visiting Bombay, I had watched a huge tanker unload American wheat, and I had reflected on how perilous was the position of people who depended for their lives on the arrival of these ships — on a life line stretching all the way to the Great Plains. Now, without causing any actual suffering, there was a chance to dramatize this danger. Let there be help. But let it be parceled out in steps — what came to be called the "short tether" policy. So it was arranged. No doubt Johnson had similar word from others, but as always one is impressed with the decisive character of one's own advice.

In the following months Johnson was criticized bitterly by Indians and by American liberals for the policy; it seemed very ungenerous. As so often, it was better to be the adviser than the person responsible.

This was almost our last encounter. The last was on April 21, 1967, or rather early the following morning. The junta in Greece had recently arrested Andreas Papandreou, the son of George Papandreou, former premier and head of the anti-royalist Center Union party. There was word, or anyhow an impression, that shortly Andreas would be executed.

Andreas Papandreou had been a graduate student in economics at Harvard and had taught at the University of Minnesota, Northwestern University and the University of California. At Berkeley he had been chairman of the department of economics. He was a good economist and a very good academic politician; those who were less skilled in those days did not endure as head of the Berkeley department. Then Andreas had abandoned his American academic career to return to Greece and to politics. His popularity in American university circles was nicely balanced by the suspicion with which he was regarded by numerous people in Washington. He was insufficiently in support of NATO, insufficiently anti-Communist and unduly inclined to attribute omnipotent wickedness to the CIA.

Through that night I received calls from across the country — Kenneth Arrow from Stanford, Leonid Hurwicz from Minnesota and Robert Dorfman at Harvard. As a former ambassador, I was presumed to have access in Washington, but of this I was a good deal less certain. Rusk would not be helpful. Nor Phillips Talbot, the ambassador in Athens. Neither of them would annoy the Greek colonels on behalf of anyone as seemingly unstalwart in his anti-Communist faith as Papandreou. Johnson was the only hope, but that was to ask help from the man whom I had deserted on Vietnam. However, if I didn't and if Papandreou were killed, my responsibility would be great. Toward midnight I decided I must give it a try.

I called Joe Califano at the White House and found him still in his office. He told me that Johnson was awake and entertaining some people in the presidential quarters. We got the details on half a page, not omitting to mention the academic concern that was being expressed for Papandreou across the country.[12] Califano took them upstairs.

In the early morning hours my phone rang once again. It was Nicholas Katzenbach, then Undersecretary of State, calling to read with a greatly audible chuckle a message he had just received from the President:

"Call up Ken Galbraith and tell him that I've told those Greek bastards to lay off that son-of-a-bitch — whoever he is."[13]

[12] Others wired the President, for he was later quoted as saying, "This is the first issue in history on which all the American economists seem to have agreed." *New York Times,* May 8, 1967.

[13] A version of this message, cleaned up with dashes, appeared in *Newsweek,* presumably leaked by one of my economist friends to whom I repeated it. Papandreou was released a little later and allowed to leave Greece. Some weeks afterward in Paris on returning to my hotel one evening, I encountered him and joined him and Irene Papas, the actress, for a drink. He told me that a copy of *Newsweek* brought casually to his jail cell by a visitor was his first indication that things were taking a turn for the better. Andreas is now leader of the major opposition party in the Greek parliament. The story here told, with slight differences in detail, is in his autobiography, *Democracy at Gunpoint: The Greek Front* (New York: Doubleday, 1970), p. 27.

29

Vietnam: The Beginning

BETWEEN ADOLESCENT EXUBERANCE and eventual disutility, an individual has at best around fifty years to come to terms with the world around him, enjoy it and respond as conscience or ambition requires to public responsibilities. It is a matter for regret if any large part of this time is preempted by some external, deep and intransigent anxiety. That is my regret as regards Indochina and in particular Vietnam.

One should not exaggerate. From 1961 when I began to face the issue until the day of the helicopters in 1975, I had many other concerns, including the books on which I will have a word in a later chapter. I did not have to work, much less fight, in that literally benighted[1] land. Nor did any member of my family. It is my impression that few sons of Harvard professors, or more generally of the American establishment, were so endangered; opposition to the war developed perceptibly when they seemed to be. Unlike many one-time friends, I was not permanently and publicly wounded by support or acquiescence in the war. I look back on those fourteen years of involvement, nonetheless, with distaste and sorrow.

*   *   *

Better than most of my colleagues in Washington, I knew this world, or rather its close counterparts, and the huge, even unbridgeable gap that divides the culture, social structure and government in Asia (Japan apart) from those in Europe and the United States. And knowing this, I was with the danger of generalizing policy and action from our world to theirs. The tendency to such generalization was and remains a major source of error.

[1] "Overtaken by dark or darkness." *American Heritage Dictionary of the English Language.*

Western industrial society has a firm economic and political structure, and within this nearly all of its people live. So, by the action of the government and directly or indirectly through corporations, unions and other organizations, these societies can be guided or even controlled. In Asia, as I knew from India, Pakistan and Ceylon, the great majority of the people live outside the structure of government and outside structured economic organizations, including that, needless to say, of the modern business enterprise. It is this detachment, indeed, that has allowed of their survival. Over most of history public authority has been deeply inimical — its agents and officers, arriving over the mud tracks or the dikes, have come for taxes, food, pillage, recruits, rarely for anything benign.

It is the nature of this quiet and quite workable anarchy that there are no instruments of power — no handles — that authority can grasp and use. The British did not govern in the Indian villages. They merely maintained order where mostly there was already order, regularized rent and taxes, traded and recruited a few soldiers to serve as mercenaries. The life of the village millions went on as before; there was little or nothing within the power of the British that could bring change. Little or nothing in the villages in the two hundred years of the Raj *was* changed.

For the Communists this lack of structure is far more serious. Communism involves a sophisticated management of industry and state. The ancient Chinese experience in and talent for organization gave Communism a limited chance in China, although in the rural parts of the country more remains the same than was ever changed. The case of India and Indian Communism, as I've earlier told, was a superb guide to what Communism would encounter in Indochina. Calling itself Communist, it would still be a village and agricultural society with only superficial control from the top and even less from Moscow or Peking. It would also be insignificant on the world scene. And, as noted, not even the most acute anti-Communist can tell a Communist jungle from a free enterprise jungle.

*   *   *

Four other factors had shaped my thoughts. In India, since Communism (or socialism) is a dream rather than a workable prospect, it invited the participation of those given to dreams. And all people have a powerful preference for their own dream. In consequence, I had come to believe that Communism was far more factional and divisive in the poor countries than conventional Cold War doctrine assumed. The notion of the great monolith so central to the system of the Dulles brothers, the Pentagon, Dean Rusk and even some of my Harvard colleagues was an artificial construct, one that served only the fashionable discussion. However, I must limit my claim here to foresight. I did not for a moment foresee the pluralism and the factionalism that, and especially in Indochina, the Communist commitment would eventually reveal.

I was also deeply impressed by the sensitivity to external influence, whatever the source, of the politicians of the new countries. I had lived, as had few others, with this sensitivity — with the pride of people who do not wish to be told what they should do either by a peripatetic economic adviser or, later, a financially endowed and presumptively powerful diplomat. Few days passed when I was ambassador when I did not give thought, this soon becoming automatic, as to how I could urge a point without seeming to be exerting influence. Contemplating Vietnam, one could only suppose that the need for such caution in face of jealously guarded independence would be an effective limitation on the role of China or the Soviet Union — and our own.

Further I had come to understand the Washington global, geopolitical or strategic mind, as variously it is called. This motivates a species of statesman, extant to this day, who should never be allowed to look at a map. Doing so and seeing Africa, Asia or Latin America — Angola, Ethiopia, the Horn of Africa, Iran, Afghanistan, Nicaragua, Chile — they ask who is in control. If not the United States, it must be the Russians. Experience of the post-colonial world is a superb antidote to the global strategic mind. It informs one deeply on the unlikelihood that people and leaders, having escaped from one form of imperial domination, will hasten to embrace another — American, Soviet or Chinese. And if, as in, say, Ethiopia, no government has ever exerted much control from inside, the real effect of external power will not be great. The ability of a country to control a people economically and culturally as well as geographically distant from its own — and without the handles provided by a developed structure of government and industry — is very limited.

Finally, in those years I was beginning to sense, although imperfectly, the dynamics of revolution in these lands. If a government is corrupt or predatory, there does not have to be a better alternative; it can be overthrown even though the alternative is much worse. The existing depredations are a matter of harsh experience. The alternative is hypothetical; it exists in promises, oratory and hope, and these always seem, until practical experience arrives, relentlessly and unqualifiedly good. Military, political, economic and inertial power may be on the side of the bad government. Liberty, achievement, honesty and progress are always, as a vision, on the side of the alternative. As later in Teheran after the Shah, it could have been argued that things in Saigon, admittedly bad, would be yet worse after the leaders we were supporting had gone. But this case could never have been persuasive.

*   *   *

My first involvement in Indochina was with Laos. Trouble there led Kennedy to ask me to advance by some weeks my departure to India in the spring of 1961. The Geneva Accords of 1954 ending the French colonial war and otherwise seeking to pacify these lands and limit foreign influence had established an International Control Commission of which Canada, Poland and India were the members, with India as chairman. Under the Accords, a neutralist government took office in Vientiane headed by Prince Souvanna Phouma, a charming and civilized man of my eventual acquaintance, who was in uneasy coalition and state of peace with the assertedly Communist forces of the Pathet Lao under Prince Souphanouvong. The Pathet Lao dominated in the northern provinces. In 1958, Prince Souvanna Phouma's neutralists were replaced by a right-wing government under Phoumi Sananikone. Although an American protégé, Phoumi Sananikone was soon replaced by a general called Phoumi Nosavan whom the CIA thought better, and he, in turn, was thrown out in 1960 by a young paratrooper named Kong Le, who brought back Prince Souvanna Phouma. A few days after Kennedy's election in 1960, Prince Souvanna was thrown out, with American connivance, by Phoumi Nosavan, a leading part being taken by J. Graham Parsons, who had previously been ambassador in Vientiane and who was now back home in charge of that part of the world in the State Department. Almost immediately the government of Phoumi Nosavan, a man of startling incompetence, began to come apart. There was no hope that he could resist the pressure of the Pathet

Lao from up north. In the spring of 1961, John F. Kennedy, having mastered the names of all the principals, explained these developments to the American people in a press conference. It was impressive, and the tapes were afterward played not for information but for amusement as the President's tongue passed faultlessly over the charming Laotian names.

Fortunately none of the developments just recounted had major effect on the people of Laos. They were protected from the aforementioned rivalries by the total absence of railroads, the near absence of roads, the happy fact that for much of its length the Mekong River is unnavigable, and by the extensive intervening forest. So they remained largely undisturbed in their rice cultivation and indolent commitment to minor narcotics and graceful conversation. Only as the armed bands of the competing generals and princes happened along were they troubled by the conflict. Of the meaning of the various and irrelevant political labels they had no knowledge. Even when fighting broke out between the opposing forces, as they were called, damage was limited by a genial convention that caused the more dangerous weapons — mortars and recoilless guns — to be fired at random, certainly without a serious effort to aim at the other side.

*   *   *

None of this distant opera was of importance to the United States. As Arthur Schlesinger observed in those years, Laos was not a dagger pointed at the heart of Kansas. Nor did President Kennedy think so. But by a process of unexamined repetition in tense and seemingly informed bureaucratic conclave, it *had* become important to many people in the State Department, the CIA and the Pentagon and to their impressionable acolytes in the foreign-policy establishment. Laos, it was said, was a vital factor in the free world; our actions there tested the leadership of the United States. Meetings were not called to inquire whether we should be in Laos; they were called only to consider what should be done in Laos. The individual who asked what we were accomplishing for ourselves in that country struck a diversionary note that was in conflict with serious business. Next time he might well be excluded. "We know what he's going to say. We've got to get on with the business."

But most of all in Laos we were subject to one of the recurrent and dangerous influences on our foreign policy — fear of the political consequences of doing the sensible thing, which in many cases is nothing much at all. While the Vientiane government of Phoumi Nosavan was militarily worthless and the people out in the country were sensibly indifferent to their rulers, to leave them to themselves was, it was said, to retreat before the march of international Communism. It was to the prospective political outcry that Kennedy reacted.

He was wrong in this assessment. Few if any votes were affected by what happened in Laos as few were lost from our eventual withdrawal from Vietnam — few, indeed, as compared with those at risk from continued involvement. But this Kennedy did not foresee. And while I was opposed to our intervention in Laos, I did not foresee it either.

*   *   *

In the spring of 1961, the only alternative to sending in the Marines, the commitment of the Royal Lao Army to nonviolence being by now thoroughly established, was to get Souvanna Phouma and his neutralists back in power and to get the International Control Commission back to Laos to help keep the peace. At White House meetings that spring, the Joint Chiefs and their chairman, General Lyman L. Lemnitzer, had assured the President that, with sufficient force, they could go in and win for Phoumi Nosavan. Pressed as to what would happen were there a major reaction by Hanoi and Peking, they said that it would be contained if they could use nuclear weapons. Kennedy was profoundly shocked and thus confirmed in the view that neutralization — the return of Souvanna Phouma — was the only solution.

A major key was Jawaharlal Nehru. He was necessary for any effort to get the International Control Commission back to Vientiane. And he seemed our best hope for persuading the Communist countries to go along with the neutralizing effort.

John Foster Dulles had equated neutrality with immorality and, by so doing, placed India beyond easy diplomatic reach. Nehru was not quickly persuaded of our change of mood. After informing myself in more detail than I wished on the politics of Laos, I addressed myself to him with much energy. Averell Harriman, passing through New Delhi, stopped also to lend his voice. At first cautiously, then with some enthusiasm, Nehru agreed to help our cause. I've always imagined that one slightly irreverent response went far to reassure him. When he asked me at the end of April 1961 how he could be sure we were serious about Souvanna and the neutral solution, that we were not still seeking somehow to extend our military sway and that of the Southeast Asia Treaty Organization, I said that we had finally learned that the Laotians were not militarily very useful, that they "had not learned to kill each other like the civilized nations." He reacted with much pleasure and almost immediately promised to go to the Soviets and to Ho Chi Minh on our behalf.[2] This, with favorable effect, he did.

With much effort elsewhere a conference on Laos was assembled at Geneva, and in the next months Harriman negotiated the return of Souvanna Phouma.[3]

* * *

During the Laos negotiations and increasingly as 1961 passed, I came to feel that our concern as regards Indochina was about the wrong country. There was a far more threatening involvement farther down the Mekong. Vietnam, divided under the 1954 Geneva Accords, was somewhat less intended by nature for obscurity than Laos, and thus it was larger in the Washington geopolitical minds. Backed by Hanoi, the Viet Cong insurrection against the government of Ngo Dinh Diem seemed far more likely to invite our intervention. I began to press Kennedy on my fears. On May 10, 1961, I wrote him that "I have reached two conclusions as the result of my concern with Laos and the Congo.[4] These jungle regimes, where the writ of government runs only as far as the airport, are going to be a hideous problem for us in the months ahead . . . The rulers do not control or particularly influence their own people; and they neither have nor warrant their people's support. As a military ally the entire

[2] Also at that meeting, as I noted at the time, he expressed the thought that there might be more trouble between the Vietnamese and the Chinese than appeared on the surface or was consistent with the Cold War vision of monolithic Communist unity.

[3] Arriving for the conference, Harriman found himself at the head of a huge delegation — around fifty in number — with an intransigent Cold War strategist as his deputy. He asked that the man be replaced by William H. Sullivan, a more amenable figure. The department protested that Sullivan was far too junior. Drawing on a knowledge of bureaucratic procedure that I observed with profit and admiration, Harriman simply reduced the size of the delegation until Sullivan was the senior.

[4] Where, at the time, there was also great geopolitical fear of some kind of Communist takeover.

Laos nation is clearly inferior to a battalion of conscientious objectors from World War I. We get nothing from their support, and I must say I wonder what the Communists get. One answer, no doubt, is that the Communists will do a better job of organizing existing leaders out. Nevertheless I am convinced that in these primitive countries we cannot always back winners and we cannot be sure that the winners we back will stay on our side. For the same reason we should never assume that anyone is lost to the Communists. We must above all face the probability of gains and losses and certainly no single loss will be decisive. Most of all we must not allow ourselves or the country to imagine that gains or losses in these incoherent lands are the same as gains or losses in the organized world, that of France or Italy — or India." [5]

Two months later, on July 11, my thoughts had passed on to Vietnam. ". . . South Vietnam is exceedingly bad. I hope, incidentally, that your information from there is good and I have an uneasy feeling that what comes in regular channels is very bad. Unless I am mistaken Diem has alienated his people to a far greater extent than we allow ourselves to know. This is our old mistake. We take the ruler's word and that of our own people who have become committed to him. The opponents are thieves and bandits; the problem is to get the police. I am sure the problem in Vietnam is partly the means to preserve law and order. But I fear that we have one more government which, on present form, no one will support." [6]

In September, back in Washington, I pressed my concerns directly with Kennedy and later added a more marginal thought:

"When I wake up at night I worry that in our first year in office we will be credited with losing Laos which we did not have, losing East Berlin which we did not have, losing East Germany which we did not have and (touchy point) with failing to persuade the world that Formosa is China. As an extreme idealist I am in favor of lost causes. But I wonder if we should lose our lost causes more than once." [7]

[5] Letter to the President in *Ambassador's Journal* (Boston: Houghton Mifflin, 1969), p. 107.
[6] Letter to the President in *Ambassador's Journal*, p. 154.
[7] Letter to the President in *Ambassador's Journal*, p. 211. My reference to Formosa was a touchy point because of my having advocated recognition of Peking and its admission to the United Nations under the two-China formula.
Everyone should react with caution to communications addressed to the President

I had little doubt as to Kennedy's agreement. It was nearly complete. The problem, as ever, was the political pressure of those clamoring for action, those wishing to do something, anything, at the price of doing the wrong thing. His words are still with me. Referring to the Bay of Pigs and the acceptance of a neutral Laos, he said, "You have to realize that I can only afford so many defeats in one year."

* * *

After the Viet Cong took Phuoc Vinh, a provincial capital sixty miles north of Saigon, in September 1961, with Diem's forces outdoing even those of Phoumi Nosavan in their Gandhian commitment to nonviolence, proposals for armed American intervention began to circulate in Washington. Kennedy decided to buy time in the usual way by sending a mission to study and report what was already known. Maxwell D. Taylor, the President's military adviser, a confident, handsome, highly cultivated paratroop general whose style greatly appealed to the Kennedys and whose systemically hard-line views were not yet fully revealed, was made head of the mission. Walt Whitman Rostow was his associate, with the certainty that he would write most of the report. Walt Rostow, a long-time personal friend of mine, was not considered a theological anti-Communist in those days. He had been kept out of the State Department, where on Kennedy's election he expected to serve, at least partly because, as I've noted, ancient FBI reports seemed to show a suspiciously accommodating taint. So, a less than obvious compromise, he had been appointed to the White House instead. My respect for Walt Rostow as an imaginative and resourceful scholar of surpassing diligence has survived many grave differences of opinion. His fault was in the ease of his accommodation to authority and the dominant political climate of the time. He had also a damaging commitment to innovative political and military design. At the time of his dispatch to Vietnam he was urging a SEATO guard of some 25,000 men, which as a practical matter would have had to be mostly American, to seal off

of the United States. The overwhelming odds are that he will never read them. However, my case could be better than some. Kennedy commented on them with frequency. And a few days after his death *Life* magazine called me to say that a short time earlier he had proposed to them that they be collected and published, presumably as worthwhile thoughts on policy in Asia. I vetoed the project because such a rush into print seemed without taste.

the northern borders of Vietnam. The seal, given the nature of the terrain and the alternative route through Laos, would have been very porous. And possibly also a commitment to combat.

Taylor, Rostow and their staff studied, went to the Philippines to write and came back to Washington with their report at about the same time — early November — that I came home with Nehru for an official visit. At Newport, Rhode Island, on November 6 at Hammersmith Farm, the estate of the President's mother- and stepfather-in-law Mr. and Mrs. Hugh D. Auchincloss, we pressed Nehru and M. J. Desai, the Indian Foreign Secretary and an old Southeast Asia hand, to help in finding a neutral solution in Vietnam. Nehru was not responsive, partly because our ideas on how to bring the Viet Cong insurrection to an end were far from precise. We asked variously for an approach by Nehru to Ho Chi Minh, a UN observer corps, a stronger International Control Commission and, more vaguely, Indian leadership in establishing a neutral belt across Southeast Asia, an idea then being urged by Chester Bowles. Some of these steps were more replete with hope than with promise. All reflected with clarity Kennedy's distaste for a more extensive military involvement.

During these discussions, or perhaps a day or so earlier, I became aware that Taylor and Rostow were urging the dispatch of troops. Back in Washington the day after the Newport meeting I went to Rostow's office in the Executive Office Building to get a copy of the report. He had one on his desk; it was classified to limit access to God and the President of the United States; specifically excluded were the other members of the Trinity. Rostow was visibly reluctant to let me see it; in this he was acting normally, for an established purpose of classification is to avoid criticism from potentially adverse readers. However, a useful informality is possible in such matters. My authorized access as an ambassador being equal to that of the authors of the report, I simply picked up the copy and walked out.

It was a thoroughly competent document on the administrative inadequacy of the Diem regime and the irrelevance of the ponderous convocation of politicians, entrepreneurs, squeeze artists and underpaid infantrymen that was called the army. It then went on to assume, but not to argue, that reform could be accomplished as an act of will by Ngo Dinh Diem. And, as I had previously heard, it proposed to send to Vietnam a modest — around 8000-man —

American armed force. This would not be the kind of naked intervention that would outwardly contravene the still exiguous ban under the Geneva Accords or that might adversely arouse world or American opinion. But the Mekong River was then in flood, a recurrent tendency of that stream, and the soldiers, with a heavy component of engineering units, would go into the Delta, the locus of the most serious insurrection, as humanely intentioned flood-control workers. This would be the publicized part of their mission. They would, however, shoot back when shot at. The real purpose was to give moral and military support to Diem and his battalions of unmotivated malingerers. Implicit in the proposal was the belief that all who heard of it, American or otherwise, would believe anything. Much other military weaponry, logistical support and combat advice would also be provided. Having read the report, I got an appointment with Kennedy to protest. He was deeply sympathetic.

In previous days he had received a recommendation from the Joint Chiefs by way of Robert McNamara and Roswell Gilpatric, the Deputy Secretary of Defense, endorsing the Taylor-Rostow proposal for armed intervention and noting that an eventual troop commitment of 205,000 men might be required, which they implied was both feasible and rather modest. And he had also in hand a memorandum from Robert McNamara and Dean Rusk urging against an immediate troop commitment, which, it noted, would have a disastrous effect on the negotiations then in progress to detach from Laos.[8] A President's life is not a simple one. Kennedy told me to go back to India by way of Saigon, talk to the people there and give him my view. He could not, I am sure, have had any doubt as to what it would be. The President plainly wanted ammunition on the other side.

As I left, McGeorge Bundy told me that the question of armed

[8] I knew generally of the Joint Chiefs' proposal at the time, and I have refreshed my recollection of the details from *The Pentagon Papers* (Boston: Beacon Press, Gravel Edition, 1971). It was a common complaint against Robert McNamara, one strongly articulated by George Ball, that he managed regularly to be on both sides of the question of intervention in Vietnam. This is not wholly surprising, assuming his intention to stay in office or his belief that he should. As Secretary of Defense he was compelled to transmit the persistently warlike designs of the Chiefs. As an adviser to the President he could, though with caution, say what he believed. Throughout the whole Vietnam controversy the three men to whom those of us opposing the war had access were George Ball, the accepted inside opponent, McGeorge Bundy and McNamara. These men, later much criticized, had the gratitude of those of us on whom they did not slam the door.

intervention in Vietnam was still unsettled. At the State Department U. Alexis Johnson, a stolid, thick-set interventionist, told me that the dispatch of troops had already been decided; my opposition and journey were futile. I decided to believe Bundy.

* * *

None could suppose my on-the-ground investigation was thorough. I spent some hours at CINCPAC (Commander-in-Chief, Pacific) in Hawaii with Admiral Harry Felt, the man in overall military command in the area, and a few more days in Vietnam with Embassy, CIA and AID officials and with General Lionel C. McGarr, the head of MAAG (the Military Assistance Advisory Group) and his officers. Although but recently arrived, the Ambassador, Frederick (Fritz) E. Nolting, Jr., a brave and attractive man, was already wholly committed to Diem and to getting to Vietnam whatever armed force might be required for his survival. But, as always in any American enterprise, there were individuals with an inescapable commitment to reality. These — lesser officers in the Embassy and the CIA — pictured the Diem regime and the Army of the Republic of Vietnam (one day to be celebrated as ARVN) as hopeless. The first was corrupt, incompetent and unpopular. So was the second.

One particular morning with General McGarr and his staff, mostly colonels, was deeply instructive. It was in a squalid room of the military headquarters. Soldiers gain political strength in the field from the tendency of civilians to be deferential, even obeisant, before the brisk military form. Those of us with the experience of dealing with the generals in World War II, as I've said before, were less vulnerable in this regard. One officer told me that operations through the jungle would not be difficult for American troops and equipment; there was little undergrowth. But another said the jungle was impassable. I pressed on the contradiction. Then, when I asked, I was given a figure of around 15,000 for the active enemy insurgents, while another officer, saying a good word for the South Vietnamese Army, estimated that it had inflicted some 17,000 casualties in the preceding ten months. I asked if any force could sustain such attrition and remain in being; at this point General McGarr lost patience and told his soldiers to shape up. There was agreement that Diem's military structure — his provincial army chiefs combined local government and political graft with military command — was unique and bad. Intelligence on insurgent operations was nonexistent.

There was further instruction from a trip by car to the north of Saigon into what later was to become famous as the Iron Triangle. This, even then, required an accompanying vehicle filled with villainous-looking protectors leaning out the sides with tommy guns.

* * *

My brief passage at an end, the Air Attaché in Saigon flew me to Bangkok. We took off steeply, for on one or two earlier occasions Viet Cong snipers sitting quietly in the heavy growth at the end of the runway had punctured the wings of low-flying planes. From Bangkok, via the "back channel" of the CIA, I sent Kennedy a summary of my conclusions, predictable as they were, in the language I could fairly well count on him to read:

"There is scarcely the slightest practical chance that the administrative and political reforms now being pressed upon Diem will result in real change . . . While situation is indubitably bad military aspects seem to me out of perspective. A comparatively well-equipped army with paramilitary formations number [ing] a quarter million men is facing a maximum of 15–18,000 lightly armed men. If this were equality, the United States would hardly be safe against the Sioux."[9] This conclusion I enlarged upon greatly the following day from New Delhi.[10]

These papers were no exercise in total prescience. I was right in seeing the danger as well as the futility in putting in troops. And my report was valid as well as mildly impassioned in holding that there was no chance that, in response to American wishes, Ngo Dinh Diem

[9] *The Pentagon Papers*, vol. II, pp. 121–122.

[10] In later years, as the Vietnam war became an all-embracing political issue in Washington, rumor circulated there of a Galbraith Report coinciding with and countering the Taylor Mission Report. Kennedy, by mentioning my communications, had contributed to this impression. I was asked repeatedly by Senator Wayne Morse about its availability and content.

There is warning here of how, even on important matters, memory can falter. My recollection was of the report that I sent from Bangkok, and since it was through the CIA to the President, it seemed impossible that copies could be exhumed. I had no thought of retaining one of my own. Had I been asked under oath how many such documents I had submitted, I would have replied perjuriously and without hesitation that there was but this one. I had forgotten about the second from New Delhi or a third written later in Washington. All eventually appeared in *The Pentagon Papers*. I read the latter with much interest, for by then I had begun to wonder how much my early doubts concerning our intervention had been improved in my memory by my later, stronger commitment to its unwisdom.

(and his relatives) would reform. However, I was wrong in suggesting that almost any alternative to Diem would be better and would turn back the Viet Cong. In this optimism I was the victim of my own evasion. In saying that the Diem regime was hopeless, which I believed, and in saying that it could not be propped up by our troops, which I believed and wanted to believe, I came close to saying, "Let the insurgents take over." But that no one could say. Such an admission was all that those arguing for intervention needed to put me in my place. A sell-out. My effectiveness would be at an end. I had to have an alternative to intervention and to Diem *and* also to the Viet Cong. From the need to persuade others that such an alternative existed, I succeeded handsomely in persuading myself.

My argument had, I believe, some bearing on Kennedy's decision not to send in troops. The authors of *The Pentagon Papers* study thought it had more to do with the President's conclusion that little was to be gained in pressing Diem to reform. Since it could have been one of my more relevant pieces of composition, the later Vietnam history considered, I reproduce here the pertinent paragraphs from my paper:

A maximum of 18,000 lightly armed men are involved in the insurrection. These are [Government of Vietnam] estimates and the factor of exaggeration is unquestionably considerable. Ten thousand is more probable. What we have in opposition involves a heavy theological dispute. Diem it is said is a great but defamed leader. It is also said he has lost touch with the masses, is in political disrepute and otherwise no good. This debate can be bypassed by agreed points. It is agreed that administratively Diem is exceedingly bad. He holds far too much power in his own hands, employs his army badly, has no intelligence organization worthy of the name, has arbitrary or incompetent subordinates in the provinces and some achievements notwithstanding, has a poor economic policy. He has also effectively resisted improvement for a long while in face of heavy deterioration. This is enough. Whether his political posture is nepotic, despotic, out of touch with the villagers and hence damaging or whether this damage is the figment of Saigon intellectuals does not bear on our immediate policy and may be bypassed at least in part.

The [South Vietnamese] Army numbers 170,000 and with paramilitary units of the civil guard and home defense forces a quarter of a million. Were this well deployed on behalf of an effective government it should be obvious that the Viet Cong would have no chance of success or takeover. Washington is currently having an intellectual orgasm on the unbeatability of guerrilla war. Were guerrillas effective in a ratio of one to fifteen or twenty-five, it is obvious that no government would be safe. The Viet Cong, it should be noted, is strongest in the Southern Delta which is not jungle but open rice paddy.

The fundamental difficulties in countering the insurgency, apart from absence of intelligence, are two-fold. First is the poor command, deployment, training, morale and other weaknesses of the army and paramilitary forces. And second while they can operate — sweep — through any part of the country and clear out any visible insurgents, they cannot guarantee security afterwards. The Viet Cong comes back and puts the arm on all who have collaborated. This fact is very important in relation to requests for American manpower. Our forces would conduct the round-up operations which the [South Vietnamese] Army can already do. We couldn't conceivably send enough men to provide safety for the villages as a substitute for an effectively trained civil guard and home defense force and, perhaps, a politically cooperative community.

*

Diem will not reform either administratively or politically in any effective way. That is because he cannot. It is politically naive to expect it. He senses that he cannot let power go because he would be thrown out. He may disguise this even from himself with the statement that he lacks effective subordinates but the circumstance remains unchanged. He probably senses that his greatest danger is from the army. Hence the reform that will bring effective use of his manpower, though the most urgent, may be the most improbable.

The political reforms are even more unlikely but the issue is academic. Once the image of a politician is fixed, whether among opposition intellectuals or peasants, it is not changed . . . Diem's image would not be changed by his taking in other non-communists, initiating some social reforms or otherwise meeting the requirements of our demarche.

Then came some sentences, not all of which I now read with pleasure. Let all be cautious in their claims to foresight.

It is a cliché that there is no alternative to Diem's regime. This is politically naive. Where one man has dominated the scene for good or ill there never seems to be. No one considered Truman an alternative to Roosevelt. There is none for Nehru. There was none I imagine for Rhee. This is an optical illusion arising from the fact that the eye is fixed on the visible figures. It is a better rule that nothing succeeds like successors.

We should not be alarmed by the Army as an alternative. It would buy time and get a fresh dynamic. It is not ideal; civilian rule is ordinarily more durable and more saleable to the world. But a change and a new start is of the essence and in considering opinion we may note that Diem's flavor is not markedly good in Asia.

A time of crisis in our policy on South Vietnam will come when it becomes evident that the reforms we have asked have not come off and that our presently proffered aid is not accomplishing anything. [American] troops will be urged to back up Diem. It will be sufficiently clear that I think this must be resisted. Our soldiers would not deal with the vital weakness. They could perpetuate it.[11]

In place of troops Kennedy sent helicopters, military assistance and advisers, and since manpower for any military enterprise must be prodigal, the numbers so sent were large. I continued to worry. In March I returned to the subject in a letter to the President: "When I am not worrying about your wife,[12] I worry about Indo-China. (Ross once told Thurber[13] in 1940 when the latter was losing his eyesight: "Thurber, I worry about you and England!") . . . I continue to be sadly out of step with the Establishment . . . We are increasingly replacing the French as the colonial military force and will increasingly arouse the resentments associated therewith. Moreover, while I don't think the Russians are clever enough to fix it that way, we are surely playing their game. They couldn't be more pleased than to have us spend our billions in these distant jungles where it does us no good and them no harm.

"Incidentally, who is the man in your administration who decides what countries are strategic? I would like to have his name and address and ask him what is so important about this real estate in the space age . . ."[14]

I then went on to propose four rules to govern our policy:

"Keep up the threshold against the commitment of American combat forces. This is of the utmost importance — a few will mean more and more and more. And then the South Vietnamese boys will go back to the farms. We will do the fighting.

"Keep [American] civilian control in Saigon. Once the military take over we will have no possibility of working out a disentanglement . . .

"We must keep the door wide open for any kind of political settlement. In particular we must keep communications open by way of the Indians and even the Russians to Hanoi. If they give any indi-

[11] *The Pentagon Papers,* vol. II, pp. 122–124.
[12] Who was about to visit India amidst a multitude of public relations risks.
[13] Harold Ross and James Thurber of *The New Yorker.*
[14] Letter to the President in *Ambassador's Journal,* pp. 310–311.

cation of willingness to settle, we should jump at the chance. Any form of disentanglement is going to bring criticism from fighting Joe Alsop as it has in Laos. But the one thing that will cause worse damage and more penetrating attack will be increasing involvement. Politics is not the art of the possible. It consists in choosing between the disastrous and the unpalatable. I wonder if those who talk of a ten-year war really know what they are saying in terms of American attitudes. We are not as forgiving as the French.

"Finally, I hold to the view, whatever our public expressions, that any alternative to Diem is bound to be an improvement. I think I mentioned once before that no one ever sees an alternative to the man in power. But when the man in power is on the way down, anything is better."[15]

* * *

In April 1962 — on April Fool's Day — I returned yet again to the issue. I was back in Washington, and Arthur Schlesinger and I were spending the day with the Kennedys in their temporary retreat, Glen Ora, near Middleburg in the Virginia equine country. While the President had a Sunday afternoon nap — and before seeing on television the film of Jacqueline's trip to India — I rehearsed my case with Schlesinger. It was that we should now seek some neutral solution. Were the Saigon government as bad as I believed, it could not survive the always seemingly superior attraction of a revolutionary alternative. Kennedy, when I addressed him, was immediately interested and asked me to pursue the matter with McNamara and Averell Harriman and to get it all down on paper. McNamara and Harriman, notably the latter, were warmly sympathetic. My brief began by noting that "We have a growing military commitment. This could expand step by step into a major, long drawn-out, indecisive military involvement." I went on to urge that we "resist all steps which commit American troops to combat action"; and then I proposed a scenario, as such things are called, for an internationally negotiated settlement. The help of the Indians would be sought. Harriman would approach the Russians. Other steps leading to a nonaligned, internationally protected government were outlined.[16]

[15] Letter to the President in *Ambassador's Journal,* pp. 311–312.
[16] A copy remained with my journal notes. Memorandum for the President in *Ambassador's Journal,* pp. 342–344.

Since Kennedy wanted it for use with our generals, I affected a brisk military style.

Neither content nor manner impressed the Joint Chiefs. A few days later on April 13, Lyman Lemnitzer, as chairman, rendered their reply. It was a model of military imperturbability as also of the required prose style:

> 5. The problems raised by Mr. Galbraith with regard to our present policy have been considered in the coordinated development of that policy. The Joint Chiefs of Staff are aware of the deficiencies of the present government of South Vietnam. However, the President's policy of supporting the Diem regime while applying pressure for reform appears to be the only practicable alternative at this time. In this regard, the views of the Joint Chiefs of Staff as expressed in JCSM-33-62 are reaffirmed.
>
> 6. It is the opinion of the Joint Chiefs of Staff that the present US policy toward South Vietnam, as announced by the President, should be pursued vigorously to a successful conclusion.[17]

*   *   *

My concern, even despair, over Vietnam continued, and I continued to look for any handle by which I might move the issue. In January 1963, the Polish Foreign Minister Adam Rapacki visited New Delhi and on January 21 sent for me for a discussion, which we had at the house of M. J. Desai. Rapacki told me, as I wrote in my journal, that "while we [the United States] probably couldn't lose in South Vietnam, we couldn't win. Meanwhile, we are forcing North Vietnam to look more and more to the Chinese for protection. This is bad. Why not get a liberal government in South Vietnam which all could support? In return, Ho Chi Minh would call off the insurrection."[18] I promptly reported the conversation to Washington where it was ignored by the State Department. Kennedy, however, saw the cable and sent word that I was to pursue the subject immediately. I could not; Rapacki by then had departed.

*   *   *

I have told of meeting with Lyndon Johnson the day after Kennedy's death. When I then urged that we were wasting our capital

---

[17]*The Pentagon Papers*, vol. II, pp. 671–672. The reader will observe that the President is strongly cited as the authority for a policy that the President is, in effect, questioning.

[18]*Ambassador's Journal*, p. 537.

and prestige on hopeless foreign policy adventures, I had Vietnam almost wholly in mind. In the next couple of years, in meetings with L.B.J. and also with McNamara and Bundy, I came back often, even tediously, to the subject. Johnson was not a great listener, although at times I thought him sympathetic. Repeatedly, as to others, he said that he was really being a force for restraint. "Ken, have you any idea what [General] Curtis LeMay would be doing if I weren't here to stop him?" But eventually and sadly I came to the conclusion that he was on a hopelessly different course. There being no seeming escape from involvement, he was accepting it. The early months of 1965 were, for me, an especially sad time. After campaigning joyously for L.B.J. and against Barry Goldwater as a warmonger, I had to watch the long-resisted introduction of combat troops and the first bombing of North Vietnam. I felt very angry. These were initiatives urged by people who had done nothing for the election of Johnson and who had no personal or emotional stake in either the President or the Democratic Party. Gradually and reluctantly I realized that the only honest course was open opposition, unpromising as that then seemed to be.

30

The Politics of
the Careful Dissent

No GREAT NATION had ever before stopped in the middle of a war to inquire whether it was necessary, possible or just. Those urging military action in Vietnam were not being reckless when they assumed that once the bands began to play, the American people would fall in line. So it had always been. And for a time in 1965 and 1966, so it seemed it would be again.

This was the prospect as I slowly came to believe that public and political opposition alone would prevent our deepening involvement — that episodic efforts at inside persuasion, however useful to one's conscience, would do no good. One of the little-celebrated powers of Presidents (and other high government officials) is to listen to their critics with just enough sympathy to ensure their silence.

One day in those early years,[1] I went down to Washington to discuss the war in Vietnam with members of the Democratic Study Group of the House of Representatives. The DSG is a convocation of the liberal members of the House; many of those present were my friends. I spoke with careful avoidance of novelty, summarizing the arguments I had originally developed with Kennedy as told in the last chapter. The later discussion was entirely given over to courteous but astringent rebuke for my deviation. In wartime one *had* to support the President. To my relief and almost to my surprise a New York congressman came to my side toward the end of the meeting. Otherwise my only support was from a former student, a Republican of American Indian antecedents from South Dakota named Ben Reifel, who, out of loyalty, had come to this alien gathering. He told

---

[1] I have no notes that retrieve the date.

those attending that his affection for his old teacher made him regret his grave disagreement.

There were also, as time passed, the sometimes inconvenient actions of one's allies. No one could be troubled by those motivated by religious conviction, old-fashioned pacifism or a deep personal dislike for the draft. But it is far from certain that those who professed a possibly unrequited love for Ho Chi Minh added strength to the cause.

There was yet another difficulty. Opposition to the war, if it were to be more than an act of personal protest, required a plan for ending it, one that would attract a political constituency. Simply to declare a victory and withdraw — the later proposal of Senator George Aiken — would not have gained one any support before 1967. One had to imagine some kind of negotiated solution. But what could be had in negotiation depended on what the other side would accept. That no one knew. So, as usual in foreign policy, supreme certainty of statement had to substitute for extreme uncertainty as to fact.

And this uncertainty persisted. Late in 1971, I made my way one day to Choisy-le-Roi outside of Paris, and there, in their modest, sparsely furnished and, I judged, thoughtfully bugged headquarters, I met with representatives from Hanoi and the National Liberation Front. I was courteously received and heard in detail of their demands, their desire for peace and their depressingly accurate views of the government and personality of Nguyen Van Thieu. I emerged no wiser as to what one could advocate as a possible bargain. To my surprise, I might add, my visit remained undisclosed. Somewhat later Pierre Salinger, then working for the election of George McGovern, made a similar visit for a similar purpose. It received wide publicity. Salinger, a rounded man, was not hospitable to my thought that for clandestine procedures the very tall are better.

*   *   *

During 1965, our active combat commitment to Vietnam was steadily enlarged, and, subject to a six-day halt in the spring, the bombing of North Vietnam was continued. Then in December Johnson suspended the air attacks and sent emissaries to various capitals — Averell Harriman to Warsaw, Foy Kohler to Moscow, Arthur Goldberg to the Vatican — to tell of his wish for an end to the war. This was called the peace offensive. Nothing resulted, but no one talking with Johnson during those months could doubt that, as his most fervent desire, he wanted peace. What he did not want, as ever, was the political outcry that would follow from seeming to bug out. And always there were the easy, heroic voices that said, "Let's get on with the job." In January 1966, I tried one final bit of persuasion, this time in a paper that had the endorsement of Arthur Goldberg, who was now at the United Nations. I entitled it "A Moderate's View of Vietnam."[2]

Memorandum for the President: Personal and Confidential

This is a conscientious attempt to see the problem of Vietnam, not in light of my own preferences or those of any particular department or agency or group, but as it concerns the Presidency and the whole country. It is a fact, overlooked by most people, that the President is the only man now dealing with this problem who has to stand election on what happens . . . We have to start from where we are with a history that we might regret but which we cannot change. Let me first lay down these propositions.

(1) We have no major national interest in Vietnam. The average American is right in thinking that it is a long way from home. As I have said before, we wouldn't give it a thought if it had gone Communist after World War II. It is a practical problem and not the focus of a holy crusade against Communism. It calls for consideration in the light of practical politics and not by anti-Communist zealots.

(2) The foregoing being true, we must keep our risks in the region at a minimum. This applies especially to any risk of war with China.

(3) On the other hand, for domestic reasons, if for no other, we cannot walk out. Too much has been said and promised . . . And while it probably makes no difference to the average Vietnamese peasant what government he lives under — whatever happens, he expects to get the shit beat out of him — we do have an obligation to the Catholics and others who have fought the Communists.

(4) While you undoubtedly have majority support in the country, you owe a lot to the feeling that you are the great restraining force in the situation . . . And there is, of course, no doubt that this is a divisive issue which robs you of some of your best, idealistic, youthful and academic support . . .

(5) This miserable conflict is monopolizing headlines that properly be-

----

[2] It is my impression, although I cannot be sure, that this was requested by L.B.J. Such requests can be serious, but they can also be a way of ending a not very welcome conversation. "That's interesting, Ken. Give me a memorandum."

long to your domestic achievements and energies that should properly go to our domestic problems.

What we do and do not do.

(1) We must give up the notion that we are going to roll back the Viet Cong and destroy them for good and all. Perhaps we could if we destroyed the country — and took the casualties. But they have controlled a lot of South Vietnam, as everyone knows, for ten years. Our object is to prevent expansion, not a roll back or a Dulles war of liberation. Moreover, if our people continue to say (I know that you have never done so yourself) that we can't compromise with the Viet Cong, we leave them no alternative but to fight it out to the bitter end.

(2) With the large manpower we have there, we should hold, along with South Vietnam forces, the cities and a solid part of the countryside that is now friendly and make it just as secure as we possibly can. And we should mount a major program for refugees and do anything possible to make life more tolerable for the other people. This kind of containment operation, if the areas are not too ambitious, will provide no insuperable problems. Casualties will be low. Then Vietnam will be off the front pages most of the time.

(3) Our military will not like this. They will press for action. So will Republicans and some of the columnists. This, once your strategy is understood, will work strongly to your advantage. Without pulling out or losing ground, you are the force for moderation and peace. You are the man who stands against impatience and a big war. A policy of holding and patience can be explained. The military must understand, here as elsewhere, that they are the instrument and not the end of policy. It is not conducted for their convenience.

(4) We, of course, keep open the offer of negotiations. Someday this will be accepted. No one, of course, knows when. But, as Churchill used to say, most wars in history have been avoided simply by postponing them.

My solution was one of the early formulations of what eventually was to be called the "enclave policy." We should withdraw our forces to the coastal and urban areas that we could hold with ease and safety and wait for negotiations. We should be prepared to wait for a long time. We would have neither victory nor defeat — nor great casualties — in the interim. It wasn't a perfect solution; it was unquestionably the best that was politically real at the time.

In those months of 1966, I was deeply engaged on *The New Industrial State*. When my work on the book was over for the day, I took up my obligatory concern about Vietnam. One has a tendency to imagine oneself alone in such a worry. It is never so. If one's own alarm deepens, one can be sure that others are having a similar response, and an event in the autumn of 1966 persuaded me that political opposition to the war was becoming a practical possibility, even a necessity.

*   *   *

Paul H. Douglas, University of Chicago economics professor, past president of the American Economic Association, former Chicago city councilor, who had gone from private to lieutenant colonel in the Marine Corps in World War II, was now senior senator from Illinois and up for re-election to a third term. His opponent, Charles H. Percy, a liberal business executive, was, as compared with Douglas, unknown. Nor was he strikingly different in his views. By any preliminary calculation, Paul Douglas, a personal and professional friend of mine, was unbeatable.

A few days before the election I received an urgent call from his principal campaign aide, Richard Wade. Paul wanted me to come to Illinois and lend a hand. My effort, predictably, was to be with the liberal suburban and university audiences where it was believed I was persuasive.

In golden autumn weather Dick Wade and I traveled by small plane across southern Illinois to Chicago. Our audiences, mostly in college or university centers, were ample. Before each I told of Douglas's devoted service to liberal economic policies, conservation, civil rights. From every audience came a barrage of questions about his support for the Vietnam war. Starting life as a pacifist and a Quaker, Paul had seen the inadequacy of his faith for dealing with Hitler and fascism. To this he had added his pride in having been one of the oldest members of the Marine Corps to see active combat. He was not a militant on Vietnam; in the Senate he spoke mostly to domestic issues. But he was unyielding in his support of the war. This was enough to evoke widespread opposition and, in the end, to defeat him.

*   *   *

A few months later, in the spring of 1967, Arthur Schlesinger, Richard Goodwin and I lunched together one day at Quo Vadis in New York. Goodwin, as I've noted, had been, with Theodore Sorensen, the most effective of John F. Kennedy's speech writers. He had remained on with Johnson to whose style, political energy and position on domestic issues he was greatly attracted. But in time he too came to realize that foreign policy and the war were dominating the scene. So he left the White House. It was of the war we talked. Schlesinger said this was the time of testing; in that last millisecond before the ultimate holocaust we should not be forced to remember that we had spent the summer on a beach.[3] We agreed that we should devote ourselves for as long as might be necessary or useful to opposing the war.

Almost immediately for me a platform presented itself, the chairmanship[4] of Americans for Democratic Action. As noted, I had been a founding member, but in later years the Democratic Party had become the major outlet for my political energies, and my identification with ADA had been, at best, episodic.

The American political graveyard is filled with the forgotten corpses of liberal organizations. ADA almost alone has survived, partly owing to the unfailing attention accorded it by Joseph L. Rauh, Jr., another of the founding members and the most effective single exponent of reform in the deeply ambiguous history of the Washington bar. His briefs on behalf of civil liberties, against abuse of power by government and against abuse of bank accounts by unions have been continuously in production for a third of a century. He is greatly and properly resented by all malefactors, for he almost always wins. Not long after I returned from India, Rauh had asked me if I would become head of ADA, and I had declined. Now, with Leon Shull, its long-time relentlessly optimistic executive director, he renewed the invitation. It would be a very good platform against the war, and I accepted. I had then to be elected by the

---

[3] In his book *Robert Kennedy and His Times* (Boston: Houghton Mifflin, 1979), Schlesinger recalls the lunch and attributes this statement to Goodwin. In my quite competent memory of the occasion and statement I have no hesitation in attributing it to Schlesinger himself.

[4] Though I am a firm supporter of women's rights, I have argued against the alteration of language to reflect, nominally, an equal access to public position. The same energy and emotion, I have urged, could better be invested in affirmative action. And the resulting words — Chairperson, Congressperson, Policeperson — have the jarring sound of any new construction. My effort failed. Once in Manhattan — Personhattan — speaking at a fund-raising gathering for women's rights under the auspices of my highly intelligent friend Gloria Steinem, I made this case. I only narrowly escaped from the hall.

annual convention early that summer, but this contest was considerably eased by the absence of opposition. There rarely was after Joe Rauh had decided.[5]

My accession to this modest authority was not without cost to ADA. It had long received the support of the more liberally disposed unions, including the United Automobile Workers and several internationals of the AFL-CIO. The AFL-CIO members were, like George Meany and the leadership, now generally in support of our involvement in Vietnam. My election became a signal for withdrawal by several of the unions, and an exceptionally ill-timed and unnecessary criticism of the union leadership in my acceptance speech didn't help.

For the next year I used ADA meetings across the country as a forum against the war. I also had an active role in another organization called Negotiations Now. And I pressed my views on other available audiences — the California Democratic Council, university groups, *ad hoc* meetings.

One of the latter, in the late summer of 1967, was exceptionally persuasive as to the prospect. It was called by local opponents of the war in the ski lodge on top of Mount Ascutney in Vermont overlooking the Connecticut River and the New Hampshire countryside beyond. The citizens of Vermont and New Hampshire are not thought easily aroused; even less so the vacationing and thus somnambulant summer residents. Expected were a few-score committed anti-war activists. When I arrived with Joe Bates of Newfane, one of the last local clock makers in New England, the mountain top was covered with cars and people. The attendance exceeded expectations by twentyfold. And it was plain from their attention and their

---

[5] ADA is a federation of state bodies of reputable strength in Minnesota, Ohio, New York, Pennsylvania, Massachusetts and a number of other northern and western states. Except as there has been word that it is dangerously radical, it is unknown in most of the South and Southwest. On the Sunday after my election (or selection), I was scheduled for a lecture in El Paso, Texas. I had also been invited as a former ambassador to speak and be the guest of honor at the annual hands-across-the-border celebration of friendship between El Paso and Ciudad Juárez, Mexico. The announcement that I had been made head of ADA struck the mayor of El Paso as a thunderbolt. He had now to face a full day of ceremony, numerous reporters and more numerous photographers with a certified radical at his side. His solution was not without resource; it was to arrange things so that the general representing nearby Fort Hood always stood in full military dress between us, the uniform serving as a disinfectant. When I became aware of the tactic, I made a point of moving in beside the mayor in a friendly fashion. It was a good day.

questions that their opposition to our being in Vietnam was angry and intense.

* * *

Serviceable as speeches might be to conscience, they did not do much to bring an end to the hostilities. Joe Rauh and I shared the view that we would be effective only as we had a presidential candidate in 1968 around whom the anti-war movement could coalesce. Then opposition would be politically reputable. And only political opposition would impress Lyndon Johnson.

But we had no candidate. During the spring and summer of 1967, we toyed with a substitute. Instead of a single spokesman, we would have a large and formidable bloc of delegates at the 1968 Democratic Convention, all strongly committed against the war. This would be called the Peace Caucus, and it would seek to write into the platform such a strong expression of opposition that not even Johnson could be indifferent. We soon discovered that it was a hopeless enterprise. Ours is the politics of people. Primary votes and party caucuses select convention delegates who are pledged to candidates, not positions.

The need for a candidate was provoking feelings of desperation elsewhere, as I had occasion to learn. In the autumn of 1967, I was on political business in Berkeley, California, and stayed overnight at the Claremont Hotel. A delegation of liberal and anti-war Democrats and members of the Peace and Freedom Party then active in opposition to the war filed into our suite; rather diffidently, their spokesman asked that I allow my name to go on the Democratic ballot. There had to be some recognized opponent of the war around whom they could rally, and I would do. I cited the Constitution; in specifying that presidential candidates must be native-born Americans, the Philadelphia fathers had specifically in mind that the post be protected from the British-born, as in my youth Canadians were. The visitors listened with seeming sorrow and filed out. On the plane to Boston the next day I reflected for the first time on the discrimination to which I was subject. A few weeks later Arthur Schlesinger called from New York to urge that I allow my name, in the absence of any other, to be entered in the New Hampshire primary. I asked my son Alan, then clerking for a California Supreme Court judge, to investigate. Perhaps the Fourteenth Amendment nullified the earlier constitutional bar.[6] He expressed the strong view that any such interpretation would be fraudulent, that in a campaign so handicapped, I would spend more time defending my eligibility than in opposing the war. In any case, the purpose of political action was to put pressure on Lyndon Johnson, and clearly such action had to be credible.

*   *   *

As the autumn of 1967 passed, the need for an anti-war candidate became ever more urgent. So one day in Washington in late October or very early November, Joe Rauh and I decided to go to Capitol Hill and look actively for a volunteer or one who could be persuaded.[7] We separated, and I went first to see George McGovern. He was sympathetic to our need but adamant as to himself. He was up for re-election in South Dakota a year hence; that would require all of his effort. (Later, in 1968, he would briefly, and not wisely, change his mind.) He thought Robert Kennedy the only chance.

I then went to see Kennedy. It was not the first time we had been over the ground. I renewed my plea, but his answer was as it had been to others and before. A candidate with a clear-cut position against the war was, indeed, needed. But people would consider his entry into the race as a personal Kennedy vendetta against Lyndon Johnson. "They would think I was running because I resented his succeeding my brother." Then to my surprise, he proposed that I go and see Eugene McCarthy who was not up for re-election in 1968. Kennedy supposed he might be giving thought to the race. This was, for me, the first serious suggestion that Gene McCarthy might be a possible candidate.

United States senators have a unique and obligatory tendency in interior decoration: colored photographs of recent Presidents with

---

[6] In 1974, Congressman Jonathan B. Bingham of New York introduced legislation calling for a constitutional amendment to remove this obstacle. It was widely interpreted as a way of allowing Henry Kissinger to run for President, but it was pointed out that it would also make me eligible, and there were less than historic references to the Kissinger-Galbraith amendment. During the summer of 1974, while it was under discussion, I was drafted by the town of Newfane to make a speech at the celebration of its bicentennial in substitution for Spiro Agnew who, for grave and unexpected reasons, had become unavailable. Reporters pressed me for my position on the Bingham amendment. I endorsed it strongly and said that it would not necessarily be my intention to have Kissinger as my Vice President.

[7] A similar voyage of persuasion was made, I subsequently learned, by Allard Lowenstein.

barely legible inscriptions asserting deeply questionable affection; similarly autographed pictures from only slightly less awesome figures, including the Reverend Billy Graham; the standard ballroom scene as the new senator, healthier in appearance than now, acknowledges his first victory with his excessively proud wife beside him; one or more pictures of the candidate waving from the door of a plane; plaques from Rotary, Kiwanis, Elks or the Veterans of Foreign Wars acclaiming the service of the statesman and advertising the group's aversion to any more substantial payment for an after-luncheon speech.

Eugene McCarthy alone avoided this detritus; his office walls were monastically unadorned. So was the furniture. He sat back of his desk with the light behind him, rather remote, one thought, from the manifold trivia of the day. Or so it seemed that morning. His desk too was bare, for Gene, both out of principle and distaste, did not do much work. In late 1967, Senator John J. "Whispering Willie" Williams of Delaware unearthed some especially exuberant communications issued by Hubert Humphrey while he was still in the Senate. They supported the sale by a Minnesota firm to the United States government at excessive cost of some secondhand machinery which was to be given as aid to India.[8] A search was made of the files at Lyndon Johnson's request for similar support by Eugene McCarthy to a Minnesota constituent. This would take the heat off his Vice President; Hubert had only been doing what any Minnesota senator would do. No letters were found. Thomas Farmer, a Washington attorney and as the general counsel for AID at the time the one who made the search, was forced to remind the White House that McCarthy did not write letters on behalf of constituents.

I had known Gene, though far from intimately, from his first weeks in the House of Representatives. Henry Reuss of Wisconsin, my OPA colleague, friend and the long-time congressman from Milwaukee, had then invited me to dinner to meet him, describing him as the most diversely talented man — economist, poet, teacher, philosopher — to be elected to the Congress in many years.

In his office that morning, McCarthy listened, I thought sympa-

---

[8] I became aware of the effort, for my name was signed routinely to telegrams from India, and some about this deal also surfaced. I was without knowledge of the transaction. That the telegrams were in opposition to this particular largesse saved me much trouble.

thetically, to my plea and told me he was coming to Boston in a few days. We would discuss it further then. I went on to speak at a significant meeting against the war at the University of Chicago — significant, for it had been organized by a group of local trade unions. There I shared the platform with an alert man of mature years who had a well-established anti-war record. He was Warren K. Billings, and he had been arrested in 1916 with Tom Mooney, the noted radical, for allegedly throwing a bomb at a Preparedness Day parade in San Francisco. He was sent or, as all now believe, railroaded to jail for many years.

Returning to Cambridge, I introduced McCarthy at a gathering of young Democrats at what was then the Continental Hotel. Afterward outside he was cheered by an impressive gathering of Harvard students whose attendance and enthusiasm were partly my inspiration: I had asked some younger colleagues to pass the word. We then adjourned to our house to consider the prospect. Among those present were Mary McCarthy, Gene's Radcliffe daughter, various members of my family and Jimmy Breslin. Breslin was distracted by learning that Charles H. Townes, the noted physicist and Nobel laureate and a tenant in our house while we were in India, had built a fallout shelter in our basement. Townes didn't think it prudent, even for a year, to be without one. Our sons, also anticipating the worst, told Breslin they were using it to stockpile food for their dog. The discussion was not prolonged. Gene had already decided to run.

*   *   *

In November 1967, I brought out a small book — more exactly a broadside or pamphlet — on the war. It was abruptly entitled *How to Get Out of Vietnam*.[9] I began by stating Dean Rusk's case, for, along with the generals, he was now the strongest defender of the war. We had gone in to resist

> . . . the announced determination to impose a world of coercion upon those not already subject to it . . . it is [an issue] posed between the Sino-Soviet empire and all the rest, whether allied or neutral; and it is posed on every continent . . .[10]

[9] New York: New American Library, 1967.
[10] Dean Rusk, *Winds of Freedom* (Boston: Beacon Press, 1962), p. 16. Quoted in *How to Get Out of Vietnam*, p. 13.

One notes that the Chinese now had primacy in this empire. Rusk had strongly reinforced the point at a news conference on October 12, 1967, at which he said that our presence in Vietnam was to stem the outward thrust of a billion Chinese now armed with nuclear weapons.

My solution in the booklet was as before — to pull back to the cities or the coastal enclaves and wait the opposition out. Substitute patience for death. As before, I did not know what Hanoi and the Viet Cong would accept. And there was the need to have a solution that was also acceptable to the largest possible political constituency in our own country. Simply to leave was not. So again the enclaves.

By now a further thought, far from unimportant in light of later developments, had come to occupy my mind. ". . . [T]here are also some millions of people in that unhappy land who for one reason or another — religious faith, political conviction, political ambition, the eager pursuit of profits, the grim pursuit of the military police — have joined our effort. We cannot simply write them off; even by majority vote we do not assign people to the sanguinary attentions of their enemies. Any solution must take account of the needs of the minority in South Vietnam who fear a takeover by the National Liberation Front and its Communist leaders." [11]

Thus added to my case for the sanctuaries was the thought that "the minimum requirement [for] the South Vietnamese . . . is that we provide a place of decent refuge for those who have joined our enterprise in Vietnam." [12]

My warning of the boat people was better than I then guessed.

*   *   *

In the next months I campaigned for McCarthy in New Hampshire, Wisconsin, Massachusetts, New York, California and wherever else it seemed useful to go. And on August 15, I served as chairman for the great culminating rally before the convention in Madison Square Garden and suffered in pain the television celebrity management that such occasions are thought to require. I suffered even more painfully from the superb indifference with which my opening and unctuous speech was received. Most of all that year I raised money.

[11] *How to Get Out of Vietnam*, pp. 9–10.
[12] Ibid., p. 38.

This is the final step in the sequence I've already noted: first and most glamorous, the writing of speeches; then the lonely addresses to audiences not worth the candidate's time; then the sighs of disappointment as one appears as the substitute;[13] finally the plea, "What we really need is some help on the money side."

Excepting possibly the massive attack by Maurice Stans, Nixon's money man, on the friendly corporate givers in 1972, money was never raised so easily as for McCarthy in 1968. The stock market had been strong for months and capital gains abundant. Many so (or otherwise) enriched felt guilt or alarm about the war and that these feelings could best be assuaged by contributions to McCarthy.

There was varied instruction and even some amusement in this effort. In the spring of 1968, Bernard Cornfeld, then at the height of his brief esteem as founding financial genius of Investors Overseas Services, the great off-shore mutual fund group, financed a meeting in Geneva on behalf of peace. Robert Maynard Hutchins organized the program. Having been much in Switzerland, I had more knowledge of the nature of the IOS support than many of those invited. I expressed my doubts. Hutchins replied that those who do good things must take their money where they find it, adding that when money passed through his hands, it became, by that act, clean. I was not wholly convinced and, since I was already in Europe, paid my own passage. In Geneva, with Senators Joseph S. Clark of Pennsylvania and William Fulbright of Arkansas, both now powerfully in opposition to the war, I heard from Chester Ronning, my former colleague in India[14] who was now acting as an intermediary with the Viet Cong and North Vietnamese, of his efforts to get negotiations under way and of the successful efforts of Washington hard-liners to frustrate them. Clark and Fulbright were angrily aroused. I also spent an afternoon on Vietnam with Martin Luther King, Jr., and his youthful assistant, Andrew Young. We agreed that the black soldiers losing their lives uselessly in Vietnam were more

[13] There are other perils in serving as a substitute. In 1964, after speaking for Robert Kennedy's senatorial campaign in New York, I was on my way to the airport one morning to return to my classes at Harvard. Stephen Smith, the candidate's manager and brother-in-law, called to plead that I go to Long Island and speak to a large audience of suburban housewives. Kennedy couldn't make it. By careful timing, I could just do it and get to class on time. Precisely as I moved onto the platform so did Senator Claiborne Pell of Rhode Island. He had received an emergency summons from someone else in the campaign organization to fill the same spot.

[14] See Chapter 27.

in need of succor than any black group in the United States. Until his death a year later, Dr. King was the nation's most effective spokesman against the war.

Howard Stein of the Dreyfus Corporation and Yura Arkus-Duntov also of Wall Street led in collecting money for McCarthy, as did Harold Willens, a deeply concerned Los Angeles textile and real estate man, and Stewart Mott, the philanthropist and General Motors heir. With one or another of these, I traveled extensively, leaving all possible poverty wherever we went. Just before the 1968 convention we united in a memorable effort under the auspices of Hugh Hefner at the *Playboy* mansion on the Chicago Near North Side. A cavernous, deeply gloomy structure in those days, it was improved by a swimming pool with glass sides so that from the adjacent bar one could watch the Bunnies swimming above.

Our money-raising effort that evening was directed at the more sporting element of Chicago liberalism. After an ear-splitting orchestra had been reduced to silence, we began, as it is called, the pitch. By this time it had become a routine. I spoke in somber terms of the war and of the bizarre and unexamined clichés that were used to justify our intervention. Stewart Mott casually indicated the scale of help that would be appropriate by citing his own donation. Harold Willens then came forward to demand and acknowledge the contributions by the system of direct assessment and taxation that has been raised to its highest level of perfection by the United Jewish Appeal.

When I had finished my part of the program, I went to the side of the room to sit with Michael Laurence, then an accomplished *Playboy* editor. He was accompanied by a lovely, slender woman with straw-colored hair and a see-through blouse from which I averted my eyes. She was, Mike said in introduction, a *Playboy* recruit from Germany.

We listened to Mott who presently, in accordance with routine, said that he himself, in light of his strong feelings, had given $100,000 to McCarthy and planned to give more.

My German companion stirred suddenly to attention and in urgent, husky accents said, "How coom he has so-o much money?"

I replied, since she seemed not to be a woman who would appreciate precision, that his father owned General Motors.

"What," she said, "is the General Motors?"

I put things within more familiar range.

"It is as if his father owned Opel. I think his father may have given him Opel for himself."

"An Opel is not such a big car."

My further explanation was more extended. She then fixed her eyes on Mott, studied him approvingly and at length and sought reassurance on one final point:

"Is he straight?"

                    *   *   *

In March and early April I went to speak in California for McCarthy and against the war. On March 31, we drove across the urban desolation to the west of Los Angeles for a speech. As I finished eating dinner, someone handed me a note; Lyndon Johnson had announced that the bombing of North Vietnam would be curtailed. And that he would not run again.

Some months after L.B.J. returned to Texas, Walter Cronkite went down to film or tape an interview with him on the highlights of his presidency for the Columbia Broadcasting System. Great preparations were made; the positioning of lights and cameras by the numerous trade unionists took, it was said, most of the day. Then, according to what I judge to be apocryphal history, the two men took their seats, microphones were attached, the requisite signals were exchanged, there was the ritualistic last-minute dab at the foreheads, and Cronkite said, "Now, Mr. President, I think the American people would like to hear the reasons back of that decision on March 31, 1968, not to run again."

"What did they expect, Walter? That bastard McCarthy came within an inch of licking me in New Hampshire and he was about to tear my ass off in Wisconsin. What else could I do?"

"Mr. President, that only took thirty seconds. We've got a whole half hour."

"All right, Walter. I'll give you the other explanation."

31

The Violent Convocation

OF THE KENNEDY BROTHERS, the one with whom I had the least ease of communication was Robert Kennedy. It was not from insufficient association. I had worked under his direction at the 1960 convention and in the campaign that followed. I saw much of him during his brother's years in office. When I had some thought on how the Kennedy Administration might do good or better, I would be told by the President, as were others, "Why don't you go and talk with Bobby?" I went down to New York to campaign for him in his Senate race in 1964, and once again, as I've already told, I sought to give the assurance to Jewish voters that no Catholic could provide and on which no Jewish advocate would be quite trusted. To some of the same audiences to which I had spoken on behalf of J.F.K. four years before, I said, "I was here in 1960 to tell you that your fears about John F. Kennedy as a Catholic were misplaced. This you now know. So you can trust me when I make the same case for his brother now." These were among the rare occasions in politics when you could know you were having effect. People who wished only to be reassured were reassured.

My distance from Robert Kennedy grew out of our different capacities for political commitment. I have always tried for a measure of detachment. I've felt that one should hold some part of one's self in reserve, never be too completely sure of being right. Let belief always be tempered by discretion. None of this suited Robert Kennedy's mood; his commitment was complete. You were either for the cause or against it, either with the Kennedys or a leper. There was no room for ambiguity, indecision or a middle ground. (It was this intensity that raised the political doubts in the liberal Jewish community.) I was never regarded by Bobby as being as completely a Kennedy man as one should be. The year 1968 was to provide unexpected evidence to this effect.

I was also regarded with uncertainty by his wife Ethel. A youthful, energetic, well-knit woman with an immediate association between thought and speech, her sense of absolutes was even greater than that of her husband. It extended notably to religion. At Kennedy gatherings at Hickory Hill in McLean, Virginia, northwest from Washington along the Potomac, prayer was obligatory before meals, and once I had the feeling, quite possibly imagined, that Ethel Kennedy had caught me smiling. It was not, I yearned to explain to her, over the fact of our devotions. Rather, I was contemplating God's surprise that so many lifelong heretics should so suddenly become so devout from being in the house of the Attorney General of the United States who was also the brother of the President.

*   *   *

In February and early March of 1968, to retrace slightly, relays of students who had bathed, shaved and laundered in unprecedented fashion descended on New Hampshire and were dispatched with hitherto unparalleled efficiency to canvass that politically harassed citizenry for Eugene McCarthy. On March 12, those who had thus kept "clean for Gene" saw their candidate receive 42.4 percent of the vote as compared with 49.5 percent for Lyndon Johnson. Presidential memoirs must, of course, be believed, and by Johnson's account this was for him a considerable victory.[1] He had already decided in his own mind not to run and thus was indifferent to the outcome. His name was not on the ballot; he had edged McCarthy with a write-in campaign. Nonetheless, by the peculiar calculus that is used to assess such events, it was in the public view a great McCarthy triumph. On the following night Arthur Schlesinger came to our house in Cambridge to consider what had happened, and during the evening Ethel Kennedy phoned to say that her husband was wavering toward candidacy. She asked Arthur to call and lend his voice in persuasion. Since Kennedy seemed a far stronger candidate than McCarthy, we both welcomed the news.

At the end of the same week I went to New York to give a fundraising speech for McCarthy at a small luncheon on Wall Street given by Benjamin J. Buttenweiser, a liberal, socially articulate banker and the son-in-law of Herbert Lehman. As always that spring it was easy;

[1] Lyndon Johnson, *The Vantage Point: Perspectives of the Presidency 1963–1969* (New York: Holt, Rinehart and Winston, 1971), p. 538.

within minutes, ten or twenty thousand dollars came in. Then I went on to repeat the effort at a larger reception for smaller amounts at the Columbia University Faculty Club on Morningside Heights. Television cameras and microphones were waiting for me in strength. My first thought was of the irresistible appeal of my oratory, but I soon learned they were there to hear the reaction of a leading McCarthy supporter to the announcement by Robert Kennedy earlier that day that he was entering the race. With crushing suddenness it came to me that I was committed to McCarthy. My speeches for him could have been forgotten. But what could not be forgotten was that hundreds of people had invested thousands of dollars in McCarthy at my behest. Money is not a negligible thing. I had made a binding contract.

While the cameras were being hauled into position, these thoughts and the consequences passed through my mind as though being sorted by a computer program. They were assisted by a Columbia professor who said, "I just heard the news. I sure hope you aren't going to desert to Kennedy." In my speech I made it clear that I was solidly with McCarthy.

A few days later I went out to speak for him in Wisconsin. There I discovered that among those most surprised by my loyalty were members of McCarthy's staff. They couldn't believe I was safe and were greatly alarmed that I had agreed to a press conference on arrival. This, obviously, involved risks of pro-Kennedy thoughts they didn't want to hear so they canceled it. It was rescheduled by higher authority, but a comely, grimly suspicious young woman came out to the Milwaukee airport to sit beside me and monitor against any surreptitious Kennedy propaganda. There being none, she seemed disappointed.

*   *   *

I was in California, as I have told, when Lyndon Johnson bowed out, and a day or two later I saw Eugene McCarthy in Los Angeles. We settled down for a talk in his rooms at the Beverly Wilshire Hotel. Political hope, the most disorienting of drugs, was working even on Gene. He made half-serious reference to the things he would do when he got to the White House and hazarded the unserious guess that a couple of hours a day would be sufficient for the job.

I was still in Los Angeles for a lecture at UCLA — political persuasion in a decent scholarly disguise — when word came that all academic functions had been canceled. Martin Luther King, Jr., had been killed. Chancellor Franklin D. Murphy, a friend with whom I had once journeyed to Russia, asked me to serve as the calming influence at a large student rally on the campus. There was some danger of disorder. I did so and dredged from my memory all available recollections of Dr. King. Then I went on to urge, as he would have done, that the effective answer to violence, whether in Memphis, Vietnam or Westwood, California, was never more of the same. Let all distinguish between the quiet, steadfast opposition that served — as on the march from Selma — and the self-indulgent rage that did not. The students, an assembly of some thousands, listened and, seeming to agree, quietly went their way.

I was to face the same task in Grant Park in Chicago in August of that year and two years later, after the Kent State slaughter, at the University of Texas at Austin and the University of Minnesota at Minneapolis.[2]

McCarthy and Kennedy met head-on in Oregon on May 28, and McCarthy won 45 percent of the vote to 39 percent. Then a week later in California, Kennedy defeated McCarthy. It was closer than had been expected or, in the euphoria of the early figures, the Kennedy forces realized. As the returns became definite in Los Angeles, Richard Goodwin, who had switched from McCarthy to Kennedy,[3] called me out of bed in Cambridge. Bobby had made it; he was going to get the nomination; it was now time for me to declare my support. My switch would be a signal to the ADA. I told Goodwin that I was sympathetic but would have to talk with McCarthy first. Then I turned on the television set to get the final results. Robert Kennedy was making his way through some crowded kitchen corridors; he had just delivered his victory statement. There was sudden

---

[2] At Austin I was called urgently from an academic lecture by the president's office to address a large and angry assembly of students in the great central concourse of the university. They were threatening to march on the Texas capitol a mile or so away, and this risked a possible confrontation with the National Guard. Without notes and without chance for prior thought I poured out my soul. Be resolute. Do not be forced to try conclusions with armed men. That night while at dinner in a local restaurant, I heard my words repeated on the radio with the comment that they had prevented bloodshed. There have been few tasks in my life that I have tackled with so little confidence. I was surprised less at the outcome than that my uncertainty had not shown.

[3] And who, after Robert Kennedy's death, returned to work most effectively for McCarthy.

movement, muffled confusion, a voice of alarm. I called Kitty from sleep; something was happening. Presently we knew that Robert Kennedy had been shot.

* * *

At St. Patrick's Cathedral I stood with others by the bier and listened to the eloquent service and the words of Edward Kennedy: "My brother need not be idealized or enlarged in death beyond what he was in life. He should be remembered simply as a good and decent man who saw wrong and tried to right it, saw suffering and tried to heal it, saw war and tried to stop it." Then we boarded the slow, sad train to Washington where, long after dark, all gathered once again on the hillside in Arlington. It seemed too much.

When it was over, I faced a commencement speech at Tufts University outside of Boston only a few hours hence. I negotiated with Nelson Rockefeller for passage on his plane to New York and then on to Boston only to discover that a specially chartered plane was taking the Harvard band back to Cambridge. I got home with only two hours to spare before going to plead in my speech against the brutal tendencies of the time. A few days later I went down to Washington again to see Gene McCarthy.

We met at his house, the large, slightly ceremonial dwelling on Woodley Road that had until recently belonged to Walter Lippmann. Gene was deeply depressed; the death of Robert Kennedy showed the hopelessness of the game. What had been real would now be pretense; what had been pleasure was now pain. Supported by Abigail, his politically acute and rather less romantic wife, I pleaded that he carry on. The banality of my argument still rings faintly in my ears. Gene remained sad and unmoved but proposed another talk in Cambridge a few days later. This we had with Coretta King and a number of McCarthy's local supporters present. His mood was better, and we went over the tasks that had still to be accomplished before the convention. After Robert Kennedy's death, however, I don't believe that Eugene McCarthy's heart was ever again wholly in the battle.

* * *

The convention that opened in Chicago on August 26 remains in the American memory as an occasion of brutality and horror. Chicago police under light blue helmets, bringing their clubs down on the heads of unkempt, frightened youngsters. Arms upheld to ward off the blows. Chemical Mace. The Illinois National Guard moving through the streets to a grim line between the dissident encampment in Grant Park and the convention headquarters in the huge, graceless Conrad Hilton Hotel just across Michigan Avenue. I remember that time as the most engaged and among the most interesting of my life. I was there for nearly ten days of press conferences, money-raising meetings, conferences on convention strategy, speechmaking, receiving advice and answering innumerable questions from other delegates. The common theme of all was a quite insupportable optimism about the prospects for the McCarthy crusade.

My appreciation of those days came partly from the circumstance that I experienced none of the violence. If you are, however marginally, a member of the Establishment or are so recognized, the police open the way whatever your views. One night I crossed Michigan Avenue from the Hilton to speak to the young demonstrators in the park. A police officer before the hotel said, "Good evening, Mr. Ambassador." The National Guard opened their ranks to let me through. From an improvised platform and using a jerrybuilt loudspeaker system I told the youngsters of our hopes and efforts at the convention amphitheater and, as I've noted, urged against answering violence with violence. Pointing to the guardsmen in the stolid line behind me, I said they were not the enemies of the anti-war forces. They too were opposed to the Vietnam war; that was why they had joined the National Guard. When I finished, the sergeant immediately in command broke ranks to follow me back to the street. I stiffened when he called to me but relaxed when he said, "Thank *you,* sir! That was the first nice thing anyone has said about us all week."

*   *   *

My headquarters as ADA chairman, McCarthy's foreign policy spokesman and, exiguously, his floor manager was on the twelfth floor of the hotel overlooking Michigan Avenue, the demonstrators and the lake.'I had learned by now that at a convention one should not try to sleep in the rooms to which one is assigned. Those with a sure design for victory or virtue will wish to see you both by day and by night; all will think it urgent. Thus you can never sleep. So I retreated for a few hours each night to a club on the Near North Side where an apartment had been arranged by a friend. My suite in the Conrad Hilton was then used as a bivouac by McCarthy's younger supporters, and it was only with difficulty that it was made habitable for daytime business. The Chicago police included these rooms in their raid on the hotel on the last night of the convention, holding that, among other manifestations, the inhabitants had urinated out the windows on the forces of law and order far below. This, contemplating conditions within the rooms, was hard to believe. Recurrently in later months I received a bill from the Hilton for damages done during the invasion. Each time I urged error in the address and asked that the charges be sent to Mayor Richard Daley. I never paid.

*　　*　　*

It was in Washington a few days before the opening of the convention that McCarthy had designated me his foreign policy spokesman. In this role I went before the Platform Committee on the evening of August 20 to urge his position (and mine) on Vietnam. It was not an easy occasion. The committee was heavy with supporters of Hubert Humphrey and defenders of the administration on the war. My opposite number at the meeting was an exceptionally moderate Dean Rusk. "It [Southeast Asia] is an area of 250 million people — almost as much as Europe . . . It seems to me that most Americans would agree on what should be fair and reasonable . . . North Vietnam and South Vietnam [should] stop the fighting and settle whatever differences they may have by peaceful means . . . Why are not these fair and reasonable ideas a reality? Because the authorities in Hanoi will not accept them . . . Unhappily no one has been willing or able to tell us what would happen if we stopped the bombing . . ."[4]

*　　*　　*

When Rusk had finished and while he was still receiving thanks for the honor he had conferred on the committee by his presence and compliments for his statesmanlike performance, he was handed a note. Soviet troops had just marched into Czechoslovakia. Rusk reported the contents of the message and, amid further applause, de-

[4]*New York Times,* August 21, 1968.

parted to see what should be done. I was left to make the case against fighting the Communists in Vietnam. It was the Chinese, not the Soviets, who were presumed to be the immediate threat in that area, but in those days Moscow was thought by most sophisticated people ultimately to control all. The members of the committee, with a few welcome exceptions, listened to me with pained tolerance. Presently to my pleasure McCarthy arrived to lend a hand.

In Chicago I had first to survive a challenge to my own right to be a delegate. My membership in the state delegation that year had come through the patronage of Edward Kennedy. Though I was the most visible McCarthy man from Massachusetts, that was not the cause of my difficulty; the delegation, although politically regular by instinct, would eventually vote 70 for McCarthy, 2 for Humphrey — a very adequate margin. My dereliction had occurred a few years earlier when I had supported Elliot Richardson, an undoubted Republican, for Attorney General, an aberration that Richardson had made notable by ascribing his victory in the election at least partly to the support of three old Kennedy hands — Jerome B. Wiesner, former scientific and technical adviser to J.F.K. and later president of MIT; Edwin O. Reischauer, my Harvard colleague and former ambassador to Japan; and myself. Now doubt was expressed that anyone so deviant was really a Democrat. I was saved by the gallant intervention of Samuel Beer, a Harvard colleague, friend and former chairman of Americans for Democratic Action, and Maurice A. Donahue, president of the Massachusetts Senate, an unquestioned regular and the holder of the Kennedy interest in the delegation. After Donahue voted for me, the others fell apppropriately into line.

McCarthy then appointed me his floor leader, a less than powerful position,[5] and soon I was enchanted to hear on television and from the press wires that, along wih other party archons, I was meeting in the back rooms. A draft of Edward Kennedy was under way. All divisions among the Democrats would thus and miraculously be healed; Kennedy could both fight the war and make the peace to the satisfaction of all. As the balloting approached, there was, indeed, one meeting in a sordid room back of the stage in the amphitheater. McCarthy had sent word that he was·willing and would re-

[5] I was never completely certain that Gene told anyone else of my designation. I was left to make my tenuous authority known as best I could.

lease his delegates to Kennedy. Our conclusion was that, even if released, they would not go. And Humphrey's delegates would not defect. Thus the power of leaders — brokers so-called — at a modern convention. It was a minor manifestation of anticlimax when Kennedy sent word that he wasn't available.

There was an interesting moment when the vote came on seating one of the two contending delegations from Alabama. The Humphrey forces had to have, or in any case, wanted the votes of the one that had only a few token blacks. Endicott Peabody, known as Chub, and the former Governor of Massachusetts, was the Humphrey voice in the Massachusetts delegation. His mother was (and remains) a noted civil rights activist who once went to jail for her views. When the choice between the Alabama delegations came to a vote, I called for a poll of the Massachusetts delegates and got a Boston television crew to stand by to film the historic moment. Placing myself beside Chub, I kept reminding him on television that his mother was watching. When his name was called, he looked wretched and abstained. It was not an act of friendship.

Since it was wholly obvious that we didn't have the votes to nominate McCarthy, our strategy was to make the strongest possible case against our Vietnam involvement to those watching the proceedings and to resist any compromise on platform language that would grace a continuation of hostilities. In politics one usually fights in order to compromise; compromise is what makes legislation and party platforms (for whatever their symbolic value) possible. But there are times when one must be completely adamant, and this was one. The war was the transcendent issue. Compromise would not only have cost us the confidence of our own supporters, it would have provided sanction for those saying the war must go on. A firm stand would require Humphrey to move toward our position during the campaign. As the platform language was debated, the urge to compromise was strong. Theodore Sorensen, speaking for the anti-war forces, was so disposed; Richard Goodwin (with others) was admirably determined. In the end the issue was carried to the floor, and in the debate and in the voting we showed our strength in defeat.

As in 1960, I made the rounds of the state caucuses. Each morning I waited outside McCarthy's room in his suite until Abigail McCarthy came out to tell me whether or where Gene was going to go. And, as before, I would hear the gasp of disappointment when I came in and the assembled delegates saw that it would not be the candidate but Galbraith. I slightly softened the blow by taking Gore Vidal with me. Early each convention morning Vidal was achieving much political celebrity by flagrantly libelous exchanges on television with William F. Buckley, Jr. In my introduction of him to the state delegations I would suggest that Vidal's congressional campaign a few years earlier in Dutchess County, New York, had established an all-time record for Democratic defeats. This Vidal would deny. "A good solid defeat but not a record." Then, unfailingly, would come the question:

"Mr. Vidal, where is your friend Mr. Buckley?"

"Mr. Buckley?" he would reply with a surprised look. "Oh, Buckley. He's over at the Wallace headquarters stitching hoods."

*   *   *

I gave up my chance to speak on the Vietnam plank, an impressive example on the convention floor of sustained, succinct, responsible debate, for the more honorific and less important assignment of putting McCarthy's name in nomination. Governor Harold Hughes of Iowa made the nominating speech; Julian Bond of Georgia and I followed. With all else, in those days, I had need to find time to write a memorable address.

I should not have bothered. There can be few tasks in politics as ungrateful as trying to attract the attention of a convention audience. And by the time I got up to speak, the television audience was gone too. The cameras were showing the climactic battle then raging between the demonstrators and the Chicago police. Nor was my speech memorable. Only once with a last-minute ad-lib did I succeed. There had been reference to McCarthy as a poet and the assertion that this was the time, instead, for practical men. Sitting immediately in front of the podium, then a Democrat, a marshal of the Johnson forces for Humphrey and an eloquent advocate for continuing the war, was John B. Connally.

"This," I said, "may not yet be the age of John Milton. But it surely isn't the age of John Wayne or John Connally."

Members of the California and New York delegations, briefly attentive, rose to shout, "Screw Connally!"

Newsmen went over to interview John; he was quoted as saying,

"Where ah come from, it sure helps to have that Galbraith agin yuh."

When my speech was over, I went to the rooms backstage and there saw the carnage downtown on television. I went back to the floor to find someone in the Humphrey command who would go to Daley and Humphrey and urge, for God's sake, that the police be called off. It was not easy. Those whom I asked, not having seen the police riot with their own eyes, were not aroused. Eventually I persuaded Robert C. Weaver, then Secretary for Housing and Urban Development, to make the effort. It was too late and perhaps, in any case, hopeless.

Humphrey was nominated by a wide margin — 1761 plus a conceptually difficult three-quarters to 601 for McCarthy and a scattering plus South Dakota for George McGovern. McGovern's quixotic effort had brought no cheers from McCarthy or from me. But respect and friendship survived, and once during those days I joined George at a press conference to describe myself as a committed McCarthy man with larger personal loyalties.

While Humphrey's victory was decisive, our defeat was far from total. We won overwhelmingly in California, Massachusetts, Wisconsin, Oregon, New Hampshire and Iowa and lost only narrowly in New York. Even Minnesota was divided. All were states that Humphrey needed for the autumn election.

* * *

Not all that week had been somber. There were touching moments and ones of characteristic absurdity. On my arrival a youthful McCarthy volunteer who had taken time off from her job as an assistant in a photo shop assumed full charge of my life. Short, with wide hips under a miniskirt, she drove my convention car around and through all traffic obstacles. In the hotel and amphitheater she strode menacingly a few paces ahead to clear the way. She disappeared when I went to get some sleep but was always waiting outside when I woke up. At the news of the final vote she broke into a flood of tears. She had expected and even assumed that McCarthy would win.

One of her achievements was to break the electronic security system at the amphitheater so that she could come, as needed, onto the floor. This she accomplished in a matter of minutes. For others the challenge of the elaborate system of guards and electronically coded passes was more formidable. One night, with Richard Goodwin and Leon Shull of ADA, I arrived at the gate behind Allen Ginsberg whom the magazine *Eye,* in an imaginative gesture to literature, had retained to cover the proceedings. His clothes, hair and beard are hard to describe — they were those less of a reporter or a poet than of an apparition. The guard at the turnstile stopped him. Ginsberg presented his press pass. The guard refused to accept it. A Chicago police captain of authoritative aspect sauntered over to learn the reason for the holdup in the line.

"What's the matter, Jack?"

"He wants to come in."

"Has he got credentials?"

"Hell, *he* ain't even got shoes."

*   *   *

It was my intention when the convention ended, and subject to some movement on the issue of the war, to support Humphrey and urge ADA to do likewise. The alternative was Nixon. But the accepted ritual of party, primary and convention politics is at odds with political credibility. One cannot have deep and ardent conflict appealing to the highest principles and then, when the issue is decided and the balloting is over, shake hands, express affection and say that the differences were all trivial. Especially was this so in 1968. By the end of the convention, I had a standing with those opposing the Vietnam involvement that was second only to McCarthy's. To have then embraced Humphrey and Muskie would have been to alienate bitterly my own constituency. Also it was far from certain that I could persuade ADA to endorse the ticket. And any prompt endorsement would have made it less necessary for Humphrey to move in our direction.

I solved the problem by becoming invisible the moment the candidates were chosen and leaving town as soon thereafter as possible. A few days later Kitty and I flew to California on the first leg of a fortuitously timed trip to New Zealand. Meanwhile passions would cool and Humphrey could move.

My strategy didn't work. Humphrey found me at the Fairmont Hotel in San Francisco just as the porter was picking up our bags to go to the airport. He was never better; his persuasion went nonstop for half an hour. Surely his old friends would now rally to him; he too had once headed ADA. I urged the need for a major movement in our direction on the war. And I argued that our strong endorsement later would be better than a divided one now. There matters remained.

On my return, as I had supposed, the Nixon specter was at work. By October, ADA was safely, if not enthusiastically, aboard. And following an encouraging anti-war speech by Humphrey in Salt Lake City the liberal and peace groups decided to coalesce at one large meeting on behalf of Humphrey and Muskie or, in any case, against Richard Nixon. It was to be at Manhattan Center, a large and deeply depressing hall on West 34th Street in New York. Shelley Winters was to preside; I was to be the main speaker; the leaders of six or eight other organizations were to affirm their support; the proceedings were all to be broadcast on radio. A long evening.

I spent the late afternoon raising money. At one party I encountered Mrs. Vijaya Lakshmi Pandit, sister of Jawaharlal Nehru, former Indian Ambassador to Washington and Moscow and former President of the General Assembly of the United Nations. She asked if she could accompany me that evening. So did Natacha Stewart Ullmann of *The New Yorker* and also Princess Irene of the Netherlands, although she later defected to a Nixon rally at Madison Square Garden. I put all of them in the care of my wife. At Manhattan Center they sat in the front row.

The speeches endured for two or three hours, and eventually at 10:45 P.M., it was my turn. There was a disturbance in front of the platform; I looked down to see a totally naked man and a handsome young woman clad only in old sneakers handing me up the head of a pig. This was an accepted mark of disfavor in those days; the decision to support Humphrey had not met with universal approval. My thought as I struggled on with my speech was that the man looked infinitely more indecent than the woman. The interlopers were quickly bundled away by the police. Outside on Broadway when the evening came finally to an end, Nan Pandit, as she is known to her friends, said, "My dear Ken, it was wonderful to see a typical American political meeting."

*   *   *

I joined Humphrey and Muskie for the closing hours of the campaign in Los Angeles and, as presumed reassurance to California liberals, was kept continuously on television and radio. One appearance was for a joint interview with a handsome daughter of Ronald Reagan, who expressed surprise at my fraternal comments on her parent as a fellow pioneer in Americans for Democratic Action. A certifiably cretinous interviewer pressed her on whether it wasn't unfair for her father and then-senator George Murphy of California, the noted song-and-dance man, to take advantage of their eminence as one-time screen actors to advance their careers in politics. She replied sensibly that to exclude actors from political life would, indeed, be discriminatory. She was surprised and at first pleased when her interrogator, turning to me for an expected disagreement, found that I warmly agreed. I had had time to frame my answer. I said I thought the problem of discrimination would be quite different: after Reagan and Murphy, screen actors would never again have a chance. How wrong!

There is, I might add, a kind of political repartee that accords its author and perhaps some others pleasure but loses votes. This was an example. "Why," viewers would ask, "does a big, smart-assed professor from Harvard have to be nasty to that nice young woman?"

When the speaking and the telethons were all over, Ed Muskie and I rode through the night in his plane to Portland, Maine, whence I went on home to vote. Muskie told me (as he had earlier told others, for I later learned there were several versions) of the day he started out from Maine on the campaign. He spoke, there was a reception afterward, and, during the idle moments on the receiving line, a Texan whom Lyndon Johnson had sent as his representative fell into conversation with Muskie's man from Aroostook County.

Asked the Texan, "You a farmer?"

The Aroostook man acknowledged that he was.

"How much land you farm?"

"Hundred acres. Potatoes."

"I farm around six thousand myself."

The man from Aroostook did not seem much impressed. Johnson's man raised the ante in an offhand way.

"That isn't really such an awful big spread where ah come from.

There's a ranch down south of San Antone, family name of Kleberg. I can give you an idea how much land that fellah has: he starts off in the morning in his car, and he ain't barely crossed his place by noon."

"I had a car like that myself once."

32

The New Industrial State and After

THE VIETNAM AGONY was far from over. With gradual detachment the war would continue for another four years. It would be another six and a half before the day of the helicopters, a day celebrated on television by the despair of those deserted and the particular anguish of Ambassador Graham Martin, once my friend and a conscientious public servant caught up in a hurricane of events and designs to which, in the manner of the organization man, he had accommodated his own convictions. The speed with which Americans put out of mind those awful days, their slight adverse political residue, are proof of how small would have been the political cost of an earlier detachment.

But now, with the Nixon Administration, my course of action was much simplified. It was no longer old friends, my own party, a President for whom I had worked, that I opposed. The only need now was to help get the Democratic Party as solidly as possible against the war (and against its Cambodia enlargement when this became known) and to work in 1972 for a candidate who would be above all ambiguity.

My opposition to the Vietnam policy of the new administration was less than absolute. I never wavered in the belief that the Vietnamization of the war was a fraud. The Saigon government and armed forces were, one knew, far too incompetent, much too commercially committed, to stand on their own. To burden such a government and army, as later in Iran, with complicated weapons and the associated requirements in repair, logistics and sophisticated organization enlarges greatly the opportunities for graft. And in the end it ensures a more resounding collapse. Weaponry, we will one day learn, must be related in its complexity to the sophistication and competence of the country that seeks to use it. The fraud of Vietnamization, however, like my own earlier arguments for the enclaves, was political cover for the larger goal of getting out. This being so, one could not object.

In Newfane after 1968, a group of friends met for summer weekends at our house and in proximity to the large and diligent beaver population by our tiny lake to consider the imminent political prospect. Richard Goodwin, Arthur Schlesinger, Jr., Gloria Steinem, Elizabeth Stevens[1] and George McGovern attended at various times. From the beginning it was assumed that McGovern would (or should) be the next presidential candidate. He had just been reelected to the Senate for six more years. As compared with McCarthy, he was more diligent and reliable, if less captivatingly artistic. No plaque marks the spot where these solemn discussions took place; for such memorials one must not lose by so wide a margin as in 1972. On this I will have a later word. Now I must retreat for a few years to consider some matters that, by my calculus, seem of at least equal importance.

*   *   *

In the autumn of 1963, I had resumed teaching at Harvard, and in the years following, my classes were large. But by one device or another I arranged to keep a hand on political matters without ever having to cancel a single session so far as I can recall. Even the airlines favored me; if once or twice they failed, it was when I was leaving Boston, not returning. However, I did not carry my share of the tedious tasks of department and university — those involved with appointments, promotions, curriculum, journals, publishing, student affairs. My influence on university matters was thus small. Then, as time passed, I began regularly to negotiate for winters off to write, and I took myself to Switzerland for three or four wholly uninterrupted months at the typewriter each year.

In the early sixties, *The McLandress Dimension*[2] on which I had

[1] A Virginia and Washington political participant of charm and liberal commitment and the wife of George Stevens, Jr., motion picture producer and film archivist, who also took part. Gloria Steinem had earlier met McGovern at our house and handled his press relations in Chicago in 1968.

[2] Boston: Houghton Mifflin, 1963. As I've said earlier, this book celebrated the scientific psychometrical studies of one Dr. Herschel McLandress. The most thought-

worked in India — my first venture into fiction — came out to generally satisfactory notices and, in 1964, *The Scotch,* which I have continued to regard as my best piece of writing. This book, as I've noted,[3] served as a bridge over the compelled idleness of ambassadorial life, the prime purpose of the writing being to fill in time. I could search my mind at length for the right adjective, phrase or characterization, for no deadline pressed. My wife was wholly unaware that the book was being written until the ceremonial family dinner at which I presented her with a copy, beautiful in its dust jacket of simulated MacDonald tartan.[4] She was, to my sorrow, a little hurt. I was leaving her out of my life. It was not my intention.

Critics commenting on *The Scotch* did not need to urge caution as to my economic and political views, for there were none there expressed. So for this, and perhaps other reasons, the reception was excellent except in Elgin County, where, as I've noted, it was regarded as an invasion of privacy. There were many translations; that Parisians, Romans and numerous Japanese should come to know of the deeper cultural life of Iona Station, Ontario, seemed a most useful thing. In Canada the book was a best seller, meaning that it sold two or three thousand copies over a period of a year or so. Canadians have a depressing tendency to resort to public libraries for their reading. My British publisher at the time, Hamish Hamilton, himself a professional Scot, refused to call the book *The Scotch* when it was published in Britain. North of the Tweed, he said, all would assume

---

ful contribution of the volume, perhaps, was the well-documented contention of Allston Wheat, a McLandress protégé, that team sports are the training ground and social foundation of socialism. They persuade the young to suppress the individualist ethic, substitute instead that of the team, accept fully the authority of captain or coach, and they do this for people at a vulnerable age. Thus socialism and team sports have developed together. Wheat's resulting Crusade for Athletic Individualism (CAI) was launched to wean American youth away from baseball, basketball and football, encouraging swimming, track, tennis singles and other individualist sports instead. A flood of letters hit *Harper's,* in which this essay was first published. Some expressed doubts. Some asked membership in CAI. More demanded the exclusion of baseball from the list of socialist sports. "When you are out there at short and the ball is coming at you, you're on your own, boy, I tell you you're on your own."

[3] Boston: Houghton Mifflin, 1964. See Chapter 25.

[4] The Galbraiths, falling, it appears deservedly, on evil days some five hundred years ago, were taken over by the stronger, more heroic and almost certainly more virtuous Clan Donald. The Galbraith clan history, which I once encountered in manuscript form, is replete with undistinguished and sordid crimes, and a distressingly large part of it was written from court records.

that it was about whisky.[5] So he turned to my description of my fellow clansmen:

> Our Scotch neighbors might be tall or short, stocky or lean, although most of them were unremarkably in between. But it was evident at a glance that they were made to last. Their faces and hands were covered not with a pink or white film but a heavy red parchment designed to give protection in extremes of climate for a lifetime. It had the appearance of leather, and appearances were not deceptive.[6]

From these words he took as his title *Made to Last.*

All who write or publish books should understand the requirements of the nonfiction title, and few do. It should tell of the contents. The buyer in the bookstore or the reader in the library needs to know what the book is about. Forgetting this, authors and publishers alike have a tendency toward what is smart, neat, euphonious or abstract. *Made to Last* was a profoundly unrevealing title. When the book appeared in a Penguin edition, this was recognized, and it became *The Non-Potable Scotch.* To my shame I at first thought this good. Three titles for one small book were too many.

*   *   *

More than all else, when I returned from India, my mind was on *The New Industrial State,* a label still undiscovered at the time and one that made no concession to cleverness. I retrieved the manuscript from the vaults of the Cambridge Trust where it had resided since my departure for New Delhi. That I thought it should be so protected is a measure of the importance I attached to it, although something should probably be attributed to the absence of Xerox machines at the time.

My purpose, to remind, was to write the economic, political and social theory of that part of the economy by now preempted by the large corporations. A thousand of the largest of these provided around half of everything manufactured and everything supplied as services by AT&T, the electric utilities, banks, railroads, airlines, in-

---

[5] He was wrong. Our Canadian reference reflected an earlier and quite proper usage. When Dr. Johnson, a wholly adequate authority, went to the Highlands, he spoke, as Boswell tells, of the Scotch.

[6] *The Scotch,* p. 13.

surance companies and department and food chains. The organization of these great enterprises had been depicted, the managerial tendencies described, and there was a large, although by no means overwhelming, body of information on managerial theory and public and regulatory policy to be sifted and cannibalized. No one, Marx and Marxists in their context apart, had perceived the economy of the giant corporations as *the* economic system. The business firm of the textbooks was still, in structure, market power, political power and motivation, the microscopic competitive firm of the Marshallian world. Were there departures, it was to the exceptional case of monopoly or oligopoly, and here both motivation and internal structure were essentially the same. Large or small, there was still the driving force of the profit-maximizing entrepreneur. Those who could believe that the neighborhood news vendor and General Motors were brothers under the skin, each similarly subordinate to larger market forces they did not control, each passive except as a voter in the affairs of the state — those who could so believe could believe anything.

Not many did. But great inertial and even less sublime forces sustained the fiction. Much economic discussion — theoretical model-building it is called — proceeds within the framework of a larger assumption that is never examined. "We assume a competitive market." The validity of the result then depends not on congruity with what exists, with reality, but on whether it derives in a valid way from the assumption.

However, there were (and are) more tendentious influences against the reality. The textbooks that convey economic instruction are an important and also for many an often disappointing source of income. The wisest course for the textbook writer is to say faithfully what has been said before with, as embellishment, some minor notes of novelty which the publisher can emphasize in his advertising. This brings the best chance of acceptance. An author who ventures boldly into the full reality, as into recognition of the world of the large corporation, takes an unacceptable risk.[7]

The risk is in challenging the beliefs of the routine teacher and in

[7] In the years immediately after World War II, Paul Samuelson did so in embracing Keynes, the national accounts — Gross National Product, National Income and their components — and the idea of macroeconomic management of the economy. He succeeded, although not without encountering a vehement attack for his departure from the old faith. No textbook writer since has been quite so courageous.

doing violence to the tranquilizing effect of the established economics. The orthodox view of the subject, as noted, made — and still makes — all producers subordinate to the market; even monopolies are held in check by their binding commitment to profit maximization. It is only that their prices are higher, a different point on the curve. If an enterprise is wholly subordinate to impersonal market forces, it has no power to deploy. It is passive in the service of consumers and the public at large. This view of economic, social and political life allowed and still allows hundreds of thousands of students to be instructed in economics each year without intruding and damaging thoughts on the way that, as a matter of inherent and organic character, the great corporation exercises power over prices, costs, technology, consumer taste, military expenditure and government policy. It is true that not all students can be so persuaded. But it is much safer that the subject of corporate power not be a matter of overt indoctrination.

This social tranquilization was not deliberately intended. It reflected the unexamined instinct of those who were at peace with the corporate economy and the power of its participants. As I've suggested before, there may be a social case for such psychic calm. Better that people be spared disturbing thought. But this one is compelled to doubt. On occasions of high ceremony university speakers proclaim the case for truth, not convenience. Their oratory should not be too obviously subordinate to their practice.

* * *

The first task in writing *The New Industrial State* was to establish the dominant role of the handful of large corporations, to show their share of total output. From this comes the bimodal character of the modern industrial economy: there are still millions of small enterprises, but half the private economy is in the hands of the large ones. It was not a difficult job. The statistics were excellent and generally irrefutable. What exists in the United States holds also in the other industrial lands. The corporate half I termed the Industrial System, an unduly bland designation that I changed to the Planning System in later editions.

The large firm seeks control of forces impinging on it; this makes planning possible. The market, inherently an unpredictable thing, must be set aside in the greatest possible measure. Prices, costs, consumer response and government policy must so far as possible be under control. If a new automobile model is to be marketed in vast numbers, after huge investment, three or five years hence, there must be some certainty as to what, within a safe range, the price will be. Similarly the major sources of supply must be assured. And the costs. And, from earnings and an appropriately close relationship with appropriately large banks, there must be knowledge that the requisite capital will be available. And when the automobile eventually appears, there must be dealers to sell it and consumers who are made to want the particular blend of originality and banality so provided. Finally there must be enough influence on the state to ensure that highways are available on which people can drive the vehicle and that no arbitrary or untoward regulation as regards safety or air pollution will inhibit its sale and use. The Chrysler Corporation shows what happens when planning fails.

That such comprehensive economic and political power is exercised is not a fit subject for either surprise or indignation. Accepting that automobiles — or rubber tires or chemicals or steel or a hundred other products — are to be produced in massive quantities as the public demands, then the need to plan and thus to control becomes essential. Economists mentally transfixed by the impersonal authority of the market protest otherwise. So do corporate spokesmen reciting the undemanding litany of the free enterprise system. The truth is accepted by those with serious operating responsibilities — corporate managements for whom planning in a controlled environment is an everyday fact and business schools which lavish much attention on planning techniques and market control.

*　　*　　*

As *The New Industrial State* took form, so did the perception of a matrix in which all parts of the modern corporate economy showed a rewarding and sometimes astonishing interrelationship. This discovery was, in many respects, the most reassuring part of the effort. Thus modern management of aggregate demand in the economy — assurance that a deficiency in effective purchasing power would not again bring a devastating depression — no longer appeared as a unique act of innovation in economic policy. Rather, it was part of the public accommodation to the needs of corporate planning. It was made necessary by the instability now inherent in the relative rigidity of corporate prices and wages and the large investment discretion now inherent in corporate decision. Management of aggregate demand sought to prevent the gross fluctuations in sales against which no individual corporation could plan. Thus it added another dimension of security to corporate planning.

Similarly the power of the corporation over prices eliminated uncertainties over labor costs, for wage increases could, after some ceremonial exchange of abuse, be conceded and passed along to the public. The union became a ministerial body exercising day-to-day surveillance on work routines and grievance procedures. Not having to fight, it ceased, not surprisingly, to be socially militant.

The explosion in university training and in research in modern times had generally been viewed as an original act of social enlightenment. More plausibly it reflected the new need of the planning system for a large supply of qualified managerial, technical and scientific personnel and a flow of usable scientific and technical innovation.

Great corporate size and the associated planning were closely interlocked with changes in the structure of the corporate enterprise. No longer could one man empowered by ownership exercise appreciable power in the organization. All important decisions required the shared knowledge and experience of many people — production men, marketing specialists, advertising geniuses, engineers, scientists, lawyers, accountants, tax experts, legislative specialists, those otherwise knowledgeable in government regulation. So the classical entrepreneur disappeared. Access to knowledge and facility in its use became the new source of power. The individual stockholder not involved in management, even the one with important holdings, became a largely passive figure. He or she might have a place on the board of directors and be heard with deference, but it was now certain that his or her uninformed ideas would promptly be forgotten.

Power, in passing to those possessed of the relevant knowledge, passed to a collectivity that I called the technostructure. This anonymous collectivity appeared as the true source of corporate authority. In their day John D. Rockefeller, J. P. Morgan, Henry Ford and Julius Rosenwald were folk figures of the first magnitude. Their capitalist power was universally celebrated and denounced. Now no one outside the immediate corporate community knows the name of the head of Exxon, Morgan Guaranty, Ford or Sears. No tremor touches the stock market when the chief executive of one of these firms retires, turns to alcohol or suffers cardiac arrest. The market accepts the reality, which is that power lies in the organization — in the technostructure.

Now there came into view one of the more pleasing contradictions of the established doctrine, and none should doubt the pleasure, even for the most compassionate scholar, in finding his professional colleagues trapped in logical conflict. In all neoclassical orthodoxy, the profit motive is vital — it is the simple muscular force moving and invigorating the whole economic machine. Yet, as the corporate system matures, power passes to the technostructure. And so visible is this process that even the orthodox have long conceded that the modern large corporation is management-controlled. But this means that profits are now pursued and maximized by people who do not get them. The nonowning managers of the corporation now work, plan, innovate and invest to increase the revenues of stockholders they do not even know. My metaphor was of a man obsessed by sex who devotes his life to enhancing the sexual opportunities of other people whom he has not met.

Reconciliation was possible by making corporate growth as well as corporate profit the goal of the technostructure. Growth means greater responsibilities and more pay for those who contribute to it. And also in the large corporation there is motivation that derives from the desire for peer approval and from the ever-present urge to identify oneself with the goals of the organization and the companion hope that by appropriate effort one can accommodate the organizational goals to one's own. I developed this view of motivation and concluded that the large corporation assimilates itself, as it grows, ever less to the profit-motivated entrepreneur, ever more to the different and unique motivation of the organization. There is nothing remarkable about this. Men did not serve in the Marine Corps in past times because of the money; they served because of their pride in being Marines. Their personalities were enhanced by their identification with the Corps. They believed that by their presence they were making it better. The more enlightened foreign service officers do not serve in the State Department for their pay; they serve because they seek the good opinion of colleagues, identify themselves with the departmental position on foreign policy or hope to adjust that policy to their own.[8] So too in the world of the large industrial corporations.

* * *

The imperatives as to the organization of large-scale production are not peculiar to capitalism. Nor is the system of motivation. I had looked at them in the Soviet Union, and, as I have earlier told, a further conclusion of high portent had emerged. Great organizations, wherever they exist, have the same or similar imperatives. The great capitalist corporation and the great socialist *combinat* have broadly the same organizational structure; they respond to the same technological needs; they stamp their demands and their culture similarly upon the communities in which they are located. Motivation — the desire for peer approval, the identification with the goals of the organization, the desire to adjust these toward one's own — are similar if not the same. Modern capitalist organization and advanced socialist organization are not in diametrical opposition. They are on a broadly convergent course — a convergence not to the inevitable power of the market but to the common requirements of technology and large-scale production, the associated organization, the common need for planning and the similar motivational forces.

* * *

There were weeks and months from autumn 1963 to autumn 1966 when, as had happened before, *The New Industrial State* captured all of my life. My thoughts were on it from morning to bedtime. New lines for exploration, new possibilities for persuasion or clarification, continued almost relentlessly to present themselves. But eventually, in late 1966, the book was finished and went in to the publisher. I had been invited by the BBC to give the Reith Lectures[9] in London

[8] One of my important sources on motivation, identification in particular, was Herbert Simon of Carnegie-Mellon University. In 1978, he won the Nobel Prize in economics for ideas that I turned to my use most gratefully.

[9] For John Charles Walsham (Lord) Reith, Director General, architect and dominating presence of the early BBC. He was dour, physically large and fearsome — Winston Churchill once called him "that Wuthering Height." I spent an evening with him in the early fifties at King's House in Kingston, Jamaica, as the guest of Sir Hugh Foot (later Lord Caradon), then the Governor of Jamaica. Reith spent the first part

that autumn, and I took the galleys with me on the plane to correct and admire. My lectures summarized various of the ideas therein. First to my surprise, then to my horror and finally to my nearly uncontrollable anger, I found that my current editor at Houghton Mifflin, ordinarily a most restrained and careful man, had decided to improve and clarify my nomenclature. Competition had become "free competition"; all references to capitalism had been revised to read "our American system of free enterprise"; the market had become the "free market." Freedom was everywhere. As a gesture of conciliation and appeasement, the publisher had nearly the whole book reset. I have been spared that kind of editorial improvement ever since.

The British public heard my thoughts with outward calm.[10] The response when the book was published[11] was everything for which I hoped and considerably more. Sales were prompt and large — in the early months over a hundred thousand in the hardcover edition. They continued through two later editions and various paperback renderings. A Senate committee under the chairmanship of Wayne Morse of Oregon called me before a large audience in the Senate Caucus Room to explain my views. Senator Russell Long drew attention to my conclusion that the modern large corporation had much discretion in setting prices and asked if this were true of the drug companies. I said yes, and he said that this being so, could they not be told to reduce their prices? This, in principle, I affirmed, and he complimented me on one of the most useful discoveries in the history of economics.

Translations of *The New Industrial State* appeared in all of the industrial countries and in the Soviet Union, Hungary, Poland and Yugoslavia. My German publisher, Droemer Knaur in Munich, a house noted for its art books and involved now to its surprise with economics, looked with special wonder at its climb up the German best-seller lists.

The orthodox reviews were as I anticipated. Robert Solow of MIT in *The Public Interest* and Scott Gordon in the University of Chicago's

---

of the evening denouncing socialism, the latter part condemning capitalism. As we went off to bed, I asked Sir Hugh what system Reith favored.

"Don't you know? He wants the whole world run by the BBC."

[10] I remember a surprising and generous telephone call to the studio from Randolph Churchill immediately after the first broadcast.

[11] Boston: Houghton Mifflin, 1967.

Journal of Political Economy were especially eloquent. This is an attention that is much to be welcomed. Such criticism advertises, perhaps unduly, one's originality. And the reviewer's indignation, outraged belief or simply his desire to destroy regularly replaces careful statement. In consequence, one can, in rebuttal, exploit miscues, errors and absurdities to great advantage while winning the attention that any vigorously polemical exchange inevitably attracts. Solow's review was especially valuable in this regard. I did what was, I believe, an accomplished hatchet job in reply, and the exchange became an obligatory item in the books of readings that economics students are given as partial relief from their textbooks.

For a more popular audience Irving Kristol in *Fortune* warned that I was undermining the whole existing rationale of capitalism. Since this was my intention, I did not reply.

The less motivated reaction was more favorable. So was the response of the students at Harvard. For some years the lectures in my principal class, Social Sciences 134, had been, as I've said, successive drafts of *The New Industrial State*. Undergraduates in large numbers had been deserting the more comprehensive but, alas, more rigorous orthodox introductory course to come to mine. After *The New Industrial State* was published, my enrollment underwent a precipitate decline because my younger colleagues in the basic course now assigned *The New Industrial State* to their students along with the conventional textbooks. I was not needed.

*   *   *

When John Stuart Mill finished his *Principles of Political Economy*, he took the manuscript to the publisher, and a fortnight or so later the printed copies went on sale. Now, with the march of progress, he would not see the finished volumes for a minimum of six months. While *The New Industrial State* was making its way through this lengthy gestation, I wrote a novel, *The Triumph*. This I had long had in mind, for only in fiction could one extract full value from the highly trained, profoundly certain, deeply solemn foreign policy experts who, aided by all available intelligence, proceed from wrong assumption to disastrous result. The statesman in my novel — Grant Worthing Campbell — guides policy in the State Department in the last days of a Central American dictator, Luis Miguel Martínez Obregón, who combines the acquisitive tendencies of Trujillo and Somoza and who rules in a capital drawn from life in Port au Prince, Santiago and Guatemala City. The dictator falls and is replaced by a worthy but ambiguous social democrat whose views and associates arouse the deepest suspicion in Washington. Desperately needed aid is refused. Instead the dictator's son, a student at the University of Michigan, is encouraged to return home where a coup by young army officers puts him in power. It is unforeseen and unfortunate that, at Ann Arbor, the young Martínez has become a radical, indeed a Communist. Arms, airlifted by U.S. planes, help him to consolidate his position. Socialization of the means of production was never so easy; his father had owned everything that amounted to anything. Title has only to be passed to the government.

Reading an early draft of *The Triumph*, Arthur Schlesinger said my love passages read like something that might have been done for research purposes at the Boston Lying-In. I took them out — took out all women, in fact. No one noticed.

When, as a play, *The Triumph* opened some distance off Broadway, love had been restored. Various of the characters went calisthenically to bed, so far as one could determine on random motivation. It was bad. Mercifully the play closed before anyone noticed.

Few labors were more pleasant than those on this novel — first in Gstaad, then over the Grand Canal in Venice, then in Deyá on Majorca. Reading what I had written each night, I had an almost orgiastic sense of creation. The characters became my companions; I walked every day on the streets of Flores, the capital of Puerto Santos, my small endangered republic. When the book was published, it went promptly onto the best-seller list. My publisher gave me an impressive certificate proclaiming my achievement; never before had one of their authors been in this enchanted company for both fiction and nonfiction in the same year. Again I break my rule against talking about money. The earnings of *The Triumph*, including the sales for two film versions that were never produced, were the same, by rough calculation, as my earnings in my first fifteen years as a full professor at Harvard.

The experience provided me also with a major insight into the bearing of history on current anxieties.

In Deyá, on the olive-tree-covered slopes down to the Mediterranean, I worked in a house that we borrowed from Ricardo Sicré, a literate Spanish banker and businessman and a friend of Robert

Graves, who lived just across the way. One afternoon as I finished work, Graves came into our living room and glanced at the *International Herald Tribune* beside my typewriter. The headline was large and black: Gamal Abdel Nasser had just closed the Gulf of Aqaba. War between Israel and Egypt now seemed inevitable.

Turning from the newspaper to me, Graves said, "You aren't worried about those Israels [sic], are you?"

I said that I was. A small country surrounded by so many hostile neighbors.

"Your generation, my dear Ken, had no preclassical history, did it?" It was not, in fact, a major subject at the Ontario Agricultural College.

Graves continued, "Do you realize that the Egyptian Army had its last military success at Kadesh against the Hittites in 1299 B.C.?"[12]

*   *   *

In 1972, I campaigned in the primaries and in the autumn for George McGovern and went as a state-wide delegate on his behalf to the Miami Convention. There I sustained a certain instinct for political disaster and contributed at least marginally to McGovern's misfortunes and later defeat.

After John F. Kennedy's death, George McGovern was my closest friend in politics, Edward Kennedy possibly excepted. He is a man of kindness, fine intelligence, humor and stubborn honesty of liberal purpose. Perhaps he was too uncompromisingly himself to be a good presidential candidate. There was George McGovern always being George McGovern.

At noon on the day following his nomination in Miami, I was briefly in my hotel room on the way to lunch with Demetrius Sakellarios, a long-time radio operator on American merchant ships and tankers and the most competently self-educated person I have ever known. It had been a somewhat exhausting morning after a long session the night before. The Massachusetts delegation, 104 strong, had been in caucus and complaining, especially to me, that its members were not being kept informed. A casual remark by McGovern

[12] When I told this story some years later to Gideon Raphael, the recently retired Director General of the Israeli Ministry of Foreign Affairs, it was solemnly disputed. Raphael said that, in fact, Ramses II was defeated, but he snatched victory from defeat in the retelling by the time he got home.

that withdrawal from Vietnam might be subject to our leaving a residual force there had added to the tension. Someone had proposed a walkout if this were policy. What was going on anyway?

Now a call came from McGovern's suite; for Vice President, George had decided on Kevin White, then as still at this writing, the mayor of Boston and the best of the modern big-city mayors. Boston has flourished during his years in the new city hall; he has made a good part of the difference. But Kevin White in 1972 had led the Muskie slate in the Massachusetts primary; when news of McGovern's choice became known, I foresaw another explosion in the delegation. On this, of all matters, my friends would believe they should have been consulted. I feared there would be a walkout from the floor. I sought out Congressman Robert Drinan, another state-wide delegate, in the next room, and he was unbelieving. "Kevin White? That's the same name as the mayor of Boston." I called McGovern and told him my fears; time was short, and he said he would go on to his next choice, which was Senator Gaylord Nelson of Wisconsin. I went to lunch and turned on television in the afternoon to hear the announcement. Nelson had declined; it would be Senator Thomas Eagleton of Missouri.

A massive assault was immediately mounted on this excellent man centering on the treatment he had undergone for an unpleasant but by no means catastrophic or even exceptional episode of mental depression. McGovern yielded and replaced him with Sargent Shriver. The campaign was damaged at the outset.

A legend has Edward Kennedy vetoing White as a rival Massachusetts politician while I served as the executioner. I had no communication of any kind with Kennedy either that day or during the convention. Nor, though he may have briefly demurred, did he object to the selection of White. The wholly effective objection was mine.

It was a mistake. Whatever passing fuss there might have been in the delegation, it would have had no lasting effect. On my return to Cambridge, I wrote to White to tell him that I was sorry for what I had done. We agreed to speak no more of the matter. Our friendship continued. In 1979, in his mayoral campaign, I endorsed him with the slogan: "You don't have to live in Boston to vote for Kevin White." Wisely, this was changed before release to "You don't have to live in Boston to be for Kevin White."

33

Last Chapter

READERS and more especially authors should be warned as to books written after sixty: the creative impulse survives more powerfully, I'm persuaded, than the critical judgment of what is written. If you continue to write, you have especially to be on guard against the tendency to plagiarize yourself. Words come to mind that are resonant in their meaning or expository power. The idea so framed is a thing of clarity and brilliance. Presently you discover, although sometimes you do not, that one reason it is so wonderful is because you have said it before.

Accepting the risk, I concluded when I had finished *The New Industrial State* that I must write one further book in the sequence with it and *The Affluent Society*. This would place the planning system — the thousand giant corporations — in the context of the economy as a whole. I would see on what terms these thousand or so giants that contribute half the national product coexist with the millions of small enterprises that contribute the other half. The book would also consider in detail the public policy required by this bimodal structure of the economy. My first thought was to explain all this in the didactic tones of a textbook. Thus I would challenge the neoclassical and Keynesian hold on undergraduate instruction. This intention I abandoned after a couple of days. There is much in the archaic textbook that is true, and this I would have to include. I found that I could not enlarge on the established truth in clear, straightforward English. It was a bore.

R. A. Butler, former Chancellor of the Exchequer and much else, whose autobiography I later introduced to American readers, was now Master of Trinity College, Cambridge. He invited me to join the college as a Fellow and there seclude myself for writing. The seclusion would not be complete; I was put down for a series of lectures in the first two terms of the 1970–71 academic year. And this allowed me as before to try out the ideas on a live audience. In October 1970, I settled into comfortable rooms in Nevile's Court — the British no longer make physical discomfort the price of academic achievement — and, when weary, allowed my eyes to wander to the Wren Library, after King's Chapel the most eloquent of Cambridge structures. Unlike Harvard where course registration implies an intention to attend and this is reinforced by examinations, lecture attendance at the English universities is voluntary. The number showing up for later lectures is a cruel measure of one's success in making the earlier ones worthwhile. I started with around 300 students; by the following spring the number was down to a third or fewer, and I heard with sympathy of a visiting American at Oxford who had started with five and ended with none at all.

The conditions for writing were rather too perfect. The porter did not pass telephone calls until after lunch. The arrival of the morning mail was a greatly welcome interruption, and it was accompanied by any important college news. "Professor Galbraith, I regret to tell you that this morning we found Professor Broad sitting at his desk. He was quite dead."[1] My lapse back into bachelorhood was not quite complete, for Kitty took an apartment in London. She had retained from our first married years a deep aversion to the self-approving male chauvinism of the English college scene. Civilized attitudes were, in fact, encroaching, but she was less than forgiving when she discovered that wives were still forbidden the Trinity High Table, although unrelated women of distinction could now come. The rule was defeated one night when the chaplain extended her an invitation while I invited the chaplain's wife.

Economics and the Public Purpose,[2] the eventual title of the third book in what the well-disposed call my trilogy, tells, among other things, how small business survives. There are limits on the toil that can be demanded in the large firm; the small businessman is at liberty to exploit himself. In this role he can be a very severe employer. In those industries, including agriculture, where people work out of sight or on unstandardized tasks, there is advantage in an arrangement that rewards diligence and punishes sloth. This is inherent in

[1] Professor C. D. Broad and Professor John Wisdom — Broad and Wisdom — were famous Cambridge philosophers.
[2] Boston: Houghton Mifflin, 1973.

the small or one-person business; it is why agriculture lends itself badly to socialism. And a final and important cause of small-business survival is the expanding industrial role of art and aesthetics. After things work well, people want them to look well. Given a sufficiency — or a plethora — of material goods, people go on to entertainment or aesthetic reward. Thus, a much ignored trend, the expanding economic importance of the artist in his various manifestations.

With rare exceptions, the artist fits badly into organization. He tends also to flock with his kind — in London, Paris, Italy generally or Los Angeles. There he sells his product — design, painting, music, whatever — as an individual or in a small business.

The mention of Italy should be especially noted. Modern Italian economic policy lays no claim to excellence or even to coherence. Neither Italian engineering nor Italian management is exceptional. Italian unions are a law unto themselves and Karl Marx. Italy, nonetheless, moves from one crisis to another on an upward curve of prosperity. That is because Italian products, out of an ancient artistic tradition, set the style for all others. This is tacitly but not openly conceded. As this is written, it is not clear that anyone can be wholly acceptable as the head of an American automobile company who does not have an Italian name.

In *Economics and the Public Purpose* I dealt also with the burdens in managing a high standard of family consumption and the resulting need to have women conditioned to this task. Above a certain income level, automobiles, houses, entertainment, adolescent recreation, clothing and social and cultural observances all require a great deal of time and attention, and old-fashioned servants quickly become unavailable when there are industrial alternatives. Since consumption can continue to expand only if there is someone to undertake the work of the modern consumers goods economy, wives, upper-income wives in particular, have become the new crypto-servant class.

The small-scale sector of the economy duly established, I went on to summarize the characteristics of the corporate or planning sector and then to contemplate the public policies by which both sectors, and more particularly the public at large, might coexist. I pleaded for public recognition of the role played by the large corporation in public and private government and defined the principal problem of public policy as that of bringing the corporate purpose into accord with the public purpose. This, in singular measure, includes the reconciliation of the private business interest in arms expenditure and weapons development and the public interest in arms control and survival. Nothing that has happened since this writing suggests a misplaced emphasis on this subject.

In *Economics and the Public Purpose* I faced but did not resolve the deep and enduring contradiction in modern industrial society. The public and the corporate purposes diverge. It is on the state that the public must rely for the assertion of the public interest. The state, however, is extensively under the control of corporate power. The head of General Motors or General Electric or General Dynamics has immediate and influential access in Washington as the ordinary citizen or smaller businessman has not. And there is a more subtle influence. What is thought to be the responsible public opinion is, at any given time, a reflection of the needs and interests of the corporate technostructure. Yet it is to a government so influenced by corporate power that one must turn for defense of the public interest. Something, one could feel, is accomplished if the contradiction is perceived. That, however, does not make it disappear.

The work on the new book had a tedious side, one that I did not foresee. I could not tell my readers to go back and read *The Affluent Society* and *The New Industrial State*. Such requests are rarely honored. So I had to summarize such as was necessary from the two previous volumes. Reviewing *Economics and the Public Purpose*, Kenneth Boulding, the least easily labeled heretic of my generation of economists and one of the most interesting, noted the repetition. I was annoyed, for I had been troubled by it myself. However, the reception of the book was not displeasing, and my work proved especially acceptable to university audiences. In books assigned for class use recurrence to earlier work is not noticed; students haven't usually read the earlier work.

*   *   *

One day in the summer of 1973, as John Dean was testifying on Watergate, a call was relayed to me in Vermont from Adrian Malone of the BBC in London. Would I consider doing a series of television programs on some unspecified economic subject, possibly the history of economics? Malone and a talented team of directors, cameramen,

sound men, lighting experts, production assistants and other crafts-
men had just accomplished a major effort on the history and
nature of science — "The Ascent of Man," written and narrated by
Jacob Bronowski. They wished now to do something similar on social science.

The call marked the beginning of a three-and-a-half-year enterprise going far from any of the preoccupations of my earlier life. If
appraised with proper solemnity, it was a dubious use of the time;
what is seen on television registers but slightly on the mind, is thus
soon forgotten, and this, one cannot doubt, is fortunate. Certainly
not much can be learned about economics from a weekly television
lecture along with some amplifying (or distracting) pictures and with
no supporting reading, discussion or concern about examinations.
Education is not that easy. But if thoughts of this sort could be
avoided, the enterprise itself — travel from Singapore to Spain, east
to Poland and over much of Western Europe, across the United
States from Boston to Los Angeles and from Minnesota to Louisi-
ana, all with extraordinarily talented and recurrently contentious
people of half my age — was profoundly interesting and often enchanting. Since it was not a task that could be combined with teaching, I met my last regular Harvard course in the autumn of 1973,
and with fewer regrets than I had expected.

Adrian Malone, with whom I spent these years, was, if such there
be, the quintessential Irishman. Of a Liverpool family whose income,
like that of Lyndon Johnson's parents, declined radically with the
telling, he was salmon-pink of hair and complexion, perceptibly
overweight and, except for occasions of extreme ceremony when he
looked uncomfortable, only partially dressed. He could not work
wearing a jacket, a necktie or a shirt that was buttoned above the
midpoint of his unduly spacious chest. With obvious effort he
achieved an impressive gruffness of manner and speech; he believed
this to reflect executive competence and command. He was an extreme male chauvinist, partly because women of intelligence sufficiently respected his ability that they would work for him regardless
of abuse. By cupping his hands around his brow, he could see any
television sequence as eventually it would appear on the screen,
along, one judged, with the resulting audience reaction. To all proposals on script, location, staging or editing he returned an outraged
no. Then after thought he would often assent. He had learned that

if he agreed too soon, he would deny himself the chance for further thought.

It was my bargain with the BBC that I would provide the ideas and the script, and my BBC colleagues — Malone, Richard Gilling, his deputy in general charge, and two assistant directors, Mick Jackson and David Kennard — would have control of illustration and scene. The bargain did not hold. My coworkers offered an infinity of useful and unuseful amendments to my thoughts; I made many suggestions, accepted and not accepted, as to how these might be illustrated.

The travel took us to Trier in the Rhineland to film at Marx's parents' house, a spacious structure partly surrounding an elegant courtyard, and to the rather more modest dwelling of Adam Smith in Edinburgh. It included the birthplace of Thorstein Veblen in southern Minnesota and, as a service to vanity, the farmhouse near Iona Station, Ontario, whence I came. We filmed on the lovely open highlands in Sutherland at the northern extremity of Scotland from which the Scotch were extruded with violence by the Highland Clearances and on the *Delta Queen* cruising down the Mississippi from Natchez.

For the winter and spring of 1976, Kitty and I took a furnished flat on Hill Street in Mayfair, and I commuted each day to Ealing and a vast BBC warehouse complex there which they called a studio for the considerable part of the production that involved stage props and artifacts. It was not quite Hollywood; there remains, even in television, a modicum of British restraint. The dressing room to which I retreated between takes was ostentatiously grim. Still, it remained a wonder that at sixty-seven one should arrive at a film studio, a place of childhood fantasy. My lifetime movement and that of Ronald Reagan have been in opposite directions.

Under the ruthless pressure of my directors, I learned for the first time to speak carefully and clearly in sentences, to give value to all appropriate consonants and to avoid the disconcerting pauses and gasping "ahs" with which my speech had previously been punctuated. Generations of Harvard students would have benefited if I had been earlier so trained. Many of my fellow professors and all politicians should get instruction from the British Broadcasting Corporation.

The more esoteric demands of theater came less easily. The series, "The Age of Uncertainty," for the many who missed both it and the accompanying book, was an abbreviated history of economic and related political ideas from Adam Smith through David Ricardo, Thomas Malthus, Karl Marx, the Americans, including the Social Darwinists and Thorstein Veblen, on down to John Maynard Keynes and after. Each of these writers we sought to place in historical context. On Marx we filmed one wintry day in the Luxembourg Gardens in Paris, the epicenter of the revolution of 1848 in which Marx's emotions and hopes were deeply engaged. (It was in this same year that with Engels he issued the *Communist Manifesto*.) My wife, for an article on our effort for *American Film,* reproduced the following interchange:

Director: Could we try that again, Professor? Just a bit more positive. That one was a bit flat.

J.K.G.: More pizzazz, you mean? How's this?

Director: Sorry, Professor, you forgot to turn away at the end.

J.K.G.: And I flubbed a word. I can do it better.

Director: Please, Professor, just a hint of a smile. Your irony may not come across.

J.K.G.: Now, Adrian, you know I can't do that. I don't want to seem to be laughing at my own jokes. It's not my style.

Director: I didn't say a laugh. I said a glint.

J.K.G.: Oh, well, I'll try.

Director: And action . . . Cut. We'll have to wait for that airplane . . . This time, Professor, you didn't stress the last sentence. You need to make your point more emphatically.

J.K.G.: I meant it to be a throwaway line. You are making me do what is not natural for me. My style is to underplay.

Director: No, Professor, it's not right there. You *must* really trust us. You know what you want to say, but, believe me, we know our television. Once more, Professor, please . . . Perfect. Professor, I'll buy that. How about you, Dick?

Co-director: Lovely.

Director: All right with you, John?

Sound recordist nods affirmatively under earphones.

Cameraman: Sorry, there's a hair in the gate.[3]

[3]*American Film,* February 1977, p. 6. A "hair in the gate" means that, on postoperative inspection, the camera lens — or something else — shows some defect. A retake is required. Briefing me on what I could expect in my new career, David Niven had warned, "Just remember that when the cameraman or the technicians bitch up, they will always say there's a hair in the gate."

In the summer of 1975, we journeyed to Tucson, Arizona, and to the Davies-Monthan Air Force Base nearby. This is the world's largest junkyard; the rows of obsolete or mothballed aircraft stretch for miles. There I spoke of the power of the military-industrial complex in our economic life, our entrapment in an ever-increasing cycle of outlay. We force action on the Soviets, they on us. So it continues. Not far from Colorado Springs at the North American Defense Command (NORAD) we made our way a mile into the mountain to see the command post positioned on great springs that is calculated to survive, however briefly, a thermonuclear strike. And in Death Valley we had the cameras roam over a terrain that gave a valid view of how the urban concentration from New Haven through New York and New Jersey to Philadelphia would look after the explosion of only four twenty-megaton bombs. How deeply the audience was impressed by this I do not know. I was sufficiently impressed to resolve that concern for nuclear disarmament would occupy as much of my time as I could find for the rest of my life.

In the summer of 1976, for the last of the programs, we gathered a cross section of the world establishment in Vermont — Henry Kissinger, then Secretary of State; Georgy Arbatov from the Soviet Union; Edward Heath, the former British Prime Minister; Jack Jones, the British trade union leader; Katharine Graham of the *Washington Post*; Shirley Williams, former British cabinet minister, and a half dozen others to discuss current issues, including how to get the weapons race under the control that, alas, still eludes mankind, to its terrible risk and potential utter sorrow. The most memorable comment during those summer days came from Kukrit Pramoj, a personal friend of many years' standing and a former Prime Minister of Thailand. After Kissinger and Arbatov had discussed the arcane issues of control as between the nuclear powers, the talk turned to proliferation. On this Pramoj had some useful observations, and especially on the condescending manner in which the great powers accepted unacceptable risks for themselves but worried about the lesser risks of proliferation for the smaller powers. He ended with a look of well-contrived concern, saying, "But let me be clear. We in Thailand do not want to have those bombs. We are a very careless people and we might let one of them *drop.*"

*   *   *

I worried greatly about having so many prima donnas in such small space for most of three days. Something was certain to go wrong; someone, in consequence, was certain to succumb to outrage. Nothing much did go wrong. Edward Heath was brought the hundred and thirty miles from Logan Airport in Boston by a local mortician who made the trip at a funereal pace of around twenty miles an hour. The press, which I had expected to react angrily to its exclusion from the proceedings — the BBC naturally sought a monopoly — did not materialize in great numbers, and those coming were deterred by the six miles of forest between our house and the village of Newfane. The Secret Service protecting Henry Kissinger was mostly dismayed by the woods — "We know about buildings, not trees." However, the army of assassins that could easily have assembled within rifle range of our august assemblage also did not materialize. The local sheriff's men aided the Secret Service in its three-day scrutiny of the forest, and one rode with Kissinger in his car when he traveled between our house and the village inn. According to a much-celebrated report, when all filming at the farm was over on Sunday, a State Department aide was waiting in Newfane to give Kissinger the parcel of weekend telegrams. In the presence of the sheriff's deputy the Secretary leafed them through and in characteristic accents rumbled, "Oh, my God. More shooting in Lebanon."

"That's out of our jurisdiction, Mr. Secretary; Lebanon is across the river in New Hampshire."

* * *

As "The Age" was made ready for airing, both some in the BBC and the American sponsors at KCET in Los Angeles were assailed by the fear that it might be thought radical. Perhaps it was. The second program of the series was on the conspicuous consumption of the Newport rich in the last century and the manners and morals of the robber barons as viewed through the sardonic lens of Thorstein Veblen. It was, by American standards, a commonplace comment on the gilded age. However, a BBC governor, a pleasantly stout man named George Anthony Geoffrey Howard, viewed the program in Vermont and was, reportedly, deeply distressed. An attack on legitimate privilege, economic predation and pillage. (Mr. Howard has since become Chairman of the Board of Governors of the BBC.) The nervousness grew when a high convocation of British conservatives imported Professor Milton Friedman all the way from the University of Chicago to lecture adversely on my economic views. Eventually the alarm subsided in England, but there was continuing and heightened concern at KCET, and the services of the Hoover Institution at Stanford University, a talent repository, even museum, of the solemn intellectual right, were engaged for the American showing. One of its recruits filmed a brief statement at the end of each of my programs explaining that I was wrong. I didn't care for this. Nor did my BBC producers. But one cannot object to free dissenting speech.

"The Age of Uncertainty," facilitated by French, German and Japanese versions, went around the world. British critics, on the whole, disapproved. They thought it overillustrated; more should have been heard, less seen. Such criticism is not easily dismissed, for Britain is the only country to have brought television to the level of an art form and, in consequence, its standards are far more rigorous than those in other countries. Perhaps also, as my BBC colleagues believed, the imaginative and at times elusive visualizations of abstract concepts clashed with the matter-of-fact tendencies of British critics. Elsewhere the series was well received, in some places with impressive acclaim.

Two books came out of the television material. When I came to prepare the program on money, I was captured by the subject and by the absence of any good history of this interesting and important artifact. A chapter-length manuscript grew to nearly 120,000 words and into a book called *Money: Whence It Came, Where It Went,*[4] a title that reflected the sad current state of what students were once told was meant to serve as an enduring storehouse of value. From the series as a whole came, inevitably, *The Age of Uncertainty.*[5] It too found a satisfactory audience at home and in foreign translations. In Japan it sold slightly more than half a million copies. My admiration of Japanese literary taste was unbounded. In the autumn of 1978, Kitty and I went to Tokyo as the guests of my publishers; never before had I realized how warm can be the response of kindly hosts when their visitor is also an earning asset.

*   *   *

[4] Boston: Houghton Mifflin, 1975.
[5] Boston: Houghton Mifflin, 1977.

I must now say a word on writing and how these and all my books got written.[6] I am thought to be an extraordinarily diligent writer, and for a while each day I am. For years I have reserved three or four hours each morning for my current book or the related reading and fact-finding, and, as convenient, I've used the rest of the day for supporting reading or thought. I've learned to close my ears to the intruding sounds of family, household and telephone and, when away from home, to ignore those of airports, airplanes and fellow travelers. I've learned to contend briefly but courteously with the seat-mate who joins me to say, "You're Doctor Galbraith. I've never read any of your books and I don't agree with your positions, but I'm sure proud to meet you."

I've also found it serviceable, as I've already indicated, to retreat on occasion and spend as much time as possible wholly alone, for without distraction one's thoughts turn automatically to the next day's work or to the unresolved problems of the morning just past. An escape of several weeks or months each year, usually to Switzerland, has contributed invaluably to every book since *The Affluent Society.*

To write adequately one must know, above all, how bad are one's first drafts. They are bad because the need to combine composition with thought, both in their own way taxing, leads initially to a questionable, even execrable result. With each revision the task eases, the product improves. Eventually there can be clarity and perhaps even grace. Anthony Trollope tells proudly in his *Autobiography* that he never sent a manuscript to his publisher without reading it over at least once with care. My commitment is to not fewer than five revisions; this, I trust sprightly, document has had six.

I have also been much helped in writing on economics by the conviction that there is no idea associated with the subject that cannot, with sufficient effort, be stated in clear English. The obscurity that characterizes professional economic prose does not derive from the difficulty of the subject. It is the result of incomplete thought; or it reflects a priestly desire to differentiate one's self from the plain world of the layman; or it stems from a fear of having one's inade-

---

[6] There were two others in these years, *The Nature of Mass Poverty* (Cambridge: Harvard University Press, 1979) to which I have already alluded and *Almost Everyone's Guide to Economics* with Nicole Salinger (Boston: Houghton Mifflin, 1978). A collection of previously published essays, *Annals of an Abiding Liberal* (Boston: Houghton Mifflin), also came out in 1979.

quacies found out. Nothing so protects error as an absence of readers or understanding.

But for the undoubted volume and the alleged quality of my writing, there is a less self-centered explanation. That is Andrea Williams. In 1958, for coping with the correspondence that came in the aftermath of *The Affluent Society* and for work on *The New Industrial State*, which I had then in mind, it occurred to me that I needed better help than the purely mechanical typing talent on which until then I had relied. I let my need be known. My first applicant was a handsome blond woman, a member of an old Rhode Island family, a recent graduate of Smith, who was of superb humor and, it later developed, of enduring tolerance. She had recently been released from marriage and was a refugee from the New York publishing subculture where she had served as personal assistant to Thayer Hobson, president of William Morrow Company. Andrea Williams and I formed a partnership that has lasted at this writing for twenty-two years. She did not, despite my best persuasion, accompany me to India. A Republican when possible, she served during those years as an aide to Elliot Richardson, then an emergent figure in Massachusetts politics, and as an editorial assistant at Houghton Mifflin, all the while awaiting my return.

Andrea has managed my office and a succession of talented assistants who have loved their employment because they loved her. She has kept a watching brief on our household economy, on our friends and their needs, on my publishing contracts and commitments, and she has assumed charge of my travel, bank account and income tax. She has regulated the tourist flow — the considerable number of travelers who, after viewing Concord, Lexington, the Old North Church and Harvard, are moved, however oddly, to view Galbraith. But most of all she has been my editor. Few writers in any language can have been so favored. My spelling is often impressionistic; my punctuation is erratic; so more rarely is my syntax; my memory, though generally good, is subject to lapse, often under conditions of the greatest certainty; my sense of taste is fallible; and so too is my impression of what is or is not clear. All these faults are corrected to near perfection by Andrea Williams. Nothing, literally nothing, that I have written for publication in the last twenty-two years has escaped her scrutiny.

The discipline for which I am sometimes admired is the clear, objective discipline of my beloved friend.

* * *

Unlike old soldiers, who fade away, politicians die, and they die twice, once just before the labored, reminding obituary, once earlier when, after losing office, they are asked to produce identification on cashing a check.

From the early seventies on, I detached myself from political matters. The Nixon Administration made few claims; the BBC was a competent distraction. And the memory of Bernard Baruch often crossed my mind as he had been in the war years — seventy, to all of us ancient but still determined to obtrude, be at the center. We thought him something of a bore. In 1976, I supported Morris Udall for President and campaigned mildly on his behalf. In 1980, with more energy, I supported Edward Kennedy. A commitment to losing causes is still a constant in my life. In 1976, I watched the convention proceedings from the stands. In 1980, I did descend briefly to give a speech on arms control:

> If we fail in the control of the nuclear arms race, all of the other matters we debate in these days will be without meaning. There will be no question of civil rights, for there will be no one to enjoy them. There will be no problem of urban decay, for our cities will be gone. So let us disagree, I trust with good humor, on the other issues that are before the Convention. But let us agree that we will tell all of our countrymen, all of our allies, all human beings, that we will work to have an end to this nuclear horror that now hovers as a cloud over all humankind.

The point is one on which I am deeply persuaded and deeply anxious to persuade. But when I had made it, I went back to the gallery. I have noticed that those who write their memoirs have difficulty in knowing when, on public matters, they should stop. The obvious stopping point is when the view is from the stands.

Index

Abt, John J., 37
Acheson, Dean, 131n, 298, 358, 359, 360
Acquisitive Society, The (Tawney), 354
ADA. *See* Americans for Democratic Action
Adams, Barbara, 350, 353
Adams, Henry, 161
Adams, R. L., 27
Adams, Sherman, 389
Adenauer, Konrad, 253
Affluent Society, The (Galbraith), 361–63, 366, 389, 448, 525, 528, 535, 536; JKG receives award for, 112n; JKG works on, 285, 347, 349, 350; publication and reception of, 313, 353–54, 361; quoted, 339–40, 450–51; in India, 366, 407n, 414
Afghan crisis (1980), 416n
Agency for International Development (AID), 159, 292, 416, 417, 472, 489
Age of Uncertainty, The (Galbraith), 534; and preceding TV series, 531–34
Agnew, Spiro, 488n
Agricultural Adjustment Administration, 25, 32, 60, 107; JKG with, 35–38, 40–41
Agriculture: as employment, attitude toward, 3, 4, 7–8, 30; and sharecropping, 4, 99; origin of colleges of, 9–10; political attitude toward, 22–25, 296; Senate Committee on, 99, 183; in India, 417–19; and socialism, 527. *See also* Economics, agricultural
Agriculture, U.S. Department of (USDA), 10, 25, 56, 84, 94, 390n; JKG with AAA of, 35–38, 40–41; Bureau of Agricultural Economics, 98; Yearbook of Agriculture, 100; and farm price supports, 102, 356 (*see also* Price controls); and meat rationing, 155; funds marketing study, 269
AID. *See* Agency for International Development
Aiken, George D., 371, 481

Airey, Colonel Richard, 1
Air Force, U.S., 106, 204, 314; and Strategic Bombing Survey, 74, 196–99, 225–26, 228, 231, 274, 275; and Air War College, 198n, 448; and B-17 (Flying Fortress), 228–29, 236; and U.S. planes in India, 415, 438; and obsolete aircraft, 532
Airlines, 71, 75; Canada-U.S. arrangements, 5–6, 444. *See also* Travel
Alcoholics Anonymous, 266
Aldrich, Winthrop, 169
Alexander, Henry C., 196, 198, 199, 226, 233
Allen, Frederick Lewis, 308
Allen, George, 120
Allen, Harold L., 187–89
Allen, Rutilus, 36
Allied Chemical Company, 116–18
Allocative inefficiency, 103. *See also* Price controls
Almost Everyone's Guide to Economics (Galbraith and Salinger), 535n
Alsop, Joseph, 383, 477
Aluminum Company of America (ALCOA), 63. *See also* Business
Amalgamated Clothing Workers, 100, 107. *See also* Trade union(s)
Ambassador's Journal (Galbraith), 306–7, 390, 393; quoted, 395, 402, 408, 409, 435, 439, 468, 476–77, 478
American Assembly, 276
American Capitalism: The Concept of Countervailing Power (Galbraith), 281n, 350, 369; quoted, 283, 284
American Dilemma, An (Myrdal), 83
American Economic Association (AEA), 27n, 31, 174, 283, 484; JKG president of, 66, 83, 156; JKG article for, 270
American Economic Review, 77
American Farm Bureau Federation (AFBF): JKG with, 98–104, 122, 418
American Film (periodical), 531